RELEVANT BUSINESS STATISTICS USING EXCEL

David W. Gerbing

School of Business Administration
Portland State University

South-Western College Publishing
an International Thomson Publishing company I(T)P®

Cincinnati • Albany • Boston • Detroit • Johannesburg • London • Madrid • Melbourne • Mexico City
New York • Pacific Grove • San Francisco • Scottsdale • Singapore • Tokyo • Toronto

Publishing Team Director: Dave Shaut
Acquisitions Editor: Charles McCormick
Developmental Editor: Jamie Gleich-Bryant
Production Editor: Mardell Toomey
Media Production Editor: Robin Browning
Production House: Omegatype Typography, Inc.
Internal Design: Joe Devine
Cover Design: Ann Small
Marketing Manager: Joe Sabatino
Manufacturing Coordinator: Sue Kirven

Library of Congress Cataloging-in-Publication Data

Gerbing, David W.
    Relevant business statistics : using Excel / David Gerbing.
        p.   cm
    Includes index.
    ISBN 0-324-00358-7
    1. Commercial statistics—Methodology—Computer programs.
  2. Microsoft Excel for Windows.   I. Title.
    HF1017.G47   1999
    519.5—dc21   98-24182
                                                CIP

1 2 3 4 5 6 7 8 9 C1 6 5 4 3 2 1 0 9 8

Printed in the United States of America

I(T)P®

International Thomson Publishing
South-Western College Publishing is an ITP Company.
The ITP trademark is used under license.

*This book is dedicated to my beautiful but crazy wife, Debbie,
and my four wonderful boys, Bradley, Michael, Patrick, and Peter.*

BRIEF CONTENTS

CONTENTS

Contents

Our personal and professional lives are filled with encounters with random, unpredictable events. Like it or not, we make virtually all of our business decisions against the backdrop of this random ebb and flow.

We never know in advance how many customers will shop at our store today, so we do not know exactly how many salespeople we need on the floor. Nor do we know the trading price of a particular stock at the end of the day, week, or month, so we do not know for sure whether to sell the stock that we own or buy more. We cannot even be sure whether our next child will be a boy or a girl, so we do not know what color to paint the baby's room.

PREFACE

Statistics is the tool for analyzing and thinking about this type of unpredictable, random variation. The manager's general goal is to make effective decisions—not to do statistics per se. Because the primary method for accomplishing effective decision making in many situations just happens to include statistical analysis, this text demonstrates the relevance of statistics for the day-to-day activities of the business manager.

To accomplish effective statistical analyses, we need to

- know the meaning of the underlying concepts,
- choose the proper analyses,
- interpret the analyses, and
- perform these analyses on the computer.

This text presents all of these topics to provide future managers with the tools needed for using statistics in their daily activities.

CENTRAL THEMES

Meaning of the Underlying Statistical Concepts

This text retains conceptual rigor while minimizing use and knowledge of mathematics. Although notation is minimized and proofs are avoided, the meaning of the underlying statistics is explained in depth. The assumption here is that statistics is a useful tool but not a panacea. An understanding of the logic underlying a statistical procedure mitigates against the overly simplistic use of the procedure.

You will find examples of these conceptual discussions throughout the text. For example, the beginning of Chapter 4 carefully develops and explains the underlying logic of statistical inference. Chapter 5 Extension discusses the implications of a type of statistical conclusion (called hypothesis testing) in the context of making business decisions. Likewise, the material in Chapter 9 explores the difficulties of obtaining accurate predictions of future events.

Relevance

Although this text provides a firm foundation in statistical inference, it also pushes students beyond the simple generation of statistics. By addressing how to apply statistical analyses, this text allows students to gain an understanding of the role that statistics will play in their business careers. Relating the numbers back to the original problem helps students see the relevance of statistics in many facets of business activity.

ORGANIZATION

The Business Application

The central organizational feature of this text is the Business Application. Each application illustrates a specific statistical concept according to a consistent, structured format. The application presents a meaningful problem expressed in plain English, followed by the data, the analysis from multiple perspectives, and a conclusion with an interpretation expressed in plain English. *The purpose of this text is to present the statistical concepts needed to provide answers to the problems presented in the Business Applications.* A Business Application accompanies each statistical concept.

Computer Usage

EXCEL INTEGRATION. The computational vehicle employed throughout the text is Microsoft Excel '97. The thoroughness of this integration proceeds along multiple tracks. Throughout the text, the obvious presentation is referred to as the Excel built-in analysis. Many, but not all, of the statistical procedures illustrated can be accomplished with preprogrammed Excel programs, which are available either as built-in functions, such as =AVERAGE(data), or from the Data Analysis option available from the Tools Menu, such as the Descriptive Statistics program. Whenever applicable, the corresponding Business Application illustrates the Excel built-in analysis.

Excel produces many of the numerative and graphical results of statistical analyses throughout the text. The primary location of the Excel instructions, however, is in the Business Applications. The output is displayed first, and detailed instructions about how to obtain the output follow. These instructions contain screen shots of the accompanying dialog boxes with the correct values entered. All menu calls and other needed information are also displayed.

CONCEPTUAL WORKSHEET. This section of a Business Application performs the statistical analysis by using Excel to implement the *conceptual* definition of the statistic of interest. Computational formulas are never displayed here (or anywhere else in the text). For example, a statistic such as the standard deviation is computed by directly implementing its definition in terms of the squared deviation for each observation. The bottom of the worksheet displays the relevant sums and means that result in the standard deviation. The Excel formulas for these computations are also displayed, so the student views both the numerical results and the formulas and data that produced those results.

Many of these conceptual worksheets, such as for the standard deviation, regression analysis, and analysis of variance, are presented in the same format. These variation tables tie into the definition of statistics as the analysis of variation. In each case, the variation table is presented in conjunction with an accompanying model. The concepts of the standard deviation, regression analysis, one-way ANOVA, and two-way ANOVA with interaction are presented in the same format.

CONTENT

Statistical Issues

QUALITY CONTROL. Quality control concepts are presented throughout the text, including the opening of Chapter 1. The concepts of common and assignable causes of variation are discussed in conjunction with the standard deviation in Chapter 3. The largest concentration of quality control material is found in the extended section of Chapter 4 on confidence intervals. The quality concept of a control chart is presented as an application of the confidence interval. Other examples of quality management are found throughout the text.

MODELS. A central theme of modern statistical analysis is the statistical model. The model explains or accounts for the values of a variable of interest—the response variable—in terms of the values of one or more variables. Traditionally, the concept of a model is introduced as, and often limited to, the explanation of regression analysis. This text integrates the concept of the statistical model throughout the text. The concept of a model is first introduced in Chapter 1. The first and simplest model is presented in Chapter 3 as an accompaniment to the standard deviation and the concept of variation. Reference to this model continues throughout Chapter 4. Chapters 8 and 9 focus on regression models, and Chapters 10 and 11 present analysis of variance, which is defined as the analysis of specific types of regression models.

When data are analyzed from the perspective of a model, the analysis proceeds from the corresponding conceptual worksheet, the variation table. Retaining a consistent format for these tables throughout the text ensures a consistent approach that enhances learning and helps the student grasp the big picture of how statistics provides tools for the study of variation.

Chapter by Chapter

CHAPTER 1. This chapter introduces the key concepts of variables and data as the first step toward demonstrating how statistics provides techniques for solving real-world problems.

CHAPTER 2. Knowledge of how often each possible value of a random variable is likely to occur leads to more effective business decisions. Students learn how to portray the values of a distribution to help them make sense of variables.

CHAPTER 3. Continuing the general theme of Chapter 2, this chapter summarizes an entire distribution and shows students more precise ways of locating the position of a value within a distribution.

CHAPTER 4. Chapter 4 moves the focus away from describing data to generalizing about the entire population represented by that data. Students are introduced to inferential statistics and learn the importance of the confidence interval.

CHAPTER 5. This chapter focuses on the form of statistical inference called hypothesis testing to identify a specific value of the unknown population mean.

CHAPTER 6. Building on the material from the previous two chapters, Chapter 6 shows students how to compare the mean of the response variable from two different groups. This discussion of statistical comparison illustrates how managers compare the performance of two different groups, products, teams, and so forth.

CHAPTER 7. Chapter 7 addresses managerial questions in which the response variable Y is categorical. The student begins the formal application of statistical inference procedures to categorical response variables, shifting from the analysis of means to the analysis of proportions.

CHAPTER 8. Here, relationships between known and unknown variables are presented. Students learn how understanding relationships between variables leads to better decision making and how regression analysis explains the extent of the influence that variables have on one another.

CHAPTER 9. This chapter extends the analysis of the four basic assumptions of regression analysis by showing the effect of outliers on the estimation of the regression model. Students also learn how to draw conclusions about the entire population using this statistical tool and to incorporate multiple predictor variables in their analysis.

CHAPTER 10. A deeper discussion of inferential statistics shows students how to evaluate the null hypothesis of equal group means for as many groups as specified. As in previous chapters, this presentation is framed in a managerial context, showing students that the goal is not just the search for differences but the attribution of causality to explain those differences. Experimental design, the collection of data classified by groups, and the accompanying statistical analysis are all addressed.

CHAPTER 11. Chapter 11 shows how the model and content presented in Chapter 10 apply when using multiple predictor variables. The advantages of more sophisticated models are discussed.

CHAPTER 12. Planning for the future is a fundamental task of every business, so this final chapter demonstrates how to use the statistical information from past events to predict future outcomes.

INSIDE EVERY CHAPTER
- **Why Do We Care?**—Each chapter opens with a brief overview of the chapter content and an explanation of its relation to previous material and its relevance to the student. This feature provides a context in which students can understand how the new material expands on what they have already learned. It also indicates how this new information is relevant to the course material and to their business studies in general.
- **Business Application**—This is one of the central organizing features of the text. For each concept, students learn how to apply the given statistical technique in order to solve a business problem.
- **Statistical Illustration**—This feature demonstrates the particular concept being presented in a step-by-step example format. All concepts are presented with the support of either a Statistical Illustration or a Business Application.
- **Exercises throughout each chapter**—Homework exercises distributed throughout each chapter (after Chapter 1) fall into one of three categories: Mechani-

cal Drill, Application, and Conceptual. The category of a specific problem is identified by one of the following tags:

Mechanical   Application   Concept

1. The Mechanical Drill exercises offer practice working with data and require little or no interpretation.
2. The Application problems follow the exact format of the corresponding Business Application and also stress interpretation. At least two application problems are included in the exercises that follow each Business Application.
3. The Conceptual problems offer the student a chance to explore the underlying concepts and may require more creativity to solve.

- **Exercises at the end of each chapter**—Additional exercises that fit the classifications of Mechanical, Applied, or Conceptual appear at the end of each chapter for additional practice. Two other elements at the end of each chapter give students the opportunity to reinforce their understanding of the chapter's concepts: (1) A series of Discussion Questions focus on the concepts and definitions presented in the chapter; and (2) The last problem of each chapter is the Integrative Analysis Problem. This problem ties together all or most of the concepts introduced in the chapter. The data are found on computer disk. Answers to this problem require computation as well as conceptual understanding and interpretation.

SUPPLEMENTS

Instructor's Manual

This supplement was written by David Gerbing and includes teaching tips and solutions.

Test Bank

The comprehensive test bank includes questions and problems of varying type and difficulty for each chapter. The goal for each test is to evaluate different levels of mastery—knowledge, comprehension, analysis, synthesis, and so on—without being difficult to grade. Test length will vary according to the quantity and difficulty of the material presented in the chapter. Professor Mohammed El-Saidi of Ferris State University, which uses an Excel approach in all business statistics courses, wrote the Test Bank; he collaborated regularly with David Gerbing to ensure integration of the materials.

Power Point Presentation Slides

The author has created a slide presentation of approximately 350 slides from his own teaching of this material. Slides include both visual material and condensed explanations of key points.

Data Disk

A disk containing the data for all problems in the text that present data for analysis is packaged with the core text book. The name of the data file for the Integrative Analysis Problem at the end of each chapter is listed as part of the problem. All other data files are identified by chapter and problem number. The data disk also contains templates for various statistical analyses not provided by Excel.

ACKNOWLEDGMENTS

I would like to thank the many reviewers whose comments and suggestions helped me prepare this textbook. Their knowledge and insightful suggestions transformed my manuscript into this comprehensive textbook.

Larry M. Austin
Texas Tech University

Steve Bajgier
Drexel University

William H. Beyer
University of Akron

Michael Broida
Miami University

John M. Charnes
University of Miami

Pete Chong
Gonzaga University

Michael Cicero
Highland Community College

Ron Coccari
Cleveland State University

Myron K. Cox
Wright State University

Rex Cutshall
Vincennes University

Terry Dalton
University of Denver

Paul W. Guy
California State University–Chico

Mark Haggerty
Clarion University

Clifford Hawley
West Virginia University

Donn Johnson
University of Northern Iowa

Don H. Mann
University of San Diego

Lee McClain
Western Washington University

Cliff Nowell
Weber State University

Rick Olson
Loyola University–Chicago

Thomas Porebski
Triton College

John Rooney
Concordia College

Hedayeh Samavati
Indiana University–Purdue/University of Ft. Wayne

Avanti Sethi
Wichita State University

Alan Smith
Robert Morris College

Don Sutterfield
Memphis State University

Stuart Warnock
University of Southern Colorado

Jeanne Wendel
University of Nevada–Reno

Steven Yourstone
University of New Mexico

David W. Gerbing

RELEVANT BUSINESS STATISTICS
USING EXCEL

Variables and Data

WHY DO WE CARE?

If you can easily imagine other activities that you could pursue at this very moment, you might ask, "Why do I care about business statistics?" Why is the study and application of statistics important in today's business environment? Why should you in particular be studying statistics? The answer is that managers are problem solvers, and solving problems is what applying statistics is all about. The field of statistics provides techniques for solving real world problems—for analyzing information to uncover and predict trends, to discover and analyze problems, and to evaluate and improve performance.

Consider the pursuit of quality. The goal of any company that aspires to world class performance and competitiveness is ever increasing customer satisfaction through continuous improvement of quality. Quality can be implemented in many different ways, but ongoing statistical analysis of data plays a vital role in the pursuit of quality for any company, large or small, manufacturing or service oriented. The more quality becomes a well-defined and formal goal of a company, the more valuable statistical analysis becomes for day-to-day operations and planning.

Management has found many other uses of statistics as well, such as for the analysis of marketing surveys or the analysis of revenues. This text presents the fundamentals of statistical knowledge used in contemporary business—knowledge that can lead to improved problem solving and better decisions at all levels of management and often, indeed, by *all* employees.

1.1 QUALITY, VARIABILITY, AND UNCERTAINTY

Successful, competitive business focuses on quality. In his influential book, *Building a Chain of Customers,* Richard Shonberger (1990, p. 67) observed, "[W]e judge total quality in two ways. One is the average (or typical) level of quality; the other is variability around the average. . . . [The goal] is improvement—better averages with less variability. . . ."

statistics
analysis of variability

These two concepts—average and variability—lie at the very heart of **statistics.** This entire text is about the analysis of variability as related to business decision making.

To achieve quality, the average must attain a desired level. When a customer must wait before obtaining service, such as the time on hold after dialing a ticket agent or the time spent waiting in line at a bank, the average should be small. For the number of miles before the tread on a tire wears out, the average should be large. For the diameter of a hole machined on a lathe, the average diameter should be neither too small nor too large.

Improving quality leads also to a consideration of the variability *around* the average. Analysis of variability is fundamental to the assessment and improvement of quality.

> *Quality improves as variability around the desired level decreases.*

A prime archenemy of quality is variation. Because no two products or services are exactly, precisely the same in every way, uncertainty necessarily accompanies every business activity. The customer placing the order does not know how long it will take to fill the order, and the machinist does not know exactly where the hole will be drilled. Some orders are processed within a day, but others require weeks; some holes are drilled very close to the correct location, but others are drilled too far off-center.

statistical thinking
recognition of the presence of variation and an attempt to understand its causes

To reduce the variability of products or services, business decision makers need to use **statistical thinking** to understand the underlying causes of variability, and then learn how to predict and control it. As we discuss in more detail later in the text, variability results from a combination of two types of causes: a large number of unpredictable and relatively minor random fluctuations and a much smaller number of more substantial, longer-term changes. In the first case, the drill press operator applies a little too much force to the drill-bit, causing the drill to jump slightly off-center. An example of a longer-term change is poor communication from the floor supervisor that leads the operator to select the wrong drill-bit, adversely affecting an entire batch of parts.

Statistics is the primary analytical tool for studying variability, and statistical thinking is indispensable to understanding and solving many business problems. Statistics is used for assessing the underlying cause of a problem and for guiding the proper response to reducing the subsequent undesirable variation. From this understanding, business decisions in the context of the ubiquitous unpredictable variation—such as when to place the order or how to manufacture the part—become more effective. Statistical analysis provides a useful means for understanding and perhaps reducing this unpredictable and often undesirable variation.

The dilemma is that the decision maker must still act without perfect information. Do you modify the production process? Do you buy the stock? What price do you charge for your product? Do you purchase the ad space? Do you invest in the land? Although many important outcomes cannot be predicted in advance, the consequences of our managerial decisions are quite real, ranging from satisfied customers and profitability to bankruptcy.

Many have found success in life by combining skill and knowledge with good luck. Statistical thinking *reduces* dependence on luck. Uncertainty and randomness do not imply a complete lack of knowledge. Many random events fit specific patterns and tendencies that can be described with the language and through the concepts of statistics. Uncertain outcomes cannot be precisely predicted, and chance can always work against us as well as for us, but we may be able to turn the odds in our favor by knowing the general patterns of outcomes.

The enhanced understanding that results from statistical thinking leads to a statistical description of the relevant information.

> *Statistical thinking facilitates decision making within an uncertain environment, such as for the reduction of variability.*

A primary tool for thinking about uncertainty and variation is something called a random variable. Before defining a random variable, we first need to introduce some related ideas.

1.2 RANDOM VARIABLES

The analysis of variability is essential for effective management and is the core concept of statistical analysis. Virtually everything of importance to the manager varies: employee salaries, quarterly returns, performance of employees, number of employees on vacation at any one time, and so forth. The study of variability begins with the concept of a variable.

Data from Variables

VARIABLES. A more efficient way to manufacture refrigerators reduces the time required to assemble refrigerators. One immediate finding from assessing manufacturing time is that each refrigerator requires a *different* amount of time to manufacture. The first refrigerator observed was assembled in 48.3 minutes, and the second refrigerator required 47.9 minutes. The variable generally assumes different values for each of these objects.

Let's introduce some formal definitions. The object of study might be fast-food hamburger outlets, employees of a specific company, consumers of a product, or the states of the United States. Each object defines a class of objects or events that may consist of a few, many, or countless instances. An **observation** could be a specific company such as Tastee Burgers, a specific employee such as George Brown, or a specific state such as California.

Each observation can be described many ways. Of particular interest are those characteristics that vary from observation to observation. The **variable** is the concept describing the characteristic that varies, such as Height. An example of a **value** of a variable is 71", the height of a specific person. More examples of variables and values appear in Table 1-1.

observation
specific instance of the object of study

variable
characteristic of an object or event with different values for different observations

value of a variable
specific instance of a variable for a single observation

Table 1-1.
Examples of variables
and values.

Object of Study	Illustrative Variables	Illustrative Values
Person	Annual salary	$38,500
	Age	46
	Gender	Female
	Job Satisfaction	Medium
Company	Number of Employees	185
	Annual Sales Revenue	$5.1 million
	State in Which Headquarters Reside	CA
	Net Quarterly Income	$1.2 million
Stock Price	Selling Price of Stock Yesterday	83 1/8
	Selling Price of Stock Today	83 5/8
	Number of Shares of Stock Traded Today	24,372
Metal Rod	Length	6.25 in
	Size of Outside Diameter	1.5 in
	Pressure before Breaking	8000 lb/sq in

A single letter for a variable name refers to a generic variable. The letter Y is chosen as the generic variable because in statistics a Y stands for the *response variable,* the variable of primary interest in the analysis. Other variables are sometimes labeled with a generic X. In real life, a meaningful name such as Age and Salary replaces a generic X or Y. Mathematicians live in the world of Xs and Ys, but managers work with Number of Defects, Employee Salaries, Assembly Time, and Taxable Income.

random variable
*specific values are
not known in
advance of the
process that
generates the values*

RANDOMNESS. The values of a **random variable** result from chance—any one value cannot be known in advance. *Advance* knowledge of the winner of the horse race, of the stock on the New York Stock Exchange that rises the most in value within one week, or of the length of the next machined part, is not possible. The values of these variables are not known until the process that sets their values has occurred. Only after the race is won, trading for the week is completed, or the part is machined can the values of the corresponding random variables be known. Each horse race or each day of trading on the stock exchange is a randomly drawn sample from an indefinitely large population of races or trading days. Thinking of a random process as a method for generating samples from a larger population is a basic concept of statistics. The terms *random variable, sample,* and *population* are at the heart of statistical analysis.

The term random variable may be new but what the term refers to is not, as seen in the examples in Table 1-2. Every reference to the generic variables X or Y in this text ultimately refers to specific applications like these.

Before moving on, it might be helpful to clarify this term. First, because all variables that we study are random variables, *variable* is a convenient abbreviation for the more formal term *random variable.* Second, the previously presented definition

Table 1-2.
More examples of random variables that give meaning to the generic and rather abstractly named variables *X* or *Y*.

Random Variable

running time of the current most popular movie

volume of sales for each salesperson

number of accidents by department of a company

mpg for a delivery truck for different weeks of the year

cost of renting a 1-bedroom apt

yearly return on a portfolio of stocks

amperage of a battery

annual income of New York City dentists

list price of next year's Honda Accord LX

weight of individual cattle in a feedlot

number of hours per day people spend watching TV

inside diameter of a metal tube machined on a lathe

labeling a randomly selected unit as acceptable or defective

price of your favorite NYSE stock at the end of the trading day

amount of cola bought by the next person at the checkout stand

gross sales in $ by salesperson John Doe during the last month

national debt at the end of the fiscal year

number of employees who call in sick tomorrow

weight of a filled cereal box

number of years that your marriage lasts

of a random variable is not the formal definition provided by mathematicians. Mathematicians who study statistics and probability generally restrict the use of the term random variable to numeric variables.

DATA. Information amenable to statistical analysis is expressed in a specific form. Statistical analysis is the analysis of **data.** Examples of data abound. One example is a list of employees from a company's marketing department that includes their salaries and their job satisfaction responses to a questionnaire. An annual list of the winning bids for government contracts in a chosen county is data, as is the list of stocks on the New York Stock Exchange with last Friday's closing prices.

How are data obtained? Sometimes others have already collected the data. The data may, for example, already reside on a central database somewhere on the Internet, ready for analysis. Or you may need to gather the data from a questionnaire administered to a sample of consumers or employees, or perhaps you can obtain the data from sources such as the newspaper or government publications.

data
observed values of one or more random variables

Data can be classified by the time period in which they were collected, either at approximately the same time, or over two or more time periods. To illustrate the first situation, samples of a new product are mailed to selected consumers on the same date, and their reactions to the product are recorded on a questionnaire returned to the company by mail. To illustrate the second scenario, a product is sampled from the production line for each day for a month, with the number of defective parts recorded for each of these days.

cross-sectional data
data collected at approximately the same time

Data from a consumer mailing on the same date are **cross-sectional data.** Sometimes the time frame within which the data are gathered is simultaneous, as in the stock prices recorded at the end of a trading day. Or, as in the consumer mailing example, the samples could have been mailed out over a period of days, and the potential consumers may respond over a month or so. In either case, however, the time frame is small enough that for purposes of analysis the data are considered to have been collected at the same time.

The cross-sectional study provides a snapshot of the topic of interest at a single point in time. Other studies focus on looking at the topic of interest over time, as in the production line example. **Time-series data,** or *historical data,* result from repeatedly observing a variable at regular intervals, such as daily, monthly, or yearly. Time-series data are ordered by a chronological sequence from the first observation to the last. The Dow Jones Industrial Average on the first day of the month for the last five years can be listed in sequence from five years ago to the present.

time-series data
data collected at different times

Time-ordered data are particularly appropriate for the analysis of a **process,** a concept at the heart of quality management and the operation of a business in general. The outcome of a process is the response variable Y.

process
repeatable sequence of events for accomplishing a specific goal

Examples of processes are easy to find. Some relatively simple processes include answering the phone, machining a metal part on a lathe, scheduling personnel for the evening shift, and entering data into the computer. A more complex process is negotiating a labor contract. An even more complex process is merging two large companies. Complex processes can be broken down into subprocesses, which in turn can often be further broken down.

Consider the process of answering the phone to record a customer's order. The sequence of events consists of the phone ringing, answering the phone, greeting the customer, answering any questions, setting up a shipping date, noting any items requested but not in stock, and then saying good-bye.

A process is attempted to achieve some goal. The process transforms some input into the desired goal, the output. The machining process begins with a solid metal cylinder and finishes with a gleaming, perfectly shaped part. The negotiation of a labor contract begins with a list of demands and constraints and finishes with a handshake and a new contract.

A key characteristic of a process is that the output of the process *varies*. When the outputs are measured, this variability can be analyzed, its sources uncovered, and decisions made and implemented to further reduce this variability, all of which furthers the ultimate goal—customer satisfaction. Reducing variability is a cornerstone of the pursuit of quality.

Regardless of whether the data are cross-sectional or time-series, data can be qualitative or quantitative (numeric). The distinction between quality and quantity is another important basis for classifying variables. Words best describe those characteristics that describe a quality of something, whereas numbers describe quantities. A statistical analysis typically involves both types of variables, which are defined in the next two sections.

Table 1-3.
Examples of categorical
variables.

Categorical Variable	Values
Gender	Male, Female
State of Residence	OR, WA, and 48 others plus DC.
Ethnicity	Caucasian, African-American, Hispanic, Native American, Other
Cola Brand Preference	Coke, Pepsi, RC, Other
Type of Payment	Cash, Check, Credit

Categorical Variables

Possible values of the variable Eye Color include Blue, Brown, Gray, and Green. Eye Color is a **categorical variable** because its values are classifications of the qualities of an object or event. All people with the quality of Blue Eyes are classified into one group, and all people with Brown Eyes are classified into another group. The categories of the variable do not reflect numerical quantities. Blue is neither larger nor smaller than Brown in the way that six is larger than two.

> **categorical variable**
> *values represent distinct, unordered categories of similar objects or events*

The key to recognizing a variable as categorical is to identify the verbal label that defines each value of the variable. For example, Gender is a categorical variable because two types of people can be classified by Gender: Male and Female. Other examples include State of Residence, Ethnic Background, and Cola Brand Preference. Representative values of these categorical variables are presented in Table 1-3.

Some categorical variables—called **binary variables**—have only two possible values, such as Male–Female, Accept–Reject, or Yes–No. Binary variables are also called *dichotomous* variables.

> **binary variable**
> *categorical variable with only two values*

The data that result from the classification of people into discrete categories such as Male and Female or choice of Cola are one of two types: **nominal** and **ordinal data.** For some categorical variables, the values are nonnumeric, but the resulting categories are characterized by a natural ordering, such as class rank indicated by Freshman, Sophomore, Junior, and Senior. Both nominal and ordinal data represent discrete categories, but in one case (nominal) the categories are unordered, and in the other case (ordinal) the categories are ordered.

> **nominal data**
> *each observation is classified into the appropriate un-ordered category of a categorical variable*

Nominal or ordinal data are most meaningfully expressed with verbal labels such as Cash, Check, and Credit. The values of a categorical variable can also be coded numerically as with a 0, 1, and 2, though the use of numeric codes for nonnumeric variables is generally not recommended. The meaning of the value Cash is clear, but does a 0 refer to a cash payment? In addition, particularly when an analysis contains many variables, someone analyzing the data may forget that the numeric codes of 0, 1 and 2 do not represent a numeric variable and perform some arithmetic on these numbers. Adding these values to compute an average, for example, is meaningless. Using meaningful names instead of arbitrary numbers conveys the meaning of the values directly, results in fewer errors when the values of the variable are entered into the computer, and also results in fewer errors during later analysis.

> **ordinal data**
> *each observation is classified into the appropriate or-dered category of a categorical variable*

Sometimes the values of a categorical variable are more naturally expressed numerically, as the number on the jersey of each football player. Although numbers define the values of the variable Jersey Number, this variable is classified as nonnumeric because the numbers define unordered categories. In this situation, the numbers represent nominal data that serve only as verbal labels that do not convey any kind of ordering. Number 55 does not indicate a better or worse player than someone with number 54.

Most studies that involve categorical variables also include numeric variables. A manager interested in the ethnicity of her company's employees would probably compare the average Salary for each of the different ethnic groups. One of these variables is the numeric variable Salary, the variable being compared across groups The other variable is a categorical variable, Ethnicity, which indicates which of the groups each person belongs to. The categorical variable is sometimes called a *grouping variable* in this context because it indicates group membership.

Continuous Variables

Examples of continuous variables include Quarterly Net Sales, Retail Price, or Box Weight. Contrast the numeric values of these variables with the values of a categorical variable such as Eye Color. A continuous variable is a theoretical abstraction described by an underlying numeric progression with an unlimited number of potential values between any two given values.[1] This progression moves from least to most, from very little or none of the characteristic of interest to very much or a maximum amount of the characteristic.

continuous variable
variable with an unlimited number of numeric values between any two values

For **continuous variables,** there is no "next" value after any given value. What number immediately follows 2 lb? Neither 2.001 lb nor 2.000001 lb nor even 2.00000001 lb immediately follows 2 lb. No matter how many zeroes are written after the decimal point, more can always be added. Continuous variables include time, weight, length, volume, and distance.

The theoretical perfect continuity of a continuous variable is never observed. In practice the values of a continuous variable are measured to a specified level of accuracy. Weight is measured, for example, to the nearest hundredth of a pound. Even for continuous variables there is a next number in the ordered sequence of corresponding measurements.

metric data
measurements of a continuous variable

The distinction between **metric data** and the nominal data introduced in the previous section is the distinction between measurement and classification. Metric data are the *measurements* of continuous variables, whereas nominal data result from the *classifications* of objects into categories.

When measuring weight to the nearest hundredth of a pound, 2.01 lb. is the measurement that immediately follows 2.00 lb. A hammer might weigh 2.01387252 lb, but when weighed to the nearest hundredth of a pound the weight of the hammer is correctly measured as 2.01 lb. The continuity that mathematically describes the values of a continuous variable is only approximated by the metric data that inevitably yield distinct categories.

We have been discussing variables and the data that result from the measurement of these variables. Next the distinction between samples and populations is presented—two different methods by which data are gathered and analyzed.

---

1. Another kind of numerical variable is a counting variable, also called a discrete random variable. Counting itself is a statistical analysis and is discussed in the next chapter.

EXERCISES

1-1. List and briefly describe six random variables of interest, at least four of which are from a business context.

1-2. For each of the random variables from 1-1, list three representative values.

1-3. Indicate whether each of the following random variables is categorical or continuous.

a. Labeling a part as Defective or Nondefective in a manufacturing process.

b. Net Quarterly Profit as reported on an income statement.

c. Gender reported in a listing of employees in a department.

d. Performance by the time required to complete a task.

1.3 PATTERNS BLURRED BY SAMPLING INSTABILITY

The practice of statistics documents and explains variability. What is the source for the data that exhibit this variability? For most analyses, the data are just one of many possible samples from a larger population. Occasionally, the data may be analyzed as a complete set without reference to a larger population. This distinction forms the basis of the two major types of statistical analyses, inferential and descriptive.

Samples from Populations

Examples of populations include all registered voters in the United States, all tractors produced at a given plant, or all employees of a company. A **population** may consist of a *fixed number of elements in a given location at a given time,* such as all the registered voters in the United States who intend to vote in the presidential election. An example of a smaller population is all M.B.A. students from a business school graduating from the new curriculum. A population may also be defined by the outcome of a *process over time,* such as cans of soup filled on the assembly line. In the case of a process, the population is defined as the output of the process over time.

> **population**
> *complete set of all existing or potential observations*

In some situations, the entire population is well defined and exists at one point in time. Given sufficient resources, the entire population can be analyzed by taking a **census.** U.S. citizens are most familiar with the ten-year census of the population of the United States by the Bureau of the Census.

> **census**
> *gathering of data on the entire population*

Analysis of the entire population is sometimes either impossible or impractical. Not all registered voters can be asked their presidential preference the day before the election, and not all potential consumers of a new product can be polled regarding the price they would be willing to pay for the product. Or, when the population consists of the outcomes of a process, such as the manufacture of a product, it is impossible to access all of the elements of the population at any one time, because some of the elements do not yet exist.

Instead of conducting a census, most analyses gather data only for a **sample** of the population, with the results of the analysis generalized to the entire population. Drawing a sample from a larger population results in the particular set of people, businesses, or counties, or whatever object is studied. A schematic representation of the relation between a population and a sample is presented in Figure 1-1. Each dot represents a single observation, such as a single company or a single employee.

> **sample**
> *subset of the population*

Figure 1-1.
A population defined by
a process and a sample
from the process, where
each dot represents a
single observation.

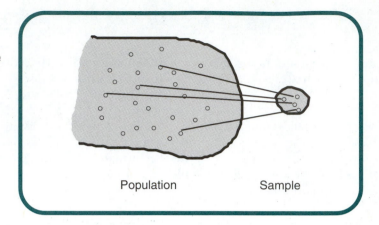

To obtain a sample from a larger population, a procedure is needed for selecting a sample. There are several different procedures for selecting the elements
that actually appear in the sample. If ten elements are to be selected, the first ten
elements encountered could be taken. Or every fifth element could be selected
until ten elements were obtained.

The elements for the most basic sampling method are randomly selected. Randomly select nine employees from the total population of 289 employees of a company, much the way in which lottery numbers are sampled by drawing numbers out
of a rotating bin. If the nine employees were truly selected as a **simple random sample,** then these nine employees were just as likely as any other nine employees to
appear in the sample. Simple random sampling is the most basic of all sampling
methods and is the sampling method assumed for the discussion of statistical inference in later chapters.

> **simple random
> sample**
> *each element of the
> population has the
> same chance of
> selection*

Descriptive versus Inferential Statistics

The relation between a sample and the population from which the sample was
drawn is crucial in most statistical analysis, and indeed, this relationship is the focus
of many applied analyses addressed throughout this text. Sometimes, however, the
goal is simply to describe the available data, without reference to a larger population. **Descriptive statistics** answer questions such as the following: What is the mean
annual salary for all employees in the company? Which ten companies listed on
the New York Stock Exchange today posted the largest gains of their stock? The
next two chapters address the techniques for describing characteristics of the data.

> **descriptive statistics**
> *summarize and
> display aspects of
> the obtained data*

Most statistical analyses, however, consider the data one of many possible arbitrary samples from a larger population or process. The conclusions of the analysis
go beyond the data, with interest focused on the entire population from which the
sample was drawn. For example, consider an analysis of the proportion of males to
females employed at a company. This analysis illustrates a focus beyond the actual
sample of employees, even if data from *all* employees at the company are included
in the analysis. The issue is not an evaluation of the gender of current employees,
but an evaluation of the *process* that hired the employees. From this more general
perspective, the current set of all employees is but one sample produced by the current hiring process. The fundamental challenge of the analysis of *sample* data is a

recognition of the fluctuations of data from sample to sample. The analyst must confront the arbitrariness of any one sample.

The results from the analysis of sample data hint at, but do not completely reveal, the truth.

Flip a coin 10 times and you might get 7 heads. But the probability of a head on any one flip is *not* .70. Flip the same coin another 10 times and 4 heads result, but the probability of a head is also not .40. Sample results present a somewhat blurred view of reality.

Why does the number of heads vary for each set of ten coin flips? The answer is that there is no answer except for pure chance. Yet the characteristics of the underlying population, such as the probability of obtaining a head on any one flip, must be estimated in the presence of sample data characterized by statistical fluctuations, or what is called *random error.* Doing **inferential statistics** is like looking at a far-off mountain with out-of-focus binoculars. You see more than you would otherwise see without the binoculars, but the details are blurred. The key issue for inferential statistics is the extent of the blur. Is the view relatively clear, or badly out of focus?

inferential statistics *estimates characteristics of an entire population from an analysis of data randomly sampled from that population*

As an example of generalizing from a sample to a population, consider a pollster who may poll only several thousand registered voters to predict the outcome of a presidential election that will be based on the preferences of millions of voters. Other than friends and spouses, no one really cares how the several thousand voters in the sample actually vote. The concern is how the millions of all voters will vote. The votes by the relatively small number of voters in the sample are of general interest only because they provide useful information about the *entire* population of voters.

The analysis of inferential statistics begins with the computation of descriptive statistics, which is then followed by the application of inferential techniques. Asking every registered voter in the country for his or her preference before a presidential election is a prohibitively expensive and unnecessary venture. Inferential statistics computed from properly sampled data provide reasonably accurate estimates of the proportion of *all* voters voting for each candidate—in this case from a sample of far less than 1% of all registered voters.

The downside of these inferential procedures is that something cannot be obtained for nothing. Some amount of uncertainty always muddies the results when we estimate a feature of a population from sample information. The statistical flux is always present when only a sample of the population is observed. The only way to obtain the exact percentage voting for a specific presidential candidate is to conduct a census of the tens of millions of registered voters. A relatively accurate estimate can be obtained from a sample of several thousand, but the estimate will not be perfect. For example, 52.4% of the sample may vote for a candidate, but in fact the true percentage across the entire population may be 52.9%. Later chapters show how to estimate the likely amount of error associated with an estimate.

Another issue in sampling is the potential difference between the *intended* population of interest and the *actual* population from which the sample was drawn.

Inferences from analysis of a sample do not *properly generalize to observations that were not eligible for inclusion in the sample.*

How will the entire student body vote for student body president? If you only interview students who frequent the student union building, the results only generalize to students who frequent the student union—not to the student body as a whole. Or, if you include only employees from the local office in the survey, results do not generalize to employees from company offices in other cities. What counts is not what you want, but what you do. The *wish* to generalize statistical results to the entire student body or to company employees in all offices does not make the generalization valid.

Overview of Statistical Analysis

The methods of statistical inference estimate characteristics of the more general population from an analysis of the variability of sample data. These population characteristics are aspects of a statistical model, an equation that describes and explains variability.

> *Much statistical analysis focuses on the construction and evaluation of a* statistical model *of a variable that accounts for the variation of the values of the variable.*

Statistics is the study of variation, and one primary understanding of variation is the identification of its sources with a statistical model. The model accounts for the value of a variable in terms of what can be estimated or known and what is error or unknown.

Consider models of the Price per Share of a stock extensively discussed in Chapters 8 and 9. What causes Price to vary from one company to another? Why is the stock of one company selling at $100 per share and the stock of another company selling at $1 per share? Consider a model in the form of a simple linear equation in which one variable, Earnings per Share (EPS), accounts for the value of another variable, Price per Share (PPS). In addition, a model always contains a random error term, which, in this example, summarizes our lack of knowledge regarding the predictability of PPS.

$$PPS = 19.69 + 5.18 \ (EPS) + error.$$

How does Price per Share vary depending on Earnings per Share? According to this model, if EPS increases by $1, PPS increases by an average of $5.18.

The presence of the random error term indicates that knowing only EPS does not completely explain the value of PPS. The value of PPS estimated by the model from the known information, the value of EPS,

$$Estimated \ PPS = 19.69 + 5.18 \ (EPS),$$

only approximates the actual value of PPS for any one company. Analysis of the model reveals the extent of the error in the estimation of PPS from EPS. Additional models can be constructed that model Price per Share in terms of other related variables, such as Dividends per Share and Book Value per Share. The inclusion of these additional variables typically leads to better estimation and improved understanding of the sources of variation.

Statistical inference estimates the characteristics of the model. Inference takes one of two forms: constructing a confidence interval or testing a hypothesis. Consider the confidence interval first.

Imagine that the percentage of voters voting for a candidate in a single sample is 52%. The actual percentage of *all* voters in the entire population voting for that candidate is probably close to but not exactly 52%. The key issue is that the sample value of the statistic is generally not equal to the corresponding true population value. Drawing another sample from the same population typically results in another sample percentage, such as 51.4%.

Any one sample percentage is not equal to the corresponding population percentage, but a sample percentage is usually close to the unknown population value. The solution to this problem is to construct an interval around the sample percentage that likely contains the unknown percentage of all voters voting for the candidate.

> A confidence interval *(e.g., ±3%) around a sample statistic (e.g., 52%) likely contains the value of the corresponding population characteristic at a given level of confidence (e.g., 95%).*

The confidence interval specifies, for example, that the true population percentage is likely within 3% of the observed value of 52%—between 49% and 55%—for a 95% level of confidence.

The width of the confidence interval communicates the precision of the estimate. A statistical estimate is useful to the extent that the sampling fluctuation from different samples is small. The ±3% interval around 52% ranges from 49% to 55%. This interval is more precise than the ±10% interval that ranges from 42% to 62%. However, the ±3% interval is less precise than the ±1% interval that ranges from 51% to 53%. One gauge of the usefulness of an estimate is the width of the confidence interval. To claim that the true population percentage is somewhere in the interval 52% ± 30% is to say almost nothing about this percentage. If the true population percentage is likely within ±1% of 52%, the sample estimate has almost exactly pinpointed the corresponding population percentage. The sample proportion is useful only to the extent that it reasonably approximates the proportion of the entire population.

The other form of statistical inference is to first hypothesize a specific value of the population parameter and then evaluate the reasonableness of this claim. To evaluate the reasonableness of the claim that 54% of the population will vote for Candidate A, see how close the corresponding percentage of a sample is to 54%. The sample value is typically *not* 54% even if the population value is exactly 54%. The question is, how close is the percentage in the sample to 54%? Hypothesis testing evaluates whether the sample percentage is close enough to consider the claim reasonable.

Suppose a sample percentage of 52% is obtained. Is the value of 52% close enough to the hypothesized value of 54% to provide support for the hypothesis?

> Hypothesis testing *evaluates whether the observed value of the statistic (e.g., 52%) is sufficiently close to the hypothesized population value (e.g., 54%) to render the hypothesis likely.*

If the observed value were 33%, the hypothesis of 54% would be abandoned without a formal statistical test. However, in many situations the outcome is not so clear, in which case the procedures of statistical inference are needed to evaluate the likelihood of the hypothesis.

To evaluate how close 52% is to 54%, formally test the hypothesis of 54% with statistical inference, computing a range of values around 54% that render this value likely or unlikely. The decision criterion regarding a hypothesized population percentage may state that if the observed percentage is more than 4% from the hypothesized value, then the hypothesis is considered unlikely. The sample statistic is close enough to the hypothesized value if it lies within 4% of the hypothesized value. In this example, the observed value of 52% would be considered consistent with the hypothesized value of 54%.

The methods of confidence intervals and hypothesis testing are closely related: *Both methods involve building intervals.* A confidence interval is constructed around the observed sample statistic such as the sample mean or proportion. The purpose of this interval is to specify a range of plausible values for the unobserved population characteristic such as the population mean or proportion. For hypothesis testing, the interval is constructed around the hypothesized value of the population characteristic. The purpose of this interval is to define what is meant by "close enough," that is, the range of values for the sample statistic that renders the hypothesis likely and the remaining values that render the hypothesized value unlikely. Both of these methods of inferential statistics are studied in depth later in this text.

This concludes our introduction to statistics. As we see next, values of a numeric variable, whether from a sample or the entire population, are described by the following kinds of information:

- a statistic that describes the middle of the values
- a statistic that describes the variability of the values around the middle
- a description of the variability of the values according to the frequencies of occurrence of each value
- when applicable, a description of the variability of the values according to their relationship to time

We look at shape and time in Chapter 2; Chapter 3 includes a discussion of the middle and variability of a distribution of values and an introduction to the normal distribution. Next, however, we introduce the primary tool—Microsoft Excel—for obtaining the computations of statistical analysis discussed throughout this text.

EXERCISES

1-4. Management of a marketing division wants to test a new brand of toothpaste in Peoria, Illinois. Your job is to sample the opinions of 250 shoppers at grocery stores throughout the city regarding the desirability of the toothpaste.

a. What is the sample of interest?
b. What is the population to which the results can be properly generalized?

1-5. Consider the following population and sample.
Population: Potential university students
Sample: Students in a high school calculus class are assigned numbers that are then randomly drawn from a hat to appear in the sample.

a. Is the intended population the same as the actual population sampled?

b. Is this a simple random sample of the population from which it was obtained, regardless of whether or not this population is the intended population?

1-6. Identify each of the following studies as either

   i) descriptive statistics
   ii) inferential statistics, confidence interval
   iii) inferential statistics, hypothesis testing

a. Examine the lengths of a sample of 10 manufactured parts to see if the average length of the parts produced by the process is 15.5 inches.
b. Post the average midterm score for this statistics class.
c. Estimate the percentage of the population that will vote for the Democratic presidential candidate.

d. Randomly select 30 babies born within the last year at the maternity ward, and estimate the birth weight of all babies born during the last year.

e. Gather a sample of 25 lightbulbs and measure the time until each bulb burns out. See if the average burn-out time is different from the goal of 400 hours?

1.4 SUMMARY

The values of a variable are generated by some random process that results in their variability. Estimating and explaining this variability is the fundamental purpose of statistical analysis. A primary means of accomplishing this task is a statistical model, an equation that identifies and relates sources of variation to explain the variation of the variable of interest.

The proper use of statistics can enhance the effectiveness of managerial decisions. Statistics provides a set of tools that help managers become better problem solvers in the presence of uncertainty. For example, in many companies the perpetual quest for quality improvement is gaining importance. Most managerial decisions are made in the presence of uncertainty. The essence of uncertainty is captured by the concept of a random variable, with values that result from a random process. The values of variables can be categorical or numeric.

Statistical analysis is performed on data, usually a random sample derived from a larger population. Nominal data result from the classification of the values of a categorical variable. Metric data result from the measurement of a continuous variable. The remaining chapters present many statistical procedures for the analysis of these data.

Analyses at the descriptive level simply describes the available data. Inferential statistics build on these descriptions to form conclusions regarding the characteristics of the larger population from which the data were randomly sampled. The underlying perspective of inferential statistics is that the obtained data comprise just one of many potential random samples. The two procedures of inferential statistics are the construction of confidence intervals around a sample estimate and a hypothesis test of an inferred population value such as the population average. The method of confidence intervals is the more general technique and should be used whenever sample estimates are used to convey information about the entire population.

Statistical analysis virtually always is accomplished with a computer. Many specialized statistics programs provide these analyses. More general spreadsheet programs such as Microsoft Excel also can accomplish many statistical analyses. Although the offerings of the spreadsheet programs are not as extensive as those found in many specialized programs, they are sufficient for many users.

1.5 KEY TERMS

binary variable *7*
categorical variable *7*
census *9*
continuous variable *8*
cross-sectional data *6*
data *5*
descriptive statistics *10*
inferential statistics *11*
metric data *8*
nominal data *7*
observation *3*

ordinal data *7*
population *9*
process *6*
random variable *4*
sample *9*
simple random sample *10*
statistical thinking *2*
statistics *2*
time-series data *6*
value *3*
variable *3*

1.6 REVIEW EXERCISES

ANALYSIS PROBLEMS

1-7. Consider the following population and sample.

Population: Potential consumers of a brand of toothpaste.

Sample: Make three copies of all twenty-six letters of the alphabet. Each copy consists of one letter per index card. Shuffle the index cards and place them in a big bowl. Blindly pick three letters out of the bowl and find the first name in the local phone book that begins with those three letters, or find the first name that alphabetically follows a name with those three letters.

a. Is the intended population the same as the actual population sampled?

b. Is this a simple random sample of the population from which it was obtained, regardless of whether or not this is the intended population?

1-8. Consider the following population and sample.

Population: Potential consumers of a brand of toothpaste.

Sample: A computer places calls to randomly dialed phone numbers (which are then followed up by a trained interviewer once a person is reached on the other end).

a. Is the intended population the same as the actual population sampled?

b. Is this a simple random sample of the population from which it was obtained, regardless of whether or not this population is the intended population?

DISCUSSION QUESTIONS

1. Why is the study of variation so important?

2. What is statistical thinking, and why is it important to managers?

3. Discuss how you could obtain a simple random sample of fifteen students to estimate the mean number of credit hours taken this term by all business majors.

4. What is the distinction between a variable and a value?

5. What is a response variable?

6. Why are the theoretical values of a continuous variable never observed in practice? What do we call the data obtained from the measurement of the values?

7. What is the distinction between nominal and metric data? For which types of variables are these data observed?

8. What information can be obtained with time-series data that is not amenable to analysis with cross-sectional data?

9. Why do we analyze data from samples when the population is of primary interest?

10. What is the distinction between descriptive and inferential statistics?

11. What is the distinction between a population and a process?

12. What is a statistical model? What is its purpose?

13. Explain how both inferential techniques of constructing confidence intervals or doing hypothesis testing involve constructing intervals. Give an example of each.

14. This entire course is about the study of two statistics. What are these statistics?

15. What is the distinction between application specific files and text files? How can you recognize this distinction?

CHAPTER 1 EXTENSION   STATISTICAL ANALYSIS USING EXCEL

E1.1 EXCEL BASICS

The following Excel worksheet is a collection of cells, each cell identified by its column, a letter, and its row, a number. For example, A1 refers to the first cell in the upper left-hand corner. Two types of information can be entered into a cell, a constant or a formula. A *constant* is either numeric, such as 5.48, or text, such as Bill Brown. Data are entered as constants. A *formula* contains references to other cells, and the value of a cell is updated as the value of the precedent cells change.

	A	B	C
1			
2			
3			

Selecting a cell or range of cells is a fundamental activity of Excel. Before performing an activity on one or more cells, such as changing the font or placing a border around the cells, you must first select the cells. Select a cell by clicking on it. Select a range of cells by clicking on the first cell in the range and then, while still holding down the mouse, dragging across the other cells and then releasing the mouse button.

Modifying Data within Cells

ENTERING INFORMATION INTO A SINGLE CELL. To enter a constant, select the cell and then simply enter the information into the cell, as with the numbers 1, 2, 3, and 4 that appear in cells A1 to A4 in the following example. Nonnumeric constants are enclosed by quotes, such as "Bill Brown."

To enter a formula, first enter an equal sign, = , as in Cell B1. Editing of the contents of a cell takes place in the edit bar at the top of the worksheet or directly in the cell itself. To enter a cell reference such as A1 into the formula, type A1 from the keyboard or simply click on Cell A1. Entering the formula =A1 + 5 into Cell B2 means that the contents of Cell B2 will equal the contents of the values of Cell A1 plus 5.

B1	▼	=	=A1+5		
	A	B	C	D	E
1	1	6			
2	2				
3	3				
4	4				

To accept the editing and move to the next cell after entering information into the current cell, use the cursor keys. Or use the Tab key to move right and the Return key to move down. Another possibility is to use the mouse to first accept the current contents by clicking on the check mark before clicking on another cell.

COPYING A FORMULA ACROSS CELLS. To copy a formula from Cell B1 across a range of cells, such as from B1 to B4, select the one cell with the formula, B1, and the remaining cells that will receive the formula.

B1	▼	= =A1+5

	A	B	C	D
1	1	6		
2	2			
3	3			
4	4			
5				

To copy the formula from Cell B1 across the selected cells, invoke the following menu sequence, which means: Choose the Edit menu, choose the Fill option from the menu, and then choose the Down option from the list of options.

Edit ➤ Fill ➤ Down

The formulas that appear in cells B1 to B4 are illustrated with italics in the following figure.

	A	B	C	D
1	1	6		
2	2	7		
3	3	8		
4	4	9		

As the expression was filled down, the cell reference A1 changed to A2, A3, and then A4, indicating the cell in the same row but the previous column. An expression such as A1 is a *relative reference,* which provides directions from the current cell to the referred cell: Stay in the same row but go back one column. If the reference to a cell in a formula should refer to a single cell regardless of the position in the spreadsheet of the current cell, then place a dollar sign ($) in front of the column and row indicators. For example, $A$1 refers to the first cell in the upper left-hand corner of the spreadsheet regardless of where the cell is referenced from throughout the spreadsheet. An expression such as $A$1 is an *absolute reference,* which does not change when the entire formula is filled down to other cells.

AUDITING A CELL FORMULA. Excel provides a helpful visual tool for identifying both the referenced cells that *lead to* the formula that defines the current cell (precedents) and the cells that *depend on* the current cell (dependents).

Click on the cell of interest (e.g., B1)
Tools ➤ Auditing ➤ Trace Precedents

	A	B
1	←—1—►	6
2	2	7
3	3	8
4	4	9

Trace Precedents yields arrows from all cells that lead into the current cell. If the Trace Dependents option is selected, all cells from which the current cell leads are marked with arrows. This tool is an invaluable aid to understanding the potentially complex relationships and formulas that define a worksheet.

INSERTING AND DELETING CELLS. An entire row, column, or specific cells can be added or removed from the worksheet. To add a row or column to the worksheet, first select the entire row or column by clicking on the corresponding row number or column letter at the beginning of the row or column. Then do the following menu sequence.

Click on the Row Number of interest
Insert ➤ Row

A similar procedure is followed when inserting an entire column.
    To insert specific cells, do the following.

Click on the Cells of interest
Insert ➤ Cells...

The resulting dialog box provides a choice of directions that cells should be shifted.

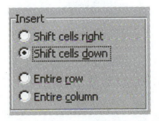

To delete rows, columns, or cells,

Click on the Row, Column, or Cells of interest
Edit ➤ Delete

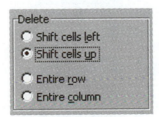

If individual cells were selected instead of an entire row or column, the accompanying dialog box appears.

NAMING CELLS. By default individual cells and cell ranges are referred to by row numbers and column letters. For example, Cell E3 is the cell in Column E and Row 3. The range of cells from Cell A1 to Cell E5 is indicated by A1:E5. To improve the readability of Excel worksheets, Excel allows individual cells and cell ranges to be named. Formulas that refer to these cells can then use the more familiar names rather than the column and row references.

To illustrate the naming of a single cell, consider a simple worksheet that multiplies some numbers by a specified constant. The value of the constant is located in Cell B1.

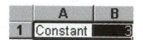

The easiest method of naming the contents of Cell B1 is to type the word Constant in Cell A1, select both cells as shown above, and then do

Insert ➤ Name ➤ Create...

This menu sequence leads to the following dialogue box. Excel automatically detects that the label is in the left column and asks for confirmation. This procedure can simultaneously be applied to a single cell, as illustrated here, or to an entire list of cells. Cell B1 can now be referred to by either the name Constant or its cell reference, $B$1.

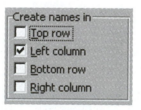

Cell names can also be applied to an entire row or column of cells. The column of numbers to be multiplied begins with the word Input. Select this cell with the label, which is Cell A3, and select the values underneath the label in Cells A4 to A8. Then repeat the preceding menu sequence to name the values.

Now the multiplication can occur in Column B with the formula

$$=\texttt{Input*Constant}$$

entered in Cells B4 to B8. The result is the following worksheet.

	A	B
1	Constant	3
2		
3	Input	Output
4	0	0
5	1	3
6	2	6
7	3	9
8	4	12

Note that the label Constant refers to a single cell and is an absolute cell reference equivalent to $B$1. The label Input refers to a cell range. A reference to Input refers to the value of Input for the given row.

Reading Data from Text Files

Data may also be read from an external file. The current universal means of transferring data between applications is with a text file. Data may also be exchanged directly between Excel and other Microsoft programs. As computer technology advances, more direct exchanges between different types of software such as spreadsheet programs and word processors will occur. Here we discuss only the universally accepted, nonproprietary format of text files.

READING TEXT FILES. Text files are the universal characters of computer programs. Text files represent information stripped down to its most basic form. These files contain no formatting codes such as for underlining or double-spacing, no special storage techniques, no extras whatsoever found in the *application specific files* saved by the usual default from an application.

The advantage of text files is that virtually any application—word processor, spreadsheet program such as Excel, database program, or statistics program—can read and write these files. Application specific files can be read only by the application that created the file or with a special translator. The icon of a document differs for text files and standard application files, as illustrated in Figure E1-1.

> **text file**
> *all individual characters (usually ASCII) include only letters, digits, punctuation, and control characters (e.g., tab, line feed).*

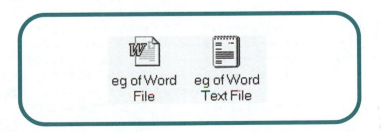

Figure E1-1.
Word icons for application and text files.

Text files can be read and written by virtually any application. Text editors such as Microsoft's Notepad program for Windows and Apple's SimpleText for Macintosh read and write only text files. Attempting to use these programs to process application specific application files results only in gibberish.

STORING DATA IN TEXT FILES. Data consist of individual characters that can be appropriately represented with a text file. The data in the text file may have been retrieved from some other source such as a mainframe database or optical scanner. Or the data may have been entered specifically for these analyses.

> **tab-delimited text file**
> *adjacent values (fields) in each row of text are separated by a tab*

Many text files are defined with adjacent values separated by a delimiter such as a space, comma, or tab. Excel can read and write text files with any character serving as a delimiter. A **tab-delimited text file** is the default, with blanks and commas other common choices. Each row of data, the data for a single observation, is called a *record*.

> **missing value**
> *value of a variable for a specific observation that is not present in the data set.*

Data collected in the "real world" usually do not have all values present for all observations on all variables. That is, usually some data are missing. Blank cells indicate **missing values** in Excel. In the corresponding text file, two delimiters with no intervening text indicate a missing data value.

An example of reading a text data file into Excel follows.

STATISTICAL ILLUSTRATION—Reading and Displaying Data with Excel

DATA

The data were entered into the word processor as in Figure E1-2. Each column lists the values of a single variable, and each row represents the values for a single observation. The → and the ¶ symbols, which print as invisible characters, result from pressing the Tab key and the Return key, respectively. Gender for Sally Jones and Salary for Bradley Kirk are missing.

The data were saved in a file called Employee. Each record in this file contains fields (values) for the variables Name, Age, Gender, Department, and Salary. This file was originally created with a word processor and saved as a text file instead of in the usual default format native to the word processor. For example, saving a file as a text file in Microsoft Word requires invoking the File → Save As . . . menu sequence and then requesting Text Only from the Save File as Type option.

Figure E1-2.
Data as entered into the word processor.

```
Last →First→Age  →  Gender     →     Dept →Salary¶
Doe →  ·John→48  →  M  →   FINC →52325¶
Jones→·Sally  →   35 →      →   ACCT →57000¶
Brown→·George   →  56 →  M  →   MKRT →43550¶
Smith→·Jane→29  →  F  →  ACCT →32470¶
Kirk→ ·Bradley  →  32 →  M  →   SALE → ¶
Downs→·Lee → 61  →  M  →   FINC →72390¶
Ritchie  →   ·Denise   →  25 →  F  →   MKRT →31750¶
Mednick  →   ·Martha  →  35 →  F  →   SALE →38420¶
Zaats→·Phil→38  →  M  →  ACCT →43450¶
```

APPLICATION—EXCEL ANALYSIS

Reading Data into Excel

Excel reads the text data from an external file beginning with the following menu sequence.

File ➤ Open

Navigate through the resulting file structure until you reach the directory with the needed file, as displayed in the following dialog box, then select and open the file.

Step 1. The resulting dialog box refers to a choice between a text file with adjacent fields separated by a delimiter such as a tab and a fixed width format in which the data for a single variable are always in the same columns for each observation.

> Original data type
> Choose the file type that best describes your data:
> ⦿ Delimited   - Characters such as commas or tabs separate each field.
> ○ Fixed width - Fields are aligned in columns with spaces between each field.

Step 2. Choose the specific delimiter and preview the data.

> Delimiters
> ☑ Tab   ☐ Semicolon   ☐ Comma   ☐ Treat consecutive delimiters as one
> ☐ Space ☐ Other: [ ]   Text Qualifier: [" ▼]
>
> Data preview
>
> | Last | First | Age | Gender | Dept | Salary |
> |-------|---------|-----|--------|------|--------|
> | Doe | John | 48 | M | FINC | 52325 |
> | Jones | Sally | 35 | | ACCT | 57000 |
> | Brown | George | 56 | M | MKRT | 43550 |
> | Smith | Jane | 29 | F | ACCT | 32470 |
> | Kirk | Bradley | 32 | M | SALE | |

Step 3. Limited options for formatting the data within each column are presented. By default Excel chooses the General format, which is appropriate for most data, so no modifications need be made in this dialog box. Any changes to this format can be made directly in the following worksheet.

	A	B	C	D	E	F
1	Last	First	Age	Gender	Dept	Salary
2	Doe	John	48	M	FINC	52325
3	Jones	Sally	35		ACCT	57000
4	Brown	George	56	M	MKRT	43550
5	Smith	Jane	29	F	ACCT	32470
6	Kirk	Bradley	32	M	SALE	
7	Downs	Lee	61	M	FINC	72390
8	Ritchie	Denise	25	F	MKRT	31750
9	Mednick	Martha	35	F	SALE	38420
10	Zaats	Phil	38	M	ACCT	43450

Reformatting the Excel Output

The appearance of the initial output can often be improved. For example, (a) salaries can be formatted in dollars, (b) the columns can be resized to reflect the width of the largest values within each field, (c) a line can be drawn under the names of the variables, and (d) the data can be sorted by last name.

(a) To format the salaries, first select the corresponding column by clicking on the F at the top of the Salary column. Next, format the values.

Format ➤ Cells... ➤ Number

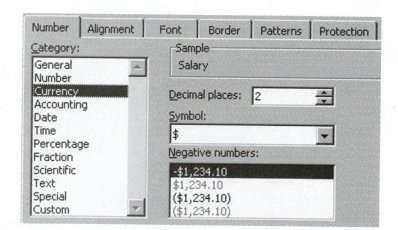

To round off the value to the nearest dollar, change the number of decimal places to 0.

(b) Clicking on the box to the left of the label for Row A selects the entire worksheet. Then doing the following menu sequence changes the column widths for the entire worksheet.

```
Format ➤ Column ➤ AutoFit Selection
```

(c) Obtain the line under the variable names by first selecting the cells in the first row—A1 to F1—that contain these names. Then either use the icon on the formatting toolbar, or do the following menu sequence.

```
Format ➤ Cells... ➤ Border
```

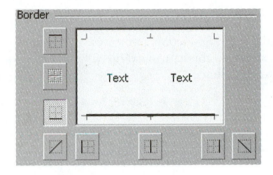

Then select the *Bottom* of the cell for adding the border.

(d) To sort the data, first select the appropriate rows or columns. If the entire worksheet consists solely of the data and variable names, then the entire worksheet can be selected, as illustrated.

```
Data ➤ Sort...
```

The specifics defining the sort are provided in the following dialog box.

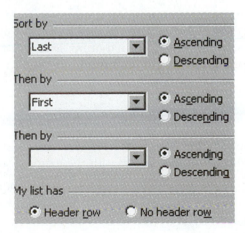

The resulting Excel output appears in Figure E1-3.

Figure E1-3.
Reformatted data.

	A	B	C	D	E	F
1	Last	First	Age	Gender	Dept	Salary
2	Brown	George	56	M	MKRT	$43,550
3	Doe	John	48	M	FINC	$52,325
4	Downs	Lee	61	M	FINC	$72,390
5	Jones	Sally	35		ACCT	$57,000
6	Kirk	Bradley	32	M	SALE	
7	Mednick	Martha	35	F	SALE	$38,420
8	Ritchie	Denise	25	F	MKRT	$31,750
9	Smith	Jane	29	F	ACCT	$32,470
10	Zaats	Phil	38	M	ACCT	$43,450

Saving the Data

To save the data, the usual Save command saves the file in the same format that the original file was read, in this case a text file. To save the data as a regular Excel file, use the Save As command.

File ➤ Save As...

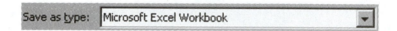

To preserve the original text file, choose a different file name for the Excel worksheet version of the data.

Print the data matrix with the following menu sequence.

File ➤ Print

The subsequent dialog box provides an option for previewing the output on the screen before printing. The following menu sequence modifies the printing options.

File ➤ Page Setup...

Page Setup allows modification of characteristics such as margins, headers and footers, and gridlines, which can be printed or invisible. Print Preview can also be selected from this option as well as directly from the File menu.

Using Excel Graphics

Excel can produce many types of graphs from data stored in a worksheet. Given the already existing data, graphing begins with the menu sequence

Insert ➤ Chart...

Or this menu sequence can be replaced by clicking on the drawing icon located on the standard toolbar.

The choice of chart is made from the following selection offered by Excel.

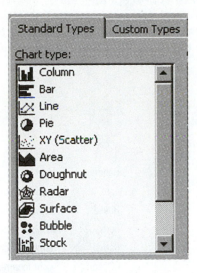

To graph the squaring function, for example, the following data were added to the worksheet. Following the preceding charting instructions, choosing the *XY (Scatter)* plotting option, and responding to several more dialog boxes results in the following graph.

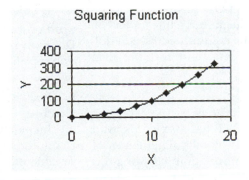

Click on the graph to edit the chart. Virtually any feature of the graph can be edited by double-clicking on that feature. To remove the gray background, for example, double-click on the background. This action results in the following dialog box. Respond by clicking None under Area.

The resulting chart has no background. Exit the chart editing mode by clicking anywhere on the worksheet except the chart.

Our introduction to Excel is now complete. The use of Excel for specific statistical analyses is illustrated throughout this text. The first example of such an analysis appears early in the next chapter on the construction of frequency distributions.

EXERCISES

E1-1. Consider the data in Figure E1-2 on page 22.

a.   What are the variables?
b.   How many observations are there?
c.   What is the value of the variable Gender for the fourth observation?

E1-2. *Enter data from the keyboard.* Consider the data in Figure E1-2 on page 22.

a.   Enter the data, including the variable names, from the keyboard into Excel (or another statistics program), and then save this information in a file with a name such as EMPLOYEE.XLS.
b.   Reformat the worksheet: Add a line under the variable names, adjust the column widths, add dollar signs to the salary data, and sort the data records by salary.

E1-3. *Read data from an existing text file.* The text data file called INTRO.DAT has 40 records, with adjacent values delimited by tabs. The names of the variables and other information regarding this file are described below. Note that the variable names are *not* part of the file.

ID:	A value from 1 to 40.
Gender:	M or F
Age:	two digit number
House:	size of respondent's house in square feet
Beds:	number of beds in respondent's house
Baths:	number of bedrooms in respondent's house
CCDebt:	debt incurred using credit cards
Income:	respondent's annual income

a.   Read the data in the INTRO.DAT file into your word processor. Add the title Intro Data at the top of the first page. Have your word processor print the data.

☞ WARNING: Do *not* save the data from your word processor over the original INTRO.DAT file. Doing so replaces a text data file with an application specific file that can only be read by your word processor (or with a special translation program).

b.   Read the text file INTRO.DAT directly into Excel (or other statistics program).
c.   Include the variable names by inserting a new row at the top of the worksheet, and then add the variable names to the relevant columns. Save the data into a new file with a name such as INTRO.XLS. Print the data.

E1.2 KEY TERMS

missing value *22*
tab delimited text file *22*
text file *21*

CHAPTER 2

Portraying the Values of a Distribution

WHY DO WE CARE?

As shown in the last chapter, understanding some characteristics of the relevant random variables is an important concern underlying successful management. One basic question about a random variable is, How often do specific values (or ranges of values) of the random variable occur? Consider the following situations.

Your job responsibilities include staffing a retail outlet. How likely is it that more than 300 customers will shop in the store today?

You got your car tuned right before the big vacation. Can you expect your car to travel more than 2,000 miles without any problems?

The new union contract provides bonuses to long-term employees. How many employees stay with the company for more than five years?

Examples of random variables include Number of Customers, Time until Breakdown, and Years Employed. Sometimes the product breaks down within several days of being fixed, and on other occasions the product may perform well for years. Of course any specific product breakdown cannot be perfectly predicted from past performance. Yet knowledge of how often each possible value of a random variable is likely to occur leads to more effective business decisions. One of the most basic ways of making sense of a variable is to assess how many times each value (or range of values) has occurred or is likely to occur.

The values of a variable may also have been gathered over time. Another basic way of making sense of such historical or time-series data is to plot the values across time. One basic goal of such a plot is to identify an underlying, systematic pattern and project the pattern into the future to forecast values. Or the goal may be to show a *lack* of pattern so that the value of the variable at each time point only represents random, chance fluctuations. This analysis is often used in conjunction with the identification of a pattern. When the correctly identified pattern is removed from the data, all that should remain is random variation.

The most basic statistical analysis is counting. Almost any data analysis includes counting the values of the variables, both categorical and continuous. The way in which a **frequency distribution** is constructed depends on whether the values of the random variable are nonnumeric categories or numbers. A distribution of nominal data results from the *classification* of the values of a categorical variable. A distribution of metric data results from the *measurement* of the values of a continuous variable. We begin with distributions of categorical variables.

2.1 DISTRIBUTIONS OF CATEGORICAL VARIABLES

Frequency distributions answer questions such as How many? or What percent? How many students in last term's statistics class received an A? How many cars did Jack sell last month? Answering questions like these is straightforward: Simply list each possible value of the variable and the number of times each value occurred. A **frequency,** designated by f, is simply a count. For example, the newly manufactured batch of refrigerators contained 28 defective refrigerators, with 183 ready for shipping.

When comparing distributions of different sample sizes, convert frequencies to **proportions** of the total number of observations. Knowing that 28 refrigerators manufactured at the Toledo plant and 33 received from the Sacramento plant are defective conveys different information to the manager than knowing the corresponding proportions. In this situation, 28 out of 183 refrigerators, or about 0.15, of the Toledo refrigerators are defective, and 33 out of 280, or only 0.09, of the Sacramento refrigerators are defective. Other examples of sample proportions include the proportion of a company's employees who are male, the proportion of sales calls that precede an order, or the proportion of callers to a mail-order business who hang up because all lines are busy. Proportions are also called *relative frequencies*.

Proportions range in value from 0 to 1. A concept closely related to the proportion is the *percentage,* which varies from 0% to 100%. The percentage is simply the proportion multiplied by 100. For example, at one company 42%, or .42, of all employees are female.

Tabular Displays

You already know how to count, so the frequency distribution example for a categorical variable is presented directly.

BUSINESS APPLICATION 2.1—Tabular Distribution of a Categorical Variable

MANAGERIAL PROBLEM

The manager of a small car dealership wants to evaluate the effectiveness of each of four salespeople. The criterion is the number of cars each salesperson sold last week.

Table 2-1.
Data

	A
1	Person
2	Bill
3	Cindy
4	Don
5	Andy
6	Don
7	Bill
8	Cindy
9	Cindy
10	Andy
11	Bill
12	Cindy
13	Cindy
14	Cindy
15	Bill
16	Bill
17	Andy
18	Bill
19	Bill
20	Bill
21	Andy
22	Andy
23	Don
24	Cindy
25	Bill
26	Cindy
27	Bill

DATA

The categorical variable Salesperson has four possible values. The salesperson responsible for each of last week's 26 sales is listed in Table 2-1 in the order of occurrence. The values are listed in a single column with a label at the top. Excel *requires* a column listing the data for this analysis.

APPLICATION—EXCEL BUILT-IN ANALYSIS

Assessing the Excel Output

The Excel frequency distribution of these data appears in Figure 2-1, with the corresponding percentages in Figure 2-2. The sample size in Figure 2-1 is labeled Grand Total.

Count of Person	
Person	Total
Andy	5
Bill	10
Cindy	8
Don	3
Grand Total	26

Figure 2-1.
Frequency distribution of the categorical variable Person.

Figure 2-2.
Frequency distribution of the categorical variable Person also expressed as proportions of the total.

Count of Person		
Person	Total	Prop
Andy	5	0.192
Bill	10	0.385
Cindy	8	0.308
Don	3	0.115
Grand Total	26	1.000

Obtaining the Frequencies

Excel refers to a frequency distribution as a *pivot table*. The Data menu contains the call to this program.

Data ➤ Pivot Table Report...

Step 1. Specify the source of the data, which is the worksheet.

Where is the data that you want to analyze?
⊙ Microsoft Excel list or database

Step 2. Specify the range of the data listed in Table 2-1. Include in this specification the label, Person, found in Cell A1. This range can be entered from the keyboard, outlined with the mouse, or it will be entered automatically if any data cell was selected before entering the Pivot Table program.

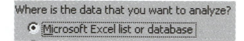

Where is the data that you want to use?

Range: Sheet1!$A$1:$A$27|

Step 3. Drag the Person box at the top right corner over to the Row area, and then drag the Person box to the Data area.

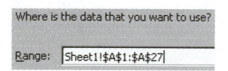

After dragging the Person box twice, the Count of Person dialog box should appear as follows. If it appears with a different label such as Sum of Person, then double-click this box and choose Count from the resulting dialog box.

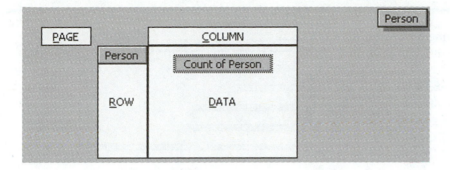

Step 4. Specify the Existing worksheet as the destination of the output, and then specify the starting cell of the output. The result is Figure 2-1.

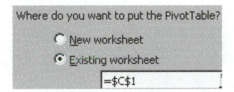

Obtaining the Proportions

By default Excel provides the frequency (counts) of each data value. The simplest way of obtaining proportions is to modify directly the frequency output, the worksheet in Figure 2-1, by adding the appropriate formula. Simply divide each frequency by the sample size.

MANAGERIAL INTERPRETATION

Bill had the most sales, 10 out of 26, or 38% of all sales. Cindy was not far behind with 31% of all sales. Don's performance was the worst of the four.

The same information contained in a tabular display of a frequency distribution can also be presented graphically, as shown next.

Graphical Displays

A graphical display of a frequency distribution is often more effective than a tabular presentation. Two widely used graphical techniques for displaying the values of categorical variables (nominal data) are the bar chart and the pie chart. Their proportions are graphed similarly.

Figure 2-3 displays the frequency distribution of a categorical variable with a **bar chart.** The gaps between the bars signify the unordered values of nominal data. The values of a categorical variable such as Country are labels that cannot be ordered from least to most or vice versa.

> **bar chart**
> *height of each bar is the frequency or proportion of the corresponding category, and adjacent bars do not touch*

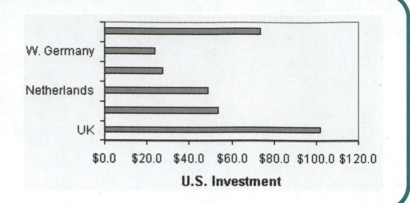

Country	Investment (millions)
UK	$101.9
Japan	$53.4
Netherlands	$49.0
Canada	$27.4
W. Germany	$23.8
All Others	$73.4

Figure 2-3.
Tabular frequency distribution and bar chart of 1989 investment in property in the United States by citizens of other countries.

Figure 2-4.
Pie chart of 1989 investment in property in the United States by citizens of other countries.

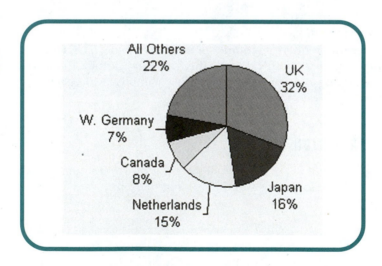

An effective bar chart can appear in many forms. In Figure 2-3 the *frequency axis* is horizontal and the *category axis* is vertical, but an equally acceptable chart could have a horizontal category axis. Another possibility is a bar chart with *two* frequency axes, one for frequencies and one for proportions. In all of these graphs, the space separating each bar indicates a nonnumeric variable.

A **pie chart** also displays the proportions of a categorical variable. Sometimes the proportion of each "slice" of the pie is explicitly labeled, and sometimes the proportion is represented only as the relative size of the slice. The pie chart in Figure 2-4 displays the same investment data presented in the bar chart from Figure 2-3. The bigger the slice of the pie, the larger the corresponding proportion.

Another example of bar and pie charts follows.

pie chart
area of each slice is the proportion of the corresponding category of the frequency distribution of a categorical variable

BUSINESS APPLICATION 2.2—Graphical Distribution of a Categorical Variable

MANAGERIAL PROBLEM

The manager of a small car dealership wants to evaluate the effectiveness of each of four sales people. The criterion is the number of cars each salesperson sold last week.

DATA

The variable Salesperson is a categorical variable with four possible values. The salesperson responsible for each of last week's 26 sales is listed in the order of occurrence in a single column, as shown in Table 2-1 of Business Application 2.1 on page 31.

APPLICATION—EXCEL BUILT-IN ANALYSIS

Assessing the Excel Output
Excel bar and pie charts of these data appear in Figures 2-5 and 2-6.

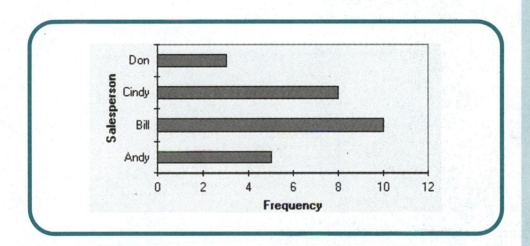

Figure 2-5.
Horizontal bar chart of last week's sales.

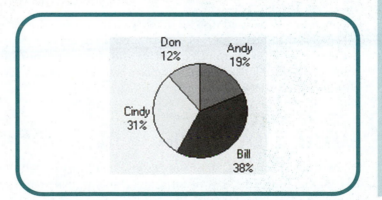

Figure 2-6.
Pie chart of last week's sales.

Obtaining the Bar Chart

First obtain the frequencies shown in Figure 2-1 on page 31.

Insert ➤ Chart...

Step 1—Chart Type. Specify a Bar chart (selected here) or a Column chart. Note that Excel refers to a chart with horizontal bars as a *bar chart*. Standard statistical usage refers to any frequency chart of categorical data as a bar chart. Next choose the Stacked Bar format.

Step 2—Chart Source. For the Data Range, specify the eight cells that contain the four names and corresponding four frequencies, shown in Figure 2-1.

Step 3—Chart Options. Name the Category axis, the Value axis, and the Chart title. Click on the Legend tab and unclick Show legend because only one variable is plotted.

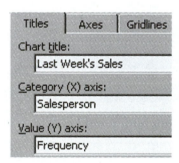

Step 4—Chart Location. Select the location as a new sheet or as an object in the current worksheet.

Obtaining the Pie Chart

A pie chart can be used instead of a bar chart. Follow the same general procedure specified for the bar chart, except request a Pie chart in Step 1. The chart in Figure 2-6 provides both the frequencies and the proportions for each value of the categorical variable. To create this chart, select the Custom Types tab in Step 1 and choose the B&W Pie.

MANAGERIAL INTERPRETATION

Bill had the most sales, 10 out of 26, which comprised 38% of all sales. Cindy was not far behind with 31% of all sales. Don's performance was the worst of the four.

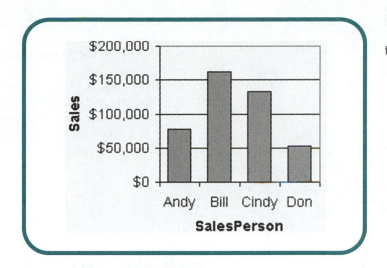

Figure 2-7.
Sales volume (in thousands of dollars) for each of the four salespeople.

The bar and pie charts from the previous example displayed the frequencies of the values of a categorical variable. However, bar and pie charts can display more than frequencies (or proportions).

The value of a continuous variable such as money may also depend on the value of a categorical variable. For example, sales people who sell primarily higher margin top-of-the line cars generate more revenue than those who sell primarily subcompacts. A bar chart of each salesperson's sales revenue complements the information provided by the frequency bar chart. For the bar chart in Figure 2-7, Andy sold $76,991, Bill sold $162,012, Cindy sold $133,065, and Don sold $52,551.

EXERCISES

2-1. Consider the number of subscribers for each of the five largest cable operators (from the *Wall Street Journal*, 3/14/90, p. B1). *Note:* This exercise provides the counts for each value of the categorical variable, so programs such as the Excel Pivot Table program are not used.

Company	Subscribers (in millions)
Tele-Communications	11.90
Time Warner	6.10
Comcast	2.63
Continental Cablevision	2.57
Cox Cable Communications	1.50

a. Construct the tabular distribution of proportions for these data.

b. Draw the bar chart for the number of subscribers by company.
c. Draw the pie chart for the proportion of subscribers by company.
d. Verbally compare the information obtained from the frequencies to the information obtained from the proportions.
e. Determine which presentation of this data you would prefer to use on an overhead projector at a business meeting. Tabular or graphical or both? Frequencies or proportions or both?

2-2. A required statistics class was targeted toward juniors. Some students put off taking the course until their senior year. Some sophomores and freshmen were allowed into the course with special permission and satisfactory advanced placement scores. The following students were in one section of the class.

Name	Class	Name	Class
Amy	Junior	Matthew	Junior
Nathan	Senior	Jason	Junior
Rebecca	Senior	Anshu	Senior
Jennifer	Junior	Dawn	Freshman
James	Junior	Jodi	Junior
Aubre	Sophomore	Chris	Junior
Susan	Junior	Jennifer	Sophomore
Frederick	Senior	Heidi	Junior
Scott	Junior	Lori	Senior

a. Construct the frequency distribution of Class with counts.
b. Construct the frequency distribution of Class with proportions.
c. Draw the bar chart for the values of Class.
d. Draw the pie chart for the values of Class.
e. Verbally compare the information obtained from the frequencies with the information obtained from the proportions.

2.2 DISTRIBUTIONS OF CONTINUOUS VARIABLES

Frequency distributions can also be constructed from metric data, which are the measurements of a continuous variable. Constructing these distributions introduces considerations in addition to those needed for the representation of nominal data. The values of a continuous variable are potentially limitless, which, as we shall see, opens up many more possibilities for portraying the corresponding frequency distribution. Another consideration is that continuous variables are numeric, with values ordered from smallest to largest.

Unlike categorical variables, there is a fundamental difference (discussed in the previous chapter) between the values of a continuous variable and the measurements of those values. This distinction between the theoretical underlying continuity and the discrete measurements of this variable forms the basis for the construction and display of the frequency distribution. The relative coarseness of the metric data approximates the smoothness of the underlying continuous distribution, yet it is the smooth distribution of the underlying continuous values that is of ultimate interest.

Constructing Distributions of Metric Data

bins
partitioning of the values of a continuous variable into a series of adjacent ranges

The limitless number of values of a continuous variable typically lead to a huge number of potential values for the corresponding metric data. Consider the variable Monthly Mortgage Payment. Monthly payments for different houses vary from several hundred dollars to several thousand dollars. Even rounding payments to the nearest dollar leaves thousands of possible values. Moreover, displaying all possible values would not effectively communicate the shape of the distribution. Unless many, many Mortgage Pymts (Payments) were considered, few specific payments such as $924 would have more than a single frequency, and many values would not occur at all. A frequency distribution of hundreds or thousands of mortgage payments is both impractical and uninformative.

width of a bin
distance from lower boundary to upper boundary of the bin

The solution to this problem of too many values is to divide the entire range of values—for example, Mortgage Pymt from $300 to $1600—into a series of adjacent intervals, usually of equal width, called **bins.** Each bin has a **width.** There is no one correct bin width, but a reasonable choice for a distribution of mortgage payments is a bin width of $100.

Table 2-2.
Bins $100 wide.

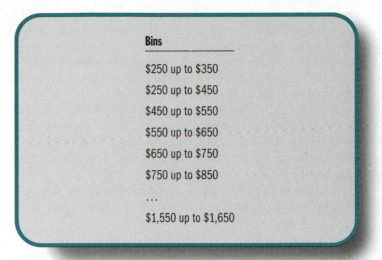

Bins

$250 up to $350

$250 up to $450

$450 up to $550

$550 up to $650

$650 up to $750

$750 up to $850

...

$1,550 up to $1,650

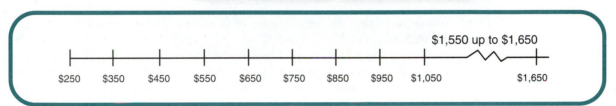

$1,550 up to $1,650

$250 $350 $450 $550 $650 $750 $850 $950 $1,050 $1,650

Figure 2-8.
Some possible bins with a
width of $100 that parti-
tion the values of the
variable Mortgage Pymt
from $300 to $1,600.

The width of the bin that extends from $650 up to $750 is

$$\$750 - \$650 = \$100.$$

Distributions are usually displayed with bins of the same width, though unequal widths can also be used. Table 2-2 illustrates some of the bins of width $100 in the range of values from $300 to $1600, and Figure 2-8 displays the bins graphically.

The smallest possible width is the unit of measurement—measuring waist size to the nearest inch implies that the resulting measurements cannot be placed in bins a quarter of an inch wide. The largest possible width is the entire range of values. In practice, bin width usually falls somewhere between these two extremes.

If all possible values of Mortgage Pymt range from $300 to $1600, then all bins together must include all possible values in this range.

Considered together, the bins encompass all *possible values of interest for the* underlying *continuous variable.*

Using bins to portray a distribution of a continuous variable represents the continuity underlying discrete metric data. To emphasize this continuity, bins that do not contain any measured values are also presented in the display of the distribution, albeit with a frequency of zero.

How do these bins relate to the construction of a frequency distribution?

Frequencies displayed in a distribution of a continuous variable are the number of values within each bin.

These bins collect values that fall within their respective boundaries.

> cutpoints of a bin
> *upper and lower boundaries of the bin*

As illustrated in Figure 2-8, a bin can be defined by its boundaries, or **cutpoints.** Consider the bin that begins at a cutpoint of $650 and extends all the way to a cutpoint of $750. Both $682 and $706 would be placed in the bin defined from $650 to $750. Similarly, both $768 and $844 would be placed in the succeeding bin that ranges from $750 to $850.

What if a value exactly equals a cutpoint? A single value can appear in only one bin, so a value that equals a cutpoint should be systematically assigned to either the lower bin or the higher bin. We follow the arbitrary convention of assigning the value to the higher bin. For example, an exact value of $650 is assigned to the bin from $650 to $750.

> midpoint of a bin
> *value in the center of the bin*

Located midway between the cutpoints is the **midpoint** of the bin, which is the value most representative of all potential values in the bin. The midpoint is calculated according to

$$midpoint = \frac{lower\ cutpoint + upper\ cutpoint}{2}.$$

As illustrated in Figure 2-9, the cutpoints of $650 and $750 define the bin with the midpoint of $700.

To construct the distribution of metric data, first choose a bin width, such as $100. Generally, choose convenient integer midpoints and cutpoints and include all values of interest, in this case from $300 to $1,600. Table 2-3 tallies the values that fall within each of the bins.

This and previous sections presented the basic concepts underlying the construction of frequency distributions of metric data. The next section pursues ways of displaying these distributions to represent the underlying continuous variable.

Displaying Distributions of Metric Data

A frequency distribution is presented in tabular or graphical format. For a continuous variable, the tabular format includes listing the adjacent bins, the midpoint

Figure 2-9. Characteristics of the bin from $650 up to $750.

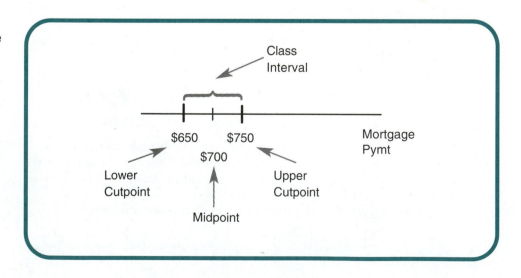

Table 2-3.
Assigning data values
to bins.

No.	Pymt		Bin Assignment
1	$1,096	⟶	Place in the $1,050 to $1,150 bin
2	$729	⟶	Place in the $650 to $750 bin
3	$873	⟶	Place in the $850 to $950 bin
4	$1,557	⟶	Place in the $1,550 to $1,650 bin
5	$704	⟶	Place in the $650 to $750 bin
6	$405	⟶	Place in the $350 to $450 bin
7	$931	⟶	Place in the $850 to $950 bin
8	$886	⟶	Place in the $850 to $950 bin
9	$637	⟶	Place in the $550 to $650 bin
10	$1,180	⟶	Place in the $1,150 to $1,250 bin
11	$605	⟶	Place in the $550 to $650 bin
12	$1,484	⟶	Place in the $1,450 to $1,550 bin
13	$952	⟶	Place in the $950 to $1,050 bin
14	$842	⟶	Place in the $750 to $850 bin

of each bin, and the corresponding frequencies and/or proportions of each bin. The information from Table 2-3 is summarized in Table 2-4. The table also includes the proportions of values within each bin. Each proportion is the corresponding frequency divided by the total number of values, 14.

A common method for graphing distributions of metric data is a **histogram.** The bars touch in a histogram to emphasize the underlying continuity of the continuous variable. The vertical axis can display either frequencies or proportions, or two axes can be included to display both frequencies and proportions. The histogram in Figure 2-10 labels the cutpoints of the bins, but labeling the midpoints instead is equally effective.

Bins with zero frequencies, such as the bin with cutpoints $450 and $550, are included in the histogram; this is easier to see in the outline of this histogram presented in Figure 2-11. Note that the histogram overlaps the horizontal axis when the frequency of the corresponding bin is zero.

An equivalent alternative to the histogram is a **frequency polygon.** Each corner of a frequency polygon is represented by the middle of the top of a bar of the corresponding histogram. An example of a frequency polygon for these data, and its relation to a histogram, appears in Figure 2-12.

The histogram or frequency polygon chosen to display the distribution of the continuous variable is like a snapshot. Before the snapshot can be taken, its graininess or sharpness, as set by the width of the bins, must first be determined. How many bins should be chosen? There is no one correct number, but the number of bins should represent a reasonable trade-off between accuracy and practicality.

histogram
displays the frequencies (or related indices such as the proportion) of metric data by the heights of touching, adjacent bars, with each bar centered over the corresponding midpoint

frequency polygon
displays the frequencies (or related indices) of metric data by corners of a polygon, with adjacent corners connected by lines

Table 2-4.
The frequency
distribution of Mortgage
Pymt.

Bin	Midpoint	Freq (*f*)	Prop (*p*)
$250 to $350	$300	0	0.000
$350 to $450	$400	1	0.071
$450 to $550	$500	0	0.000
$550 to $650	$600	2	0.143
$650 to $750	$700	2	0.143
$750 to $850	$800	1	0.071
$850 to $950	$900	3	0.214
$950 to $1,050	$1,000	1	0.071
$1,050 to $1,150	$1,100	1	0.071
$1,150 to $1,250	$1,200	1	0.071
$1,250 to $1,350	$1,300	0	0.000
$1,350 to $1,450	$1,400	0	0.000
$1,450 to $1,550	$1,500	1	0.071
$1,550 to $1,650	$1,600	1	0.071
		14	1.000

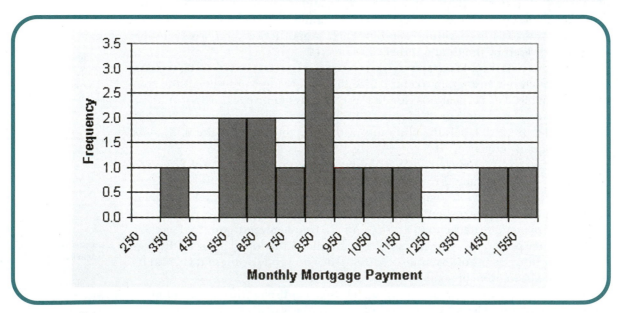

Figure 2-10.
Histogram of the 14
monthly mortgage
payments.

If the bins are too wide, accuracy is lost as the snapshot of the distribution becomes too grainy. If the bins are too narrow, the number of bins may become unwieldy, and, moreover, many of the bins may have zero frequencies. Too many bins and the view is too sharp and lacks perspective. The goal is not to obtain the most

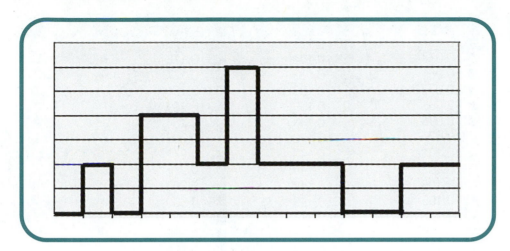

Figure 2-11.
Outline of the histogram
of the 14 monthly
mortgage payments,
emphasizing that bins
with zero frequencies
are included.

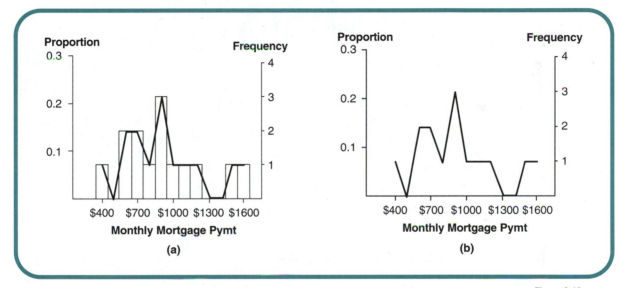

Figure 2-12.
The histogram (gray)
and the superimposed
frequency polygon
(black) are shown in (a).
Only the frequency
polygon appears in (b).

precise representation possible but the most *useful* representation. As with most of life, final decisions represent compromises. Most distributions are usually best displayed with between 5 and 15 bins, as illustrated next.

BUSINESS APPLICATION 2.3—Frequency Distribution of a Continuous Variable

MANAGERIAL PROBLEM

A well-known large manufacturer of machined parts[1] recently implemented statistical methods to improve quality. One critical part has been particularly difficult to

---

1. These data are from a manufacturing application performed at a real company. The company, however, wishes to remain anonymous.

Table 2-5.
Sorted values above a fixed reference point, measured to 0.001 of an inch.

	A
1	Meas
2	0.037
3	0.051
4	0.072
5	0.085
6	0.095
7	0.096
8	0.101
9	0.103
10	0.105
11	0.106
12	0.107
13	0.108
14	0.108
15	0.116
16	0.117
17	0.119

	A
18	0.123
19	0.124
20	0.133
21	0.133
22	0.139
23	0.140
24	0.140
25	0.143
26	0.146
27	0.149
28	0.153
29	0.154
30	0.156
31	0.159
32	0.163
33	0.168
34	0.172

	A
35	0.175
36	0.176
37	0.177
38	0.181
39	0.189
40	0.234
41	0.236
42	0.241
43	0.276
44	0.293
45	0.300
46	0.321
47	0.336
48	0.395
49	0.400

manufacture properly. In over ten years of manufacturing this part, the company has endured an unacceptably high level of scrap and rework. To better understand and control sources of undesired variation, measurements of a critical dimension—length—were obtained from 48 test parts. The long-term goal is to minimize variability of output even when all parts are acceptable, but any value 0.300 and above exceeds the engineering specification, resulting in a nonfunctional part that must be scrapped.

DATA

The 48 values in Table 2-5 are the measurements after completion of the machining process expressed in how many thousandths of an inch the measurement is above a fixed reference point. For convenience, these values are sorted from the smallest to the largest value. This sort is *not* required for the accompanying analyses.

APPLICATION—EXCEL BUILT-IN ANALYSIS

Assessing the Excel Output

As a first step toward understanding process variability, obtain the histogram of this distribution. Management first considered constructing a frequency distribution in which the bin width is as small as possible: a measurement unit of 0.001. A measured value such as 0.037 represents all possible distances from 0.0365 up to 0.0375.

The frequency distribution based on this bin width, however, provides a poor representation of these values. One problem with the bin size of 0.001 is the large number of zero frequencies. The measurements vary all the way from 0.037 to 0.400, yet most of the values between these two extremes—such as 0.038, 0.039—simply do not occur. Another problem is that this frequency distribution is too long for convenient display. To illustrate these problems, Figure 2-13 displays the fre-

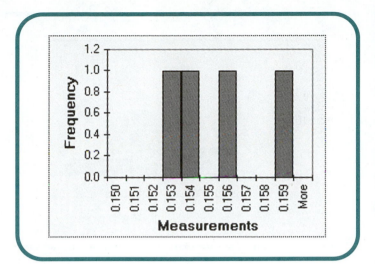

Figure 2-13.
Partial modified
Excel histogram for
a bin width of .001
(only including
values from 0.150
to 0.159).

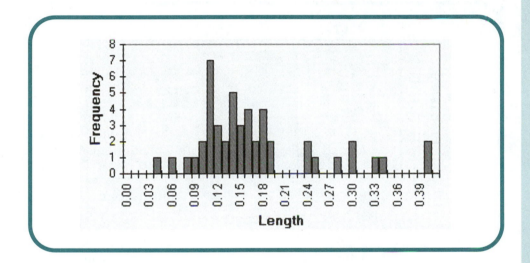

Figure 2-14.
Modified histogram
for a bin width of
.01.

quency distribution of these measurements. To conserve space, only the values from 0.150 to 0.159 are listed.

Before grouping approximately equal values into bins, select the bin width. Figures 2-14, 2-15, and 2-16 illustrate three possible groupings.

Specifying the Bins

To construct a frequency distribution of a continuous variable, enter the *upper* boundary or cutpoint of each bin onto the worksheet. Generally, somewhere between 5 to 15 bins adequately portray the distribution. One way to enter cutpoints is with the Series feature. First enter a descriptive label, and then enter the ending value of the first bin, as in Cells B1 and B2.

Figure 2-15.
Modified histogram
for a bin width of
.05.

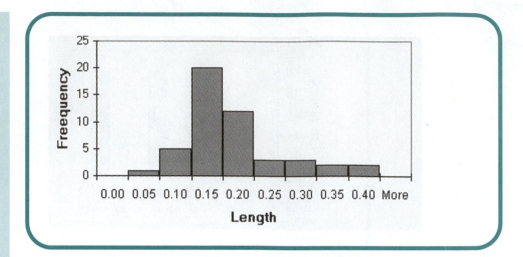

Figure 2-16.
Modified histogram
for a bin width of
.10.

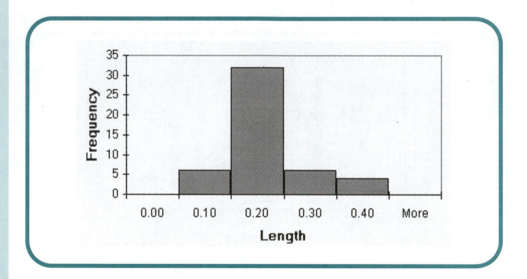

Select the first data value, in this case 0.00. Then invoke the menu sequence

Edit ➤ Fill ➤ Series...

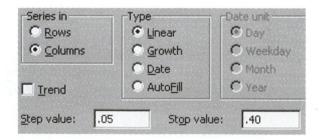

Respond to the accompanying dialog box to enter all remaining upper cutpoints of the succeeding bins. The Step Value defines the width of each bin.

The result is the accompanying complete set of upper cutpoints for all bins. For example, the 0.10 in Cell B4 marks the end of the bin that varies from beyond 0.05 up to 0.10.

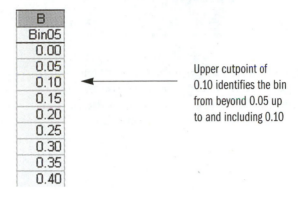

Upper cutpoint of 0.10 identifies the bin from beyond 0.05 up to and including 0.10

Obtaining the Histogram

Call up the frequency distribution program with the following menu sequence and resulting dialog box.[2]

$$Tools \ \blacktriangleright \ Data\ Analysis...\ \blacktriangleright\ Histogram$$

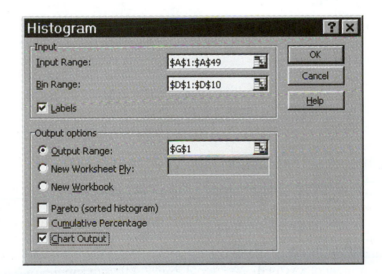

Despite the label Excel provides, the resulting chart is not a histogram because gaps separate adjacent bars. To obtain a true histogram, modify the chart computed by Excel. Double-click on one of the bars, select the Options tab, and set

2. The Data Analysis option does not appear under the Tools menu in the default installation of Excel. If this option is not present, select the Add-Ins . . . option under Tools and check the Analysis Toolpack box. If that possibility is not present in the Add-Ins . . . dialog box, then return to the procedure that initially installed Excel and add the Data Analysis option.

Gap Width to zero. (Excel 5 users invoke the 1 Column Group . . . option under the Format menu to change Gap Width.)

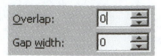

Unfortunately, the numeric values on the horizontal axis of the resulting histogram are not correctly displayed. These values are the bin upper cutpoints, but Excel plots each cutpoint in the middle of each bar of the histogram as if it were a midpoint. To correct this, copy the graph and paste into a drawing environment such as that provided by Microsoft Word. Use the Word Paste Special command found under the Edit menu to specify that the histogram be pasted as a Picture. Double-click on the histogram, and then select each of the numeric values by clicking on each value while holding down the Shift key. Then slide the numeric values on this axis to the right to align each value under the upper cutpoint instead of the midpoint.

Remove the gray background by double-clicking on the background and selecting None for Area. Remove the redundant legend and title by selecting each object and pushing the Delete key.

STATISTICAL PRINCIPLE

The distribution based on the bin width of the precision of measurement, .001, does not reveal the important characteristics of the distribution of measurements. This display of the data has too many possible values to list conveniently, and too many values did not occur. The most generally useful frequency distribution of measurements for these data is with a bin width of .05. The bin width of .01 reveals too much detail and the bin width of .10 obscures too much information.

MANAGERIAL INTERPRETATION

Most of the parts are within tolerance, but five of the 48 measurements exceed the unacceptable value of 0.300. All five values are outliers or potential outliers. Perhaps the cause of this undesirable variation can be identified. It is possible that some specific characteristic of the machining process differed from that of the acceptable parts. Perhaps only the second shift machinist manufactured them, or a different cutting tool was used, or material from a different supplier was used only for these five parts. Further substantive study of the machining process is needed to uncover the cause of this undesirable variation.

For most data sets, organizing metric data with bins effectively approximates the distribution of the underlying continuous variable. The bins group similar values so that the total number of bins considerably reduces the total number of in-

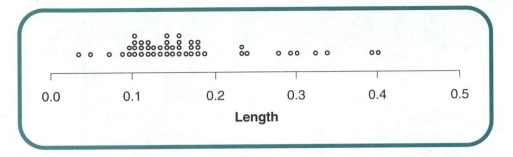

Figure 2-17.
A dit plot of the data
from the previous
example.

dividual values. This grouping solves the problem of having too many data values to display conveniently or meaningfully.

Some data sets, however, are small. Either not much data was available or excessive expense prevented the collection of more than a small number of values. For small data sets, alternative graphical displays of a continuous variable called **dit plots** display each *individual* value of the distribution. A common symbol used in the dit plot is the dot. As the dots pile up, they begin to resemble the bars on a histogram. The higher the stack, the greater the frequency of the corresponding value, as shown in Figure 2-17.

To recapitulate, with or without bins the construction of any frequency distribution includes a list of the values of a variable and the associated frequencies. From these frequencies, proportions may be computed. For a continuous variable, cumulative proportions and cumulative frequencies may also be computed. These calculations are the subject of the next section.

> **dit plot**
> *displays each individual data value with a graphical symbol that is stacked to indicate repeated occurrences of approximately equal values*

Calculating Cumulative Distributions

Unlike the values of categorical variables, the numeric values of a continuous variable can be sorted from smallest to largest or vice versa before frequencies are computed. Questions such as the following can then be answered.

How many parts are *at least* .300 inch wide?

How many monthly mortgage payments are *at most* $1,000?

Cumulative frequency questions contain phrases such as *at least* or *at most*. Because cumulative frequency distributions also apply to proportions, a continuous variable can be represented by four different distributions: frequencies, proportions, cumulative frequencies, and cumulative proportions. Table 2-6 illustrates all four types of frequencies.

Figure 2-18 plots these cumulative distributions. Frequencies are either zero or positive, so the cumulative distribution has a characteristic pattern of moving uphill or staying at the same level when moving from left to right along the variable axis.

The cumulative distribution is useful when we are interested in the number or percentage of the observed values that lie *below* or *above* a specified value. What is the value of the distribution in which half of the values are below the specified value and half of the values are above it? To obtain an approximate answer to this

> **cumulative frequency of the value of a continuous variable**
> *sum of the frequencies of all values up to and including the value*

Table 2-6.
The frequency distributions of Mortgage Pymt.

Bin (lb)	Midpoint	Freq (f)	Prop (p)	Cum. Freq.	Cum. Prop
$250 to $350	$300	0	0.000	0	0.000
$350 to $450	$400	1	0.071	1	0.071
$450 to $550	$500	0	0.000	1	0.071
$550 to $650	$600	2	0.143	3	0.214
$650 to $750	$700	2	0.143	5	0.357
$750 to $850	$800	1	0.071	6	0.429
$850 to $950	$900	3	0.214	9	0.643
$950 to $1,050	$1,000	1	0.071	10	0.714
$1,050 to $1,150	$1,100	1	0.071	11	0.786
$1,150 to $1,250	$1,200	1	0.071	12	0.857
$1,250 to $1,350	$1,300	0	0.000	12	0.857
$1,350 to $1,450	$1,400	0	0.000	12	0.857
$1,450 to $1,550	$1,500	1	0.071	13	0.929
$1,550 to $1,650	$1,600	1	0.071	14	1.000

Figure 2-18.
Cumulative histogram and frequency polygon for the mortgage payment data.

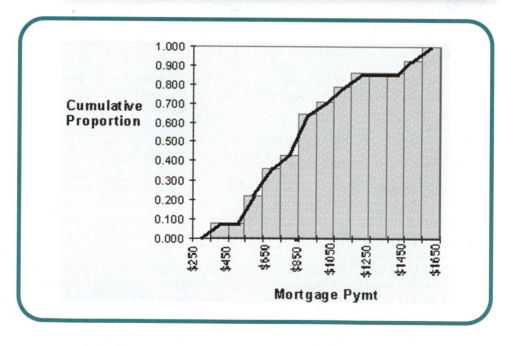

question, identify the value of the distribution with the specified cumulative proportion. Figure 2-19 illustrates that approximately half of the values are smaller than $840 and that approximately half of the values are larger.

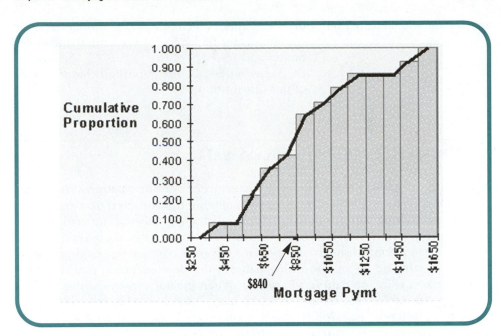

Figure 2-19.
The value $840 has a
cumulative proportion of
0.5, the middle value in
the distribution of
mortgage payments.

EXERCISES

2-3. Complete the remainder of this table.

Mechanical

Bin	Midpt	Freq	Propor-tion	Cum Freq	Cum Prop
	60	1			
	70	4			
	80	17			
	90	30			
	100	35			
	110	24			
	120	12			
	130	2			

2-4. The following data represent scores on three different quizzes by five students. Do this analysis by hand, without the computer.

Application

	Y_1	Y_2	Y_3
Bill	0	2	3
Jim	4	5	2
Sally	2	3	3
Sue	1	7	5
Jeff	4	3	5

a. Assume that Y_3 is a continuous variable. Display in tabular form the frequency distribution for frequencies, proportions, cumulative frequencies, and cumulative proportions. Include the bins and corresponding midpoint. Use a bin width that is the same as the precision of measurement, which is 1 unit.

b. Plot the histogram of the frequencies for Y_3.

c. Plot the frequency polygon of the frequencies for Y_3.

d. Plot the dit plot of the frequencies for Y_3.

e. Determine which of the plots provides the most useful characterization of the distribution and why?

f. Verbally describe the characteristics of this distribution.

2-5. The following 25 family incomes were randomly sampled from a recent census.

Application

$3,810	$20,005	$11,150	$2,860
$31,790	$1,255	$2,805	$9,460
$3,205	$11,005	$10,005	$23,570
$19,055	$6,915	$6,815	$33,010
$52,535	$32,500	$25,005	$8,220
$30,240	$84,810	$14,385	$5,110
$10,005			

Compute the histograms for these data with a bin width of

a. $5,000
b. $10,000
c. $20,000

d. Determine which bin width most effectively communicates the shape of the underlying distribution and why?
e. Verbally describe the important characteristics of this distribution.

2.3 TIME-SERIES PLOTS OF PROCESS DATA

time-series plot
displays the values of the process output in the order in which the values occurred

A primary use of time-ordered data is to detect trends or other patterns that occur over time. Managers who become adept at analyzing time-ordered data are able to uncover underlying patterns in the presence of chance statistical fluctuations. Are gross revenues rising? Is March the lowest month for sales each year? Is customer satisfaction increasing over time? Or, conversely, the interest might focus on establishing the *lack* of an underlying pattern, the demonstration that the time-ordered data exhibit no pattern whatsoever. When the correctly identified pattern is removed from the data, all that should remain is random, chance variation.

Several different types of relatively sophisticated statistical analyses can accomplish this search for patterns, but often a simple charting of the data such as a **time-series plot** reveals the underlying patterns. A key to analyzing a time series is to understand the form of any underlying pattern of the data ordered over time. The underlying patterns are presented next.

trend component *T* of a time series *Y*
long-term, gradual increase or decrease of the variable Y

This pattern potentially consists of several different components, all of which combine to yield the observed values of the time series. A time-series analysis can isolate each component and quantify the extent to which each component influences the form of the observed data. If the individual components of a time series are isolated and identified, a forecast can project the underlying pattern into the future.

cyclical component *C* of a time series *Y*
gradual, long-term, up-and-down potentially irregular swings of the variable Y

The most basic time-series component is long-term growth or decline called a **trend component.** The form of the trend pattern may be linear or nonlinear, as illustrated in Figure 2-20. A linear trend pattern such as in (a) and (b) of Figure 2-20 is the most commonly encountered trend pattern.

The **cyclical component** modifies the trend component. For most business and economic data, the cyclical component is measured in periods of many years. This component reflects broad, irregular swings on either side of the trend line, as illustrated in Figure 2-21.

seasonal component *S* of a time series *Y*
regular, relatively short-term repetitive up-and-down fluctuations of the variable Y

In addition to the trend and cyclical components, time-series data may include a **seasonal component.** For much business and economic data, the seasonal component is measured in quarters of the year, literally the four seasons of winter, spring, summer, and fall. Two seasonal components in the absence of cycles are illustrated in Figure 2-22.

error component *E* of a time series *Y*
random increase or decrease of the variable Y over time

The trend, cyclical, and seasonal components combine to form the pattern underlying the time-series data—the values of *Y* ordered over time—though not all three of these components characterize every data set. An important purpose of time-series analysis is to isolate each of these three components and demonstrate how each affects the value of *Y* over time, including forecasts. The identification of this pattern, the predictable aspect of a time series, however, is complicated by the presence of an **error component.**

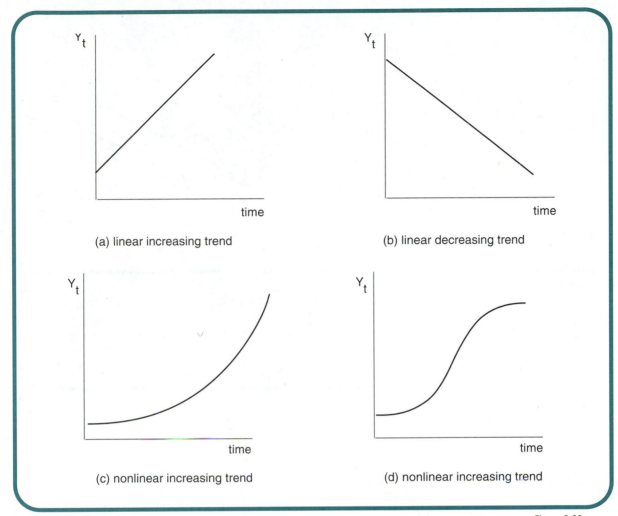

(a) linear increasing trend

(b) linear decreasing trend

(c) nonlinear increasing trend

(d) nonlinear increasing trend

Figure 2-20.
Four types of trend patterns.

Because all time series include random error, pure trend, cyclical, and seasonal components or combinations of these components are observed together with the error component.

The specific combination of trend, cyclical, or seasonal components that defines the underlying pattern of a time series is observed in the presence of random error.

The forecast is based on the underlying pattern delineated from the random error or noise that obscures this pattern. Isolating the pattern is a central goal of a time-series analysis.

The stable, predictable component of a time series is the specific combination of trend, cyclical, and seasonal components that characterizes the particular time series. How do these components combine to result in a value of Y_t? One of two models accounts for the underlying pattern, an *additive* model or a *multiplicative*

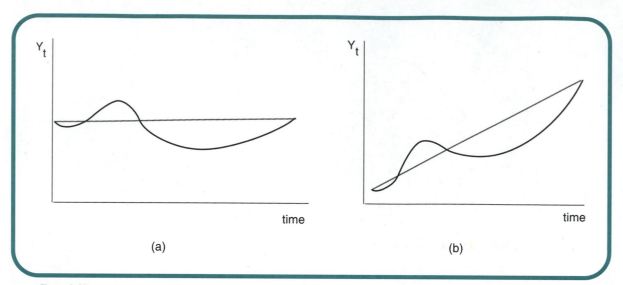

Figure 2-21.
Two time series consist-
ing of the same cyclical
component imposed on
(a) no trend and (b) a
positive linear trend.

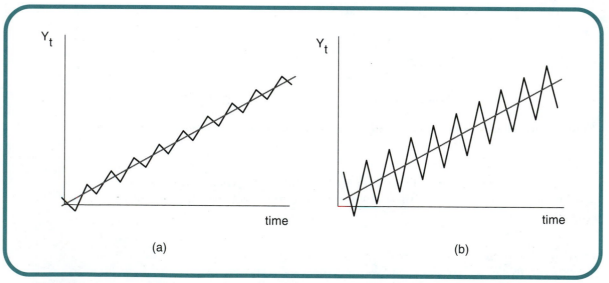

Figure 2-22.
Two seasonal patterns
imposed on the same
trend.

model. The additive model expresses Y_t as the sum of the trend, cyclical, seasonal, and error components.

$$
\underset{\text{data}}{\boxed{Y_t}} = \underset{\text{predictable}}{\boxed{T_t + C_t + S_t}} + \underset{\text{random}}{\boxed{E_t}}
$$

Additive model of time-series data:

The cyclical, seasonal, and error components are each a fixed number of units above or below the underlying trend. For example, if the seasonal component is −$12.89 and there is no cyclical component, then the effect of that season is to lower Y_t $12.89 *below* the value that considers only the trend. If the error component is $4.23 at time t, then the effect of error on Y_t is an increase of $4.23 above the combined influence of trend and seasonality.

The multiplicative model explains the value of Y at time t as a product of the individual components.

$$Y_t = T_t \cdot C_t \cdot S_t \cdot E_t$$

data   predictable   random

For the multiplicative model, the C, S, and E components are expressed as percentages above or below the underlying trend. Each percentage is a ratio with values above or below the baseline 1. The trend component T is expressed in the original units of Y, and the C, S, and E ratios modify the underlying trend by multiplication to yield the actual data. With the multiplicative model, the larger the trend, the stronger the influence of the remaining components. For the additive model, the influence of a given value of C, S, or E is the same for *all* values of T.

To illustrate, consider a time series with no cyclical component C and a seasonal component for the third quarter of $S_3 = 1.2$, which means that Y is 20% above the annual average during this season. Assume that the trend at Time 3 is $T_3 = 5$. The stable component of Y_3 from the multiplicative model is the combination of trend and seasonality, or $(5)(1.2) = 6.0$. The next third quarter is at Time 7, so $S_3 = S_7 = 1.2$. What if the trend has increased to $T_7 = 10$? The stable aspect of Y_7 is $(10)(1.2) = 12.0$. The seasonal component of 20% increased the trend at Time 3 by 1 unit, and at Time 7 the *same* seasonal component increased the larger trend by 2 units.

The forecast is based on the identification of the underlying stable component, free of the obscuring error.

The forecast extends into the future the stable pattern of trend, cyclical, and seasonal components underlying the historical data.

Figure 2-23 presents examples of stable patterns that reflect different combinations of trend, cyclical, and seasonal components embedded in the presence of random errors. Each example presents an underlying stable pattern in the context of little random error and then considerably more random error.

A more complex time series involves a combination of trend and seasonality in the presence of random error, as shown in Figure 2-24.

The most general type of time series is influenced by all four components, a stable pattern consisting of trend, cyclical, and seasonal components observed in the presence of the random error component, as shown in Figure 2-25.

How is the stable pattern detected in the presence of the random error, and how are the specific components that contribute to the pattern isolated from each

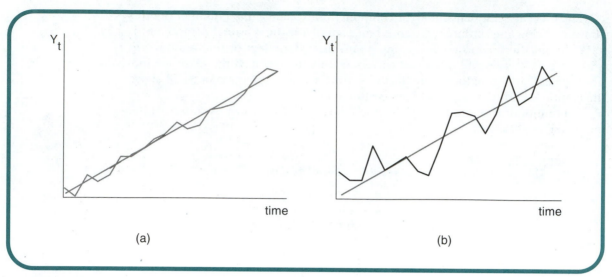

Figure 2-23.
Two time series with the same linear trend in the presence of little additive random error (a) and considerably more random error (b).

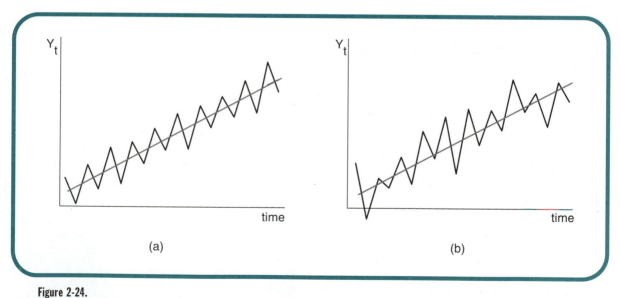

Figure 2-24.
Two time series with the same additive seasonal component imposed on the same linear trend in the presence of (a) little additive random error and (b) considerably more random error.

other? Although sophisticated methods for accomplishing these tasks are beyond the scope of this discussion, fortunately a simple visual inspection often provides much of this information, though in qualitative form, as illustrated next.

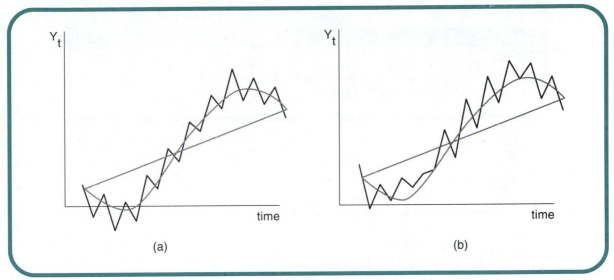

Figure 2-25.
Two time series with the same trend, cyclical, and seasonal components with (a) no random error and (b) additive random error that perturbs the pattern in (a).

BUSINESS APPLICATION 2.4—Time-Series Plot

MANAGERIAL PROBLEM

A mail-order company depends on its phone response to customer inquiries and orders. Management at one mail-order company was concerned that some orders and potential customers were lost because of inadequate service. The study of this problem included recording the number of seconds that callers were placed on hold at various times throughout the business day.

DATA

Every two hours over four days, management monitored the number of seconds that individual customers were placed on hold at a mail-order firm. The data appear in Table 2-7.

APPLICATION—EXCEL GRAPHICS

Assessing the Excel Output
The breaks in Figure 2-26 represent times that the business is closed. No data are collected each day from 5 P.M. to 9 A.M.

	A	B	C	D	E	F	G	H	I	J	K	L	M	N	O	P	Q	R	S	T	U
1	Day			1					2					3					4		
2	Hour	9	11	1	3	5	9	11	1	3	5	9	11	1	3	5	9	11	1	3	5
3	Sec on Hold	0	12	3	28	7	2	9	5	22	6	0	13	4	29	4	0	7	5	19	7

Table 2-7.
Number of seconds individual customers were placed on hold.

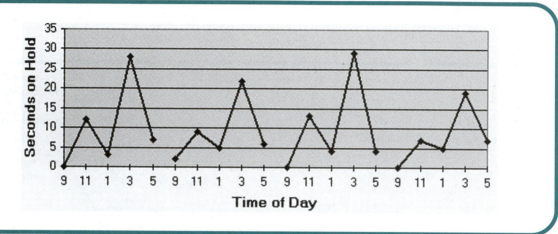

Figure 2-26.
Number of seconds that individual customers were placed on hold, plotted every two hours over four days.

Obtaining the Graph

Obtain the time-series plot with an Excel Line chart.

Insert ➤ Chart...

Select the region on the sheet for the graph to appear.

Step 1—Chart Type. Specify a Line chart, which is for a categorical (nonnumeric) horizontal axis. Then choose a format, such as the line with markers to display each data value.

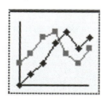

Step 2—Chart Source. For Data Range, specify the cells that include the values for the vertical axis, the Seconds on Hold. Click on the Series tab and specify the numeric values for the Category (X) labels, Hour.

Data range: =Sheet1!$B$3:$U$3

Category (X) axis labels: =Sheet1!$B$2:$U$2

Step 3—Chart Options. Select the Legend tab and then unclick the Show legend checkbox to remove the redundant legend. Select the Titles tab, and name the *X* and *Y* axes as well as the chart.

☐ Show legend

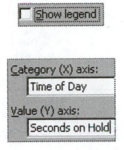

Category (X) axis:

Time of Day

Value (Y) axis:

Seconds on Hold

Step 4—Chart Location. Specify the location of the chart, either on a new sheet or as an object on the current worksheet.

To obtain a break in the curve, click on one of the line segments, which selects the entire curve. Clicking one more time on a line segment to be removed selects just that corresponding data value. Double-clicking on the selected line segment opens a dialog box. Select the Patterns option that offers the accompanying choice for a Line. Selecting None removes the line segment.

Line
◯ Automatic
◉ None
◯ Custom

MANAGERIAL INTERPRETATION

As can readily be seen from the time-series plot of this process, a delay occurs each day around 3 P.M. Management needs to address this problem. One possible solution is to schedule more employees at that time to better serve the customers.

A visual inspection of a time series can reveal underlying patterns, as in the previous example. More formal statistical procedures for the analysis of a time series can also be used, some of which are introduced later in this text. Understanding the nature of trends is an important component of the manager's ability to make business decisions.

EXERCISES

Application

2-6. Consider the following gross national product (GNP) data (in billions of 1992 dollars).

Year	1980	1981	1982	1983	1984	1985
Trade Deficit	12,226	13,547	13,961	14,998	16,508	17,529

Year	1986	1987	1988	1989	1990
Trade Deficit	18,374	19,323	20,605	21,984	23,416

Year	1991	1992	1993	1994	1995
Trade Deficit	24,447	25,373	26,589	27,541	

a. Construct the time-series plot of the GNP.
b. Determine which value of GNP you predict (roughly) for 1996 from these data and why.
c. Plot the time-series plot of the changes in GNP.
d. After examining this plot, decide whether you are as confident about your prediction of GNP in 1996 and why or why not.

Application

2-7. The following data represent the greeting card industry as a whole (Annual Survey of Manufacturers). The variable named Production is the number of hours of employment in production. The other variable is the Value Added by Manufacture to the cost of materials, that is, the difference between the selling price of the manufactured goods and the cost of raw materials used in their manufacture.

	1982	1983	1984	1985	1986
Production (mil hr)	20.2	21.0	18.4	17.7	19.3
Value Added ($ mil)	1,349	1,611	1,667	1,895	2,036

	1987	1988	1989	1990
Production (mil hr)	21.7	19.0	20.8	23.7
Value Added ($ mil)	2,204	2,279	2,554	2,828

a. Create a time-series plot of Production, expressed in millions of hours.
b. Create a time-series plot of Value Added by the manufacturer of the product, expressed in millions of dollars.
c. Briefly describe the pattern of these two variables over time. What do these trends imply about the use of paid labor in the production process? Justify your answer.

Application

2-8. Consider the following annual U.S. merchandise trade deficit, listed in billions of dollars.

Year	1983	1984	1985	1986	1987
Trade Deficit ($ bil)	57.5	107.9	132.1	152.7	152.1

Year	1988	1989	1990	1991	1992
Trade Deficit ($ bil)	118.6	109.6	101.7	65.4	84.5

Year	1993	1994	1995
Trade Deficit ($ bil)	115.6	151.1	159.6

a. Create a time-series plot of Trade Deficit.
b. Sketch by hand the approximate trend component of this time series.
c. Briefly describe the pattern of this variable over time.

Mechanical

2-9. The pattern of annual gross revenues for a growing business is provided below for the last 40 years (random errors were removed for clarity).

1.02	2.82	4.23	3.24	2.56
6.12	9.88	8.97	9.20	17.25
23.28	18.69	18.60	35.12	44.98
31.90	24.32	35.28	40.22	27.41
21.46	31.05	32.46	19.44	12.78
26.50	38.10	31.40	29.64	51.74
65.62	49.84	47.22	85.30	104.96
71.77	52.94	74.48	82.56	54.82

a.   Plot the time series.
b.   Determine which time period has the largest value.
c.   Answer the question, If gross revenues are increasing over time, why does the largest value not parallel the last time period?

2-10. For the data in Exercise 2-9, hand sketch the

Mechanical

a.   trend component
b.   cyclical component
c.   seasonal component

2-11. A time-series analysis estimated a multiplicative model. At a specific time, the trend component is 259. At that time

Mechanical

period, the model estimates a seasonal component of 1.14, and an error component of .93. No cyclical component was present.

a.   Does the seasonal component raise or lower the data value around the underlying trend? Why? What is the combined effect of trend and seasonality at time period?
b.   Does the error component raise or lower the data value around the underlying trend and seasonal component? What is the actual value of Y at that time period?

2.4 SUMMARY

Our primary interest in statistics is solving problems that require decision making in the presence of uncertainty. The essence of *uncertainty* is captured by the concept of a random variable. A random variable in formal mathematics is a numeric variable with values set by a random process, though we have seen that the values of categorical variables can also be determined randomly so that they too can be considered random variables.

Applying statistics requires collecting data, which result from the measurement of the values of the relevant random variables for a given sample. Distributions for categorical variables are expressed in terms of frequencies and proportions, with corresponding graphic displays that include bar and pie charts. Frequency distributions for continuous variables involve grouping similar values into bins, the graphic display of which is a histogram or frequency polygon. For data sets with relatively few values, dit plots may be more appropriate.

Data for continuous variables can be analyzed with frequency distributions by displaying frequencies and proportions as well as the corresponding cumulative distributions. Data collected over time can be displayed with a histogram as well as with a time-series plot that illustrates time-dependent patterns such as seasonal cycles.

2.5 KEY TERMS

bar chart *33*
bins *38*
cumulative frequency *49*
cutpoints *40*
cyclical component *52*
dit plot *49*
error component *52*
frequency *30*
frequency distribution *30*

frequency polygon *40*
histogram *40*
midpoint *40*
pie chart *34*
proportion *30*
seasonal component *52*
time-series plot *52*
trend component *52*
width *38*

2.6 REVIEW EXERCISES

ANALYSIS PROBLEMS

2-12. A company's sales for last year were $139,342 in the Northeast Region, $89,297 in the Southeast Region, $118,638 in the Northwest Region, and $93,371 in the Southwest Region.

Mechanical

    a. Compute the proportion of total sales volume for each region.

    b. Draw the bar chart for the sales volume of each region.

    c. Draw the pie chart for the sales volume of each region.

    d. Verbally compare information obtained from the frequencies with information from the proportions.

2-13. Last year a certain university had 1,409 freshmen, 1,366 sophomores, 1,093 juniors, and 899 seniors.

Mechanical

    a. Compute the proportion of students in each class.

    b. Draw the bar chart for the number of students in each class.

    c. Draw the pie chart for the number of students in each class.

    d. Verbally compare information obtained from the frequencies with information from the proportions.

2-14. A statistics professor needed to know what operating system her students used on their personal computers so that compatible software could be ordered. The data follow.

Mechanical

Name	OS	Name	OS
Bill	Win 3.1	Brady	Mac
Scott	Win 95	Mat	Mac
Jennifer	Mac	Ryan	Win 95
Jason	Win 95	Beth	Win NT
Audra	Mac	Kara	Win NT
Dave	Win 3.1	Craig	Win 3.1
Jean	Win 95	Tracy	Win 95
Sally	Win NT	Kristan	Mac

    a. Construct the frequency distribution of OS with counts.

    b. Construct the frequency distribution of OS with proportions.

    c. Draw the bar chart for the values of OS.

    d. Draw the pie chart for the values of OS.

    e. Verbally compare information obtained from the frequencies with information from the proportions.

2-15. For the family income data in Exercise 2-5, using a bin width of $10,000 display with histograms the

Mechanical

    a. cumulative frequencies

    b. cumulative proportions

2-16. For the family income data in Exercise 2-5, display the dit plot.

Mechanical

2-17. Complete the remainder of this table.

Mechanical

Bin	Midpt	Freq	Propor-tion	Cum Freq	Cum Prop
	60	1			
	70	4			
	80	17			
	90	30			
	100	35			
	110	24			
	120	12			
	130	2			

2-18. Grocery prices were compared for two chains of stores: Tasty Foods and Best Price Groceries. The prices were compared by shopping for the identical 20 items at each of the 12 Tasty Foods stores and the 15 Best Price Groceries stores in the city. The respective prices at the two stores follow.

Mechanical

Tasty Foods

$75.92 $86.56 $75.26 $73.67 $76.00 $78.35
$70.19 $74.59 $64.88 $72.74 $77.76 $76.08

Best Price Groceries

$64.69 $81.06 $86.33 $81.19 $94.96 $78.96 $73.53 $76.54
$85.84 $66.21 $79.94 $70.22 $70.81 $78.69 $93.03

a. Construct a separate histogram of prices for each chain.

b. Determine how the cost of groceries compares at these stores,

2-19. The assessed values of 24 houses in a single neighborhood were gathered and reported in thousands of dollars. Some of the houses bordered on a lake, and these houses tended to have a much higher value than the other houses.

Mechanical

182   195   137   769   127   216   138   222
202   202   159   836   181   155   194   238
209   1197   161   128   169   136   132   156

Display in tabular form the distribution of frequencies and proportions of these prices.

a. Use a bin width of 100 (thousand dollars).

b. Determine how many houses are on the lake.

c. Use a bin width of 100 (thousand dollars) for all houses with an assessed value of approximately $500,000 or below, and bins of $2,000,000 dollars for houses with larger values.

d. Compare the values from a and c. Which set of bins provides the most useful display of the underlying distribution? Why?

2-20. For the assessed value of housing data in Exercise 2-19,

Mechanical

  a. Plot the cumulative distributions of frequencies and proportions.

  b. Determine how many houses have an assessed value of less than $200,000.

  c. Determine which assessed value is closest to cutting off the bottom third of the distribution of assessed values.

2-21. The percentage correct on the statistics midterm exam follows.

Mechanical

84	91	98	87	91	74	87	86
84	96	89	88	96	79	72	83
76	90	88	91	66	82	90	81

Construct the histogram of these values using a bin width of

  a. 10 percentage points

  b. 5 percentage points

  c. 2 percentage points

  d. 1 percentage point

  e. Determine which bin width you prefer and why.

  f. Describe the shape of this distribution in terms of the resulting grades.

2-22. The times in seconds required to assemble a fixture appear below for 48 different fixtures.

Mechanical

135	125	114	116	129	115	117	132
117	121	123	112	104	121	115	115
136	102	114	111	129	119	135	115
104	118	136	115	116	131	116	124
96	114	118	134	137	128	110	126
110	119	119	111	115	118	98	116

Construct the histogram of these values using a bin width of

  a. 20 seconds

  b. 10 seconds

  c. 5 seconds

  d. Determine which bin width you prefer and why.

  e. Describe the shape of this distribution in terms of the resulting times.

2-23. A small manufacturing company is planning retirement option plans for its employees. As part of this preparation, the company analyzes the ages of its 35 employees, which are listed below.

Mechanical

38	33	42	28	33	56	24	60	24
39	44	58	52	28	36	33	40	45
64	33	34	56	20	35	38	42	29
51	34	22	34	23	44	39	61

Construct the histogram of these values using a bin width of

  a. 15 years

  b. 10 years

  c. 5 years

  d. Determine which bin width you prefer and why.

  e. Describe the shape of this distribution in terms of the resulting ages.

2-24. For the age data in the previous exercise,

   a. Construct the cumulative histogram using a bin width of 5 years.

   b. Determine how many employees are less than 30 years old.

   c. Calculate how many employees will retire within 5 years if the retirement age is 65.

2-25. To develop a checkout system that better served his customers, a manager measured 20 checkout times at a cash register. These times are recorded below in minutes.

0.04	1.82	5.01	4.36	0.19	2.29	3.33
2.42	2.05	6.26	2.94	4.67	6.40	2.32
0.28	0.94	2.94	3.86	2.46	0.93	

Construct the histogram of these values using a bin width of

   a. 30 seconds

   b. 15 seconds

   c. 10 seconds

   d. Determine which bin width you prefer and why?

   e. Describe the shape of this distribution in terms of the resulting times.

2-26. Following is a listing of the tax receipts gathered by the U.S. government from 1980 to 1996. The values are in billions of dollars.

Year	1980	1981	1982	1983	1984	1985
Taxes	517.1	599.3	617.8	600.6	666.5	734.1

Year	1986	1987	1988	1989	1990	1991
Taxes	769.1	854.1	909.0	990.7	1,031.3	1,054.3

Year	1992	1993	1994	1995	1996
Taxes	1,090.4	1,153.5	1,257.7	1,355.2	1,426.8

   a. Create a time-series plot of tax receipts.

   b. Sketch by hand the approximate trend component of this time series.

   c. Briefly describe the pattern of this variable over time.

2-27. Following is a listing of the deficit generated by the U.S. government from 1980 to 1996. The values are in billions of dollars.

Year	1980	1981	1982	1983	1984	1985
Deficit	73.8	79.0	128.0	207.8	185.4	212.3

Year	1986	1987	1988	1989	1990	1991
Deficit	221.2	149.8	155.2	152.2	221.2	269.4

Year	1992	1993	1994	1995	1996
Deficit	290.4	255.1	203.1	163.9	145.6

   a. Create a time-series plot of the deficit.

   b. Sketch by hand the approximate trend component of this time series.

   c. Briefly describe the pattern of this variable over time.

Mechanical

2-28. The following data are the Gross Sales and Net Income of a growing company.

	1990	1991	1992	1993	1994	1995
Sales ($ mil)	117.3	335.1	583.4	983.5	1516.9	1918.2
Net Income ($ mil)	12.6	39.5	61.3	77.5	64.8	61.7

	1996	1997	1998
Sales ($ mil)	117.9	335.4	583.6
Net Income ($ mil)	12.2	39.6	61.7

a. Create a time-series plot of Sales.

b. Create a time-series plot of Net Income.

c. Briefly describe the trend of these two variables over time. What do these trends imply about the growth of the company during this period? Justify your answer.

Mechanical

2-29. A time-series analysis estimated an additive model. At a specific time, the trend component is 24. At that period, the model estimates a seasonal component of 10 and an error component of -14. No cyclical component was present.

a. Does the seasonal component raise or lower the data value around the underlying trend? Why? What is the combined effect of trend and seasonality at that period?

b. Does the error component raise or lower the data value around the underlying trend and seasonal component? What is the value of Y at that period?

Mechanical

2-30. A time-series analysis estimated a multiplicative model. At a specific time, the trend component is 67. At that period, the model estimates a seasonal component of .96 and an error component of 1.14. No cyclical component was present.

a. Does the seasonal component raise or lower the data value around the underlying trend? Why? What is the combined effect of trend and seasonality at that period?

b. Does the error component raise or lower the data value around the underlying trend and seasonal component? What is the actual value of Y at that period?

DISCUSSION QUESTIONS

1. When should the distribution of a variable be displayed in terms of proportions instead of frequencies?

2. Why do bar charts but not histograms have gaps between the bars?

3. How do you determine which bin to assign a value to when the value falls on a cutpoint of a bin?

4. Why are cumulative distributions not appropriate for the analysis of categorical variables?

5. What problem is encountered when too many bins are used to display a frequency distribution of a continuous variable?

6. What problem is encountered when too few bins are used to display a frequency distribution of a continuous variable?

7. How can frequencies and proportions be displayed on the same graph?

8. When is a dit plot preferred over a histogram?

9. What information does a time-series plot add to the information provided by a histogram?

10. What information does a histogram add to the information provided by a time-series plot?

11. What are the three systematic components of a time-series?

12. What are the distinctions between the additive model and the multiplicative model of a time series?

INTEGRATIVE ANALYSIS PROBLEM

A small brewery had two bottling machines. The file BEER.DAT contains the measured volumes of 53 randomly sampled purportedly 12 oz bottles from the two machines: 27 from the first machine and 26 from the second. The corresponding two variables in the data file are labeled Machine and Volume. A third variable, Number, indicates the order in which the bottles were sampled from each bottling machine at approximately equal intervals.

a. Count the number of bottles that have more than 12 oz and less than 12 oz from each machine. Plot these four values with a bar chart.

b. Plot the histogram of all 53 volumes using .2 oz bin widths.

c. Plot the histogram of all 53 volumes using .1 oz bin widths.

d. Determine which bin width you prefer and why.

e. Plot the histograms separately of the 27 bottles from the first machine and the 26 bottles from the second machine. Choose a bin width, but use the same bin width for both machines.

f. Comment on the relative performance of the two machines.

g. Plot the time series of the measured volumes for the first machine.

h. Plot the time series of the measured volumes for the second machine.

i. Comment on the relative performance of the two machines based on the analysis of the time-series data as well as the histograms.

j. What recommendations do you make to management regarding the performance of the two machines?

CHAPTER 2 EXTENSION   DENSITY DISTRIBUTIONS

E2.1 DENSITY DISTRIBUTIONS

The width of the bins must be chosen *arbitrarily* before you construct a histogram or frequency polygon. Although some choices are better than others, different bin widths provide differently shaped histograms. The arbitrariness of bin width implies that the corresponding frequencies and proportions are also somewhat arbitrary, with larger bin widths generally leading to larger frequencies and proportions per bin.

Different histograms of the same or related data may have different bin widths, and sometimes a *single* histogram may contain different bin widths. When reporting income, a few large incomes may be placed in a bin of \$100,000–\$1,000,000, and much smaller bins such as from \$10,000–\$20,000 may be used for the much more frequently occurring smaller incomes.

How should the problem of differing bin widths be addressed? Instead of plotting frequencies or proportions, plot **densities** when bin widths differ. Data are found in relatively high concentrations around values with high density. Values with low density occur in regions of a distribution with relatively low concentrations of data.

A continuous variable such as Weight and the measurements of such a variable are two distinct concepts. Mathematics can specify densities precisely for the values of an abstract continuous variable. These theoretical densities can be estimated from metric data. First we apply the concept of density to the metric data that result from the measurement of a continuous variable, and then we discuss densities directly for a continuous variable.

density
relative concentration of values around a specific value of a continuous variable

Density of Metric Data

density of a bin
$density = \dfrac{proportion\ in\ bin}{width\ of\ bin}$

The **density**[1] **of a bin** is the corresponding proportion p relative to the bin width. Density of Weight can be expressed as the proportion of values per pound, and Density of Time as the proportion of values per hour. Choose the unit to express bin width for convenience, but use the same unit for all bins. If inches is chosen as the unit for the first bin, then inches should be used for the computation of the densities of all bins.

To illustrate, consider a distribution of Income in which one bin \$5,000 wide has a proportion of .25, and another bin \$10,000 wide has a proportion of .30. The unit chosen for computing the density of this particular bin width could be \$1, which would make the first bin \$5,000 wide. The densities of the bins computed with this width are

$$density = \frac{.25}{5000} = .00005 \quad and \quad density = \frac{.30}{10000} = .00003$$

The proportion of families per \$1 of income is .00005 for the first bin and .00003 for the second bin.

Alternatively, the unit of bin width could be \$5,000, in which case the first bin is 1 unit wide and the second bin is 2 units wide. The densities of the bins are

$$density = \frac{.25}{1} = .25 \quad and \quad density = \frac{.30}{2} = .15$$

The proportion of families per \$5,000 of income is .25 for the first bin and .15 for the second bin. Different choices of bin widths yield equivalent results, but some choices yield more convenient numbers. The value .25 is easier to write than .00005.

Because of different bin widths, a comparison of density for these two bins is more meaningful than a comparison of their respective proportions. The potentially

1. More formally, the proportion (sample probability) divided by the width of the bin is called *probability density*.

misleading proportion of values in this latter bin is larger, but the more meaningful density is considerably smaller because of the larger bin width. In this case, the narrower bin has a larger proportion of values *relative* to the width of the bin.

In summary, frequency distributions for three types of indices can be constructed from metric data. Histograms constructed with frequencies, proportions, or densities all have the same shape, distinguished only by the scaling of the frequency axis. The density histogram is the most general of the three types of histograms because it adjusts not only for differences in sample sizes, which is also true for proportion histograms, but also for differences in bin widths. Histograms that display proportions only adjust for unequal sample sizes.

The following theorem further illustrates the generality of the density histogram.

The total area of the bars in a density histogram is 1.0.

The sum of the areas is 1.0 regardless of sample size, number of bins, width of each bin, or the value of each proportion p.

$$\text{area of a bar} = \text{density} * \text{width} = (p/\text{width}) * \text{width} = p.$$

The sum of the proportions is 1.0, so the area of all the bars is 1.0.

Distributions of density for metric data are illustrated in the following example.

BUSINESS APPLICATION E2.1—Distribution of Densities for Metric Data

MANAGERIAL PROBLEM

An advertising manager for a national brand was interested in the differences in Household Income for different ethnic groups such as Whites and Blacks. Examining government statistics printed in the *Statistical Abstract of the United States, 1994*, p. 464, the manager discovered that the frequency distributions for incomes are displayed with bins of unequal widths. How should these data be displayed to facilitate comparison of Household Income across the two ethnic groups?

DATA

Table E2-1 displays the money income of 82,083 White families and 11,190 Black families from 1992.

APPLICATION—CONCEPTUAL WORKSHEET

Excel does not provide a specific program for computing densities, though they are easily computed from the worksheet, as shown in Figure E2-1. Density was computed as the percentage of families per $1,000 of Household Income. To compute density, divide each of the given percentages (shaded in gray) by the corresponding bin width. The last bin for income, $75,000 and up, has no bin width and, therefore, no density.

From this worksheet, Excel computed the graph of the densities for Blacks and Whites in Figure E2-2.

Table E2-1.
Percent distribution
of money Income of
Households for
Whites and Blacks
in 1992.

Bin	% of Whites	% of Blacks
$0 up to $10,000	12.5	30.5
$10,000 up to $15,000	9.1	12.2
$15,000 up to $25,000	16.7	18.3
$25,000 up to $35,000	15.1	13.2
$35,000 up to $50,000	17.7	12.8
$50,000 up to $75,000	17.0	8.8
$75,000 up	11.9	4.2

Figure E2-1.
Density for White
and Black 1992
Household Income
(in thousands).

	A	B	C	D	E	F
				White		*Black*
1						
2	Width	Bin	Prop	Density	Prop	Density
3	10	10	12.5	1.25	30.5	3.05
4	5	15	9.1	1.82	12.2	2.44
5	10	25	16.7	1.67	18.3	1.83
6	10	35	15.1	1.51	13.2	1.32
7	15	50	17.7	1.18	12.8	0.85
8	25	75	17.0	0.68	8.8	0.35
9		More	11.9		4.2	
10			100.0		100.0	

APPLICATION—EXCEL GRAPHICS

Assessing the Excel Output

Figure E2-2.
Density of 1992
Income for White
and Black
Households.

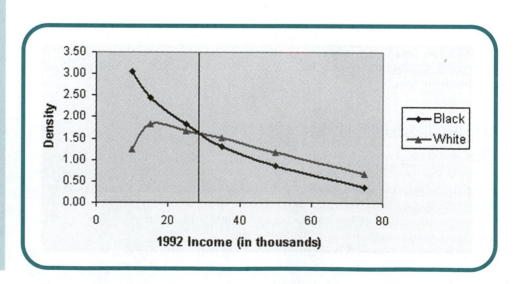

Obtaining the Graph

Insert ▶ Chart...

Step 1—Chart Type. Specify an *X Y* (Scatter) chart, which is for a numeric horizontal axis. Select the format that connects the points with line segments, or the format that joins them with a smooth curve.

Step 2—Chart Source. Specify the cells for the Data Range that include the densities for White and Black and then specify the bins for the horizontal axis. Include the labels for each column of data.

Data range: =$D$2:$D$8,$F$2:$F$8,$B$2:$B$8

This discontiguous selection is accomplished with the mouse by holding down the Control key (Windows) or the Command key (Mac) when making a new selection. Or enter each data range from the keyboard, and separate the data ranges with commas. The first two series are plotted, and the last series is automatically listed as labels on the *X*-axis.

Step 3—Chart Options. Under the Titles tab, name the *X* or horizontal axis and the *Y* or vertical axis.

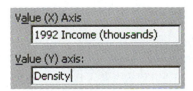

Value (X) Axis

1992 Income (thousands)

Value (Y) axis:

Density

Step 4—Chart Location. Specify a new sheet for the graph or place the graph in the current worksheet (Sheet1).

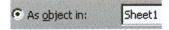

⊙ As object in: Sheet1

STATISTICAL PRINCIPLE

Because of different bin widths, comparing density for these two distributions is more meaningful than comparing their respective proportions. The structure of these frequency data does not emerge until the proportions are expressed in terms of bins of common width. In this example, the unit of the densities is percent of Households for every $1,000 bin of Income. To illustrate, consider Figure E2-3, an enhanced section of Figure E2-2.

Figure E2-3.
The bin $1,000 wide around the income of $10,000 contains about 1.25% of White Household Incomes.

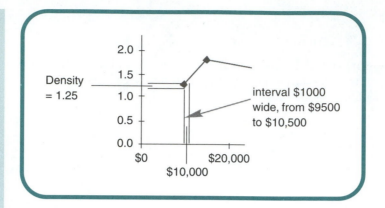

A bin $1,000 wide can be constructed around any value of the distribution, and the corresponding percentage of observations that lies within the bin can be calculated directly from the graph. These densities only approximate the actual densities of the underlying theoretical variable. Bins that describe densities of continuous variables have an infinitesimally small width (as described by the tools of calculus).

MANAGERIAL INTERPRETATION

Black Incomes are concentrated almost three times as much as White Incomes at the lowest Income levels. As Income increases, the concentration of Black Incomes steadily decreases. The concentration of White Incomes is the largest around $15,000, and then also steadily decreases as Income increases. The concentration of Black Incomes is larger than the concentration of White Incomes for Incomes approximately less than $22,000. White Incomes are found at higher concentrations for values larger than about $22,000.

The frequency, proportion, and density computed from metric data estimate a theoretical value of a continuous variable. Each theoretical value within the bin is approximated as the computed frequency, proportion, and density of the *entire* bin. The frequency, for example, assigned to a bin from 50°F to 55°F reflects the frequency of all values in the bin, such as 52°, 51°, and 54.5°. The narrower the bin, the better the approximation of the frequency for the individual values within the bin. The next section explores how to make the bin width infinitesimally small.

Density of Continuous Variables

Using statistics to analyze information requires moving back and forth between mathematical abstractions, such as the normal curve, and the practical realities of the corresponding metric data. As discussed in the previous chapter, continuous variables are mathematical abstractions, the exact values of which are never observed. The theoretically correct value of Weight is not 4 lb, nor 4.2 lb, nor even 4.2372398523728241 lb. A *theoretical* distribution of individual values of a continuous variable cannot be expressed with frequencies or proportions because the bin assigned to each individual value has no width.

Although the probability of any value from a theoretical continuous distribution is zero, each value can be assigned a density. The individual bars of a his-

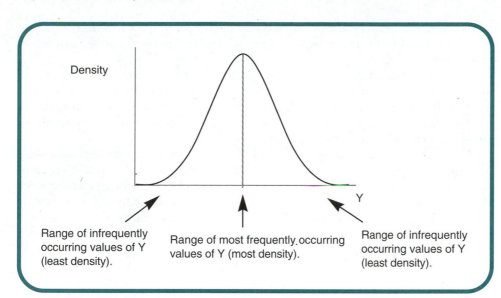

Figure E2-4.
Population densities of
the normally distributed
continuous variable *Y*.

togram or the jagged edges of a frequency polygon are smoothed out in the expression of the densities of the underlying continuous variable.

> *The distribution of density for a continuous variable is the mathematical abstraction of a perfectly smooth curve.*

A high density for a value means that more data tend to be located in a bin around the value than in a bin of the same size for another value with lower probability density.[2]

The distribution of a continuous variable *Y* corresponds to the population distribution, and the distribution of metric data that results from the measurement of this variable provides a sample estimate of the population densities. The continuous distribution that business decision makers find most useful is the normal distribution, which forms the foundation of much theoretical and applied statistical analysis. Plotting the densities of a normally distributed variable *Y* results in the smooth curve—or normal curve—in Figure E2-4. The total area under the curve is 1.0.

The densities of a normally distributed variable *Y* are specified precisely by an equation[3] that depends on the values of the population mean μ_Y and standard deviation σ_Y. The range of values of *Y* around the middle is the densest region of data. The further a value is from the middle, the less likely it is that data in a bin around that value will occur. This drop-off of density is rather rapid, so that data rarely occur in a bin far from the middle of a normal distribution.

2. Those with a calculus background around may recognize a probability density as the limit of a process in which the size of the bin around a value of *Y* goes to zero, resulting in an infinitesimally small interval. Density is calculated for increasingly narrow intervals until, at the limit, density is computed for the infinitesimally small point, the value of *Y*. Probability is computed as the definite integral over an interval of the densities of *Y*.

3. The probability density function for the normal distribution (which you need *not* memorize unless you happen to enjoy that sort of thing) is

$$f(Y \mid \mu, \sigma) = \frac{1}{\sigma\sqrt{2\pi}} \exp\left\{ -\frac{1}{2}\left(\frac{Y-\mu}{\sigma}\right)^2 \right\}.$$

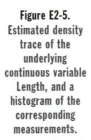

density trace
smooth curve display of density, analogous to a histogram with infinitely thin bars

stripe plot
direct display of density with a set of vertical lines, one line for each occurrence of a value

The relation between measurements and the theoretical distribution of the underlying continuous variable becomes explicit by "smoothing" out the histogram or frequency polygon.

A **density trace** can follow a specific distribution such as the normal curve, or the density trace can best characterize the data without a prior specification of the form of the function. The mathematical bases of the various methods for obtaining the density trace are beyond the scope of this presentation, but computer technology makes these methods accessible.

There are also other graphical displays of a continuous variable, including **stripe plots.** If a distribution contains too many data values, the "stripes" blend into each other, resulting in an uninformative rectangle of black. For a small or moderate data set, however, the stripe plot efficiently displays the approximate form of the underlying distribution. Denser regions of the horizontal axis are darker because of the larger number of vertical lines, and a much smaller number of lines characterize less dense regions, as illustrated below.

STATISTICAL ILLUSTRATION—Graphical Density Estimates

DATA

The data are from Business Application 2.3 for constructing a frequency distribution and histogram for a continuous variable. Excel does not provide a density trace (Figure E2-5) or stripe plot (Figure E2-6).

DENSITY TRACE

The algorithm that computes the density trace in Figure E2-5 is considerably more sophisticated than simply connecting the tops of the histograms with smooth

Figure E2-5. Estimated density trace of the underlying continuous variable Length, and a histogram of the corresponding measurements.

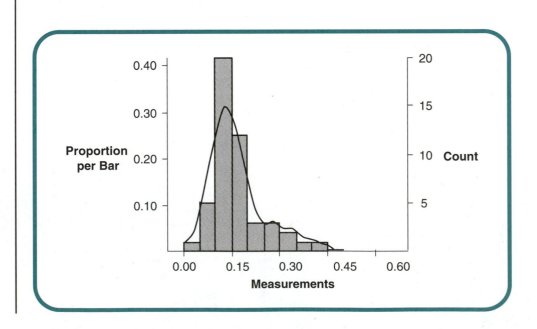

curves. For example, the histogram bar for the metric data that span the bin from .010 to .015 is much higher than adjacent bars. Because the algorithm considers the height of these adjacent bars when estimating density over any one bin, the height of the estimated density curve is less than the height of this corresponding bar of the histogram. Similarly, the density trace is higher than the histogram bar for the .025–.030 bin.

DISPLAYING DENSITY DIRECTLY

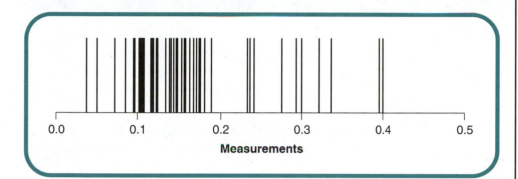

**Figure E2-6.
A stripe plot of the measurement of length.**

STATISTICAL PRINCIPLE

A histogram is a graphical estimate of the population density of a continuous variable. The specific shape of the histogram depends, in part, on the widths of the bins. A better estimate of shape is an explicit estimate of the underlying smoothed density curve, which avoids the arbitrariness associated with bin width. The estimated smoothed density curve demonstrates the form of the underlying distribution more clearly than does any one particular histogram.

The stripe plot is a direct display of density. Values that correspond to higher levels of density lie in darker areas. Less dense areas have fewer stripes. The smoothed curve density estimate in Figure E2-5 peaks between .10 and .15, which corresponds to the darkest region in the stripe plot in Figure E2-6.

The analysis of distributions discussed so far focused on graphical displays. Next we introduce statistics that summarize important characteristics of a distribution.

E2.2 SUMMARY

Data for continuous variables can be analyzed with frequency distributions by displaying frequencies, proportions, and densities; the corresponding cumulative distributions can also be displayed. Proportions adjust the raw frequencies for sample size, and densities adjust the proportions for bin width. That is, the size of the proportion does not depend on the size of the sample, and the size of the density does not depend on the size of the bin used to group the original frequencies.

E2.3 KEY TERMS

density *68*   density trace *74*
density of a bin *68*   stripe plot *74*

E2.4 REVIEW EXERCISES

ANALYSIS PROBLEMS

Mechanical

E2-1. For Exercise 2-19 from the last section, compute

   a. densities

   b. cumulative densities

Concept

E2-2. For the data in Exercise 2-5, based on a bin width of $10,000, display in graphical form your best guess regarding the shape of the underlying density function of the

   a. proportions

   b. cumulative proportions

Application

E2-3. The following percentages of Household Incomes for Blacks, reported in constant 1992 dollars, are based on a sample size of 6,180,000 for 1970, 8,847,000 for 1980, and 10,671,000 for 1990. (*Source: Statistical Abstract of the United States, 1994,* p. 464)

Bin	1970	1980	1990
$0 up to $10,000	27.9	12.9	11.8
$10,000 up to $15,000	13.4	8.8	8.4
$15,000 up to $25,000	22.4	17.4	16.8
$25,000 up to $35,000	15.5	16.3	15.4
$35,000 up to $50,000	12.2	19.5	18.2
$50,000 up to $75,000	7.2	16.5	16.9
$75,000 up	1.5	8.6	12.4

   a. Plot the three density frequency polygons (or histograms).

   b. Draw a conclusion about the distribution of Income in Black families over these three decades.

Application

E2-4. The following percentages of 1992 Household Incomes for Hispanics were obtained from *Statistical Abstract of the United States, 1994,* p. 464. These values are based on a sample size of 6,626,000.

Bin	%
$0 up to $10,000	20.4
$10,000 up to $15,000	12.6
$15,000 up to $25,000	20.8
$25,000 up to $35,000	16.3
$35,000 up to $50,000	14.5
$50,000 up to $75,000	10.5
$75,000 up	5.0

a. Plot the density frequency polygon (or histogram) of these data.

b. Compare this density analysis with the comparable figures for Whites and Blacks presented in Business Application E2.1 on page 70. What do you conclude about the comparison of Income in White, Black, and Hispanic families during 1992?

DISCUSSION QUESTIONS

1. When should the distribution of a continuous variable be displayed in terms of densities instead of proportions?

2. What is the advantage of using an estimated smoothed density curve to illustrate the distribution of the underlying continuous variable instead of the histogram of the corresponding metric data?

3. What are the differences in shape between a frequency polygon and the corresponding smoothed density curve?

4. Contrast the two ways of portraying density: smoothed density curves and stripe plots.

CHAPTER

3

Numerical Summaries of a Distribution

WHY DO WE CARE?

This chapter continues the general theme of the previous chapter: summarizing an entire distribution of values. A distribution with tens, hundreds, or thousands of values is too large for us to grasp its most important features simply by scanning all values. The previous chapter demonstrated how to display the shape of the entire distribution with a table or a graph. This chapter introduces statistics that describe important characteristics of a distribution of numerical values. The overall purpose remains the same—to summarize a mass of data by efficiently and concisely conveying the important properties of the distribution of a random variable.

Another useful analysis describes the position of a single value *within* a distribution. After examining the distribution of salaries for your department, you might wonder where your own salary falls within that distribution. The most obvious answer to such a question would be something like "seventh from the top." This chapter introduces more precise ways of locating the position of a value within a distribution.

3.1 MIDDLE OF A DISTRIBUTION

One of the most useful properties of a distribution is its middle. Though *middle* can be defined many ways, the three most common definitions are the mean, the median, and the mode. We begin with the mean.

Arithmetic Mean

> **arithmetic mean**
> *sum of a list of values divided by the number of values*

You are probably already familiar with the **arithmetic mean,** often called simply the *mean,* or its more colloquial name, the *average.* There are many different types of means, but by far the most widely used is the arithmetic mean.

Expressing the definition of the mean with statistical notation requires the uppercase Greek letter sigma, Σ, which indicates the sum of a list of numbers. To indicate the sum of five salaries, write

$$\sum Y = \$48{,}750 + \$35{,}250 + \$38{,}840 + \$52{,}330 + \$45{,}280$$

$$= \$220{,}450$$

Whenever you see a $\sum$ think *sum of a list of numbers.*

Also used to define the mean is *n,* the number of values in the sample. A single sample may consist of 10 values, in which case $n = 10$, or 3,623 values, in which case $n = 3{,}623$. In general, a sample consists of *n* values.

The three-pronged equal sign, $\equiv$, is useful here. This modified equal sign means "by definition." The usual two-pronged equal sign, $=$, means "by derivation." Using $\equiv$ indicates that the left-hand side of an equation is declared equal to the right-hand side, that is, equal by declaration or definition. There is no derivation such as an algebraic rule to figure out. The left-hand side of the equation is simply an abbreviation for a more complicated symbol string on the right-hand side of the equation. Using both $\equiv$ and $=$ avoids the confusion that results from referring to two concepts, definition and derivation, by the same name.

The name of the variable with a bar on top indicates the sample mean, such as $\overline{Y}$ for the variable *Y.* The definition of $\overline{Y}$ can now be expressed with statistical notation and applied to the five salaries:

$$\overline{Y} \equiv \frac{\sum Y}{n} = \frac{\$220{,}450}{5} = \$44{,}090.$$

A more detailed example follows.

STATISTICAL ILLUSTRATION—Mean

The 1992 closing Price per Share (PPS) of 10 publicly traded companies was recorded. What is the mean Price per Share?

APPLICATION—CONCEPTUAL WORKSHEET

The mean is the sum of the values divided by the number of values. This definition is illustrated in the following worksheet for the PPS values in cells C3 through C12.

	A	B	C
1			PPS
2		Company	Y
3	1	PHIL. SUBURBAN CORP	16.00
4	2	TULTEX CORP	8.63
5	3	CALMAT CO	22.50
6	4	TANDY CORP	24.50
7	5	NICOR INC	49.75
8	6	OKLAHOMA GAS & ELECTRIC	34.13
9	7	FAMILY DOLLAR STORES	17.25
10	8	IMO INDUSTRIES INC	6.50
11	9	RTZ PLC	41.38
12	10	TORO CO	13.00
13		Sum	233.64
14		Sample size	10
15		Mean	23.36

The sum and sample size are obtained with the Excel SUM and COUNT functions. The following excerpt from the worksheet displays these formulas.

	B	C
13	Sum	=SUM(C3:C12)
14	Sample size	=COUNT(C3:C12)
15	Mean	=C13/C14

APPLICATION—TRADITIONAL NOTATION

Mean PPS for these 10 companies is

$$\overline{Y} \equiv \frac{\sum Y}{n} = \frac{233.64}{10} = 23.36.$$

APPLICATION—EXCEL BUILT-IN ANALYSIS

Excel computes the mean directly with either the Descriptive Statistics program accessed via the Tools → Data Analysis menu sequence, or the built-in function,

```
=AVERAGE(number1,number2, . . . ).
```

Using this function, the mean of the 10 PPS values in cells C3 through C12 is obtained with

```
=AVERAGE(C3:C12),
```

which results in the value 23.36 appearing in the cell in which the formula is entered.

The same definition of a mean applies to both a population and a sample from the population. In terms of notation, uppercase N replaces lowercase n to indicate population size, and the lowercase Greek letter mu, μ, represents the population mean. The population mean is

$$\mu_Y \equiv \frac{\sum Y}{N}.$$

For clarity, μ_Y explicitly designates the mean of variable Y. Representing population values with Greek letters and the corresponding sample statistics with Roman letters is a widely accepted convention.

When computing the arithmetic mean, each value in the distribution receives the same weight. Some values may merit more emphasis than others, however, such as the final exam counting twice as much as the midterm. In this situation, the important values may be weighted more than the remaining values in the computation of the mean. The weight for a value can be any number such as 1; 2; 8.63; or 1,000, though the resulting weighted mean is meaningful only if the chosen weights are meaningful.

> **weighted mean**
>
> $$\overline{Y}_{WT} \equiv \frac{\sum wY}{\sum w}$$
>
> *for each value of Y and its associated weight, w*

The **weighted mean** for Y is the sum of each value of Y multiplied by its associated weight, which is divided by the sum of the weights. The arithmetic mean is a special case of the weighted mean in which the weight for each variable equals 1. In this case, the denominator, or the sum of the weights $\sum w$, is just $1 = n$. For the numerator, each (wY) term is just $(1Y) = Y$. The result is the usual arithmetic mean.

To illustrate the weighted mean, consider the variable Test Score. Suppose Joe received an 87 on the first exam and only a 79 on the second. After studying particularly hard, he raised his score to 97 on the final, which was weighted twice as much as either of the two exams. Because the final was worth two exams, Joe raised his final course score to 90 for an A. The 90 was computed as a weighted mean,

$$\overline{Y}_{WT} = \frac{(1)87 + (1)79 + (2)97}{1 + 1 + 2} = \frac{360}{4} = 90.$$

The weighted mean is computed as if there were two separate scores of 97, with four scores overall instead of three. Other applications of the weighted mean are explored throughout the text.

For some distributions, the mean is not always an appropriate index of the middle because it is not a "typical value" of the distribution. To illustrate, consider the following five salaries sorted in ascending order,

$35,250 $38,840 $45,280 $48,750 $52,330.

These salaries range from a low of $35,250 to a high of $52,330. The mean of these five salaries is $44,090, which is close to the value that lies in the middle of the distribution, $45,280.

Now consider a distribution of salaries identical to the previous distribution with only a single change—the last value is $252,330 instead of $52,330:

$35,250 $38,840 $45,280 $48,750 $252,330.

> **outlier of a distribution**
>
> *value considerably different from most other values*

The value of $252,330 is far removed from the remaining values and would be considered an outlier. In statistical analysis, **outliers** require special examination. An extreme value may result from a simple mistake. The data entry person may hit an extra 2, changing $52,330 to $252,330. The solution to this outlier is simply to identify and correct the mistake. In other situations, however, the outlier was correctly measured and recorded. What to do then?

The key consideration is the analysis of the process that generated the outlier. Is the outlier from the same population as the other values, or does its discrepant value indicate that some other population has been sampled? Salaries in the range of $30,000 to $50,000 are likely generated by a different process than a salary of a quarter million. Is the point of the analysis to investigate salaries of hourly workers or of vice presidents and CEOs? Most meaningful analyses would separate the two sets of employees because the process that generates these sets of salaries differs considerably.

What are the numerical consequences of combining a vice president's salary with the typical hourly worker's salary? By increasing only one value in the distribution by $200,000—from $52,330 to $252,330—the mean increases from $44,090 to $84,090, a number *not* representative of any one value in the distribution. The mean salary of $84,090 does not resemble any of the four moderate salaries, nor does it approximate the one large salary.

Trimmed Mean and Median

Two other descriptions of the middle of a distribution address this problem of the potential unrepresentativeness of the mean: trimmed mean and median. To compute the **trimmed mean,** trim the specified number of values off each side of the distribution. This specified number is expressed in terms of the proportion of all values trimmed from the distribution. When *percent* = .10, the trimmed mean is $\overline{Y}_{.10}$, with .05 trimmed off each side.

> **trimmed mean of a distribution,**
> $\overline{Y}_{percent}$
> *mean of remaining values after the smallest percent/2 and largest percent/2 values (rounded to the nearest integer) are discarded*

What happens when the number of values trimmed from each side is computed from *percent/2,* and the resulting number is not an integer? Computing $\overline{Y}_{.10}$ for a sample of size $n = 34$ yields the number to trim from each side as $(.05)(34) = 1.70$. A common convention is to round the resulting value down to the nearest integer. Rounding 1.70 down to the nearest integer results in one value trimmed from each side of the distribution.

The trimmed mean is an example of a weighted mean, in which *percent/2* of the values at either end of the distribution are weighted 0 and all remaining values are weighted 1. Either a value is included in the calculation of the trimmed mean or it is not. The extreme version of the trimmed mean trims all but the middle value of the distribution. The **median,** the single value in the middle of a sorted distribution or the average of the two values closest to the middle, is retained with a weight of 1. All other values are weighted 0. For example, the median of the following distribution of 5 salaries is $45,280. Two salaries are smaller than $45,280 and two are larger. To show this, sort the distribution and rank the values from largest to smallest.

> **median of a distribution**
> *value that falls in the middle when all individual values are arranged in numerical order*

Rank	5	4	3	2	1
Y	$35,250	$38,840	$45,280	$48,750	$52,330

The median is the value with rank of $.5(n + 1)$. With sample size n equal to five, $.5(n + 1) = .5(6) = 3$. The value with rank 3 is $45,280.

For the second distribution with the largest value of $252,330, the median is more representative of the typical value than is the mean. As shown in Figure 3-1,

Figure 3-1.
Location of the median
for a distribution in
which data are more
concentrated for small
values than for large
values.

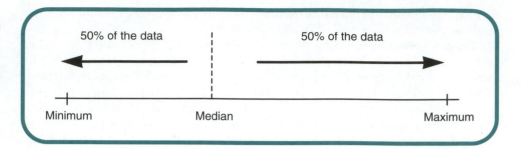

the data are concentrated at the lower end of the distribution. Except for the one large value over $200,000, the remaining values are much closer to the median of $45,280 than to the mean of $84,090.

Finding the middle of the distribution of sorted salaries in the previous example was easy because the size of the distribution was an odd number, 5. When the sample size is odd, a specific number falls in the middle. What happens if the size of the distribution is even, such as the following distribution of four salaries?

Rank	4	3	2	1
Y	$35,250	$38,840	$45,280	$48,750

Of the two numbers in the middle of this distribution, $38,840 and $45,280, which one is the median? The answer is neither. Again, the median is the value with the rank of $.5(n + 1) = .5(5) = 2.5$. What value has a rank of 2.5? The answer is the value midway between the values with a rank of 2, $45,280, and a rank of 3, $38,840. The median of this distribution is

$$\text{median} = \frac{\$38{,}840 + \$45{,}280}{2} = \$42{,}060.$$

When the distribution contains an even number of values, the median is the average of the two middle values.

The advantage of the trimmed mean and the median compared with the mean is apparent from these examples. Both the trimmed mean and the median remain the same when a single value toward the high end or the low end of the distribution is changed (assuming there are enough values for some trimming to occur). When outliers are present, both the trimmed mean and the median better represent the values in the middle of distributions than does the mean.

BUSINESS APPLICATION 3.1—Mean, Trimmed Mean, and Median

MANAGERIAL PROBLEM

A realtor wanted to describe the affluence of a particular neighborhood to a potential buyer in terms of household income. Because one very rich person lived in the neighborhood, the realtor knew that the mean would not be close to most, if any, of the values in the distribution, so the trimmed mean and median were also computed.

DATA

The distribution of 10 incomes, sorted from smallest to largest, follows.

	A	B	C	D	E	F	G	H	I	J
1	1	2	3	4	5	6	7	8	9	10
2	$29,750	$35,250	$38,840	$42,440	$44,320	$45,000	$45,280	$48,750	$52,330	$55,390,000

APPLICATION—TRADITIONAL STATISTICAL NOTATION

Mean

The mean is computed as

$$\overline{Y} = \frac{\$29{,}750 + \$35{,}250 + \ldots + \$52{,}330 + \$55{,}390{,}000}{10}$$

$$= \$5{,}577{,}196$$

Trimmed Mean

The sample size, 10, is so small that the .10 trimmed mean, $\overline{Y}_{.10}$, is the same value as the usual mean, $\overline{Y}$. Instead, the .20 trimmed mean is computed with .10 trimmed off both ends of the sorted distribution.

$$\text{Number to trim per side} = \text{round down}(.10n)$$

$$= \text{round down}(.10(10)) = \text{round down}(1) = 1.$$

Lopping off one value on each side of the distribution, the trimmed mean is the mean of the remaining eight values:

$$\overline{Y}_{.20} =$$

$$\frac{\$35{,}250 + \$38{,}840 + \$42{,}440 + \$44{,}320 + \$45{,}000 + \$45{,}280 + \$48{,}750 + \$52{,}330}{8}$$

$$= \$44{,}026.25.$$

Median

The median is the number exactly in the middle of the sorted values,

$$Y_{\text{median}} = \text{value with rank of } .5\,(n+1) = .5\,(10+1) = 11/2 = 5.5.$$

This distribution has an even number of values ($n = 10$), so the median is the average of the two values closest to the middle, those ranked 5 and 6:

$$Y_{\text{median}} = \frac{\$44{,}320 + \$45{,}000}{2} = \frac{\$89{,}320}{2} = \$44{,}660.$$

EXCEL BUILT-IN ANALYSIS

Excel computes the average and median directly with either the Descriptive Statistics program accessed via the Tools → Data Analysis menu sequence or the built-in functions,

```
=AVERAGE(data) and =MEDIAN(data).
```

The trimmed mean is available only as a built-in function,

```
=TRIMMEAN(data,proportion_to_trim).
```

These statistics for the 10 household income values in Cells A2 to J2 are obtained with

$$=\text{AVERAGE}(\text{A2}:\text{J2})$$

$$=\text{MEDIAN}(\text{A2}:\text{J2})$$

$$=\text{TRIMMEAN}(\text{A2}:\text{J2},.20)$$

which results in values of \$5,577,196, \$44,660, and \$44,026.25 appearing in the respective cells in which each formula is entered.

MANAGERIAL INTERPRETATION

The salaries range from a low of \$29,750 to a high of approximately 55 million dollars. The trimmed mean is \$44,026 and the median is \$44,660, both similar in value to the middle-class incomes. The mean of about 5½ million represents *neither* the four middle-class incomes nor the single extremely large income.

Mode

> **mode of a distribution**
> *value that occurs most frequently*

The **mode** is another indicator of the middle of a distribution. A retailer may not care that the mean waist size of the pants sold in his store is 32.89 or even that the median value is 32.5. What is of greater interest is that the waist size 32 was the waist size most desired by his customers during the last year. The retailer can then ensure that plenty of size 32s are available when the fall clothing appears in his store.

On a given day, eight size 32s were sold, eight size 34s were sold, and fewer pants were sold for all other sizes. What is the mode for the pants size sold on that day? In case of a tie for the largest frequency of two values, the distribution is *bimodal*. Similarly, if three values are tied for the largest frequencies, the distribution is *trimodal*. A single mode distribution is *unimodal*. If no value appears more than once, the mean and the median can be straightforwardly computed, but the mode does not exist.

If the data are available only in the form of a frequency distribution with different data values collapsed into the same class interval, the mode of the original data cannot be computed because only the midpoints of each class are known. For most frequency distributions, however, the inability to compute the mode of the original data is of little consequence. Who cares if 259 size 32s but "only" 258 pairs of size 34s were sold? Technically, if these are the two largest frequencies, the mode is 32, but this piece of information alone can be misleading because almost as many size 34s were also sold.

> **modal class of a frequency distribution**
> *bin with the largest number of values*

For frequency distributions, the interest shifts from the frequency of a single value to the frequency of each bin or class interval. For example, suppose bins are of width four, and the bin containing sizes 32–36 has 648 values, more than any other bin. The 32–36 class bin is the **modal class.** Any differences between the 32, 33, 34, 35, and 36 sizes are irrelevant within this grouping.

Comparing the Mean, the Median, and the Mode

The mean, the median, and the mode provide complementary perspectives of the middle of a distribution. One index may be more appropriate than another for a specific distribution, but generally all three indices are reported. The comparison

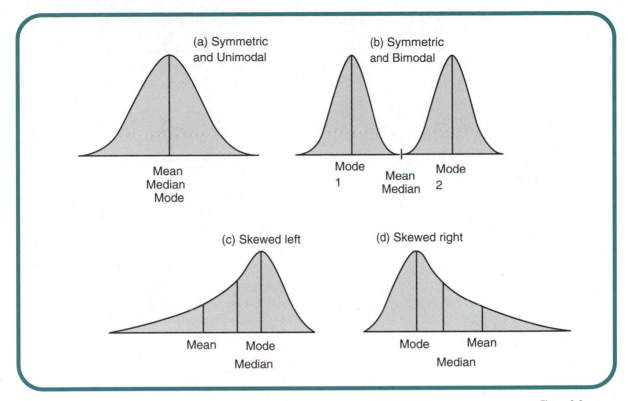

Figure 3-2.
Distributions of differing
skewness.

of their values provides more information regarding the distribution than is available from each statistic separately. By comparing all three values, the approximate shape of the distribution can often be reconstructed, as shown in Figure 3-2.

The distributions illustrated in Figures 3-2a and 3-2b are symmetric. Holding a mirror along the vertical axis of a **symmetric distribution** produces a reflection identical to the half of the distribution covered by the mirror. For a unimodal symmetric distribution as illustrated in Figure 3-2a, the mean, the median, and the mode are all equal. A bimodal symmetric distribution such as in Figure3-2b has a mode that differs from the mean and the median, which are the same value.

A skewed distribution is not symmetric, so that one side has a "tail." The tail represents a small number of either very large or very small values. For a skewed-left distribution (Figure 3-2c), some very small values and fewer or no very large values balance out the small values. Similarly, a skewed-right distribution (Figure 3-2d) has a small number of very large values.

For the skewed-left distribution, the mean is smaller than either the median or the mode because the small values pull the mean away from the median and the mode. The mode is at the highest point of the distribution, the region of most frequently occurring values. The median for the skewed-left distribution is between the mean and the mode because the small values in the tail of the distribution pull the median to the left of the mode to a smaller extent than the mean. Similar logic applies to the skewed-right distribution.

Knowing that the modal class of the dollar value of contracts sold for the past quarter is $85,000, the median is $93,000, and the mean is $102,000 provides much

> **symmetric distribution**
> *graph of a distribution in which the right side reflects the left side*

information regarding the effectiveness of the sales force. Knowing also that the smallest value was only $60,000 and the largest value was $165,000 tells even more about last quarter's performance. The mean is larger than the median and the mode, so the distribution is skewed right. Thus, we know that a small number of salespeople are doing very well and few, if any, salespeople are doing poorly.

EXERCISES

3-1. These data are scores on three quizzes by five students:

	Y_1	Y_2	Y_3
Bradley	0	2	3
Tyler	4	5	2
Dotty	2	3	3
Jordanne	1	7	5
Jeff	4	3	4

Compute the mean of Y_2 with

a. a conceptual worksheet
b. traditional formulas
c. a statistical analysis built into a computer program

3-2. For the data in Exercise 3-1, compute the

a. median of Y_2
b. mode of Y_2

3-3. The following data are the Gross Sales and Net Income of a new computer manufacturer from 1991 to 1995.

	1991	1992	1993	1994	1995
Sales ($ mil)	1918	1902	2661	4071	5284
Net Income ($ mil)	61	154	218	400	454

a. What are the average sales and the average net income for these five years?
b. What are the median sales and the median net income for these five years?
c. How do sales compare to income? Are any trends over time discernible?

3-4. Fred bought 180 shares of XYZ stock for 47⅛, 100 shares of High Flyer for 25⅞, and 250 shares of Blue Sky for 32½. One year later, he sold these stocks for 44, 37⅝, and 58¼, respectively. (Stock prices are expressed to the nearest one-eighth of a dollar.)

a. How much did Fred spend buying the stocks? What was the average price of the three stocks?
b. How much did Fred sell the stocks for? What was the average selling price of the three stocks?
c. What is the average difference in buying and selling price?

3.2 VARIABILITY INDICES

You may be intrigued by the variability of values of many different distributions. Why do salaries among managers differ? Why do some phone calls to the order department get answered immediately and at other times customers are placed on hold for varying lengths of time? The more the stock price fluctuates, the riskier the investment.

People are prime examples of the principle that variability is everywhere. Consider the time it takes two employees, Jim and Bob, to assemble five brackets:

Jim: 5.6   5.9   6.0   6.2   6.3 min.
Bob: 4.0   4.0   5.0   7.0   10.0 min.

These two employees averaged the same number of assembled brackets over the same time span, 6.0. Although the means of the two distributions are identical, however, the distributions are not. Jim's assembly times approximately equal one another, whereas Bob's are more dispersed. A statistic that summarizes variability is larger for Bob's times than for Jim's.

The analysis of variability is central to improving quality. As discussed in Chapter 1, successful quality management reduces variability of process output. For a bank's customers, variability translates into inconsistency of service times, so that some customers standing in line become annoyed at waiting too long for service. For the machine shop, variability means inconsistency in the dimensions of machined parts, so that some parts may not fit into the completed assembly. Many processes can be identified within any company. The output of these processes always varies—the values of a random variable differ.

A starting point for the analysis of variability is an assessment of the *amount* of variability. To accomplish this assessment, two types of variability indices are introduced next. The simplest index of variability is based on the distance between *two* values of the distribution. Other variability indices are computed from *all* values.

Range

The simplest index of variability is the **range.** If the values in the distribution are all approximately equal to each other, the range is small. A large range means more variability, at least among some of the values.

> **range of a distribution**
> *positive difference between the smallest and largest values*

The primary problem with the range is that it is calculated from only two values, the largest and the smallest. All other values in the distribution are ignored, so the range reflects no other aspects of variability. To illustrate this problem, consider the following two distributions.

| Distribution A: | 10 | 80 | 90 | 100 | 110 | 120 | 190 |
| Distribution B: | 10 | 15 | 20 | 100 | 180 | 185 | 190 |

Both distributions have the same range, $190 - 10 = 180$ (as well as the same mean and median of 100), yet the distributions are quite dissimilar. Most of the values from Distribution A are close to the mean and the median of 100, except for the very smallest value, 10, and the largest value, 190. For Distribution B, all values except the mean and the median of 100 are close to either the smallest value of 10 or the largest value of 190.

More sophisticated indices of variability, the variance and the standard deviation, are introduced in the following sections. These indices play a central role throughout statistical theory and practice.

Deviation Scores

The fundamental concept underlying variability for a numerical variable is the distance of each value from a specified target. For the variance and the standard deviation statistics, the target is the mean. The **mean deviation** is the distance of each value from the mean. Therefore, a deviation score indicates how far and in what direction a particular value is from the mean. If the value of Y is above the mean, the corresponding deviation score is positive. For $\overline{Y} = 10$ and $Y = 12$,

> **mean deviation**
> *original value minus the mean,*
> $Y - \overline{Y}$

$$Y - \overline{Y} = 12 - 10 = 2.$$

Negative deviation scores correspond to values of Y below the mean. For $\overline{Y} = 10$ and $Y = 8$,

$$Y - \overline{Y} = 8 - 10 = -2.$$

A value of Y that exactly equals the mean has a deviation of zero.

How does the deviation score reflect variability? If the values are bunched up around the mean with little variability, the deviations are small. Distributions with greater variability have larger deviations around the mean.

The mean deviation is our first encounter with transformed variables. The deviation score is transformed algebraically, by subtracting a constant (the sample mean) from each value of an existing variable. **Transformed variables** are encountered throughout statistical analysis. An example follows.

> **transformed variable**
> *new variable created from existing variables*

STATISTICAL ILLUSTRATION—Variable Transformations

DATA

Table 3-1 shows how mean deviations reflect variability for the distributions of bracket assembly times of two employees, Jim and Bob. Both distributions have the same mean of 6 minutes. Each mean deviation is computed by subtracting the mean of its respective distribution from the given completion time (e.g., for Jim's Bracket #1, $5.6 - 6.0 = -0.4$). The deviation with the largest magnitude for Jim's times is -0.4, whereas the largest deviation for the more variable distribution of Bob's times is 10 times as large, 4.0.

STATISTICAL PRINCIPLE

Each original score has a corresponding deviation score. For example, Bob completed Bracket #4 in 7.0 min and had a corresponding deviation score of 1.0 min for that bracket. The distinction is that the values of the original variable Y are measured and the values of the deviation score $Y - \overline{Y}$ are computed.

Table 3-1.
The transformed variable $Y - \overline{Y}$.

Bracket	Jim Y	Jim $\overline{Y}$	Jim $Y - \overline{Y}$	Bob Y	Bob $\overline{Y}$	Bob $Y - \overline{Y}$
1	5.6	6.0	-0.4	4.0	6.0	-2.0
2	5.9	6.0	-0.1	4.0	6.0	-2.0
3	6.0	6.0	0.0	5.0	6.0	-1.0
4	6.2	6.0	0.2	7.0	6.0	1.0
5	6.3	6.0	0.3	10.0	6.0	4.0
Sum			0.0			0.0

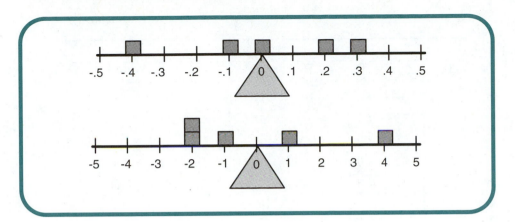

Figure 3-3.
Mean as the balance
point.

A statistic is needed that summarizes the variability of the entire distribution of all the original values. One such possibility is the mean of all the deviation scores. The means for the two respective sets of mean deviations in the bracket example are

$$\text{Jim:} \quad \overline{Y} = \frac{-0.4 - 0.1 + 0.0 + 0.2 + 0.3}{5} = \frac{0}{5} = 0$$

$$\text{Bob:} \quad \overline{Y} = \frac{-2.0 - 2.0 - 1.0 + 1.0 + 4.0}{5} = \frac{0}{5} = 0.$$

For both employees, the respective mean deviations add up to 0, so the corresponding means are also 0. Is this coincidence? The mean is the one number for which, when subtracted from all values of the distribution, the resulting deviations add up to 0. Figure 3-3 illustrates the mean as the *balance point* (center of gravity) of a distribution because all positive deviations exactly cancel out the negative deviations.

The average deviation score cannot serve as a statistic for evaluating the variability of a distribution because it is always zero. How should this problem be addressed? The answer follows.

Population Variance

One possibility for eliminating the problem of the zero sum of deviation scores is to define another transformed variable with only positive or zero values. The *absolute deviation* simply eliminates the accompanying negative signs, and the *squared deviation* squares each deviation. The squared deviation is generally preferred. Not only is the absolute deviation more difficult to work with than the squared deviation, but the squared deviation is intimately related to the normal curve.

Table 3-2 illustrates these squared deviations. Consistent with the previous analyses of these data, the squared deviations for Jim's times are much smaller than for Bob's times. The largest squared deviation score for Bob (16) is 100 times larger than the largest such score for Jim (0.16).

The sum of squares, .30 for Jim and 26.00 for Bob, is the sum of the squared deviations around the mean. The terms "sum of squares of Y" or "SSY" abbreviate the wordier "sum of squared deviations of Y." Statistics is the study of variability, and the **sum of squares** is the most basic and fundamental expression of variability for a numerical variable. The larger the SSY, the larger the *total* variation of the original values around the mean.

sum of squares SSY for variable Y
sum of the squared deviations around the mean

Table 3-2.
The transformed variable, $(Y - \overline{Y})^2$, and the resulting sum of squares.

Bracket	Jim				Bob			
	Y	$\overline{Y}$	$Y - \overline{Y}$	$(Y - \overline{Y})^2$	Y	$\overline{Y}$	$Y - \overline{Y}$	$(Y - \overline{Y})^2$
1	5.6	6.0	-0.4	.16	4.0	6.0	-2.0	4.00
2	5.9	6.0	-0.1	.01	4.0	6.0	-2.0	4.00
3	6.0	6.0	0.0	.00	5.0	6.0	-1.0	1.00
4	6.2	6.0	0.2	.04	7.0	6.0	1.0	1.00
5	6.3	6.0	0.3	.09	10.0	6.0	4.0	16.00
Sum			0.0	0.30			0.0	26.00

SSY is a sum, so the more values, the larger the sum. The size of the SSY reflects both variability and the number of values to sum. To assess only variability, compute the mean of the squared deviations, or the *mean square* of Y.

The **population variance** is computed with each data value deviated from the population mean, μ_Y. The population variance is denoted by a squared lowercase Greek letter sigma, σ^2, or σ_Y^2, to explicitly indicate the variance of Y:

> **population variance of a distribution of Y**
> *mean of the squared deviations, the* mean square

$$\sigma_Y^2 \equiv \frac{\sum (Y - \mu_Y)^2}{N} \equiv \frac{SSY}{N}.$$

The population variance is *not* the mean of the original data Y, but the mean of the squared deviations $(Y - \mu_Y)^2$.

Sample Variance and Standard Deviation

The same reasoning defines both the population variance σ_Y^2 and the sample variance s_Y^2. When computing the variance of a sample, however, the population mean μ_Y is usually not known in advance, so the deviations are computed around the sample mean, $\overline{Y}$, instead of around μ_Y. This apparently straightforward substitution introduces another complication: One statistic $\overline{Y}$ is needed to compute another statistic s_Y^2.

First compute the sample mean, $\overline{Y}$. Then use $\overline{Y}$ to compute the deviation scores needed for the computation of another statistic, the sample variance. Computing the sample variance requires a statistic previously computed from the *same* data. Computing one statistic and then making a second pass through the same data to compute a second statistic is fudging a bit, because using information from the first pass through the data to compute a statistic in the second pass in effect uses up or locks up a "piece of data."

To illustrate, refer back to the previous example with Bob's five assembly times of 4, 4, 5, 7, and 10 min. These data sum to 30 min. with a sample mean of $\overline{Y} = 6$. Given knowledge of this sum (or mean) and any four values of this distribution, such as the first four values, the fifth and final assembly time of 10 can be deduced:

$$4 + 4 + 5 + 7 + \boxed{} = 30.$$

Using $\overline{Y}$ in the computation of the sample variance s_Y^2 results in one less *independent* piece of data. One data value is locked in when the sample variance is computed using the sample mean previously computed from the same data. Given $\overline{Y}$ from the first pass through the data, only four values are free to vary for the second pass through the data when computing SSY.

The concept of **degrees of freedom,** which is the number of observations not locked in, or free to vary, plays an important role in many statistical analyses. For the computation of the sample variance s_Y^2, one other statistic—the sample mean $\overline{Y}$—is required. The effective sample size for the sample variance is the actual sample size n reduced by one,

$$df = n - 1.$$

degrees of freedom
of a statistic
*effective sample size,
or the number of
values free to vary
after other statistics
are computed from
the same data*

For statistics other than the sample variance, *df* may assume values such as $n - 2$ and so forth, depending on the number of "recycled" statistics previously estimated from the same data.

As discussed in Chapter 1, interest typically focuses not on the particular sample from which the statistic was computed but on the larger population from which the sample was obtained. To provide the best estimate of the population variance from sample data, compute the **sample variance** with the effective sample size $n - 1$, the degrees of freedom, instead of with sample size n,

$$s_Y^2 \equiv \frac{\sum (Y - \overline{Y})^2}{n - 1} \equiv \frac{\text{SSY}}{df}.$$

sample variance
*sum of the squared
deviations divided
by degrees of freedom*

An alternate notation for the variance s_Y^2 is MSY, or mean square of *Y*, which emphasizes that the variance is the mean of the squared deviations.

Both the population variance and the sample variance are the mean of squared deviation scores. In both cases, the mean is based on the *effective* sample size. For the population, the effective sample size is N, and for a sample with unknown μ_Y, the effective sample size is the degrees of freedom, $n - 1$.

One more transformation beyond the variance is useful for describing variability. A problem with the variance is that squaring the mean deviations also squares the units of measurement. For example, instead of expressing variability in lb for measurements of weight, the variance expresses variability in terms of squared lb, a unit of little intrinsic interest. Variability is expressed with the same measurement units as the original variable by unsquaring the variance. The population **standard deviation** is σ, and the sample standard deviation is *s*. The notation

$$\sigma_Y = \sqrt{\sigma_Y^2} \text{ or } s_Y = \sqrt{s_Y^2}$$

standard deviation
*square root of
variance*

explicitly refers to the standard deviation of the variable *Y*.

An example of computing and interpreting the standard deviation follows. The conceptual worksheet presented in this example for computing the sum of squares follows the form used throughout this text.

Statistics is the study of variability, and the sum of squares is the basic unit of variability for numerical data.

Each worksheet that computes a sum of squares is labeled for the specific variable of interest, such as price per share (PPS). Each worksheet is also labeled with the generic description of each of the variables in the worksheet.

Response	Center	Deviation from Cntr	Squared Deviation

The Response is the variable of interest. The Center is the value from which the deviations are computed. For the computation of the standard deviation, the center is the mean of the variable Y. The Deviation from Center and the Deviation Squared also appear in the table.

BUSINESS APPLICATION 3.2—Standard Deviation

MANAGERIAL PROBLEM

The 1992 closing Price per Share (PPS) of 10 publicly traded companies was recorded. What is the standard deviation of these prices?

APPLICATION—CONCEPTUAL WORKSHEET

	A	B	C	D	E	F
1			Response	Center	Deviation from Cntr	Squared Deviation
2			PPS	Mean PPS	mean deviation	squared deviation
3		Company	Y	$\bar{Y}$	$Y-\bar{Y}$	$(Y-\bar{Y})^2$
4	1	PHIL. SUB. CORP	16.00	23.36	-7.36	54.23
5	2	TULTEX CORP	8.63	23.36	-14.73	217.09
6	3	CALMAT CO	22.50	23.36	-0.86	0.75
7	4	TANDY CORP	24.50	23.36	1.14	1.29
8	5	NICOR INC	49.75	23.36	26.39	696.22
9	6	OK. GAS & ELECTRIC	34.13	23.36	10.77	115.91
10	7	FAMILY DOL. STORES	17.25	23.36	-6.11	37.38
11	8	IMO INDUSTRIES INC	6.50	23.36	-16.86	284.39
12	9	RTZ PLC	41.38	23.36	18.02	324.58
13	10	TORO CO	13.00	23.36	-10.36	107.41
14		Sum	233.64		0.00	1839.25
15		Effective sample size	10			9.00
16		Mean	23.36			204.36
17		SQRT of Mean				14.30
18						
19						14.30

From this worksheet, the sum of Y is 233.64 for a sample size of 10, which yields a sample mean of 23.36. The analysis of the squared deviations yields a sum of squares of 1,839.25 for 9 degrees of freedom, a variance of 204.36 and a standard deviation of 14.30.

The following excerpt from the worksheet displays the cell formulas for computing the sum, sample size, mean, and square root. Also displayed are the deviation from the mean and the deviation squared for the last observation in Row 13.

	B	C	D	E	F
13	TORO CO	13	=$C$1	=C13-$C$16	=E13^2
14	Sum	=SUM(C4:C13)		=SUM(E4:E13)	=SUM(F4:F13)
15	Effective sample size	=COUNT(C4:C13)			=COUNT(F4:F13)-1
16	Mean	=C14/C15			=F14/F15
17	SQRT of Mean				=SQRT(F16)
18					
19					=STDEV(C4:C13)

APPLICATION—TRADITIONAL NOTATION

Mean PPS is 23.36. The mean deviation for the first company, Philadelphia Suburban Corp, is

$$Y - \overline{Y} = 16.00 - 23.36 = -7.36.$$

Most of the effort in calculating the standard deviation is obtaining the sum of squares, the sum of the squared deviations for *all* of the observations,

$$\text{SSY} = \sum (Y - \overline{Y})^2 = 1839.25.$$

The calculation of the corresponding variance quickly follows:

$$s_Y^2 \equiv \frac{\sum (Y - \overline{Y})^2}{n - 1} \equiv \frac{\text{SSY}}{df} = \frac{1839.25}{9} \approx 204.36$$

The square root of this variance is the standard deviation,

$$s_Y \equiv \sqrt{s_Y^2} = \sqrt{204.36} \approx \$14.30.$$

APPLICATION—EXCEL BUILT-IN ANALYSIS

Excel computes the standard deviation directly with either the Descriptive Statistics program accessed via the Tools → Data Analysis menu sequence, or the function

=STDEV(number1,number2,...).

The 10 PPS values in the preceding table are in Cells C4 through C13. The estimated standard deviation is obtained from the built-in function,

=STDEV(C4:C13),

which results in the value 14.30 appearing in Cell F19 in the previous worksheet.

STATISTICAL PRINCIPLE

The standard deviation, $14.30, is much smaller than the corresponding variance, $204.36. The standard deviation is expressed in dollars, whereas the variance is expressed in squared dollars.

MANAGERIAL INTERPRETATION

The magnitude of a value is the distance from zero, positive or negative. The size of the standard deviation indicates the typical magnitude of the deviations from the mean. These magnitudes range from $0.86 to $26.39, and this range of magnitudes is summarized by the value of the standard deviation, $s_Y = \$14.30$.

As noted previously, one reason for the wide use of the standard deviation as an indicator of variability is that the standard deviation is expressed in the same units as the original variable *Y*. Another powerful reason for using the standard deviation is its relation to the normal curve, as discussed next.

The Standard Deviation and the Normal Curve

An important property of the standard deviation is its relation to the family of normal distributions. Figure 3-4 illustrates two normal distributions. Both normal distributions are bell-shaped. Most values occur in the middle of the distribution; values very far from the middle are rare.

The population mean μ_Y and the population standard deviation σ_Y jointly define a specific normal distribution. The standard deviation of any normal distribution specifies ranges over which different percentages of values occur. For example, 95% of the values of *any* normal distribution lie within 1.96 (or about 2) standard deviations of the mean.

According to the **empirical rule,** almost all values of a normally distributed variable are close to the mean, spanning only six standard deviations (6σ). As illustrated in Figure 3-5, normally distributed values more than two standard deviations from

empirical rule
virtually all values of a normally distributed variable— 99.73%—lie within three standard deviations of either side of the mean

Figure 3-4.
Two normal distributions (curves) with the same mean but different standard deviations.

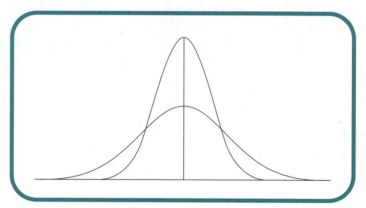

Figure 3-5.
Range of values of a normally distributed variable in terms of standard deviations from the mean.

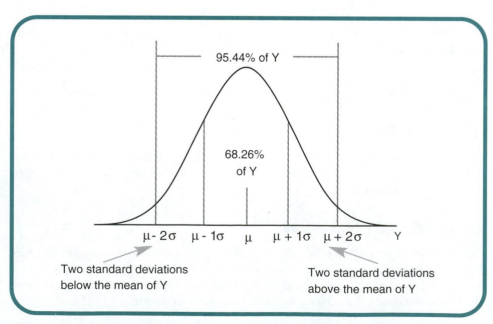

the mean are infrequent, and more than two-thirds (68.26%) lie within a single standard deviation of the mean.

The standard deviation of a normal distribution is precisely interpreted. The percentage of values between any two endpoints can be specified, such as 68.26% of values within one standard deviation of the mean. Although the standard deviation is useful for describing the variation of almost any numerical distribution, the standard deviation of normally distributed data contains information regarding the percentage of values that lie between any two endpoints.

STATISTICAL ILLUSTRATION—Generating Normal Curve Data

What are some representative values from a normal distribution with $\mu_Y = 50$ and $\sigma_Y = 10$?

APPLICATION—EXCEL BUILT-IN ANALYSIS

Excel simulates sampling from specified distributions with the Random Number Generation program accessed via the Tools → Data Analysis menu sequence. Calling up this program results in the following dialog box and resulting output. In this example, 15 data values are sampled for a single variable. The dialog box specifies that the data are from a normal distribution with a mean of 50 and a standard deviation of 10.

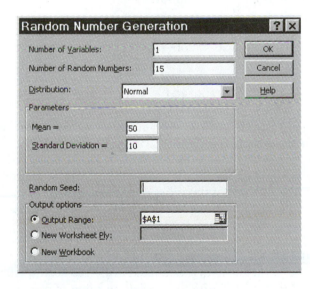

STATISTICAL PRINCIPLE

The data range from 28.94 to 66.09. One standard deviation is 10, so two standard deviations is 20. Two standard deviations down from the mean of 50 is 30, and two above the mean is 70. Even for this small data set of only 15 normal observations, rough compliance with the normal distribution was obtained. Both the minimum and the maximum values of the distribution are approximately two standard deviations on either side of the mean. Larger samples would provide even greater compliance.

Next, the concept of analyzing a set of values all generated by the same process is further refined.

Common and Assignable Causes of Variation

The standard deviation can be computed from any set of numeric data. For example, the standard deviation can be computed from five randomly sampled stock prices from the NYSE combined with the GMAT scores of five randomly sampled MBA students. However, the sample mean of these 10 values does not correspond to a population mean of interest, so their standard deviation is of little interest. Although computationally straightforward, the mean of five stock prices and of five GMAT scores has no meaningful interpretation. Instead of representing a sample from a single interesting population, these 10 values actually represent two distinct populations of interest, with two distinct processes generating their values.

Statistics such as the mean and the standard deviation are most meaningfully interpreted for data sampled from the *same* population in which a single process generates all the data. Although each data value Y potentially differs from other values, a constancy underlies all values from the same process. The mean and the standard deviation of the population from which each data value is drawn are the *same* for all values of Y. Statistical models account for this constancy, as well as for the resulting variation. A model specifies sources of variation for the output (response) of an ongoing process, or the response variable Y. These sources of variation contribute either to a stable, known component or to an unexplained component. This unexplained component is random error.

The standard deviation portrays variation in terms of deviations around a constant mean. The **stable-process model,** which generates the values of the response variable Y, is expressed as Actual Response = Population Mean + Random Fluctuation, or

> **stable process model**
> *actual response Y is the sum of the population mean and random error*

$$Y = \mu_Y + \varepsilon, \text{ with constant } \sigma_\varepsilon.$$

If the population value μ_Y is not known, the sample value $\overline{Y}$ serves as its estimate, with corresponding sample error e replacing the population error E.

The model specifies that the stable component underlying each value of Y is the unchanging population mean response, μ_Y. The model does not account for deviations from μ_Y. Random fluctuations of the value of Y around the center, μ_Y, are unexplained by the model and so represent the estimated source of error e. The variability of these fluctuations is constant across all values of Y.

The value of μ_Y is identical for all values of response Y, so the *only* source of variability of Y specified by the model of a stable process is the unpredictable random error ε. Suppose the population mean μ_Y is estimated as $\overline{Y} = 23.26$. If the first replicaton of the process yielded $\varepsilon = -7.26$, then the resulting value of Y is 16.00. If the second replicaton yielded $\varepsilon = 1.14$, then $Y = 24.40$. The value of ε is random, so both the values of ε and ultimately of the response Y are also unpredictable, known only after the data value is sampled. Figure 3-6 plots these deviations around the center from the process of sampling 10 price per share values.

What contributes to the size of these error terms, ε, and ultimately of Y? Why does one coin toss result in a head and another toss of the same coin result in a tail? Why does one person hired turn out to have the ideas that contribute to en-

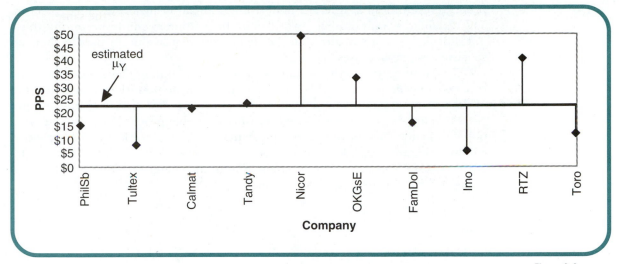

Figure 3-6.
Deviations of the 10 company PPS values from the estimated mean.

hanced profitability, and yet another person hired with the same expectations leaves the company in only a few months having contributed nothing? Sometimes the answer is that there is no answer. From the limited information available, the combined influences of unexplained and unaccounted for variables, which the model designates as chance fluctuations, contribute to the final outcome.

We do know, however, that the value of the error term underlying each data value reflects the cumulative effects of many relatively small chance fluctuations. **Common causes** are numerous, small random influences that jointly influence all values of response Y.

Consider the common causes that influence the process of drilling a hole in a machined part. Inevitably the holes differ from each other on a variety of criteria, including the distance from the center of the actual hole to the center of the desired location. Exactly where the center of a particular hole is located depends on many factors such as the sharpness of the drill, the amount of lubricant on the drill, the angle at which the operator is standing relative to the drill, the firmness of the fixture in which the part is clamped into place, the mental alertness of the operator at that particular point in time, and even the humidity and temperature of the room.

Many changing factors contribute to the random variability ε of every hole drilled. Yet all outputs of the process—the drilled holes—are sampled from the same population with the same mean and standard deviation. Because the population mean μ_Y is a constant, the only source of variability from output to output is the random variation ε.

The stable-process model does *not* describe the generation of all values of output Y whenever the underlying mean or variance *differs* for some of the output. In this situation, a special or **assignable cause**—a transitory, relatively influential source of variability—applies to some but not all of the outputs. Perhaps the person who usually runs the drill press is on vacation, and a poorly trained temporary employee is drilling instead. Or perhaps a defective lot of metal was received. Each of these influential anomalies temporarily changed the structure of the

common causes
random contributions to the variability of all process output

assignable cause
influences only some of the output of a process

process, resulting in a different underlying population mean, variance, or both. The variability of only those holes drilled by the temporary employee, or only those holes drilled in parts made from the defective metal, is due in part to their respective assignable causes.

The presence of assignable causes changes the defining characteristics of the process. A **stable process** yields varying output, but the underlying characteristics of the process, the population mean and the standard deviation, remain constant. Note that a stable process is not necessarily a desirable process, because the variation may be too large or the process mean may be too high or low. A stable process is simply one without assignable causes.

To assess the extent of the variation around the center with the standard deviation, first specify the population mean.

stable process
process with only common cause variation

> *Specifying the population mean of interest includes a consideration of the underlying sources of variation.*

For example, the manager of a fleet of trucks wants to know the average fuel mileage of the trucks, so the response variable Y is fuel mileage. The issue is that each time the same truck follows the same route, fuel mileage varies.

Much of this variation is due to cumulating the many relatively small, unaccountable random influences on fuel mileage. The specific truck, the brand of fuel, the flow of traffic along the route, the temperature and humidity, the mechanical condition of the engine, and other factors all contribute to the value of Y, or the specific fuel mileage obtained from a tank of fuel. Each of these relatively minor influences is typically not measured, but their cumulative impact results in a specific value of ε each time a route is driven. The different values of ε that result from driving the same route at different times account for the random variation of Y.

However, the fleet contains two types of trucks: big trucks and little trucks. The most obvious and pronounced source of variation in fuel mileage among trucks is truck size. Big trucks get considerably worse fuel mileage than little trucks. Because this source of variation is identifiable (assignable) and systematic, it should be explicitly included in the model apart from the error term.

To meaningfully assess the mileage of the fleet and the corresponding variability, consider the two types of trucks as defining two separate populations, each with its own underlying population mean. A substantial, identifiable source of variation, such as type of truck, usually comprises the stable component of the model. For the stable-process model, this stable component is the respective population mean fuel mileage for one type of truck, μ_Y. Two versions of the model are specified, one for the big trucks and one for the little trucks. Assessing fuel mileage for a different type of truck shifts the analysis to a different population with a different value of μ_Y.

Variation implies that different values are different distances from the mean of the entire distribution. Analogous to the way in which inches or centimeters assess height, this distance of a value from the mean can be expressed in terms of the standard deviation. This idea is central to statistical analysis and is explored further in the next section.

EXERCISES

 3-5. The following data are the number correct on a quiz for five students:

	Score
Bradley	2
Tyler	5
Dotty	3
Jordanne	7
Jeff	3

Compute the standard deviation of Score with the

a. conceptual worksheet
b. traditional formulas
c. statistical analysis built into a computer program

 3-6. The following data represent the Gross Sales and the Net Income of a new computer manufacturer from 1991 to 1995.

	1991	1992	1993	1994	1995
Sales ($ mil)	1918	1902	2661	4071	5284
Net Income ($ mil)	61	154	218	400	454

a. What are the standard deviation of Sales and the standard deviation of Net Income for these five years?
b. Is the standard deviation an effective summary of the variability of these distributions? Why or why not?

 3-7. Using a computer program such as Excel, generate 100 normally distributed data values with a population mean of 100 and a standard deviation of 15.

a. What percentage of values of this distribution are more than 30 units (two standard deviations) above and below the mean?
b. Is the result in (a) consistent with data from a normal distribution? Why or why not?

 3-8. About 95% of the values of a normally distributed variable lie within two standard deviations of the population mean, μ_Y, which means that about 95% of the values span a range of 4 standard deviations, or 4σ. Accordingly, the standard deviation can be approximated from the range of a sample of normally distributed values, or

$$\sigma \approx \text{Range}/4.$$

To evaluate the effectiveness of this approximation, use a computer program such as Excel to generate 100 normally distributed values with a mean of 100 and a standard deviation of 15. Sort the 100 values from smallest to largest.

a. Calculate the range of the data for the first 10 values.
b. Use the above approximation to estimate σ from these 10 values. How close is the approximation to the true value of 15?
c. Calculate the range of the data for all 100 values.
d. Use the above approximation to estimate σ from these 100 values. How close is the approximation to the true value of 15?
e. Suggest how the approximation should be modified to increase its accuracy for large samples.

3.3 RELATIVE POSITION OF A VALUE IN A DISTRIBUTION

The sample standard deviation, s_Y, summarizes the variability of an entire distribution of values. A related issue is the distance of a *single* value from the middle. How does a score of 88% on an aptitude test compare to the other scores? A not very precise answer is, "Near the top" or "Somewhere near the middle." A more precise answer to this question is the *z-value*.

A variable can be measured in any of several different units. Financial results can be expressed in terms of dollars, marks, lira, and so forth. Length is measured in feet, inches, or millimeters. In these examples, each unit applies to only specific kinds of dimensions, such as inches to height and dollars to money. A unit applicable to *any* numeric variable is the standard deviation.

z-value of Y

number of standard deviations a value Y is from the mean

A **z-value** indicates the relative position of an observation within the distribution. A transformed variable, Z, defines a distribution of z-values transformed from the original values. If $Z = -1.2$, then the corresponding value of Y is 1.2 standard deviations *below* the mean of Y. If $Z = 0.4$, then the corresponding value of Y is 0.4 standard deviations *above* the mean.

The expression for the Z-transformation follows directly from its definition. For either population values or sample statistics, the variable Z is

$$Z_Y \equiv \frac{Y - \mu_Y}{\sigma_Y} \text{ or } Z_Y \equiv \frac{Y - \overline{Y}}{s_Y}.$$

To compute Z_Y, first compute the mean and the standard deviation of Y. Then, subtract the mean from the value and divide by the standard deviation.[1]

Z-values rescale the original variable without changing the shape of the underlying distribution. The same histogram is obtained whether height is measured in inches, centimeters, or the number of standard deviations from the mean. The histogram remains the same; only the variable axis is rescaled to indicate a new unit of measurement. The unit affects the scale used to display the corresponding distribution but not the shape of the distribution. The same number of people who are 71" tall are also 5'11" tall.

We have shown three transformations of the variable Y: deviations, squared deviations, and Z. Each of these transformations is a variable, with its own mean and standard deviation. The mean of a population distribution of z-values is 0 and the standard deviation of this distribution is 1.

BUSINESS APPLICATION 3.3—z-Value

MANAGERIAL PROBLEM

Different aptitude tests were given to two different groups of newly hired employees to assist in their job placement. To assess how well each employee did on the test, management could either examine each employee's number (or percentage) correct, or each z-value. Each group consisted of 18 employees.

DATA

Group A:

    54 58 54 55 56 57 57 54 57 56 54 59 56 56 60 56 55 54

Group B:

    80 80 78 74 69 65 62 60 55 54 52 52 47 45 43 36 33 23

---

1. A linear transformation of one variable (X) to another (Y) takes the form $Y = bX + a$. Examples include converting inches to millimeters and Y to Z, where $b = \frac{1}{\sigma_Y}$ and $a = \frac{\mu_Y}{\sigma_Y}$.

For the first test, the scores exhibited little variability; everyone scored at least 54 correct out of 60 possible, or 90%, on the test. For the second test, scores varied over a much wider range; for example, the lowest score was only 23 correct out of 80, or 28.75%.

APPLICATION—TRADITIONAL NOTATION

For both distributions, the deviation score for a value of $Y = 60$ is $+4$. That is, because the mean of the two distributions is the same, 56, an original score of 60 has the same deviation score in either distribution. However, the standard deviation of the first distribution, 1.782, is considerably smaller than for the second distribution, 16.606. Accordingly, $Y = 60$ is many more standard deviations from the mean in the first distribution than in the second. The z-value for $Y = 60$ is much larger in the first distribution. For example, for the first employee in Group A, Z is

$$Z_Y \equiv \frac{Y - \overline{Y}}{s_Y} = \frac{60 - 56}{1.782} = 2.24.$$

Table 3-3 presents all z-values for Group A. Compare these z-values with the z-values for Group B, which are found in Table 3-4.

Table 3-3. Group A: Z defined from $\overline{Y} = 56$, $s_Y = 1.782$.

Employee	Number Right, Y	$Y - \overline{Y}$	$Z \equiv \dfrac{Y - \overline{Y}}{s_Y}$	% Right $= Y/60$
1	60	4	2.24	100.00
2	59	3	1.68	98.33
3	58	2	1.12	96.67
4	57	1	0.56	95.00
5	57	1	0.56	95.00
6	57	1	0.56	95.00
7	56	0	0.00	93.33
8	56	0	0.00	93.33
9	56	0	0.00	93.33
10	56	0	0.00	93.33
11	56	0	0.00	93.33
12	55	-1	-0.56	91.67
13	55	-1	-0.56	91.67
14	54	-2	-1.12	90.00
15	54	-2	-1.12	90.00
16	54	-2	-1.12	90.00
17	54	-2	-1.12	90.00
18	54	-2	-1.12	90.00

Table 3-4.
Group B: Z **defined**
from $\bar{Y} = 56$,
$s_Y = 16.606$.

Employee	Number Right, Y	$Y - \bar{Y}$	$Z \equiv \dfrac{Y - \bar{Y}}{s_Y}$	% Right $= Y/60$
1	80	24	1.45	100.00
2	80	24	1.45	100.00
3	78	22	1.32	97.50
4	74	18	1.08	92.50
5	69	13	0.78	86.25
6	65	9	0.54	81.25
7	62	6	0.36	77.50
8	60	4	0.24	75.00
9	55	-1	-0.06	68.75
10	54	-2	-0.12	67.50
11	52	-4	-0.24	65.00
12	52	-4	-0.24	58.75
13	47	-9	-0.54	56.25
14	47	-11	-0.66	53.75
15	43	-13	-0.78	45.00
16	36	-20	-1.28	41.25
17	33	-23	-1.39	28.75
18	23	-33	-1.99	90.00

APPLICATION—EXCEL BUILT-IN ANALYSIS

To compute Z_Y for a value of Y, first compute the mean and the standard deviation of the entire distribution. The Excel Standardize function computes Z_Y for a single value of Y,

```
=STANDARDIZE(Y,mean,SD).
```

For example,

```
=STANDARDIZE(C3,$C$22,$C$23)
```

standardizes the value in Cell C3, where the mean of the distribution is stored in $C$22 and the standard deviation is in $C$23. Applying this formula to the entire distribution of Y results in the distribution of z-values.

STATISTICAL PRINCIPLE

Z indicates the *relative* standing of the corresponding Y value. Although everyone in Group A received at least 90% correct, the z-values range all the way from -1.12 to 2.24. Ninety percent correct is good performance in absolute terms, but relative to the entire distribution, 90% correct is 1.12 standard deviations *below* the mean. Only when the scores are more variable does 90% result in a positive *z*-value, as in the scores for Group B.

MANAGERIAL INTERPRETATION

Aptitude test scores differ depending on whether the scores are expressed in absolute or relative terms. An applicant with 90% correct has a negative *z*-value if 90% is a low score relative to the others. Depending on the test and the specific nature of the job, 90% could indicate excellent aptitude. The performance of the other test takers could be irrelevant in terms of job placement. In other situations, as with a surplus of employees for a position, employees scoring low on a test relative to everyone else, regardless of their absolute scores, would be assigned a different job.

The following section combines concepts presented in this and the previous section. The concept of probability is introduced in the context of applying *z*-values to the normal distribution.

EXERCISES

 3-9. The following data represent the Gross Sales and the Net Income of a new computer start-up from 1991 to 1995.

Application

	1991	1992	1993	1994	1995
Sales ($ mil)	1918	1902	2661	4071	5284
Net Income ($ mil)	61	154	218	400	454

a. What are the *z*-values of sales and net income for these five years?
b. What do these values indicate about the pattern of sales and net income?

3-10. Roughly draw a normal curve. On this drawing, indicate approximately where

Mechanical

a. $z = -1.00$
b. $z = 1.50$
c. $z = -0.2$
d. $z = 5.5$

 3-11. The first 25 space shuttle flight launch temperatures are presented below to the nearest 5 degrees Fahrenheit, sorted from lowest to highest value.

Application

```
30  55  60  60  65  70  70  70  70
70  70  70  70  70  70  75  75  75
75  80  80  80  80  80  85
```

a. Standardize these data with a conceptual worksheet.
b. Standardize one of these values with traditional formulas.
c. Standardize these data with the built-in analysis of a computer program.
d. Determine how many standard deviations below the mean the launch temperature (30°) was on the day of the shuttle explosion.
e. Make a recommendation based on your analysis of these data.

 3-12. Using a computer program such as Excel, generate 100 normally distributed data values with a population mean of 100 and a standard deviation of 15.

Mechanical

a. Sort the data from the smallest to the largest values. Standardize this sorted data.
b. Determine what percentage of values of this distribution have *z*-values larger than 2.0 or smaller than −2.0.
c. Determine whether the result in (b) is consistent with data from a normal distribution and why or why not.

3.4 NORMAL DISTRIBUTION PROBABILITIES

The last two sections introduced two important concepts, standard deviation and z-values. This section demonstrates that the standard deviation is the basic unit for calibrating a normal distribution.

Probability

probability
degree of certainty that an event will occur

The study of probability is the study of the **probability** of events. How are the probabilities of events assigned? What is the probability that the next applicant is male, that the next employee on the list called in sick, or that the contents of the next cereal box weighs between 11.9 and 12.1 oz? The probability of an event is denoted as P(event), so the probability of the cereal box weight is written as $P(11.9 < Y < 12.1)$.

Probabilities range from zero to one, inclusive. A probability of 0.0 for an event means the event will not occur, and a probability of 1.0 means that the event will occur. Numbers between 0.0 and 1.0 reflect varying degrees of likelihood that the event will occur. The probability that a coin tossed into the air will land on heads is 0.5, which means that it is just as likely that a heads will be obtained on the next flip as that it won't.

Unlike the probability of a single value of data, the probability of a single *theoretical* value of a continuous variable is zero. So how can probabilities of continuous variables be computed?

Probabilities for a continuous random variable are computed for a range of values— or interval—of the random variable.

Consider a normally distributed Y with $\mu_Y = 100$ and $\sigma_Y = 15$. For the single value $Y = 115$,

$$P(Y = 115) = 0.$$

Figure 3-7 illustrates that the probability that a randomly sampled value of Y is less than 115 is

$$P(Y < 115) \approx .84.$$

The probability of a single value is zero, so the expressions

$$P(Y < 115) = P(Y \leq 115) \approx .84$$

are equivalent. The geometric interpretation of probability is area under the curve, so the total area is 1.00.

Normal Curve Probabilities

Normal curve probabilities are obtained with integral calculus. For convenience, these probabilities are tabled in Appendix A and provided by many computer programs. The probabilities in the table are for z-values, the number of standard deviations a value is from its mean. Appendix A gives the probabilities for $Z < z$,

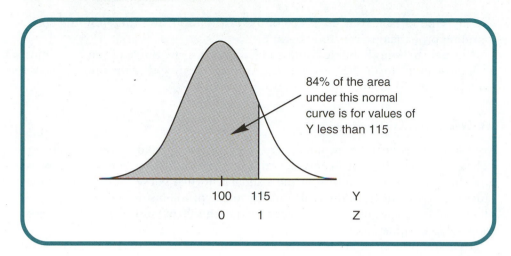

Figure 3-7.
For normal Y with $\mu_Y =$
100 and $\sigma_Y = 15$, the
probability that a
randomly selected Y is
less than 115 is about
.84.

84% of the area
under this normal
curve is for values of
Y less than 115

100	115	Y
0	1	Z

Z	Cumul. Prob.
1.20	0.8849
1.21	0.8869
1.22	0.8888
1.23	0.8907
1.24	*0.8925*
1.25	0.8944
1.26	0.8962
1.27	0.8980
1.28	0.8997

Table 3-5.
The probability that a
normally distributed Z is
less than 1.24 is 0.8925.

where z is the constant of interest between -4 and 4 and where Z is a random variable, or the Z-transformation of the variable of interest, Y. For example, the **cumulative normal probability** for $Z = 1.24$, $P(Z < 1.24)$, is the probability that a randomly sampled value from a normally distributed Y is less than 1.24 standard deviations above its mean μ_Y.

To find $P(Z < 1.24)$ using the cumulative normal probabilities listed in Appendix A and the excerpt in Table 3-5, first identify the value of the constant z, 1.24. The accompanying probability, 0.8925, is available directly from the table. The probability is .8925 that a randomly sampled value of a normally distributed variable Y is less than 1.24 standard deviations above the mean μ_Y.

The probabilities of interest are usually not for Z but for the original random variable Y. When using a table, $P(Z < z)$ is the vehicle for finding $P(Y < y)$. First convert Y to Z, which has the same effect as converting feet to inches. A new scale

**cumulative normal
probability of a value**
*area under the
normal curve less
than (to the left of)
the value*

describes the variable, but the shape of the distribution, and therefore the corresponding probabilities, remain the same.

Normal curve probabilities can be obtained from any range of values, not just from those of the form $P(Y < y)$. Finding probabilities in either the upper or lower tail of a normal distribution is demonstrated next.

New Events from Existing Events

Normal curve probability problems are often not as straightforward as the preceding problem. Many problems require some reformulation before the desired probability can be obtained from the standard normal curve table. Probabilities can be read directly from the table only for those problems of the form $P(Z < z)$. All probabilities must ultimately be expressed in this form before using the normal curve table in Appendix A.

To accomplish these transformations, define two new events from the original events: the complement and the union. We also show how to compute the probabilities of these new events from the probabilities of existing events. The complement is presented first.

A complement of an event defines a new event. For our purposes, an event is a continuous random variable's range of values. For example, Event A could be the values of Y greater than 115. The **complement** of an event is everything left over from the original event. If Event A is $Y \geq 115$, the complement of A is $Y < 115$.

> **complement of Event A**
> *all values of the variable not in A*

Because the probability of the range of all possible values is one, the sum of the probabilities of an event and its complement is one. This property is restated in the following theorem. This theorem is used repeatedly in computing normal curve probabilities.

> *The probability of the complement of Event A is $1 - P(A)$.*

Another way of defining a new event is through the union of two existing events. The **union** consists of all values in A only, in B only, and those in *both* A and B. The union of two events A and B is written as [A *or* B] because a value of Y is included in the union if it is in A *or* if it is in B *or* it is in both.

> **union of Events A and B, Event [A or B]**
> *all values in A and all values in B*

Consider the probability of the union. The union of Events A and B includes all values of Y in A, so the probability of the union, $P(A \text{ } or \text{ } B)$, is at least as large as $P(A)$. This union also includes all the values of Y in B, so $P(A \text{ } or \text{ } B)$ is at least as large as $P(B)$. Further, some of the values of Y can be in both Event A and Event B. However, in the applications of primary interest to us, Events A and B are **mutually exclusive events;** the values of Y are either in Event A or Event B but not both. For example, $Y > 10$ and $Y < 5$ are mutually exclusive events.

> **mutually exclusive events**
> *events with no values in common*

The probability of the union of two mutually exclusive events is easily computed if the probability of each of the two events is known.

> *probability of the union of mutually exclusive events A and B*
>
> $$P(A \text{ } or \text{ } B) = P(A) + P(B)$$

An example that illustrates the complement and the union follows.

BUSINESS APPLICATION 3.4—Normal Distribution Probability

MANAGERIAL PROBLEM

When beginning a project to minimize variability of the output of the length of a machined bushing, management noted that the bushing would not be functional if it was over 12.450 inches long or shorter than 12.370 inches. After thousands of these bushings had been manufactured, the population was determined to be normal with a mean length of 12.416 inches and a standard deviation of 0.018. What proportion of manufactured parts is defective in terms of length?

APPLICATION—TRADITIONAL NOTATION

The probability that a part is too short is the *lower-tail probability* $P(Y < 12.370)$:

$$P(Y < 12.370) = P\left(\frac{Y - \overline{Y}}{s_Y} < \frac{12.370 - 12.416}{0.018}\right) = P(Z < -2.56).$$

This probability is read directly from the normal curve probability table in Appendix A as 0.0052.

The probability that a part is too long is the *upper-tail probability* $P(Y > 12.450)$. Use the complement rule to reexpress this *greater than* probability statement in the form of a *less than* probability from Appendix A:

$$P(Y > 12.450) = 1 - P(Y < 12.450).$$

This probability is

$$P(Y < 12.450) = P\left(\frac{Y - \overline{Y}}{s_Y} < \frac{12.450 - 12.416}{0.018}\right)$$
$$= P(Z < 1.89) = 0.9706.$$

The probability that a randomly sampled part is too long is

$$P(Y > 12.450) = 1 - 0.9706 = 0.0294.$$

The *combined probability*, the probability of the union of these two mutually exclusive events that a part is too long or too short, is

$$P[Y < 12.370 \quad or \quad Y > 12.450] = P(Y < 12.370) + P(Y > 12.450)$$
$$= 0.0052 + 0.0295 = 0.0348.$$

APPLICATION—EXCEL BUILT-IN ANALYSIS

The Excel function for cumulative (lower-tail) normal probabilities is

$$=\texttt{NORMDIST(Y,Mean,SD,1)},$$

where the "1" for the last value in the list[2] is a flag that specifies the cumulative probability for the value Y.

---

2. A "0" for the last value in the list requests the density of the value Y, which is the value on the vertical axis of the normal curve. Plotting a range of these densities results in a normal curve.

The probability that a part is too short, $P(Y < 12.370)$, is

$$=\text{NORMDIST}(12.370,12.416,.018,1),$$

which returns the value 0.0053.

The probability that a part is too long is the upper-tail probability $P(Y > 12.450)$. Cumulative probabilities are *less than* probabilities. Use the complement rule to reexpress this as a *greater than* probability,

$$=1-\text{NORMDIST}(12.450,12.416,.018,1),$$

which returns the value 0.0295.

The probability of the union of these two mutually exclusive events is the sum of the individual probabilities,

$$= 0.0053 + 0.0295.$$

The cell in which this sum is performed returns the value 0.0348.

MANAGERIAL INTERPRETATION

About 3½% of the parts manufactured with this process have defective lengths.

To recap, the typical probability problem that relies on a normal curve table (instead of a computer) first involves converting from Y to Z. For cumulative probabilities, whether from a table or a computer, manipulate the complements and unions where necessary so that the problem can be expressed in terms of probabilities of the form $P(Z < z)$. Appendix A lists the corresponding probabilities of the standard normal curve table.

The next section uses the normal curve table "in reverse."

Quantiles

The z-value is one gauge of the relative position of an observation within a distribution. Another gauge of relative position is the proportion of observations equal to or smaller than the value of interest, or a **quantile.** To compute a quantile, first sort the values of the distribution from smallest to largest. Then count the number of values below the value of interest and convert to a percentage or proportion.

Suppose 35 students took a multiple-choice exam with 60 questions. Out of the 35 students, 30 had a score of 56 or lower. Because $30.00/35.00 = 0.86$, 56 is the .86 quantile. That is, 86% of the class obtained a score of 56 or lower. Sometimes the .86 quantile is referred to as the 86th *percentile*. Percentiles are formed by dividing up a distribution into 100 ordered groups, with the same proportion of observations in each of the groups, just as the median divides up a sorted distribution into four groups of equal proportions.

Quantiles of particular interest are given special names. The .50 quantile is the median, the .00 quantile is the minimum, and the 1.00 quantile is the maximum. Sometimes a distribution is divided into quarters. The .25 quantile is the first quartile and the .75 quantile is the third quartile. The median is also the second quartile.

Quantiles can be applied to the values of any distribution, including normal distributions. The normal curve problems encountered previously involved finding the probability given a value of Y or Z. To reverse this process, find the value of Y that cuts off a specified percentage of the distribution. For example, the value of Y that

*q*th quantile Y_q of a value
value with q percent of values less than or equal to Y_q

cuts off .75 of a specified normal distribution is the .75 quantile. For these *inverse normal curve probability* problems, the value of *Y* is obtained from the given probability.

To solve this type of problem, first identify the relevant probability *within* the body of the table, and then locate the *z*-value that corresponds to this probability. Convert the obtained value of *Z* to the quantile *Y* to obtain the cutoff value of interest.

BUSINESS APPLICATION 3.5—Normal Curve Quantiles

MANAGERIAL PROBLEM

As part of a project to minimize variability of the length of a machined bushing, management wanted to know the length at which only 10% of the bushings were as short or shorter (the .10 quantile). After the manufacture of thousands of these bushings, the population was determined to be normal with a mean length of 2.416 inches and a standard deviation of 0.018.

APPLICATION—TRADITIONAL NOTATION

Z Value

Z	Cumul. Prob.
-1.30	0.0968
-1.29	0.0985
-1.28	0.1003
-1.27	0.1020
-1.26	0.1038

The normal curve probability table in Appendix A lists the cumulative probability for each *z*-value. As seen in the accompanying excerpt from the *z*-table, the closest value within the body of the table to .10 is .1003. The corresponding *z*-value for the .10 quantile is $z = -1.28$.

Y Value

The .10 quantile of any normal distribution is 1.28 standard deviations below the mean. One standard deviation is 0.018, so 1.28 standard deviations is (1.28) (0.018) = 0.023 inches. The length 1.28 standard deviations below the mean of 2.416 is

$$Y = 2.416 - (1.28)(0.018) = 2.416 - 0.023 = 2.393.$$

APPLICATION—EXCEL BUILT-IN ANALYSIS

The Excel function for calculating the specified quantile of a normal curve is the inverse normal curve function,

```
=NORMINV(Probability,Mean,SD),
```

where Probability specifies the lower-tail cutoff probability for the specified population mean and the standard deviation.

The .10 quantile of the normal distribution with $\mu_Y = 2.416$ and $\sigma_Y = 0.018$ is obtained from Excel with

$$=\text{NORMINV}(.10,2.416,0.018),$$

which returns a value of 2.393.

MANAGERIAL INTERPRETATION

Ten percent of the bushings have a length of 2.393 inches or shorter.

We have now introduced and discussed many fundamental statistical concepts. We have presented the concept of a frequency distribution, defined some basic summary statistics, and discussed how to use a normal curve table to compute normal curve probabilities. The study of inferential statistics begins in the next chapter.

EXERCISES

3-13. Let Y be the time it takes a light bulb from a certain manufacturer to burn out, where $\mu_Y = 700$ hr, $\sigma_Y = 44$ hr, and Y is normal. Using both the normal curve table in Appendix A and a computer program, find the probability that the burn-out time for a randomly selected light bulb is

a. less than 660 hr
b. more than 730 hr
c. less than 660 hr or more than 730 hr

3-14. Let Y be the time it takes a lightbulb from a certain manufacturer to burn out, where $\mu_Y = 700$ hr, $\sigma_Y = 44$ hr, and Y is normal. Using both the normal curve table in Appendix A and a computer program, find the period of time in which

a. 80% of the lightbulbs will burn out (.80 quantile)
b. 90% of the lightbulbs will burn out (.90 quantile)

3.5 SUMMARY

This chapter presented descriptions of the middle of a distribution that include the mean, the median, and the mode. The mean is the balancing point, the median is the value in the middle of the sorted distribution, and the mode is the most frequently occurring value. The mean is sensitive to outliers, a relatively small number of values that differ greatly from the other values. The median is insensitive to outliers, as is the trimmed mean, which discards the largest and smallest values before computing the mean.

The first variability statistic introduced is the range, which is the difference between the largest and smallest values. The second type of variability statistic is the variance and its square root, the standard deviation. The standard deviation is the primary unit for expressing the distance of a value from the mean, particularly for a normally distributed variable. The variance and standard deviation are computed from the deviations of each value from the mean.

The effective sample size for computing the sample versions of the variance and the standard deviation is not the original sample size but the sample size minus one. The reason for this adjustment is that the sample mean is first computed, and then this informa-

Name	Population Value	Statistic
mean	μ_Y (mu)	$\overline{Y}$
std dev	σ_Y (sigma)	s_Y

Table 3-6.
Notation used
throughout this text.

tion is applied to the same data to compute the deviation values needed for the sample variance or the standard deviation.

This chapter also showed how to locate the position of a value within a distribution with quantiles (or percentiles) and z-values. The qth quantile is the value of the distribution that has $q\%$ of the distribution below it in value. The number of standard deviations from the mean, the z-value, is used to compute probabilities of ranges of normally distributed variables. The inverse probability turns the probability question around, providing a value (quantile) from the specified probability.

Using the notation in Table 3-6, the following chapters rely extensively on the mean and the standard deviation to describe both sample and population data.

The Z transformation and the normal curve probabilities are used extensively throughout much of statistical inference. Expressing the distance of a value from its mean in terms of standard deviations is central to statistical inference, as discussed in the next chapter.

3.6 KEY TERMS

arithmetic mean *80*
assignable cause *99*
common causes *99*
complement *108*
cumulative normal probability *107*
degrees of freedom *93*
empirical rule *96*
mean deviation *89*
median *83*
modal class *86*
mode *86*
mutually exclusive *108*
outlier *82*
population variance *92*

probability *106*
quantile *110*
range *89*
sample variance *93*
stable process *100*
stable process model *98*
standard deviation *93*
sum of squares *91*
symmetric distribution *87*
transformed variable *90*
trimmed mean *83*
union *108*
weighted mean *82*
z-value *102*

3.7 REVIEW EXERCISES

ANALYSIS PROBLEMS

Mechanical

3-15. At the men's clothing department of a popular department store, the following number of customers purchased clothing during a recent week:

$$Y_{\text{SUN}} = 130 \quad Y_{\text{MON}} = 173 \quad Y_{\text{TUE}} = 182 \quad Y_{\text{WED}} = 199$$

$$Y_{\text{THR}} = 178 \quad Y_{\text{FRI}} = 214 \quad Y_{\text{SAT}} = 245$$

a. Compute the mean number of customers per day.

b. Compute the standard deviation of the number of customers per day.

3-16. In one college course, two exams and a final were given. The final was weighted three times as much as either of the two exams.

a. Joe scored 88%, 82%, and 91%, respectively, on the three tests. What is Joe's percentage across all three tests?

b. Sally scored 91%, 89%, and 86%, respectively, on the three tests. What is Sally's percentage across all three tests?

3-17. Last term a student took four college courses. He got a B in the first course, which was a 3-credit course. He got an A in the second course, worth 4 credits. The third course resulted in a C and was worth 2 credits. The final course was also 3 credits and resulted in another A. Assuming a 4-point grading system with an A worth 4 points, a B worth 3 points, and a C worth 2 points, what is the student's GPA?

3-18. Consider the following three distributions.

Distribution 1:	35	37	38	43	44
Distribution 2:	73	77	89	91	99
Distribution 3:	198	199	201	204	206

a. Just by looking at these distributions, *without* any calculations, which sample is characterized by the most variability? Why?

b. What is the standard deviation of each of the distributions?

c. Which value from these distributions has the largest deviation score?

d. Do the formal calculations confirm your intuition?

3-19. For the three distributions in the preceding exercise, compute the z-scores. Use this information to describe the variability of each of the distributions.

3-20. For these seven test scores,

94% 85% 84% 79% 77% 73% 69%,

a. compute the z-values.

b. determine whether the top score or the bottom score is farthest from the mean.

3-21. To develop a checkout system that better served his customers, a manager measured 20 checkout times at a cash register. These times are recorded below in minutes.

| 0.04 | 1.82 | 5.01 | 4.36 | 0.19 | 2.29 | 3.33 | 2.42 | 2.05 | 6.26 |
| 2.94 | 4.67 | 6.40 | 2.32 | 0.28 | 0.94 | 2.94 | 3.86 | 2.46 | 0.93 |

a. Compute the mean checkout time.

b. Compute the standard deviation of checkout times.

c. Determine if these values are acceptable. What do the mean and standard deviation imply about customers' shopping experiences?

3-22. A small manufacturing company is planning retirement option plans for its employees. As part of this preparation, the company analyzes the ages of its 35 employees, which are listed below.

38	33	42	28	33	56	24	60	24	39	44	58
52	28	36	33	40	45	64	33	34	56	20	35
38	42	29	51	34	22	34	23	44	39	61	

a. Compute the mean age.

b. Compute the standard deviation of ages.

c. Determine what the mean and standard deviation imply about the company's retirement planning.

3-23. Grocery prices were compared for two chains of stores—Tasty Foods and Best Price Groceries—by shopping for the identical 20 items at each of the 12 Tasty Foods and the 15 Best Price Groceries in the city. The respective prices at the two stores are listed below.

Tasty Foods

$75.92	$86.56	$75.26	$73.67	$76.00	$78.35
$70.19	$74.59	$64.88	$72.74	$77.76	$76.08

Best Price Groceries

$64.69	$81.06	$86.33	$81.19	$94.96	$78.96
$73.53	$76.54	$85.84	$66.21	$79.94	$70.22
$70.81	$78.69	$93.03			

a. What are the mean and the standard deviation of prices at Tasty Foods?

b. What are the mean and the standard deviation of prices at Best Price Groceries?

c. Which store has the most consistent pricing? For shoppers who patronize only one chain, at which chain are shoppers more likely to be surprised at their grocery bills if they go to another store in the same chain?

3-24. Because the mean of the deviation scores is always zero, the sum of the positive and negative deviations cannot serve as an indicator of variability. The standard deviation is based on the concept of the squared deviation score. The deviations are squared to remove the negative sign from negative deviations and because squaring the deviations ties into the normal curve. If the normal curve is not of interest, the negative sign of each negative deviation can be removed simply by dropping it. That is, use the absolute value of each deviation instead of the squared deviation when computing the variability index. The index based on the magnitude (absolute value) of the deviations is the mean absolute deviation, or MAD.

a. Compute MAD for the Tasty Foods data from the previous problem.

b. Compare the value of the largest absolute value of the deviations to the value of the largest squared deviation. Which is larger? Why?

c. Compare the value of MAD to the standard deviation. Which is larger? Why?

3-25. Consider the mpg obtained on the last trip over identical routes for the same model of delivery truck. Of the eight trucks in your fleet, the following miles per gallon were obtained.

19.8	14.5	19.2	18.9	17.5	22.4	19.7	20.9

Compute the z-values for all of the mpg values to determine if any one truck is performing much worse relative to the others, thereby indicating that special maintenance may be needed.

3-26. Using a computer program such as Excel, generate 100 normally distributed data values with a population mean of 50 and a standard deviation of 10.

   a. Sort the data from the smallest to the largest values. Standardize this sorted data.

   b. Determine what percentage of this distribution's values have z-values larger than 2.0 or smaller than −2.0.

   c. Determine whether the result in (b) is consistent with data from a normal distribution and why or why not.

3-27. The mean SAT score for 827 students who applied to a college was 1,048 with a standard deviation of 122.

   a. What values of the distribution cut off one standard deviation above and below the mean?

   b. What values of the distribution cut off two standard deviations above and below the mean?

   c. What values of the distribution cut off three standard deviations above and below the mean?

3-28. If the distribution of 827 SAT scores with the mean 1,048 and the standard deviation 122 is normally distributed, what percentage of scores lie within

   a. one standard deviation of the mean

   b. two standard deviations of the mean

   c. three standard deviations of the mean

3-29. Roughly draw a normal curve. On this drawing, indicate approximately where

   a. $z = -2.00$

   b. $z = 0.50$

   c. $z = -0.5$

   d. $z = 2.5$

3-30. For a normally distributed variable with $\mu_Y = 50$ and $\sigma_Y = 10$, what percentage of values are less than

   a. 35

   b. 50

   c. 58

3-31. For a normally distributed variable with $\mu_Y = 50$ and $\sigma_Y = 10$, what is the

   a. .10 quantile

   b. .50 quantile

   c. .90 quantile

3-32. For a normally distributed variable with $\mu_Y = 250$ and $\sigma_Y = 30$, what percentage of values is less than

   a. 300

   b. 250

   c. 150

3-33. For a normally distributed variable with $\mu_Y = 250$ and $\sigma_Y = 30$, what is the

Mechanical

    a. .20 quantile

    b. .60 quantile

    c. .95 quantile

DISCUSSION QUESTIONS

1. What is the meaning of the uppercase Greek letter sigma in statistical analysis?
2. What do the symbols $\overline{Y}$ and μ_Y represent? How are the underlying concepts related? Which of the two is more easily computed in most circumstances? Why?
3. Why is the usual definition of the mean a special case of the more general definition of a weighted mean?
4. When does the median provide useful information beyond that provided by the mean?
5. When does the trimmed mean provide more useful information than the mean?
6. How useful are the mean, the median, and the mode when applied to categorical data?
7. Why is the deviation score such an important concept in quantifying variability?
8. Why is the degrees of freedom also called the effective sample size?
9. Why is the sample standard deviation computed dividing by sample size minus one?
10. What is the unit of measurement used to calibrate a normally distributed variable?
11. What is the relation between quantiles and percentiles?
12. For a normal distribution, why is knowing the z-value of a score equivalent to knowing the score's quantile?
13. Why are the operations of the complement and the union needed to compute normal curve probabilities?
14. What is the relation between a normal curve probability and an inverse normal curve probability?

INTEGRATIVE ANALYSIS PROBLEM

Competitive manufacturers attempt to minimize the time lag between ordering materials from suppliers and receiving those materials. Management is interested in analyzing this time lag in deliveries from one of its major suppliers.

Two variables in the data file DELVTM.DAT indicate the date the order was placed to the supplier and the date on which the order arrived. The data extend for 24 deliveries, one per month for two years.

a. Plot the distribution of delivery times. Verbally describe the primary characteristics of this distribution.

b. Compute the z-values of the distribution.

c. Determine how many values are outliers or potential outliers and what these values are.

d. Compute the mean and the median of this distribution.

e. Determine why the mean and the median are so different.

f. Compute the standard deviation of the distribution.

g. Determine how many standard deviations from the mean the largest value of the distribution is.

h. Compute the mean and the median without the largest value.

i. Compute the standard deviation without the largest value.

j. Compare the mean computed with all data values and the mean computed with the largest data value deleted. Do the same for the standard deviation.

k. Decide which questions you would ask regarding delivery times when talking with the supplier's management.

l. Determine how you would state your conclusions regarding this analysis if the largest shipping time was due, in part, to the rare event of the courier, UPS, initially shipping the order to the wrong address.

CHAPTER 3 EXTENSION   QUARTILES AND BOX PLOTS

E3.1 INTERQUARTILE RANGE AND BOX PLOTS

quartiles of a distribution
values that divide a sorted distribution into four sections with the same number of values in each section

The median of a distribution is the value in the middle when all of the values (including values that occur more than once) are sorted in numerical order. The median is the number that separates the smallest half of the values from the largest half. But why stop at halves? Another useful way to break up a distribution is to divide it into fourths, or **quartiles.** The first quartile (Q_1) has the smallest one-fourth of the values below it and the largest three-fourths above it. The second quartile (Q_2) is the median. The third quartile (Q_3) has three-fourths of all values below it. These statistics are sometimes called *order statistics* because the values of the distribution must first be ordered before these statistics can be computed.

rank of a value
observation number of the value beginning with one for the smallest value, with ties assigned the average rank for that value

The computation of the quartiles begins by sorting the data from smallest to largest and then **ranking** the values. After the initial ranks are listed, the final ranks are assigned by resolving ties. Consider a distribution with only four values: 2, 5, 5, 9. Before considering ties, the value two has a rank of 1, the first five has a rank of 2, the second five a rank of 3, and the nine has a rank of 4. Ties are assigned the average rank of the value. The rank of a five in the distribution is the average of 2 and 3, or 2.5.

Given the ranks, the calculation of all quartiles is similar, where n is the number of values.

1st quartile = value with a rank of .25 $(n + 1)$

2nd quartile or median = value with a rank of .5 $(n + 1)$

3rd quartile = value with a rank of .75 $(n + 1)$

If the rank is not an integer, then the quartile is computed as the fraction of the distance between the values at the corresponding ranks. For example, if the sample size is $n = 62$, then the rank of the first quartile is .25 (63) = 15.75. The value of the first quartile lies *between* the values with ranks of 15 and 16. The quartile is the value with a rank of 15 plus three-fourths of the distance between the values with ranks 15 and 16, as illustrated in Figure E3-1. If the value with rank 15 is 33.0 and the value with rank 16 is 35.4, then the distance between these values is 2.4. Three-fourths of this distance is .75 (2.4) = 1.80, so the first quartile is 33 + 1.80 = 34.80.

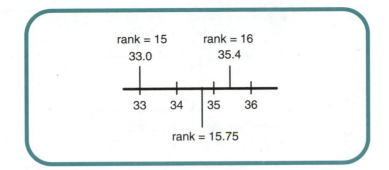

Figure E3-1
The value 34.80 has a
rank of 15.75, which is
.75 of the distance
separating the values
with ranks 15 and 16.

A useful index of the variability of a distribution is defined in terms of quartiles. The **interquartile range** is the range of the middle 50% of the values. The range of the entire distribution is less useful as an index of variability because it is computed only from the two most extreme values, the largest and the smallest. Computation of the IQR involves values embedded *within* the distribution, meaning the first and third quartiles. The values of the minimum, maximum, first quartile, and third quartile all depend in part on the particular sample observed, so their values differ for different samples. However, the minimum and maximum vary more from sample to sample than do the quartiles, so the IQR is a more reliable index of variability than the range.

> **interquartile range
> (IQR)**
> *positive difference
> between the first and
> third quartiles*

The IQR and other aspects of the distribution are illustrated graphically with a box plot. The basic **box plot** is constructed from only five values of the distribution, called a *5-number summary* by its inventor, John Tukey. Together, the minimum, first quartile, median, third quartile, and maximum provide much information about the shape of the distribution. The length of the box portrays the IQR.[1] The longer the box, the larger the IQR.

Tukey defined two versions of box plots. Figure E3-2 illustrates the simpler version.

Sometimes box plots are called box-and-whisker plots because the lines drawn from the box to the minimum and maximum values are called whiskers. In the version of the box plot illustrated in Figure E3-2, the whiskers extend from the first and third quartiles all the way out to the minimum and maximum, respectively. The range of the distribution is the length of the box plus the length of the two whiskers extending out from each side of the box.

> **box plot of a
> distribution**
> *the narrow edges of
> a box defined by the
> first and third
> quartiles, and a
> line parallel to these
> edges through the
> median, with
> perpendicular lines
> extending out from
> the edges*

A second version of a box plot provides more information useful for detecting outliers. As shown in Figure E3-3, the whiskers for this version do not extend out to the extreme values but stop at the end of the data that do not include any outliers. *Potential outliers* are values more than 1.5 IQRs from the edges of the box (first and third quartiles) but within 3.0 IQRs of these edges. Values more than 3.0 IQRs out from the box's edges are *outliers*. The symbols * and 0 display potential outliers and outliers, respectively.

Each whisker extends to the most extreme data value within 1.5 IQRs of the box's edges. In essence, the whiskers end before the outliers begin.

---

1. To be precise, the edges of a box plot are called hinges instead of the first and third quartiles. The lower hinge is the median of the smallest 50% of the sorted values, and the upper hinge is the median of the largest 50% of the sorted values. For most distributions, these values differ slightly if at all from their quartile counterparts. For simplicity, we refer only to quartiles.

Figure E3-2.
Example of the first version of a box plot.

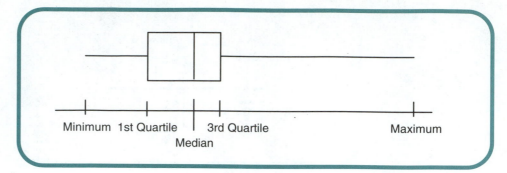

Figure E3-3.
Example of the second version of a box plot.

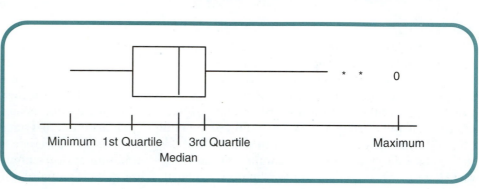

Figure E3-4.
Histogram (with estimated density function) and box plot of the same skewed distribution of family worth.

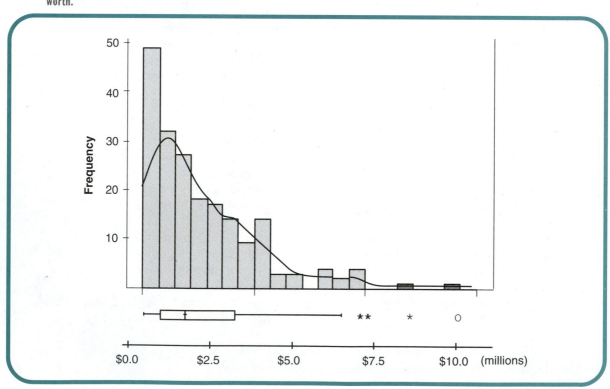

Figure E3-4 illustrates the financial worth of 210 families. In this figure, a histogram of the distribution is superimposed on top of the corresponding box plot. The distribution is skewed because many more families have lower assessments than higher assessments. The short side of the box, which ranges from the first quartile of $0.54 million to the median of $1.27 million, occurs on the lower side of the distribution, the side with the greater density. The tail of the distribution is represented by the long side of the box from the median to the third quartile of $2.76 million. The outliers represent larger financial worth close to $10,000,000.

BUSINESS APPLICATION E3.1—Box Plot and Outlier Detection

MANAGERIAL PROBLEM

A well-known large manufacturer of machined parts[2] recently implemented statistical methods to improve quality. One critical part has been particularly difficult to manufacture properly. In over 10 years of manufacturing this part, the company has endured an unacceptably high level of scrap and rework. To better understand and control sources of undesired variation, measurements of a critical dimension from 48 test parts were taken. The long-term goal is to minimize variability of output even when all parts are acceptable, but any value 0.300 and above exceeds the engineering specification, resulting in a nonfunctional part that must be scrapped.

DATA

The 48 values in Table E3-1 are the measurements after completion of the machining process, expressed in how many thousandths of an inch the measurement is above a fixed reference point. For convenience, these values are sorted from the smallest to the largest value. This sort is not required for the accompanying analyses.

	A			A			A
1	Meas		18	0.123		35	0.175
2	0.037		19	0.124		36	0.176
3	0.051		20	0.133		37	0.177
4	0.072		21	0.133		38	0.181
5	0.085		22	0.139		39	0.189
6	0.095		23	0.140		40	0.234
7	0.096		24	0.140		41	0.236
8	0.101		25	0.143		42	0.241
9	0.103		26	0.146		43	0.276
10	0.105		27	0.149		44	0.293
11	0.106		28	0.153		45	0.300
12	0.107		29	0.154		46	0.321
13	0.108		30	0.156		47	0.336
14	0.108		31	0.159		48	0.395
15	0.116		32	0.163		49	0.400
16	0.117		33	0.168			
17	0.119		34	0.172			

Table E3-1. Sorted values above a fixed reference point, measuring to 0.001 of an inch.

2. These data are from a manufacturing application performed at a real company. The company, however, wishes to remain anonymous.

APPLICATION—TRADITIONAL NOTATION

Ordering the Statistics

The minimum and maximum values can be read directly from the sorted data above. The first value is .037 and the last value is .400.

One-half of the 48 values is 24, so the median lies between the 24th and 25th largest values, .143 and .146, respectively. The median is

$$\text{Median} = \frac{.143 + .146}{2} = .1445.$$

The value .1445 has 24 values below it and 24 values above it.

Quartiles divide the distribution into fourths. The first quartile Q_1 is the value with a rank of $.25\,(n + 1) = .25\,(49) = 12.25$. As shown below, the value closest in rank to 12.25 is .108, which occurs twice and has a rank of 12.5, the average of 12 and 13. So Q_1 is almost .108. The distance between the ranks of 11 and 12.5 is 1.5, and 12.25 is 1.25/1.50 of this distance, or 0.833. The distance from 0.107 and 0.108 is .001, and 0.8333 of this distance is 0.00083. So Q_1 is about $0.107 + 0.00083 = 0.1078$.

Meas	Rank
0.106	10
0.107	11
0.108	12.5
0.108	12.5
0.116	14
0.117	15

The third quartile Q_3 is the value with a rank of $.75\,(n + 1) = .75\,(49) = 36.75$. That is, Q_3 is located three-fourths of the distance between the values with ranks 36 and 37, .177 and .181. The distance between these values is $181 - .177 = .004$, so Q_3 is .75 of this distance above .177,

$$Q_3 = .177 + .75\,(.004) = .177 + .003 \approx 0.180.$$

The interquartile range is

$$\text{IQR} = Q_3 - Q_1 = 0.180 - 0.1078 = .072.$$

Detecting the Outliers

Potential outliers lie between $3.0 * \text{IQR}$ and $1.5 * \text{IQR}$ below Q_1 or above Q_3. Identifiable outliers lie beyond $3.0 * \text{IQR}$ below Q_1 or above Q_3.

$$1.5 * \text{IQR} = 1.5 * .072 = .108$$

$$3.0 * \text{IQR} = 3.0 * .072 = .216.$$

Moving down 1.5 IQRs from the first quartile and up 1.5 IQRs from the third quartile results in

$$Q_1 - (1.5 * \text{IQR}) = .108 - .108 = .000$$

$$Q_3 + (1.5 * \text{IQR}) = .1798 + .108 \approx .288.$$

Moving down 3.0 IQRs from the first quartile and up 3.0 IQRs from the third quartile results in

$$Q_1 - (3.0 * IQR) = .108 - .216 = -.108$$

$$Q_3 + (3.0 * IQR) = .1798 + .216 \approx .396.$$

For these data, potential outliers are values that fall within the ranges

$$-.108 \text{ to } .000 \text{ or } .288 \text{ to } .396.$$

No potential outliers fall below Q_1, but five values are larger than .288 and smaller than .396.

Values readily identified as outliers are less than $-.108$ and greater than .396. No values are negative, but two values are larger than .396.

Obtaining the Box Plot

The height of the box is not important, but boxes are usually drawn so that their height is smaller than their width, the IQR. The *'s represent potential outliers, and the 0's represent outliers.

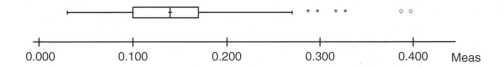

APPLICATION—EXCEL BUILT-IN ANALYSIS

Assessing the Excel Output

Excel provides four columns of output, as shown in Table E3-2. One of these columns is a copy of the original data. The other columns are labeled Point, Rank, and Percent, which is the percentile of each value. Unfortunately, Excel defines rank differently from the common usage, so that neither the Point nor the Rank columns contain the ranks as typically defined. For reference, the Excel output in Table E3-2 is listed next to a column labeled True Rank.

First, consider the Rank column. The Excel ranks are in the opposite order from that typically encountered. Excel defines the first rank as the largest value, whereas most applications define the first rank as the smallest value. Second, the ranks of tied values are not resolved by averaging the preliminary ranks, or the initial ranking that does not account for ties. Instead, Excel takes the minimum of the preliminary ranks of the tied values. For example, the value 0.108 occurs twice. The preliminary ranks of these values are 12 and 13, which averages to their true rank of 12.5. Excel lists these ranks as 36. If ties were resolved by averaging, the ranks of 0.108 would actually be 36.5, the average of 36 and 37.

How is the True Rank obtained, in which the ranks follow the usual order with ties resolved according to the conventional method? The column labeled Point contains the preliminary ranks in their usual order with the smallest value assigned a rank of 1. Initially, create the True Rank column as a copy of the Point column. The problem with this initial ranking is that multiple occurrences (rows) of the *same* value of *Y* have *different* ranks. Resolve these ties by averaging the initial ranks or Points of observations that have the same value. For small data sets such as the

True Rank	Point	Y	Rank	Percent
1	1	0.037	48	.00%
2	2	0.051	47	2.10%
3	3	0.072	46	4.20%
4	4	0.085	45	6.30%
5	5	0.095	44	8.50%
6	6	0.096	43	10.60%
7	7	0.101	42	12.70%
8	8	0.103	41	14.80%
9	9	0.105	40	17.00%
10	10	0.106	39	19.10%
11	11	0.107	38	21.20%
12.5	12	0.108	37	23.40%
12.5	13	0.108	36	23.40%
14	14	0.116	35	27.60%
15	15	0.117	34	29.70%
16	16	0.119	33	31.90%
17	17	0.123	32	34.00%
18	18	0.124	31	36.10%
19.5	19	0.133	30	38.20%
19.5	20	0.133	29	38.20%
21	21	0.139	28	42.50%
22.5	22	0.140	27	44.60%
22.5	23	0.140	26	44.60%
24	24	0.143	25	48.90%

True Rank	Point	Y	Rank	Percent
25	25	0.146	24	51.00%
26	26	0.149	23	53.10%
27	27	0.153	22	55.30%
28	28	0.154	21	57.40%
29	29	0.156	20	59.50%
30	30	0.159	19	61.70%
31	31	0.163	18	63.80%
32	32	0.168	17	65.90%
33	33	0.172	16	68.00%
34	34	0.175	15	70.20%
35	35	0.176	14	72.30%
36	36	0.177	13	74.40%
37	37	0.181	12	76.50%
38	38	0.189	11	78.70%
39	39	0.234	10	80.80%
40	40	0.236	9	82.90%
41	41	0.241	8	85.10%
42	42	0.276	7	87.20%
43	43	0.293	6	89.30%
44	44	0.300	5	91.40%
45	45	0.321	4	93.60%
46	46	0.336	3	95.70%
47	47	0.395	2	97.80%
48	48	0.400	1	100.00%

Table E3-2.
Ranks computed by Excel and the true ranks.

following, this averaging of the preliminary ranks is accomplished quickly by applying the Average function wherever a tie occurs. For example, the value of $Y = 0.108$ occurs twice. The values of Point for these two observations are 12 and 13, so the rank of these values is 12.5.

Obtaining the Ranks

Tools ➤ Data Analysis ➤ Rank and Percentile

Selecting Rank and Percentile results in the following dialog box.

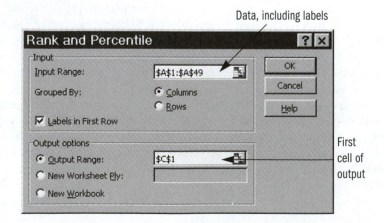

Ordering the Statistics

Excel computes quartiles with the built-in function Quartile, with format

$$=\texttt{QUARTILE(data,specific\_quartile)}.$$

The specific quartile is an integer from 0 to 4. For example, the expression

$$=\texttt{QUARTILE(A2:A49,3)}$$

displays the third quartile for the data in the first column from the second through the forty-ninth row.

	C	D	E
1	Quartile	Value	Label
2	0	0.037	Min
3	1	0.108	Q1
4	2	0.145	Median
5	3	0.178	Q3
6	4	0.400	Max

Note that the value of Q_3, .178, does not follow the traditional definition. Q_3 is usually defined as the value with a rank of

$$.75\,(n + 1) = .75\,(49) = 36.75.$$

The value with this rank is .180.

Obtaining the Box Plot

Excel does not provide box plots.

MANAGERIAL INTERPRETATION

Most of the parts are within tolerance, but 5 of the 48 measurements are greater than or equal to the unacceptable value of 0.300. All five values are outliers or potential outliers. A sixth value is also a potential outlier but does fall within the acceptable tolerance. Perhaps some specific cause of this undesirable variation can be identified. Maybe only the second shift machinist manufactured the parts, or a different cutting tool was used, or material from a different supplier was used only for these five parts. Further substantive studf the machining process may uncover the cause of this undesirable variation.

The groundwork of describing sample data has now been established. The next chapter builds on these concepts to introduce statistical inference.

E3.2 SUMMARY

Compute the interquartile range from a distribution with the values sorted in ascending or descending order. Interquartile range is the difference between the first and third quartiles.

These quartiles appear in a box plot with the median and the largest and smallest values. The box plot requires only five values—the minimum, 25th perecentile or first quartile, 50th percentile or median, 75th percentile or third quartile, and the maximum.

E3.3 KEY TERMS

box plot *119*   quartiles *118*
interquartile range (IQR) *119*   rank *118*

E3.4 REVIEW EXERCISES

ANALYSIS PROBLEMS

Mechanical

E3-1. The following data, presented in a previous problem, represent three differ-ent quiz scores by five students:

	Y_1	Y_2	Y_3
Bradley	0	2	3
Tyler	4	5	2
Dotty	2	3	3
Jordanne	1	7	5
Jeff	4	3	4

For Y_2 compute the range using

a. a conceptual worksheet

b. traditional formulas

c. statistical analysis built into a computer program

Mechanical

E3-2. For the data in the previous exercise, compute the interquartile range using

a. a conceptual worksheet

b. traditional formulas

c. a statistical analysis built into a computer program

Application

E3-3. In January 1986, all those aboard the space shuttle Challenger died when the booster rocket exploded. The Challenger's flight was the 25th shuttle launch. The temperatures for these 25 launches are presented below to the nearest 5 degrees Fahrenheit, sorted from lowest to highest value. The only below-freezing flight was the Challenger.

30	55	60	60	65	70	70	70	70	70	70	70	70	70	70	75
75	75	75	80	80	80	80	80	85							

Later analysis revealed that a part of the booster rocket called the O-rings failed due, in part, to the cold temperature. Unfortunately, NASA engineers did not perform several basic statistical analyses before launch that would have led to the detection of a problem.[3]

Do what NASA did not do. Draw a box plot of these data and identify any outliers. Which temperature on this plot represents that of the Challenger? What would you recommend given these data?

E3-4. For the grocery store price data in Exercise 3-23,

   a. Compute the IQR for the prices at each of the two stores.

   b. Draw a box plot for the prices at each of the two stores.

   c. Determine whether there are any outliers or potential outliers in these two sets of data.

   d. Given your answers to (b) and (c), decide whether analysis of these data should proceed without further investigation of the validity of the data.

E3-5. Consider the miles per gallon obtained on the last trip over identical routes for the same model of delivery truck. Of the eight trucks in your fleet, the following mpg's were obtained.

   19.8   14.5   19.2   18.9   17.5   22.4   19.7   20.9

   a. Use outlier analysis based on the IQR to determine if any one truck is performing much worse relative to the others, thereby indicating that special maintenance may be needed.

   b. Compute the z-values for all of the mpg values to determine if any one truck is performing much worse relative to the others, thereby indicating that special maintenance may be needed.

   c. Compare your answers from the IQR analysis and z-value analysis. Does one method provide more information than the other method for these data?

E3-6. Analysis of a sample of data yielded the following values: $Q_1 = 112$, $Q_2 = 120$, and $Q_3 = 169$.

   a. What do these quartile values reveal about the underlying distribution?

   b. Where does the value 110 lie relative to the other values in the distribution?

   c. Where does the value 125 lie relative to the other values in the distribution?

   d. What is the interquartile range, IQR?

   e. How would you interpret the value of IQR?

E3-7. The following statistics describe a distribution.

$\overline{Y} = 3.124$ median $= 3.266$ $s_Y = 2.636$

min $= 0.123$ max $= 8.940$ $Q_1 = 0.730$ $Q_3 = 4.085$

   a. Draw a box plot of the distribution.

   b. Determine whether there are outliers in the distribution.

   c. Determine whether the distribution is skewed.

---

3. For more information regarding this analysis, see Frederick Lighthall's article "Launching the Space Shuttle Challenger: Disciplinary Deficiencies in the Analysis of Engineering Data" in *IEEE Transactions on Engineering Management, 38*(1), February 1991.

DISCUSSION QUESTIONS

1. How does the concept of a quartile compare to the median?

2. What distinguishes a sorted distribution from a ranked distribution?

3. How is the interquartile range an index of variability?

4. What five values are needed for the construction of a box plot?

5. What are the two versions of box plots?

6. How does a box plot aid in the detection of outliers?

7. What is the distinction between potential outliers and actual outliers?

CHAPTER 4

Confidence Interval around a Mean

WHY DO WE CARE?

The previous chapters demonstrated how to describe and summarize data. Our focus now shifts to inferential statistics—from merely summarizing data to generalizing to the entire population. We have a fresh point of view but not necessarily different data. Instead of just describing, we now want to infer population characteristics such as the value of the unknown population mean.

Using a sample mean to estimate an unknown population mean presents a problem: A sample mean generally does not equal the corresponding population mean. Stated differently, the estimate is wrong. More useful is the knowledge of how *close* the estimate is likely to be to the corresponding population value. That is, the estimate should include a range of values that likely contains the true population mean. This range of values around the sample statistic—a margin of error—is called a *confidence interval*. From a sample proportion of 52%, a pollster concludes that 52% ± 3% of *all* voters will vote for Smith. From a sample mean of 12.03 oz, the quality control manager concludes that the average weight of the cereal in *all* the cereal boxes is 12.03 oz ± .09 oz.

Confidence intervals move the interpretation of the sample mean beyond simply describing the sample to generalizing about the entire population. The votes of several thousand people in the pollster's sample are of little interest except for the information these data provide regarding the voting tendencies of the entire population. The crucial issue is the *amount* of information that the sample statistic conveys about the population. To claim that 52% ± 20% of *all* voters intend to vote for Smith is to claim almost nothing at all. The interval 52% ± 0.5% communicates much more information. The same sample percentage, 52%, is useful in one situation and potentially misleading in the other.

4.1 SAMPLE MEAN AS A RANDOM VARIABLE

Statistical inference generalizes information from a sample of values of the response variable Y to the entire population from which the sample was drawn. The focus of analysis shifts from the observed sample to the larger population. The confidence interval around a sample statistic likely contains the corresponding unknown population value. To construct a confidence interval around a sample mean $\overline{Y}$, we need the range of values over which $\overline{Y}$ varies. To accomplish this, consider a process that can be repeated again and again.

Random Variation

The study of inference begins with an analysis of the possible sample outcomes from a population or process. Repetitions of the same process yield different results. Each repetition of the process (or more generally, different samples from the same population) generates another value of the response variable Y.

Random output from repeatable processes is part of our daily lives. Consider the following examples.

1. Price of your favorite NYSE stock at the end of the trading day.
2. Amount of cola bought by the next person at the checkout stand.
3. Gross sales by salesperson John Doe during the last month.
4. National debt at the end of the fiscal year.
5. Number of employees who call in sick on a given day.
6. Fuel mileage obtained from the last tank of fuel.

Each outcome of a process sets the value of the response variable Y, the variable of interest. Y varies because each repetition of the process generates a random component not predictable in advance. Underlying all outcomes of the process is the population mean μ_Y. Each repetition generates some random fluctuation around μ_Y that results in a value of response Y being larger, smaller, or equal to μ_Y. The stable-process model introduced in the previous chapter describes the relation of the mean and the random fluctuation to a value of the response Y. This model specifies that the value of Y is the underlying population mean plus a random fluctuation, or

$$Y = \mu_Y + \varepsilon, \text{ with constant } \sigma_\varepsilon.$$

Flip a coin. Only after the flip can you know whether the response—the process output—is a head or a tail.

The concept of a repeatable procedure with unpredictable outcomes lies at the very core of statistical inference. Do the same thing again and again, such as repeatedly drawing a random sample from the same population, and potentially obtain a different value of $\overline{Y}$ each time. The following analysis provides more information about the variation of the sample mean, $\overline{Y}$.

Standard Error of the Sample Mean

Consider a response variable of interest Y—fuel mileage for a fleet of trucks, weight of the contents of cereal boxes, family income within a specified zip code—or any of thousands of other possibilities of interest to the business decision maker. Suppose that the value of the population mean μ_Y is unknown. The problem is that management wants to know the value of μ_Y—the average fuel mileage of the *entire* fleet of trucks, the average weight of the contents of cereal boxes from a day's production, or the average income of *all* families within the zip code. To estimate the value of μ_Y, draw a sample of size n from the population of Y and compute $\overline{Y}$. How close is the known value of the sample mean $\overline{Y}$ to the unknown value of the population mean μ_Y?

In practice, only a single $\overline{Y}$ is computed from a single sample. From the perspective of statistical inference, this sample is only one arbitrary sample out of many possibilities that could have occurred. Because of chance—random, unpredictable statistical fluctuations—$\overline{Y}$ is close to the unknown population mean μ_Y for some samples and far away for others.

> *The sample mean $\overline{Y}$ is a random variable with values that vary randomly from sample to sample.*

A specific value of $\overline{Y}$ is the outcome of a process that could be repeated again and again from sample to sample. This value of $\overline{Y}$ for any one sample cannot be predicted in advance. Understanding that the value of $\overline{Y}$ randomly varies for different samples from the same population is crucial to understanding inferential statistics.

STATISTICAL ILLUSTRATION—Sample Mean as a Random Variable

DATA—FIRST SAMPLE

An investor believes that lumber prices will soon increase dramatically. Before this anticipated increase occurs, she wants to purchase a tract of forested land with thousands of trees. To estimate the amount of potential lumber on this tract, measure 10 randomly selected tree diameters to the nearest tenth of an inch. The resulting ten diameters are

Y: 23.9   22.8   19.1   22.4   17.7   24.9   21.3   17.3   21.2   19.2

with $= \overline{Y} = 21.0$, and $s_Y = 2.6$.

DATA—EIGHT SAMPLES

In actual applications of statistical inference, only one sample is collected. For illustrative purposes, hypothetically more samples could be collected. A second, hypothetical random sample of 10 different trees results in another 10 measurements.

Y: 23.8   30.6   24.6   22.6   21.2   19.5   25.4   17.4   22.4   22.5

The new sample statistics are $\overline{Y} = 23.0$, and $s_Y = 3.6$.

Hypothetically, this process of repeated sampling could be invoked many times. In this example, obtain eight samples with 10 trees each ($n = 10$) from the same population. Next, compute the eight sample means and standard deviations, as reported in Table 4-1.

Table 4-1.
Tree Diameters Y in
inches from one
actual sample and
seven hypothetical
samples of size 10
($n = 10$).

Tree	Actual Sample 1	Hypothetical Samples 2	3	4	5	6	7	8
1	23.9	23.8	18.7	25.4	20.8	13.8	26.7	21.8
2	22.8	30.6	12.1	19.9	14.1	26.9	23.7	27.7
3	19.1	24.6	21.2	27.7	18.9	13.6	20.4	23.9
4	22.4	22.6	12.2	24.0	27.2	26.5	19.3	24.0
5	17.7	21.2	24.8	17.7	27.7	8.5	20.3	19.6
6	24.9	19.5	20.5	10.3	12.6	19.9	17.3	22.2
7	21.3	25.4	13.1	27.8	24.6	26.8	18.7	20.8
8	17.3	17.4	19.0	20.7	30.7	23.4	17.8	24.0
9	21.2	22.4	18.9	12.2	16.5	12.4	26.8	13.0
10	19.2	22.5	18.0	17.6	27.9	22.2	14.2	24.7
$\bar{Y}$	21.0	23.0	17.8	20.3	22.1	19.4	20.5	22.2
s_Y	2.6	3.6	4.2	6.0	6.4	6.8	4.1	3.9

ANALYSIS

Although the eight sample means approximately equal one another, their values differ, ranging from 17.8 to 23.0. $\bar{Y}$ is a response variable with eight distinct values in this example.

   $\bar{Y}$:   21.0   23.0   17.8   20.3   22.1   19.4   20.5   22.2

As for any random variable, each sample of $\bar{Y}$'s has a mean and a standard deviation. The mean of these eight $\bar{Y}$'s is 20.79. The sample standard deviation of $\bar{Y}$ is 1.68, a value considerably less than any of the eight sample standard deviations of the original variable Y, which range from 2.6 to 6.8.

STATISTICAL PRINCIPLE

Any one sample yields only a single value of $\bar{Y}$. When moving from sample to sample, however, $\bar{Y}$ is a random variable with its own distribution, mean, and standard deviation. In practice only one sample is collected, so only the first sample mean, $\bar{Y} = 21.0$, would be observed. If multiple samples were collected, however different sample means would be obtained.

The unknown population mean μ_Y is of primary interest. The value of μ_Y is unknown, however, so the manager estimates how close a *particular* sample mean, $\bar{Y}$, is likely to be to the unknown value of μ_Y.

Estimating the likely range of distances of $\overline{Y}$ from μ_Y requires knowledge of the distribution of the random variable $\overline{Y}$.

Using $\overline{Y}$ to estimate the unknown value of μ_Y requires two random variables, Y and $\overline{Y}$.

In a descriptive statistics analysis, only one $\overline{Y}$ is computed from the data. From the perspective of inference, however, $\overline{Y}$ is a random variable. Any random variable has its own population distribution with its own shape, mean, and standard deviation. A distribution of any statistic is called a sampling distribution. In particular, the sampling distribution of the mean is the distribution of all possible sample means. Although the name of this distribution begins with the word "sampling," the distribution is a population distribution based on all possible values of the sample statistic $\overline{Y}$. **The sampling distribution of the mean** is the population distribution of the sample mean over repeated samples.

Each possible sample size yields a different distribution of sample means. Repeatedly sampling from a population with samples of size 5 yields a different distribution of sample means than repeated samples from the *same* population with a sample size of 1,000. Sample means from samples of size 1,000 are typically close to each other in value, whereas sample means from samples of size 5 fluctuate considerably more.

sampling distribution of the mean
population distribution of the response variable $\overline{Y}$ based on all possible samples for a single sample size

STATISTICAL ILLUSTRATION—Comparing Distributions of Sample Means

DATA

Eight samples of tree diameters were taken from three different tracts of forested land. In this example, all tracts have the same population mean of $\mu_Y = 21.4$ in. The means of each of the eight samples from each population follow.

$\overline{Y}$s from Population A:	11.7	22.9	24.8	16.2	29.1	21.6	17.4	24.6
$\overline{Y}$s from Population B:	21.0	23.0	17.8	20.3	22.1	19.4	20.5	22.2
$\overline{Y}$s from Population C:	20.2	20.8	20.4	21.1	20.6	21.6	20.1	21.7

The eight sample means from Population B are taken from the previous example. The other two sets of eight means are new.

ANALYSIS

To understand the differences among these three sets of samples and resulting set of sample means, consider the following question.

From which population is a single sample mean $\overline{Y}$ likely to provide the best estimate of the underlying population mean, μ_Y?

To answer this question, examine the descriptive statistics computed from the eight means for each of the three populations in Table 4-2.

Table 4-2.
Descriptive statistics
computed from three
sets of sample means.

	n	Mean	SD	Min	Max
Statistics for Population A $\overline{Y}$'s	8	21.04	5.60	11.70	29.10
Statistics for Population B $\overline{Y}$'s	8	20.79	1.68	17.80	23.00
Statistics for Population C $\overline{Y}$'s	8	20.81	0.61	20.10	21.70

The sample means approximately equal each other, but the standard deviations of these three samples differ dramatically. The values of $\overline{Y}$ fluctuate wildly from 11.70 to 29.10 in the first sample, and from only 20.10 to 21.70 in the third sample. The sample standard deviation of each of these distributions of sample means is

computed with sample means from Population A: $s_{\overline{Y}} = 5.60$
computed with sample means from Population B: $s_{\overline{Y}} = 1.68$
computed with sample means from Population C: $s_{\overline{Y}} = 0.61$.

CONCLUSION

From which population is the one sample drawn that likely provides the best estimate of the corresponding μ_Y? The answer is Population C. The standard deviation $s_{\overline{Y}}$ is the smallest for the samples drawn from that population, so the $\overline{Y}$'s tend to be close to each other. Any one $\overline{Y}$ is likely to be closer to the unknown μ_Y.

What is the value of this unknown μ_Y? The value cannot be pinpointed exactly, but the distribution of $\overline{Y}$ over repeated samples provides a clue. The value of μ_Y is probably within the range of $\overline{Y}$. For Population C, the range of $\overline{Y}$ is from 20.10 to 21.70, which defines a kind of confidence interval. The unknown value of μ_Y is likely found within this interval.

In real life, however, multiple samples are usually not available. The next sections show how to compute a confidence interval from information available in only a single sample.

When the population standard deviation of $\overline{Y}$, $\sigma_{\overline{Y}}$, is small, the values of $\overline{Y}$ are close to one another, increasing the likelihood that any one randomly chosen sample mean is close to the unknown population mean, μ_Y. For larger $\sigma_{\overline{Y}}$, the values of $\overline{Y}$ are more spread out. The standard deviation $\sigma_{\overline{Y}}$, the **standard error of the mean,** reflects the typical amount of error using $\overline{Y}$ to estimate μ_Y. A standard error is simply the standard deviation of a statistic over repeated samples. Next, the importance of the standard error of $\overline{Y}$ is developed further.

standard error of the
mean
population
standard deviation
of $\overline{Y}$, $\sigma_{\overline{Y}}$

Distribution of the Sample Mean

The distribution of $\overline{Y}$ can be constructed from repeated samples of the population of Y with constant mean μ_Y. This distribution provides information for how close

$\overline{Y}$ is likely to be to μ_Y. However, in practice usually only a single sample is available. Fortunately, the properties of the population distribution of $\overline{Y}$—mean, standard deviation, and shape—are obtained from the information from only a single sample. Applying the following three theorems is the key to obtaining this information about multiple samples from only a single sample.

Consider the shape of the distribution of $\overline{Y}$. The population distribution of $\overline{Y}$ is normal if the distribution of Y is normal. The somewhat surprising and extremely powerful result expressed by the **central limit theorem** is that the distribution of $\overline{Y}$, except for very small samples of less than 20 or so, is approximately normal even if Y is *not* normal[1]. The central limit theorem is one of the most important theorems in statistics.

As discussed in Chapter 3, the standard deviation of any normal distribution is the natural unit for expressing the distances of individual values from their mean. When distance is expressed in terms of standard deviation for a normally distributed variable, the percentage of values between any two values is known. For example, 68.26% of all normally distributed values lie within a single standard deviation of their population mean μ_Y and 95.44% of all values lie within two standard deviations of μ_Y.

central limit theorem, distribution of $\overline{Y}$
random variable $\overline{Y}$ is approximately normally distributed (except for small samples of nonnormal Y)

> The standard error of the mean $s_{\overline{Y}}$ is the unit for measuring the distance of the sample mean $\overline{Y}$ from the population mean, μ_Y.

Because in most situations $\overline{Y}$ is approximately normal, probability statements about normally distributed variables apply to $\overline{Y}$ as well.

The usual method of calculating a standard deviation is from the sum of squares of sample data, which for $s_{\overline{Y}}$ would require obtaining multiple samples in order to obtain multiple values of $\overline{Y}$. Fortunately, the standard error of the mean is easily estimated without resorting to multiple samples. Information about the variability of the variable Y *within* a single sample provides information about the variability of the statistic $\overline{Y}$ *across* multiple samples, as illustrated in Figure 4-1.

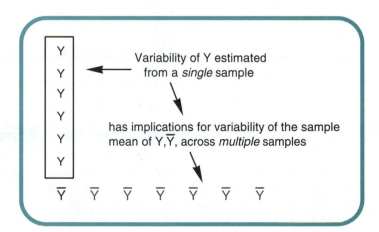

Figure 4-1.
Information from one sample provides information for the variability of the sample mean across samples.

---

1. More generally, *any* weighted sum of a set of variables approximates a normal distribution except for very small samples from nonnormal distributions. The sample mean is a weighted sum in which the weight of each variable is $\frac{1}{n}$. The sum of a set of values is also a weighted sum with each variable weighted 1.

Figure 4-2.
Distribution of the
sample mean from four
different populations
and three different
sample sizes.

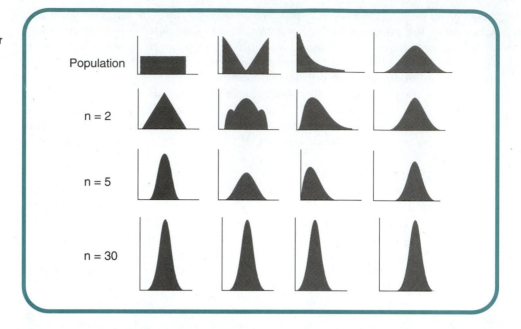

Population

n = 2

n = 5

n = 30

Standard deviation (error) of the sample mean:

$$\sigma_{\overline{Y}} = \frac{\sigma_Y}{\sqrt{n}}$$

Because the sample size n is in the denominator of this expression, larger sample sizes lead to smaller standard errors for a given value of σ_Y.

As the sample size n grows, the values of $\overline{Y}$ gather more tightly around μ_Y. The standard deviation (error) of $\overline{Y}$ is always less than the standard deviation of Y. When computing $\overline{Y}$, large values of Y in the sample tend to cancel out small values.

Obtaining the mean of the sample means is simple.

mean of the sample mean:
$$\mu_{\overline{Y}} = \mu_Y$$

No surprise here. The mean of the sample means is the original mean.

Figure 4-2 illustrates these three results for four distributions of Y. These distributions show the standard deviation of $\overline{Y}$ decreasing as n increases with a constant value of $\overline{Y}$. Notice how quickly each distribution of $\overline{Y}$ approaches normality as sample size n increases, even for distinctly nonnormal populations. Only the sampling distributions from the asymmetric population distribution are not approximately normal by a sample size of five.

The next section develops the logic of confidence intervals further by establishing the range of variation of $\overline{Y}$ around a *known* value of the population mean, μ_Y. The succeeding section flips this problem around, using this newfound knowledge to construct a confidence interval about $\overline{Y}$ to estimate the *unknown* value of μ_Y.

EXERCISES

4-1. The population mean and the standard deviation of Y are 20 and 3, respectively. For samples of a fixed size $n = 25$ drawn from this population, what is the

a. population mean of the sample means over repeated sampling?
b. population standard deviation of the sample means?

a. $n = 10$
b. $n = 25$
c. $n = 100$
d. $n = 500$
e.   Graph the relationship between sample size and $\sigma_{\overline{Y}}$ for these four values of sample size. What is the relationship between sample size and the standard error of the sample mean, $\sigma_{\overline{Y}}$?
f.   State what this relationship implies about the estimation of the population mean from a sample mean.

4-2. For $\sigma_Y = 18$, compute the standard error of the mean $\sigma_{\overline{Y}}$ for

4.2 TYPICAL VARIATION OF THE SAMPLE MEAN

The issue is that $\overline{Y}$ does not equal μ_Y. Instead, $\overline{Y}$ is a random variable centered around μ_Y. How far is a single value of $\overline{Y}$ from μ_Y? Any one randomly sampled $\overline{Y}$ could be close to or far from μ_Y. The size of the confidence interval is the *typical* range of these distances, or **sampling errors.** Before constructing a confidence interval around $\overline{Y}$, we must know the probable size of these errors.

> **sampling error of the mean**
> $\overline{Y} - \mu_Y$

Defining Typical Variation of Distances

No upper and lower bounds constrain the values of a normally distributed continuous variable—100% of the variation ranges from the infinitely small to the infinitely large. However, most values of a normally distributed variable are close to the mean, so a more useful question addresses the range of *typical* variation of $\overline{Y}$. Typical can be defined many ways. The most common definition is 95%. For any normally distributed random variable, including $\overline{Y}$, 95% of the values fall within 1.96 standard deviations of the population mean.

Our primary concern is not the value of $\overline{Y}$ per se, but rather the sampling error—$\overline{Y} - \mu_Y$, the distance of the obtained value of $\overline{Y}$ from μ_Y. The size of $\overline{Y} - \mu_Y$ is meaningfully interpreted for the normally distributed $\overline{Y}$ when expressed in terms of its standard deviation (error).

> *Distance of $\overline{Y}$ to μ_Y, the Z transformation of $\overline{Y}$:*
> $$Z_{\overline{Y}} \equiv \frac{\overline{Y} - \mu_Y}{\sigma_{\overline{Y}}}, \ \textit{with standard error } \sigma_{\overline{Y}} = \frac{\sigma_Y}{\sqrt{n}}.$$

This gauge of sampling error, $Z_{\overline{Y}}$, is computed from known values of μ_Y and σ_Y.

As noted in Chapter 3 and illustrated in Figure 4-3, the Z transformation does not change the shape of the distribution of the underlying random variable, in this

Figure 4-3.
The 95% range of
variation of $\overline{Y}$ and the
range of distances $Z_{\overline{Y}}$
from the population
mean, μ_Y.

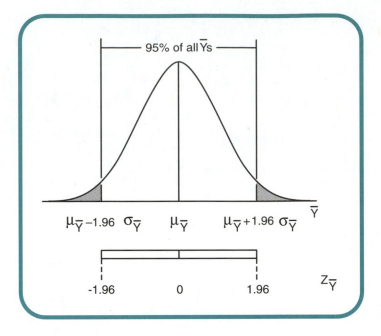

case $\overline{Y}$. The same graph illustrates both the distribution over repeated sampling of values of $\overline{Y}$ and the distribution of distances of $\overline{Y}$ from μ_Y, $Z_{\overline{Y}}$. The only distinction is a rescaling of the variables.

Of course, 5% of all values of $\overline{Y}$ or $Z_{\overline{Y}}$ are *not* within this range of typical variation. The lower end of this typical range of variation cuts off 2.5% of the left-hand tail at -1.96 standard errors, and the upper end cuts off 2.5% of the right-hand tail at 1.96 standard errors, which is the .975 quantile. That is, 5% of all $Z_{\overline{Y}}$ distances are either larger than 1.96 or smaller than -1.96. The .025 **cutoff value** for the right-hand tail of the standard normal distribution is written as

**cutoff value of a
distribution**
*cuts off a specified
percentage of the
values*

$$z_{.025} = 1.96.$$

Z is the standardized response variable and $z_{.025}$ is a constant equal to 1.96.

STATISTICAL ILLUSTRATION—Variation of the Sample Mean around the Known Population Mean

PROBLEM

A sample of size $n = 90$ is drawn from the population of the response variable Y with $\mu_Y = 100$ and $\sigma_Y = 28$. Within which values of the sample mean $\overline{Y}$ do 95% of all sample means of such samples fall?

CALCULATIONS

$\overline{Y}$ is normally distributed with $\mu_Y = 100$. The standard error is

$$\sigma_{\overline{Y}} = \frac{28}{\sqrt{90}} = \frac{28}{9.49} = 2.95.$$

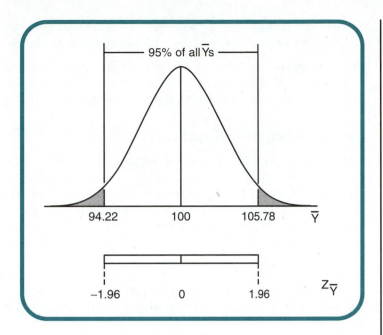

Figure 4-4.
The 95% range of
typical variation for
sample means with
$n = 90$, $\mu_y = 100$,
and $\sigma_y = 28$ is
between 94.22 and
105.78 in terms of Y,
and between −1.96
and 1.96 in terms
of Z.

The interval around the population mean μ_Y is computed from the normal distribution cutoff value of $z_{.025} = 1.96$. The size of 1.96 standard errors for this particular distribution of Y is

$$(1.96)(\sigma_{\overline{Y}}) = (1.96)(2.95) = 5.78.$$

The bounds of the interval on either side of μ_Y are 1.96 standard errors above and below μ_Y,

Lower bound: $\mu_Y - (1.96)(\sigma_{\overline{Y}}) = 100 - 5.78 = 94.22$

and

Upper bound: $\mu_Y + (1.96)(\sigma_{\overline{Y}}) = 100 + 5.78 = 105.78.$

STATISTICAL PRINCIPLE

As illustrated in Figure 4-4, if random samples of size 90 are drawn repeatedly from a population with $\mu_Y = 100$ and $\sigma_Y = 28$, 95% of the $\overline{Y}$'s would fall between 94.22 and 105.78. The range of typical variation of $\overline{Y}$ over multiple samples can be established from the information contained within a single sample. This range is 1.96 standard errors on either side of the population mean.

The previous example displayed the sampling distribution of $\overline{Y}$ for $n = 90$ (from a population with mean 100 and standard deviation 28). There is a different sampling distribution for each sample size. The larger n is, the smaller the standard error of $\overline{Y}$. The following two important facts needed for the construction of a confidence interval around a sample mean have now been established.

1. $\overline{Y}$ is a random variable computed from random samples from the same population and sample size.

2. The interval defined by moving 1.96 standard errors $\sigma_{\overline{Y}}$ in both directions around the population mean, μ_Y, contains 95% of all $\overline{Y}$'s.

Before constructing a confidence interval around a sample mean to estimate the unknown value of μ_Y, one more issue must be addressed. In practice, when estimating an unknown value of μ_Y, the value of σ_Y is also usually not known.

Estimating Typical Variation of Distances in Practice

To compute a confidence interval, we need the typical range of distances that $\overline{Y}$ varies around μ_Y. The standard error of the mean is the key to computing this range of distances. The problem is that when the population mean, μ_Y, is unknown, usually the population standard deviation σ_Y is also unknown. If σ_Y is not known, the population standard error $\sigma_{\overline{Y}}$ cannot be computed. What do you do? When σ_Y is not known, use the best available estimate, which is the standard deviation estimated from the sample, s_Y.

The *actual* standard error of the mean is $\sigma_{\overline{Y}}$. Using the sample estimate s_Y in place of the population value σ_Y results in the *estimated* standard error. The **estimated standard error** $s_{\overline{Y}}$ is computed from the estimated standard deviation of Y, s_Y.

When $\sigma_{\overline{Y}}$ is not known, the sampling error $\overline{Y} - \mu_Y$, is expressed in terms of *estimated* standard errors $s_{\overline{Y}}$. This new statistic, $t_{\overline{Y}}$, is the **t-value,** the distance of $\overline{Y}$ from μ_Y in terms of *estimated* standard errors. The expression for $t_{\overline{Y}}$ follows.

> **estimated standard error of the sample mean**
> $$s_{\overline{Y}} = \frac{s_Y}{\sqrt{n}}$$

> **t-value of a sample mean**
> *number of estimated standard errors that separate the sample and the population means*

$$\text{Distance of } \overline{Y} \text{ to } \mu_Y\text{: } t \text{ transformation of } \overline{Y}\text{:}$$
$$t_{\overline{Y}} \equiv \frac{\overline{Y} - \mu_Y}{s_{\overline{Y}}} \text{ , where } s_{\overline{Y}} = \frac{s_Y}{\sqrt{n}}.$$

Both t and Z gauge distance. The distinction is that $Z_{\overline{Y}}$ is defined with the *known* population standard error $\sigma_{\overline{Y}}$, and $t_{\overline{Y}}$ is defined with the standard error estimated from the data.

Why bother defining a new statistic? Specifying a confidence interval around the sample mean requires knowing the typical range of distances of this sample mean from the population mean.

> *Based on the standard error* estimated *from the data, the distribution of t across repeated samples provides the typical (e.g., 95%) range of distances of $\overline{Y}$ from μ_Y.*

Actually, a qualification is in order. In small samples, $\overline{Y}$ is normally distributed only when Y is normally distributed. So, in small samples, the distribution of $t_{\overline{Y}}$ precisely follows the t-distribution only for a normally distributed Y. Unless Y is decidedly nonnormal, however, the distribution of $t_{\overline{Y}}$ approximates the t-distribution very well.

Replacing σ_Y with s_Y changes the behavior of the resulting statistic, $Z_{\overline{Y}}$ or $t_{\overline{Y}}$, across repeated samples. $Z_{\overline{Y}}$ is the distance of $\overline{Y}$ from a *known* μ_Y in terms of standard errors. The statistic $t_{\overline{Y}}$ is this distance in terms of *estimated* standard errors $s_{\overline{Y}}$.

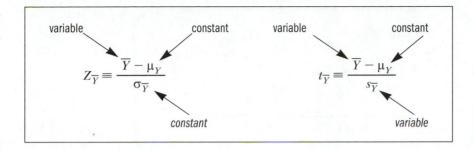

To establish the range of sampling variability for $Z_{\overline{Y}}$ and $t_{\overline{Y}}$, consider that the population values μ_Y and σ_Y are constant for each sample drawn from that population, but the sample statistics $\overline{Y}$ and s_Y vary for each sample. When constructing the distribution of $Z_{\overline{Y}}$ distances across repeated samples, the only change from sample to sample is the value of $\overline{Y}$. However, the $t_{\overline{Y}}$ distance for each sample involves two sources of variability—both $\overline{Y}$ and $s_{\overline{Y}}$ change from sample to sample. Accordingly, any t-distribution is more variable than the corresponding distribution of $Z_{\overline{Y}}$'s.

Although there is only one standard normal distribution, each sample size n yields a different t-distribution. Each distribution is identified by the degrees of freedom of the sample standard deviation s_Y,

$$df = n - 1,$$

as defined in Chapter 3. The distribution of $t_{\overline{Y}}$ distances across repeated samples with known μ_Y is almost but not quite the same as the distribution of $Z_{\overline{Y}}$ distances with known μ_Y. A t-distribution is also bell-shaped and symmetric with a mean of zero. The larger the df, the more similar the corresponding t-distribution and the standard normal distribution, as illustrated in Figure 4-5.

What values of a t-distribution define the typical range of variation for the distances of $\overline{Y}$ from μ_Y? For the 95% range of variation, one of these values cuts off 2.5% of the upper tail of the t-distribution, and the other value cuts off 2.5% of the lower tail. The notation $t_{.025}$ denotes the upper-tail cutoff, as illustrated in Figure 4-6.

Table 4-3 lists $t_{.025}$ cutoff values for various t-distributions. Each of these distributions defines the range of typical variation of $\overline{Y} - \mu_Y$ distances in terms of

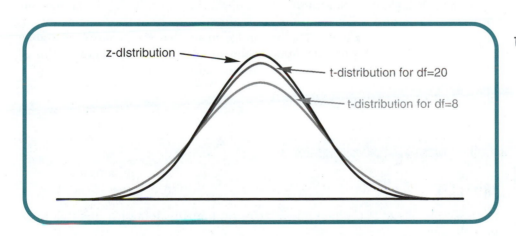

Figure 4-5.
The normal *z*-distribution compared to two *t*-distributions.

Figure 4-6.
The value of *t* that cuts off 2.5% of the corresponding *t*-distribution.

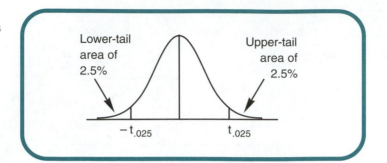

df	1	2	3	10	20	30	60	120	200	Normal
$t_{.025}$	12.70	4.30	3.18	2.23	2.09	2.04	2.00	1.98	1.97	1.96

Table 4-3.
Representative values of $t_{.025}$ illustrating the 95% range of variation of the distances of $\overline{Y}$ from μ_Y in terms of the estimated standard error $s_{\overline{Y}}$.

estimated standard errors. The table also illustrates the similarity of Z and t for large sample sizes, with 1.96 the minimum baseline value from the normal distribution.

How are these values from different *t*-distributions interpreted? For all sample sizes, the interval that contains 95% of the *t*-values is wider than the corresponding interval of *z*-values constructed with knowledge of σ_Y. Particularly in small samples, using $s_{\overline{Y}}$ in place of $\sigma_{\overline{Y}}$ exacts a price. As seen in Table 4-3, for $df = 1$, 95% of $\overline{Y}$'s vary between -12.70 and 12.70 estimated standard errors from μ_Y. At $df = 20$, the 95% range of variation of t drops to between -2.09 and 2.09. By $df = 200$, the distributions of $t_{\overline{Y}}$ and $Z_{\overline{Y}}$ are almost identical, with respective 95% cutoffs at 1.97 and 1.96. The distributions of $Z_{\overline{Y}}$ and $t_{\overline{Y}}$ become approximately equal as df increases, but the sampled values of $Z_{\overline{Y}}$ and $t_{\overline{Y}}$ are not precisely equal until the sample becomes the *entire* population—when s_Y becomes σ_Y.

A more detailed table of *t*-cutoff values appears in Appendix B. The *t*-table lists the values of *t* in the interior of the table with the corresponding percentages listed across the top of each column. The reason for this is that each row of the *t*-table briefly summarizes the *entire t*-distribution for the corresponding degrees of freedom. By contrast, the normal curve table devotes an entire page to the values of a single distribution. The last row of the *t*-table in Appendix B presents values from the standard normal distribution.

STATISTICAL ILLUSTRATION—Inverse *t*-Distribution Probabilities

PROBLEM

For a sample of size 101, what value of *t* cuts off the *t*-distribution at the following probabilities?

a. Two-tail probability: $P(t < -t_{.025}) + P(t > t_{.025}) = 0.05$
b. Upper-tail probability: $P(t > t_{.05}) = 0.05$
c. Lower-tail probability: $P(t < -t_{.05}) = 0.05$

CALCULATION FROM t-DISTRIBUTION TABLE

For $n = 101$,

$$df = n - 1 = 101 - 1 = 100.$$

Obtain the probabilities from the row of the t-table in Appendix B that begins with $df = 100$.

	Upper-Tail Area						
$df = n - 1$	0.400	0.250	0.100	0.050	0.025	0.010	0.005
100	0.254	0.677	1.290	1.660	1.984	2.364	2.626

a. $P(t < -t_{.025}) + P(t > t_{.025}) = 0.05$
   The total area under both tails of the t-distribution for $df = 100$ specified by this problem equals 0.05. The corresponding cutoff value of t cuts off 0.025 of the distribution for each tail. Read the value of $t_{.025}$ directly from the table as 1.984.

b. $P(t > t_{.05}) = 0.05$
   Read the value of $t_{.05}$ directly from the table as 1.660.

c. $P(t < -t_{.05}) = 0.05$
   Convert the tabled value of $t_{.05} = 1.660$ to $-t_{.05} = -1.660$.

EXCEL BUILT-IN ANALYSIS

To obtain the value of t for a given tail probability, use the Excel inverse t-distribution function,

```
= TINV(probability,df).
```

The form of this function does not follow the same form as the normal distribution inverse function NORMINV introduced in Chapter 3. Instead of providing a value based on the cumulative probability, TINV provides a t-value for a specified *tail* probability. TINV provides the cutoff value of t that results in the specified probability when totaled across both tails of the distribution.

a. $P(t < -t_{.025}) + P(t > t_{.025}) = 0.05$
   The positive and negative values of $t_{.025}$ cut off the lower tail and upper tail of the distribution for a *total* probability of 0.05. Specifying a two-tailed probability of 0.05 with $df = 100$,

```
=TINV(.05,100)
```

returns a value for t_{cutoff} of 1.98, with 0.025 probability in each tail.

b. $P(t > t_{.05}) = 0.05$

To obtain only an upper-tail cutoff for a specified probability with TINV, multiply the desired probability by two. The cutoff value of t for a .05 probability in the upper tail only is obtained from

$$=\text{TINV}(.10,100),$$

which returns a value of 1.66 for t_{cutoff}.

c. $P(t < -t_{.05}) = 0.05$

To obtain only a lower-tail cutoff for a specified probability with TINV, multiply the desired probability by two. Further, TINV returns only positive values, so the negative sign must be explicitly added. The cutoff value of t for a .05 probability in the lower tail only is obtained from

$$=-\text{TINV}(.10,100),$$

which returns a value of -1.66 for $-t_{.05}$.

Obtaining the interval that defines the range of typical variation of the distances of $\overline{Y}$ from μ_Y is *not* a method for statistical inference. Constructing this interval around μ_Y calls for deductive reasoning from the known population mean to describing probabilities of obtaining specific values from this population. Fortunately, we can use this knowledge of the range of $\overline{Y}$ to develop a method for estimating an unknown population mean. The next section accomplishes this task by reasoning inductively from the sample to the population, using the data to infer the unknown value of the population mean.

EXERCISES

 4-3. A sample of size 50 is drawn from the population of the response variable Y with $\mu_Y = 500$ and $\sigma_Y = 30$.

a. What values of $\overline{Y}$ define the range that includes 95% of all means of such samples?
b. Is this a probability (deduction) problem or an inference problem? Why?

 4-4. The population mean is 50. A sample of size 25 yields a sample mean of 57.84 and a sample standard deviation of 5.90.

a. What is the value of $t_{\overline{Y}}$, the number of estimated standard errors that $\overline{Y}$ is from μ_Y?
b. What is the probability of obtaining a value of t that is as large or larger than the value obtained in (a)?

 4-5. What value of t cuts off 1% of the t-distribution in the right-hand tail for

a. $n = 5$
b. $n = 50$
c. $n = 200$
d. What is the relationship between cutoff values from a t-distribution and the sample size?

 4-6. At each specified df, tabled t-distributions such as those in Appendix B, or computer programs, provide cutoff t-values for tail probabilities.

a. At $df = 20$, obtain the cutoff t-values for tail probabilities of .010, .020, .025, .030, .040, and 0.50 from the printed t-table in Appendix B. Can this be done? Why or why not?
b. At $df = 20$, obtain the cutoff t-values for tail probabilities .010, .020, .025, .030, .040, and 0.50, as well as the standard .010 and .050 with a computer program. Can this be done? Why or why not?
c. Determine whether the computer or a printed table is preferred source of information for t-distribution probabilities and why.

Table 4-4.
Deduction and induction
compared.

| Deduction → from a model of the population to the data | deduce probabilities of observing specified values of the data from the *known* population characteristics |
| Induction → from the data to a model of the population | infer *unknown* population characteristics from statistics computed from the observed data |

4.3 CONFIDENCE INTERVAL AROUND A SAMPLE MEAN

Statistical inference involves a change of perspective from the previous section, a change from deduction to induction. Deduction begins with the known characteristics of the population and derives probabilities of obtaining intervals of randomly sampled values from that population. If the population is normal with $\mu_Y = 100$ and $\sigma_Y = 15$, what is the 95% range of variation of the distances of $\overline{Y}$ from μ_Y for $n = 50$?

Deduction is the foundation of statistical inference. The deductive rules of probability set up the problem of statistical inference, an example of induction. Statistical inference turns the problem around, as shown in Table 4-4. The value of an unknown population parameter is *inferred* from statistics computed from randomly sampled data. If $\overline{Y} = 103$ and $s_Y = 14$, what are the most likely values of the process or population mean μ_Y?

Now that the range of typical variation of the sample can be computed, statistical inference in the form of a confidence interval may be introduced.

Defining the Confidence Interval

The most fundamental form of statistical inference is the **confidence interval.** Confidence intervals are needed because a sample statistic such as $\overline{Y}$ only approximately equals the corresponding population value such as μ_Y. Although sample data do not reveal the exact value of μ_Y, the confidence interval calculated from these data *likely* contains the unknown value μ_Y.

How is the confidence interval obtained? The key piece of information is the typical range of variation of $\overline{Y}$. Statistical inference flips the perspective of probability around, placing an interval around $\overline{Y}$, as in Figure 4-7.

> **confidence interval around the sample mean** $\overline{Y}$
> *range of values that likely contains the unknown population mean, μ_Y*

If the typical range of variation constructed around the population mean contains the sample mean, then the same *interval around the sample mean contains the population mean.*

In practice, σ_Y is usually estimated from s_Y, requiring the use of the *t*-distribution. The cutoff for the 95% range of variation is the somewhat larger value from the relevant *t*-distribution cutoff $t_{.025} \approx 2$ instead of $z_{.025} = 1.96$ from the normal distribution. This cutoff value $t_{.025}$ is then multiplied by the estimated standard error of the mean $s_{\overline{Y}}$. To form the confidence interval, add $t_{.025}s_{\overline{Y}}$ to $\overline{Y}$ and subtract $t_{.025}s_{\overline{Y}}$ from $\overline{Y}$.

Figure 4-7.
The size of the
confidence interval
around the sample mean
is the range of typical
variation of the sample
mean around the
population mean.

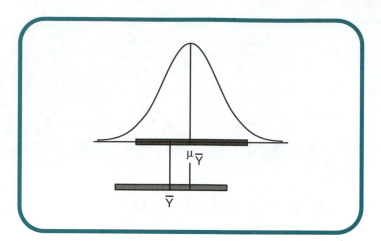

Figure 4-8.
The general 95%
confidence interval
around a sample mean.

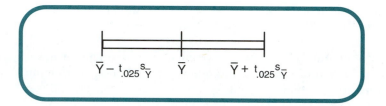

$$95\% \text{ confidence interval around a sample mean:}$$
$$\overline{Y} \pm t_{.025}s_{\overline{Y}}, \text{ where } t_{.025} \approx 2$$

Figure 4-8 illustrates this confidence interval around $\overline{Y}$.

The size of the confidence interval is often expressed in terms of its half-width, the precision of its estimate. For a 95% confidence level, the **maximum error** that can be made and still contain μ_Y is $t_{.025} \approx 2$ standard errors from $\overline{Y}$. The confidence interval is $\overline{Y} \pm E$.

maximum error E
furthest distance the population mean μ_Y can be from the sample mean $\overline{Y}$ and still lie within the confidence interval

$$\text{Maximum error for a 95\% level of confidence:}$$
$$E \equiv t_{.025}(s_{\overline{Y}}), \text{ where } t_{.025} \approx 2$$

To further illustrate the meaning of the confidence interval around $\overline{Y}$, think of repeatedly sampling from the population of Y and separately computing the 95% confidence interval around *each* sample mean.

The 95% confidence interval around each sample mean, $\overline{Y}$, for the same sample size n contains the population mean μ_Y for 95% of all random samples.

To illustrate, compute the six confidence intervals in Figure 4-9 from six samples (assuming a known σ_Y for simplicity). By chance, the fifth sample mean $\overline{Y}$ is more

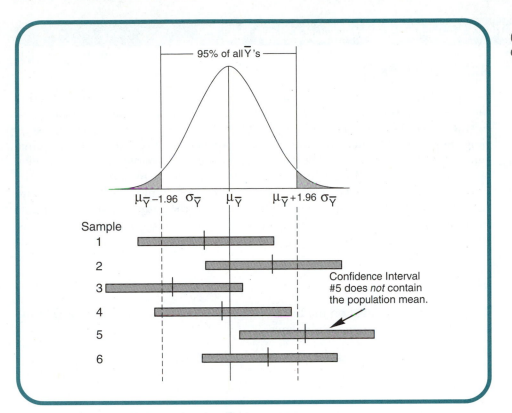

Figure 4-9.
Computation of six 95%
confidence intervals for
the population mean.

than 1.96 standard errors from the population mean, so the confidence interval constructed around the fifth sample mean does not contain the population mean, μ_Y. In practice, of course, only one corresponding confidence interval is computed from a single sample. The analyst does not know if the one available confidence interval missed the target.

In Figure 4-9 the population standard deviation σ_Y is known, so all confidence intervals are the same size. In practice, variability of both $\overline{Y}$ and s_Y contribute to the size of the interval. Not only are different confidence intervals centered over different $\overline{Y}$'s, as in Figure 4-9, but their lengths differ as well.

The **confidence level** specifies the probability that the population mean μ_Y will lie in any one interval. Before obtaining the sample, the probability is 95% that any one confidence interval will contain the population mean. After obtaining the sample, however, either the interval contains μ_Y or it does not, so the concept of probability precisely interpreted does not apply. The more precise phrasing is that the confidence level is 95%.

The level of confidence indicates the degree of certainty of capturing the unknown μ_Y. The flip side of the confidence level is the error rate, or **alpha.** The confidence level and the error rate add up to 1.0, or 100%.

An illustration of the calculation and interpretation of a confidence interval around the sample mean follows.

confidence level (e.g., 95%)
probability that any one confidence interval around the sample mean will contain the population mean

alpha α (e.g., 5%)
probability that any one confidence interval around the sample mean will not contain the population mean

BUSINESS APPLICATION 4.1—Confidence Interval around a Sample Mean

MANAGERIAL PROBLEM

Competitive manufacturers attempt to minimize the time lag between ordering materials from suppliers and receiving those materials. At one firm, management decided that one of several criteria used to evaluate suppliers is that average shipping time should be no more than 7½ days. Management realized that individual values might be larger or smaller than 7½, but the overall average should be smaller. What is the average delivery time of a specific supplier during the last year?

To predict future performance, assess past delivery times. Yet the past is of no inherent interest for management decisions about the future. Last year's sample mean is just one random outcome from a larger population; it only approximates the unknown population mean.

DATA

To name this data range on the Excel spreadsheet, first select the 15 cells with the Time data and do the menu sequence,

$$\text{Insert} \; \blacktriangleright \; \text{Name} \; \blacktriangleright \; \text{Define...}$$

Then specify the name *data*.

Time	8.4	9.9	10.0	8.9	9.7	8.1	7.8	5.2	9.4	5.7	7.9	6.5	9.8	7.8	6.2

ASSUMPTIONS

Computation of the confidence interval requires the assumption of a specific statistical model: The *only* source of variability of response *Y* is random error. That is, assume that the population mean and the standard deviation remain unchanged so that the supplier's shipping procedures applied to all of last year's 15 deliveries. Only random fluctuations obtained from repeated use of this procedure should lead to differences in shipping times, as specified by the stable-process model introduced in the previous chapter.

This analysis does not include shipping times measured more than one year ago because the assumption of unchanged shipping practices becomes less tenable as more time lapses. The population should consist only of values that result from random variation of the *current* process. If management changed shipping procedures, then the population from which the data are sampled also changes. If there was some substantive change in the way that orders are processed or packages wrapped or the way in which the parts are inspected, then data from the outdated procedure should not be included in the analysis. Changing the shipping procedures implies that both random error and a changing population mean or standard deviation contribute to the variability of shipping times. Including data for analysis generated by different shipping procedures would not assist in extrapolating the analysis of *current* procedures into the future.

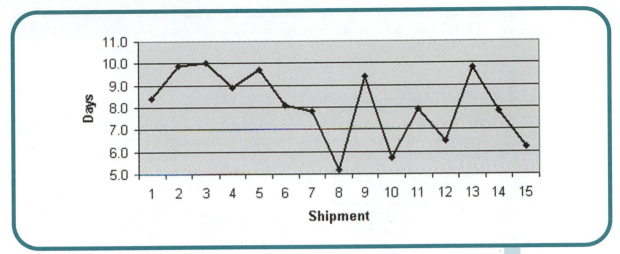

Figure 4-10.
Time-series plot of
shipping times,
assuming
approximately equal
intervals between
shipments.

The time-series plot of the shipping times for last year's 15 deliveries appears in Figure 4-10. Examination of this time series reveals an apparently stable process. The plot exhibits no obvious patterns such as a steady increase or decrease in shipping times, or a substantial shift in shipping times that occurred at one point in time. Apparently the stable-process model, which specifies random variation around the process mean, could account for these data.

At least one more assumption remains. The small sample size of 15 requires the assumption of normally distributed delivery times. If the population does not follow a normal distribution, particularly if it is asymmetric, then the *t*-distribution will not provide accurate cutoff values for constructing the width of the confidence interval. The histogram of these delivery times is shown in Figure 4-11.

Obviously, these 15 response values do not exactly conform to a normal distribution, but in small samples such as this, exact conformance is rare. For this distribution, if only one of the values in the 9.5 to 10.0 bin was in the 6.5 to 7.0 bin,

Figure 4-11.
Histogram of the
15 delivery times
with a bin width
of 0.5 days.

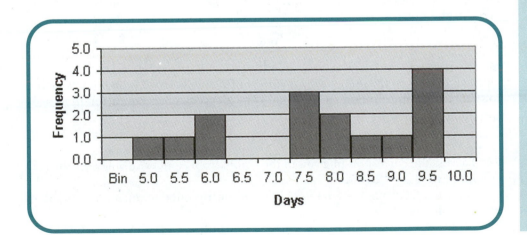

the data would be almost as normal as possible for this small sample. For this reason, the distribution is considered to be reasonably consistent with the normal distribution. In particular, there are no outliers in this data set.

APPLICATION—CONCEPTUAL WORKSHEET

This conceptual worksheet is excerpted from the Excel template provided with this text called MeanInference. (The complete worksheet provides both an estimate of the population mean with a confidence interval around the sample mean as well as a test of an hypothesized value of the population mean.)

Description	Name	Value	Formula
count of data	n	15	COUNT(data)
mean of data	mean	8.087	AVERAGE(data)
standard dev of data	stdev	1.587	STDEV(data)
standard error of mean	sterr	0.410	stdev/SQRT(n)
confidence level	level	0.95	
t cutoff value	tcut	2.145	TINV(1-level,n-1)
precision	E	0.879	sterr*tcut
lower bound of conf int	LB	7.21	mean-E
upper bound of conf int	UB	8.97	mean+E

This worksheet refers to cells with cell names, such as StErr for Standard Error, instead of the more cryptic references such as D6. The Excel section in Chapter 1 demonstrates how to name these cells.

APPLICATION—TRADITIONAL NOTATION

For these 15 values, $\overline{Y} = 8.087$ days and $s_Y = 1.587$ days. The estimated standard error of the mean $s_{\overline{Y}}$ is

$$s_{\overline{Y}} = \frac{s_Y}{\sqrt{n}} = \frac{1.587}{\sqrt{15}} \approx 0.410 \text{ days.}$$

Next, find the cutoff value of t for a 95% confidence interval, which corresponds to .025 of the distribution in each tail. The degrees of freedom for the corresponding t-distribution is

$$df = n - 1 = 14.$$

Read across the corresponding row in the t-table from Appendix B. Under the .025 column, find $t_{.025} = 2.145$.

The distance from $\overline{Y} = 8.09$ to either end of the interval, E, is 2.145 standard errors, which is

$$E = 2.145\,(s_{\overline{Y}}) = 2.145\,(0.410) = 0.879 \text{ days.}$$

The 95% confidence interval is E added to and subtracted from $\overline{Y}$, or 8.087 ± 0.879 days.

$$\text{Lower Bound:} \quad \overline{Y} - 2.145\,(s_{\overline{Y}}) = 8.087 - 0.879 = 7.21 \text{ days}$$

and

$$\text{Upper Bound:} \quad \overline{Y} + 2.145\,(s_{\overline{Y}}) = 8.087 + 0.879 = 8.97 \text{ days}$$

We can be confident that the actual *average* delivery time is somewhere between 7.21 days and 8.97 days. This confidence interval is

$$8.97 - 7.21 = 1.76 \text{ days}$$

wide.

APPLICATION—EXCEL BUILT-IN ANALYSIS

Excel provides a built-in function called CONFIDENCE for computing a confidence interval. Unfortunately, this function only uses the z-cutoff value instead of the t-cutoff value. That is, the confidence function requires either a known population standard deviation or a large sample size.

MANAGERIAL INTERPRETATION

The average delivery time of last year's 15 deliveries was 8.09 days, yet management decreed that an average of no more than 7½ days is acceptable. Assuming the 15 data values represent random variation from the same process, however, an actual average delivery time as low as 7.21 days is plausible. Perhaps the obtained sample mean of 8.087 days is so large simply because of chance sampling fluctuation. Or perhaps the true average is considerably larger than 7½ days, but the resulting interval that estimates the true average delivery time is so large that even values as low or lower than 7½ are plausible.

The results of this statistical analysis are inconclusive. These results do not provide sufficient evidence for rejecting the supplier. Before finding another supplier, perhaps provide this supplier more opportunity to demonstrate a sufficiently small delivery time.

Up to this point, only 95% confidence intervals have been constructed. The next section discusses the construction of intervals with any specified level of confidence, such as 90% or 99%.

Choosing the Level of Confidence

Ninety-five percent is only one possible level of confidence. For the same data, larger levels of confidence such as 99% yield wider intervals, and smaller levels such as 90% yield narrower intervals. What is the most appropriate width of the confidence interval? The width of the interval can be tailored to the specific problem, though for most purposes a 95% confidence level suffices. The problem in choosing the size of the interval is that both larger and smaller intervals have desirable and undesirable properties.

Larger intervals have the desirable property that they are more likely to contain μ_Y. Unfortunately, the larger the interval, the less precise the estimate. Consider the largest possible (theoretical) interval. The population mean μ_Y is guaranteed to fall between negative infinity to positive infinity, but who cares? By asking for everything, you get nothing.

Smaller intervals have the desirable property of providing a more precise, more useful range. Unfortunately, the smaller the interval, the more likely that μ_Y falls outside the interval. Consider the smallest possible interval, a single value of $\overline{Y}$, for which the probability is zero. For a theoretical distribution of a continuous variable, $\overline{Y}$ is guaranteed not to equal the population mean μ_Y. Real life metric data are not so precise, but the conclusion remains. The smaller the confidence interval, the smaller the probability that the population mean is contained within the interval.

The only distinction in the computation of confidence intervals at confidence levels other than 95%, such as 99% or 90% confidence levels, is the use of a cutoff value different from $t_{.025}$. For the 90% confidence interval around $\overline{Y}$, divide the corresponding error rate of 10% into two 5% pieces, one piece for each tail of the distribution.

$$90\% \text{ confidence interval around a sample mean:}$$
$$\overline{Y} \pm t_{.05} s_{\overline{Y}}, \text{where } t_{.05} \geq 1.65$$

Similarly, the $t_{.005}$ cutoff value applies to a 99% confidence interval because the 1% error is distributed .5% or .005 in each tail.

$$99\% \text{ confidence interval around a sample mean:}$$
$$\overline{Y} \pm t_{.005} s_{\overline{Y}}, \text{where } t_{.005} \geq 2.58$$

The three most commonly used confidence levels are 90%, 95%, and 99%.

In summary, the confidence interval should be wide enough to likely contain μ_Y, but small enough to provide a reasonably precise estimate.

A desirable confidence interval is narrow with a high confidence level.

The goal is to obtain a precise estimate with a high probability of containing the population mean, a goal usually met with a 95% level of confidence.

STATISTICAL ILLUSTRATION—Confidence Level

PROBLEM

The previous business application computed the 95% confidence level for mean delivery time as 7.21 days to 8.97, which is 1.76 days wide. What is the size of this interval for other confidence levels?

90% CONFIDENCE LEVEL

This interval was computed from 15 time points, so $df = n - 1 = 14$. For the 90% confidence level, $t_{.05} = 1.76$. The previously computed standard error is $s_{\overline{Y}} = 0.410$. The maximum error E is

$$E = t_{.05}s_{\overline{Y}} = (1.76)(0.410) = 0.722.$$

The resulting interval is

Lower Bound: $\overline{Y} - E = 8.087 - 0.722 = 7.365$ days,

and

Upper Bound: $\overline{Y} + E = 8.087 + 0.722 = 8.809$ days.

We can be 90% confident that the actual average delivery time is somewhere between 7.37 days and 8.81 days. This confidence interval is

$$8.809 - 7.365 = 1.44 \text{ days}$$

wide.

99% CONFIDENCE LEVEL

This interval was computed from 15 time points, so $df = n - 1 = 14$. For the 99% confidence level, $t_{.005} = 2.977$. The previously computed standard error is $s_{\overline{Y}} = 0.410$. The maximum error E is

$$E = t_{.005}s_{\overline{Y}} = (2.977)(0.410) = 1.221.$$

The resulting interval is

Lower Bound: $\overline{Y} - E = 8.087 - 1.221 = 6.866$ days,

and

Upper Bound: $\overline{Y} + E = 8.087 + 1.221 = 9.308$ days.

We can be 99% confident that the actual average delivery time is somewhere between 6.87 days and 9.31 days. This confidence interval is

$$9.308 - 6.866 = 2.44 \text{ days}$$

wide.

STATISTICAL PRINCIPLE

The larger the confidence level, the wider the corresponding confidence interval. In this example, as the confidence level increased from .90 to .95 to .99, the width of the corresponding interval increased from 1.44 to 1.76 to 2.44 days. Larger intervals provide an enhanced likelihood of containing the unknown μ_Y, but they also provide less precise estimates of μ_Y.

The confidence interval communicates the same amount of information regardless of the level of confidence. For the same data, raising the level of confidence does not provide any more information than lowering the confidence level. Only so much information can be wrung out of the data. Each specific confidence level represents a trade-off between the probability of containing μ_Y and the precision of the estimate.

The way to provide a more precise estimate is to gather more data to reduce the standard error of the mean. Next we show how to estimate the sample size needed to achieve the specified precision for a confidence interval around a sample mean.

EXERCISES

4-7. The local state patrol office is interested in knowing how fast cars are traveling on a stretch of interstate freeway at 2 P.M. The speed limit is 60 mph. A sample of 51 cars revealed a mean speed of 64.7 mph with a standard deviation of 4.3 mph.

a. Construct the 95% confidence interval around $\overline{Y}$ using a conceptual worksheet.
b. Construct the 95% confidence interval around $\overline{Y}$ using traditional formulas.
c. Interpret the meaning of this confidence interval.
d. Determine whether the size of the interval is small enough to provide useful information regarding the speed of cars on this stretch of interstate freeway.
e. Determine what other information would be useful for this evaluation.

4-8. A random sample of the length of telephone calls at a local telephone exchange revealed a mean of 4.2 minutes with a standard deviation of 2.7 minutes for a sample of 176 calls.

a. Construct the 95% confidence interval around $\overline{Y}$ using a conceptual worksheet.
b. Construct the 95% confidence interval around $\overline{Y}$ using traditional formulas.
c. Interpret the meaning of this confidence interval.

4-9. A manufacturer of automobile tires was interested in knowing how long a certain brand of tires lasted. Past experience

dictated that the population standard deviation of usable tire wear is 2,539 miles, but the population mean is unknown. From a sample of 28 tires, the sample mean was 36,720 miles.

a. Construct the 95% range of variation around $\overline{Y}$.
b. Interpret the meaning of this range of variation.
c. Determine why this interval is described as a "range of variation" instead of a "confidence interval".

4-10. Twenty random samples of size 15 were obtained from a normal distribution with a mean of 50 and a standard deviation of 10. From the size, mean, and standard deviation of each sample, the corresponding 95% confidence interval was computed. The lower bound (LB) and upper bound (UB) of each interval are listed in the following table.

	1	2	3	4	5	6	7
LB	39.58	45.27	49.49	41.63	40.21	45.69	45.55
UB	49.61	56.55	60.98	53.31	52.37	56.56	57.64

	8	9	10	11	12	13	14
LB	45.03	42.65	45.02	36.94	42.80	41.77	47.44
UB	53.97	56.99	53.70	49.20	54.27	53.07	56.08

	15	16	17	18	19	20
LB	41.93	44.74	44.18	43.74	39.69	47.28
UB	53.16	56.48	53.97	52.21	50.55	61.54

a. Identify the confidence intervals that do *not* contain the population mean.

b. Determine on average how many confidence intervals computed from 20 samples will *not* contain the population mean for a 95% confidence level. Are the results of these samples consistent with that expectation?

c. Compute the widths of the confidence intervals for the first and second samples. Why do they differ?

d. Calculate the mean of the second sample.

e. Calculate the standard deviation of the third sample.

4-11. An automobile tire manufacturer is developing a new brand of tires. From a sample of 15 of these tires after 50,000 miles of simulated use, the mean amount of remaining tread was .381 inches with a standard deviation of .047 inches. Construct and interpret the

a. 99% confidence interval around the sample mean.

b. 95% confidence interval around the sample mean.

c. 90% confidence interval around the sample mean.

d. Compute and compare the widths of these confidence intervals. What are the advantages and disadvantages of each?

4-12. To satisfy the IRS, estimate the total value of 8,725 boxes of toys stored in a warehouse. A random sample of 120 boxes is taken, yielding a mean value of $47.92 with a standard deviation of $8.34. The total estimated value is

$$(\$47.92)(8725) = \$418,102.00.$$

The lower and upper bounds of an accompanying confidence interval around the sample mean are multiplied by 8,725 to obtain a confidence interval of the total inventory value. Construct and interpret the

a. 99% confidence interval around the sample mean and the total value.

b. 95% confidence interval around the sample mean and the total value.

c. 90% confidence interval around the sample mean and the total value.

d. Plot the width of each confidence interval in terms of the confidence level. Interpret the relationship.

4-13. The actual standard error of the mean, $\sigma_Y/\sqrt{n}$, is based on an implicit assumption. Usually the entire sample is obtained at one time, so that each sampled element is not returned to the population for potential resampling. When the size of the population is finite, that is, of fixed size N, the standard error is modified as

$$s_{\overline{Y}} = \frac{s_Y}{\sqrt{n}} \sqrt{\frac{N-n}{N-1}}.$$

The expression $\sqrt{(N-n)/(N-1)}$ is called the *finite correction factor*, with values ranging from zero (if $n = N$) to one (if $n = 1$). As the sample size n gets closer and closer to the population size N, the value of the correction factor becomes smaller and smaller, which reduces the standard error $\sigma_{\overline{Y}}$.

To estimate the mean tree diameter on a lot of 100 trees, the diameter of each tree in a sample of 20 trees was measured, yielding a sample mean of 15.3 inches and a standard deviation of 3.9 inches. Construct and interpret the 95% confidence level of mean tree diameter.

4-14. What is the value of the finite correction factor, defined in the previous problem, when

a. $n = 4, N = 20$

b. $n = 4, N = 100$

c. $n = 4, N = 1000$

d. What conclusion can be drawn regarding the importance of the finite correction factor from the answers to (a), (b), and (c)?

4.4 SAMPLE SIZE AND PRECISION

How can a high level of confidence and a small confidence interval be realized simultaneously? The answer is straightforward: Increase the sample size. All other factors the same, increasing sample size decreases the width of the confidence

Figure 4-12.
Maximum error and the
size of the confidence
interval.

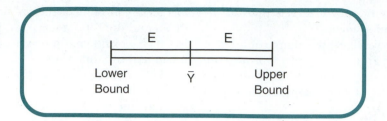

interval. To reduce the size of the confidence interval for estimating an unknown μ_Y, reduce the standard error,

$$\sigma_{\overline{Y}} = \frac{\sigma_Y}{\sqrt{n}} \, .$$

Reducing $\sigma_{\overline{Y}}$ means either reducing σ_Y or increasing the sample size n. In some manufacturing processes, quality can be increased by reducing the variability of a critical dimension's measurements, leading to a reduced σ_Y. But typically the size of σ_Y is beyond the manager's control, leaving the alternative of increasing n.

How precise is a given confidence interval? Precision is expressed as one-half of the interval's width, or the largest discrepancy between $\overline{Y}$ and either end of the interval. This distance is the maximum error, E, illustrated in Figure 4-12.

For a 95% level of confidence and known σ_Y, compute E from $z_{.025} = 1.96$ and the standard error $\sigma_{\overline{Y}}$,

$$E \equiv 1.96\sigma_{\overline{Y}} = 1.96\left[\frac{\sigma_Y}{\sqrt{n}}\right].$$

Larger sample sizes n lead to narrower confidence intervals. For example, for a standard deviation of 28 and a sample of size 5,

$$E = (1.96)\left(\frac{28}{\sqrt{5}}\right) = (1.96)(12.52) = 24.54.$$

Increasing sample size to 25 yields

$$E = (1.96)\left(\frac{28}{\sqrt{25}}\right) = (1.96)(5.60) = 10.98,$$

resulting in a considerably smaller interval $\overline{Y} \pm E$. To obtain a smaller confidence interval for a given confidence level, pay more money to collect a larger sample. What is true for all of life remains true with statistics; there is no free lunch.

To show the sample size needed for a specific level of precision, rearrange the expression for the precision E to solve for the required sample size,

$$n_\sigma = \left[\frac{(1.96)\sigma_Y}{E}\right]^2.$$

The symbol for sample size, n, is subscripted with a σ as n_σ because its computation requires the population standard deviation σ_Y. The problem with using this expression in practice is the by now familiar problem that if μ_Y is not known, then σ_Y is probably not known either, in which case n_σ cannot be computed.

The best solution to this problem of the unknown σ_Y is to obtain a comparatively small preliminary sample and estimate σ_Y with the resulting sample value s_Y. Substituting s_Y for σ_Y results in

$$n_s = \left[\frac{(1.96)s_Y}{E} \right]^2.$$

The problem with applying this expression is the sampling fluctuation of s_Y. By design, the preliminary sample should be smaller than the actual sample needed to obtain the desired precision. Yet, particularly in small samples, s_Y fluctuates greatly from sample to sample. By chance, a particularly small value of s_Y relative to the true value of σ_Y may be obtained, which would result in an estimate of n_s too low to obtain the desired level of precision.

The best available protection against obtaining a small value of s_Y by chance is an upward adjustment of the estimated n_s. The protection against a value of s_Y that is too low can never be complete, but a reasonable degree of protection can be attained. The following adjustments provide the protection for a 70%, 90%, and 99% probability of obtaining the needed sample size n to achieve the specified precision E for a 95% level of confidence.[2]

Required sample size to obtain the specified precision E for a 95% confidence level around a mean with unknown σ_Y:

$$.70\ probability: \quad n = 1.054n_s + 4.532$$
$$.90\ probability: \quad n = 1.132n_s + 7.368$$
$$.99\ probability: \quad n = 1.242n_s + 10.889$$

$$where\ n_s = \left[\frac{(1.96)s_Y}{E} \right]^2.$$

The larger the desired probability of actually achieving the precision E when the confidence interval is computed, the larger the sample size.

To illustrate, consider a situation in which the initial estimate of sample size n_s yielded a value of 50 for a 95% confidence interval. For a .70 probability of obtaining a 95% confidence level at the desired level of precision, the needed sample size is actually 57. This value increases to 65 and then to 68 for probabilities of .90 and then .99, respectively. If the sample size was only the initial estimate of $n_s = 50$, the actual probability of obtaining the desired level of precision for a 95% confidence interval is only .43.

The expressions for upward adjustment at confidence levels of 90% and 99% are almost identical to those equations shown for a 95% level of confidence. To obtain the value of n_s, choose the appropriate critical value from the z-distribution, 1.645 for the 90% confidence level or 2.576 for the 99% confidence level. If a value of n_s under 100 is obtained, the needed sample size n for a confidence level of 90% is generally one less than the value obtained for the 95% confidence level, and n is generally one more for the 99% confidence level. For values of n_s over 100, the resulting adjustment to the value of n_s can be considered identical to the adjustments for the 95% confidence level.

This upward adjustment of the initial estimate n_s is needed because two statistics—$\overline{Y}$ and s_Y—vary from sample to sample. The estimation of the needed value

2. Most textbooks fail to report this upward adjustment, which is explained in Kupper and Hafner (1989). These equations reported here for the upward adjustment (and for the following discussion on the sample size for the mean difference) were obtained by a regression analysis (Chapter 8) of the values in the tables reported by Kupper and Hafner.

of n to achieve sufficient precision must account for sampling fluctuations (sampling error) of *both* of these statistics. The level of confidence refers to the likelihood that the unknown population mean μ_Y lies within the confidence interval. When using s_Y to estimate the needed value of n to achieve the specified precision, the probability that the resulting confidence interval will achieve the desired level of precision for the sample size n must also be specified.

In summary, to estimate the needed sample size, follow these three steps:

1. Obtain the estimate s_Y, such as from a preliminary sample.
2. Compute the initial estimate of sample size n_s.
3. Adjust the sample size upward to protect against an unusually low value of s_Y.

Following these three steps still does not guarantee that the needed sample size will be obtained. These steps can be repeated with increasingly more accurate values of s_Y until the population mean is estimated with the desired precision.

E is the specified level of precision, the cutoff value $t_{.025}$ corresponds to the 95% confidence level, and s_Y can be estimated from a preliminary pilot sample. From these values, the needed sample size n is easily computed, as illustrated in the following application.

BUSINESS APPLICATION 4.2—Setting n for a Precise Estimate of the Mean

MANAGERIAL PROBLEM

The previous business application constructed a confidence interval around the mean delivery time of the last 15 shipments from a single company. Unfortunately, management deemed inadequate the obtained precision of estimation of 0.879 days. How many more shipments must be sampled before there is a .90 probability of achieving a precision of half a day or less?

DATA

The initial sample of 15 shipments yielded 1.587 days as an estimate of the population standard deviation.

APPLICATION—CONCEPTUAL WORKSHEET

The following conceptual worksheet for calculating the needed sample size is the Excel template called CISampleSize.

Description	Name	Value	Formula
standard deviation	stdev	1.587	
desired precision	E	0.5	
z cutoff for 95% confidence level	zcut	1.96	
initial sample size	ns	38.70	((zcut*stdev)/E)^2
needed sample size	n	**51.18**	1.132*ns+7.368

APPLICATION—TRADITIONAL NOTATION

The cutoff value from the z-distribution that defines the 95% range of variation is $z_{.025} = 1.96$, and the desired level of precision for estimating the unknown population mean μ_Y is $E = .5$. From this information, compute the initial estimate of the needed sample size for a confidence level of 95%,

$$n_s = \left[\frac{(z_{.025})s_Y}{E} \right]^2 = \left[\frac{(1.96)(1.587)}{.5} \right]^2 \approx 38.70.$$

To account for the sampling fluctuation of s_Y, this value n_s is adjusted upward to protect against a small value of s_Y being obtained by chance. To provide a 90% probability of obtaining the desired precision,

$$n = 1.132n_s + 7.368 = 1.132\,(38.70) + 7.368 = 51.18.$$

There is a .90 probability that the desired level of precision, $\pm .5$ day, will be obtained for a confidence interval calculated from a sample of 52 shipments at a confidence level of 95%. Fifteen shipments have already been sampled, so an additional 37 shipments are needed to ensure a reasonable degree of certainty of obtaining a confidence level with the desired level of precision.

EXCEL BUILT-IN ANALYSIS

Excel does not provide an analysis for computing the needed sample size to obtain the desired level of precision in the estimation of the unknown population mean.

MANAGERIAL INTERPRETATION

For a 95% level of confidence, there is a 90% probability that the level of precision obtained with a confidence interval from a sample of 52 shipments will be within the specified level of 0.5 day. Only in 10% of such samples should the influence of chance result in a sample size too low to provide the sufficient precision. If the obtained value of precision falls short of the desired level, the revised sample size can be computed from the new data by repeating the preceding procedure.

Unfortunately, data from an additional 37 shipments may not be available. The first 15 data values represented delivery times for the last year. If the data are available, one possibility is to use data for the last two or three years instead of just the last year. Before using this data to construct a confidence interval, a time-series analysis would reveal whether changes in shipping procedures occurred during this time.

In the last sections, we estimated the value of a population mean from an interval around the sample mean. Next we consider an application of confidence intervals to time-series analysis in the pursuit of quality control.

EXERCISES

4-15. The FDA requires that a cold break-fast cereal manufacturer provide an esti-mate of the weight of the cereal in its packages labeled 346 grams. A preliminary sample of 14 boxes provides a sample mean of 344 grams and an estimated standard deviation of 1.7 grams. For a .90 probability of succeeding, calculate how large a sample is required to obtain an estimate with a 95% confidence level to the nearest

a.   gram
b.   half a gram
c.   quarter of a gram
d.   tenth of a gram

e.   Draw conclusions about the relationship of the precision of estimation to the sample size needed to obtain that level of precision.

4-16. The accounting department of a large national trucking company needs to know the average miles per gallon of their large, interstate trucks. The estimate is to be within 2 mpg. Measurements based on a preliminary sample size of 10 trucks provided a sample mean of 9.4 mpg and an estimated standard deviation of 1.9 mpg. For a .90 probability of succeeding, how large a sample is required to obtain an estimate with a 95% confidence level?

4.5 SUMMARY

Repeat the same procedure and get a different result. Each sample yields a different sample mean, $\overline{Y}$. In statistics this repeatable procedure is drawing a random sample, which includes the outcomes of a process generated over time. Using $\overline{Y}$ to estimate the unknown population mean μ_Y requires a *known* distribution of $\overline{Y}$ over repeated sampling. Statistical inference of μ_Y involves not only the distribution of Y but also the distribution of $\overline{Y}$ gathered over many, usually hypothetical, repetitions of a random experiment. The central limit theorem shows that, except for very small samples from nonnormal populations, the distribution of $\overline{Y}$ is approximately normal. Further, the population mean of the variable $\overline{Y}$ equals the population mean of the original variable Y, $\mu_{\overline{Y}} = \mu_Y$, so μ_Y refers to the mean of both distributions.

The standard deviation of $\overline{Y}$, $\sigma_{\overline{Y}}$, is called the standard error of the mean because its size directly indicates the likely range of expected error when $\overline{Y}$ estimates μ_Y. In practice, *both* the population values of μ_Y and σ_Y are usually not known, so the standard error of the mean is estimated with

$$s_{\overline{Y}} = \frac{s_Y}{\sqrt{n}} \ .$$

Using an estimated standard error to estimate an unknown μ_Y introduces another source of error: Both $\overline{Y}$ and s_Y vary from sample to sample. When using $s_{\overline{Y}}$, the family of *t*-distributions provides the cutoff values that define a given range of variation of $\overline{Y}$, such as 95%. There is a separate *t*-distribution for each degree of freedom, where

$$df = n - 1.$$

The larger the *df*, the closer the shape of the corresponding *t*-distribution to the shape of the standard normal distribution. For sizes of 200 or greater, the cutoff values from a *t*-distribution and from a *z*-distribution are typically equal to within two decimal digits, though the corresponding *t*-cutoff is always somewhat larger.

The 95% confidence interval is constructed around the sample mean by moving $t_{.025} \approx 2$ standard errors on either side of the mean:

μ_Y is likely in the interval $\overline{Y} \pm t_{.025} s_{\overline{Y}}$, where $t_{.025} \approx 2$ and $s_{\overline{Y}} = \frac{s_Y}{\sqrt{n}}$.

The resulting confidence interval is a range of values that likely contains the unknown population mean at a specified level of confidence.

The sample size needed to achieve a desired level of precision in the estimation of μ_Y can be calculated so that the width of the confidence interval is small enough to obtain the desired accuracy: however, additional resources are usually not committed to gathering a sample size larger than needed. This calculation in practice is usually done with an unknown value of the population standard deviation, which must be estimated from a comparatively small preliminary sample. When the minimum sample size is computed from the sample standard deviation, the result is adjusted upward to protect against a small chance value of the sample standard deviation.

4.6 KEY TERMS

alpha *147*
central limit theorem *135*
confidence interval *145*
confidence level *147*
cutoff value *138*
estimated standard error of the
    sample mean *140*

maximum error *146*
sampling distribution of the mean *133*
sampling error *137*
standard error of the mean *134*
t-value *140*

4.7 REVIEW EXERCISES

ANALYSIS PROBLEMS

4-17. The population mean and the standard deviation of *Y* are 34 and 8, respectively. For samples of a fixed size *n* = 16 drawn from this population, what is the

    a. population mean of the sample means over repeated sampling?

    b. population standard deviation of the sample means?

4-18. A sample size of 50 is drawn from the population of the response variable *Y* with $\mu_Y = 100$ and $\sigma_Y = 28$. Within which values do 95% of all sample means of such samples fall?

4-19. A sample size of 28 is drawn from the population of the response variable *Y* with $\mu_Y = 100$ and $\sigma_Y = 15$.

    a. What are the values of $\overline{Y}$ within which 95% of all sample means will fall?

    b. Is this a problem of probability or inference? Why?

4-20. The population mean is $8,027. A sample size of 33 yields a mean of $7,975 and a standard deviation of $149.

    a. What is the value of *t,* the number of *estimated* standard errors the sample mean is from the population mean?

    b. What is the probability of obtaining a value of *t* that is as small or smaller than the obtained value (from [a])?

    c. What is the probability of obtaining a value of *t* that is as large or larger than the obtained value (from [a])?

4-21. For a confidence level of 95%, find the corresponding

Concept

    a. *z*-cutoff

    b. *t*-cutoff for *n = 10*

    c. *t*-cutoff for *n = 20*

    d. *t*-cutoff for *n = 40*

    e. What is the relationship between the cutoff values of z or t and the corresponding confidence interval?

4-22. For a sample size of 15, what value of t cuts off the t-distribution at the following probabilities?

Mechanical

    a. $P(t > .40)$

    b. $P(t > .10)$

    c. $P(t < .05)$

4-23. For a sample size of 50, what value of t cuts off the t-distribution at the following probabilities?

Mechanical

    a. $P(t > .40)$

    b. $P(t > .10)$

    c. $P(t < .05)$

4-24. What is the value of t for a sample size of 16 that cuts off the upper or lower tail of the t-distribution at

Mechanical

    a. $P(t > ?) = .40$ **b.** $P(t < ?) = .40$ **c.** $P(t > ?) = .025$

4-25. What is the value of t for a sample size of 30 that cuts off the upper or lower tail of the t-distribution at

Mechanical

    a. $P(t > ?) = .10$ **b.** $P(t < ?) = .10$ **c.** $P(t > ?) = .05$

4-26. What is the average salary of the CEO of a company with gross earnings between 1 and 10 million dollars? A random sample of the salary of CEOs from 89 such companies revealed a mean salary of $188,000 with a standard deviation of $24,230. Construct and interpret the meaning of the mean salary for a confidence level of

Application

    a. 95%

    b. 99%

    c. Determine whether this is a problem of probability or inference and why.

4-27. A machine shop is bidding on a specific part that needs a hole drilled through the center. How long, on average, does it take to drill a hole through this part? Ten drilling times are presented below.

Application

4.12	4.20	4.30	3.67	3.56
4.10	3.23	3.78	3.03	3.20

Construct and interpret the meaning of the confidence interval around the mean drilling time for a confidence level of

    a. 90%

    b. 95%

    c. 99%

    d. When constructing a 95% confidence interval, the approximate value of the *t*-cutoff is 2. How close is the approximation in this example? How do you explain this discrepancy?

4-28. The number of hours required for each newly manufactured lightbulb to burn out is supposed to be 500 hr. The burn-out times for 30 lightbulbs follow:

520.53	473.77	504.36	499.03	461.46	475.44	465.11	496.94
509.24	492.36	497.89	469.87	492.63	467.70	504.41	477.69
491.72	485.71	518.69	482.25	487.91	493.32	513.07	485.84
501.06	447.10	545.06	519.39	480.96	477.48		

    a. Construct the 95% confidence interval of the mean burn-out time.

    b. Interpret the meaning of the confidence interval.

    c. Determine whether the confidence interval includes the targeted 500 hr. Is the 500 hr target a plausible value of the population mean?

4-29. A steel company produced a custom batch of 87 castings. The mean carbon content of the steel in these castings was estimated by testing a sample of 10 castings. The obtained mean was 2.1% with a standard deviation of .2%. Construct and interpret the meaning of the confidence interval around the mean carbon content for a confidence level of

    a. 90%

    b. 95%

4-30. There are 23 convenience stores in town. A random sampling of 6 of these stores noted the price of a gallon of 2% milk. The mean price was $2.27 with a standard deviation of 8¢. Construct and interpret the meaning of the confidence interval around the mean price of a gallon of 2% for a confidence level of

    a. 90%

    b. 95%

4-31. An automobile manufacturer improved the engine on its most popular model to increase gas mileage. A sample of 26 cars revealed a mean of 31 mpg with a standard deviation of 2.4. Construct and interpret the meaning of the confidence interval around the mean mpg for a confidence level of

    a. 90%

    b. 95%

4-32. The manager at the local Really Quick Lube wanted to know how long an oil change took on average. He recorded the lengths of 49 oil changes, obtaining a mean of 15.7 minutes with a standard deviation of 1.9 min. Construct and interpret the meaning of the confidence interval around the mean length of an oil change for a confidence level of

    a. 90%

    b. 95%

4-33.   Motivated by a desire to improve service, a manager at a mail-order clothing store measured the time it took to respond to 29 randomly sampled telephone orders. She obtained a mean of 8.2 sec with a standard deviation of 5.4 sec. Construct and interpret the meaning of the confidence interval around the mean sec for a confidence level of

   a.   90%

   b.   95%

   c.   Given the size of the standard deviation, and assuming an approximately normal distribution of wait times, what are the larger values of response times in this distribution?

   d.   What should the manager do in addition to improving the mean response times?

4-34.   How much television do elementary schoolchildren watch? A sample of 38 children revealed a mean of 3.9 hr per day with a standard deviation of 2.1 hr. Construct and interpret the meaning of the confidence interval around the mean hours of TV watched for a confidence level of

   a.   90%

   b.   95%

4-35.   The contents of 95 randomly sampled 12 oz cans of tomato sauce were weighed. The mean weight was 11.97 oz with a standard deviation of 0.02 oz. Construct and interpret the meaning of the confidence interval around the mean weight for a confidence level of

   a.   90%

   b.   95%

   c.   Is the assumption of a normal distribution of weight required? Why or why not?

4-36.   A developer is considering building a shopping mall in a growing suburb. Before beginning this project, she wants to know the mean family income for the residents of this region estimated to within $2,000 of the true (population) mean at a 95% level of confidence. After selecting an initial sample of 20 families, the population standard deviation was estimated as $7,429. How many families should be sampled for a .90 probability to obtain the desired level of precision at a 95% level of confidence?

4-37.   A new lubricant is supposed to extend the life of the drill-bit used to drill holes in metal parts. To estimate the mean life of the drill-bits with the new lubricant within 1 hr, a preliminary sample of 18 drill-bits revealed a mean life of 16.4 hr with a standard deviation of .9 hr. For a .90 probability of achieving the desired precision, how large a sample is required to obtain an estimate for a 95% confidence level?

4-38.   The selling price of a brand of washing machine soap varies according to the type of store and the part of the country in which the store is located. An advertising manager needs to know the average cost of the soap to within 5¢. A preliminary sample size of 20 prices provided a sample mean of $6.40 and an estimated standard deviation of 15¢. For a .90 probability of achieving a precision of 5¢, how large a sample is required to obtain an estimate for a 95% confidence level?

4-39. The quality control manager for a machine shop needs to estimate the mean outside diameter of several thousand recently manufactured bushings from one batch. The estimate is to be within .001 of an inch. A preliminary sample size of 28 provides a sample mean of 2.791 in. and an estimated standard deviation of .0024 in. For a .90 probability of achieving a precision of .001 in., how large a sample is required to obtain an estimate for a 95% confidence level?

4-40. A manager at a car rental firm wants to estimate the average distance each of its cars is driven. The estimate is to be accurate to within 10 miles. A preliminary sample size of 20 cars provided a sample mean of 87 miles and an estimated standard deviation of 21 miles. For a .90 probability of succeeding, how large a sample is required to obtain an estimate for a 95% confidence level?

4-41. Using a computer program such as Excel, generate eight samples of 10 values each. The data in each sample are normally distributed with a population mean of 50 and standard deviation of 10.

    a. Compute the estimated standard error for each sample.

    b. Compute the standard deviation of the eight sample means based on the average squared deviation score.

    c. Determine how the estimated standard errors compare to the standard deviation of the eight sample means. How should this standard deviation compare to the estimated standard errors?

4-42. Using a computer program such as Excel, generate 10 samples of 10 values each. The data in each sample are normally distributed with a population mean of 10 and standard deviation of 1.

    a. Compute the confidence interval around each sample mean at the 95% confidence level.

    b. Determine whether all intervals contain the population mean.

    c. Calculate how many, on average, of the 10 intervals you would expect to contain the population mean.

DISCUSSION QUESTIONS

1. What is the difference between a probability problem and a statistical inference problem?

2. If our primary goal is to develop and understand the methods of statistical inference, why bother learning some principles of probability?

3. Why is the standard error of the mean such a convenient unit of measurement for indicating how far a sample mean is from a known population mean?

4. When is the sample mean *not* normally distributed?

5. Why is the *t*-statistic called a distance measure? What distance does this statistic assess?

6. For any one application, only one row of the *t*-table is used. Why?

7. How does the family of *t*-distributions resemble the normal distribution?

8. How is the standard error of the mean estimated in practice?

9. When is a *t*-distribution used in place of the distribution of $Z_{\overline{Y}}$?

10. When is the *t*-distribution for all practical purposes the same as the normal distribution of *z*-values? Support your answer with representative values of these distributions.

11. What is the primary information provided by the confidence interval?

12. What is the purpose of a time-series analysis of the data *before* computing a confidence interval?

13. How does the chosen level of confidence affect the size of the resulting confidence interval?

14. Why does a 100% confidence interval yield a meaningless confidence interval?

15. How is sample size related to the width of a confidence interval?

16. How is the confidence level related to the width of a confidence interval?

17. For a given data set, why does a 99% confidence interval not provide any more information than a 95% confidence interval?

18. After computing the 95% confidence interval, what new information is needed to compute the 99% confidence interval?

19. What is the primary practical difficulty when computing the needed sample size to obtain a desired level of precision with a confidence interval?

20. Why does the initial estimate of the sample size required to obtain a sufficient level of precision need to be adjusted upward?

INTEGRATIVE ANALYSIS PROBLEM

The director of obstetrics at a local hospital wants to estimate average birth weight during the last year to within ±¼ lb. For convenience, the director obtained the birth weights (lb) of 26 randomly selected babies from the many hundreds of babies born during the year. These weights are the values of the variable Weight in the data file BIRTHWT.DAT.

a. Determine the unit of analysis. From which population is this sample drawn?

b. Determine the single best numerical estimate of the mean birth weight of all the babies born during the last year at this hospital.

c. Decide whether you must make any assumptions regarding the shape of the distribution of birth weights to compute a confidence interval.

d. Evaluate the reasonableness of these assumptions with a plot of the distribution.

e. Determine which statistical model presumably describes all of the data from which the confidence interval is computed.

f. Construct the 95% confidence interval around $\overline{Y}$ with a conceptual worksheet.

g. Construct the 95% confidence interval around $\overline{Y}$ with traditional formulas.

h. Interpret the meaning of this confidence interval.

i. Determine whether this result is sufficiently precise and why or why not.

j. Recommend sample size.

k. Determine what conditions must apply for this confidence interval to be applicable for describing mean birth weight in future years.

CHAPTER 4 EXTENSION   QUALITY CONTROL

E4.1 QUALITY CONTROL

Confidence intervals play a role in the pursuit of quality and customer satisfaction beyond that of statistical inference. A primary statistical analysis for the improvement of quality is the control chart, a time-series plot of the sample means of the process output. A confidence interval constructed around this set of means provides information regarding the underlying causes of the resultant variability of a process; this information is necessary to increase quality by reducing variation. Only when management understands the underlying causes of variation can it take appropriate action to reduce this undesirable variation. The result of variation reduction is that costs go down, quality goes up, and, ultimately, the customer is more satisfied.

Variability of Output

The purpose of business is straightforward: Make a product or perform a service that the customer purchases at a price that is higher than the cost of providing the product or service. Yet variation in the outcome of the product or service is inevitable. Some of this variation results in completely unacceptable products or services; other variation results in marginally acceptable output. The goal is to narrow the range of variation in order to achieve quality output virtually all of the time.

Thinking statistically is a key tenet of quality management. One conclusion drawn from statistical thinking is, Do it right the first time.

> *Improve the process by understanding the* causes *of variation, and then adjust these causes to reduce variation.*

Quality cannot be added after the process—the product or service—is completed. Inspection can distinguish between the good and the bad, but the bad must be reworked or discarded. Quality management focuses not on putting a bandage on what went wrong but on adjusting and fixing the process to decrease variability. Information needed to achieve this goal of understanding the causes of variation includes an analysis called Statistical Process Control, or SPC.

To understand SPC, we must first understand the causes of variability.

REASONS FOR VARIABILITY. The output of a process is the variable Y. Improving quality means, in part, reducing the variability of Y, which first requires an understanding of its underlying causes. As discussed in Chapter 3, variability results from two types of causes—common causes and assignable causes. The effective response for reducing variability depends on the type of cause.

Common causes are inherent to the process. Why did the particular set of 10 coin flips yield six heads on 10 flips? Why was the particular hole drilled .009" too far to the left? Why did more customers than there were available phone lines call in at 2:28 P.M., yet at 2:24 P.M. half of the phone operators were idle?

Reduce variation by controlling some of the chance, or previously random common causes. Perhaps the procedure for drilling the hole did not take into account the placement of the hose that distributes a continual flow of lubricant to the part. By chance, perhaps sometimes the lubricant flowed onto the drill several inches above the hole, and at other times the lubricant flowed directly on the hole being drilled. Does this chance variation influence the output of the process, including the closeness of the hole to the desired center? If the answer is yes, then the process should be changed so that the lubricant always flows at the same angle and level for each part. Reducing this source of variation reduces the variability of the output, resulting in more consistent, accurate placement of the drilled hole.

STABLE AND UNSTABLE PROCESSES. Changing the process to reduce variability requires identifying uncontrolled, random sources of variation and then preventing some of these sources from varying. Before the analysis of sources of variation common to all process output begins, however, the process should be stable. The output varies, but the process should not. A changing, unstable process is not amenable to analysis of uncontrolled sources of variation common to all output, because the sources of variation are themselves changing.

The output of any process necessarily varies, but the causes of this variation for a process in control are stable across time. As defined in Chapter 3, variability of a stable process is due only to common causes, each a relatively minor influence on process variability that contributes to the variability of all output. A stable process is also called a *process in control*. The underlying process mean μ_Y and the standard deviation σ_Y of a stable process are constant across successive output.

A stable process can be described with the statistical model introduced in Chapter 3 called the stable-process model. This model specifies the actual value of Y in terms of the underlying population mean and chance fluctuation: $Y = \mu_Y + \varepsilon$, with constant σ_ε. The issue for quality control is whether the stable-process model correctly describes the process output. When the process mean and the standard deviation remain constant, the variability of the output is due only to a combination of many small common influences, summarized as the error term e, that jointly influence the value of Y.

When is a process *not* in control? The answer is, whenever assignable causes are present. The presence of an assignable cause implies that there is no one process that generated all the data. Instead, a different process generated at least some of the data, for example a temporary employee who answered the phone only some of the time, or a different shipment of metal castings used in only some of the parts. This different process, which includes the assignable cause, has a different population mean or standard deviation than the process that generated the values of the remaining output. A process not in control, an unstable process, is subject to additional sources of variability beyond the usual randomness of a stable process. First removing the assignable causes of unwanted variation reduces variability of an unstable process.

Before the variability of a process can be reduced, management must understand the extent to which the underlying variability is due to assignable causes and to common causes. Correcting problems due to assignable causes is usually straightforward—spend more time training the temporary employee or do not accept any more metal from the supplier who provided the defective shipment. To reduce undesirable variability due to common causes, a redesign or revision of the entire process is required. The assignable causes can be fixed directly, but the process itself is modified in response to the variability that is due to common causes.

The preceding discussion established that an unstable process—a process out of control—should not be adjusted. Instead, the assignable causes should be identified and removed. A related principle is that a somewhat large random fluctuation should not initiate adjustment if the fluctuation is attributable to the common causes of variation in process output.

TAMPERING. A common mistake, called **tampering,** is to attempt to fix or adjust an aspect of the process that does not need fixing. Adjusting the wrong aspect of a process with the goal of reducing variability can result in exactly the opposite result. The process is not stable if temporary assignable causes are present. Adjusting the manufacturing procedure for all employees to compensate for the errors introduced by a temporary employee or a defective batch of metal is worse than time wasted. Consider a temporary employee drilling a hole in a metal part or machining a substandard batch of metal. Only when the usual employees are working or the proper metal is used should the process be analyzed for adjustment and modification. To reduce variability due to the common causes, the process must have settled down so that *only* common causes are randomly operating.

> **tampering**
> *adjusting a process either in reaction to*
> *(a) assignable causes, or*
> *(b) normal chance deviations,*
> increases *variability*

The other form of tampering treats a chance occurrence as a systematic part of the process. The output of all processes is subject to a normal range of variability and fluctuation due to the joint contribution of the common causes. Adjusting the process in reaction to moderate deviation due only to random fluctuation leads to increased variability. Perhaps purely by chance the last three holes were drilled to the right of center. Adjusting the drilling set up to account for these chance deviations leads to more erratic output than does leaving the process alone.

EXERCISES

E4-1. Classify each of the following sources of variation as being common causes or assignable causes, and explain why.

a. dayshift operator had a poor night's sleep
b. temperature 1° warmer than average
c. measuring device randomly overreads or underreads true value
d. metal used during the night shift has a deficient carbon content

E4-2. The population mean of the process output is $\mu_Y = 100$. The process is stable.

Provide 10 reasonable values of the random error term *e* that lead to a process with

a. small output variation
b. large output variation

E4-3. For the error values in Exercise E4-2, list the corresponding output values of Y for

a. small output variation
b. large output variation

Control Chart of the Sample Mean

By itself, being in control does not define a successful process. Even when the process is in control, variation of output may be so large that individual products or services may not meet design specification. Once the process is stable, the sources of variability can be studied and perhaps changed to reduce variability. Achieving control of a process is a necessary but not final step to increasing quality. How to assess this stability is discussed next.

CONSTRUCTING THE CONFIDENCE INTERVAL. Because variation of the output of a process in control is attributable only to random influences, the output has no repeatable pattern over time. According to the central limit theorem from Chapter 4, the means of the output of random variable Y should randomly vary around the population mean in a normal distribution. Individual sample means should not lie too far from the population mean, sample means should not gradually increase or decrease, and output should not follow any cycle or other pattern. Any such violation of this pattern of randomness implies that the variability of output is not due solely to normal variation of a stable process, but rather to an underlying lack of stability due to one or more assignable causes.

> **control chart of a statistic**
> *time-series plot of the statistic that includes the average value of the statistic and confidence limits around the average*

The **control chart** is the basis for assessing the randomness of output. A control chart, constructed for statistics such as the sample mean or sample standard deviation, assesses whether the output from a process acts as random output from a single distribution. The control chart is a primary statistical tool of quality control procedures.

Consider a stable process that outputs a continuous variable Y, such as distance, time, length, or weight.* The same underlying parameters μ_Y and σ_Y for *all* output imply an approximately normal distribution of the sample mean $\overline{Y}$. Virtually all of the variation of a stable process falls within a set of limits. If the process is in control, 68% of sample means are within one standard error of the population mean, and 99% of the sample means are within 2.57 standard errors of the mean—this is true today, tomorrow, and for as long as the process remains stable.

The $\overline{Y}$'s from a stable process are independent of each other, so the size of one $\overline{Y}$ is unrelated to the size of the previous values or succeeding values. This variation of Y differs when the process is out of control. The output of an unstable process exhibits some pattern as μ_Y or σ_Y, or both, change. The output fluctuates wildly, or it exhibits systematic, transitory tendencies such as a steady increase or decrease of mean values over time. The population values μ_Y and σ_Y are *not* the same for all values of Y for a process out of control.

As with any time series, the primary analysis is the search for detectable patterns. For a control chart, the presence of such patterns indicates a process out of control.

> *For a process with output Y, any violation of normally distributed random variation of $\overline{Y}$ around the population mean, μ_Y, or its estimate provides evidence that the process is* not *in control.*

*Regardless of the shape of the distribution of Y.

n	2	3	4	5	6	7	8	9	10	15	20	25
a	1.250	1.125	1.083	1.063	1.050	1.042	1.036	1.031	1.028	1.018	1.013	1.010

Table E4-1.
Adjustment factor a for estimating σ_Y from $\bar{s}_Y$.

The next section examines in more detail these violations from normally distributed random variation. The most obvious violation is a sample mean that lies more than three standard errors from the overall average. Other violations include patterns such as a gradually increasing sample mean over time.

To evaluate the stability of a process with a control chart, take at least 20 samples of the same size with at least $n = 5$ elements each. Consider first the control chart for the mean. The sample mean $\overline{Y}$ is plotted as a time series over all samples. The best estimate of the underlying population mean μ_Y from these data is the mean of the 20 or more sample means, which is expressed on a control chart by the **centerline.** From the overall mean $\overline{\overline{Y}}$ and the corresponding estimate of the population standard deviation σ_Y, construct the confidence interval. An estimate of σ_Y, is the mean of the 20 or more sample standard deviations, $s_{\overline{Y}}$. A *preliminary* version of the 99.73% confidence interval,

centerline
horizontal line in a control chart that represents the mean of all the sample means, $\overline{Y}$

$$\overline{\overline{Y}} \pm 3\,\frac{\bar{s}_Y}{\sqrt{n}} \;,$$

is constructed around $\overline{\overline{Y}}$ with this information.

Why is this expression for the confidence interval around the overall sample mean only preliminary? The mean of the distribution of sample variances s_Y^2 is the population variance σ_Y^2, but the mean of the distribution of sample standard deviations s_Y is *less than* the corresponding population value σ_Y. For all but small samples, this downward bias is inconsequential, but control charts are typically constructed with samples as small as $n = 5$. To correct this underestimation, the sample value $\bar{s}_Y$ is adjusted upward by multiplying by the corresponding correction factor a from Table E4-1. The smaller the sample size, the larger the correction.[1]

The confidence interval is constructed from the usual expression introduced in Chapter 4, given the upward adjustment of replacing $\bar{s}_Y$ with $(a)(\bar{s}_Y)$. The upper and lower **control limits** define the 99.73% confidence interval around the overall mean $\overline{\overline{Y}}$. A different confidence level is obtained by substituting the appropriate value for 3 in the preceding expression.

control limits for the sample mean
$$\overline{\overline{Y}} \pm 3a\,\frac{\bar{s}_Y}{\sqrt{n}}$$

An example of a control chart for a process in control is presented next.

---

1. The adjustment for the estimate of the population standard deviation of a normally distributed variable is to multiply the sample standard deviation by $1 + \frac{1}{4(n-1)}$.

BUSINESS APPLICATION E4.1—Control Chart of $\overline{Y}$ for a Process in Control

MANAGERIAL PROBLEM

Is the manufacturing process of lightbulbs in control regarding burn-out times?

DATA

Twenty samples were taken of six lightbulbs each. The time in hours from being turned on until burnout was recorded for each bulb. The burn-out times for these $20 \times 6 = 120$ lightbulbs appear in Table E4-2 under Items within the Sample.

APPLICATION—EXCEL GRAPHICS

Assessing the Excel Output
The control chart produced with Excel appears in Figure E4-1.

Obtaining the Means and Standard Deviations
First calculate the means and standard deviations for each of the 20 samples with the AVERAGE and STDEV functions. Enter these functions in Cells H3 and I3 to compute these statistics for the data in Cells B3 through G3, the six data values for the first sample. Copy these formulas through row 22, such as with the Edit ➤ Fill Down menu sequence.

Table E4-2. Burn-out times for 20 samples of six lightbulbs each.

Sample		Items within the Sample				
	1	2	3	4	5	6
1	497.73	508.39	495.38	503.87	481.68	493.15
2	487.02	508.02	502.53	485.48	506.62	490.68
3	498.98	498.15	481.43	494.05	516.53	484.46
4	506.18	487.27	495.19	498.60	496.92	494.66
5	502.16	497.89	502.30	487.50	506.54	506.76
6	502.56	490.16	515.71	499.87	510.36	474.69
7	509.32	498.04	484.88	511.65	497.13	512.41
8	481.99	487.62	486.37	493.81	492.89	496.99
9	489.85	515.40	503.10	489.42	498.10	496.70
10	511.95	498.89	511.28	496.81	477.91	516.74
11	489.08	497.61	493.98	498.29	498.49	481.67
12	487.57	507.01	516.00	498.29	495.11	525.38
13	491.87	491.50	506.37	498.69	468.17	482.35
14	511.33	492.64	486.88	509.02	510.65	490.16
15	513.60	494.86	494.31	513.55	471.65	510.59
16	500.03	493.50	503.01	498.61	520.97	490.66
17	504.46	511.30	502.98	489.75	513.60	504.12
18	495.84	492.63	501.98	498.20	507.03	502.83
19	485.46	490.83	510.19	505.30	495.17	494.12
20	491.48	501.36	486.04	493.09	502.47	510.79

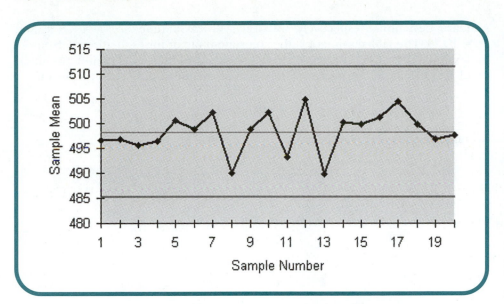

Figure E4-1.
Control chart for
sample means.

Table E4-3.
The mean and the
standard deviation
for each sample.

	H	I	J	K	L
1				for Means	
2	Mean	SD	CL	UCL	LCL
3	496.70	9.26	498.28	511.44	485.12
4	496.73	10.16	498.28	511.44	485.12
5	495.60	12.52	498.28	511.44	485.12
6	496.47	6.14	498.28	511.44	485.12
7	500.53	7.18	498.28	511.44	485.12
8	498.89	14.77	498.28	511.44	485.12
9	502.24	10.84	498.28	511.44	485.12
10	489.95	5.56	498.28	511.44	485.12
11	498.76	9.66	498.28	511.44	485.12
12	502.26	14.28	498.28	511.44	485.12
13	493.19	6.69	498.28	511.44	485.12
14	504.89	14.05	498.28	511.44	485.12
15	489.83	13.30	498.28	511.44	485.12
16	500.11	11.37	498.28	511.44	485.12
17	499.76	16.39	498.28	511.44	485.12
18	501.13	10.70	498.28	511.44	485.12
19	504.37	8.35	498.28	511.44	485.12
20	499.75	5.21	498.28	511.44	485.12
21	496.85	9.23	498.28	511.44	485.12
22	497.54	8.98	498.28	511.44	485.12

Obtaining the Control Limits

From these statistics, obtain the centerline and upper and lower control limits, as shown in Table E4-3. First, in Cells H23 and I23, as illustrated in the following excerpt from the worksheet, compute the means of *all* 20 sample means and *all* 20 standard deviations, respectively, with the AVERAGE function, $\overline{\overline{Y}} = 498.28$ and $\overline{S}_Y = 10.23$. The tabled value of a, the adjustment factor for estimating σ_Y from $\overline{s}_Y$, for a sample size of six, is 1.050. Calculate the control limits, the confidence interval of size ± 3 standard errors, on either side of the mean of the sample means.

$$\overline{\overline{Y}} \pm E \text{ where } E = 3a \frac{\overline{s}_Y}{\sqrt{n}} .$$

Accomplish these calculations on the worksheet as follows.

	G	H	I
23		498.28	10.23
24			
25	E	13.156	
26			
27	UCL	511.432	
28	LCL	485.121	

	G	H	I
23		=AVERAGE(H3:H22)	=AVERAGE(I3:I22)
24			
25	E	=(3*1.05*I23)/SQRT(6)	
26			
27	UCL	=H23+H25	
28	LCL	=H23-H25	

Constructing a Control Chart—Sample Means
The first version of the chart includes only the plot of the sample means.

Insert ➤ Chart...

STEP 1—CHART TYPE. Specify a Line chart, the Excel chart type for a categorical horizontal axis. Select the format that displays the line with markers at each data value.

STEP 2—CHART SOURCE. Specify the Data Range as the 20 sample means.

Data range: =H$2:$H$22

STEP 3—CHART OPTIONS. Name the axes and the chart. Select the Gridlines option, and remove the gridlines by unchecking the Major gridlines checkbox under the Value axis.

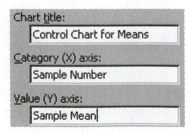

STEP 4—CHART LOCATION. Specify that the chart be placed on a new worksheet or on the current worksheet.

Next, change the format of the values and the scale of the vertical axis. Double-click on the vertical axis and then click on the Number tab.

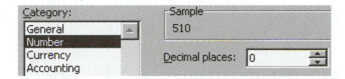

Then click on the Scale tab.

Value (Y) axis scale

Auto

☐ Minimum: 480

☐ Maximum: 515

Constructing a Control Chart—Upper Control, Lower Control, and Centerlines

To add the two control lines and the centerline to the chart, add three columns next to the cell means, J3 through L22. The control lines, 511.44 and 485.12, and the centerline, 498.28, are all the same value for each of the 20 samples, as shown in columns J, K, and L in Table E4-2. Each column contains one of the three values repeated 20 times. To plot the corresponding lines, first select the cells that contain the constants for each of the three lines, J3 through L22. Move the mouse over this selection until the cursor changes into an arrow at the edge of the selection, and then drag the entire selection over to the chart and release the mouse button.

When the upper control, lower control, and centerline are initially added to the chart, they assume the same format as the existing line, which plots each point as well as each line that connects successive points. They are also different colors. Modifying the Line attribute and Marker attribute, as specified in the following dialog box, changes these three lines to black, smooth lines.

Double click on the UCL line

Select the *Patterns* tab

```
                    Click  on  the  CL  Line
          Edit  ➤  Repeat  Format  Data  Series
                    Click  on  the  LCL  line
          Edit  ➤  Repeat  Format  Data  Series
```

To further customize the graph, change the Weight of the Line in the previous dialog box to double thickness for the upper and lower control lines.

APPLICATION—TRADITIONAL NOTATION

The mean of the sample means and the mean of the sample standard deviations are

$$\overline{\overline{Y}} = \frac{9965.54}{20} = 498.28 \text{ hr} \qquad and \qquad \overline{s}_Y = \frac{204.64}{20} = 10.23 \text{ hr},$$

respectively. The coefficient a from the previous table for a sample size of six is 1.050. The control limits—the confidence intervals of size ± 3 standard errors—on either side of the mean of the sample means are calculated from

$$\overline{\overline{Y}} \pm 3a \, \frac{\overline{s}_Y}{\sqrt{n}} \, ,$$

where

$$3a \, \frac{\overline{s}_Y}{\sqrt{n}} = \frac{(3)\,(10.23)}{\sqrt{6}} \, (10.23) = (1.287)\,(10.23) = 13.156.$$

The control limits are

$$\text{UCL} = 498.28 + (1.287)\,(10.23) = 498.28 + 13.16 = 511.44$$

and

$$\text{LCL} = 498.28 - (1.287)\,(10.23) = 498.28 - 13.16 = 485.12.$$

The corresponding confidence intervals for ± 1 and ± 2 standard errors are similarly calculated.

MANAGERIAL INTERPRETATION

The control chart exhibits the usual range of variation and lack of patterns expected with a stable process, that is, a process free of assignable causes. No substantive significance should be given to the cause of Sample 13, for which the sample mean of $\overline{Y} = 489.83$ is further than any other sample from the overall mean.

Given this conclusion, management can study the process from the perspective of recentering μ_Y and reducing σ_Y. A process in control is not necessarily a desirable process, because the mean may be wrong or the process may generate too much variability, but the process is amenable to further study to address problems such as these.

The previous example illustrated a control chart of the sample mean for a process in control. The next section shows how to identify a process out of control.

IDENTIFYING A PROCESS OUT OF CONTROL. The random processes that characterize a stable process do not generate repeatable patterns and rarely generate values far from the mean. To facilitate the search for deviations from common causes, each side of the control chart is divided into three zones. The regions between three standard errors and two standard errors of the center define Zone A. Zone B comprises the regions within two standard errors and one standard error. Zone C defines the regions within a single standard error of the center. A variety of patterns based on these three zones is very unlikely output of a stable process.

1% rule
a control chart pattern with a probability of less than 1% given a stable process indicates a potential out-of-control process

The analysis of control charts is, in part, the search for these and other patterns as specified by the **1% rule.** The nature of data, and of the statistical analysis of data, is that improbable events do occasionally occur. The occurrence of a pattern in the control chart does not prove that the process is out of control, but the occurrence does indicate a likely possibility.

Perhaps the most obvious deviation from randomness is the detection of a single point beyond Zone A. Because 99.73% of all values from a stable normal distribution are within three standard deviations of the mean, just one $\overline{Y}$ outside of this range indicates a potential out-of-control process. Expressed another way, for 10,000 sample means generated by a stable normal process, only about 27 of these sample means are more than three standard errors from μ_Y. An example of such an outlier appears in the following control chart.

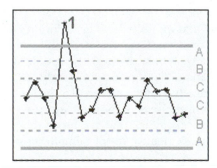

Test 1.   One point beyond Zone A.

Certain patterns of outliers are also very unlikely. One unlikely pattern is two out of three points in succession within Zone A or beyond, which means beyond two standard errors of the centerline. Also unlikely is the occurrence of four out of five points in a row within a single Zone B or beyond, with means more than a single standard error on one side of the centerline. Another unlikely pattern is the occurrence of eight consecutive points beyond a single standard error in either direction of the centerline. Points that complete these patterns are labeled 5, 6, or 8, respectively, in the following control charts using previously established nomenclature.

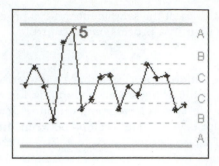

Test 5. Two out of 3 consecutive
points in one Zone A or beyond.

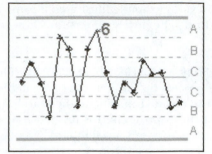

Test 6. Four out of 5 consecutive
points in one Zone B or beyond.

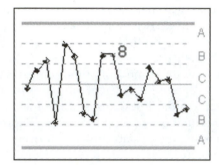

Test 8.   Eight consecutive points
beyond either Zone C.

A sequence of means that exhibits *too little* variation can also indicate the violation of normally distributed random output. As illustrated in the figure labeled Test 7, 15 consecutive means all lie within a single standard error of the centerline. By themselves, the 15 means in the figure do not indicate a process out of control. In the context of all 20 means, however, these 15 means vary too little relative to the remaining 5 means. Or, expressed another way, the sample means at the beginning and the end of the sequence that are more than a single standard error from the mean vary too much relative to the remaining sample means.

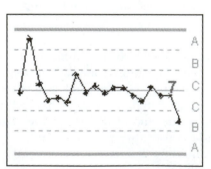

Test 7.   Fifteen consecutive points in
either Zone C.

Other tests for assignable causes do not involve the confidence intervals indicated by the zone nomenclature. These tests only compare the value of each sample mean with the preceding sequence of values. A stable process would only rarely generate six sample means in a row that either are all increasing or all decreasing. Obtaining nine sample means in a row all on one side of the centerline, or in an oscillating pattern of 14 consecutive points, would also rarely occur with a stable system. These three patterns are illustrated in the following control charts.

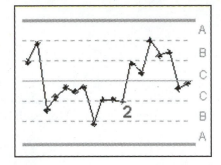

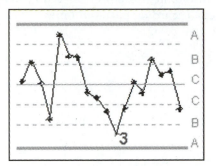

Test 2.   Nine points in a row on same side of center line.

Test 3.   Six consecutive points all increasing or decreasing.

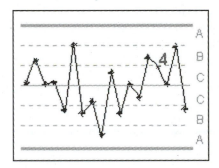

Test 4.   Fourteen consecutive points alternating up or down.

A stable process can exhibit many other unlikely patterns. For example, 10 of 11 sample means in a row on one side of the center line, or 12 of 14 sample means in a row, are both unlikely patterns. An experienced analyst of control charts can detect patterns in the data without first using the computer to identify these patterns. Moreover, no computer program is able to identify all possible patterns generated by out-of-control processes.

What is the proper managerial response to a process out of control? When the statistical analysis indicates an out-of-control process, the manager needs to identify the assignable cause. Also, the control chart should then be rerun without the deviant sample means. The deviant sample means imply that the underlying population mean or standard deviation are not constant for all values, which implies that the sample estimates of these population values are not meaningful when the deviant data values are included. Only when the control chart is of a process in control can the range of variation due to common causes be assessed.

An example of a control chart that indicates a probable assignable cause follows.

BUSINESS APPLICATION E4.2—Control Chart of $\overline{Y}$ for a Process Out of Control

MANAGERIAL PROBLEM

A lightbulb manufacturer studied burn-out times. Is the manufacturing process in control regarding burn-out times?

DATA

As in the previous example, a lightbulb manufacturer conducted a process control study of burn-out times. Twenty samples were taken of six lightbulbs each. The time in hours from being turned on until burnout was recorded for each bulb.

CONTROL CHART

The time series of the resulting 20 sample means, plus horizontal lines for the UCL, LCL, centerline, and zones, results in Figure E4-2.

    This control chart indicates that sample mean 15 failed Test 5 for assignable causes. Test 5 is the detection of two out of three points in a row in Zone A or beyond. In this case, sample means from the fourteenth and fifteenth samples are both more than two standard errors from the centerline. On the basis of this evidence, the process appears to be out of control.

Figure E4-2.
A sample mean control chart of a process out-of-control for 20 sample means of lightbulb burn-out times.

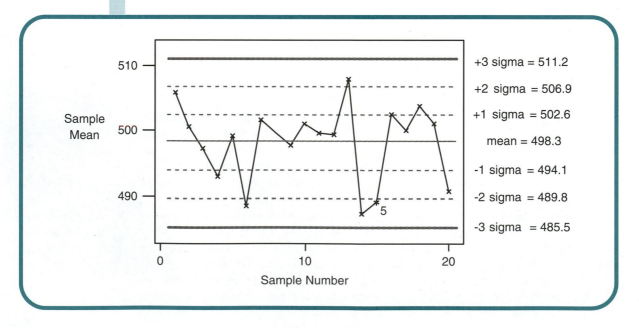

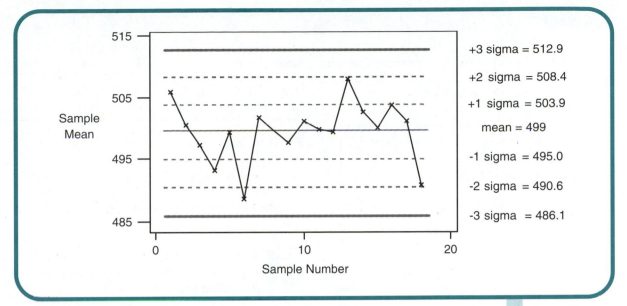

Figure E4-3.
A sample mean control chart of the process for the 18 remaining sample means of lightbulb burn-out times.

REVISED CONTROL CHART

To assess the stability of the process for the remaining 18 samples, a new control chart was created just for those samples, as shown in Figure E4-3.

The remaining 18 sample means appear to have been sampled from a process in control.

MANAGERIAL INTERPRETATION

Investigating further, management discovered that the filaments were obtained from a substitute subcontractor only on the days the lightbulbs from the fourteenth and fifteenth samples were manufactured. Apparently, the filaments provided by the substitute contractor were not of the same quality as the filaments ordinarily used. The result was the manufacture of lightbulbs that burned out more quickly than the other lightbulbs.

This substitute contractor will either no longer be a vendor for the company, or the subcontractor must provide sufficient assurance that only quality filaments will be supplied.

Control charts can be created for a variety of statistics and even for individual observations. The following section introduces the control chart for the sample standard deviation, followed by the control chart for individual observations.

EXERCISES

E4-4. Does the following control chart indicate a stable or an unstable process with respect to the mean? Why?

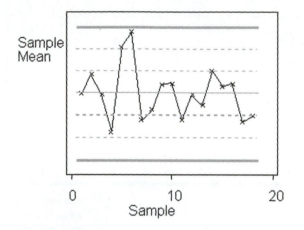

E4-5. A bottle-filling company fills 12 oz pop bottles. Management wanted to assess whether the bottle-filling process was stable and to assess the range of variation. To answer this question, the weight of the liquid was collected for 10 different samples, each sample consisting of six filled pop bottles. Each sample was randomly collected from all of the output of the day. The resulting means and standard deviations are shown below.

Sample	1	2	3	4	5
Mean	11.987	11.979	11.971	11.959	12.043
SD	0.074	0.076	0.075	0.136	0.148

Sample	6	7	8	9	10
Mean	12.005	12.005	12.009	11.942	11.986
SD	0.100	0.131	0.088	0.140	0.099

a. Generate the control chart for the sample mean.
b. Determine whether the process is in control with respect to the mean and why or why not.
c. Make a recommendation regarding this process.

E4-6. The following control chart indicates an unstable, out-of-control process according to a variety of criteria.

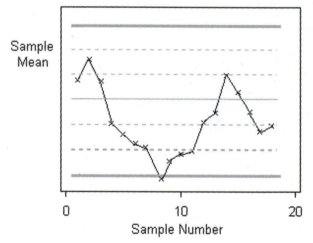

Identify the different ways that the process is out of control.

Other Control Charts

A process can be out of control when either the underlying population mean or the underlying population standard deviation is not the same for all output. The control chart of the mean is used to assess the stability of the center of the process. The control chart of the standard deviation, introduced next, is used to assess the stability of the variability of the process, regardless of the patterning of the sample means.

CONTROL CHART OF THE SAMPLE STANDARD DEVIATION. The control chart of the sample mean in Figure E4-4 indicates that the mean of the process is under control. However, the accompanying control chart in Figure E4-5 constructed for the sample standard deviation from the *same* data indicates that the variability of the process is out of control.

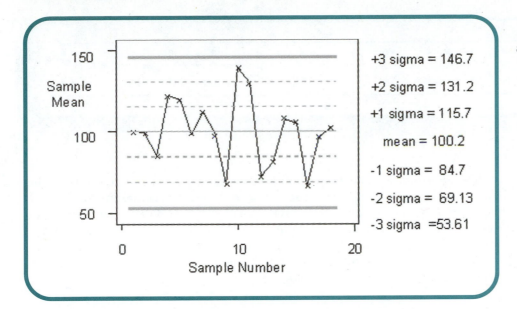

Figure E4-4.
A control chart of $\bar{Y}$ for a process with the mean in control.

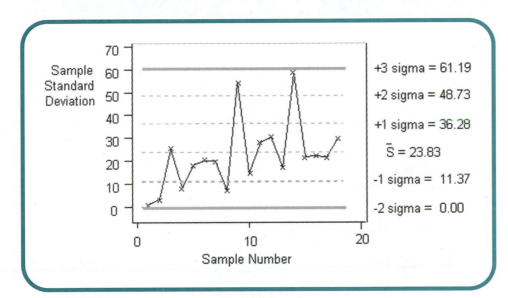

Figure E4-5.
A control chart of s_y indicating that variability is out of control, characterized by increasing values of s_y.

How is the control chart of the sample standard deviation constructed? A key piece of information for constructing a confidence interval for any statistic is the standard error of the statistic over repeated sampling. The confidence interval around the estimated standard deviation s_Y depends on the size of the standard error of the standard deviation across repeated sampling. Although the mathematics of this relationship are more complex than we want to deal with here, this relationship is described in Table E4-4 for the coefficient c. Given the tabled value, which reflects the standard error, the ±3 standard error **control limits for the sample standard deviation** are easily computed from the estimated standard deviation. Similar confidence bounds are computed for 1 and 2 standard errors by substituting for the 3 in the expression for the control limits.

> **control limits for the sample standard deviation**
> $$\bar{s}_Y \pm (3c)\bar{s}_Y$$

n	2	3	4	5	6	7	8	9	10	15	20	25
c	0.677	0.496	0.422	0.363	0.323	0.294	0.272	0.254	0.238	0.191	0.164	0.141

Table E4-4.
Adjustment factor c for calculating control limits around $\bar{s}_Y$.

The appearance of the sample standard deviation control chart is similar to the control chart for the sample mean already introduced. The centerline for the sample standard deviation control chart is the average standard deviation of the 20 or so samples. The sample standard deviations are plotted as a time series around the centerline, and the control limits are also added to the figure.

An example of the construction and interpretation of a sample standard deviation control chart is presented next.

BUSINESS APPLICATION E4.3—Control Chart of s_Y for a Process in Control

MANAGERIAL PROBLEM

Is the manufacturing process of lightbulbs in control regarding the variability of burn-out times?

DATA

Twenty samples were taken of six lightbulbs each. The burn-out times for these $20 \times 6 = 120$ lightbulbs, as well as the corresponding sample means and standard deviations, appear in Table E4-2.

APPLICATION—EXCEL GRAPHICS

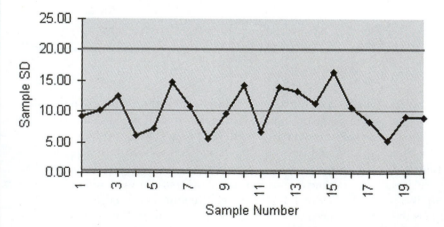

The control chart exhibits the usual range of variation and lack of patterns expected with a stable process, that is, a process free of assignable causes.

APPLICATION—CONCEPTUAL WORKSHEET

The mean of the sample standard deviations is

$$\bar{s}_Y = 10.23 \text{ hr.}$$

The tabled value of the coefficient c for a sample size of six is 0.323. Calculate the control limits—the confidence intervals of size ±3 standard errors—on either side of the mean of the sample means from

$$\bar{s}_Y \pm E \text{ where } E = (3c)\bar{s}_Y.$$

The accompanying worksheet illustrates these calculations.

	H	I
23	498.28	10.23
24		
25	E	9.915
26		
27	UCL	20.147
28	LCL	0.317

23	=AV	=AVERAGE(I3:I22)
24		
25	E	=3*0.323*I23
26		
27	UCL	=I23+I25
28	LCL	=I23-I25

APPLICATION—TRADITIONAL NOTATION

The mean of the sample standard deviations is

$$\bar{s}_Y = \frac{204.64}{20} = 10.23 \text{ hr.}$$

The coefficient c from Table E4-3 for a sample size of six is 0.323. Next, calculate the control limits, the confidence intervals of size ±3 standard errors, on either side of the mean of the sample means,

$$\bar{s}_Y \pm (3c)\bar{s}_Y,$$

where

$$(3c)\bar{s}_Y = (3)(.323)(10.23) = (.970)(10.23) = 9.915.$$

The control limits are

$$\text{UCL} = 10.23 + (.970)(10.23) = 10.23 + 9.915 = 20.15$$

and

$$\text{LCL} = 10.23 - (.970)(10.23) = 10.23 - 9.915 = 0.32.$$

Compute corresponding confidence intervals in the same way for ±1 and ±2 standard errors.

MANAGERIAL INTERPRETATION

Given that the process is in control, as assessed for both the mean (in a previous example) and the standard deviation, management can study the process from the perspective of reducing variation. Although a process in control is not necessarily a desirable process—the mean may be wrong or the process may generate too much variability—the process is now amenable to further study.

The next topic is the construction of a control chart not for a statistic such as a sample mean or standard deviation but for individual observations.

CONTROL CHART OF INDIVIDUAL OBSERVATIONS. The control charts already introduced in this chapter all share a common feature. Each plotted value in the chart was a statistic, either a sample mean or a sample standard deviation. A particularly useful property of the sample mean is that these means are normally distributed according to the central limit theorem.

In some situations, however, a control chart constructed from individual observations is more practical, or even necessary. Data may become available very slowly so that there is not sufficient time to collect enough data to form individual samples. Or data collection may be too expensive. Running a lightbulb until burnout is feasible, but subjecting expensive computer systems to destructive conditions is not.

The immediate problem encountered when constructing a control chart from individual observations is the estimation of process variation. The sample size is only one, and any index of variation such as the standard deviation cannot be estimated from a single observation. Yet the standard deviation should not be estimated from all of the data, because its value could be changing over time. The solution to this problem is to estimate the standard deviation at a single time from the value at that time and one or more adjacent values.

Using data from multiple time periods to estimate the standard deviation for a single time period involves a trade-off. More data values minimize sampling error, yet fewer values minimize the number of different time periods used to estimate the standard deviation at a single time. In practice, the minimum number of data values, two, is used for the estimation of the standard deviation. Estimate the standard deviation at each specific time from only the current value and the immediately preceding value.

Another issue is that the sampling error for the standard deviation of very small samples is very large. With such a small sample size, the standard deviation is more effectively estimated with the range, which is the positive difference between the largest and smallest values in the sample. The **moving range** for two time periods, R_2, is the positive difference between the value of Y at the current time period and the value of Y at the previous time period.

> **moving range**
> *range computed across successive time periods*

Estimate the standard deviation from the average of all the moving ranges and a coefficient d,

$$s_{\overline{Y}} = \frac{\overline{R}_2}{d}.$$

The corresponding 99.73% confidence interval is

$$\overline{Y} \pm 3s_{\overline{Y}} \qquad \text{or} \qquad \overline{Y} \pm \frac{3}{d}\,\overline{R}_2.$$

For a moving range computed over two time periods, $d = 1.128$, so the confidence interval becomes

$$\overline{Y} \pm \frac{3}{1.128}\,\overline{R}_2 = 2.66\overline{R}_2,$$

which defines the upper and lower control limits for the control chart of individual observations.

An example follows.

BUSINESS APPLICATION E4.4—Control Chart of $\overline{Y}$ with Individual Observations

MANAGERIAL PROBLEM

A lightbulb manufacturer studied burn-out times. Is the manufacturing process in control regarding burn-out times?

DATA

Ideally, 100 or so lightbulbs would have been available for study so that multiple samples of at least size 5 could be obtained. Unfortunately, only 25 bulbs were available for study. The following table records the burn-out times of these 25 bulbs. (For illustrative purposes, these are the first 25 values from the previous examples of control charts for the mean and the standard deviation.)

APPLICATION—CONCEPTUAL WORKSHEET

Control Limits

The mean of the individual observations Y and the mean moving range of length two are

$$\overline{Y} = \frac{7439.11}{15} = 495.94 \text{ hr}$$

and

$$\overline{R}_2 = \frac{167.76}{15} = 12.74 \text{ hr.}$$

	A	B
1	Y	MR
2	497.73	
3	508.39	10.66
4	495.38	13.01
5	503.87	8.49
6	481.68	22.19
7	493.15	11.47
8	487.02	6.13
9	508.02	21.00
10	502.53	5.49
11	485.48	17.05
12	506.62	21.14
13	490.68	15.94
14	498.98	8.30
15	498.15	0.83
16	481.43	16.72
17	495.94	12.74

	A	B
15	498.15	=ABS(A14-A15)
16	481.43	=ABS(A15-A16)
17	=AVERAGE(A2:A16)	=AVERAGE(B2:B16)

The value of the coefficient d, the adjustment factor for calculating s_Y from the moving range of size 2, is 1.128. Calculate the control limits, the confidence intervals of size ± 3 standard errors, on either side of the mean,

$$\overline{\overline{Y}} \pm E \text{ where } E = \frac{3}{d}\,\overline{R}_2.$$

Accomplish these calculations on the worksheet as follows.

	A	B
17	495.94	12.74
18		
19	E	33.89
20		
21	UCL	529.84
22	LCL	462.05

	A	B
17	=AVERAGE(A2:A16)	=AVERAGE(B2:B16)
18		
19	E	=(3/1.128)*B17
20		
21	UCL	=A17+B19
22	LCL	=A17-B19

The control limits are 462.05 and 529.84.

Control Chart

The control chart for the individual observations is a time-series plot of those individual values that include the centerline and the upper and lower control limits. Business Application E4.1, the control chart for the mean, provides the details for obtaining the control chart. In summary, construct the control chart as an Excel Line chart. Select the format that plots the individual points and connects the lines. Add the control lines as straight lines by first adding their constant values to each of the 20 rows of the worksheet that contain data. Select these values, move the cursor to the end of the selection so that it turns into an arrow, and drag them to the chart. Select each line and remove the markers that indicate individual points.

MANAGERIAL INTERPRETATION

On the basis of these 15 observations, the process appears to be stable. Ideally, however, more data would be collected so that observations could be grouped into samples of at least size five.

Figure E4-6.
A sample mean control chart of a process in control for 15 individual observations.

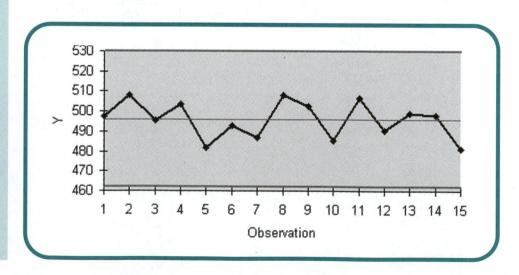

The model for a process in control, the stable process model, consists of only a constant mean and a random error term. More complex models are considered in succeeding chapters, and for all of these models, the analysis of modeling errors for individual observations is facilitated by constructing a control chart of the individual errors. Methods developed for one type of statistical analysis—quality control—generalize to many more applications.

The control chart is a primary statistical tool for evaluating the stability of a process. More is needed, however, to ensure quality than just a process in control, as discussed in the next section.

EXERCISES

E4-7. Consider the pop bottle-filling data from Exercise E4-5.

Application

a. Generate the control chart for the sample standard deviation.
b. Determine whether the process is in control with respect to the standard deviation and why or why not.
c. Make a recommendation to management regarding this process.

E4-8. A company could only produce one complex assembly per day. Because of the small number of finished assemblies, con-

Application

trol charts of individual observations (instead of statistics such as the mean and standard deviation) were established for a variety of dimensions. The lengths (inches) of the first 25 assemblies appear in the following table.

49.71	48.08	48.14	48.50	50.87	47.00
50.57	51.56	50.93	49.52	51.33	50.13
51.18	50.53	52.16	50.90	49.87	49.75
50.00	48.70				

Is the process in control?

Process Capability

Variation must also be considered in terms of specified limits. Any variation from the desired value is unwanted, but at some level the variation is so large that it is completely unacceptable.

Statistical analysis of a process is done for a reason—to guide decision making. The natural range of any normally distributed variable is an important consideration in the assessment of the quality of manufactured parts. Studying how the process *actually* performs, however, differs from an analysis of how we *desire* the process to perform. Quality improves as variability of output decreases, so the long-term goal is the continual reduction of this variability. However, most products or services are described by specifications that limit the range of variability so severely that any output that exceeds the specifications is completely unacceptable.

These specifications, which apply, for example, to each dimension of a manufactured part, are the upper specification limit (USL) and the lower specification limit (LSL). Most dimensions are constrained both ways. Traditionally, output was either considered acceptable or unacceptable. Acceptable output satisfied all specifications, and unacceptable output failed one or more specifications. Figure E4-7 illustrates this dichotomous evaluation procedure. The more modern quality control approach defines *any* deviancy from the target value as a loss of quality, so the goal of reducing process variation is never complete. According to this view, there can never be too much quality.

Figure E4-7.
Traditional all-or-none quality loss function, and the more modern quality control loss function that defines any deviation from the target as a loss.

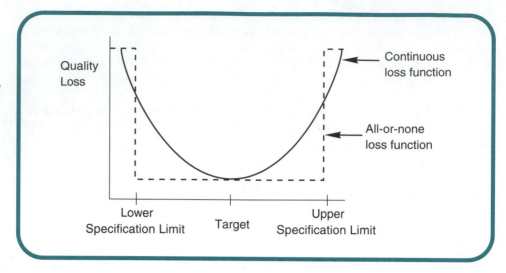

Though the quality emphasis is on the continued reduction in variability, process specifications cannot be ignored. The process output, such as a machined part, is acceptable only if the corresponding dimension falls within the specification limits. The **specified range of variation** of the relevant dimension must be between USL and LSL.

What we need are indices that account for **process capability** but at the same time provide a more continuous measure of quality than provided by a simple accept–reject classification. These indices are based on the specification limits, the specified range of variation. This range of variation, illustrated in Figure E4-8, is 6σ for normally distributed variables.

Compare the specified and actual ranges of variation with their ratio to obtain a **process capability index.** Desirable values of C_p are greater than one, which indicates that the *specified* range of variation is larger than the *obtained* range of variation. The ultimate goal is to continually reduce variability of output; therefore, the larger the C_p index, the better the results.

Unfortunately, C_p is not influenced by the process mean. The actual range of variation may be small and well within the specified range of variation, but the output of the process is unacceptable if the actual mean is far from the desired mean. Consider the extreme case in Figure E4-9, in which the actual range of variation is small but all output is unacceptable. C_p only demonstrates whether a process is capable *if* it were centered over the nominal value.

We need an additional index that takes into consideration both variation and middle. The logic underlying this revised process capability index is that half of the distribution, or 3σ, lies on either side of the actual mean $\overline{Y}$. Further, *each* half of the distribution should lie within the corresponding specification limit, a condition violated in Figure E4-10.

When the specification limits properly contain the actual range of variation, the distance of the process mean to the specification limit is more than 3σ. Again, compare these values with a ratio to form a new process capability index.

specified range of variation
Upper Spec Limit—Lower Spec Limit

process capability
Upper Spec Limit—Lower Spec Limit

process capability index C_p
ratio of the specified to the actual range of variation:
$$C_p = \frac{USL - LSL}{6\sigma}$$

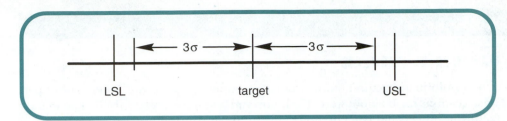

Figure E4-8.
A process centered on
the target that yields a
distribution of output
that is within the
specification limits.

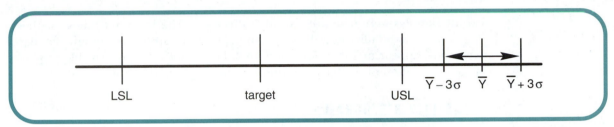

Figure E4-9.
A large C_p value but
virtually 100%
unacceptable output.

Figure E4-10.
Off-center process with
variation that exceeds
lower specification limit.

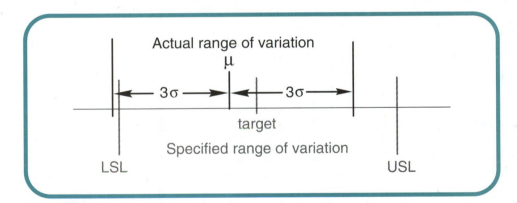

This **process capability index** reflects both middle and variation. Choosing the smaller of the two values indicates the capability of the process on the side in which the actual mean is closest to the corresponding specification limit, which is the furthest distance from the desired center. C_{pk} is always equal to or smaller than C_p, depending on the distance of the obtained mean $\overline{Y}$ from the specified center. The greater the value of the index the better, but the process is capable only when $C_{pk} > 1$.

An example of applying these capacity indices is presented next. Often these indices are supplemented with a graphical analysis such as a histogram labeled with the specification limits, which is called a *capability histogram.*

**process capability
index C_{pk}**
*ratio of the distance
of the mean from the
nearest specification
limit to half of the
range of variation:*
$C_{pk} = minimum\ of$
$$\frac{\mu - LSL}{3\sigma}\ and$$
$$\frac{USL - \mu}{3\sigma}$$

BUSINESS APPLICATION E4.5—Process Capability

MANAGERIAL PROBLEM

A lightbulb manufacturer studied burn-out times in which the lower and upper specifications for burnout were 470 hours and 530 hours, respectively. The manufacturing process has been demonstrated to be in control, but is it capable?

DATA

Twenty samples were taken of six lightbulbs each. The burn-out times for these $20 \times 6 = 120$ lightbulbs, as well as the corresponding sample means and standard deviations, appear in Tables E4-2 and E4-3. Figure E4-11 compares the obtained range of variation of the burn-out times to the specification limits.

CAPABILITY HISTOGRAM

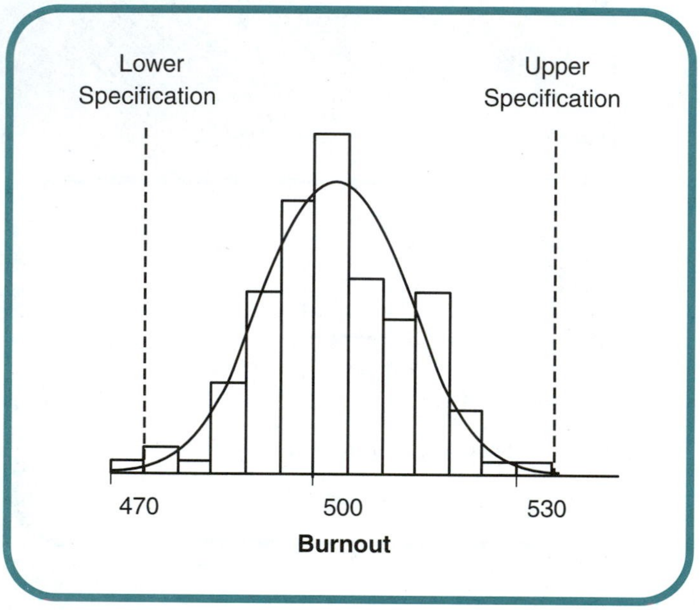

Figure E4-11.
Process capability histogram with a range of variation that exceeds the specification limits.

CAPABILITY INDICES

Obtain the summary statistics $\overline{Y} = 498.28$ and $s_Y = 10.602$ for these data.

$$C_p = \frac{USL - LSL}{6s} = \frac{530 - 470}{(6)(10.602)} = \frac{60}{63.612} = .94$$

and

$$C_{pk} = \text{minimum of } \frac{\overline{Y} - LSL}{3s} \text{ and } \frac{USL - \overline{Y}}{3s}$$

$$= \text{minimum of } \frac{498.28 - 470}{(3)(10.602)} \text{ and } \frac{530 - 498.28}{(3)(10.602)}$$

$$= \text{minimum of } .89 \text{ and } 1.00 = .89.$$

A problem is that both process capability indices are below 1.00, indicating a process that yields output beyond the specification limits.

MANAGERIAL INTERPRETATION

The process is stable or in control as shown in an earlier analysis, but it is not capable. Some burn-out times are below the lower limit, resulting in a product not satisfactory to the customer. None of the sample outcomes exceeded the upper limit, but the largest values were close, allowing the possibility for this value to be exceeded in other samples.

The continual goal of process refinement is to reduce variability around the target value, but for this process, variability reduction is urgent.

All processes should be monitored on a regular basis to reduce the variation of output. A process that is not capable, however, requires immediate attention because some output exceeds the process specification.

EXERCISES

E4-9. Consider the pop bottle-filling data from Exercise E4-5. The overall summary statistics are $\overline{Y} = 11.989$ and $s_Y = .105$. Determine, according to C_p and C_{pk}, whether the process is capable for

a. USL = 13.0 LSL = 11.0

b. USL = 12.5 LSL = 11.5

c. USL = 12.1 LSL = 11.9

E4-10. The breaking point for a metal part is engineered to be between 345 and 355 lb. The process summary statistics are $\overline{Y} = 352.1$ and $s_Y = 1.4$. Is the process capable?

E4.2 SUMMARY

The control chart, a primary statistical tool of quality management, applies confidence intervals to management decision making. Constructing and analyzing control charts of a process accomplish several objectives. Analysis indicates whether the process is stable or unstable, identifies assignable causes, and establishes the expected range of variation.

Two kinds of causes contribute to the variability of the output of a process—common causes and assignable causes. Common causes are fundamental to the nature of the process and contribute to the variation of *all* output. Assignable causes apply only to *some* of the output, in effect changing the underlying distribution for these output. A process is stable, or in control, when only common causes are operating, that is, when only a single mean with a constant random error variance contributes to the generation of each value of Y. When management wants to decrease variability of output, only a process in control should be adjusted or modified.

We first introduced the sample mean control chart, which is a time-series plot of sample means with a confidence interval constructed around the mean of the sample means. This confidence interval is defined by the upper and lower control limits, plotted as horizontal lines on the chart. Any pattern of sample means that indicates a lack of randomness also implies the existence of underlying assignable causes, because the population mean of all of the output is not the same.

A process is also out of control or unstable when the population variability of the output changes over time. Assess the constancy of the variability of the output in part with a control chart for the sample standard deviation. If insufficient data are available, control charts may also be constructed from individual observations. In this situation, the standard deviation at each time period is estimated from the average moving range, computed as the positive difference between each observation and its immediate predecessor.

A process should be in control before you proceed with the fundamental task of adjusting the process to minimize output variation. However, being in control is not a sufficient criterion for generating desirable output. In addition, the manufactured parts or the provided service must all be within the design specifications. The C_p and C_{pk} indices provide crucial information for the assessment of variability.

E4.3 KEY TERMS

1% rule *177*
centerline *171*
control chart *170*
control limits for the sample standard
     deviation *183*
control limits for the sample mean *171*

moving range *186*
process capability *190*
process capability index C_p *190*
process capability index C_{pk} *191*
specified range of variation *190*
tampering *169*

E4.4 REVIEW EXERCISES

ANALYSIS PROBLEMS

E4-11. Everyone in a community is concerned about the quality of drinking water. Water can contain many different types of impurities. To study the variation in water quality, a company collected 10 different samples of six assessments each. The resulting means of the parts per million of one of these impurities are shown below.

Sample	1	2	3	4	5	6	7	8	9	10
Mean	4.1	4.0	2.8	4.0	2.9	2.8	2.2	1.8	2.4	3.3

  a. Generate the control chart for the sample mean.

  b. Determine whether the process, in control with respect to the mean and why or why not.

  c. Make a recommendation to management regarding this process.

E4-12. The timely processing of orders is a central concern for most companies. To study the variation in the time of order processing, a company collected 12 different samples of five orders each. The resulting means and standard deviations (hr) of the time until the order is processed are shown below.

Sample	1	2	3	4	5	6	7	8	9	10	11	12
Mean	6.9	7.4	5.5	5.0	6.3	6.1	7.0	8.4	5.8	6.8	7.1	5.6
SD	.36	.20	.39	.47	.22	.31	.46	.52	.39	.41	.62	.32

    a. Generate the control chart for the sample mean.

    b. Generate the control chart for the sample standard deviation.

    c. Determine whether the process is in control and why or why not.

    d. Make a recommendation to management regarding this process.

E4-13. The diameters of a shaft in an automobile's drive train are a critical quality component. A manufacturer of these shafts wants to construct control charts to analyze the variation of these diameters.

Application

Sample	1	2	3	4	5	6	7	8	9	12
Mean	4.002	3.991	4.010	4.006	3.997	3.989	4.001	3.992	3.999	3.991
SD	.001	.002	.002	.001	.003	.004	.002	.001	.001	.003

    a. Generate the control chart for the sample mean.

    b. Generate the control chart for the sample standard deviation.

    c. Determine whether the process is in control and why or why not.

    d. Make a recommendation to management regarding this process.

E4-14. A critical dimension on a guidance system for commercial aircraft was assessed over 20 successive installations.

Application

61	8	17	53	87	10	57	56	93	52
33	24	18	53	16					

Is the process in control? Why or why not?

E4-15. Assembly time in days was available for only 24 instances of the manufacture of a complex radar assembly.

Application

10.56	8.98	10.31	10.96	9.58	10.87	10.11	9.63
10.02	10.57	6.99	9.24	10.71	11.61	11.34	11.25
11.18	9.93	9.98	9.41	8.30	9.48	9.98	9.08

Is the process in control? Why or why not?

E4-16. The inside diameter of a metal bearing should be between 1.120 and 1.125 in. The process summary statistics for the manufacturing process are $\overline{Y} = 1.123$ and $s_Y = .0024$. Is the process capable?

Application

Application

E4-17. The weight of dog food bags labeled 50 lb are supposed to be between 49 lb and 51 lb. The process summary statistics are $\overline{Y} = 50.14$ and $s_Y = .51$. Is the process capable?

Application

E4-18. The average breaking strength of a metal part is supposed to be between 220 and 230. The process summary statistics are $\overline{Y} = 220.4$ and $s_Y = 1.6$. Is the process capable?

DISCUSSION QUESTIONS

1. What are the differences between common causes of variability and assignable causes of variability?

2. Why should a process be in control before you adjust the process to minimize variation?

3. If a process in control is stable, why does the output vary?

4. What is the statistical model for a process in control?

5. What is tampering?

6. Why is a control chart based on the concept of a confidence interval?

7. What does the central limit theorem have to do with control charts of the sample mean?

8. Why is the expression for the control limits for a control chart of the mean modified from the usual expression for a confidence interval?

9. What is the fundamental criterion for identifying a process out of control?

10. What is the purpose of identifying Zones A, B, and C in a control chart?

11. What is an example of a pattern that indicates an out-of-control process in terms of deviancy from the overall mean?

12. What is an example of a pattern that indicates an out-of-control process in terms of the relation of the sample means to each other, regardless of their distance from the overall mean?

13. How does the control chart for the sample standard deviation complement the control chart for the sample mean?

14. Under what condition does the sample standard deviation tend to underestimate the corresponding population standard deviation?

15. When is a control chart for individual observations typically used?

16. What is a moving range and why is it used in the computation of a control chart of individual observations?

17. What is the difference between process stability and process capability? Is either possible without the other?

18. What is a quality loss function? Provide two examples.

INTEGRATIVE ANALYSIS PROBLEM

One-liter cans of oil should contain close to one liter of oil. Too much oil and the company wastes money. Too little oil and customers or regulatory agencies complain. To monitor the process of filling the cans, six oil cans were sampled at each hour and their contents measured. The data file OIL.DAT contains the amount of overfill or underfill of each can for 25 successive hours.

a. Compute the mean and standard deviation of each of the 25 samples.

b. Generate the control chart for the sample mean.

c. Generate the control chart for the sample standard deviation.

d. Determine whether the process is in control and why or why not.

e. Variation of the volume of each can should not exceed .02 liter. Is the process capable?

f. Make a recommendation to management regarding this process.

Hypothesis Test of a Mean

WHY DO WE CARE?

Sometimes interest focuses on a *specific* value of the unknown population mean. Has the goal of mean burnout time of 400 hr for the lightbulbs been achieved? Does the new model of cars achieve the claimed 35 mpg? Each of these values is an hypothesized value of an unknown characteristic—the population mean—of the population. The hypothesis test is the form of statistical inference that evaluates how close the sample mean is to the hypothesized value. If the sample mean is far from the hypothesized value, the manager has strong evidence that the process that generates the output is not attaining the desired center, so adjustment is needed.

5.1 LOGIC OF HYPOTHESIS TESTING

The type of statistical inference called the confidence interval estimates the value of the population mean. This interval centers the estimated range of variation of the sample mean over the obtained sample mean. Sometimes, however, the focus is on a specific value of the population mean, such as the ideal value specified by the engineering specifications. The other form of statistical inference, the hypothesis test, takes the same estimated range of the sample mean and centers it over the specific value of interest.

Hypothesized Value

Hypothesis testing evaluates the distance separating a sample statistic, such as the sample mean, from the hypothesized population value, such as the population mean.

> *The hypothesized value is considered reasonable only if the sample mean is close to the hypothesized population mean.*

Comparing the sample value to the hypothesized value renders the hypothesized value reasonable or unreasonable. Sometimes management wants to support the hypothesis, but often the goal is to reject the hypothesized value.

Consider the hypothesis that the average mpg for a new car model is 35.0 mpg. Even if the hypothesized value of 35.0 mpg is correct, the resulting sample mean will probably *not* equal 35.0 mpg. Suppose a sample mean of 34.6 mpg was obtained, a value that is close to but not precisely equal to 35.0 mpg. Is 34.6 mpg close enough to 35.0 mpg that 35.0 mpg is considered reasonable? Evaluate closeness in terms of standard errors. If 35 mpg really is the correct population value, then 95% of all sample means lie within about two standard errors on either side of 35 mpg.

The hypothesized value of the population mean is μ_0. As presented at the beginning of Chapter 3, the sample mean and the (unknown) population mean of response variable Y are $\overline{Y}$ and μ_Y, respectively. The hypothesized value of the mean μ_0 is assumed correct for purposes of the hypothesis test.

> *The distance separating the sample mean $\overline{Y}$ from the hypothesized population value μ_0 is given in standard errors.*

test statistic of the sample mean

$$Z_{\overline{Y}} = \frac{\overline{Y} - \mu_0}{\sigma_{\overline{Y}}} \ or$$

$$t_{\overline{Y}} = \frac{\overline{Y} - \mu_0}{s_{\overline{Y}}}$$

The number of standard errors separating $\overline{Y}$ from μ_0 is given by the **test statistic of the sample mean,** either $Z_{\overline{Y}}$ or $t_{\overline{Y}}$. The distinction between $Z_{\overline{Y}}$ and $t_{\overline{Y}}$ is the distinction between using the actual population standard error of the sample mean $\sigma_{\overline{Y}}$ or its sample estimate $s_{\overline{Y}}$.

The size of the test statistic, $Z_{\overline{Y}}$ or $t_{\overline{Y}}$, shows how likely it is that $\overline{Y}$ came from a population with the hypothesized value μ_0 as its mean, assuming the value of μ_0. Because $\overline{Y}$ is approximately normally distributed, if $Z_{\overline{Y}}$ or $t_{\overline{Y}}$ is much larger than about two, then the observed $\overline{Y}$ and the hypothesized μ_0 are too far apart to render μ_0 plausible.

On the basis of an hypothesis test, conclude either that

(a) the sample mean is too many standard errors from the hypothesized value, so reject the hypothesized value, or

(b) the sample mean is close to (consistent with) the hypothesized value, so do not reject the hypothesized value.

Failure to reject the hypothesized value does not prove that this value is correct. Rather, failure to reject is evidence that the hypothesized value is reasonable, as are other values close to the hypothesized value.

Null Hypothesis

Suppose the mean manufacturing time for a machined part is hypothesized as 50 min. To evaluate this claim, the manufacturing time of 95 randomly selected parts was measured, yielding a sample mean $\overline{Y}$ of 175 min and an estimated standard deviation s_Y of 10 min. This much larger value of $\overline{Y}$ than μ_0 demonstrates the unreasonableness of the hypothesized value μ_0 *without* a formal test. Whatever the value of the population mean μ_Y, it is considerably larger than 50 min.

The hypothesis test quantifies this conclusion by calculating the number of standard errors that separate $\overline{Y}$ and μ_0. For this example, the test statistic is

$$t_{\overline{Y}} = \frac{\overline{Y} - \mu_0}{s_{\overline{Y}}} = \frac{175 - 50}{\dfrac{10}{\sqrt{95}}} = 121.84.$$

The observed $\overline{Y} = 175$ min is an *extremely* unlikely 121.84 estimated standard deviations from the hypothesized value of 50. If the hypothesized value were true, obtaining a value that is as far as 121.84 standard errors from 50 would be an event of extraordinarily low probability. For example, the probability of obtaining a normally distributed value larger than just 8 standard errors from the hypothesized value is only 0.00000000000000067. When the sample results are unlikely assuming the hypothesized value, reject the hypothesized value.

If the sample mean were instead $\overline{Y} = 51$ min with $s_Y = 10$ min, these data would be consistent with the hypothesized value of 50 min. This sample mean is close to the hypothesized value of 50 min. The following test statistic demonstrates the consistency of $\overline{Y}$ and μ_0,

$$t_{\overline{Y}} = \frac{51 - 50}{\dfrac{10}{\sqrt{95}}} = .97.$$

The sample mean $\overline{Y} = 51$ min is only .97 estimated standard errors larger than the hypothesized value of 50 min, well within the range of 95% variation for $\overline{Y}$ around $\mu_Y = 50$.

No hypothesized value (such as $\mu_0 = 50$ min) is definitely proved true or false. Whether in statistics or any other area of life, we observe evidence regarding the likelihood of a claim.

Hypothesis testing does not *prove conclusively that any one population value is correct, because reasonable alternate values always exist.*

Evidence that supports one claim also supports other claims. For example, $\mu_Y = 50$ min provided a reasonable explanation for obtaining $\overline{Y} = 51$ min, but so does $\mu_Y = 52$ min. There are always alternate values of the mean that account for the same data. The hypothesis test is more successful at demonstrating that something does not exist than at demonstrating that it does exist.

Also, the hypothesized value μ_0 is not necessarily the value that management *wants* to be true. Indeed, management often deliberately sets out to reject μ_0. In the previous example, 50 min might have been the old population mean manufacturing time before the new manufacturing process was implemented. In this case, management wants the new process to diminish the mean, so that a sample mean much lower than 50, such as $\overline{Y} = 35$ min, would be obtained. The hypothesized value μ_0 is the baseline for evaluating change, but ideally change did occur after installation of the new process.

> **null hypothesis H_0**
> *specifies potential values of the population mean μ_Y when the hypothesized value μ_0 is not rejected*

Hypothesis testing is typically framed in terms of the **null hypothesis** and the alternative hypothesis, respectively denoted as H_0 and H_1. For the nondirectional tests discussed in this section, in which values of $\overline{Y}$ larger or smaller than μ_0 are of interest, the null hypothesis is simply that the population mean equals the hypothesized value, or H_0: $\mu_Y = \mu_0$. The null hypothesis for the previous example is H_0: $\mu_Y = 50$ min.

> **alternative hypothesis H_1**
> *specifies potential values of the population mean μ_Y when the hypothesized value μ_0 is rejected*

The **alternative hypothesis** H_1 specifies all values of μ_Y not specified by H_0. Values larger *or* smaller than the hypothesized mean μ_0 are typically of interest. Rejecting the hypothesized value μ_0 simply rejects μ_0 as a potential value of μ_Y, so *all* values other than μ_0 are considered. If H_0: $\mu_Y = \mu_0$ is rejected, the alternative hypothesis H_1: $\mu_Y \neq \mu_0$ is accepted. For example, H_1: $\mu_Y \neq 50$ min.

In these examples, the sample mean $\overline{Y} = 50$ was either obviously far away or obviously close to the hypothesized value μ_0. Other situations are more subtle and require that we perform a more detailed analysis of $t_{\overline{Y}}$ before we conclude whether μ_0 is reasonable. This more detailed analysis is discussed next.

EXERCISES

5-1. A manager at a mail-order clothing business was concerned that the amount of time customers were placed on hold before talking to a salesperson, an average of 24.7 seconds, was too long. With the objective of lowering this time, he changed the procedure for answering calls. To see if these changes lowered (or inadvertently raised) the hold time, he observed a random sample of incoming calls. For this hypothesis test,

a. state the null hypotheses
b. state the alternative hypotheses

5-2. A parking garage next to a shopping mall was recently remodeled. Before the remodeling, the average parking time was 118 min. A random sample was obtained to see if any changes in mean parking time occurred after the remodeling. For this hypothesis test,

a. state the null hypotheses
b. state the alternative hypotheses

5.2 CONDUCTING THE HYPOTHESIS TEST

Hypothesis testing begins with a problem expressed in ordinary language and completely free from statistical jargon. Any manager without formal understanding of statistics should be able to understand the statement of the **substantive problem.** For example: Did the new manufacturing process lower the manufacturing time? The attempt to answer the substantive question (in words, without statistical jargon) is the objective of the study. Statistics is a tool for pursuing this answer.

substantive problem
a question or concern expressed in the language of business for which management wants an answer

Range of Typical Variation around the Hypothesized Value

The hypothesis test assesses the distance between $\overline{Y}$ and μ_0 in terms of the standard error (deviation) of $\overline{Y}$. This hypothesized value μ_0 is the key to the test. The null hypothesis $H_0: \mu_Y = \mu_0$ is assumed to be true. All calculations proceed from this assumption.

> *The hypothesis test assumes a sampling distribution of $\overline{Y}$ centered on the hypothesized value μ_0.*

Assuming the hypothesized μ_0 is correct, what is a reasonable value of $\overline{Y}$? "Typical" usually refers to the range of variation of $\overline{Y}$ over repeated samples around μ_0 that contains 95% of all $\overline{Y}$'s. The size of this range is expressed in standard errors. If $\overline{Y}$ is within about two standard errors of μ_0, it is close to μ_0, otherwise $\overline{Y}$ is in the **rejection region.** If $\overline{Y}$ is out of this range, it is considered far away from μ_0, rendering μ_0 unreasonable. We indicate an unreasonable μ_0 by accepting the alternative hypothesis for this (nondirectional) test, $H_1: \mu_Y \neq \mu_0$.

The cutoff values of the test statistic define the range of typical variation for a particular hypothesis test and, by implication, the rejection region. Obtain the exact cutoff values from the corresponding t or Z distribution. As discussed in the previous chapter, in practice the estimated standard deviation s_Y replaces the (usually) unknown population value σ_Y; in which case, obtain the cutoff values from the t-distribution. For a 95% range of typical variation (which leaves 2.5% of the t-values in the upper and lower tails, respectively), $t_{.025} \approx 2$. The size of $t_{\overline{Y}}$ relative to the cutoff values such as $t_{.025}$ and $t_{.05}$ dictates whether μ_0 is rejected, as illustrated in Figure 5-1.

rejection region for a test
values in the tails of the distribution of the test statistic centered on the hypothesized value

Specifying the cutoff values of the test statistic demonstrates whether the sample mean $\overline{Y}$ lies in the rejection region or in the range of typical variation consistent with the hypothesized value. The answer to the question of whether $\overline{Y}$ is in the rejection region is a simple yes or no. The topic of the next section, the p-value, provides a more informative statement.

p-Values

Before computers, cutoff values were routinely calculated when hypothesis tests were conducted. Now, however, the **p-value** is generally used instead to evaluate the closeness of $\overline{Y}$ to μ_0. Assuming the hypothesized value μ_0, compute the p-value from the data to indicate the reasonableness of the sample mean $\overline{Y}$. Instead of comparing the observed $t_{\overline{Y}}$ to the cutoff values, the p-value provides the probability of obtaining a $\overline{Y}$ as far or farther from the assumed μ_0 as the observed $\overline{Y}$.

The hypothesized value is rejected only when the p-value is less than α.

p-value
probability of obtaining a sample result more extreme than the obtained test statistic, assuming the hypothesized value

> *Reject the hypothesized value for a small p-value, such as a value less than $\alpha = .05$.*

Figure 5-1.
A two-tailed rejection region for $\alpha = .05$, illustrating the values of the test statistic $t_{\overline{Y}}$, renders the hypothesized value μ_0 unlikely.

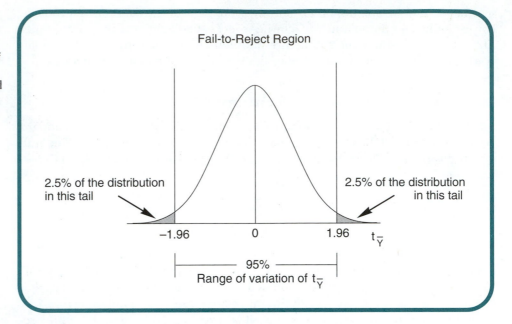

Figure 5-2.
The obtained value of $t_{\overline{Y}} = 2.06$ lies in the rejection region; $p = (.02)(2) = .04 < \alpha = .05$.

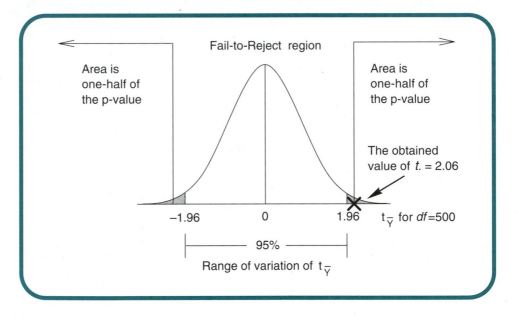

When the p-value is less than α, $t_{\overline{Y}}$ lies in the rejection region, so the p-value is sufficiently small to render the hypothesized value unlikely. The value of α defines the criterion of *unreasonableness* in terms of probability. The p-value indicates the obtained level of unreasonableness. A small p-value indicates that the obtained result is unlikely, assuming that μ_0 is correct.

For the hypothesis tests considered here, μ_0 is rejected for both much larger values of $\overline{Y}$ as well as much smaller values. Of course, the obtained $t_{\overline{Y}}$ lies in only one tail of the t-distribution. Suppose that in an actual data analysis problem $t_{\overline{Y}} = 2.06$. As illustrated in Figure 5-2, for $df = 500$, 2% of the area of the corre-

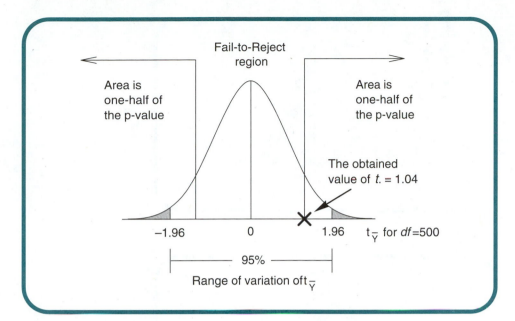

Fail-to-Reject region

Area is one-half of the p-value

Area is one-half of the p-value

The obtained value of $t. = 1.04$

−1.96   0   1.96 $t_{\overline{Y}}$ for $df=500$

95%

Range of variation of $t_{\overline{Y}}$

Figure 5-3.
The obtained value of $t_{\overline{Y}} = 1.04$ is *not* in the rejection region; $p = (.15)(2) = .30 > \alpha = .05$.

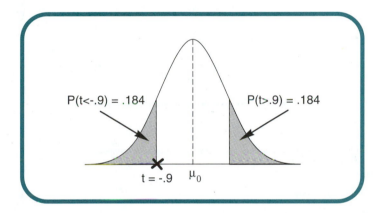

$P(t<-.9) = .184$ $P(t>.9) = .184$

$t = -.9$ μ_0

Figure 5-4.
The *p*-value is $.184 + .184 = 0.37$, indicating that $\overline{Y}$ is close to the hypothesized value.

sponding *t*-distribution lies to the right of $t_{\overline{Y}} = 2.06$. This means that the probability of obtaining a *t*-value of 2.06 or greater, assuming that the hypothesized value μ_0 is correct, is only .02. But μ_0 is just as unlikely for a deviation the same size in the opposite direction for $t_{\overline{Y}} = -2.06$. Accordingly, the *p*-value is *twice* the cutoff value of $t_{\overline{Y}}$ obtained in just one tail of the distribution. Assuming that μ_0 is correct, the probability of obtaining $t_{\overline{Y}}$ more extreme than 2.06 *or* −2.06 is $p = (.02)(2) = .04$.

Figure 5-3 illustrates a scenario with an obtained value of $t_{\overline{Y}} = 1.04$ that is not within the rejection region. Fifteen percent of all *t*-values from this distribution are as large or larger than 1.04. The *p*-value, the probability of obtaining $\overline{Y}$ at least 1.04 estimated standard errors in *either* direction from the hypothesized value μ_0, is $(.15)(2) = .30$. This probability is much too high to reject μ_0 given the criterion of $\alpha = .05$. In this example, the obtained $\overline{Y}$ is consistent with μ_0. More examples of different *p*-values appear in the Figures 5-4 through 5-7.

Computing a *p*-value requires a more detailed knowledge of a *t*-distribution than is generally available from a printed table. To compute a *p*-value, the area in

Figure 5-5.
The *p*-value is .382 +
.382 = 0.76, indicating
that $\overline{Y}$ is very close to
the hypothesized value:
P > α, so do not
reject μ₀.

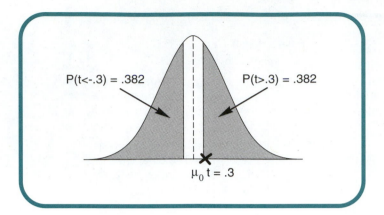

Figure 5-6.
The *p*-value is .002 +
.002 = 0.004, indicating
that $\overline{Y}$ is very far from
the hypothesized value:
P < α, so reject μ₀.

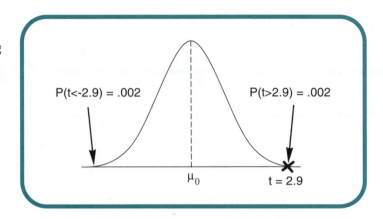

Figure 5-7.
The *p*-value is .067 +
.067 = 0.13, indicating
that $\overline{Y}$ is not too close to
the hypothesized value:
P > α, so do not
reject μ₀.

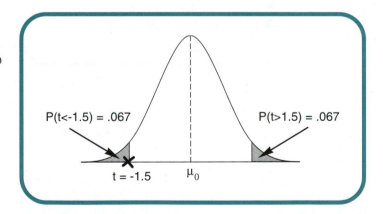

the tails of the corresponding *t*-distribution must be available for *any* value of *t*, not just the probabilities of the special cutoff values such as .05 and .01 usually found in a *t*-table. Computer programs compute *t*-probabilities directly, providing for more exact probability statements. Virtually every statistics computer program provides a *p*-value instead of a *t*-cutoff value for evaluating the null hypothesis.

A primary advantage of the p-value approach is that it provides more information than the simple yes–no conclusion of the cutoff value approach. This information encourages the realization that we never know for sure whether our decision to reject or not reject μ_0 is correct. We do know, however, that a large p-value such as .94 more clearly indicates consistency with the hypothesized value than does a small p-value such as .0002.

Also, remember that failing to reject the hypothesized value does not prove that value. Evaluating a result of $p = .0501$ against $\alpha = .05$ technically leads to the failure to reject μ_0, but realistically we have little confidence in this decision. The null hypothesis may genuinely be incorrect, but the test may have failed to detect this difference, as we discuss in detail later. An important managerial decision based on an hypothesis test that fails to reject the hypothesized value requires additional analysis and information before management can conclude that no change from the hypothesized value occurred. Sometimes the appropriate conclusion from an hypothesis test is to seek more information provided by a larger, revised sample.

Conclusion

Statistical significance is central to hypothesis testing. *Statistically discernible* is a more descriptive term than *statistically significant,* but the latter term is well embedded in statistical usage. Statistical significance simply means that the hypothesized value is rejected—the actual population mean of the response variable is probably not the hypothesized value. Statistical significance should not be confused with practical significance, which is the difference between the actual mean μ_Y and the hypothesized value μ_0 that is real and large enough to be meaningful.

> **statistically significant (discernible) result**
> *hypothesized value is rejected*

A statistically significant result implies that the actual value of the population mean μ_Y is not the hypothesized value μ_0. However, the difference between μ_Y and μ_0 may be too small to be of practical use. If implementing a new manufacturing process reduced the population mean manufacturing time from 50.0 min to 49.99 min, who cares? Such a modest gain in efficiency may not justify the cost of implementation.

After all the computations have subsided, what is the bottom line? Both the substantive hypothesis and the **substantive conclusion** must be expressed in language that is absolutely free from statistical jargon. The question of interest and the resulting conclusion must be understandable to someone who knows the business issues but who is mercifully oblivious to the technical aspects of statistical analysis.

> **substantive conclusion**
> *answers the substantive question of interest to management, free from all statistical jargon*

Did the new manufacturing process make a difference? Remember that when the null hypothesized value is not rejected, the null hypothesis is not proved true but only demonstrates consistency with the data. Instead, the proper conclusion is that no difference from the null value is detected. When the null hypothesis is rejected, however, the correct conclusion is that apparently the process does make a difference.

Sometimes the p-value is close to $\alpha = .05$, such as a p-value of .048 or .061. In terms of placing confidence in the resulting decision, a p-value of .048 instills little more confidence than a p-value of .051. The distinction, of course, is that the first p-value is below the $\alpha = .05$ threshold, whereas the second value is not. In circumstances such as obtaining a p-value of .048, the rejection of the null hypothesis should be qualified, with emphasis on the word "apparently."

BUSINESS APPLICATION 5.1—Nondirectional Test of a Mean

MANAGERIAL PROBLEM

The weight of the cereal in a cereal box is claimed to be 350 grams. If the machine that fills the boxes is adjusted so that more than 350 g tend to be put in the box, money is wasted. If the average amount of cereal is less than 350 g, the company may encounter unhappy consumers as well as liability for false advertising. Is 350 g the average weight of the contents of the boxes?

STATISTICAL HYPOTHESIS

Null hypothesis H_0: $\mu_Y = 350$ g.
Alternative hypothesis H_1: $\mu_Y \neq 350$ g.

DATA

These 25 weights are named *data* on the Excel worksheet, a random sample of cereal boxes from a day's production, measured to the nearest tenth of a gram.

Weight									
348.3	346.1	351.3	353.5	349.4	349.6	349.7	346.8	351.2
349.0	353.7	351.7	351.1	351.8	352.8	356.0	349.1	347.5
351.9	355.5	351.8	349.5	355.5	348.2	350.5		

APPLICATION—CONCEPTUAL WORKSHEET

The worksheet uses the name of each statistic (see Chapter 1) instead of the cell location such as A2. Calculate the *p*-value with the TDIST function, which provides the tail probability for the corresponding value of *t* at the specified degrees of freedom. The form of the function is

$$=\texttt{TDIST(t,df,tails)},$$

where *t* is the obtained value of the *t*-distribution $t_{\overline{Y}}$ with degrees of freedom *df*. The value of *tails* is set at 2 for a simultaneous consideration of both tails.

The calculations of the *t*-test for the hypothesized value of 350 appear in the following worksheet. This conceptual worksheet is excerpted from the Excel template called MeanInference that is provided with this text. (The complete worksheet provides both an estimate of the population mean with a confidence interval around the sample mean, as well as a test of an hypothesized value of the population mean.)

Description	Name	Value	Formula
count of data	n	25	*COUNT(data)*
mean of data	mean	350.860	*AVERAGE(data)*
standard dev of data	stdev	2.660	*STDEV(data)*
standard error of mean	sterr	0.532	*stdev/SQRT(n)*
hypothesized value	mu0	350	
t statistic	t	1.617	*(mean−mu0)/sterr*
p-value, two-tailed	pvalue	**0.119**	*TDIST(ABS(t),n−1,2)*

APPLICATION—TRADITIONAL NOTATION

From the measured 25 weights, calculate the following descriptive statistics: $\overline{Y} = 350.86$ g and $s_Y = 2.66$ g. The estimated standard error of the mean $s_{\overline{Y}}$ is,

$$s_{\overline{Y}} = \frac{s_Y}{\sqrt{n}} = \frac{2.66}{\sqrt{25}} = .532.$$

The number of estimated standard errors the observed $\overline{Y}$ is from the hypothesized mean μ_0 is

$$t_{\overline{Y}} = \frac{\overline{Y} - \mu_0}{s_{\overline{Y}}} = \frac{350.86 - 350}{.532} = 1.62.$$

The sample mean $\overline{Y} = 350.86$ g is 1.62 estimated standard errors from the hypothesized population value of 350 g.

The approximate p-value can be obtained by reading from the body of the t-table, the relevant portion of which is excerpted below.

df	0.100	0.050
24	1.318	1.711

In this table, the probability of obtaining a t-value larger than 1.318 is listed as .10, and the corresponding probability for t-value 1.711 is .05. Because $t_{\overline{Y}} = 1.62$, the corresponding probability cutoff is between .10 and .05, somewhere around .06. That is, approximately 6% of all t-values will be larger than 1.62 for a sample of size 25.

However, deviations as large as 1.62 estimated standard errors on *either* side of the hypothesized value are of interest. So the cutoff probability[1] obtained from the t-table is multiplied by two to obtain the p-value,

$$p\text{-value} = (.06)(2) = .12.$$

Given $\mu_Y = 350$ g, 12% of all observed values of $t_{\overline{Y}}$ for a sample size of 25 will be 1.62 or more estimated standard errors from 350.

APPLICATION—EXCEL BUILT-IN ANALYSIS

Excel does not provide a direct method for calculating the one-sample t-test.

STATISTICAL PRINCIPLE

Although relatively small, an event with a probability of .12 is not sufficiently fluky to suggest that the hypothesized value is unreasonable. The usual definition of "unreasonable" is that which would only occur $\alpha = .05$ of the time or less over repeated sampling.

---

1. The exact p-value obtained from a computer program for $t = 1.62$ and $df = 24$ is 0.1182.

MANAGERIAL INTERPRETATION

Is the average population weight of cereal boxes 350 g? Statistical methods cannot answer this question with certainty, but the sample mean of 350.86 g is close enough to 350 to provide credence to a claim of 350 g. The sample mean was on the high side, but not high enough as to render 350 g unlikely.

We have just completed our tour of the basic concepts underlying the hypothesis testing of means. The previous chapter presented the concept of the confidence interval. The next section relates the two forms of statistical inference, confidence intervals and hypothesis tests.

EXERCISES

5-3. With the following p-values and α levels, would you reject or fail to reject the null hypothesis?

Mechanical

a. p-value $= 0.02$ and $\alpha = 0.10$
b. p-value $= 0.02$ and $\alpha = 0.01$
c. p-value $= 0.00001$ and $\alpha = 0.01$

5-4. What is the approximate p-value for the following values of $t_{\overline{Y}}$ for a two-tailed test?

Mechanical

a. $df = 67$, $t_{\overline{Y}} = 1.00$
b. $df = 4$, $t_{\overline{Y}} = -2.17$
c. $df = 28$, $t_{\overline{Y}} = -0.19$

5-5. A manager at a mail-order clothing business was concerned that the amount of time customers were placed on hold before talking to a salesperson, an average of 24.7 seconds, was too long. With the objective of lowering this time, he changed the phone system and the procedure by which calls are answered. To see if these changes lowered (or inadvertently raised) the hold time, he observed the wait times for a random sample of 39 incoming calls, obtaining a sample mean of 20.60 seconds with a sample standard deviation of 9.95 seconds. Does an hypothesis test indicate that a change probably occurred?

Application

5-6. A parking garage next to a shopping mall was recently remodeled. Before the remodeling, the average parking time was 118 min. A sample of the parking time of 28 cars after the remodeling revealed a sample mean of 123.54 min and a standard deviation of 29.75 min. Does an hypothesis test indicate that a change in average parking time occurred after remodeling?

Application

5-7. The null hypothesis is that $\mu_Y = 100$. A sample of 25 reveals a mean of 95. Compute the p-value and state the outcome of the hypothesis test for $\alpha = 0.05$ for a sample standard deviation of

Concept

a. 1
b. 2
c. 5
d. 10
e. Graph the sample standard deviations and corresponding p-values.
f. Determine the relation between the sample standard deviation and the rejection of the null hypothesis.
g. Determine what this relationship implies for the business decision maker when the null hypothesis is *not* rejected.

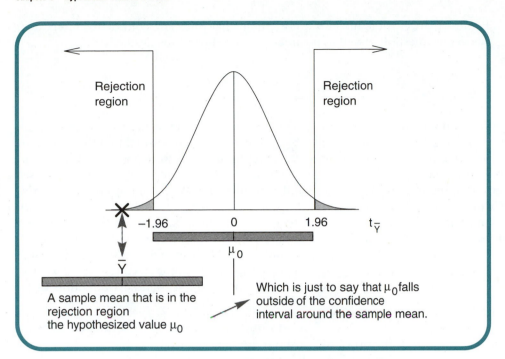

Figure 5-8.
Ninety-five percent range of variation around the sample mean (confidence interval), and the same range of variation around the hypothesized value.

5.3 HYPOTHESIS TESTS AND CONFIDENCE INTERVALS

In Figure 5-8 a sample mean $\overline{Y}$ lies in the rejection region defined by the 95% range of variation of $\overline{Y}$ around the hypothesized value μ_0. With $n = 500$, the 95% range of variation is computed from $t_{.025} = 1.96$. In this figure, a confidence interval computed from the *same* 95% range of variation is constructed around the sample mean $\overline{Y}$. If $\overline{Y}$ falls in the rejection region, the corresponding confidence interval constructed around $\overline{Y}$ will *not* contain μ_0.

This argument applies to any hypothesized value μ_0: A confidence interval constructed around a sample statistic is more general than any one particular hypothesis test. A specific hypothesis test evaluates a single hypothesized value μ_0. The construction of a confidence interval is equivalent to evaluating many individual hypothesis tests of different proposed values of μ_0.

> *Hypothesis testing is a specific case of the more general concept of a confidence interval.*

Any value of the hypothesized value μ_0 that lies within the confidence interval constructed around $\overline{Y}$ is not rejected by the corresponding test of μ_0.

The confidence interval provides information that complements the information provided by the hypothesis test. The hypothesis test evaluates the reasonableness of an hypothesized mean, whereas the confidence interval shows where the population mean probably lies. Particularly when the hypothesized value μ_0 is rejected, knowing the range of values that likely contain the population mean μ_Y can be informative. If the mean is not μ_0, then what is it? The confidence interval answers this question as well as it can be answered from the available data.

EXERCISES

5-8. Competitive manufacturers attempt to minimize the time lag between ordering materials from suppliers and receiving those materials. At one firm, management decided that one of several criteria used to evaluate suppliers is that average shipping time should be no more than 7½ days. Management realizes that individual values might be larger or smaller than 7½, but the overall average should be smaller. For a sample of 15 shipments, the sample mean was 8.087 with a standard deviation of 1.587.

a. Conduct the hypothesis test on the specified maximum value of 7½ days.
b. In Business Application 4.1 from the previous chapter, the computed confidence interval is 7.21 to 8.97. Relate the interpretation of this interval to the hypothesis test. Are the two methods of statistical inference consistent?

5-9. A manager at a mail-order clothing business was concerned that the amount of time customers were placed on hold before talking to a salesperson, an average of 24.7 seconds, was too long. With the objective of lowering this time, he changed the phone system and the procedure by which calls are answered. To see if these changes lowered (or inadvertently raised) the hold time, he observed a random sample of 39 incoming calls, obtaining a sample mean of 19.1 seconds with a sample standard deviation of 8.5 seconds.

a. Construct the 95% confidence interval around the sample mean.
b. Determine whether this interval contains the value of 24.7. Relate this answer to the hypothesis test conducted on these data from Exercise 5-5.

5.4 DIRECTIONAL HYPOTHESIS TESTS

In the hypothesis tests presented up to this point, large differences of more than about two standard errors of $\overline{Y}$ from the hypothesized value μ_0 in *either* direction render μ_0 implausible. For example, sample mean weights of the contents of cereal boxes that are much larger than 350 g or much smaller than 350 g lead to the rejection of 350 g as a reasonable value of the population mean. These hypothesis tests are called *nondirectional tests* or two-tailed tests because the rejection region is in both tails of the *t*-distribution.

In some applications, however, interest focuses on values of $\overline{Y}$ that are either only much larger than μ_0 or only much smaller than μ_0. Perhaps management is not concerned if a little extra cereal gets in the box but is very concerned if the weight of the box tends to be far below the advertised value of 350 g. In this case, management is focused on deviations from the hypothesized value μ_0 in one direction only. The mechanics and logic of these *directional* hypothesis tests are similar to that of the previously studied nondirectional tests. The evaluation of the reasonableness of an hypothesized value μ_0 remains the objective of a directional test, but the unreasonable values of $\overline{Y}$ occur in one direction only.

> *The rejection region of a directional test is in only one tail of the sampling distribution of the test statistic.*

For a 5% rejection region, all 5% is concentrated in one tail instead of dividing up the 5% into 2.5% in each of two tails. For example, for the 95% range of variation

Rejection Region	Null Hypothesis	Alternative Hypothesis
Both Tails	$\mu_Y = \mu_0$	$\mu_Y \neq \mu_0$
Lower Tail	$\mu_Y \geq \mu_0$	$\mu_Y < \mu_0$
Upper Tail	$\mu_Y \leq \mu_0$	$\mu_Y > \mu_0$

Table 5-1.
Possible null and alternative hypotheses.

of $\overline{Y}$ for the normal distribution, the two-tailed cutoff value is $z_{.025} = 1.96$, but the one-tailed value is the smaller $z_{.05} = 1.65$.

Mechanics of a Directional Test

The only change in moving from a nondirectional to a directional test is the calculation of the p-value. For a directional test, the p-value is just the probability of obtaining a result as large (or small) as $t_{\overline{y}}$. That is, the t-cutoff for $t_{\overline{y}}$ is *not* multiplied by two to compute the p-value as it is for nondirectional tests.

The rejection region corresponds to the alternative hypothesis. If the rejection region is in the lower tail, then the alternative hypothesis is $H_1: \mu_Y < \mu_0$. Suppose a regulatory agency evaluates the weight of the contents of cereal boxes to ensure that the claim of an average of 350 g of cereal is met. From the point of view of the regulatory agency, the only result of interest is when the average weight is below 350 g, so the alternative hypothesis is written as $H_1: \mu_Y < 350$ g. For a directional test with the rejection region in the lower tail, the null hypothesis corresponds to all values as large or larger than μ_0, that is, $H_0: \mu_Y \geq \mu_0$. The null hypothesis for this example is $H_0: \mu_Y \geq 350$ g.

Similarly, placing the rejection region in the upper tail, $H_1: \mu_Y > \mu_0$ specifies that μ_Y is larger than the hypothesized value μ_0. The corresponding null hypothesis is $H_0: \mu_Y \leq \mu_0$. Table 5-1 summarizes this information.

Regardless of whether the test is nondirectional or directional, the focus is always the hypothesized value μ_0. The test always evaluates how far μ_0 is from $\overline{Y}$. The issue is whether the rejection region is in one tail or two. Is unreasonableness defined in one direction only or both directions?

An example of a directional hypothesis test follows. The Excel worksheet for accomplishing this test is not provided, because the worksheet is so similar to that in the previous business application.

BUSINESS APPLICATION 5.2—Directional Test of a Mean

MANAGERIAL PROBLEM

Suppose a car manufacturer claims that a certain model of its cars gets at least 40 mpg. When evaluating the accuracy of this claim, the EPA is not interested in whether the average mileage is greater than 40. The EPA is quite content to have the cars obtain an average of 45 mph when the manufacturer claims 40. The problem occurs when the manufacturer claims too much, such as claiming a mean of at least 40 when the actual population mean is 35.

The EPA is only interested in the unreasonableness of the hypothesized value of 40 mpg for values of the mean smaller than 40. If the manufacturer claims that a certain model of automobile obtains 40 mpg, then the EPA must accept that a single $\overline{Y}$ might be less than 40 and still be consistent with the manufacturer's hypothesis. Indeed, if the claim is true, then exactly half of all possible $\overline{Y}$'s are less than 40. The question the EPA must ask is: How much smaller than 40 mpg can the sample mean become before the hypothesized value of 40 becomes unreasonable?

The burden of proof rests on the EPA. If $\overline{Y}$ is larger than 40, no statistical test is necessary. If $\overline{Y}$ is not too much less than 40, the EPA still cannot reject the manufacturer's claim. Only if $\overline{Y}$ is substantially less than 40, in terms of the estimated standard error, can the EPA dispute the claim.

STATISTICAL HYPOTHESES

Null hypothesis H_0: $\mu_Y \geq 40$ mph.
Alternative hypothesis H_1: $\mu_Y < 40$ mph.

DATA

The EPA randomly samples 20 cars off the assembly line during several weeks of production. After testing each car under identical conditions, the following mpg's were obtained.

```
40.0   39.4   39.5   39.0   39.4   39.9   39.6   39.6   39.9   39.9
38.9   40.7   39.7   40.1   39.8   39.8   39.8   40.6   40.1   40.0
```

CALCULATION FROM DESCRIPTIVE STATISTICS

From these 20 mpg's obtained from 20 different cars, the following descriptive statistics were computed: $\overline{Y} = 39.78$ mpg and $s_Y = .44$ mpg. Calculate the estimated standard error of the mean $s_{\overline{Y}}$ as

$$s_{\overline{Y}} = \frac{s_Y}{\sqrt{n}} = \frac{.44}{\sqrt{20}} = .098.$$

From this standard error and the difference of the hypothesized mean μ_0 from $\overline{Y}$, calculate the observed value of t.

$$t_{\overline{Y}} = \frac{\overline{Y} - \mu_0}{s_{\overline{Y}}} = \frac{39.78 - 40}{.098} = -2.24.$$

The sample mean of $\overline{Y} = 39.78$ mpg is 2.24 estimated standard errors below the hypothesized population value of 40 mph.

EVALUATION OF t USING THE CUTOFF VALUE

For $n = 20$, the corresponding cutoff value of t for $\alpha = .05$, with a lower-tail rejection region, is $t_{.05} = -1.73$. This result is illustrated in Figure 5-9. The observed value of t is smaller than -1.73, so reject the hypothesized value of 40.

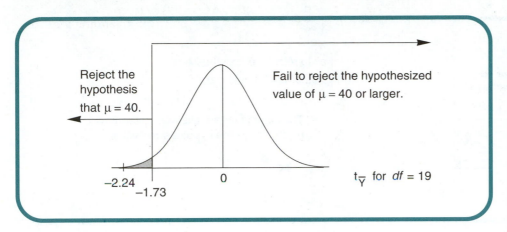

Figure 5-9.
Rejection region for
directional test of
$\mu_0 = 40$.

EVALUATION OF t USING THE p-VALUE

If the hypothesized value of $\mu_Y = 40$ mpg is true, what is the probability of obtaining a t-value as large or larger than 2.24 or as small or smaller than –2.24? The approximate p-value can be obtained by reading the t-table "backward," the relevant portion of which is excerpted below.

df	0.025	0.010
19	2.093	2.539

From this table, the probability of obtaining a t-value larger than 2.093 is listed as .025 and the corresponding probability for 2.539 is .01. Because the observed t-value is –2.24, the corresponding probability cutoff is between .025 and .010; midway is about .018. That is, only approximately 1.8% of all t-values will be smaller than –2.24 for a sample of size 20. Because this is a directional test, this cutoff probability is also the p-value[2] (multiplication by two is not needed).

Given $\mu_Y = 40$ mpg, only about 1.8% of all observed values of t for a sample size of 20 will be 2.24 or more estimated standard errors below 40 mpg.

MANAGERIAL INTERPRETATION

The sample mean of 39.78 mpg is only .22 mpg below the claimed 40 mpg. However, this distance is large enough for the EPA to conclude that the actual population mpg is apparently below 40.

In the previous application, the EPA had to show that the obtained $\overline{Y}$ is *considerably* less than 40 mpg (in terms of standard errors) before concluding that the population mean μ_Y is less than 40. In general, whether the hypothesis is evaluated as a directional or a nondirectional test, the hypothesized value μ_0 is given the benefit of the doubt, whereas the burden of proof is carried by the party attempting to reject μ_0.

2. The exact p-value obtained from a computer program for $t = -2.24$ and $df = 19$ is 0.019.

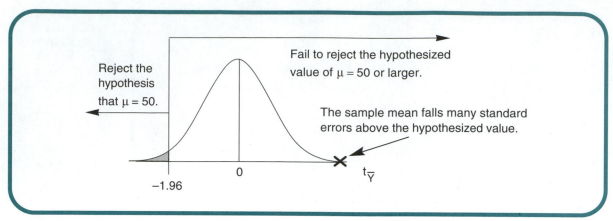

Figure 5-10.
A sample mean that falls in the opposite direction of the rejection region for a directional hypothesis test.

> *The burden of proof rests on the claimant who attempts to reject the hypothesized value.*

To show the hypothesized value μ_0 as unlikely, the obtained sample mean $\overline{Y}$ must not just be below or above μ_0, but must be *significantly* below or above μ_0. The hypothesized value μ_0 is on trial in hypothesis testing, to be displaced only by strong evidence.

Inappropriate Directional Tests

In the previous application, the EPA evaluated the claim that average mpg of a specific automobile model is 40. The EPA only cares about sample means that are too far under 40 to render 40 a reasonable population value, so this is a valid application of a directional hypothesis test. Values that are close to 40 or far above 40 are ignored in the sense that the EPA need not take any action.

A directional test is *inappropriate* when the rejection region is placed only on the side in which management wants the outcome to occur, but deviations in either direction are of interest. If a new manufacturing process is intended to decrease production times, a manager might be tempted to evaluate this claim by setting up a directional test in which the hypothesized value was the old mean production time. The goal would be to reject the hypothesized value by obtaining a sample mean much smaller than the old mean. With this approach, the rejection region of this test is in only the lower tail of the z- or t-distribution. The observed $\overline{Y}$ either falls in this rejection region or it does not, so all that can be concluded from this directional test is that the new process does or does not yield *lower* production times.

The problem here is that although management may intend for the new mean to be smaller, but it is actually interested in deviations from the hypothesized value in *either* direction. If the sample mean was much larger than the old mean, as illustrated in Figure 5-10, management would prefer to conclude that the new process had the opposite effect than that desired.

> *If managerial implications follow from both high values and low values of the sample mean $\overline{Y}$, the corresponding hypothesis test is nondirectional.*

When setting up a directional test, the rejection region should be the *only* direction of interest—not just what is desired. If, in this example, management was willing to interpret a very large $\overline{Y}$ as indicating that the new process was worse, then in fact the test is nondirectional, with a rejection region in each tail.

Our introduction to hypothesis testing is now complete. The next chapter applies both forms of statistical inference—the confidence interval and hypothesis testing—to the evaluation of the *difference* between two means.

EXERCISES

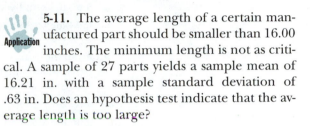

5-10. The manager of the local department store will be promoted if the mean annual income of the store's credit card customers is at least $33,000 per year. A sample of 44 credit card customers yields a sample mean of $33,606.75 with a sample standard deviation of $3,788.28. Does an hypothesis test indicate that the manager gets the promotion?

5-11. The average length of a certain manufactured part should be smaller than 16.00 inches. The minimum length is not as critical. A sample of 27 parts yields a sample mean of 16.21 in. with a sample standard deviation of .63 in. Does an hypothesis test indicate that the average length is too large?

5.5 SUMMARY

Hypothesis testing evaluates the reasonableness of an hypothesized population value such as a population mean. The evaluation is based on the closeness of the hypothesized population mean to the obtained sample mean. Closeness is expressed in terms of actual or estimated standard errors from the hypothesized value. In practice, only the estimated standard error computed from the sample standard deviation is available, so the corresponding test statistic is the *t*-statistic. For the more common nondirectional test, the *p*-value is the probability of obtaining a result as deviant as the obtained *t*-statistic in either direction from the hypothesized mean. A small *p*-value, which is less than the α criterion usually equal to .05, indicates that the obtained sample mean is unlikely given the hypothesized mean, so reject the hypothesized mean.

Traditionally the hypothesis test is framed in the language of the null and alternative hypotheses. The test can be nondirectional (two-tailed), in which differences are examined in both directions, or directional (one-tailed), which focuses on a greater than or less than difference. The corresponding alternative hypothesis is framed accordingly. The alternative hypothesis corresponds to the rejection region, which can be on either side (either $\mu_Y < \mu_0$ or $\mu_Y > \mu_0$) or both sides of the hypothesized value ($\mu_Y \neq \mu_0$). The null hypothesis includes the range of values not included by the alternative hypothesis.

5.6 KEY TERMS

alternative hypothesis *202*
null hypothesis *202*
p-value *203*
rejection region *203*

statistically significant *207*
substantive conclusion *207*
substantive problem *203*
test statistic *200*

5.7 REVIEW EXERCISES

ANALYSIS PROBLEMS

5-12. Does a school's average SAT score equal 600? For this hypothesis test,
   Mechanical
   a. state the null hypotheses
   b. state the alternative hypotheses

5-13. Does the average length of time spent training for the job equal 48 hours? For this hypothesis test,
   Mechanical
   a. state the null hypotheses
   b. state the alternative hypotheses

5-14. From the perspective of a consumer advocacy group, does the average number of miles obtained by a new model of automobile tire last 50,000 miles before tread is worn down to 1/16 of an inch? For this hypothesis test,
   Mechanical
   a. state the null hypotheses
   b. state the alternative hypotheses

5-15. Would you reject or fail to reject the null hypothesis for the following p-values and α levels?
   Mechanical
   a. p-value = 0.06 and $\alpha = 0.05$
   b. p-value = 0.06 and $\alpha = 0.10$
   c. p-value = 0.04 and $\alpha = 0.05$

5-16. Would you reject or fail to reject the null hypothesis for the following p-values and α levels?
   Mechanical
   a. p-value = 0.04 and $\alpha = 0.10$
   b. p-value = 0.04 and $\alpha = 0.01$
   c. p-value = 0.0001 and $\alpha = 0.01$

5-17. With the following p-values and α levels, would you reject or fail to reject the null hypothesis?
   Mechanical
   a. p-value = 0.08 and $\alpha = 0.05$
   b. p-value = 0.08 and $\alpha = 0.10$
   c. p-value = 0.02 and $\alpha = 0.03$

5-18. What is the approximate p-value for the following values of $t_{\bar{Y}}$ for a two-tailed (nondirectional) test?
   Mechanical
   a. $df = 39$, $t_{\bar{Y}} = -0.98$
   b. $df = 55$, $t_{\bar{Y}} = 1.19$
   c. $df = 31$, $t_{\bar{Y}} = -1.94$

5-19. What is the approximate p-value for the following values of $t_{\bar{Y}}$ for a one-tailed (directional) test?
   Mechanical
   a. $df = 9$, $t_{\bar{Y}} = 1.34$
   b. $df = 100$, $t_{\bar{Y}} = -1.21$
   c. $df = 35$, $t_{\bar{Y}} = -0.40$

5-20. What is the approximate *p*-value for the following values of $t_{\bar{Y}}$ for a two-tailed (nondirectional) test?

  a. $df = 15$, $t_{\bar{Y}} = 0.49$

  b. $df = 100$, $t_{\bar{Y}} = 2.09$

  c. $df = 35$, $t_{\bar{Y}} = -1.43$

5-21. What is the approximate *p*-value for the following values of $t_{\bar{Y}}$ for a one-tailed (directional) test?

  a. $df = 97$, $t_{\bar{Y}} = 2.05$

  b. $df = 44$, $t_{\bar{Y}} = -3.26$

  c. $df = 39$, $t_{\bar{Y}} = -4.84$

5-22. Data entry for a widely used company form supposedly produces an average of 15 forms per hour. Management wants to know how average performance compares to this criterion. A sample of 20 employees yielded a sample mean of 14.1 forms per hour with a standard deviation of 2.5. Does an hypothesis test indicate that a change occurred?

5-23. Consider the information given in Exercise 5-22.

  a. Construct the 95% confidence interval around the sample mean, and then do an informal hypothesis test on the basis of this confidence interval. That is, determine whether the hypothesized mean value falls within the confidence interval, and then interpret the result.

  b. Determine whether the results from this and Exercise 5-22 are consistent or inconsistent and why.

5-24. The quality control manager at a cereal plant needs to keep the weight of the cereal in the boxes at 12 oz, though the weight of the cereal in any individual box will only be approximately 12 oz. A sample of 40 boxes yields a mean weight of 11.9 oz with a standard deviation of .13 oz. Does an hypothesis test indicate that there is sufficient evidence to support the contention that the population weight is 12 oz?

5-25. Consider the information given in Exercise 5-24.

  a. Construct the 95% confidence interval around the sample mean, and then perform an informal hypothesis test on the basis of this confidence interval. That is, determine whether the hypothesized mean value falls within the confidence interval, and then interpret the result.

  b. Determine whether the results from this and Exercise 5-24 are consistent or inconsistent and why.

5-26. As a test of the effectiveness of a sales incentive, 55 employees were randomly chosen to receive a bonus if average sales increased $5,000 from last year's average of $85,478. The sales figures for these 55 employees averaged $92,049 with a standard deviation of $7,328. Does an hypothesis test indicate that there is sufficient evidence to support the contention that sales achieved an average of $90,478?

5-27. The manager at the local Really Quick Lube wanted to reduce the average length of an oil change to 15 minutes. He recorded the lengths of 49 oil changes, obtaining a mean of 15.7 min with a standard deviation of 1.9 minutes.

  a. Conduct an hypothesis test to evaluate the claim of 15 minutes.

b. Given that the sample mean was larger than 15 minutes, determine how this result can be reconciled with the outcome of the hypothesis test.

5-28. Cans of dog food are advertised as containing 12 oz of the product. A random sample of 25 cans revealed a mean weight of 10.97 oz. Does an hypothesis test indicate sufficient evidence to support the contention that the population weight is 12 oz? Conduct the test with a

a. standard deviation of .02 oz

b. standard deviation of .2 oz

c. standard deviation of 2 oz

d. standard deviation of 20 oz

e. What is the effect of the standard deviation of the variable of interest on the *p*-value and on the rejection or acceptance of the null hypothesized value?

f. Does failure to reject the null hypothesized value imply that the hypothesized value is true? Answer this question using the information in (a) through (d).

5-29. Use a computer program such as Microsoft Excel to generate 10 samples of 25 normally distributed values, each having a population mean of 75 and a standard deviation of 5.

a. Compute the 10 sample means and standard deviations. What are the ranges of these two statistics across the 10 samples?

b. Compute the *p*-value of the hypothesis test of the true population mean for each of the 10 samples. What is the range of *p*-values across the 10 samples?

c. For $\alpha = .05$, determine whether the true value of $\mu_Y = 75$ would be rejected in any of the samples.

d. Use these results to comment on the following statement: Sampling fluctuation is the heart and soul of statistical inference.

5-30. A computer program (Microsoft Excel) generated the following 10 values from a normal distribution with a population mean of 50 and a standard deviation of 8. The corresponding sample statistics are $\overline{Y} = 42.23$ and $s_Y = 10.16$.

54.46   25.95   36.44   48.17   39.25   30.78   55.16   46.88   34.98   50.20

a. Perform the hypothesis test on the true population mean of 50.

b. Determine whether the value of 50 is rejected or accepted?

c. Explain this result in terms of random sampling.

5-31. A human resources manager wants to test the claim that the average dental expense of all employees is less than $400, though she would also be interested in knowing if the average was greater than $400. A routine expense involves routine procedures such as cleaning and cavity filling, and does not include major procedures such as root canals. A sample of 27 employees resulted in the following data.

$678.79	$267.43	$406.43	$164.55	$308.41	$824.01	$623.88
$1,067.96	$244.65	$446.08	$591.58	$294.03	$282.02	$240.37
$460.57	$366.81	$355.20	$343.40	$246.37	$243.80	$330.98
$187.99	$262.02	$294.17	$398.66	$194.94	$477.03	

a. Does an hypothesis test indicate a change in the average dental expense from $400?

b. Calculate and interpret the corresponding confidence interval.

c. Determine if the results of the two inferential procedures are consistent.

d. Determine which procedure provided more information and why.

5-32. A mail-order company suspects that shipments have gotten heavier than in the past. The old mean shipping weight was 15.8 lb. Data from a random sample of 25 packages follow.

15.4	18.1	17.2	20.7	14.5	22.3	19.0	15.6	25.1	14.7
16.9	10.7	12.3	13.1	15.8	9.2	14.5	16.9	15.2	19.3
15.1	21.0	16.1	8.8						

a. Determine if an hypothesis test indicates a change in the average shipping weight from 15.8 lb.

b. Calculate and interpret the corresponding confidence interval.

c. Determine if the results of the two inferential procedures are consistent.

d. Determine which procedure provided more information and why.

5-33. The percentage of nickel in a batch of steel should be 1.3%. A sample of 30 different batches resulted in a sample mean of 1.5% nickel with a standard deviation of 0.4%. Does an hypothesis test indicate that the target value of 1.3% is consistent with the data?

5-34. Samples of ten 50-gallon oil drums yielded a sample mean of 49.4 gal. with a standard deviation of 0.6 gal. Does an hypothesis test indicate that 50 gal. is a reasonable value?

5-35. The production goal of soap manufactured per hour is 2,000 lb. A sample of the amount of soap manufactured during 10 different randomly sampled hours revealed a sample mean of 1,976 lb and a standard deviation of 48 lb.

a. Does an hypothesis test indicate that the goal is consistent with the data?

b. How do you explain this result? Use the value of the sample standard deviation as part of your answer.

c. What recommendation do you make regarding the soap manufacturing process?

5-36. A quality control engineer wants to maintain a mean burn-out time of lightbulbs of 750 hours. A sample of 50 lightbulbs reveals a mean of 758.3 hr with a standard deviation of 24.2 hr.

a. Use an hypothesis test to test the plausibility of the target of 750 hr.

b. Make a recommendation about what action the company should take regarding the size of the standard deviation. Include in your answer a discussion of the results of your hypothesis test.

5-37. A parking garage next to a shopping mall was recently remodeled. Before the remodeling, the average parking time was 118 min. A sample of the parking time of 28 cars after the remodeling revealed a sample mean of 126 min and a standard deviation of 32 min. Did average parking time change after re-modeling?

    a. Construct the 95% confidence interval around the sample mean.

    b. Determine whether this interval contains the value of 118. Relate this answer to the hypothesis test conducted on these data from Exercise 5-6.

Application

5-38. The FTC monitored a beer producer to ensure that bottles labeled 12 oz contained at least 12 oz. A random sample of 45 bottles resulted in a mean of 11.88 oz with a standard deviation of .24 oz. Does an hypothesis test justify the producer's claim?

Application

5-39. An advertising company claims that retail stores using its advertisements will experience increased sales of at least 5% in two weeks due to the appearance of the advertisements. A sample of 25 stores that purchased the advertisements indicated a mean level of increased sales of 4.2% with a standard deviation of 1.8%. Does an hypothesis test justify the advertiser's claim?

Application

5-40. A trade organization monitored a company's steel cable to ensure compliance with the minimum stated tensile strength of 3,500 lb. A random sample of 45 cables resulted in a mean of 3,488 lb. with a standard deviation of 8.3 lb. Does an hypothesis test justify the producer's claim?

Application

5-41. An automobile manufacturer claims its EPA rating of a new model for highway driving is at least 39 mpg. The EPA test of 49 models of the car results in a mean of 37.4 mpg and a standard deviation of 5.2. Is there sufficient evidence to conclude that the manufacturer's claim for the car is correct?

Concept

5-42. An automobile manufacturer claims its EPA rating of a new model for highway driving is at least 39 mpg.

    a. The EPA test of 49 models of the car results in a mean of 37.4 mpg. The population standard deviation is known to be 5.2. Is there sufficient evidence to conclude that the manufacturer's claim for the car is correct?

    b. Identify the difference between the information given in this problem and the previous problem. How does this difference affect the resulting hypothesis test?

Application

5-43. The FTC monitored a beer producer to ensure that bottles labeled 12 oz contained at least 12 oz. A random sample of 45 bottles resulted in a mean of 11.88 oz with a standard deviation of .24 oz. Is the producer's claim justified?

DISCUSSION QUESTIONS

  1. What is the relation between the null hypothesis and the alternative hypothesis?

  2. In hypothesis testing, why is the sampling distribution of the mean centered on the hypothesized value?

  3. What are the different methods for defining the rejection region?

  4. What is meant by "close" in terms of comparing the sample mean $\overline{Y}$ to the hypothesized value of the population mean μ_0?

  5. Why does an hypothesis test involve *both* an obtained value of t, $t_{\overline{Y}}$, and a tabled t-value, such as $t_{.025}$, yet a confidence interval only involves a tabled t-value?

  6. Why is the p-value more useful than the observed value of t when evaluating an hypothesis test?

7. Why does a large p-value indicate greater consistency with the null hypothesis than a small p-value?

8. Why does the p-value assessment of an hypothesis test provide more information than a reject–no reject conclusion?

9. Why is the cutoff value multiplied by two to compute the p-value for a nondirectional test, but not for a directional test?

10. Confidence intervals and hypothesis tests both involve the construction of intervals approximately ± 2 estimated standard errors in width. Define and compare these intervals for these two forms of statistical inference.

11. How can a confidence interval be used to construct an hypothesis test?

12. Why is the confidence interval a more general form of statistical inference than an hypothesis test?

13. What is the primary piece of information obtained from an hypothesis test that is *not* obtained from a confidence interval when evaluating the plausibility of a specific value?

14. How does the use of a confidence interval to evaluate a specific value corroborate the claim that the null hypothesis is not rejected for the corresponding hypothesis test?

15. What is the distinction between a directional and a nondirectional test?

16. When is an hypothesis test incorrectly specified as a directional test?

17. A directional hypothesis test specified a mean of at least 15. The sample mean is 15.78. Should the hypothesis test proceed? Why or why not?

INTEGRATIVE ANALYSIS PROBLEM

The county assessed the average of single-family homes within a single neighborhood of a large city at $109,880. The neighborhood association questions the accuracy of this assessment; it draws a random sample of 42 homes and reevaluates with an independent assessment. The valuations of these 42 homes are found in the data file HOMES.DAT.

a. State the null and alternative hypotheses that evaluate the county's assessment.

b. Identify the assumptions regarding normality that must be satisfied in order to perform the hypothesis test.

c. Determine whether the test statistic would be based on the z-distribution or the t-distribution and why?

d. Calculate the t-value for the hypothesis test at $\alpha = .05$.

e. Calculate the p-value for the hypothesis test at $\alpha = .05$.

f. Determine whether the county's mean assessed value is reasonable given the alternative assessments and why or why not?

g. Compute the 95% confidence interval for the unknown population mean.

h. Determine if the mean assessed value of the county is within this interval.

i. Compare the results of the hypothesis test and the confidence interval. Do the results of these two methods of statistical inference agree? Why or why not?

j. A consumer group is concerned that property taxes are too high. Representatives from this group are interested only in whether the true assessed mean value is smaller than the mean value maintained by the county. How does the resulting hypothesis test differ from the test done by the neighborhood association?

k. Perform this revised hypothesis test. What is the primary conclusion?

l. Determine how the conclusions of the two hypotheses test compare and why.

CHAPTER 5 EXTENSION   POWER ANALYSIS

E5.1   MAKING DECISIONS WITH HYPOTHESIS TESTS

There are two ways to be fooled:
One is to believe what isn't so;
the other is to refuse to believe what is so.

Soren Kierkegaard

Binary Decisions

A binary decision presents only two choices from which the decision maker may choose. Each day we encounter many binary decisions. Do you go to your 1:00 class? Do you take an umbrella with you to the game? Do you cross the street now or wait until the car down the road has passed by? On a somewhat grander scale, do John and Jane marry? On the grandest scale of them all, do you reject or not reject the hypothesized value?

A typical problem for many managers is whether to make a specific investment. If market share and unit sales will increase, an investment in additional manufacturing capacity is warranted. If growth is small or the market is stagnant, however, current capacity suffices.

As shown in Figure E5-1, the manager made a correct decision if growth was predicted, the investment was made, and growth occurred. A correct decision was also made if growth was not predicted, so no investment was made, and growth did not occur. However, these two correct decisions are matched by two errors. Predicting growth and investing was the wrong choice if growth did not occur. Similarly, predicting lack of growth and not investing was the wrong choice if growth did occur. Both of these errors lead to negative consequences. In the first case, money was invested in unused and unneeded manufacturing capacity. In the second case, market share was lost because not enough product could be manufactured to meet demand.

> *A binary decision has four possible outcomes: two correct decisions and two incorrect decisions.*

For any binary decision, there are two ways to be right and two ways to be wrong.

Type I Errors

Hypothesis testing is another example of a binary decision, with two ways to be right and two ways to be wrong. In the context of hypothesis testing, the two errors are called Type I and Type II errors, as illustrated in Figure E5-2. To understand the meaning of these errors, think conditionally. That is, "Now, *if* the hypothesized value really is true . . . " or "Now, what *if* the hypothesized value really is false . . . ".

One type of hypothesis testing error is a **Type I error.** A Type I error occurs when the sample mean $\overline{Y}$ is in the rejection region but the hypothesized value is, in fact, true. Setting the rejection region defines the region of values of $\overline{Y}$ that render the hypothesized value μ_0 unlikely. However, an unlikely value of $\overline{Y}$ does not disprove the hypothesized value, because fluky results still occur, albeit infrequently.

> **Type I error**
> *falsely rejecting a*
> *true null hypothesis*

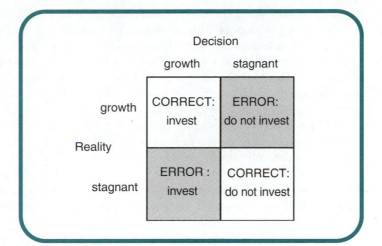

Figure E5-1.
Four possible outcomes resulting from a binary decision.

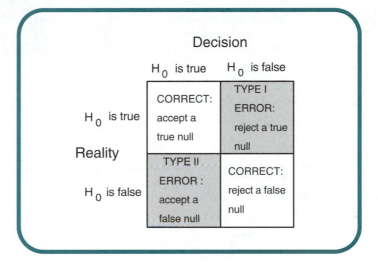

Figure E5-2.
The four possible outcomes of an hypothesis test.

The computation of the probability of a Type I error is straightforward. How often will a sample mean fall in the rejection region when in fact the hypothesized value μ_0 is true? The answer depends on α. If $\alpha = .05$, these unlikely events occur precisely 5% of the time. The probability of a Type I error is determined by setting the value of α.

Note that from the analysis of a single sample, the analyst does not know if a Type I error did or did not occur. If the true value of μ_Y were known, there would be no point to hypothesis testing. However, what is known is that if the hypothesized value μ_0 is true, then for a 5% rejection region, 5% of the time μ_0 will be incorrectly rejected if the hypothesis test were repeated many times.

The other type of error, a Type II error, is introduced next.

Power and Type II Errors

The hypothesized value μ_0 is false whenever μ_0 does not *exactly* equal the true population mean μ_Y, that is, whenever $\mu_0 \neq \mu_Y$. Consider a store that was remodeled with the goal of increasing the average purchase from \$30. The hypothesized value of \$30 (no change) is false if indeed remodeling changed μ_Y to \$40, \$35, \$31, or even \$30.01. Unfortunately, even though remodeling may have made a difference, by chance the sample mean $\overline{Y}$ can still be too close to $\mu_0 = \$30$ to statistically detect this difference. The hypothesis of $\mu_0 = \$30$ might appear reasonable given the data, even though in actuality a change from this value did occur. When this happens, the analyst errs, failing to detect a real change from the hypothesized value.

A **Type II error** occurs when the hypothesized value μ_0 is false but the sample mean $\overline{Y}$ is so close to μ_0 that μ_0 is considered reasonable. An error is made by *not* rejecting a false null hypothesis. The probability of a Type II error is called β.

For each different value of μ_Y, a different probability of a Type II error is obtained—the further the true μ_Y is from the hypothesized μ_0, the easier it is to detect the difference. Suppose remodeling was an absolutely huge success, so that average sales increased all the way from $\mu_Y = \$30$ to $\mu_Y = \$65$, with $\sigma_{\overline{Y}}$ equal to \$2 for both values of μ_Y. Such a dramatic change in the average consumer purchase—an increase of \$35—would virtually always be detected by an hypothesis test. For $\mu_0 = \$30$, the value of β is quite low if indeed $\mu_Y = \$65$. The resulting sample mean $\overline{Y}$ from this new distribution centered on $\mu_Y = \$65$ would inevitably be far larger than the hypothesized value of $\mu_0 = \$30$, as illustrated in Figure E5-3. In fact, 95% of $\overline{Y}$'s would vary between $(1.96)(\$2) = \$3.92$ on either side of the true mean of \$65, so very few $\overline{Y}$'s would be much below \$61.

Instead of $\mu_Y = \$65$, consider the alternate situation illustrated in Figure E5-4, an increase in average sales to only $\mu_Y = \$35$. With the actual mean so much closer to the hypothesized value, the value of β is considerably higher. The closer the ac-

Figure E5-3.
The hypothesized and actual distributions of $\overline{Y}$, illustrating that a Type II error would virtually never occur in this situation because the actual range of variation of the sample mean does *not* overlap the fail-to-reject region.

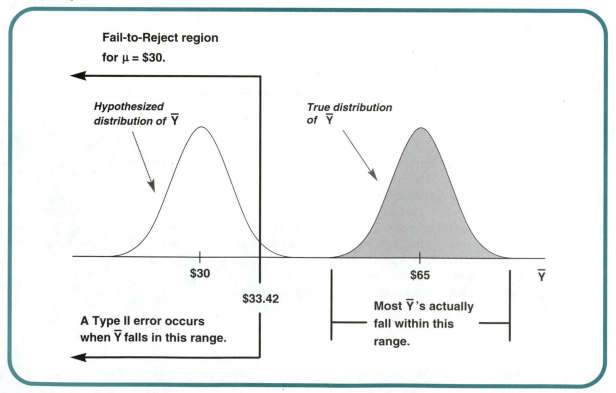

Fail-to-Reject region for $\mu = \$30.$

Hypothesized distribution of $\overline{Y}$

True distribution of $\overline{Y}$

\$30   \$65 $\overline{Y}$

\$33.42

A Type II error occurs when $\overline{Y}$ falls in this range.

Most $\overline{Y}$'s actually fall within this range.

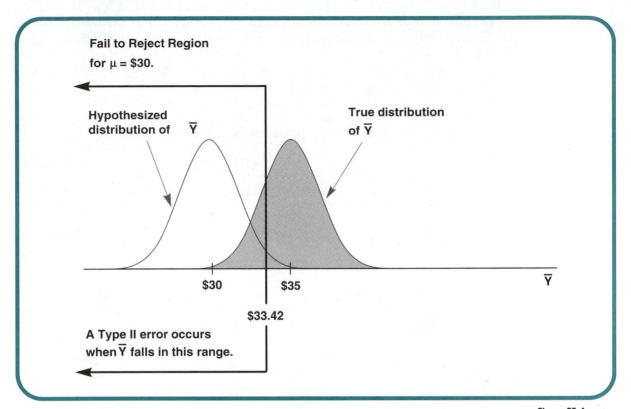

Fail to Reject Region
for μ = $30.

Hypothesized
distribution of $\overline{Y}$

True distribution
of $\overline{Y}$

$30 $35 $\overline{Y}$

$33.42

A Type II error occurs
when $\overline{Y}$ **falls in this range.**

Figure E5-4.
The hypothesized and
actual distributions of
the sample mean,
illustrating that a Type II
error is probable in this
situation because the
actual range of variation
of the sample mean and
the fail-to-reject region
overlap.

tual μ_Y is to the hypothesized value μ_0, the more difficult it is to reject μ_0. The sample mean $\overline{Y}$ may be so close to μ_0 that $\overline{Y}$ falls within the fail-to-reject region constructed around μ_0, resulting in a Type II error.

When the hypothesized value μ_0 is false and is in fact rejected, the correct decision has been made. The probability of making the *correct* decision with a false μ_0 is the power of the test to detect the difference between μ_0 and μ_Y. **Power** is the probability of correctly rejecting a false null hypothesis. The false hypothesized value is either correctly rejected or not. These two decisions are complementary events, so power $\equiv 1 - \beta$. When the hypothesized value μ_0 is false, power shows the probability of making the correct decision, and β shows the probability of a Type II error.

Of course the actual value of μ_Y is not known, for if it were known there would be no point to the hypothesis test. As we will see throughout the remainder of this chapter, however, knowing the probability of a Type II error for one or more alternative values of μ_Y provides practical information for real-world applications of hypothesis testing. Type II error analysis provides a series of *what if* scenarios. What if the true mean is _____? Would such a difference from the hypothesized value likely be detected?

The computation of β follows directly from the definition of a Type II error.

power of an
hypothesis test
probability of
correctly detecting a
specified true
difference from a
false hypothesized
value

> To compute β, *find the cutoff value(s) of* $\overline{Y}$ *that define the fail-to-reject region assuming* μ_0, *and then find the probability that* $\overline{Y}$ *falls within this region given a specific alternative value of* μ_Y.

For nondirectional tests, the fail-to-reject region lies between two rejection regions, so two cutoff values are required, whereas directional tests require only one cutoff value.

The only computational wrinkle here is that the fail-to-reject and rejection regions are not expressed in terms of t-values but in terms of the sample mean $\overline{Y}$. Corresponding to each cutoff value of t such as $t_{.05}$ is a cutoff value of $\overline{Y}$ such as $\overline{Y}_{.05}$. Obtained values of $\overline{Y}$ larger (or smaller) than $\overline{Y}_{.05}$ lead to the rejection of μ_0. This cutoff value is easily obtained from $t_{.05}$.

> *Cutoff value of the sample mean* ($\alpha = .05$):
> $$\overline{Y}_{.05} = \mu_0 + (t_{.05})(s_{\overline{Y}})$$

For example, if a cutoff t-value in a particular problem is 1.96, the corresponding value of $\overline{Y}_{.05}$ is

$$\overline{Y}_{.05} = \mu_0 + (1.96)(s_{\overline{Y}}).$$

To state this expression in words, the cutoff value of $\overline{Y}$ that defines the fail-to-reject and rejection regions is 1.96 estimated standard errors above the hypothesized value for this particular example. For a nondirectional test, this is the only cutoff value to consider.

Computing β requires two steps, each step presuming a specific point of view. The first step assumes that the hypothesized value μ_0 is the correct value of the population mean. The second step assumes a specific alternative value of μ_Y as the correct population mean. For simplicity, these concepts are illustrated only for a directional test, but the same principles apply to nondirectional tests as well.

Step 1. *Find the fail-to-reject region in terms of $\overline{Y}$ given the hypothesized value* μ_0. Set up the hypothesis test of μ_0. Assume that the hypothesized value of the population mean μ_0 is correct, and compute $\overline{Y}_{.05}$, which defines the fail-to-reject and rejection regions.

Step 2. *Find the probability of obtaining $\overline{Y}$ in the fail-to-reject region given the assumed value of* μ_Y. Assume a value of the population mean μ_Y, which, with the standard error, defines a likely range of values that contains $\overline{Y}$. Compute the probability of obtaining a value of $\overline{Y}$ within the fail-to-reject region defined by $\overline{Y}_{.05}$.

The following example illustrates this two-step process of computing β. The Excel worksheet that provides Type II errors is demonstrated in a more general example later in the chapter.

BUSINESS APPLICATION E5.1—Type II Error Probability

MANAGERIAL PROBLEM

After refining an engine design to increase power, the question of interest is whether the refinement leads to an increase in the average mpg beyond the previous average of 30 mpg. The hypothesized value of 30 mpg is rejected if the sample mean is substantially larger than 30 mpg. Assume that the real increase was 5 mpg. What is the probability that the hypothesized value will incorrectly *not* be rejected given a true mean of 35 mpg?

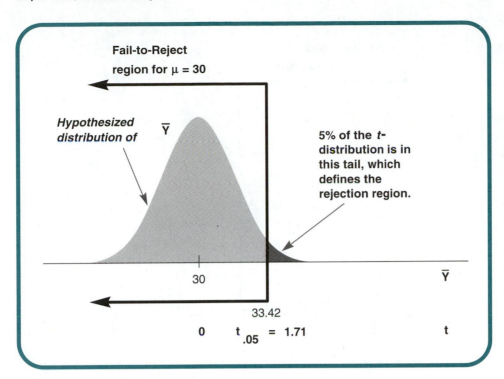

Figure E5-5.
The one-sided fail-
to-reject region for
$\mu_0 = 30$ mpg.

DATA

The sample size for the hypothesis test is $n = 25$ with $s_Y = \$10$.

STEP 1: FIND THE FAIL-TO-REJECT REGION IN TERMS OF $\overline{Y}$

Assuming $\mu_0 = 30$ mpg, find $\overline{Y}_{.05}$ illustrated in Figure E5-5. More power leads only to increased mpg, so this is a one-tailed test, with the rejection region defined by the right-side tail. The fail-to-reject region is everything to the left of the rejection region. The cutoff value for t with $\alpha = .05$ is $t_{.05} = 1.71$. All values of $\overline{Y}$ less than 1.71 standard errors above the hypothesized mean lead to not rejecting the hypothesis that $\mu_Y = \$30$.

What is $\overline{Y}_{.05}$? That is, what value of $\overline{Y}$ corresponds to $t = 1.71$? Because $n = 25$ and $s_Y = \$10$, the estimated standard error of the mean $s_{\overline{Y}}$ is

$$s_{\overline{Y}} = \frac{s_Y}{\sqrt{n}} = \frac{\$10}{\sqrt{25}} = \$2.$$

The cutoff value of $\overline{Y}$ is 1.71 standard errors above $\mu_0 = 30$:

$$\overline{Y}_{.05} = 30 + (1.71)(2) = 30 + 3.42 = 33.42.$$

Any $\overline{Y} < 33.42$ leads to not rejecting the hypothesized value of 30 mpg.

STEP 2: FIND PROBLEM OF OBTAINING A $\overline{Y}$ IN THE FAIL-TO-REJECT REGION

The second step illustrated in Figure E5-6 answers the question, what is the probability that $\overline{Y} < \$33.42$? The answer depends on the assumed alternative value of

Figure E5-6.
The fail-to-reject
region derived from
the false
hypothesized value
in the context of
the *real* distribution
of $\overline{Y}$ centered on
$\mu_Y = 35$ mpg.

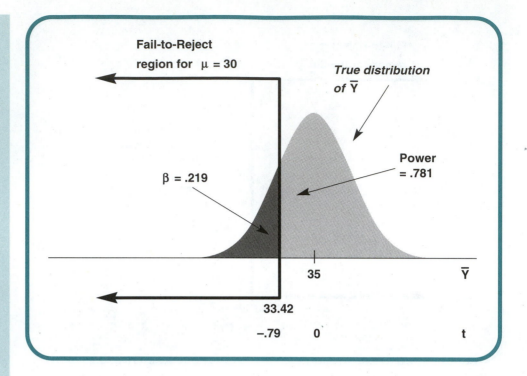

μ_Y. In this example, $\mu_Y = 35$. Note that this is just the usual kind of probability problem that we have solved many times before. To find the probability, first find the corresponding t-value for 33.42 from this distribution *centered on 35*.

$$t_{\overline{Y}} = \frac{\overline{Y}_{.05} - \mu_Y}{s_{\overline{Y}}} = \frac{33.42 - 35.00}{\dfrac{10}{\sqrt{25}}} = \frac{-1.58}{2} = -0.79.$$

What percentage of the t-distribution lies to the left of $t = -0.79$?

$$P(\text{Type II error}) \equiv \beta = P(t < -.79) = P(\overline{Y} < 33.42).$$

From the t-table for $df = 24$, find that $\beta \approx 0.2$. (The exact value is 0.219.) If the population mean is $\mu_Y = 35$, almost 22% of the time the hypothesized value of $\mu_0 = 30$ would be *incorrectly* not rejected. On the positive side, the power of the test to detect this difference is calculated as

$$\text{Power} = 1 - \beta = 1 - 0.219 = 0.781.$$

Seventy-eight percent of the time the hypothesized value of 30 mpg would be correctly rejected.

COMPARE STEPS 1 AND 2

The probability of a Type II error has been computed as .219, but for illustrative purposes Figure E5-7 combines both of the previous figures. This probability is seen as the region of the distribution centered on $\mu_Y = 35$ that overlaps the fail-to-reject region based on the evaluation of the hypothesized value $\mu_0 = 30$.

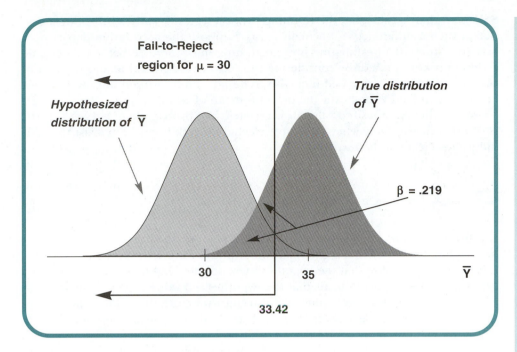

Figure E5-7.
The two distributions from which the probability of a Type II error is computed. One distribution is centered on the hypothesized value $\mu_0 = 30$ mpg, and the other is centered on the presumed actual value of the population mean $\mu_Y = 35$ mpg.

MANAGERIAL INTERPRETATION

If this identical study were repeated again and again, 78% of the studies would correctly detect an increase in mpg from 30 to 35 mpg.

The computation of the probability of a Type II error requires that a specific value of the population mean μ_Y first be specified, and yet the fact that μ_Y is unknown is the point of the entire hypothesis testing process. What is the practical impact of knowing the probability of a Type II error for only assumed instead of known values of μ_Y? This question is addressed in the next section, which focuses on the systematic analysis of a wide range of alternative values of μ_Y, including the smallest meaningful difference.

Power Curves and Practical Significance

Falsely failing to reject the hypothesized value of 30 mpg does not concern management if refinement increased the real mean to only 30.01 mpg. From the manager's perspective, failure to detect a change is not a meaningful error if remodeling increased average retail sales only .01 mpg. From a purely statistical perspective, however, a Type II error literally occurs *whenever* $\mu_Y \neq \mu_0$ and μ_0 is not rejected.

When the null hypothesized value is false, it is false to some specific degree. The focus here is the comparison between any change from μ_0 to μ_Y, so that $\mu_Y \neq \mu_0$, and a change large enough to matter. A Type II error concerns management only when a difference of $\overline{Y}$ from μ_0 large enough to be **practically significant** is not detected. Of particular interest is the **smallest meaningful difference** large enough to be practically significant. Management should be aware of the

practical significance
the difference of μ_Y from the hypothesized value μ_0 large enough to be meaningful

smallest meaningful difference (SMD)
smallest difference of μ_Y from μ_0 of practical significance

SMD and then ensure that the resulting hypothesis test is sufficiently powerful to detect such a difference if it actually exists. Suppose the accounting department was given the task of estimating how much mpg must increase before the engine redesign is not justified. By considering the cost of reengineering and the cost of business lost due to increased fuel costs, redesign is not justified if it increases average mpg at least 2 mpg over the previous mean of 30 mpg.

When the hypothesized value μ_0 is rejected, the probability of a Type II error is of no concern. Only when μ_0 is not rejected does the possibility exist that this failure to reject may be incorrect.

> *Whenever the hypothesized value μ_0 is not rejected, the power of the hypothesis test for the smallest meaningful difference should be evaluated.*

If this power is low, management should not conclude that a real change did not occur simply because of failing to reject the hypothesized value μ_0. Rather, management should conclude that the hypothesis test did not lead to a conclusion for or against. Failure to reject means that the hypothesized value is consistent with the data, but many other related values are also consistent with these data. The logic of the hypothesis test succeeds best when the hypothesized value μ_0 is rejected.

To more fully comprehend the implications of a Type II error, its probability can be computed over a range of plausible values of μ_Y. In addition to the smallest meaningful difference $\mu_Y = 32$, what is the probability of a Type II error and the associated power if $\mu_Y = 36$, or $\mu_Y = 37$, or whatever? The **power curve** systematically shows how the power of a test depends on the specific alternative values of the actual population mean μ_Y. For example, as the value of the presumed actual mean μ_Y increases, the probability that $\overline{Y} \leq 33.42$ decreases. The further μ_Y is from μ_0, the larger the power of the hypothesis test.

power curve
graph of the power of an hypothesis test for a range of specific alternative values of the population mean μ_Y

BUSINESS APPLICATION E5.2—Power Curve

MANAGERIAL PROBLEM

How likely is the hypothesis test to detect the effect of engine refinement on mpg for a range of plausible values of the unknown population mean μ_Y?

APPLICATION—CONCEPTUAL WORKSHEET

The given information, provided in gray on the following worksheet, is the sample size, standard deviation, hypothesized value, and alpha level. From this information, compute the standard error and the corresponding cutoffs for t, $t_{.05}$, and the sample mean, $\overline{Y}_{.05}$, that define the fail-to-reject region.

n	stdev	mu0	alpha	stderr	tcut	meancut
25	10	30	0.05	2.000	1.711	33.422

stderr	tcut	meancut
=stdev/SQRT(n)	=TINV(alpha*2,n-1)	=mu0+tcut*sterr

MU	t	Beta	Power
30.01	1.705	0.949	0.051
31	1.210	0.881	0.119
32	0.710	0.758	0.242
33	0.210	0.582	0.418
33.42	0.000	0.500	0.500
34	-0.290	0.387	0.613
35	-0.790	0.219	0.781
36	-1.290	0.105	0.895
37	-1.790	0.043	0.957
38	-2.290	0.016	0.984
39	-2.790	0.005	0.995

Table E5-1.
Probabilities of Type II error (β) for $\mu_0 = \$30$, $n = 25$, $s_{\bar{y}} = 2$.

The probability of a Type II error β varies according to the true value of the population mean, labeled MU in Table E5-1. The given range of values is from just above the hypothesized value of 30 up to 39.

The formulas for t and Power are just simple arithmetic.

Formula for t: `=(meancut-MU)/stderr`

Formula for Power: `=1-beta`

The formula for β (or Beta) requires cumulative t-distribution probabilities, which are obtained from the probabilities provided by the Excel TDIST function. This function is defined as

`=TDIST(t, df, number_of_tails)`

where the number of tails is 1 or 2. Instead of a lower-tail or cumulative probability, the TDIST function returns the upper-tail probability for only positive values of t and zero. For these nonnegative values of t, obtain the cumulative probability by subtracting the TDIST result from 1. For negative values of t, obtain the tail probability for the positive counterpart of t, $-t$. Given the symmetry of the t-distribution, this upper-tail probability equals the corresponding lower-tail probability for the corresponding negative value of t. To choose these different actions depending on the sign of t, use the Excel *if* statement.

Formula for Beta:

`=IF (t>=0, 1-TDIST (t, DF, 1), TDIST (-t, DF, 1))`

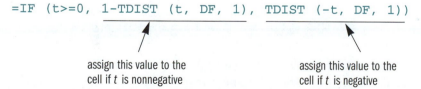

assign this value to the   assign this value to the
cell if t is nonnegative   cell if t is negative

This problem, with a rejection region in the upper-tail, requires the calculation of cumulative probabilities. Power problems for a one-tail hypothesis with the rejection region in the lower-tail require one minus the cumulative probability. Power problems for two-tailed tests require the simultaneous probability assessment for two tails. Either of these alternatives requires modification of the above formula for β to obtain the correct probability.

Figure E5-8.
The power curve
for $n = 25$.

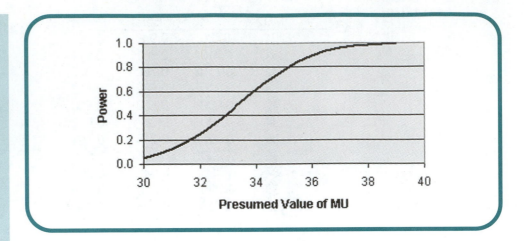

APPLICATION—EXCEL GRAPHICS

Assessing the Excel Output

The information from the previous table is plotted in Figure E5-8, in which power is expressed as a function of the presumed value of μ_Y. This plot is a power curve.

Obtaining the Power Curve

Insert ➤ Chart...

Step 1—Chart Type. Specify a XY (Scatter) chart, which is for a numeric horizontal axis. Select the format that connects the points with live segments, or the format that joins them with a smooth curve.

Step 2—Chart Source. Specify the cells for the Data Range. First list the values of Power for the Y-axis (Cells B6 through B16), enter a comma, and then enter the cell range for the data for the X-axis, which are MU (Cells E6 through E16). Do not include the labels in these cell ranges.

Data range: =Sheet1!$B$6:$B$16,Sheet1!$E$6:$E$16

Step 3—Chart Options. Click the Legend tab and uncheck the Show legend box. Click the Titles box to provide the titles for the Y and X axes.

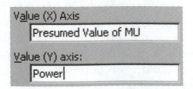

Step 4—Chart Location. Specify that the chart be placed on a new worksheet or on the current worksheet.

The displayed chart scales the *X*-axis from 0 to 50. To enhance readability, the values should range from 30 to 40. To change this scaling, double-click on the *X*-axis, select the Scale tab, and enter the changes into the following dialog box.

Value (X) axis scale

Auto

☐ Mi<u>n</u>imum: 30

☐ Ma<u>x</u>imum: 40

MANAGERIAL INTERPRETATION I

Table E5-1 illustrates the relationship between the probability of a Type II error, β, and the presumed mean μ_Y over a range of alternative values of μ_Y. When μ_Y is as large as 39 or larger, β becomes negligible, so correctly rejecting the hypothesized value of 30 is a virtual certainty.

For values of the unknown population mean closer to 30, however, there is a reasonable chance that the difference between the actual population mean and the hypothesized value of 30 will *not* be detected. Of course, if the real mean is 30.01, then falsely failing to reject the hypothesized value that $\mu_0 = 30$ does not present a problem. However, for the smallest *meaningful* difference of an increase in mpg from 30 to 32, β increases to .758. If average mpg increased 2, in this study this difference would *fail* to be detected by the statistical test three out of four times. Management should be aware of which minimal difference is actually important, and then ensure that the resulting test is sufficiently powerful to detect such a difference if it actually exists.

INCREASE POWER

Type II error can be minimized, and, conversely, power can be increased by increasing sample size. If a difference of only 2 is important enough to discern, then the analyst can choose a sample size sufficiently large to detect a difference of 2. To illustrate how the probability of a Type II error can be *decreased* by increasing sample size, consider the previous situation using all the same values except that sample size *n* is 100 instead of 25.

THE FAIL-TO-REJECT REGION

First define the fail-to-reject region with the new cutoff value of 1.66 and the new estimated standard error of

$$s_Y = \frac{s_Y}{\sqrt{n}} = \frac{10}{\sqrt{100}} = 1.$$

Because

$$\overline{Y}_{.05} = 30 + (1.66)(1) = 31.66,$$

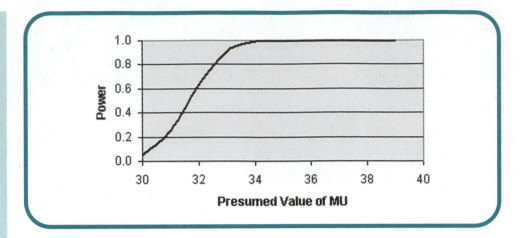

Table E5-2.
Probabilities of
Type II error for
$\mu_0 = \$30$,
$n = 100$, $s_{\bar{Y}} = 1$.

MU	t	Beta	Power
30.01	1.650	0.949	0.051
31	0.660	0.745	0.255
32	-0.340	0.367	0.633
33	-1.340	0.092	0.908
33.42	-1.760	0.041	0.959
34	-2.340	0.011	0.989
35	-3.340	0.001	0.999
36	-4.340	0.000	1.000
37	-5.340	0.000	1.000
38	-6.340	0.000	1.000
39	-7.340	0.000	1.000

any $\bar{Y} \leq 31.66$ leads to the failure to reject the hypothesized value that $\mu_0 = 30$. Based on this information, a power curve analysis for a sample size of 100 instead of 25 is presented in Figure E5-9 for the same hypothesis test in the previous example. The data are in Table E5-2.

MANAGERIAL INTERPRETATION II

The resulting table and curve illustrate the increase in power that results from a larger sample size. For the minimally important difference of 2, power increases from 0.24 for $n = 25$ to 0.63 for $n = 100$. As usual, the path to a more precise analysis is more data. Decisions based on statistical analysis are decisions based on an analysis of random events, with the caveat that the more data you have, the less you have to rely on chance.

Power analysis demonstrates that the real issue for the manager is not statistical significance but rather making decisions. Hypothesis tests can provide useful information regarding these decisions, but tests alone do not necessarily provide the answers management needs. Whether or not an hypothesis test is statistically significant is not the issue.

> A "significant" result may reflect a real difference between hypothesized and actual values too small to be useful.

Or, consider a result that does not achieve statistical significance.

> An "insignificant" result may result from a test with too little power to detect a meaningful existing difference.

For an hypothesis test to provide information useful for managerial decision making, the test must be sufficiently powerful to detect the smallest discrepancy between the hypothesized and actual values of the mean that management deems useful.

EXERCISES

Application
E5-1. The mean accounts receivable of a certain company should be at least $525; anything less than $500 is dangerously low for the company's financial health. Thus, a value of $525 is still comfortable, but at least $500 is absolutely necessary. To test the hypothesis that the mean accounts receivable is at least $525, a sample yielded $\overline{Y} = \$520$, $s_Y = \$52$, and $n = 84$. No statistical difference was found between sample and hypothesized values ($t = -.88$), yet the true mean might still be lower than the cutoff of $500. What is the probability of failing to detect a true value of the mean as low as $500 when evaluating an hypothesized mean of $525?

Application
E5-2. To see how much time viewers spent watching TV ads, 110 randomly selected households had time meters installed, with which they monitored their TV watching. The results were a mean of 9.2 minutes of television ads watched during the day, with a standard deviation of 4.0 minutes.

a. If the real population mean is 9.5, compute the probability of a Type II error of performing a statistical test in which the hypothesized range of values is that 10 or more minutes were watched during the day.

b. If the real population mean is 8.5, compute the probability of a Type II error of performing a statistical test in which the hypothesized range of values is that 10 or more minutes were watched during the day.

c. Calculate the power curve for this scenario for a range of population means from 7 to 10.

E5.2 SUMMARY

Two kinds of errors can be made when conducting an hypothesis test. Type I error, with probability α, is rejecting the hypothesized value as unreasonable when in fact it is correct. Type II error, with probability β, is failing to detect a difference from the hypothesized value when in fact such a difference exists. Power is the complement of the probability of a Type

II error in that power and the probability of a Type II error add to 1.00. Power analysis is useful for analyzing the sensitivity of an hypothesis test to detect such a real difference. The power of a test to detect the smallest difference that is of practical importance should be calculated, particularly if the hypothesized value is not rejected. If this power is small, the failure to reject the hypothesized value may have more to do with the deficiency of the test than with reality. The standard method of increasing power is to increase sample size.

Rejecting or not rejecting the hypothesized value provides the manager with useful information, but this is often not all of the information the manager needs to make an informed decision. A "significant" result may reflect a real difference between hypothesized and actual values too small to be useful, and an "insignificant" result may result from a test with too little power to detect a meaningful difference that does in fact exist. Hypothesis testing, power analysis, and the collection of additional information form a nearly complete collection of statistical tools that underlie informed decision making.

E5.3 KEY TERMS

power *227*

power curve *232*

practical significance *231*

smallest meaningful difference (SMD) *231*

Type I error *224*

Type II error *226*

E5.4 REVIEW EXERCISES

ANALYSIS PROBLEMS

Application

E5-3. The quality control manager at a cereal plant needs to keep the weight of the cereal in the boxes at 12 oz, though the weight of the cereal in any individual box will only be approximately 12 oz. A sample of 40 boxes yields a mean weight of 11.9 oz with a standard deviation of .13 oz. Is there sufficient evidence to conclude that the population weight is 12 oz? If the true mean is 11.95 oz, what is the probability of not detecting this change?

Application

E5-4. A company assembles a product that uses many lightbulbs. A sample of 25 bulbs is obtained from an incoming shipment of 10,000 bulbs. If the mean burn-out time of these 10,000 bulbs is less than 800 hr, the shipment will be returned to the supplier. The sample reveals a mean burn-out time of 798.2 hr with a standard deviation of 2.9 hr. What is the probability of not detecting this deviation under 800 hr when

a. the true mean burn-out time is 799 hr

b. the true mean burn-out time is 795 hr

c. the true mean burn-out time is 790 hr

DISCUSSION QUESTIONS

1. What is meant by "close" in terms of comparing the sample mean $\overline{Y}$ to the hypothesized value of the population mean μ_0?

2. How is power related to Type II error?

3. Why is the probability of a Type I error never calculated?

4. What is the relation between sample size and the power of an hypothesis test?

5. When is a statistically significant result in which the hypothesized value is rejected *not* of interest?

6. When is the probability of a Type II error of concern to the manager?

7. If the analyst does not know the value of the population mean, what is the value of the "what if" scenarios in which the power of the hypothesis test is evaluated against different potential values of the mean?

8. What is the smallest meaningful difference? Why is the analysis of power against this alternative important?

Evaluating a Mean Difference

WHY DO WE CARE?

The two previous chapters provided the tools for comparing the mean of a variable to a fixed value, answering questions such as, "Is the average weight of the cereal in the cereal box at 350 g?" An extension of this procedure is to compare the mean of the response variable from one group with the mean of the same variable from a second group. Instead of taking a single sample to evaluate against the fixed value, gather two separate samples.

Managers often compare the performance of one group with another group on response variables such as product share, satisfaction, cost, salary, or time. Questions such as "Which group has the most satisfaction, or the least cost, or the highest salary?" confront most managers on a regular basis. Examples of these comparisons appear in Table 6-1.

The difference between the sample means of the two groups is calculated directly, but the real issue of interest is the difference between the *population* means.

Table 6-1.
Comparing differences
between population
means.

Groups to Compare	Variable Compared	Question of Interest
parts made with the old vs. the new manufacturing processes	tolerances	Does the new process increase quality?
different mutual funds	rate of return	Does one mutual fund have a higher rate of return than another fund?
package color of retail display	dollar volume of sales	Does a bright orange package affect sales differently than a bright red package?
students at two different MBA programs	salary of first job after completing the MBA	Do students from one program have higher starting salaries than students from the other program?
mail-order customers vs. in-store customers	dollar volume of sales	Do in-store customers purchase more than mail-order customers?

6.1 CONFIDENCE INTERVAL FOR A MEAN DIFFERENCE

A confidence interval constructed around the difference between sample means specifies a range of likely values that contains the corresponding population mean difference. The process of constructing the confidence interval follows the same procedure used to estimate a single population mean μ_Y with a confidence interval around $\overline{Y}$. The difference between two population means $\mu_1 - \mu_2$ is estimated with a confidence interval around the difference between two sample means, $\overline{Y}_1 - \overline{Y}_2$. The size of the sample for the first group is n_1, and the second sample is of size n_2.

Sample Mean Difference as a Variable

independent samples
individual values in one sample are not linked to individual values in the other sample(s)

Consider two **independent samples** of the response variable Y, which is the variable such as length, price, salary, or sales that is compared across the two groups. Values of Y for the two samples are labeled Y_1 and Y_2, respectively. An example of independent samples includes groups of MBA students at two different schools in which the students at one school are selected without regard to the students in the other school. The order of the values in one sample is irrelevant to the order of the values in the other sample. The alternative would be to match the students on some variable such as GMAT score. When one student is selected from one school, then a student with approximately the same GMAT score is selected from the other school. This situation is an illustration of *dependent* samples, a concept further explored at the end of this chapter.

Consider two samples drawn from populations Y_1 and Y_2, respectively, which have the same mean of 10. The sample mean of the first group $\overline{Y}_1$ is 9.1 and the sample mean from the second group $\overline{Y}_2$ is 10.6. That is,

$$\mu_1 = \mu_2 = 10, \text{ but } \overline{Y}_1 = 9.1 \text{ and } \overline{Y}_2 = 10.6.$$

Expressed in terms of mean differences,

$$\mu_1 - \mu_2 = 0, \text{ but } \overline{Y}_1 - \overline{Y}_2 = -1.5.$$

Although the population mean difference is zero, the ubiquitous random error prevalent in sample data resulted in random fluctuations around the population value. These particular sample means differed by -1.5 because $\overline{Y}_1$ is 1.5 units smaller than $\overline{Y}_2$.

The issue is again one of repeated sampling. Different sets of samples yield different mean differences, even when the populations have the same mean. In practice, take only one sample from each population but consider hypothetical additional samples from each of these two populations with the same mean. Suppose the second set of samples yielded a mean difference of -0.9. Suppose a third set of samples yielded a mean difference of +1.7, and so on. The sample means $\overline{Y}_1$ and $\overline{Y}_2$ are both random variables, and so is their difference, $\overline{Y}_1 - \overline{Y}_2$, a random variable across repeated samples. As with any random variable, this distribution of differences has its own shape, mean $\mu_{\overline{Y}_1 - \overline{Y}_2}$, and standard deviation $\sigma_{\overline{Y}_1 - \overline{Y}_2}$, which is the standard error of the mean difference.

What is the range of typical variation of these sample mean differences around the population mean difference? The distribution of these differences over repeated samples, illustrated in Figure 6-1, provides a baseline for evaluating the size of the sample mean difference. Inference of the difference of population means $\mu_1 - \mu_2$ follows from knowledge of the distribution of the sample means $\overline{Y}_1 - \overline{Y}_2$.

The issue is not the observed sample mean difference but the underlying, *unknown* population mean difference. The more interesting issue is not a description of the samples but an inference that compares the respective populations from which the samples were drawn. The sample means differ, as usual, but what is the difference in population means, if any? The inferential analysis that constructs the

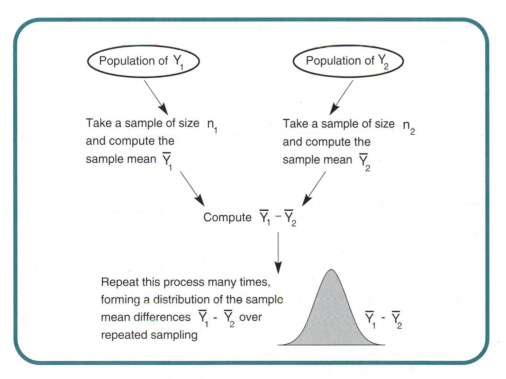

Figure 6-1.
The distribution of mean differences over repeated sampling.

confidence interval around the sample mean difference provides the answer to this question, couched within the qualifications of probability.

Interpreting the Confidence Interval

The standard error is the key concept that shifts the level of analysis from description to inference. The single obtained sample mean difference $\overline{Y}_1 - \overline{Y}_2$ is only one possibility from an entire distribution of possible mean differences. The construction of the confidence interval requires that we know the variation of this distribution as described by the standard error of this mean difference, estimated as $s_{\overline{Y}_1 - \overline{Y}_2}$.

> *95% confidence interval around a sample mean difference:*
> $$\overline{Y}_1 - \overline{Y}_2 \pm t_{.025} s_{\overline{Y}_1 - \overline{Y}_2}, \text{ where } t_{.025} \approx 2$$

The confidence interval around a sample mean difference follows the same form as the confidence interval around a sample mean. The distinction is that the variable $\overline{Y}_1 - \overline{Y}_2$ replaces the variable $\overline{Y}$.

How is this confidence interval around $\overline{Y}_1 - \overline{Y}_2$ interpreted? The confidence interval contains the probable values of the population mean difference $\mu_1 - \mu_2$. As with any confidence interval, size is a key aspect. The narrower the interval, the more precise the estimate.

Also of interest is the relation of the size of one population mean to the other. Each value within the confidence interval represents a negative difference, a zero difference, or a positive difference. That is, each value satisfies one of three possibilities: $\mu_1 > \mu_2$, $\mu_1 = \mu_2$, or $\mu_1 < \mu_2$.

> *A confidence interval around a sample mean difference estimates the extent of the population mean difference, which provides evidence of the size of one population mean to the other.*

When $\mu_1 = \mu_2$, the population means are equal, which means that the mean difference $\mu_1 - \mu_2$ is zero. The location of the value of zero relative to the confidence interval around the sample mean difference is of particular interest.

If the confidence interval around the sample mean difference *includes* zero, then no difference between means is a reasonable possibility. A difference may actually exist, but when zero lies in the interval, all three possibilities—$\mu_1 > \mu_2$, $\mu_1 = \mu_2$, or $\mu_1 < \mu_2$—also fall within the interval, so no consistent difference among population means is detected.

Suppose $\overline{Y}_1 = 5.25$ and $\overline{Y}_2 = 4.00$, which yields a sample mean difference of $\overline{Y}_1 - \overline{Y}_2 = 1.25$. When calculated from the corresponding standard error, as shown in the next section, the corresponding confidence interval in Figure 6-2 stretches from -1.1 to 3.7. If the population mean difference is -1.1, then the first population group mean is 1.1 units *smaller* than the second population group mean. If the population mean difference is 3.7, however, then the ordering of the population means is reversed—the first group mean is 3.7 units *larger* than the second group mean. The value of 0 is also in this interval, in which case both population means are *equal*. All values within the confidence interval are plausible, so no conclusion can be drawn from this analysis regarding the relative sizes of the population group means. The population mean of the first group may be smaller than, equal to, or larger than the population mean of the second group.

If all of the values within the confidence interval are positive or all are negative, the value of zero is outside of the confidence interval. In this case, one population

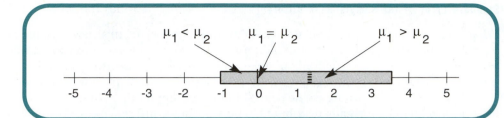

Figure 6-2.
The confidence interval around $\overline{Y}_1 - \overline{Y}_2 = 1.25$ includes zero, so there may be no difference between the population means or either population mean may be larger than the other.

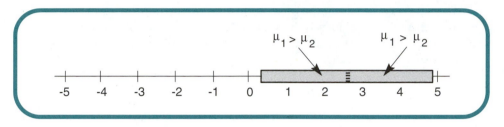

Figure 6-3.
The confidence interval around $\overline{Y}_1 - \overline{Y}_2 = 2.67$ contains only positive values, so the population mean for Group 1 is probably larger than the corresponding mean for Group 2.

mean is apparently larger than the other. The confidence interval estimates the potential magnitude of this difference. Figure 6-3 presents the situation in which $\overline{Y}_1 = 8.00$ and $\overline{Y}_2 = 5.33$. The resulting mean difference is $\overline{Y}_1 - \overline{Y}_2 = 2.67$. All values in the resulting confidence interval around the sample mean difference of 2.67 are positive. The lower bound of this confidence interval is 0.2 and the upper bound is 4.9, so the first group mean is anywhere from 0.2 to 4.9 units larger than the second group mean.

This section demonstrated how to interpret the confidence interval around a sample mean difference. The next section shows how to obtain the confidence interval.

EXERCISES

6-1. Consumer preferences of two different versions of a product are compared on a scale that ranges from 0 to 5. The resulting confidence interval around the sample mean difference $\overline{Y}_1 - \overline{Y}_2$ is from -1.4 to -1.9. Interpret this confidence interval.

Application

6-2. The retail price of similar products from two different manufacturers is compared based on a sample of the first product from a variety of stores and a sample of the second product from a different set of stores. The resulting confidence interval around the sample mean difference $\overline{Y}_1 - \overline{Y}_2$ is from \$4.32 to –\$1.12. Interpret this confidence interval.

Application

6.2 OBTAINING THE CONFIDENCE INTERVAL

The missing piece of the information in the previous presentation is the standard error of the mean difference. Knowledge of the distribution of these sample mean differences, including the actual standard deviation $\sigma_{\overline{Y}_1 - \overline{Y}_2}$ or its estimate $s_{\overline{Y}_1 - \overline{Y}_2}$, provides information that is needed in constructing a confidence interval around $\overline{Y}_1 - \overline{Y}_2$. A discussion of this estimate follows.

Standard Error of the Sample Mean Difference

What are the shape, mean, and standard deviation (error) of this new variable $\overline{Y}_1 - \overline{Y}_2$? The population mean of the difference of two variables is simply the difference between the corresponding population means. The respective population means of $\overline{Y}_1$ and $\overline{Y}_2$ are μ_1 and μ_2, so the population mean of the new variable $\overline{Y}_1 - \overline{Y}_2$ is $\mu_1 - \mu_2$. According to the central limit theorem, both $\overline{Y}_1$ and $\overline{Y}_2$ are at least approximately normally distributed. The sums and differences of normally distributed variables are normally distributed, so the new variable $\overline{Y}_1 - \overline{Y}_2$ is also at least approximately normally distributed around $\mu_1 - \mu_2$.

What is the expression for the population standard error $\sigma_{\overline{Y}_1 - \overline{Y}_2}$? The variance of the difference of two variables is the sum of the variances of each variable. The variables are sample means, $\overline{Y}_1$ and $\overline{Y}_2$, so the standard deviation is the square root of the sum of the individual variances, or

$$\sigma_{\overline{Y}_1 - \overline{Y}_2} = \sqrt{\sigma^2_{\overline{Y}_1} + \sigma^2_{\overline{Y}_2}}.$$

The variance of a sample mean is the square of its standard error (deviation), which leads to the following expression.

Standard error of the mean difference:

$$\sigma_{\overline{Y}_1 - \overline{Y}_2} = \sqrt{\frac{\sigma^2_1}{n_1} + \frac{\sigma^2_2}{n_2}}$$

The standard error of the mean difference—the gauge of the extent of sampling variability—is computed directly from the population variances of the two groups σ^2_1 and σ^2_2.

As before, in practice the values of the population standard deviations σ_1 and σ_2 are usually not known. Instead of calculating the actual standard error of the mean differences $\sigma_{\overline{Y}_1 - \overline{Y}_2}$ from σ_1 and σ_2, calculate the *estimated* standard error $s_{\overline{Y}_1 - \overline{Y}_2}$ from the sample standard deviations s_1 and s_2. There are two different methods for calculating $s_{\overline{Y}_1 - \overline{Y}_2}$. The traditional method discussed next assumes equal population variances. The alternative allows unequal variances.

For the traditional method, assume that both populations have the same unknown variance $\sigma^2_1 = \sigma^2_2$ regardless of the values of their means. Why assume equal variances? The logic of building a confidence interval is based on the distances over repeated sampling of the sample distance statistic around the corresponding *known* population value. The sample statistic, or the distance of the sample mean difference from the known population mean difference, is

$$\frac{(\overline{Y}_1 - \overline{Y}_2) - (\mu_1 - \mu_2)}{s_{\overline{Y}_1 - \overline{Y}_2}}.$$

Only when the population variances of the two groups are equal, with two normally distributed populations, does the distribution of this distance statistic follow the *t*-distribution. Fortunately, if the population variances are not too widely discrepant, and particularly when sample sizes are approximately equal, then the consequences of violating the assumption of equal population variances are minor.

Assuming normally distributed populations and equal population variances, the two sample variances s^2_1 and s^2_2 estimate the same population variance. Refer to the single population variance that describes the population of Y_1 and of Y_2 as σ^2_Y. How is σ^2_Y estimated? The estimate is the average of the two sample variances.

The simple average of s_1^2 and s_2^2 is not the best available estimate of σ_Y^2 when sample sizes are unequal. The estimate obtained from the larger sample should carry more weight. With unequal sample sizes, compute a *weighted* average of the two sample variances, where the weight for each sample is its degrees of freedom, df_1 and df_2, respectively.

> *Weighted average of the sample variances:*
> $$s_{\text{avg}}^2 \equiv \frac{df_1 s_1^2 + df_2 s_2^2}{df_1 + df_2}$$

Recall from Chapter 3 that for the sample standard deviation, $df = n - 1$.

Assuming equal population variances, s_{avg} replaces both σ_1 and σ_2 in the expression for the actual standard error of the mean difference $\sigma_{\overline{Y}_1 - \overline{Y}_2}$. The result is the estimated standard error.

> *Estimated standard error of the mean difference—equal population variances:*
> $$s_{\overline{Y}_1 - \overline{Y}_2} = \sqrt{\frac{s_{\text{avg}}^2}{n_1} + \frac{s_{\text{avg}}^2}{n_2}}$$

This standard error is the estimated standard deviation of the sample mean difference across repeated sampling.

The 95% confidence interval is approximately two estimated standard errors on either side of the sample mean difference. The exact multiplier is the $t_{.025}$ cutoff of the corresponding *t*-distribution for the appropriate *df*. The cutoff values $-t_{.025}$ and $t_{.025}$ define the typical range of variation of the distances of each sample mean difference from the known population mean difference in terms of the estimated standard error $s_{Y_1 - \overline{Y}_2}$:

> *df for the t-cutoff value—equal population variances:*
> $$df = (n_1 - 1) + (n_2 - 1)$$

The degrees of freedom for this cutoff value is the sum of the *df* of each sample.

Before considering the following example, note the distinction between demonstrating a difference between two groups and asserting that group membership *causes* this difference.

> *The t-test for independent groups can establish a difference between population means, but statistical computations alone do not establish causality.*

As discussed in more detail at the beginning of Chapter 10, to support a causal inference, each individual observation should be randomly assigned to one of the groups. With random assignment, there is no difference on average between any variable across the two groups except for membership in the different groups.

Consider an example in which random assignment was *not* followed. Suppose only male employees were assigned to one type of training program and only female employees to the other type of training program. A demonstrated population mean difference of the amount learned could imply that one training program is better than the other. On the other hand, a demonstrated population difference could imply that men and women learn differently. The method of obtaining the samples is a crucial determining factor in drawing the conclusion that group membership, such as participation in one type of training program, has a causal influence on the variable of interest, such as amount of information learned.

BUSINESS APPLICATION 6.1—Confidence Interval around the Mean Difference

MANAGERIAL PROBLEM

Competitive manufacturers attempt to minimize the time lag between ordering materials from suppliers and receiving those materials. At one firm with two suppliers, is the delivery time of materials longer for one supplier than for the other?

The goal of the analysis is not to describe what happened last year (descriptive statistics), but to infer what *will* happen next year (inferential statistics). Last year's sample mean difference is just one random outcome from a larger population and only approximates the unknown population mean difference. What range of values likely contains this population mean difference?

DATA

The 19 delivery times from the first supplier (S1) and the 15 delivery times from the second supplier (S2) are listed below.

S1	8.7	7.3	9.1	10.5	9.1	9.2	10.2	9.9	13.7	9.0	8.3	10.7	8.4	7.7
	11.1	10.5	9.4	8.7	10.4									

S2	8.4	9.9	10.0	8.9	9.7	8.1	7.8	5.2	9.4	5.7	7.9	6.5	9.8	7.8
	6.2													

To facilitate a causal inference that any detected population mean difference is due to the type of supplier, orders were randomly assigned to each supplier. After this random assignment, there are no population average differences between the two groups on any variable except for choice of supplier. Variables such as weight or dollar value of the shipments have equal population means across the two groups.

ASSUMPTIONS

As discussed in the first business application in Chapter 4, computation of the confidence interval requires the assumption of a specific statistical model: The *only* source of variability of response Y is random error. That is, assume the population mean and standard deviation remain unchanged so that the supplier's shipping procedures applied to all of last year's deliveries. Only random fluctuations obtained from repeated use of this procedure should lead to differences in shipping times, as specified by the stable-process model introduced in Chapter 3.

To informally evaluate this model, the time-series plot of the shipping times for the second supplier were presented in the first business application in Chapter 4. The time series-plot for the new data presented here, the shipping times for Supplier 1, are presented below. These data also appear to reflect random deviations around the mean of a stable process.

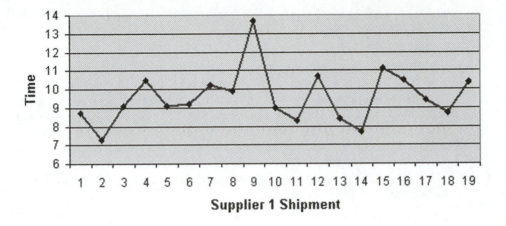

EXCEL GRAPHICAL ANALYSIS

Assessing the Excel Output and Analysis

Histograms of the distributions of shipping times for each of the two samples are displayed on the same graph in Figure 6-4. These histograms provide a visual comparison of the two sets of times.

This graphical comparison helps identify outliers. One value for supplier S1, 13.7, is particularly large relative to all other values for either company. The integrity of this value should be checked to guard against a possible coding error. Or, an atypical event generated by a weird, infrequent set of circumstances may have occurred that slowed one specific shipment, in effect changing the process for that shipment. If such an atypical event would likely not occur again in the future, then this value may not represent the natural variation that results from the shipping process.

The goal of the analysis is to predict future performance. Therefore, including a value in the analysis sampled from a different population process that will probably not repeat in the future obscures any predictability obtained from the remaining data. Deciding whether this value has been sampled from the same process as the other values is a decision made not with statistics but with a substantive investigation into the cause of this large variation. Analysis can proceed,

Figure 6-4.
Shipping times
(days) for suppliers
S1 and S2.

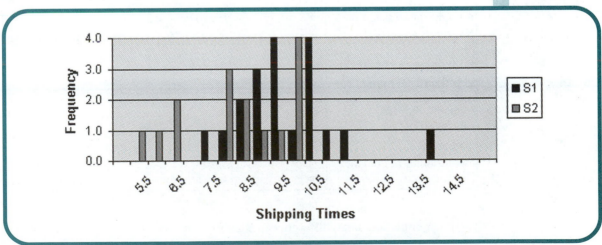

assuming that this value is correctly coded and properly sampled from the same population as the other values.

Obtaining the Output

The Excel Histogram program generated the histograms as described in Business Application 2.3. The bins (class intervals) varied from 5.00 to 14.00 in increments of 0.5. The Histogram program was run separately to obtain the corresponding frequencies for S1 and S2. The Histogram program also created the initial histogram for S1. The histogram for S2 was added to this graph by selecting the frequencies for S2 and dragging the selection onto the top of the graph. Most elements of the graph—such as the plot area, the individual axes, and the data series—were customized by double-clicking on the specific element and then responding to the resulting dialog box.

APPLICATION—CONCEPTUAL WORKSHEET

To name the data ranges on the Excel spreadsheet, first select the cells with the S1 data and do the menu sequence

Insert ➤ Name ➤ Define...

The specify the name "data1." Follow the same procedure for the S2 data, naming the corresponding cells "data2."

This conceptual worksheet is excerpted from the Excel template that is called MeanDiffInference provided with this text. (The complete worksheet also provides an hypothesis test of no population mean difference.)

Description	Name	Value	Formula
count of group1 data	nn1	19	COUNT(data1)
mean of group1 data	mean1	9.574	AVERAGE(data1)
stand dev of group1 data	sd1	1.447	STDEV(data1)
count of group2 data	nn2	15	COUNT(data2)
mean of group2 data	mean2	8.087	AVERAGE(data2)
stand dev of group2 data	sd2	1.587	STDEV(data2)
sample mean difference	diff	1.487	mean1-mean2
average sample variance	avgvar	2.280	(((nn1-1)*(sd1^2))+((nn2-1)*(sd2^2)))/df
total degrees of freedom	df	32	nn1+nn2-2
stand error of mean diff	sterr	0.522	SQRT((avgvar/nn1)+(avgvar/nn2))
confidence level	level	0.95	
t cutoff value	tcut	2.037	TINV(1-level,df)
precision	E	1.062	sterr*tcut
lower bound of conf int	LB	**0.42**	diff-E
upper bound of conf int	UB	**2.55**	diff+E

The population mean difference probably lies between 0.42 days and 2.55 days.

APPLICATION—TRADITIONAL NOTATION

Assuming equal population variances, average the two sample variances, weighting each sample with its df. The df for each group is

$$df_1 = n_1 - 1 = 19 - 1 = 18 \text{ and } df_2 = n_2 - 1 = 15 - 1 = 14.$$

The estimated single error variance of the two populations is

$$s_{avg}^2 = \frac{df_1 s_1^2 + df_2 s_2^2}{df_1 + df_2} = \frac{(18)1.45^2 + (14)1.59^2}{18 + 14} = 2.29.$$

Now substitute $s_{avg}^2 = 2.29$ into the expression for the standard error of the mean difference.[1]

$$s_{\overline{Y}_1 - \overline{Y}_2} = \sqrt{\frac{s_{avg}^2}{n_1} + \frac{s_{avg}^2}{n_2}} = \sqrt{\frac{2.29}{19} + \frac{2.29}{15}} = \sqrt{0.12 + 0.15} \approx .52.$$

The degrees of freedom for the t-statistic is the sum of the degrees of freedom for each sample,

$$df = df_1 + df_2 = 18 + 14 = 32.$$

The .025 cutoff value of t, for a 95% confidence interval with $df = 32$, is 2.037.
    The maximum error of estimation, or precision, is 2.037 standard errors,

$$E = 2.037 \, (s_{\overline{Y}_1 - \overline{Y}_2}) = 2.037 \, (.522) = 1.062.$$

To compute the confidence interval, add and subtract E from the sample mean difference of 1.48,

$$\text{Lower Bound: } (\overline{Y}_1 - \overline{Y}_2) - 2.037 \, (s_{\overline{Y}_1 - \overline{Y}_2}) = 1.487 - 1.062 = 0.42$$

and

$$\text{Upper Bound: } (\overline{Y}_1 - \overline{Y}_2) + 2.037 \, (s_{\overline{Y}_1 - \overline{Y}_2}) = 1.487 + 1.062 = 2.55.$$

APPLICATION—EXCEL BUILT-IN ANALYSIS

Excel does not provide a means to compute directly the confidence interval around a sample mean difference. However, some of the needed values computed in the conceptual spreadsheet in Figure 6-5 can be obtained from the t-Test Two-Sample Assuming Equal Variance program accessed via the Tools → Data Analysis menu sequence. This program provides the descriptive statistics—n, $\overline{Y}$, and s_Y—for each sample, plus the average variance and the critical t-value. The actual calculation of the confidence interval still requires you to enter formulas for the remaining information into the worksheet.

---

1. Computing the corresponding average standard deviation is informative:

$$s_{avg} = \sqrt{s_{avg}^2} = \sqrt{2.29} = 1.51.$$

As it must, the average standard deviation s_{avg} lies between $s_1 = 1.45$ and $s_2 = 1.59$.

MANAGERIAL INTERPRETATION

For the two samples of data collected, the average of supplier S2's delivery times was 1.48 days smaller than the corresponding average for supplier S1. The subsequent inferential analysis demonstrated that supplier S2's average delivery time is likely between .42 and 2.54 days faster than supplier S1's. Because even the smallest difference in this interval, .42, is larger than 0, supplier S2 apparently provides faster delivery service than supplier S1.

This conclusion assumes that the same process generated all data values for supplier S1, including the single large shipping value of 13.7. If additional fact-finding verifies that this large value is due to an anomaly not likely to be repeated in the future, then this large data value biases the analysis of supplier S1's performance in terms of future prediction.

In some situations, the variabilities of the two samples are so discrepant that the equality of population variances cannot be assumed. The appropriate estimated standard error in this situation is presented next.

Unequal Population Variances

When the population variances are unequal, the average variance does not accurately portray either population variance, so compute the estimated standard error of the sample mean difference $s_{\overline{Y}_1 - \overline{Y}_2}$ differently.

> *Estimated standard error of the mean difference—unequal population variances:*
> $$s_{\overline{Y}_1 - \overline{Y}_2} = \sqrt{\frac{s_1^2}{n_1} + \frac{s_2^2}{n_2}}.$$

For this version of the estimated standard error of the mean difference, substitute each sample variance directly into the expression for the actual standard error.

When the population variance estimates are not too discrepant, the differences between the methods of estimating $s_{\overline{Y}_1 - \overline{Y}_2}$ are typically small. Consider the estimated standard error that does *not* assume equal population variances. Applying this estimate to the data in the previous example yields

$$s_{\overline{Y}_1 - \overline{Y}_2} = \sqrt{\frac{s_1^2}{n_1} + \frac{s_2^2}{n_2}} = \sqrt{\frac{1.45^2}{19} + \frac{1.59^2}{15}} = \sqrt{.11 + .17} \approx .53.$$

This value is close to the previous result of .52 obtained from assuming equal population variances.

The distance separating the sample mean difference $\overline{Y}_1 - \overline{Y}_2$ from the population mean difference $\mu_1 - \mu_2$ is expressed in terms of estimated standard errors $s_{\overline{Y}_1 - \overline{Y}_2}$. Unfortunately, when the individual population variance estimates are substituted directly into the expression for the standard error, the resulting distance statistic

$$\frac{(\overline{Y}_1 - \overline{Y}_2) - (\mu_1 - \mu_2)}{s_{\overline{Y}_1 - \overline{Y}_2}}$$

does not follow the *t*-distribution or any other known distribution over repeated sampling. This distance statistic does, however, *approximate* the *t*-distribution when the corresponding degrees of freedom is calculated as follows.

$$df \text{ for the t-cutoff value—unequal population variances:}$$

$$df = \frac{(n_1 - 1)(n_2 - 1)}{(n_1 - 1)(1 - c)^2 + (n_2 - 1)c^2} , \text{ where } c = \frac{\dfrac{s_1^2}{n_1}}{\dfrac{s_1^2}{n_1} + \dfrac{s_2^2}{n_2}}$$

Applying this expression to the data from the previous example results in $df = 28.77$. When using the *t*-table with a noninteger *df*, the fractional part is truncated, such as from 28.77 to 28.

This expression for *df* when allowing for unequal population variances yields a smaller value than that obtained from the simpler $df = (n_1 - 1) + (n_2 - 1)$ when assuming equal population variances. For example, $df = 28.77$ versus $df = 32$ from the previous example. The *t*-value that cuts off the upper 2.5% of the corresponding *t*-distribution for $df = 28$ is 2.045, so the maximum error, or precision, is

$$E = 2.045\,(s_{\overline{Y}_1 - \overline{Y}_2}) = 2.045\,(.53) = 1.08.$$

When assuming equal variances in the previous example, the resulting maximum error is $E = 1.06$, so the resulting confidence interval computed from this unequal variance method is only slightly wider, 0.40 to 2.56 instead of 0.42 to 2.54.

How discrepant can the sample variances and sample sizes become before we abandon the equal population variances assumption? There is no exact answer to this question, and the statistical tests that guide this decision are difficult to interpret meaningfully. We do know, however, that only when both the sample variances *and* the sample sizes are widely discrepant does violation of the equal population variances assumption invalidate the use of the *t*-distribution in practice.

In practice, confidence intervals using both methods can be obtained easily from the computer, and the results of the two analyses can be compared. As long as both sample sizes are approximately equal, little difference will usually separate the sizes of the corresponding confidence intervals. For substantially different results, the wider, more conservative interval that results from *not* assuming equal variances can then be adopted.

One more topic regarding our study of confidence intervals around a mean remains. Next we show how to calculate the needed sample size to achieve the desired level of precision for the confidence interval.

EXERCISES

6-3. Management was considering relocating to one of two cities in different parts of the country. One factor in the decision is the annual snowfall. The amount of snowfall in each city for the last 10 years is displayed below.

Application

City A	38.17	33.41	30.17	34.94	42.09
	41.11	29.60	39.59	41.98	60.49

City B	30.35	43.28	48.77	38.89	32.67
	60.70	60.05	46.76	59.97	47.41

Is there sufficient evidence to conclude that the two cities have differing amounts of snowfall?

a. Evaluate the stable-process model for each sample of data. What do you conclude?
b. Construct and interpret the 90% level of confidence.
c. Construct and interpret the 95% level of confidence.
d. Construct and interpret the 99% level of confidence.

6-4. Model A and Model B are relatively comparable automobiles. In preparing a statewide advertising campaign for Model B, the ad agency wanted to know if the average selling price for Model B in the state was less than the average selling price of Model A. The mean selling price for Model B at 15 dealers randomly sampled statewide was $14,440 with a standard deviation of $378. The mean selling price of Model A at 18 dealerships was $14,890 with a standard deviation of $420.

a. Assuming equal population variances, compute the 95% confidence interval of this mean difference with a conceptual worksheet.
b. Assuming equal population variances, compute the 95% confidence interval of this mean difference with traditional formulas.
c. Interpret the width of the confidence interval.
d. Determine whether no difference between population means is a plausible value and why or why not.

6-5. A record company executive wants to know if the average play length of rock-and-roll singles differs from that of country and western singles. To provide an answer to this question, she selects 10 country and western singles along with 9 rock-and-roll singles.

C&W	3.80	3.30	3.43	3.30	3.03
	4.18	3.18	3.83	3.22	3.38
R&R	3.88	4.13	4.11	3.98	3.98
	3.93	3.92	3.98	4.67	

a. Plot the two distributions of data on the same graph.

b. Compute the 95% confidence interval around the sample mean difference.
c. Interpret the range of values that probably contains the true difference.
d. Determine whether average play length differs.

6-6. The sample means for two groups are 97 and 102, and the respective *population* standard deviations are 11.5 and 9.7. The respective sample sizes are 55 and 46.

a. Compute the standard error for the difference of the two sample means.
b. State whether you pooled the group standard deviations to compute the standard error and why or why not.

6-7. Assume equal population variances.

a. Suppose $s_1 = 6$, $s_2 = 8$, and $n_1 = 50$, $n_2 = 50$. Calculate both the simple average of the sample variances and the weighted average that yields the estimate of the common population variance.
b. Suppose $s_1 = 6$, $s_2 = 8$, and $n_1 = 25$, $n_2 = 75$. Calculate both the simple average of the sample variances and the weighted average that yields the estimate of the common population variance.
c. Compare the simple averages obtained from (a) and (b). Are they the same or different? Why?
d. Compare the estimates of the common population variance from (a) and (b). Are they the same or different? Why?

6-8. Managers from a company with a large sales force want to evaluate the effectiveness of two types of sales presentations. Twenty randomly chosen salespeople are trained in one type of presentation, and 20 more randomly chosen salespeople are trained in the other type. After one-month of sales, the average gross revenue obtained with the first type of presentation is $1,806,821 with a standard deviation of $276,379. Comparable figures for the second type of presentation are $1,498,361 and $387,640 respectively.

a. Assuming equal population variances, compute the 95% confidence interval of this mean difference with a conceptual worksheet.
b. Assuming equal population variances, compute the 95% confidence interval of this mean difference with traditional formulas.

c. Interpret the width of the confidence interval.
d. Determine if no difference between population means is a plausible value, and why or why not.

 6-9. Consider the comparison of effectiveness of two types of sales presentations from Exercise 6-8.

a. State whether you would expect the confidence interval computed *without* assuming equal variances to differ from the interval computed with the assumption and why or why not.

b. Compute the confidence interval of the difference *without* assuming equal population variances. The degrees of freedom is 73.89.

c. Determine whether the confidence intervals computed from the two different variance assumptions are comparable. What primary feature distinguishes the two intervals?

6.3 SAMPLE SIZE AND PRECISION

How can a high level of confidence and a small confidence interval be realized simultaneously? Whether using a confidence interval to estimate either an unknown population mean μ_Y or an unknown population mean difference $\mu_1 - \mu_2$, the answer is the same: Increase the sample size. All other factors the same, increasing sample size decreases the width of the confidence interval. The following sections provide expressions for computing the sample size needed for obtaining a specified level of precision.

The logic of calculating the needed sample size to obtain a sufficiently precise estimate of a population mean difference is the same as the logic of calculating the estimate of a single population mean. However, the problem for two samples in its most general form is complex. Large sample sizes for one group offset smaller sample sizes for the other group, so all different combinations of sample sizes would need consideration. To obtain a more manageable problem, assume equal sample sizes, so that only one sample size n need be computed. Equal population variances $\sigma_1^2 = \sigma_2^2 \equiv \sigma_Y^2$ are also assumed, resulting in the following expression for the standard error of the mean difference.

$$\sigma_{\overline{Y}_1 - \overline{Y}_2} = \sqrt{\frac{\sigma_1^2}{n_1} + \frac{\sigma_2^2}{n_2}} = \sqrt{\frac{\sigma_Y^2}{n} + \frac{\sigma_Y^2}{n}} = \sqrt{2}\,\frac{\sigma_Y}{\sqrt{n}}\,.$$

Use this simplified expression for the standard error in the estimation of the needed sample size.

The width of the confidence interval depends on the common sample size. For a 95% level of confidence, the maximum error or precision of the confidence interval around the sample mean difference is

$$E \equiv 1.96\sigma_{\overline{Y}_1 - \overline{Y}_2} = 1.96\sqrt{2}\,\frac{\sigma_Y}{\sqrt{n}}.$$

Rearranging this equation to solve for the needed n for *each* sample yields the following result:

$$n_\sigma = 2\left[\frac{(1.96)\sigma_Y}{E}\right]^2.$$

As with the previous discussion in Chapter 4, the symbol for sample size, *n*, is denoted as n_σ because the population standard deviation σ_Y is needed for the computation of sample size. The required sample size of *each* sample for estimating a difference between two means is *twice* that needed for estimating a single mean, assuming a common variance and sample size.

Again, the best solution to this problem of the typically unknown σ_Y is to obtain a preliminary sample and obtain a sample estimate of σ_Y. The best estimate of the common population variance is the weighted average of the two sample variances, which is the average estimate s_{avg} defined previously. Substituting s_{avg} for σ_Y results in the following equation:

$$n_s = 2\left[\frac{(1.96)s_{avg}}{E}\right]^2.$$

The problem with this equation is again the sampling fluctuation of s_{avg}. By chance, a particularly small value of s_{avg} relative to the true value of σ_Y may be obtained, which would result in an estimate of n_s too low to obtain the desired level of precision.

The best available solution to the fluctuating s_{avg} problem is to adjust n_s upward to protect against obtaining a small value by chance. The equations presented below provide the protection for a 70%, 90%, and 99% probability of obtaining the needed sample size n to achieve the specified precision E for a 95% level of confidence around the sample mean difference.

> *Required sample size to obtain the specified precision E for a 95% confidence level around a mean difference with unknown σ_Y:*
>
> *.70 probability:* $n = 1.039 n_s + 2.921$
> *.90 probability:* $n = 1.099 n_s + 4.863$
> *.99 probability:* $n = 1.175 n_s + 7.526$
>
> *where* $n_s = 2\left[\dfrac{(1.96)s_{avg}}{E}\right]^2.$

Suppose the initial estimate of sample size n_s for each sample yielded a value of 50. For a .70 probability of obtaining a 95% confidence level at the desired level of precision, the needed sample size is actually 55. This value increases to 60 and then to 67 for probabilities of .90 and then .99. For the initial estimate of $n_s = 50$, the actual probability of obtaining the desired level of precision for a 95% confidence interval is only .45.

The equations for upward adjustment at confidence levels of 90% and 99% are almost identical to the equations reported here for a 95% level of confidence. For values of n_s under 100, the needed sample size n for a confidence level of 90% is generally identical to or occasionally one less than the value obtained for the 95% confidence level. For the 99% confidence level, n is generally one more. For values over 100, there is virtually no difference in the adjustments.

EXERCISES

6-10. At one firm with two suppliers, is the delivery time of materials longer for one supplier than for the other? The estimate of the difference between supplier mean delivery times should likely be within half a day of the true value. To calculate the sample size needed to answer the question, preliminary samples were obtained to estimate the assumed common variance.

The delivery times for the last 19 shipments from one supplier (1) and the last 15 shipments from the other supplier (2) were recorded. The resulting value of $s_{avg} = 1.51$ days was obtained for a mean difference of 1.48 days. For a .90 probability of succeeding, how large a sample from each supplier is required to obtain an estimate with a

a.   95% level of confidence?
b.   99% level of confidence?

6-11. A manufacturing company evaluated the time required to perform a machining operation using one of two different techniques. The estimate of the difference between manufacturing times should be within one second of the true value. To calculate the sample size needed to determine this difference, preliminary samples were obtained to estimate the assumed common variance. The machining times for the last 15 parts from Method 1 and the last 15 parts from Method 2 were recorded. The resulting value

Application

of $s_{avg} = 2.36$ sec was obtained for a mean difference of 1.39 sec. For a .90 probability of succeeding, how large a sample from each technique is required to obtain an estimate with a 95% level of confidence?

6-12. For groups of size 20 each, the respective sample means are 10 and 12. What is the size of the confidence interval around the mean difference if the respective sample standard deviations are both

Concept

a.   5
b.   3
c.   1
d.   .5
e.   What is the relationship between the sample standard deviations and the width of the confidence interval?
f.   Approximately what value of the sample standard deviations is needed to support a difference between the two population means?

6.4 HYPOTHESIS TEST OF A MEAN DIFFERENCE

This section introduces the test of the null hypothesis of equal population means on response variable Y across two groups. As with the confidence interval, groups are defined by a categorical variable with at least two values or levels. Measurements of Y are taken for a sample of observations from each group—employees, companies, manufactured parts, counties, and so forth.

Before presenting this hypothesis test, consider the similarity of this test to the inferential procedures already presented. The key statistic underlying the procedures of inferential statistics—confidence intervals and hypothesis tests—is the standard error. The calculations of confidence intervals and hypothesis tests are based on the standard error in conjunction with the corresponding cutoff of the t-distribution, such as $t_{.025} \approx 2$ for an error rate of $\alpha = 5\%$.

Consider the sample mean. From Chapter 4 we know the standard error of the sample mean and its estimate, respectively, as

$$\sigma_{\overline{Y}} = \frac{\sigma_Y}{\sqrt{n}} \text{ and } s_{\overline{Y}} = \frac{s_Y}{\sqrt{n}} \, .$$

Using this simple expression and a value of $t_{.025} \approx 2$, the confidence interval (see Chapter 4) and hypothesis test (see Chapter 5) are easily constructed.

confidence interval:

sample mean $\pm$ $(t_{.025})$ (standard error of the sample mean)

hypothesis test:

compare $t_{\overline{Y}} = \dfrac{\text{sample mean} - \text{hypothesized mean}}{\text{standard error of sample mean}}$ to $t_{.025}$.

Reject the hypothesized mean for $\alpha = .05$ when the observed sample mean is further than about two standard errors from the hypothesized population value—that is, when the magnitude of $t_{\overline{Y}}$ is larger than $t_{.025} \approx 2$. For either the confidence interval or the hypothesis test, the exact value of $t_{.025}$ depends on the specific value of α, the sample size, the directionality of the test, and whether the standard error is known (z) or estimated (t).

How are confidence intervals and hypothesis tests for the mean difference constructed? As discussed previously in this chapter, the sample mean and the sample mean difference are random variables across samples with their own mean, standard deviation, and shape. The primary distinction between a confidence interval for a mean and a mean difference is simply that the mean difference replaces the mean in the corresponding expression. The 95% confidence interval around the sample mean difference is

confidence interval:

  sample mean difference $\pm$ ($t_{.025}$) (standard error of the sample mean difference).

The same result applies to the hypothesis test. For the hypothesis test of the mean difference, simply replace the mean with the mean difference.

To set up the corresponding hypothesis test, begin with two independent samples of measurements of the response variable *Y,* one sample for each level of the grouping variable. "Independent" means that individual values in one sample are not linked to individual values in the other sample. The sample mean difference is $\overline{Y}_1 - \overline{Y}_2$, and the hypothesized mean difference is $\mu_1 - \mu_2$, which the null hypothesis usually specifies as equal to zero. The standard error of the mean difference is $\sigma_{\overline{Y}_1 - \overline{Y}_2}$, which is estimated by $s_{\overline{Y}_1 - \overline{Y}_2}$. The distance of the sample mean difference from the hypothesized value in terms of the number of estimated standard errors is the t statistic, $t_{\overline{Y}_1 - \overline{Y}_2}$, as shown below.

hypothesis test:

  compare

$$t_{\overline{Y}_1 - \overline{Y}_2} = \frac{\text{sample mean difference} - \text{hypothesized mean difference}}{\text{estimated standard error of sample mean difference}}$$

  to $t_{.025}$.

Conducting an hypothesis test requires the sample mean difference computed from the data, the hypothesized mean difference specified by the analyst, and the standard error of the mean difference estimated from the data.

t-Tests of the Mean Difference

First consider the traditional *t*-test of a mean difference. This test statistic is *exactly* distributed as *t,* although at the cost of an additional assumption. As shown previously in this chapter, assuming equal population variances, the weighted mean of the two sample variances s_{avg}^2 estimates the single variance underlying both populations. Each sample's degrees of freedom serves as the sample's weight,

$$s_{avg}^2 = \frac{df_1 s_1^2 + df_2 s_2^2}{df_1 + df_2} .$$

The resulting test statistic $t_{\overline{Y}_1 - \overline{Y}_2}$ is the number of *estimated* standard errors that the sample mean difference $\overline{Y}_1 - \overline{Y}_2$ is from the hypothesized mean difference $\mu_1 - \mu_2$.

t-test statistic for difference of two population means:

$$t_{\overline{Y}_1 - \overline{Y}_2} = \frac{(\overline{Y}_1 - \overline{Y}_2) - (\mu_1 - \mu_2)}{\sqrt{\dfrac{s_{avg}^2}{n_1} + \dfrac{s_{avg}^2}{n_2}}}$$

The degrees of freedom for $t_{\overline{Y}_1 - \overline{Y}_2}$ is the sum of the degrees of freedom for each group, $df = (n_1 - 1) + (n_2 - 1)$.

The independent samples *t*-test of the mean difference also requires that the populations from which each sample were taken are normally distributed for the resulting distance statistic to be distributed as *t*. Fortunately, the distribution of the distance statistic,

$$\frac{(\overline{Y}_1 - \overline{Y}_2)}{s_{\overline{Y}_1 - \overline{Y}_2}},$$

does not markedly differ from the corresponding *t*-distribution if the corresponding populations only roughly approximate the normal distribution. If equal variances cannot be assumed, then calculate the estimated standard error directly from the two sample standard deviations s_{Y_1} and s_{Y_2}. The corresponding distance statistic is called t'.

t'-test statistic for difference of two population means:

$$t'_{\overline{Y}_1 - \overline{Y}_2} = \frac{(\overline{Y}_1 - \overline{Y}_2) - (\mu_1 - \mu_2)}{\sqrt{\dfrac{s_1^2}{n_1} + \dfrac{s_2^2}{n_2}}}$$

The computed df' based on the expression on page 253 is usually not an integer, so when using a *t*-table to obtain probability values, df' is truncated. When evaluating an obtained value of the t'-statistic with $df' = 19.6$, truncate 19.6 to 19, so use the $df = 19$ row in the *t*-table.

As with the hypothesis tests of a single mean presented in the previous chapter, the evaluation of the plausibility of the null hypothesis of the mean difference, whether using the *z*-test, *t*-test, or t'-test, is based on the *p*-value. The **p-value** indicates the reasonableness of the sample mean difference given the hypothesized population mean difference, which is usually zero. If the *p*-value is small, such as less than .05, the null hypothesis is judged improbable and is rejected.

An example of an hypothesis test of a mean difference based on independent samples follows. This example is a reanalysis of the data presented earlier in the chapter for the confidence interval around the sample mean difference.

> **p-value for a two-sample hypothesis test**
> *probability of obtaining a difference between sample means as large or larger than the observed difference, assuming the hypothesized difference of population means*

BUSINESS APPLICATION 6.2—Mean Difference with Independent Samples

MANAGERIAL PROBLEM

Modern manufacturers attempt to minimize the time lag between ordering materials from suppliers and receiving those materials. At one firm with two suppliers, is the delivery time of materials longer for one supplier than for the other?

STATISTICAL HYPOTHESES

Null hypothesis H_0: $\mu_1 - \mu_2 = 0$.
Alternative hypothesis H_1: $\mu_1 - \mu_2 \neq 0$.

DATA

The delivery times last year for all 19 shipments from one supplier (A) and all 15 shipments from the other supplier (B) were recorded in Figure 6-5 with the corresponding histogram in Figure 6-4. To facilitate a causal inference that any detected population mean difference is due to the type of supplier, orders were randomly assigned to each of the suppliers. Because of random assignment, there should be no average differences in orders or any other variable such as weight or dollar value of the shipment between the two groups except for the choice of supplier.

Is the observed difference of 1.48 days too large, assuming equal population means? To answer this question, compute the number of standard errors that separate the difference of 1.48 from the hypothesized difference of 0.

APPLICATION—CONCEPTUAL WORKSHEET

This conceptual worksheet of the hypothesis test of no population mean difference is excerpted from the Excel template called MeanDiffInference that is provided with this text. (The complete worksheet also estimates the population mean difference with a confidence interval.) The second to last line of this worksheet calculates the distance of the sample mean difference from the hypothesized value of zero, which is the observed value of t. The last line calculates the corresponding p-value with the TDIST function. This function only accepts positive values of t, so in general include the ABS function for obtaining the absolute value of the t-statistic.

Description	Name	Value	Formula
count of group1 data	nn1	19	COUNT(data1)
mean of group1 data	mean1	9.574	AVERAGE(data1)
stand dev of group1 data	sd1	1.447	STDEV(data1)
count of group2 data	nn2	15	COUNT(data2)
mean of group2 data	mean2	8.087	AVERAGE(data2)
stand dev of group2 data	sd2	1.587	STDEV(data2)
sample mean difference	diff	1.487	mean1-mean2
average sample variance	avgvar	2.280	(((nn1-1)*(sd1^2))+((nn2-1)*(sd2^2)))/df
total degrees of freedom	df	32	nn1+nn2-2
stand error of mean diff	sterr	0.522	SQRT((avgvar/nn1)+(avgvar/nn2))
t statistic	t	2.851	diff/sterr
p-value	p-value	**0.008**	TDIST(ABS(t),df,2)

The p-value is less than 0.05, so reject the null hypothesis of no difference in delivery times for the two companies.

APPLICATION—EXCEL BUILT-IN ANALYSIS

Unlike with the confidence interval, Excel does provide a built-in analysis for the corresponding hypothesis test of the mean difference. However, this analysis only applies to problems that include the original data. If only the six summary statistics are available, then the previous worksheet is needed to obtain the p-value.

Assessing the Excel Output

The p-value of about 0.008 is considerably less than 0.05, so reject the null hypothesis of equal population means.

t-Test: Two-Sample Assuming Equal Variances

	S1	S2
Mean	9.574	8.087
Variance	2.093	2.520
Observations	19	15
Pooled Variance	2.280	
Hypothesized Mean Diff	0	
df	32	
t Stat	2.851	← t-statistic
P(T<=t) one-tail	0.004	
t Critical one-tail	1.694	← p-value for two-tailed t-test
P(T<=t) two-tail	**0.008**	
t Critical two-tail	2.037	

Obtaining the Output

Select the menu sequence

Tools ➤ Data Analysis...

Next, select the t-Test Two-Sample Assuming Equal Variances program or the t-Test Two-Sample Assuming Unequal Variances program.

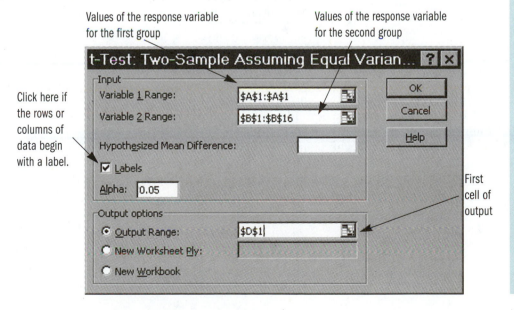

Values of the response variable for the first group

Values of the response variable for the second group

Click here if the rows or columns of data begin with a label.

First cell of output

APPLICATION—TRADITIONAL NOTATION

Calculating the *t*-Value

The denominator of the *t*-statistic is the standard error of the difference between sample means, assuming equal variances. To compute this standard error, first average the two sample variances to obtain a single average variance term, weighting each sample by its *df*. The *df* for each group is

$$df_1 = n_1 - 1 = 19 - 1 = 18 \quad \text{and} \quad df_2 = n_2 - 1 = 15 - 1 = 14.$$

The estimated error variance is

$$s_{\text{avg}}^2 = \frac{df_1 s_1^2 + df_2 s_2^2}{df_1 + df_2} = \frac{(18)\,1.45^2 + (14)\,1.59^2}{18 + 14} = 2.29.$$

Substitute the estimated error variance of 2.29 into the formula for the standard error of the mean difference.

$$s_{\overline{Y}_1 - \overline{Y}_2} = \sqrt{\frac{2.29}{19} + \frac{2.29}{15}} = \sqrt{0.12 + 0.15} \approx .52.$$

The number of estimated standard errors that the sample mean difference is from zero is

$$t_{\overline{Y}_1 - \overline{Y}_2} = \frac{(\overline{Y}_1 - \overline{Y}_2) - (\mu_1 - \mu_2)}{s_{\overline{Y}_1 - \overline{Y}_2}} = \frac{1.48 - 0}{.52} = 2.85.$$

The degrees of freedom for the test statistic $t_{\overline{Y}_1 - \overline{Y}_2}$ is the sum of the degrees of freedom for each sample,

$$df = df_1 + df_2 = 18 + 14 = 32.$$

Calculating the *p*-Value

Assuming the null hypothesis of equal population means, what is the probability of obtaining a *t*-value as large as $t = 2.85$ for $df = 32$? The closest *df*'s from the *t*-table in Appendix B are 30 and 40. The corresponding values of *t* closest to $t = 2.85$ are listed below.

df	0.10	.005
30	2.46	2.75
40	2.42	2.70

The observed value of t, 2.85, cuts off the area under the curve of the *t*-distribution for $df = 32$ somewhere beyond 0.005. If the null hypotheses is true, the probability of obtaining a value of t at least as large as $t = 2.85$ is very small.

For a two-tailed test, the same probability is applied to both tails. What is the probability of obtaining a *t*-value smaller than -2.85 *or* larger than 2.85? The *p*-value is twice the value of the probability cutoff for one tail obtained from the *t*-table. The exact *p*-value (obtained with a computer) is .008.

Reject the null hypothesis of no difference between population means because

$$p \approx .01 < \alpha = 0.05.$$

The *p*-value is small, so the sample mean difference is too many standard errors away from the hypothesized population value of no difference to consider no difference plausible.

MANAGERIAL INTERPRETATION

The delivery time for the first company tends to be more than the delivery time for the second company.

The t'-test, which does *not* assume equal variances, can be used in place of the t-test. Compute the standard error of the mean difference directly from each estimated sample variance,

$$s_{\overline{Y}_1 - \overline{Y}_2} = \sqrt{\frac{s_1^2}{n_1} + \frac{s_2^2}{n_2}} = \sqrt{\frac{1.45^2}{19} + \frac{1.59^2}{15}} = .528.$$

Now compute t',

$$t'_{\overline{Y}_1 - \overline{Y}_2} = \frac{(\overline{Y}_1 - \overline{Y}_2) - (\mu_1 - \mu_2)}{s_{\overline{Y}_1 - \overline{Y}_2}} = \frac{(9.57 - 8.09) - (0)}{.528} = 2.80.$$

The rather elaborate expression for *df* from earlier in the chapter yields 28.78. When using the t-table in Appendix B, truncate this value to 28. The resulting p-value of approximately .01 was obtained using the same procedure as illustrated above for the t-test. For both test statistics, as is usually the case, the same conclusion was reached: reject the null hypothesized value of no difference between the population means.

Another issue to consider is the confidence interval. For the previous example, the null hypothesized value was rejected. If the population mean difference is not zero, then what is it?

In the preceding example, the confidence interval ranges from 0.42 to 2.54, which does not include the null hypothesized value of zero. Consequently, the null hypothesized value of no difference is rejected from either the perspective of the hypothesis test or that of the confidence interval. Further, the confidence interval states that the average delivery time of the first supplier is anywhere from almost half a day to two and a half days longer than that of the second supplier.

Regardless of the outcome of the hypothesis test, the confidence interval provides potentially useful information. The hypothesis test ends with either a do not reject or a reject. The confidence interval provides a *range* of plausible values for the unknown population value, in this case the difference between the population means. Both the confidence interval and the hypothesis test are based on a common set of assumptions, which are examined next.

Assumptions

The validity of the independent samples t-test for the mean difference and the corresponding confidence interval depends on the three assumptions in Table 6-3 being at least reasonably well satisfied.

Generally, computer programs do not automatically check the validity of these assumptions when performing a t-test. Nor is it even possible for the computer to evaluate the validity of Assumption 2, because this assumption is based on the way in which the data were collected instead of on any numerical properties of the data.

Assumption 3 is the equal variances assumption. If this assumption is known to be false or appears to be false, then the standard error computed from the average of the two standard deviations should not be used. Unfortunately, statisticians

Table 6.3.
Assumptions underlying an independent samples *t*-test.

> 1. The two populations are normal.
>
> 2. The samples are independent of one another.
>
> 3. The variances of the two populations are equal.

are unable to provide the size of the maximum discrepancy of the sample group variances that would disqualify the use of the *t*-distribution. What *is* known is that the equal variances assumption becomes less and less tenable as the sample variances become more unequal and also as the sample sizes become more unequal. The population variances are rarely exactly equal, but as long as they are approximately equal, the resulting probabilities from the *t*-distribution are reasonably accurate. However, radically different standard deviations or variances, particularly when the sample sizes are also unequal, result in a test statistic that is not well approximated by the *t*-distribution.

Most computer programs compute both estimated standard errors that underlie the t and t' statistics and the corresponding confidence intervals. In most cases, the choice of either statistic leads to the same decision regarding the hypothesized mean difference, and the size of the confidence intervals are virtually the same. In practice, use the computer to compute both t and t'. Only when these statistics lead to different conclusions is the issue of which to interpret important, and this situation does not occur often in practice.

The next section presents the analysis of a single significant difference between means when the two samples are dependent instead of independent.

EXERCISES

6-13. A paint company claimed that its best exterior paint dried faster than the highest quality exterior paint offered by its leading competitor. A random sample of 25 different houses was painted with its paint, and 23 different houses were painted with the competitor's paint.

Ours	5.70	4.28	5.48	6.08	4.83	5.99	5.30	4.86	5.21
	5.71	2.64	4.52	5.84	6.65	6.41	6.33	6.50	5.14
	5.18	4.67	3.67	4.73	5.18	4.37	3.95		

Theirs	6.57	6.50	5.38	6.50	5.24	5.15	4.49	4.05	4.70
	5.69	5.55	3.97	5.34	5.97	8.22	3.92	5.90	3.69
	6.92	6.06	5.39	6.62	4.90				

a. Compute and compare the summary statistics of the drying times of both groups.

b. Graph the histogram of both groups on the same plot.
c. Determine how the *sample* drying times compare.
d. Using the accompanying data, test the hypothesis that the paints yielded identical drying times.
e. Determine how the *population* drying times compare.
f. State the managerial implication of failing to perform the inferential test.

6-14. A new assembly process was developed with the goal of reducing assembly time. Sixteen employees were tested using the old method and 19 different employees were tested using the new method. The mean assembly time for the old method was 31.1 sec, a time reduced all the way down to 14.6 sec for the new method. The respective standard deviations for the old and new methods are 59.4 sec and 43.1 sec.

a.   Test the hypothesis that the new method improves assembly times (assume equal variances).
b.   Determine whether the result is surprising, and explain your findings.
c.   Make a recommendation based on your explanation regarding future studies comparing the old and new methods.

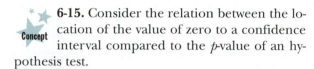

6-15. Consider the relation between the location of the value of zero to a confidence interval compared to the *p*-value of an hypothesis test.

a.   The confidence interval ranges from -.26 to -9.70. What is your best guess for the *p*-value of the corresponding hypothesis test? Why?
b.   The confidence interval ranges from -3.73 to 3.91. What is your best guess for the *p*-value of the corresponding hypothesis test? Why?

c.   The confidence interval ranges from -3.73 to -3.91. What is your best guess for the *p*-value of the corresponding hypothesis test? Why?

6-16. For groups of size 20 each, the respective sample means are 10 and 12. What is the *p*-value of the hypothesis test of the mean difference if the respective sample standard deviations are both

a.   5
b.   3
c.   1
d.   .5
e.   What is the relationship between the sample standard deviations and the *p*-value?
f.   Approximately what value of the sample standard deviations is needed before the null hypothesis of no difference is rejected?

6-17. The sample means for two groups are 15 and 18, and the respective *population* standard deviations are 2 and 2.5. The respective sample sizes are 94 and 92. Compute the corresponding *z*-test statistic for the equality of population means.

6.5 DEPENDENT-SAMPLES ANALYSIS

In our study of group differences up to this point, the values in one group were sampled independently of the values in the other group—the order of the values within each group was irrelevant. The only information needed to construct a confidence interval or conduct the hypothesis test is the sample size, mean, and standard deviation of the response variable for each group.

Data may also be gathered according to a block design in which the samples are dependent on each other. A **block** could be the data values of the same person before training and after training, or a block could consist of happiness measures from two different people—a husband and a wife—in a study of marital happiness. Collecting data in blocks implies that the samples are not independent of each other. Each data value in one group is linked to a corresponding value in the same block in the other group.

A typical **dependent samples** scenario is a pre- and postanalysis. Consider Assembly Time, measured for each employee. A new assembly procedure is introduced, and then Assembly Time is measured again for each employee. Did the new procedure speed up assembly? The data in this situation are organized by blocks of employees: *Each* employee has a corresponding data value in *each* sample. The data value for the first person before the new procedure is introduced is matched with his or her value after the procedure is introduced. For a dependent-samples test, the data values are explicitly matched across the samples.

> **block of matched observations**
> *each data value in one group is linked to a corresponding data value in the other group(s)*

> **dependent samples**
> *data for the samples are collected in blocks*

The analysis of these dependent samples, or what are sometimes called *paired samples,* is straightforward. Both independent-samples and dependent-samples analyses address the population difference between the two groups. The dependent-samples analysis directly analyzes the mean of a transformed variable—the difference between values for *each* individual. The independent-samples analysis, on the other hand, evaluates the *overall* difference between the group means.

> *Dependent-samples analysis assesses change at the individual level, whereas independent-samples analysis assesses change at the aggregate level.*

Collecting blocks of data that define a dependent-samples analysis is often more difficult than collecting independent samples, but as we shall see, the dependent-samples test is typically the more powerful of the two and is usually preferred.

A dependent-samples analysis begins with a **difference score.** The direction of subtraction is irrelevant. The direction can be chosen to yield generally positive differences, or, if the analysis is a pre- and postanalysis, the premeasurement can be subtracted from the postmeasurement to indicate the direction of change for each block.

difference score for each block
$$Y_{diff} \equiv Y_{1st\ score} - Y_{2nd\ score}$$

The dependent-samples hypothesis test is a version of the one-sample *t*-test introduced in Chapter 5. This test is performed on the mean of the *difference scores* for each block.

> *t-test statistic for dependent-samples:*
> $$t_{diff} = \frac{\overline{Y}_{diff} - \mu_{diff}}{s_{\overline{Y}_{diff}}}, \ where \ s_{\overline{Y}_{diff}} = \frac{s_{diff}}{\sqrt{n}}$$

The null hypothesis for this test is that the population mean of the difference scores, μ_{diff}, is some specified constant, usually zero. If a positive or negative change did occur, then the value of t_{diff} will tend to be significantly larger or smaller than the hypothesized value of zero. Particularly when the null hypothesis is rejected, the confidence interval around the sample mean of the difference scores $\overline{Y}_{diff}$ should be obtained to estimate the value of the underlying population difference.

The following example illustrates the dependent-samples *t*-test with the corresponding confidence interval around the estimated difference.

BUSINESS APPLICATION 6.3—Mean Difference with Dependent Samples

MANAGERIAL PROBLEM

A manager wanted to choose the faster of two Assembly processes. Each employee's assembly time would be measured for each process.

STATISTICAL HYPOTHESES

Null hypothesis H_0: $\mu_{diff} = 0$ (Assembly Times are equal for both groups).
Alternative hypothesis H_1: $\mu_{diff} \neq 0$ (Assembly Times differ)

DATA

Seven employees assembled parts using the old method, one at a time. After thorough training in the new method, the employees then assembled the same type of part using the new method. The data for each employee are presented below, measured to the nearest hundredth of a minute. Each employee contributes a block of matched data, which is shaded in gray.

	B	C	D
	Empl	Proc. A	Proc. B
1			
2	1	17.37	10.37
3	2	14.59	12.19
4	3	16.94	15.14
5	4	24.28	16.08
6	5	16.16	17.06
7	6	21.11	18.61
8	7	22.19	21.49

Contrary to the independent-samples test, the same observation (employee) generates data for both processes, Process A and Process B.

EXCEL GRAPHICAL ANALYSIS

Assessing the Excel Output

The chart shows a decrease in Assembly Times for all but Employee 5. The accompanying statistical analysis assesses the likelihood that this pattern generalizes to the entire population and is not just a chance statistical fluctuation.

Obtaining the Output

Insert ➤ Chart...

Step 1—Chart Type. Specify a Column chart, which is for a categorical (nonnumeric) horizontal axis. Then choose a format, such as the clustered column, that compares values across categories.

Step 2—Chart Source. Specify the cells that include the data, which are the two columns of the response variable *Y* with the labels.

Data range:	=Sheet1!$C$1:$D$8

Step 3—Chart Options. Name the chart and the axes.

Chart title:
Comparison of Two Processes

Category (X) axis:
Employee

Series (Y) axis:
Time

Step 4—Chart Location. Specify the location of the chart, either on a new sheet or as an object on the current worksheet.

APPLICATION—CONCEPTUAL WORKSHEET

This conceptual worksheet is excerpted from the Excel template called MeanInference that is provided with this text. This is the same worksheet from which excerpts were presented in Chapters 4 and 5, with the addition of the employee data and the computed difference scores. The seven difference scores serve as the data for the construction of the confidence interval and the hypothesis test. In the following worksheet, these seven scores are called Diff, as specified by the Insert ➤ Name ➤ Define menu sequence performed on the selected cells.

Empl	Proc. A	Proc. B	Diff
1	17.37	10.37	7.00
2	14.59	12.19	2.40
3	16.94	15.14	1.80
4	24.28	16.08	8.20
5	16.16	17.06	-0.90
6	21.11	18.61	2.50
7	22.19	21.49	0.70

Description	Name	Value	Formula
count of data	n	7	COUNT(Diff)
mean of data	mean	3.100	AVERAGE(Diff)
standard dev of data	stdev	3.305	STDEV(Diff)
standard error of mean	sterr	1.249	stdev/SQRT(n)
confidence level	level	0.95	
t cutoff value	tcut	2.447	TINV(1-level,n-1)
precision	E	3.056	sterr*tcut
lower bound of conf int	LB	0.04	mean-E
upper bound of conf int	UB	6.16	mean+E
hypothesized value	mu0	0	
t statistic	t	2.482	(mean-mu0)/stderr
p-value, two-tailed	pvalue	0.048	TDIST(ABS(t),n-1,2)

The confidence interval of the mean of the differences indicates that the second process averages from 0.04 to 6.16 minutes faster than the first process. Or, the null hypothesis of no difference between processes is rejected for $\alpha = 0.05$, yielding the conclusion that the second process is faster.

APPLICATION—EXCEL BUILT-IN ANALYSIS

Assessing the Excel Output

Excel does not compute the confidence interval around the sample mean of the differences, but Excel does calculate the hypothesis test.

t-Test: Paired Two Sample for Means

	Proc. A	Proc. B
Mean	18.949	15.849
Variance	12.817	14.146
Observations	7	7
Pearson Correlation	0.596	
Hypothesized Mean Diff	0	
df	6	
t Stat	2.482	← t-statistic
P(T<=t) one-tail	0.024	
t Critical one-tail	1.943	
P(T<=t) two-tail	0.048	← p-value for two-tailed t-test
t Critical two-tail	2.447	

Reject the null hypothesis of no difference because, for a two-tailed test, $p \approx .047 < \alpha = 0.05$. Because the p-value is so small, the observed mean is relatively far from the hypothesized value in terms of estimated standard errors. The obtained p-value, however, is just under the 0.05 cutoff.

Obtaining the Output

Tools ➤ Data Analysis... ➤ t-Test: Paired Two Sample for Means

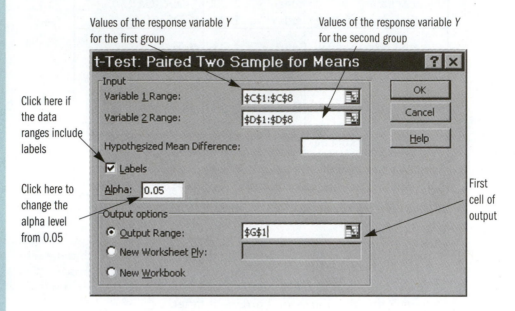

Values of the response variable Y for the first group

Values of the response variable Y for the second group

Click here if the data ranges include labels

Click here to change the alpha level from 0.05

First cell of output

STATISTICAL PRINCIPLE

The p-value from this nondirectional (two-tailed) hypothesis test is under .05, which leads to a literal rejection of the null hypothesis of no difference. However, this conclusion is not unequivocal given that $p = .047$, which is only .003 below .05. This equivocation from the hypothesis test is matched by the size and location of the confidence interval. The mean decrease may be over 6 min, or as small as .05 min, that is, just barely larger than zero.

MANAGERIAL INTERPRETATION

Process B tends to yield faster Assembly Times than does Process A, though the decrease is not necessarily substantial. The average decrease in Assembly Times with the new process is likely somewhere in the range of a low of .05 min to a high of 6.15 min. If greater precision in this estimate is desired, then a larger sample should be gathered.

The study in the previous example could have been designed for an analysis with either an independent- or a dependent-samples t-test. Instead of taking seven employees and measuring their assembly times for both processes, 14 randomly sampled employees could then each have been randomly assigned to one of the two processes. This later study would have resulted in two independent samples of employees, and the independent-samples t-test would have been appropriate for the analysis of the resulting data.

So why choose one version of the test over the other? Look what happens when we analyze the data from the previous example as if it were collected from two independent groups.

STATISTICAL ILLUSTRATION—Independent-samples *t*-test (reanalyzing dependent-samples data)

PROBLEM

A manufacturing engineer wanted to evaluate two processes for assembly time. The engineer had seven employees assemble parts using the old method, one at a time. After thorough training in the new method, the employees then assembled the same type of part using the new method.

DATA

The data are presented below, measured to the nearest hundredth of a minute, accompanied by the descriptive statistics of each group in Table 6-5. For the purposes of this analysis, the two measurements from each employee are not linked. Each employee's data appears on two separate lines in the independent-samples representation of the data. For example, the data for the first employee appear in both Row 1 and Row 8, because, for purposes of this analysis, data in these two rows could have come from different employees.

Empl	Process	Time
1	A1	17.37
2	A1	14.59
3	A1	16.94
4	A1	24.28
5	A1	16.16
6	A1	21.11
7	A1	22.19
8	A2	10.37
9	A2	12.19
10	A2	15.14
11	A2	16.08
12	A2	17.06
13	A2	18.61
14	A2	21.49

Table 6-3.
Descriptive statistics.

Group	n	Mean	SD
A1	7	18.95	3.58
A2	7	15.85	3.76

CALCULATION OF t FROM DESCRIPTIVE STATISTICS

$$s^2_{\text{avg}} = \frac{(n_1 - 1)s_1^2 + (n_2 - 1)s_2^2}{(n_1 - 1) + (n_2 - 1)} = \frac{(7 - 1)3.58^2 + (7 - 1)3.761^2}{(7 - 1) + (7 - 1)} = 13.48$$

$$s_{\overline{Y}_1 - \overline{Y}_2} = \sqrt{\frac{13.48}{7} + \frac{13.48}{7}} = \sqrt{1.93 - 1.93} \approx 1.96$$

$$t_{\overline{Y}_1 - \overline{Y}_2} = \frac{(\overline{Y}_1 - \overline{Y}_2) - (\mu_1 - \mu_2)}{s_{\overline{Y}_1 - \overline{Y}_2}} = \frac{3.10 - 0}{1.96} = 1.58$$

CALCULATION OF THE p-VALUE

Assuming that the null hypothesis of equal population means is true, what is the probability of obtaining a t-value as large as $t = 1.58$ for $df = 12$? The corresponding values of t closest to $t = 1.58$ for $df = (n_1 - 1) + (n_2 - 1) = 12$ are

df	.100	.050
12	1.36	1.78

If the null hypothesized value is true, the probability of obtaining a value of t at least as large as $t = 1.58$ is about .074.

For a two-tailed test, the same probability of .074 is applied to *both* tails, so $p \approx .074 + .074 \approx .15$. The exact p-value (obtained with a computer) is .140. The null hypothesis of no difference between population means is not rejected, because $p \approx .15 > \alpha = .05$. The p-value is not very small, so the observed mean is reasonably close to the hypothesized value.

STATISTICAL PRINCIPLE

The independent-sample analysis of these data detected no difference between assembly times for the two processes. Note that this conclusion is the opposite of that obtained from the more appropriate and more powerful dependent-samples analysis of these data.

What happened in the previous example? For the dependent-samples analysis, $p = 0.048$, which led to the rejection of the hypothesis of equality and to the substantive conclusion that Process B yields faster assembly times than Process A. Yet when these same data were analyzed by the independent-samples t-test, $p = 0.140$, so the hypothesis that assembly times for the two processes are identical was not rejected. No difference between assembly times was detected.

The reason for this discrepancy in results is the large variability across assembly times for different employees—*regardless* of the processes used to assemble the parts. Some employees are faster than others. For example, Employee #2 has the best assembly times, and Employee #4 has the slowest times. In the independent-samples analysis, this large variation of times *within* the group masks the differences *between* the processes. In the dependent-samples analysis, this variability is explicitly accounted for and neutralized by measuring the times for both processes by each employee, and then directly analyzing the resulting differences.

For the same sample size, the smaller the standard deviation of the variable analyzed, the smaller the standard error of the mean. The group standard deviations and the average standard deviation of the response variable Y are

$$s_1 = 3.58, \ s_2 = 3.76, \text{ and } s_{avg} = 3.67,$$

respectively. The standard deviation of the difference scores is

$$s_{diff} = 3.31.$$

This reduction in variability from $s_{avg} = 3.67$ to $s_{diff} = 3.31$ is due to eliminating the assembly time differences among employees. Each employee yields a block of matched data; Employee is the blocking variable for this design. Instead of evaluating the difference between group means, the dependent-samples analysis focuses directly on the difference between the two scores for each employee. The fact that Employee #1's difference score is 7.00 min does not imply assembly times of 17.37 min and 10.37 min. The employee could be comparatively slow with times such as 20 min and 13 min, or comparatively fast with times such as 12 min and 5 min.

A dependent-samples test in which the blocking variable is related to the response variable is more likely to detect an actual difference between groups. This additional power was demonstrated by the previous two examples, in which the dependent-samples analysis led to the rejection of the hypothesis of equal population means, but the independent-samples analysis did not have enough power to reject this false null hypothesis. The direct analysis of change for each observation with a dependent-samples analysis is usually preferred to the analysis of mean differences with an independent-samples analysis.

The two-group t-tests for both independent samples and dependent samples can be generalized to as many groups as specified. This more general statistical procedure, referred to as ANOVA, is covered later in the text. Next, however, we consider a different type of generalization. Comparing two groups, such as males and females, according to a quantitative variable of interest, such as salary, is the comparison of two variables. One variable is categorical, with two levels, and the other variable is continuous. The next chapter considers the comparison of two categorical variables.

EXERCISES

Application

6-18. The manager of a weight-reduction program weighed 10 participants before the program began and then again after the program was completed. The following weights were recorded for the evaluation of the effectiveness of the program.

Person	1	2	3	4	5
Before	220	187	265	314	219
After	206	189	254	289	215

Person	6	7	8	9	10
Before	172	183	202	298	174
After	163	180	202	291	163

a. Plot the sets of two scores for each person on the same graph.
b. Construct the confidence interval.
c. Conduct the hypothesis test.
d. Determine if the program is effective.

6-19. A long-distance telephone company claimed that by switching to its services, costs would decrease. To evaluate this claim, the manager responsible for making this decision had samples of the last eight monthly company phone bills analyzed. The actual costs of using the current phone company and the costs claimed by the new company are listed below to the nearest dollar.

Month	1	2	3	4
Current	$7420	$6493	$7234	$8334
New	$7336	$6421	$7298	$8314

Month	5	6	7	8
Current	$6216	$6149	$8337	$7209
New	$6228	$6151	$8329	$7177

a. Plot the sets of two scores for each company on the same graph.

b. Construct the confidence interval.

c. Conduct the hypothesis test.

d. Determine if the services provided by the new company are less costly.

6-20. Reanalyze the data in the previous problem with an independent-groups *t*-test.

a. How does this result, in terms of observed *t*-value and *p*-value, compare with the corresponding values obtained from the dependent-groups analysis?

b. How do you explain the differences?

6.6 SUMMARY

To assess the difference between two population means, draw a sample from each population and compute the difference between the sample means. A confidence interval can be constructed around the sample mean difference. The confidence interval contains plausible values of the population mean difference. To interpret this confidence interval, focus on the value of zero, which corresponds to *no* difference in population means. When zero is in the confidence interval, a difference between population means is not detected. The population means could be equal, or either mean could be larger than the other. When zero is *not* in the confidence interval, all plausible mean differences are positive or negative, so one population mean is apparently larger than the other population mean.

The confidence interval that probably contains the population mean difference is about two standard errors on either side of the sample mean difference. The standard error of the mean difference is estimated either by assuming equal population variances or by allowing unequal variances. These confidence intervals around the sample mean difference are illustrated below.

$$95\% \text{ confidence interval around the sample mean difference:}$$

$$\mu_1 - \mu_2 \text{ is likely in the interval } \overline{Y}_1 - \overline{Y}_2 \pm t_{.025} s_{\overline{Y}_1 - \overline{Y}_2}, \text{ where } t_{.025} \approx 2$$

$$\text{Two ways of computing the estimated standard error } s_{\overline{Y}_1 - \overline{Y}_2}:$$

$$(a) \text{ allow for unequal population variances, } s_{\overline{Y}_1 - \overline{Y}_2} = \sqrt{\frac{s_1^2}{n_1} + \frac{s_2^2}{n_2}}$$

$$(b) \text{ assume equal population variances, } s_{\overline{Y}_1 - \overline{Y}_2} = \sqrt{\frac{s_{avg}^2}{n_1} + \frac{s_{avg}^2}{n_2}}$$

$$\text{where } s_{avg}^2 = \frac{df_1 s_1^2 + df_2 s_2^2}{df_1 + df_2}$$

The sample size needed to achieve a desired level of precision in the estimation of $\mu_1 - \mu_2$ can be calculated to satisfy two opposing criteria. The width of the confidence interval is small enough to obtain the desired precision, but in practice additional resources are not committed to gathering a sample size larger than needed. In practice, this calculation is usually done with the unknown value of the population standard deviation estimated from a comparatively small preliminary sample. When the minimum sample size is computed from the sample standard deviation, the result is adjusted upward to protect against a small chance value of the sample standard deviation.

The two forms of statistical inference are confidence intervals and hypothesis testing. This chapter presented three different independent-samples hypothesis tests for evaluating the observed difference between the sample means of two groups. Even though the sample means differ, the purpose of these tests is to see if the respective *population* means differ. These tests can be used in conjunction with the confidence interval. Particularly when the null hypothesis is rejected so that a mean difference in the response variable is inferred across the two groups, a confidence interval around the sample mean difference estimates the extent of this population difference.

The three test statistics are Z, t, and t', defined as follows.

$$Z_{\overline{Y}_1 - \overline{Y}_2} = \frac{(\overline{Y}_A - \overline{Y}_B) - 0}{\sqrt{\dfrac{\sigma_A^2}{n_A} + \dfrac{\sigma_B^2}{n_B}}}$$

$$t'_{\overline{Y}_1 - \overline{Y}_2} = \frac{(\overline{Y}_A - \overline{Y}_B) - 0}{\sqrt{\dfrac{s_A^2}{n_A} + \dfrac{s_B^2}{n_B}}}$$

$$t_{\overline{Y}_1 - \overline{Y}_2} = \frac{(\overline{Y}_A - \overline{Y}_B) - 0}{\sqrt{\dfrac{s_{avg}^2}{n_A} + \dfrac{s_{avg}^2}{n_B}}},$$

where $s_{avg}^2 = \dfrac{(n_A - 1)s_A^2 + (n_B - 1)s_B^2}{n_A + n_B - 2}$.

Each of these test statistics indicates the number of standard errors or estimated standard errors that the sample mean difference is from the hypothesized mean difference. This hypothesized mean difference is specified as zero in the preceding expression of the tests.

The denominators for the tests are related, but each is unique. For the z-test, the population variance of each respective group must be known. For the t'-test, the two sample variances separately estimate their corresponding population variances. For the t-test, the most widely used test of the three, the two sample variances are averaged (weighted by their respective df). This single average variance estimates the assumed common population variance across the two groups. For large samples with equal variances, the three tests yield almost identical results.

Data obtained from designs with dependent samples produced matched observations for each value of the blocking variable. For dependent samples with only two groups, the key is to calculate the difference of the two measurements for each block. The mean of these difference scores, $\overline{Y}_{diff}$, can be analyzed with a confidence interval or an hypothesis test. The confidence interval is about two standard errors on either side of the sample mean of the differences. The hypothesis test of no mean difference is

$$t_{\text{diff}} = \frac{\overline{Y}_{\text{diff}} - 0}{\frac{s_{\text{diff}}}{\sqrt{n}}}.$$

This dependent-samples test analyzes differences directly instead of through the analysis of aggregate differences provided by the independent-samples test.

6.7 KEY TERMS

block *265*   independent samples *242*
dependent samples *265*   *p*-value *259*
difference score *266*

6.8 REVIEW EXERCISES

ANALYSIS PROBLEMS

6-21. The time spent waiting in line before getting service at two different branches of a bank was assessed. The resulting confidence interval around the sample mean difference $\overline{Y}_1 - \overline{Y}_2$ is from .21 min to .46 min. Interpret this confidence interval.

6-22. The gas mileage of two competing models of automobiles was measured. The resulting confidence interval around the sample mean difference $\overline{Y}_1 - \overline{Y}_2$ is from -1.1 mpg to 2.9 mpg. Interpret this confidence interval.

6-23. The cost of groceries at two national chains of grocery stores was measured using identical groceries bought at samples of each of the two stores. The resulting confidence interval around the sample mean difference $\overline{Y}_1 - \overline{Y}_2$ is from -$4.13 to $1.46. Interpret this confidence interval.

6-24. Management wanted to evaluate the effectiveness of a new process for entering data onto forms. Measurements of the number of forms entered in an hour by 28 data entry personnel with the old process are recorded below. The measurements for a sample of 21 different employees after a series of new training sessions are also recorded below.

Old	21.7	27.4	21.0	30.4	27.9	26.0	29.5	24.5	23.6	28.5	18.3
	23.5	23.8	24.4	19.3	21.2	28.5	23.0	27.1	34.9	28.1	24.87
	22.2	27.5	23.6	27.2	26.1	21.1					
New	22.1	22.8	19.9	19.9	22.3	22.2	17.9	21.9	18.4	18.3	20.6
	19.4	15.6	23.0	25.0	15.2	24.4	18.0	15.9	26.4	25.8	

Is there sufficient evidence to conclude that the mean number of forms entered per minute increased?

    a. Evaluate the normality of the data with a histogram of each sample. How crucial is this evaluation for these data?

    b. Construct and interpret a 95% level of confidence.

    c. Conduct and interpret an hypothesis test with $\alpha = .05$.

    d. Determine if the results of the confidence interval and hypothesis test agree, and why or why not.

Application

6-25. Ratings of two different teachers for a specific course were compared. The first teacher taught 14 sections of the course and the second teacher taught 10 sections of the course. The course ratings are on a 10-point scale. A 10 means "absolutely wonderful" and a 1 means "absolutely terrible." The first teacher received a mean course rating of 8.1 with a standard deviation of 1.3. The second teacher received a mean course rating of 8.3 with a standard deviation of 0.9. Is there sufficient evidence to conclude that students perceive one teacher more highly than the other with a

    a. 90% level of confidence

    b. 95% level of confidence

    c. 99% level of confidence

Application

6-26. Two different methods of instruction were used in a management training program. Managers were randomly assigned to either the traditional classroom-lecture method (CLM) or the computer assisted instruction method (CAI). None of the managers was familiar with the material at the beginning of training, and at the end of training all participants were tested to evaluate their learning. The scores for 52 CLM and 38 CAI managers are recorded below.

CLM	93	87	82	91	78	81	100	73	91	73	87
	92	100	100	77	85	82	88	93	65	82	83
	100	70	83	87	90	81	99	82	72	82	73
	92	88	95	91	100	91	81	83	95	82	84
	97	84	87	90	79	72	87	82			
CAI	76	93	65	75	73	87	79	93	76	67	78
	93	75	76	89	77	83	60	75	78	92	94
	87	72	84	72	79	79	73	76	78	62	77
	87	76	85	76	66						

Is there sufficient evidence to conclude that the two designs lead to different levels of learning?

    a. Construct and interpret a 95% level of confidence.

    b. Conduct and interpret an hypothesis test with $\alpha = .05$.

    c. Determine if the results of the confidence interval and the hypothesis test agree, and why or why not.

Application

6-27. Management at a mail-order firm wanted to improve the response time of payment for those customers who received merchandise before payment. When they receive the merchandise, the customer is informed that payment is due immediately, so most payments are received with a few weeks. However, the issue is whether adding a stamp to the envelope sent to the customer to return payment would speed up the process. To evaluate this question, an experiment was conducted in which 29 randomly selected customers did not receive a stamp on the envelope and 35 randomly selected customers received a stamp. The time in days in which their payment was received is recorded below. Those few customers who didn't pay without additional collection efforts were not included in this analysis.

No Stamp	18	8	11	12	9	12	15	29	10	11	7	8
	11	7	21	13	3	10	14	9	7	9	0	10
	8	12	12	10	22							
Stamp	8	27	6	8	6	19	8	14	8	9	16	24
	9	3	12	10	8	11	7	16	10	23	6	6
	6	2	3	16	5	9	16	10	7	4	9	

Is there sufficient evidence to conclude that the presence of a stamp speeds up the return of payment?

   a. Conduct and interpret a 95% level of confidence.

   b. Conduct and interpret an hypothesis test with $\alpha = .05$.

   c. Determine if the results of the confidence interval and the hypothesis test agree, and why or why not.

6-28. Starting salaries were compared for graduating students from two M.B.A. programs. One of the programs recently began to emphasize quality management, and the other program retained the traditional content. The respective mean starting salaries for the programs with and without quality management content are \$43,740 ($n = 28$, SD = \$3,125) and \$41,688 ($n = 31$, SD = \$3,767). Is there sufficient evidence to conclude that the mean starting salaries differ for the two programs?

   a. Conduct and interpret a 95% level of confidence.

   b. Conduct and interpret an hypothesis test with $\alpha = .05$.

   c. Determine if the results of the confidence interval and the hypothesis test agree, and why or why not.

6-29. Management wanted to assess the relative job satisfaction of its men and women employees. Using a job satisfaction inventory that yielded scores from 0 to 100 for maximum satisfaction, the data showed that 241 men averaged 88.2 with a standard deviation of 4.3, and 202 women averaged 87.8 with a standard deviation of 5.1 Use an hypothesis test to assess if there is a difference in job satisfaction for men versus women.

6-30. Assume equal population variances.

   a. Suppose $s_1 = 10$, $s_2 = 15$, and $n_1 = 30$, $n_2 = 30$. Calculate both the simple average of the sample variances and the weighted average that yields the estimate of the common population variance.

   b. Suppose $s_1 = 10$, $s_2 = 15$, and $n_1 = 15$, $n_2 = 45$. Calculate both the simple average of the sample variances and the weighted average that yields the estimate of the common population variance.

   c. Compare the simple averages obtained from (a) and (b). Are they the same or different? Why?

d. Compare the estimates of the common population variance from (a) and (b). Are they the same or different? Why?

Application

6-31. To determine if tires manufactured with new materials last longer than tires manufactured the old way, a tire manufacturer had nine test cars outfitted with identically sized tires. One randomly chosen front wheel of each car had one type of tire and the other front wheel had the other type. All nine cars were driven for many tens of thousands of miles (on a test machine), and the mileage at which each tire reached $\frac{1}{16}''$ tread was recorded.

Car	1	2	3	4	5	6	7	8	9
Old	42,771	42,534	43,858	43,538	44,063	38,840	40,458	41,840	42,481
New	45,010	44,446	45,749	46,031	46,215	41,547	42,677	43,326	44,476

Is tire wear affected by the choice of materials?

a. Analyze these data graphically. What do you conclude?

b. Analyze these data with a dependent-samples confidence interval.

c. Analyze these data with a dependent-samples t-test.

d. Compare the two analyses. What do you conclude?

Application

6-32. To improve safety at its eight manufacturing plants, management instituted a new training program. To evaluate the effectiveness of this program, the average daily loss of employee work hours was measured before and after instituting the program.

Plant	1	2	3	4	5	6	7	8
Before	4.2	3.7	6.9	5.5	3.8	2.1	6.7	5.0
After	3.9	4.2	4.7	5.1	4.1	2.0	6.7	4.4

Does the training program affect safety as measured by the loss of employee work hours?

a. Analyze these data graphically. What do you conclude?

b. Analyze these data with a dependent-samples confidence interval.

c. Analyze these data with a dependent-samples t-test.

d. Compare the two analyses. What do you conclude?

Concept

6-33. Reanalyze the data in the previous exercise with an independent-groups t-test.

a. How does this result, in terms of observed t-value and p-value, compare with the corresponding values obtained from the dependent-groups analysis?

b. How do you explain the differences?

Application

6-34. A soda water company developed a new cola. Potential consumers tasted the new cola and the leading competitor's cola. Half of the tasters drank the new cola first and half drank the other cola first. Tasters rated the products on a scale from 1 (yucky) to 10 (extremely tasty).

Store	1	2	3	4	5	6	7
Ours	7	8	6	8	9	10	8
Theirs	6	8	7	6	9	9	9

Is one cola perceived as tastier than the other?

a. Analyze these data graphically. What do you conclude?

b. Analyze these data with a dependent-samples confidence interval.

c. Analyze these data with a dependent-samples *t*-test.

d. Compare the two analyses. What do you conclude?

Application

6-35. A manager for a leading laundry detergent manufacturer wanted to compare the average retail price of his firm's detergent with a competitor's average price. The manager gathered the price of the two detergents from seven different stores.

Store	1	2	3	4	5	6	7
Ours	$3.14	$2.99	$3.09	$2.99	$3.29	$3.13	$2.99
Theirs	$3.10	$2.99	$3.19	$2.89	$3.19	$3.29	$2.99

Is there a difference in the price of the two brands of detergent?

a. Analyze these data graphically. What do you conclude?

b. Analyze these data with a dependent-samples confidence interval.

c. Analyze these data with a dependent-samples *t*-test.

d. Compare the two analyses. What do you conclude?

Concept

6-36. For the data in the previous exercise,

a. Determine why the laundry detergent data were analyzed as dependent samples.

b. Analyze these data with an independent-samples confidence interval.

c. Compare the width of the confidence intervals from the dependent-samples and independent-samples analyses. Are they different? Why?

DISCUSSION QUESTIONS

1. What is the distinction between independent and dependent samples?

2. How is the confidence interval around a mean difference interpreted if the interval includes zero?

3. What are the two different methods by which the estimated standard error of the sample mean difference is calculated?

4. What is the primary practical difficulty when computing the needed sample size to obtain a desired level of precision with a confidence interval?

5. How does the equation for computing the required sample size to obtain a sufficient level of precision for estimating a mean compare to the equation for estimating a mean difference?

6. How is the independent-samples *t*-test similar to the *t*-test that evaluates a single mean (introduced in the previous chapter)?

7. What is the difference between the *t*-test and the *t'*-test?

8. When is the equal variances assumption important in the analysis of mean differences?

9. What is a block of data?

10. How does randomization proceed in a design that uses blocks?

11. How is the dependent-samples *t*-test similar to the *t*-test that evaluates a single mean?

12. What is the advantage of analyzing data collected with dependent samples with a dependent-samples test instead of an independent-samples test?

13. When does a dependent-samples *t*-test *not* do as well compared to the independent-samples version of the test?

INTEGRATIVE ANALYSIS PROBLEM

The owner of two restaurants wanted to compare the average price of a meal at Restaurant A with the average price of a meal at Restaurant B. The data are found in the file called RESTR.DAT. Thirty-eight receipts at Restaurant A and 42 Restaurant B receipts were recorded. Do customers spend more money at one restaurant than at the other?

Restaurant A costs

14.66	9.47	13.85	15.98	11.46	15.70	13.18	11.60
12.88	14.71	2.94	10.34	15.18	18.12	17.25	16.95
17.60	12.60	12.77	10.88	7.25	11.12	12.76	9.81
7.91	16.33	16.13	12.16	16.11	12.36	12.08	10.12
8.79	10.75	13.69	13.29	8.55	12.66		

Restaurant B costs

12.95	19.59	8.38	13.53	7.78	16.21	13.97	12.22
15.41	10.93	10.07	14.45	5.35	10.01	10.31	10.80
6.20	7.93	14.52	9.58	13.26	20.26	14.09	11.20
8.87	13.59	10.12	13.32	12.30	7.83	13.32	14.04
11.12	11.16	13.52	13.44	9.17	13.11	9.63	9.53
11.88	10.68						

a. Construct a histogram of each data set.

b. Examine the data for outliers.

c. Compute the sample size, mean, and standard deviation for each sample.

d. Determine whether a reasonable justification can be made for assuming equal variances.

e. Compute the 95% confidence interval around the mean difference, assuming equal variances.

f. Interpret the confidence interval. Is a difference between the costs of meals detected with this confidence interval?

g. Determine the *p*-value for the hypothesis test of no difference between costs for the two restaurants.

h. Interpret the hypothesis test.

i. Compare the results of the confidence interval and the hypothesis test. Do they lead to the same conclusion? What different types of information do these two forms of statistical inference provide in this problem?

j. Determine whether choice of restaurant is related to cost of the meal.

Analysis of Categorical Variables

WHY DO WE CARE?

A common form of data that managers are interested in is responses to questionnaires administered to other managers, employees, or consumers. Responses to questions such as "Would you buy this product" can be answered with a "Yes" or a "No" response. Or a statement such as "I like this product" could be responded to with "Agree," "No Opinion," or "Disagree" responses. Each set of responses defines a categorical variable, the first with two values and the second with three values. The analysis of this questionnaire data from many different people is the analysis of the proportion of responses for each of the values of one or more categorical variables.

Previous chapters presented a variety of issues of interest to managers regarding the statistical inference of means. These same issues apply to the analysis of categorical variables as well. Most questions regarding means also apply to proportions. Constructing a confidence interval around a proportion, evaluating the difference between two or more proportions, or examining the simultaneous relationship of a categorical grouping variable with a categorical response variable are as interesting to management as the corresponding questions regarding the means of numeric variables.

Further, metric data from the measurements of continuous variables are often presented in grouped categories. Although income may have been measured originally to the nearest dollar or hundred dollars, it may be reported in large summary categories such as Low ($10,000 to $25,000), Medium ($25,000 to $40,000), and so forth. In this situation, the analysis of a continuous variable is reduced to the analysis of data classified into categories.

This chapter addresses managerial questions about a categorical response variable Y. Previous chapters presented statistical inference of the mean for a numeric response variable or a mean difference of two numeric response variables. We are now ready to apply statistical inference to categorical response variables.

7.1 MAKING INFERENCES REGARDING THE SAMPLE PROPORTION

Eye color is a categorical variable because its values are discrete, nonnumeric labels such as Blue, Brown, and Green. The proportion of occurrence for a value of a categorical variable, such as the proportion of people with Brown eyes is also a mean, as shown next. Because proportions are means, constructing a confidence interval around a sample proportion follows the same basic logic as the confidence interval around the sample mean. The key insight here is the indicator variable.

Indicator Variables

> **indicator variable (or dummy variable)**
> *variable with values only of 0 and 1, which respectively represent no occurrence and occurrence of the category of interest*

To show that the proportion is a mean, suppose that 300 out of a sample of 500 people have Brown eyes. That is, the sample proportion p is .60. Suppose the first and second people have Brown eyes, the third person does not, the fourth person does, and so on. To compute a sample mean from these data, define a new variable Y. This transformed variable—or **indicator variable**—has a value of 1 for every eye color of Brown and a 0 for any other color. Compute the sample mean from the indicator variable Y as

$$\overline{Y} = \frac{\sum Y}{n} = \frac{1 + 1 + 0 + 1 + \ldots + 0 + 1}{500} = \frac{300}{500} = .60 = p.$$

That is, $\overline{Y} = p$. The summation of the values of Y, the numerator of the mean, is just a counting of the number of people with Brown eyes. The result is that the mean of the indicator variable Y is the proportion of 1's, which in this example is the proportion of people in the sample with Brown eyes.

This result is quite general. When applied to population or sample data, respectively, this relationship is

$$\mu_Y \equiv \frac{\sum Y}{N} = \pi \quad \text{or} \quad \overline{Y} \equiv \frac{\sum Y}{n} = p,$$

where π is the population proportion. One way to obtain the proportion is to count the values of a categorical variable in a frequency distribution (Chapter 2). The proportion can also be obtained from the mean of the corresponding indicator variable, such as the mean of these 500 values of 0 and 1.

The standard deviation of any variable Y, including an indicator variable Y, can be obtained from the usual expressions based on squared deviations,

$$\sigma_Y \equiv \sqrt{\frac{\sum (Y - \mu_Y)^2}{N}} \quad \text{or} \quad s_Y \equiv \sqrt{\frac{\sum (Y - \overline{Y})^2}{n - 1}}.$$

However, the standard deviation of an indicator variable Y can also be expressed in terms of the proportion of successes.

The population standard deviation of indicator variable Y is

$$\sigma_Y = \sqrt{\pi(1 - \pi)},$$

with corresponding sample standard deviation

$$s_Y = \sqrt{p(1 - p)}\sqrt{\frac{n}{n - 1}}.$$

This expression for s_Y contains $\sqrt{\dfrac{n}{n - 1}}$, which is algebraically equivalent to dividing the sum of squared deviations by $n - 1$ instead of by n.

For 300 Brown eyes out of a sample of 500, the estimated standard deviation of indicator variable Y is

$$s_Y = \sqrt{.6(1 - .6)}\sqrt{\frac{500}{499}} = \sqrt{.24}\sqrt{1.002} = \sqrt{.24048} \approx .49.$$

If the proportion is known, then the standard deviation of the indicator variable Y can be computed directly, without applying the more general but also more cumbersome expression based on the squared deviations.

Confidence Interval around a Sample Proportion

The sample mean $\overline{Y}$ is a random variable with a normal distribution. The sample proportion p is a special example of the sample mean, so it also is a random variable that varies from sample to sample. Consider the eye color example. From a sample of 500, 300 people had Brown eyes. Although the sample proportion is $p = .60$, the corresponding population proportion π is unknown. Presumably π is somewhere around .60, though another sample of 500 voters might yield $p = .59$, a third sample might yield $p = .64$, and so forth. To use p as the basis for inference, follow the usual procedure for any random variable of interest: Find its mean, standard deviation (error), and distribution shape over repeated samples, just as $\overline{Y}$ was analyzed in Chapter 4.

When constructing a confidence interval around the sample proportion p, the proportion is either given or computed from the data. The calculation of s_Y follows from p. Once s_Y is known, compute the estimated standard error of the proportion (mean) from the usual expression,

$$s_{\overline{Y}} = s_p = \frac{s_Y}{\sqrt{n}}.$$

What is true for the mean is true for the proportion.

In large samples, the distribution of the sample proportion p is *approximately* normal. How large should sample size n be before this approximation is attained?

The answer depends on how close the proportion is to its extreme values of 0 or 1. The closer p is to .5, the smaller the value of n required.

> When $np > 5$ and $n(1 - p) > 5$, p is approximately normal.

Expressed in terms of frequencies, np is simply the frequency of occurrences and $n(1 - p)$ is the frequency of nonoccurrences. When these conditions are met, normal curve probabilities can be used to establish the range of typical variation of p.

Given knowledge of the distribution of p, a confidence interval around p is constructed with the same techniques that place such an interval around the sample mean. When p is (approximately) normal, about 95% of all 95% confidence intervals around a *sample* proportion will contain the population proportion π.

> 95% confidence interval around a sample proportion:
> $$p \pm 1.96 s_p$$

This expression for a confidence interval around a sample proportion is almost identical to the corresponding expression for the sample mean. Unlike the analysis of metric data, however, even when σ_p is *not* known, the analysis of proportions assumes the normal distribution when $np > 5$ and $n(1 - p) < 5$. Accordingly, when assuming normality, use the $z_{.025} = 1.96$ cutoff to define the range of typical variation of the sample statistic of interest, which in this case is the proportion.

An example of a confidence interval around a sample proportion follows.

BUSINESS APPLICATION 7.1—Confidence Interval around a Sample Proportion

MANAGERIAL PROBLEM

Does the hiring policy for management positions yield the same proportion of male and female employees? The goal is to evaluate the policy instead of just the proportion of female employees hired from the most recent group of applicants.

DATA

Approximately the same number of males and females applied for the open management positions within a company, yet out of 93 people hired, 42 (45.2%) were female.

APPLICATION—CONCEPTUAL WORKSHEET

The data from which the calculations are based in the following conceptual worksheet are shaded in gray. This conceptual worksheet is excerpted from the Excel template called *PropInference* that is provided with this text. (The complete worksheet provides both an estimate of the population proportion with a confidence interval around the sample proportion as well as a test of an hypothesized value of the population proportion.)

Description	Name	Value	Formula
number of occurrences	n_occr	42	
sample size	n	93	
sample proportion	p	0.452	n_occr/n
sample standard deviation	stdev	0.500	SQRT(p*(1-p))*SQRT(n/(n-1))
both values must be	np	42	n*p
greater than 5	n(1-p)	51	n*(1-p)
confidence level	level	0.95	
standard error of the prop	sterr	0.052	stdev/SQRT(n)
z cutoff	zcut	1.960	-NORMINV((1-level)/2,0,1)
precision	E	0.102	sterr*zcut
lower bound of conf interval	LB	**0.350**	p-E
upper bound of conf interval	UB	**0.553**	p+E

APPLICATION—TRADITIONAL NOTATION

First check the normality assumption. The proportion of female employees hired during the last year is p, and n is sample size. From these 93 values with 42 successes, the sample proportion is

$$p \equiv \frac{\text{\# of occurrences}}{n} = \frac{42}{93} = .452.$$

If np and $n(1-p)$ are both larger than 5, then p is approximately normally distributed,

$$np = (93)(.452) = 42$$

$$n(1-p) = (93)(1-.452) = 51$$

Both values are larger than 5, so calculate the confidence interval with normal curve probabilities.

The estimated standard deviation of the corresponding indicator variable Y is

$$s_Y = \sqrt{p(1-p)}\sqrt{\frac{n}{n-1}}$$

$$= \sqrt{.452(1-.452)}\sqrt{\frac{93}{93-1}} = .500.$$

Calculate the estimated standard error of the mean (proportion) $s_{\overline{Y}}$ as

$$s_{\overline{Y}} = \frac{s_Y}{\sqrt{n}} = \frac{.500}{\sqrt{93}} \approx .052.$$

Next, find the cutoff value of Z for a 95% confidence interval, which corresponds to .025 of the distribution in each tail, $z_{.025} = 1.96$, which is the .975 quantile. The distance E from the sample proportion $p = .452$ to either end of the interval is 1.96 standard errors,

$$E = 1.960(s_{\overline{Y}}) = 1.96(.052) = .102.$$

Calculate the confidence interval by adding and subtracting E from $\overline{Y}$, where the sample mean $\overline{Y}$ is the same as the proportion p.

$$\text{Lower Bound: } \overline{Y} - 1.96\,(s_{\overline{Y}}) = .452 - .102 = .350$$

and

$$\text{Upper Bound: } \overline{Y} + 1.96\,(s_{\overline{Y}}) = .452 + .102 = .553$$

The population proportion π is likely between .350 and .553, with a 95% level of confidence. This confidence interval is

$$.553 - .350 = .203$$

wide.

APPLICATION—EXCEL BUILT-IN ANALYSIS

Although Excel does not directly compute a confidence interval around a sample proportion, the calculations for this statistic can be easily entered directly into the conceptual worksheet, as previously illustrated.

STATISTICAL PRINCIPLE

The evaluation of hiring policy bias is not limited to the description of any one sample. The goal is not to evaluate a particular sample of 93 people but to evaluate a general policy as implemented on *any* randomly selected group of applicants. Interest does not focus on the sample $p = .425$ as much as on the unobserved population proportion π, which is the proportion of females that would be hired with this process in the entire *population* of potential applicants.

The population proportion π is the value obtained if the random experiment of hiring 93 different people were repeated many times under identical circumstances. From only one sample of data, π cannot be identified exactly. However, the range that likely contains π is the 95% confidence interval around the sample proportion p.

MANAGERIAL INTERPRETATION

The true population proportion of women hired is probably somewhere between .35 and .55, as illustrated in Figure 7-1. In particular, this range includes .5, so the

Figure 7-1.
The confidence interval around the sample proportion .45.

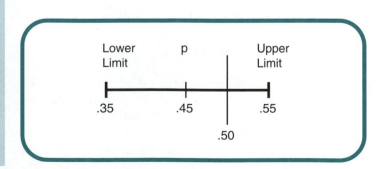

data are consistent with the assertion that an equal number of males and females are being hired in the population as a whole.

This result does not *prove* that the same number of males and females are being hired, but it does not render this value unlikely either. A larger sample size, or perhaps different kinds of data, such as that obtained from an analysis of the procedures used to screen applicants, may possibly provide additional information regarding the proportions of males and females hired.

The previous example focused on whether the confidence interval around the sample proportion contained the proportion $\pi = 0.5$. Testing a specific population value is an example of the form of statistical inference called hypothesis testing. The previous example demonstrated that a confidence interval provides a test of an hypothesized value of the proportion. The next section presents the formal hypothesis test of a proportion.

Hypothesis Tests of a Proportion

A proportion is simply a special case of a mean of the corresponding indicator variable Y with values of 0 and 1. That is, $\mu_Y = \pi$ for the population or $\overline{Y} = p$ for the sample. The hypothesized value remains μ_0, also referred to in this context as the population proportion π_0. The null hypothesis for a nondirectional test of a proportion is

$$H_0: \pi = \pi_0,$$

where π_0 is a constant between .00 and 1.00 inclusive.

For hypothesis testing of a proportion, focus on the *population* standard deviation σ_Y instead of on the sample standard deviation. The value of the population proportion π *determines* the population standard deviation σ_Y,

$$\sigma_Y = \sqrt{\pi(1 - \pi)},$$

which means that

$$\sigma_p = \sigma_{\overline{Y}} = \frac{\sigma_Y}{\sqrt{n}} = \sqrt{\frac{\pi(1 - \pi)}{n}}.$$

Assuming that π_0 is the correct value of the population proportion π implies a known standard error of the proportion σ_p.

Z-test statistic for the population proportion:

$$Z_p = \frac{p - \pi_0}{\sigma_p}, \text{ where } \sigma_p = \sqrt{\frac{\pi_0(1 - \pi_0)}{n}}$$

When σ_Y is known, use the z-distribution to obtain the cutoff value.

To perform the hypothesis test, after stating the null and alternative hypotheses, calculate the actual sample proportion p and the population standard deviation consistent with the null hypothesis σ_p. Next, compute the test statistic Z_p. Last, compute the p-value of the Z-test statistic, or the corresponding critical value, to formally evaluate the null hypothesis.

BUSINESS APPLICATION 7.2—Nondirectional Test of a Proportion

MANAGERIAL PROBLEM

An electrical equipment manufacturer received a shipment of circuit boards from a supplier. The company will not accept this shipment if the proportion of defective boards is greater than 3%, and management wants to commend the supplier if the proportion of defective boards is less than 3%. Management wants to know if the proportion of defective boards in the entire shipment of 16,000 is more or less than 3%, but testing all of the boards would be prohibitively expensive. Instead, a random sample of boards is tested.

STATISTICAL HYPOTHESIS

Null hypothesis H_0: $\pi = .03$.
Alternative hypothesis H_1: $\pi \neq .03$.

DATA

From a random sample of 200 boards (out of 16,000), 8 boards were defective.

NORMALITY ASSUMPTION

From these 200 values and 8 occurrences, the sample proportion is

$$p \equiv \frac{\text{\# of occurrences}}{n} = \frac{8}{200} = 0.04 \text{ boards.}$$

First make sure that p is approximately normally distributed. To do this, verify that the following two conditions are met:

$$np > 5 \quad \text{and} \quad n(1 - p) > 5.$$

In this case, both

$$np = (200)(0.04) = 8$$

and

$$n(1 - p) = (200)(1 - 0.04) = 192$$

are larger than 5, so proceed with the assumption of normality.

APPLICATION—CONCEPTUAL WORKSHEET

The data from which the calculations are based are shaded in gray. This conceptual worksheet is excerpted from the Excel template called *PropInference* that is provided with this text. (The complete worksheet provides both an estimate of the population proportion with a confidence interval around the sample proportion as well as a test of an hypothesized value of the population proportion.)

Description	Name	Value	Formula
number of occurrences	n_occr	8	
sample size	n	200	
sample proportion	p	0.040	n_occr/n
sample standard deviation	stdev	0.196	SQRT(p*(1-p))*SQRT(n/(n-1))
both values must be	np	8	n*p
greater than 5	n(1-p)	192	n*(1-p)
hypothesized proportion	pi0	0.03	
implied standard error	stderr0	0.012	SQRT((pi0*(1-pi0))/n)
observed value of Z	z	0.829	(p-pi0)/stderr0
upper tail cutoff of observed Z	uptail	0.204	1-NORMDIST(ABS(z),0,1,1)
two-tailed p-value	p-value	**0.407**	2*uptail

APPLICATION—TRADITIONAL NOTATION

The standard deviation of the corresponding indicator variable Y consistent with H_0 is

$$\sigma_Y = \sqrt{\pi_0 (1 - \pi_0)}$$

$$= \sqrt{0.03\,(1 - 0.03)} = 0.171 \text{ boards.}$$

Calculate the standard error of $\overline{Y}$ as

$$\sigma_p = \sigma_{\overline{Y}} = \frac{\sigma_Y}{\sqrt{n}} = \frac{0.171}{\sqrt{200}} \approx .012 \text{ boards.}$$

The calculation of the test statistic follows:

$$Z_p = \frac{p - \pi_0}{\sigma_p} = \frac{.04 - .03}{.012} = 0.83.$$

EVALUATION OF Z USING THE CUTOFF VALUE

The .025 cutoff is $z_{.025} = 1.96$. If in actuality μ_Y really does equal .03, then 95% of all sample means will lie within 1.96 standard errors of .03. If the obtained Z-value is larger than 1.96 or smaller than –1.96, the hypothesized value of .03 is considered unreasonable. However, $Z_p = 0.83$ is *less than* 1.96 in magnitude, so p is within the 95% range of variation around .03. That is, the data are consistent with the hypothesized value.

EVALUATION OF Z USING THE p-VALUE

Assuming that the null hypothesis is true, what is the probability of obtaining a Z-value larger than 0.83? From the Z-table, if the null hypothesized value is true, the probability of obtaining a value of Z at least as large as $Z = 0.83$ in magnitude is about .20.

Because this is a two-tailed test, apply the same probability of .20 to both tails. What is the probability of obtaining a Z-value smaller than -0.83 *or* larger than 0.83? The p-value is twice the value of the cutoff for one tail,

$$p\text{-value} \approx .203 + .203 \approx .41.$$

The data are consistent with the hypothesized value because the sample value of p is within the 95% range of variation around .03.

APPLICATION—EXCEL BUILT-IN ANALYSIS

Excel does not calculate a one-sample hypothesis test for the population proportion, but the calculations for this statistic can be easily entered directly into the worksheet, as previously shown.

MANAGERIAL INTERPRETATION

The data indicate that a 3% failure rate is a reasonable value for all 16,000 circuit boards received in the shipment.

The previous example was an hypothesis test that compared a sample proportion to an hypothesized value. The next section introduces tests that involve differences among two or more proportions.

EXERCISES

7-1. Consider five people: Bill, Jim, Sally, Sue, and Jeff.

Mechanical

a. Create the indicator variable for the value Male of the categorical variable Student.
b. Compute the proportion of males in the data set according to the definition of proportion (from the beginning of Chapter 2).
c. Compute the proportion of males in the data set according to the definition of the mean of the indicator variable Male.
d. Compute the standard deviation of the indicator variable Male.

7-2. Among 115 randomly selected adults from the local metropolitan area, 11 were unemployed. Construct and interpret the meaning of the confidence interval around the unemployment rate for a confidence level of

Application

a. 99%
b. 95%

7-3. The quality control manager for a machine shop wants to estimate the proportion of defective bushings from a batch of several thousand recently manufactured. A sample size of 40 yielded 6 defective bushings. Construct and interpret the meaning of the confidence interval around the proportion of defective bushings for a confidence level of

a. 99%
b. 95%

7-4. A grocery store chain is considering offering dinnerware at special prices to its customers but only if the customers are interested in the product. Management will offer the dinnerware if more than 10% of customers will purchase it. As a pilot test, the dinnerware is offered at three stores, and 16 out of 125 of customers purchased the dinnerware. Are more (or less) than 10% of all customers interested in the dinnerware?

Application

7-5. During the past five years, 38% of the applicants to an MBA program have been female. After an extensive advertising campaign targeting females, the school administration wondered if the percent of female applicants had changed. Of the 126 applicants to next year's class, 52 are female.

a. Determine if the percentage of female applicants changed with an hypothesis test.
b. Construct the 95% confidence interval around the sample proportion.

c. Determine if this interval contains the value of .38 and interpret the result.

7-6. Seventy-eight potential consumers of your company's latest product were asked if they would be likely to purchase the product at a price of $99.99. Fifty-three respondents answered yes. Test the hypothesis that two-thirds of all potential consumers would likely purchase the product.

7.2 COMPARING PROPORTIONS ACROSS TWO OR MORE SAMPLES

This section demonstrates how to evaluate the differences among the proportions of two or more groups. The test is based on a new statistic that has many applications for the analysis of categorical variables. Before presenting the statistical issues, however, first consider a prominent application of these analyses—the analysis of survey data.

Surveys

How does management know the child-care needs of the company's employees, or which group retirement plant employees favor, or which supervisor is most liked? Questions such as these are answered by conducting a **survey**—asking a sample of employees and tabulating the results. Designing and administering a set of questions regarding issues such as child-care needs to each employee in the sample is an example of conducting a survey.

> **survey**
> *systematic process of obtaining information from a population*

Survey data can be collected a variety of ways, such as by mail, telephone, or personal interview. Mail surveys work best when they are targeted to a specific group of interested people rather than to the general public. Most people do not bother to fill out a questionnaire unless they have a specific interest in the topic addressed by the survey. The telephone provides a relatively inexpensive means for obtaining information, particularly when the available phone numbers are representative of the corresponding population of interest. Personal interviews are more expensive but necessary for complex questionnaires.

Surveys can also be classified by their content. Some surveys measure attitudes and opinions. These surveys contain statements such as

A personal income tax should be replaced by a national sales tax.

    Strongly   Disagree   Agree   Strongly
    Disagree   Agree

Other surveys measure aspects of a person's personality or interests with statements such as

I prefer to stay home at night instead of going to a party.

    Almost   Sometimes   Almost
    Always   Never

Other survey statements may focus on demographic characteristics such as ethnic background, or other facts of a person's life such as personal income.

How are survey data analyzed? Some data analysts attach numerical scales to structured questionnaire responses, as illustrated in the two statements in the previous paragraph. For example, a Strongly Disagree can be coded as a 1, a Disagree coded as a 2, an Agree coded as a 3, and a Strongly Agree coded as a 4. The advantage of this approach is that statistics such as the mean and standard deviation can be computed for each question. The mean response to a question coded on a scale from 1 to 4 could be 3.4, for example, which indicates that most people tended to agree or strongly agree with the statement.

Other analysts prefer to code structured responses to statements on a survey as categorical variables. These analysts argue that such responses are not truly numeric. Instead of analyzing the responses of a single variable in terms of means and standard deviations, they analyze the proportion of responses to each response category. For example, what proportion of people chose the response Strongly Agree?

What about the relationship between *two* categorical variables. Do people who want to replace the income tax with a sales tax tend to vote Democratic or Republican? Do people who prefer to stay home at night instead of going out tend to prefer expensive, trendy clothes or more basic, inexpensive clothes? Answering questions such as these is based on the analysis of the relationship between two categorical variables, the topic of the next section.

Two-Way Contingency Tables

> **two-way contingency table**
> *frequencies of the occurrence of each combination of the values of two categorical variables*

Categorical variables have a limited set of values, so the possible number of pairs of values of two categorical variables is usually small. A **two-way contingency table** displays the relationship, simply listing the number of occurrences—the frequencies—of each potential *pair* of values. Contingency tables are also called *cross-tabulation tables* or *cross-tabs tables*. A table is identified by the number of levels of each of the categorical variables. For example, a 3 × 2 table defines six individual cells: three levels of one categorical variable and two levels of the other. The data for each of the cells are frequencies.

A contingency table provides the answer to a simple question such as, "Which supplier has the greater percentage of defective parts?" The contingency table in Figure 7-2 illustrates the differences in the good and defective parts of two companies. Company *A* provided 6 defectives (and 146 acceptable parts) out of 152 parts, a sample proportion of defectives of $p_A = 0.0395$. Company *B* supplied 10 defectives (and 137 acceptable parts) out of 147 parts for a sample proportion of defectives of $p_B = 0.0680$. Although the sample proportions are reasonably discrepant, can the corresponding population proportions be shown to be different?

The two groups represent two distinct populations, defined as the two companies, from which the corresponding samples were derived. Company is the *grouping variable,* because the value of Company defines the group that the part is assigned to. Quality is the *response variable* in this analysis, defined as the two response categories, Accept and Defective.

Chi-Square Test

The analysis of contingency table data requires the marginal frequencies, the row and column totals, plus the grand total. Figure 7-3 illustrates these marginals for a

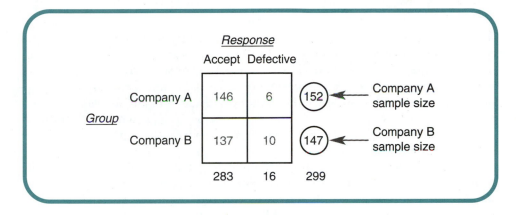

Figure 7-2.
Two-way contingency table of Company and Quality of Part.

Figure 7-3.
Marginal totals for the two-way contingency table of Company and Quality of Part.

contingency table with only two groups, Companies A and B, and two responses, Accept and Defective. The marginal totals for the two companies are their respective sample sizes.

The inferential statistical analysis of these contingency table data is called the χ^2 **test of homogeneity.** The null hypothesis for this test specifies equal population proportions of defective parts across the two groups, or, equivalently, equal population proportions of acceptable parts. If π is the *population* proportion of defective parts, the null hypothesis is that the proportion of defective parts for Company A, π_A, is the same as the proportion of defective parts for Company B, π_B. That is, H_0: $\pi_A - \pi_B = 0$.

The distinguishing feature of a contingency table that is subject to the test of homogeneity is that the responses are analyzed for two or more groups of observations. Each group is a sample from a *separate* population, and each corresponding marginal total is equal to the sample size of the respective group. These sample sizes are established *before* data analysis begins.

A crucial assumption must be met before the analyst can conduct the χ^2 test.

> *The χ^2 test is valid only when all cell frequencies are larger than five.*

This assumption is a version of the requirement that both $np > 5$ and $n(1 - p) > 5$ must be true before the sample proportion p, computed from a single sample of

test of homogeneity of distributions
evaluates the null hypothesis of identical proportions at each level of the categorical response variable across samples

Table 7-1.
Computing the observed
value of the chi-square
χ^2 statistic.

Description	Formula
1. For each cell, subtract the expected frequency from the observed frequency	$O - E$
2. For each cell, square the difference.	$(O - E)^2$
3. For each cell, divide the squared difference by the expected frequency	$\dfrac{(O - E)^2}{E}$
4. Sum the preceding term over all cells	$\chi^2_{obs} = \Sigma \left[\dfrac{(O - E)^2}{E} \right]$

size n, is normally distributed. The proportion p is simply the frequency of occurrences of the value of interest divided by the sample size n. That is, $np > 5$ means that the frequency of occurrences is greater than five. Similarly, the frequency of nonoccurrences must also be greater than five for the sample proportion to be approximately normally distributed. For contingency tables of any size with any specified number of groups, all cell frequencies must be greater than five to properly proceed with the χ^2 test, a requirement (barely) met by these data, in which the smallest cell frequency is six.

The test for homogeneity is just one application of a general procedure for the analysis of categorical response variables. This general procedure compares the observed frequency for each cell (the data) with the frequency expected from the null hypothesis. Assuming a true null hypothesis of no difference in population proportions, $\pi_A - \pi_B = 0$, the **chi-square statistic** approximately follows what is called the chi-square, or χ^2, distribution over repeated samples. The observed value of chi-square, χ^2_{obs}, is calculated from the contingency table and is compared with the χ^2 distribution over repeated samples.

Table 7-1 outlines the steps for computing χ^2_{obs}.

What are the expected frequencies of defective parts for each company assuming the null hypothesis of no difference in the proportions across groups? First obtain the estimated proportion of defective parts common to both companies under the null hypothesis. Out of 299 parts over both groups, 15 were defective, so the overall proportion of defective parts is

observed chi-square
statistic χ^2_{obs}
sum of the quantity
of the squared
difference of
observed and
expected frequencies
divided by the
expected frequency

$$p_{DFCT} = \frac{16}{299} = 0.0535.$$

Company A had 152 parts, so the frequency of defective parts most consistent with the null hypothesis for Company A is 5.35% of 152, or

Company A: $n_{DFCT} = (p_{DFCT})(152) = (0.0535) = 8.134.$

The frequency of defective parts for Company B most consistent with the null hypothesis is

Company B: $n_{DFCT} = (p_{DFCT})(147) = (0.0535) = 7.866.$

Because the sample sizes for the two groups differ, the expected frequencies differ under the null hypothesis of the *same* proportion of defective parts for both companies.

Similarly, calculate expected frequencies for the two cells that display the counts for the acceptable parts. From these observed and expected frequencies, calculate the χ^2 statistic as outlined in the preceding table.

		Obs	Exp	Diff	Diffsq	DfSq/Exp
Cmp	Quality	O	E	$O - E$	$(O - E)^2$	$(O - E)^2/E$
A	GOOD	146	143.866	2.134	4.553	0.032
A	BAD	6	8.134	-2.134	4.553	0.560
B	GOOD	137	139.134	-2.134	4.553	0.033
B	BAD	10	7.866	2.134	4.553	0.579
		299				**1.203**

The computed χ^2 statistic for the given contingency table is $\chi^2_{obs} = 1.203$. Interpret this value within the context of the entire distribution of such values obtained with repeated sampling from the same two populations. This repeated sampling would occur given the null hypothesis of no difference in the proportion of defective parts from the two companies.

What is the shape of the χ^2 distribution? As with t-distributions, there is a family of χ^2 distributions, one distribution for each degree of freedom. The degrees of freedom is the number of expected frequencies that are free to vary given the row and column marginal totals.

> *df for a contingency table with r rows and c columns:*
> $$df = (r - 1)(c - 1)$$

For a 2×2 contingency table, $df = (1)(1) = 1$. Set the row and column marginal totals; there is only one expected frequency for a 2×2 table that can be obtained before the values of the remaining three expected frequencies are fixed. Although the unnumbered table above displays four expected frequencies, one for each cell, only one of these is free to vary. Once any one of these expected frequencies is known, the values of the remaining frequencies are determined from the marginals.

Only the right-hand tail of the χ^2 distribution is of interest because all values of the distribution are positive. How extreme is the obtained value of $\chi^2_{obs} = 1.203$ for $df = 1$? As shown in Figure 7-4, the p-value is .273, which renders the obtained value reasonable given the null hypothesis of no difference. This figure also shows that this observed value is well below the .05 cutoff value, obtained from Appendix C, of $\chi^2_{.05} = 3.841$, so the null hypothesis cannot be rejected. The observed proportion of defects from the two companies is not sufficiently different to support the conclusion that Company B does a better job.

The shape of the χ^2 distribution for $df = 1$ does not represent the shape of other χ^2 distributions, as illustrated in Figure 7-5. As df increases, the χ^2 distribution approximates a normal distribution, with some skew in the right-hand tail.

Our completed example of the χ^2 test of homogeneity involved only two groups, with a response variable defined by only two levels. In this example, no difference in the proportion of defective parts is equivalent to no difference in the proportion of good parts. The χ^2 test can, however, be applied much more broadly.

Figure 7-4.
The χ^2 distribution for
$df = 1$, and the observed
and $.05\chi^2$ values.

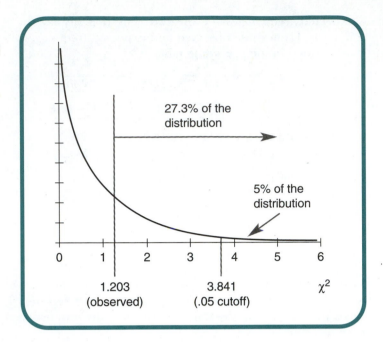

Figure 7-5.
Three chi-square
distributions.

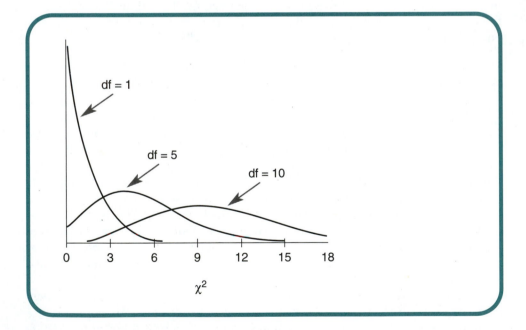

The test applies to as many groups as specified for as many response categories as is applicable. The observed value χ^2_{obs} is calculated the same way for these tests. First, assume the null hypothesis of no difference at *each* level of the response variable, compute the corresponding frequencies expected from this assumption, and then obtain the observed χ^2 statistic and *p*-value by comparing the observed and expected frequencies.

Strength of Relationship

Evaluation of the null hypothesis of no group differences indicates whether there is a relationship between the grouping and response variables. An hypothesis test, however, does not demonstrate the *strength* of this relationship. The strength of a relationship refers to the predictability of the value of one variable from another variable. Does knowledge of the value of one variable lead to a successful prediction of knowledge of the value of the other variable?

Consider again the two categorical variables Company and Quality. If you know the company that shipped the part, how successfully can you predict the quality of the part? Consider the extreme example in which the relationship between Company and Quality is perfect. All parts shipped by Company *A* are defective, and all parts shipped by Company *B* are acceptable. Or, stated in terms of proportions of defective parts, $p_A = 1.00$ and $p_B = 0.00$. In this situation, knowledge of the value of one variable, Company, leads to perfect prediction of the second variable, Quality. If you know the company, you know the quality.

Now consider the other extreme with unrelated variables. In this case, $p_A = p_B$. The proportion of defective parts from each company is the same, so knowledge of the company provides no predictive knowledge regarding quality. The null hypothesis would not be rejected in this situation.

Actual data analysis, of course, typically results in situations between these two extremes. The sample proportions are usually not equal, so some relationship between the variables is indicated in the sample data. When the null hypothesis is rejected with a small *p*-value, such as less than 0.05, the sample proportions are sufficiently distinct from each other that a relationship between the variables is concluded to exist in the population.

As shown below, however, the size of the *p*-value reflects both the strength of the relationship and the sample size. For very large samples, even weak relationships are detected with small *p*-values. A new statistic is needed that reflects only the degree to which the variables are related.

Cramer's V indicates strength of association between the two categorical variables that define the contingency table. Cramer's V ranges from 0 to 1, with a 0 indicating no relationship and a 1 indicating a perfect relationship. Values of Cramer's V above .6 are usually interpreted as indicating a strong relationship. Values between .4 and .6 indicate a reasonably strong relationship, and values between .2 and .4 indicate a moderate relationship. Values between .1 and .2 indicate a weak relationship, and values below .1 indicate that the two categorical variables are virtually not related. Of course, the value of Cramer's V calculated from a sample is only an estimate of the value that would be calculated if the entire population was available.

> **estimated Cramer's V**
> $$\hat{V} = \sqrt{\frac{\chi^2}{MN}},$$
> *where M is the smaller of r − 1 or c − 1, and N is the total sample size*

To illustrate, consider the previous example in which 152 parts were sampled from Company *A* and 147 parts were sampled from Company *B*. Cramer's V is zero when 31 parts from Company *A* are defective and 30 defective parts come from Company B. In this case, the respective sample proportions are identical at .20 to within rounding error. If 51 defectives are from Company *A* and only 30 from Company B, the respective sample proportions are .34 and .20, which leads to a Cramer's V of 0.148. When the sample proportions are as discrepant as .60 and .07, Cramer's V jumps to 0.561. Finally, if all 152 parts from Company *A* are defective, and all 147 parts from Company *B* are acceptable, Cramer's V indicates a perfect relationship at 1.00.

Table 7-2.
Required sample size to reject the null hypothesis for the specified strength of association between grouping and response variables.

Cramer's V	Needed N
0.500	15
0.400	24
0.300	43
0.200	96
0.100	384
0.050	1,536
0.010	38.400

Examining the expression for Cramer's V helps to clarify the distinction between a rejected null hypothesis and the size of the relationship. Algebraically rearranging terms from the expression for Cramer's V results in the following expression for sample size N:

$$N = \frac{\chi^2}{V^2 M}.$$

For a sufficiently large sample, a significant χ^2_{obs} can be obtained for *any* strength of association, no matter how small. Consider a 2×2 contingency table, so that $M = 2 - 1 = 1$. Df is 1 and the corresponding .05 cutoff is $\chi^2_{.05} = 3.84$. Table 7-2 shows that for a strong relationship between the grouping and response variables, only a small sample size is needed to correctly reject the null hypothesis. This table also shows, however, that even for a strength of relationship as small as .01, the null hypothesis tends to be rejected for a sample size of 38,400 or more.

The following example of the test of homogeneity and Cramer's V also involves two groups, but it generalizes to three levels of the response variable.

BUSINESS APPLICATION 7.3—Test of Homogeneity

MANAGERIAL PROBLEM

A clothing manufacturer specializes in a line of outdoor wear for touring motorcyclists, those who ride large motorcycles for long distances. Most of those who purchase this riding gear own Honda Gold Wing or BMW motorcycles.

One source of sales is at motorcycle trade shows and rallies. When attending one of these shows or rallies, management wants to stock the specific products most likely to sell to the owner of the corresponding type of motorcycle. Three types of nylon jackets are available; the difference is in the thickness of the weave, which is 1,000 denier, 500 denier, or 200 denier. The trade-off is between the protection against falls offered by the extremely thick, heavy, and rigid 1,000 denier versus the light, compact 200 denier material from which most ordinary outdoor jackets are constructed. Is the thickness of the material worn by the rider related to the type of his or her motorcycle?

STATISTICAL HYPOTHESIS

Null hypothesis H_0 of equal population proportions *within* each response category:

for 200 denier (LITE), $\pi_{HONDA,200} = \pi_{BMW,200}$

for 500 denier (MED), $\pi_{HONDA,500} = \pi_{BMW,500}$

for 1,000 denier (THICK), $\pi_{HONDA,1,000} = \pi_{BMW,1,000}$

Alternative hypothesis H_1: At least one set of proportions is not equal.

DATA

The number of sales from last summer of each type of jacket and motorcycle were recorded (found in the file JACKET.DAT).

	A	B
1	Bike	Jacket
2	BMW	LITE
3	Honda	MED
4	Honda	MED
5	BMW	MED
6	BMW	MED
7	Honda	MED
8	BMW	THICK

	A	B
1023	Honda	THICK
1024	Honda	THICK
1025	BMW	LITE
1026	BMW	THICK

APPLICATION—EXCEL BUILT-IN ANALYSIS

Contingency Table

The body of the table lists the six observed frequencies for combinations of Bike and Jacket in Cells E3 to G4. The three column totals and two row totals are listed at the right and bottom margins of the table.

Count of Jacket	Jacket			
Bike	LITE	MED	THICK	Grand Total
BMW	129	134	155	418
Honda	232	197	178	607
Grand Total	361	331	333	1025

Obtaining the Contingency Table

Excel calls a contingency table a *pivot table*. Access the program from the Data menu.

Data ➤ PivotTable Report...

Step 1. Specify the source of the data, which is the worksheet.

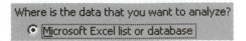

Step 2. Specify the range of the data, including the labels. This range can be entered on the keyboard, or it will be entered automatically if any data cell was selected before entering the Pivot Table program.

Step 3. Define the rows and columns of the pivot table. First drag the Bike box at the top right corner over to the Row area, and then drag the Jacket box at the top right corner to the Column area. Finally, drag the same Jacket box at the top right corner over to the Data area.

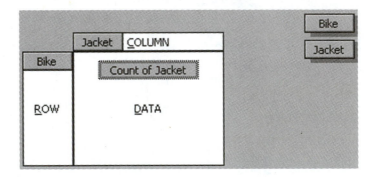

Step 4. Specify the starting cell of the output.

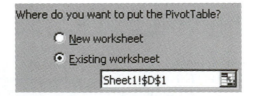

Computing Expected Frequencies

Excel does not calculate the expected frequencies under the null hypothesis required by the χ^2 test. Instead, calculate these frequencies from the information in the contingency table. First verify that all observed frequencies are five or above, in which case analysis can proceed.

Copy the value labels and marginal frequencies from the contingency table to another location. The data in the cells of the table will also be copied, but this information can be deleted by selecting these cells in the new table and pushing the Delete key. Be careful *not* to copy the variable labels Bike and Jacket. Variable labels define the range of cells as a contingency table (or pivot table in Excel terminology), and the individual cells of a pivot table cannot be modified.

	D	E	F	G	H
8		LITE	MED	THICK	Grand Total
9	BMW				418
10	Honda				607
11	Grand Total	361	331	333	1025

Assuming the null hypothesis of equal group population proportions *within* each response category, each expected frequency is the product of the corresponding row and column marginals divided by the total frequency. For example, for BMW owners with jackets of 200 denier (LITE), the expected frequency is

$$\text{expected freq. for BMW owners with LITE jackets} = \frac{(361)(418)}{1025} = 147.22.$$

A formula to calculate the expected frequency given the null hypothesis can be entered individually into each of the six cells. Or the following formula can be entered into the BMW,LITE cell.

```
=(E$11*$H9)/$H$11.
```

The $ sign indicates that the row or column reference should be held constant while filling down or filling right. Using the $ allows the formula in the cell to be filled right into the selected cells with the menu sequence Edit ➤ Fill ➤ Right and filled down with Edit ➤ Fill ➤ Down. All six expected frequencies follow.

	D	E	F	G	H
8		LITE	MED	THICK	Grand Total
9	BMW	147.22	134.98	135.80	418
10	Honda	213.78	196.02	197.20	607
11	Grand Total	361	331	333	1025

Test of Homogeneity

From these expected frequencies and observed frequencies, calculate the *p*-value of the observed χ^2 statistic χ^2_{obs} with the Excel χ^2 test function, CHITEST. This function is defined in terms of the range of actual (observed) frequencies and the expected frequencies,

```
=CHITEST(actual_values,expected_values).
```

The function call in this example is

```
=CHITEST(E3:G4,E9:G10),
```

which yields a p-value for χ^2_{obs} of 0.0150. The null hypothesis of equal group population proportions within each response category is rejected for $\alpha = .05$. The preference for the thickness of the nylon used to construct the jacket depends on the type of motorcycle owned.

Strength of Association

Excel does not provide an index of the strength of association such as Cramer's V. The calculation of Cramer's V requires the test statistic χ^2_{obs}. The CHITEST function provides the corresponding p-value, but not the value of the test statistic. To obtain χ^2_{obs}, use the inverse χ^2 function on the obtained p-value, which is

$$=\text{CHIINV(probability,df)}.$$

The p-value is stored in cell B22, with degrees of freedom

$$df = (3-1)(2-1) = (2)(1) = 2.$$

The function call,

$$=\text{CHIINV(B22,2)},$$

returns 8.4033, so $\chi^2_{obs} = 8.4033$.

Cramer's V also requires the total number of observations, $N = 299$, and the smaller of the number of rows minus one and the number of columns minus one, which is $M = r - 1 = 1$. The estimate of Cramer's V is

$$\hat{V} = \sqrt{\frac{\chi^2}{MN}} = \sqrt{\frac{8.403}{(1)(1025)}} = 0.0905.$$

APPLICATION—TRADITIONAL NOTATION

The previous Excel section presented the observed frequencies and expected frequencies under the null hypothesis. From these expected and observed frequencies, compute the χ^2 statistic χ^2_{obs} for the test of homogeneity.

Bike	Denier	Obs O	Exp E	Diff $O-E$	Diffsq $(O-E)^2$	DfSq/Exp $(O-E)^2/E$
HONDA	THIN	232	213.8	18.2	331.88	1.552
HONDA	MED	197	196.0	1.0	0.97	0.005
HONDA	THICK	178	197.2	-19.2	368.68	1.870
BMW	THIN	129	147.2	-18.2	331.88	2.254
BMW	MED	134	135.0	-1.0	0.97	0.007
BMW	THICK	155	135.8	19.2	368.68	2.715
						8.403

χ^2_{obs} is 8.403. The corresponding cutoff value from Appendix C for $\alpha = .05$ with $(3-1)(2-1) = 2$ degrees of freedom is 5.99. Reject the null hypothesis of equal group population proportions. The preference for the thickness of the nylon used to construct the jacket depends on the type of motorcycle owned.

EXCEL GRAPHICAL ANALYSIS

Assessing the Excel Output

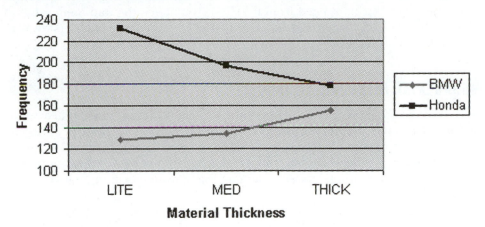

In this sample, motorcycle type and material preference are related. Honda users had a stronger preference for thinner material, and BMW users had a stronger preference for thicker material. The previous analysis demonstrated that this relationship generalizes to the population.

Obtaining the Output

Construct a line chart of these frequencies from the contingency table. Begin with the following menu sequence.

Insert ➤ Chart...

Step 1—Chart Type. Specify a Line chart, which is for a categorical (nonnumeric) horizontal axis. Then choose a format, such as the line with markers, to display each data value.

Step 2—Chart Source. For Data Range, specify the cells in the three rows and three columns that include the frequencies and the corresponding labels.

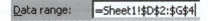

Step 3—Chart Options. Click on the Titles tab and name the Category and Value axes.

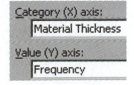

Step 4. Specify the location of the chart, either on a new sheet or as an object on the current worksheet.

The resulting Excel chart was modified by changing the scale of the vertical axis. The original scale ranged from 0 to 250. To change the minimum value to 100, double-click on the vertical axis, choose the Scale tab, and enter 100 next to the minimum prompt.

MANAGERIAL INTERPRETATION

BMW owners are more likely to choose the protection offered by the heavy-duty jackets made out of the thicker material, and Honda owners are more likely to prefer the compactness and lightness of the thinner, more flexible material. Although the relationship is somewhat weak, this trend in last summer's data apparently generalizes to future summers as well, assuming that consumers do not change their underlying preferences.

The previous example illustrated the test of homogeneity for two populations, with three levels of response within each population. The same technique generalizes to any specified number of populations and response levels. When the null hypothesis of no difference in proportions across populations is rejected, and the number of populations is larger than two, tests are needed to isolate where the differences occurred. Presentation of these tests is beyond the scope of this text, but there is a variety of possibilities.

This section showed how to use the χ^2 distribution to test for homogeneity of proportions across groups. However, the χ^2 distribution has more applications, as shown in the next section.

EXERCISES

7-7. Last year a survey revealed that 29% of all business undergraduates had access to a computer at home. This year the survey showed that 245 of 743 students had access to their own computer. Was there a change from last year to this year in the percentage of students with access to a home computer?

7-8. Last year, a radio station had 23% of the market. After increasing advertising, a sample of 150 listeners revealed that 38 listened to the station. Did market share increase?

7-9. An advertising manager placed ads in three different magazines. Two weeks after subscribers received the magazine, some subscribers to each (and only one) of the magazines were asked if they remembered the ad well, a little, or not at all. The data appear in the following contingency table.

		Response Remember...		
		Well	Little	None
	Magazine A	170	215	156
Group	Magazine B	80	67	39
	Magazine C	104	113	99

The goal is to evaluate potential differences in recall for the different magazines. Answer this question with a

a. chi-square test, including a statement of the null hypothesis

b. strength of association index

7-10. For the analysis of a 4×3 contingency table, what sample size is needed to reject the null hypothesis at the $\alpha = .05$ level when Cramer's V is

a.   .50
b.   .25
c.   .10

d.   What is the relationship between sample size and Cramer's V in terms of rejecting the null hypothesis?

e.   Why should Cramer's V always be reported when the null hypothesis is rejected?

7.3 EVALUATING PROPORTIONS IN ONE SAMPLE

The previous application of the χ^2 (chi-square) statistic compared proportions at each level of response across all groups. Each group was a sample from a distinct population. This section introduces two applications of the χ^2 statistic that involve only a *single* sample. Although the computation of χ^2_{obs} from a contingency table is the same for the previously covered test of homogeneity as it is for the tests introduced in this section, the meaning of the tests differs. For these one-sample tests, there is no grouping variable, only response variables. The first χ^2 test introduced in this section examines the association between two response variables. The second test focuses on the goodness of fit of a set of frequencies for a response variable to a specified distribution. We begin with a discussion of independence, which provides the needed background for understanding these tests.

Independent Events and Joint Events

INDEPENDENCE. The concept of independence is crucial to many aspects of statistical analysis. Two coin flips are **independent events** because whether the first coin lands heads or tails has no effect on whether the second coin lands heads or tails. We can express the independence of these events by using the language of **conditional probability.**

The | notation in the margin definition box means "given that" or "if." Two coin flips are independent events because

$$P(\text{head on flip 2} \mid \text{head on flip 1}) = P(\text{head on flip 2}).$$

That is, the probability of getting a head on the second flip is the *same* whether a head was obtained on the first flip or not.

Events that are not independent are dependent. For example, suppose you draw two cards from a shuffled card deck and you do *not* put the first card drawn back into the deck. The probability of drawing an ace for the second card is different depending on whether you drew an ace for the first card. There are 52 cards and 4 aces, so the *unconditional* probability of an ace is

$$P(\text{ace on first draw}) = \frac{4}{52} = .0769.$$

After the first draw, 51 cards remain. If you drew an ace the first time, then only 3 aces remain, so the probability of an ace appearing on the second draw is the conditional probability

$$P(\text{ace on second draw} \mid \text{an ace on first draw}) = \frac{3}{51} = .0588.$$

If you did not draw an ace the first time, then all 4 aces are left in the deck of the remaining 51 cards, so the probability of drawing an ace is

$$P(\text{ace on second draw} \mid \textit{not} \text{ an ace on first draw}) = \frac{4}{51} = .0784.$$

> **independent events**
> *occurrence or nonoccurrence of one event has no effect on the probability of the occurrence of the other event*

> **conditional probability of Event B on Event A, P(B | A)**
> *probability of event B given the outcome of event A*

Drawing cards from a deck without replacing the drawn cards and reshuffling results in a series of dependent events.

> *The conditional probability of a dependent event changes depending on what events previously occurred.*

In this example, the probability of drawing an ace on the second draw depends on whether an ace was drawn on the first draw.

In this text we deal almost entirely with independent events. The concept of a random experiment depends on repeated, independent repetitions of the experiment. The outcome of one repetition of the random experiment does not affect the outcomes of other independent repetitions.

JOINT EVENTS AND INTERSECTION. A pattern of joint events can also define a new event. If you sample two parts from the production line, what is the probability of obtaining one acceptable part *and* one defective part? In other words, what is the probability of an **intersection** between these two events?

> **intersection of Events A and B, Event [A *and* B]**
> *all values in both A and B*

Event [*A and B*] is the joint event that occurs when both *A* and *B* occur. Compute the probability of the joint event simply by multiplying the probabilities of the constituent independent events.

> If *Events A and B are independent, then the probability of their intersection is* $P(A$ and $B) = P(A)P(B)$.

An example illustrating this probability rule[1] follows.

STATISTICAL ILLUSTRATION—Probability of the Intersection of Independent Events

Only 60% of the computer chips produced by a specific manufacturer are good. If two chips are randomly sampled from the production line at two different time intervals, what is the probability that the first chip is defective *and* that the second chip is good?

The quality of the two chips is assumed to be independent because the chips were randomly selected from the production line at two different times. To compute the probability of this joint event, all we need is the probability of each of the two individual events. The probability of a good chip is 0.6. By the complement rule, the probability of a defective chip is

$$P(\text{defective chip}) = 1 - P(\text{good chip}) = 1 - 0.6 = 0.4.$$

Applying the probability rule for the intersection of independent events yields

$$P(\text{1st chip defective } and \text{ 2nd chip good}) = (0.4)(0.6) = 0.24$$

Almost one-fourth of all samples of two chips from the production line will produce a defective first chip and a good second chip.

---

1. The more general form of the preceding theorem applies to both dependent and independent events, but because we do not need to use this more general and more complex form, we do not present it in this text.

Note that in this problem the arbitrarily specified *order* of the chips was important; we were interested in samples in which the first chip was defective and the second chip was good.

The concept of independence is applied to categorical variables in the next section.

Testing Independence of Two Categorical Variables

Understanding the relationship between variables is vital to successful business decision making. For instance, is gender related to the number of promotions? That is, does knowing a person's gender lead to a better estimate of the number of promotions than not knowing gender?

Categorical variables are unrelated when their values are **independent.** When *A* and *B* are independent, the probability of an event—the response at a level of categorical variable *A*—is the same at *all* levels of variable *B*.

Consider the response to the third level of *A*, A_3 or three promotions, as illustrated in Figure 7-6. If *B* has two levels, Male and Female, then all conditional probabilities of event A_3 equal the unconditional probability.

$$P(A_3) = P(A_3 \mid B_1) = P(A_3 \mid B_2).$$

The probability of a third promotion is the same for males as it is for females *if* number of promotions and gender are independent. If these relationships hold for all levels of *A*, then variables *A* and *B* are independent—the level of *B* does not change the probability of any level of *A*.

The statistical test of the independence of two variables is based on the χ^2 distribution. Given the expected frequencies, this test is computationally identical to the test of homogeneity introduced in the previous section. Let A_i be the event of the *i*th response level of *A*, and B_j be the *j*th response level of *B*. Variables *A* and *B* are independent when the probability that both A_i and B_j occur—the joint event—is equal to the product of the probabilities of the separate events. The null hypothesis of independence is

$$H_0\text{: } P(A_i \text{ and } B_j) = P(A_i)P(B_j) \text{ for } all \text{ levels of } A \text{ and } B.$$

Figure 7-7 illustrates these relationships for a true null hypothesis in which variable *A* has three levels and variable *B* has two levels. The key aspect of the null hypothesis is that the joint probabilities, or the expected probabilities *within* the body of the table, are obtained from the marginal probabilities.

> **independence of categorical variables A and B**
> *proportion of the* total *population at any response level of A equals the proportion at* each *of the response levels of B*

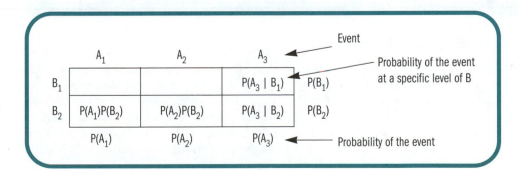

Figure 7-6.
Conditional and unconditional probabilities of event A_3.

Figure 7-7.
Cell probabilities
expected from the null
hypothesis of
independence.

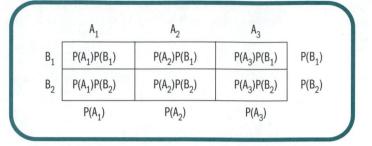

	A_1	A_2	A_3	
B_1	$P(A_1)P(B_1)$	$P(A_2)P(B_1)$	$P(A_3)P(B_1)$	$P(B_1)$
B_2	$P(A_1)P(B_2)$	$P(A_2)P(B_2)$	$P(A_3)P(B_2)$	$P(B_2)$
	$P(A_1)$	$P(A_2)$	$P(A_3)$	

test of independence
*evaluates the null
hypothesis that two
categorical variables
are unrelated, or
independent*

In sample data, the marginal population probabilities (or proportions) are estimated by the sample proportions. For example, $P(A_1)$ is estimated by the proportion of all observations at level A_1, which is the marginal frequency of A_1 divided by the total sample size. Once all marginal probabilities are obtained, calculate the joint probabilities consistent with the null hypothesis to perform the **test of independence.**

From the expected frequencies, calculate χ^2_{obs} the same as for the test of homogeneity. Obtain each expected frequency by multiplying the corresponding expected probability by the total sample size. Calculate the sum of each of the squared differences between the observed and expected frequencies with each squared difference divided by the expected frequency. Calculate the degrees of freedom as $(r-1)(c-1)$.

Conceptually, the tests of homogeneity and independence have different meanings. The test of homogeneity is based on *multiple* samples from multiple populations. The marginal for each of the groups represents the group sample size and is fixed before data analysis begins. The samples are obtained, the sample sizes are set, and then the responses are analyzed for each of the samples. In contrast, the test of independence is based on analyzing the relation between attributes of two categorical variables for a *single* sample. For the test of independence, all marginals are random variables, their values determined during data analysis.

An example of the test of independence follows. Note that the test of independence illustrated below is computationally identical to the previously illustrated test of homogeneity. Because the Excel procedures for these tests are identical, the Excel inputs in this example are not presented in detail, as they were in the previous example.

BUSINESS APPLICATION 7.4—Test of Independence

MANAGERIAL PROBLEM

A large consumer products company that offers different brands of laundry detergent wants to market each brand to a distinct market segment. Management hypothesized that more "sophisticated" consumers purchase detergent on the basis of "rational" considerations such as the ecological issues, the amount and type of whiteners in the detergent, and the appropriateness of the detergent for the local water hardness. The "regular" consumer's purchase is hypothesized to be more impulsive, based on considerations such as price and package color.

To gather evidence for or against this alleged market segmentation, consumers of the company's products were surveyed regarding the sophistication of their laundry procedures and knowledge. For example, one question assessed the extent to which the consumer tailored the water temperature to the type of wash. Some consumers carefully sort their laundry into white, colors, and delicate, and then wash in hot, warm, or cold water, respectively; others just throw the most recent pile of laundry into the washer, paying little or no attention to temperature. Another question queried knowledge about local water hardness. Does the consumer know whether the local water is hard, medium, or soft?

Management wanted to know how many people can be categorized in a specific market segment based on their responses to the survey. Management also wanted to know whether questions such as these are related, in other words, indicative of a more global construct of laundry washing sophistication. If some people tend to provide the "sophisticated" answer to a core group of questions, then responses to these questions could define this market segment.

STATISTICAL HYPOTHESIS

Null hypothesis H_0: knowledge of water hardness and varies water temperature are independent

Alternative hypothesis H_1: knowledge of water hardness and varies water temperature are dependent (associated)

DATA

Responses were collected from 107 people (found in the file WATER.DAT). The values for varies temperature begin with a digit so that they will be placed in order in the subsequent contingency table. Excel alphabetizes the values, and the categories should be listed in order of magnitude: Always, Some, and Rare.

	A	B
1	Hardness	Temp
2	No	3Rare
3	No	3Rare
4	No	2Some
5	No	1Always
105	No	2Some
106	No	3Rare
107	Yes	1Always
108	No	1Always

APPLICATION—EXCEL ANALYSIS

Contingency Table

Excel calls a contingency table a *pivot table;* obtain it from the Data menu.

Data ➤ PivotTable...

Step 1. Specify the source of the data, which is the worksheet.

Step 2. Specify the range of the data, including the labels.

Step 3. First drag the Hardness box at the top right corner over to the Row area, and then drag the Temp box at the top right corner to the Column area. Finally, drag the same Temp box at the top right corner over to the Data area.

Step 4. Specify the starting cell of the output.

Count of Temp	Temp			
Hardness	1Always	2Some	3Rare	Grand Total
No	21	28	29	78
Yes	15	9	5	29
Grand Total	36	37	34	107

Expected Frequencies

First verify that all observed frequencies are five or above. Then compute the expected frequencies from the expected probabilities.

Assuming the null hypothesis of independence, each expected probability is the product of the corresponding row and column marginal probabilities. For example, for the response category Know Water Hardness *and* Always Adjust Water Temperature, the probability of occurrence assuming independence is estimated as

$$p_{know,always} = p_{know} p_{always} = \left(\frac{29}{107}\right)\left(\frac{36}{107}\right) = (.271)(.336) = 0.091.$$

Figure 7-8 presents all six expected joint probabilities and the corresponding marginals.

The expected frequency for the response category Know Water Hardness *and* Always Adjust Water Temperature is

$$\text{Expected Freq} = (n)\, p_{know,always} = (107)(.091) = 9.737.$$

The following worksheet lists all six expected frequencies and associated marginal frequencies in Cells E9 to G10.

	1Always	2Some	3Rare	Grand Total
No	26.24	26.97	24.79	78
Yes	9.76	10.03	9.21	29
Grand Total	36	37	34	107

Test of Independence

From these expected frequencies and observed frequencies, calculate the *p*-value of the observed χ^2 statistic χ^2_{obs} with the Excel χ^2 test function CHITEST. This function is defined in terms of the range of actual (observed) frequencies and the expected frequencies,

```
=CHITEST(actual_values,expected_values).
```

The function call in this example is

```
=CHITEST(E3:G4,E9:G10),
```

	Adjust water temperature			
	Always	Sometimes	Rarely	
Know hardness	.091	.094	.086	.271
Do not know hardness	.245	.252	.232	.729
	.336	.346	.318	1.000

Figure 7-8. Expected probabilities of each response (margins), and the corresponding joint probabilities (cells) assuming independence.

which yields a p-value for χ^2_{obs} of 0.036. Reject the null hypothesis of no association between knowledge of water hardness and varies water temperature for $\alpha = .05$.

Strength of Association

Excel does not provide an index of the strength of association between the variables such as Cramer's V. The observed value of χ^2, χ^2_{obs} is needed to compute Cramer's V. To obtain χ^2_{obs}, use the inverse χ^2 function CHIINV on the p-value for $df = (3-1)(2-1) = 2$, which returns $\chi^2_{obs} = 6.654$.

To estimate Cramer's V, note that the total number of observations is $N = 107$, and the smaller of the number of rows minus one and the number of columns minus one is $M = r - 1 = 2 - 1 = 1$. Estimate Cramer's V as

$$\hat{V} = \sqrt{\frac{\chi^2}{MN}} = \sqrt{\frac{6.654}{(1)(107)}} = \sqrt{0.0622} = 0.249.$$

APPLICATION—TRADITIONAL NOTATION

Calculate χ^2_{obs} from the given expected frequencies and observed frequencies.

		Obs	Exp	Diff	Diffsq	DfSq/Exp
Hrdns	Temp	O	E	$O - E$	$(O - E)^2$	$(O - E)^2/E$
Yes	Always	15	9.76	5.2	27.49	2.817
Yes	Some	9	10.03	-1.0	1.06	0.105
Yes	Rarely	5	9.21	-4.2	17.77	1.928
No	Always	21	26.24	-5.2	27.49	1.047
No	Some	28	26.97	1.0	1.06	0.039
No	Rarely	29	24.79	4.2	17.77	0.717
		107				**6.654**

The observed value of χ^2 is 6.654. The corresponding cutoff value from Appendix C for $\alpha = .05$ with $(3-1)(2-1) = 2$ degrees of freedom is 5.99. Reject the null hypothesis of independence.

EXCEL GRAPHICAL ANALYSIS

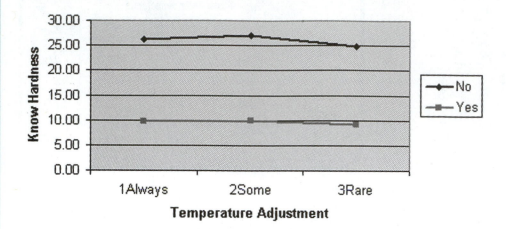

In this sample, people who did not know their water hardness were less likely to adjust the water temperature, and those who knew their water hardness were more likely to vary water temperature. The inferential statistics analysis demonstrated that this relationship generalizes to the population.

To obtain the graph of this relationship, follow the procedures for a Line chart as illustrated in the previous Business Application.

MANAGERIAL INTERPRETATION

This analysis supports the concept of a market segment defined by relatively "sophisticated" users of laundry detergent. People who do not know their water hardness are less likely to adjust the water temperature, and those who know their water hardness are more likely to pay attention to water temperature.

Many users of χ^2 tests confuse tests of homogeneity with tests of independence. Probably the central reason for the confusion is that the calculations for the analysis of two-way contingency tables are identical. In both cases, the expression for the expected cell frequency is

$$\text{expected frequency} = \frac{(\text{row total})(\text{column total})}{\text{sample size}}.$$

The method of data collection, the conceptual status of the variables, and the interpretation of the results, however, differ for the two tests. The test of homogeneity is focused specifically on the group differences, with samples from the distinct populations taken *before* data analysis begins. One variable is the grouping variable, and the other variable is the response variable. For the test of independence, however, only one sample is taken, and the number of observations in each group is known only after data analysis begins. Both variables in the test of independence are response variables.

Another issue in the analysis of contingency table data is the distinction between metric data that result from measurements and nominal data that result from classification. Many contingency tables are constructed from variables that represent crude measurement of an underlying continuous variable instead of from the classification based on a truly categorical variable. Salary could be analyzed with a contingency table represented by rough categories such as low, medium, and high. This variable would be more effectively analyzed using analyses appropriate for continuous variables. Classifying values for variables such as years of employment or salary into only three categories inefficiently discards much information in subsequent statistical analyses.

The next section introduces another application of the χ^2 statistic.

Testing Goodness of Fit

The χ^2 statistic compares observed frequencies of the values of categorical variables with the frequencies expected assuming the null hypothesis. The first application of the χ^2 statistic already introduced assesses differences in proportions across two or more samples. The second application assesses the independence of the two categorical variables from a single sample.

The application of the χ^2 statistic introduced here, the χ^2 **goodness-of-fit test,** assesses the closeness of the observed frequencies to the expected frequencies from a specified probability distribution. The values of the variable are either categorical or, if continuous, partitioned into categories.

> **goodness-of-fit test**
> *evaluates the likelihood that the data were generated by a specified probability distribution*

How good is the fit of the data to what is expected from a specified distribution, such as the normal distribution or the uniform distribution? The data are of a single categorical variable, so the corresponding table of data consists of only a single row or a single column. If no population values are estimated from the data, so that only the population proportion for each category is estimated, then the degrees of freedom for this test is the number of categories minus one.

A common application of the χ^2 goodness-of-fit test is to compare the fit of the data to the uniform distribution, which is the distribution specifying that all values of the categorical variable occur with *equal* probability. For this application, the null hypothesis specifies equal proportions, but this is *not* the multigroup test of equal proportions described in a previous section. The test of homogeneity evaluated the equality of proportions across groups. This goodness-of-fit test evaluates the equality of proportions across all the response levels for a single group.

BUSINESS APPLICATION 7.5—Goodness of Fit

MANAGERIAL PROBLEM

Management at New Cola Company believed that they had developed a truly better tasting cola than that provided by the two dominant cola companies, Brand X and Brand Y. To support their claim, they conducted taste tests. Each potential consumer in the study tasted all three colas, though the identity of each cola was hidden. Each person was asked to select the best tasting cola.

STATISTICAL HYPOTHESES

Null hypothesis H_0: All three colas are equally preferred.

Alternative hypothesis H_1: At least one cola is preferred more than the others.

DATA

The number of choices of each type of cola was recorded. Data were collected from 164 people.

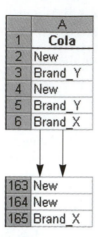

APPLICATION—EXCEL ANALYSIS

Contingency Table

The three observed frequencies for combinations of cola are listed within the body of the table, and the total sample size is listed at the bottom of the table.

	C	D
1	Count of Cola	
2	Cola	Total
3	Brand_X	47
4	Brand_Y	53
5	New	64
6	Grand Total	164

Obtaining the Contingency Table

Data ➤ PivotTable Report...

Step 1. Specify the source of the data, which is the worksheet.

Where is the data that you want to analyze?
⦿ Microsoft Excel list or database

Step 2. Specify the range of the data, including the label. This range can be typed in, or it will be entered automatically if any data cell was selected before entering the PivotTable program.

Range: $A$1:$A$165

Step 3. First drag the Cola box at the top right corner over to the Row area, and then drag the same Cola box at the top right corner to the Data area.

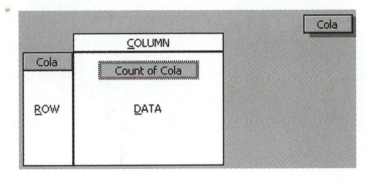

Step 4. Specify the starting cell of the output.

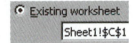

Goodness-of-Fit Test

If cola preference does not differ, then the expected number of the 164 people who endorse each cola is the same for all three levels of the response variable,

$$E = \frac{164}{3} = 54.67.$$

Add this value to the worksheet for each level of the response variable.

	C	D	E
1	Count of Cola		
2	Cola	Total	Expected
3	Brand_X	47	54.667
4	Brand_Y	53	54.667
5	New	64	54.667
6	Grand Total	164	

Excel's χ^2 test function, CHITEST, provides the p-value of the test. This function is defined in terms of the range of actual (observed) frequencies and the expected frequencies,

        =CHITEST(actual_values,expected_values).

The function call in this example is

        =CHITEST(D3:D5,E3:E5),

which yields a p-value for χ^2_{obs} of 0.257. The null hypothesis of equal population proportions *cannot* be rejected, because $p \geq \alpha = .05$.

APPLICATION—TRADITIONAL NOTATION

Calculate the sample χ^2 statistic from the following table.

	Obs	Expected	Deviation	Dev. Sq.	DfSq/Exp
	O	E	$O-E$	$(O-E)^2$	$(O-E)^2/E$
New	64	54.67	9.33	87.11	1.59
X	47	54.67	-7.67	58.78	1.08
Y	53	54.67	-1.67	2.78	0.05
	164	164.00	0.00		**2.72**

All expected number of occurrences are greater than five, so the statistic

$$\sum \left[\frac{(O-E)^2}{E} \right] = 2.72$$

may be evaluated according to the χ^2 approximation. For $3 - 1 = 2$ degrees of freedom, the corresponding cutoff value for $\alpha = .05$ is 5.99, as obtained from Appendix C. The null hypothesis of equal population proportions cannot be rejected.

EXCEL GRAPHICAL ANALYSIS

Assessing the Excel Output

The sample proportions differ, and, indeed, New Cola was preferred more often than the traditional colas. The preceding analysis, however, could not support the generalization of these sample differences to the population. Calculation of the contingency table provides the numbers needed for further analysis. A bar graph of the three frequencies, as illustrated in Figure 7-9, provides a visual display of the sample differences among cola preferences.

Figure 7-9.
Observed and expected frequencies of cola preference.

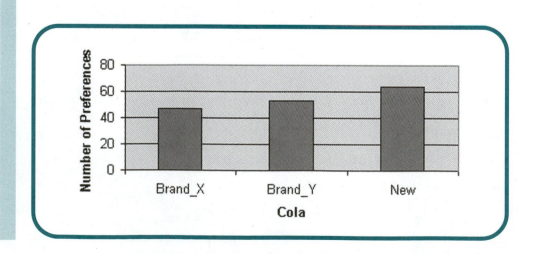

Obtaining the Chart

To obtain this chart, begin with the following menu sequence.

Insert ➤ Chart...

Step 1—Chart Type. Specify a Column chart or Bar chart, which is Excel terminology for a bar chart of a categorical variable with either vertical or horizontal bars, respectively. Choose a format, which is the clustered column that compares values across categories.

Step 2—Chart Source. Specify the cells for the Data Range that contain the data values and corresponding frequencies.

Data range: =Sheet1!$C$2:$D$5

Step 3—Chart Options. Under the Titles tab, name the axes and provide a chart title. Click on the Legend tab and uncheck the Show legend checkbox.

Step 4. Specify the location of the chart, either on a new sheet or as an object on the current worksheet.

MANAGERIAL INTERPRETATION

Unfortunately, management's initial excitement about the preliminary examination of the data did not survive formal statistical analysis. Despite the differences in sample proportions, this analysis did not demonstrate any difference between cola preferences. A difference could still exist, but this analysis did not uncover it.

The previous example illustrated the χ^2 goodness-of-fit test for the uniform distribution. However, this goodness-of-fit test is quite general. The expected frequencies specified by the null hypothesis can be derived for *any* distribution. Instead of specifying the .33 probabilities of response for each of the three categories in the previous example, the analyst could have hypothesized that the response to New Cola would be preferred twice as often to the responses of either of the other two colas. Under this hypothesis, the corresponding expected frequencies would be .50, .25, and .25. These proportions could be converted to frequencies simply by multiplying each proportion by sample size.

Applications of the goodness-of-fit procedure also include well-known distributions such as the normal distribution. In these cases, obtain the expected probabilities directly from a table of probabilities such as those found in the appendices or a computer program. For continuous variables, partition the values into intervals and assign a probability to each interval.

Table 7-3.
Expected frequencies for
$n = 400$ from a normal
population with a mean
of 50 and a standard
deviation of 10.

Interval	Expected Probability	Expected Frequency
75 up to 80	0.005	1.94
70 up to 75	0.017	6.62
65 up to 70	0.044	17.62
60 up to 65	0.092	36.74
55 up to 60	0.150	59.95
50 up to 55	0.191	76.58
45 up to 50	0.191	76.58
40 up to 45	0.150	59.95
35 up to 40	0.092	36.74
30 up to 35	0.044	17.62
25 up to 30	0.017	6.62
20 up to 25	0.005	1.94

To illustrate, consider a normal distribution with a mean of 50 and a standard deviation of 10. To evaluate the goodness-of-fit of data to this distribution, first define intervals (categories) such as five units wide on either side of the mean. The expected probabilities for each interval are the corresponding normal curve probabilities. Convert these probabilities to frequencies by multiplying each probability by the sample size, as illustrated in Table 7-3 for a sample size of $n = 400$. Calculate the χ^2_{obs} statistic as before from both the observed frequencies and the expected frequencies, which here are based on the normal curve probabilities.

The expected frequencies in Table 7-3 were computed from a normal distribution with a specified mean and standard deviation. What if the specific normal distribution is not specified, and instead the question is simply if the sample data conform to a normal distribution, whatever the mean and standard deviation might be? Before the expected frequencies can be computed, the mean and standard deviation of the normal distribution must first be specified. When not provided as part of the null hypothesis, these values must first be estimated from the data and the expected frequencies calculated from these estimated values. As we have seen in Chapter 3, however, using sample estimates from the same data to obtain other estimates reduces the degrees of freedom.

> *Degrees of freedom for χ^2 goodness-of-fit test:*
> $df = num.\ categories - num.\ estimated\ values - 1$

When no population values are estimated from the data, the degrees of freedom is one less than the number of categories.

EXERCISES

7-11. A baseball player is hitting .300 (averaging three hits in every 10 at-bats). In a recent game, the player comes to bat four times, and either gets a hit (H) or is out (O). What is the probability of

a. the simple event, OHOH, in the order specified
b. the simple event, OOOH, in the order specified

7-12. Compute the expected frequencies of each cell below from the marginal probabilities given the null hypothesis of independence.

	Much	Some	None	
A				199
B				47
C				255
	38	64	17	

7-13. Nineteen men and 15 women are in Department A. Department B has 33 men and 20 women. Are gender and department independent? Answer this question with a chi-square test of independence and the strength of association.

7-14. After being given some dice, Jim wanted to check that each die was fair, that is, that the probability of obtaining any one of the six sides of each die was the same. The following data were recorded for one of the dice.

Side	1	2	3	4	5	6
Freq	8	7	12	13	9	15

Is the die fair? Answer this question with a chi-square test of independence and the strength of association.

7.4 SUMMARY

The statistical analysis of a categorical response variable is based on the proportion of values that occur for each category. This chapter presented two primary techniques for the analysis of proportions: z-tests of the corresponding indicator variables and χ^2 (chi-square) tests. The indicator variable for each level of response is coded with values 1 and 0 representing the occurrence and nonoccurrence, respectively, of the level of interest. The mean and standard deviation of an indicator variable are directly obtained from the proportion of occurrences of the corresponding category. Sample proportions are sample means of the corresponding indicator variables.

For sufficiently large samples, when np and $n(1 - p)$ are both larger than five, the sample proportion is approximately normally distributed. By analyzing the corresponding indicator variable, the standard inference procedures can be applied to proportions from large samples. A confidence interval around a sample proportion or the hypothesis test that the population proportion equals a specified value are easily computed using the same techniques applied to the sample means. The primary difference between the procedures is that the cutoff values for the distribution of sample proportions are obtained from the normal distribution instead of the t-distribution, a difference of little practical importance for large samples. Further, the hypothesized value of the population proportion determines the value of the population standard deviation.

The χ^2 tests presented in this chapter compare the observed frequencies with the corresponding expected frequencies for each combination of values (cell). The test of homogeneity tests differences of proportions across each response level for different groups. The responses on a categorical variable are recorded for two or more groups of observations and organized into a contingency table, which displays the frequencies for each cell. The groups are defined by a categorical grouping variable, and the sample sizes are set before the analysis begins. The null hypothesis specifies that the population proportions for each level of response are identical across groups. The test of independence is computationally identical to the test of homogeneity. The expected frequencies for each cell given the null hypothesis are computed from the marginal frequencies. However, the meaning and interpretation of the tests differ. The test of independence is a one-sample test in which both categorical variables are response variables. Groups *could be* defined for the different levels of one of the response variables and observations separately sampled before assessing the responses. But the sampling plan for the test of independence is to sample from a single group and assess all frequencies and marginals as part of the data analysis.

The tests of homogeneity and independence both involve analyzing frequencies and proportions for all combinations of values for two categorical variables. The associated χ^2 tests are tests of a null hypothesis of no relation. A strength of association index supplements the hypothesis test. Ranging from zero to one, Cramer's V assesses the degree of association for two categorical variables and is a straightforward function of the observed χ^2 value and sample size.

The expression for Cramer's V shows how the χ^2 test of homogeneity or independence can reject the null hypothesis of no relation for a large sample size, yet the strength of the relation can be very small. For large sample sizes, small values of Cramer's V can still lead to the rejection of the null hypothesis. This is the same issue addressed in Chapter 5 under the topic of practical versus statistical significance.

The third and last χ^2 test introduced in this chapter is the one-sample goodness-of-fit test. This test involves only a single variable, so the resulting table of data is only a single row or column. The expected frequencies are computed from the null hypothesis, which can be based on any specified probability distribution. The distribution can be from the well-known families such as the uniform or the normal, or it can be customized to the context of the study. To test the goodness of fit for a continuous distribution such as the normal, partition the values of the response variable into adjacent categories.

7.5 KEY TERMS

chi-square statistic *296*
conditional probability *307*
Cramer's V *299*
goodness-of-fit test *315*
independence *309*
independent events *307*

indicator variable *284*
intersection *308*
survey *293*
test of independence *310*
two-way contingency table *294*
χ^2 test of homogeneity *295*

7.6 REVIEW EXERCISES

ANALYSIS PROBLEMS

Mechanical

7-15. At the Favorite Music Store, 12 compact discs were requested for special order today. The discs were classified as

rock rock jazz rock classical jazz rock classical
rock rock jazz rock

a. Create the indicator variable for the value Rock.

b. Compute the proportion of Rock requests according to the definition of proportion (from the beginning of Chapter 2).

c. Compute the proportion of Rock requests according to the definition of the mean of the corresponding indicator variable.

d. Compute the standard deviation of the indicator variable Rock.

7-16. At the local business school, 14 undergraduates declared their major today from among the following choices: Marketing, Management, Finance, and Accounting. The majors were

   mrkt   mgmt   finc   mgmt   acct   mrkt   finc   mgmt   mgmt   finc
   acct   acct   mgmt   mrkt

a. Create the indicator variable for the value Acct.

b. Compute the proportion of Acct declarations according to the definition of proportion (from the beginning of Chapter 2).

c. Compute the proportion of Acct declarations according to the definition of a mean (from the beginning of Chapter 3).

d. Compute the standard deviation of the indicator variable Acct.

7-17. Thirty-eight randomly selected employees out of 74 polled advocated converting to a union shop. Construct and interpret the meaning of the confidence interval around the proportion of employees advocating converting to a union shop for a confidence level of

a. 99%

b. 95%

7-18. A random sample of 150 consumers revealed that 88 preferred your company's product over the competition's. Construct and interpret the meaning of the confidence interval around the proportion of consumers who prefer your product for a confidence level of

a. 99%

b. 95%

c. Determine if more than 50% of consumers support your company's product and why or why not.

7-19. A supplier claims that only 4% of all shipped parts do not meet specifications. To evaluate this claim, a sample of 50 parts uncovers three defective parts.

a. Construct and interpret the meaning of the confidence interval around the proportion of defective parts for a confidence level of 95%.

b. Determine if the supplier's claim is supported by the data.

7-20. A manager claimed that the proportion of Speedy convenience stores in a state is 27% of all convenience stores. A random sampling of 107 stores revealed that 36 stores were Speedy stores. Use an hypothesis test to assess if the data support the claim.

7-21. Twenty-three of the 45 students in a college class are female. Test the hypothesis that the process by which students enter the class yields the same proportion of males and females.

7-22. A candidate for political office wants to know the percentage of the electorate planning to vote for her. The obtained sample of 284 voters yielded 148 votes for this candidate.

    a. Compute and interpret the 95% confidence interval around the sample proportion.

    b. Determine whether it is reasonable that less than 50% of *all* voters intend to vote for her even though the observed sample percentage is larger than 50%.

7-23. The proportion of accounts receivable that were past due at our favorite company used to hover right around 12%. After more stringent conditions for receiving goods and services without advance payment were implemented, 19 out of 180 accounts were past due. Does it appear that the new policy changed the percentage of past due accounts?

7-24. Classify each of the following analyses as a test of homogeneity or a test of independence. Provide the rationale for the classification. Analyze the relation of

    a. rejection of mortgage applications at three different banks to a random sample of 30 applications from each bank

    b. gender to the vote for one of three presidential candidates in a sample of 200 voters

    c. highest degree earned (high school, college, graduate) to type of job in a sample of 350 workers

    d. quality of the part depending on the machine that made the part to a random sample of 15 parts from each of four machines

7-25. In 1974 the National Football League decided to break ties with an overtime quarter. The team that wins a coin toss is awarded first possession of the ball during overtime. Of the first 192 games, 11 were still tied at the end of the overtime quarter, so these games ended in a tie. Of the remaining 181 games, the winner of the coin toss won 92 games and the loser won 89. Based on the data from these 181 games in which a winner was decided in the overtime period, is the winner of the coin toss more likely to win the game?

7-26. An advertiser wants to know if there is a difference between the proportion of males and females who watch a certain TV show. A random sample of 125 males reveals that 49 watch the show on a regular basis, and 46 out of a sample of 115 females watch the show. Is there a difference in the proportions of males and females in the viewing audience?

7-27. An auditor noticed that out of 142 mortgage loan applications made during the last six months at Bank A, 26 were rejected. At nearby Bank B, 28 applications were rejected out of a total of 188. At Bank C, 19 applications were rejected out of a total of 109. Is there a difference in the proportions of rejected applications at these banks?

7-28. An airline manager wants to evaluate any potential differences between no-shows on weekday versus weekend flights. Of 1,492 weekday travelers, 121 failed to show. Of 341 weekend travelers, 26 failed to show. Based on these data, is there a difference in the proportions of no-shows for weekday and weekend flights?

7-29. Of 236 parts made with Machine A, 18 were defective. Of 212 parts made with Machine B, 15 were defective. Other than different machines, the parts were manufactured under comparable circumstances. Is there a difference between machines in the proportion of manufactured defective parts? Answer this question with a test of homogeneity and the corresponding strength of association.

7-30. For the analysis of a 5 × 2 contingency table, what sample size is needed to reject the null hypothesis at the $\alpha = .05$ level when Cramer's V is

   a. .60

   b. .30

   c. .15

   d. Plot the relationship between sample size and Cramer's V.

   e. Summarize this relationship verbally.

7-31. Some pharmaceutical researchers evaluated the side effects of three drugs that accomplished the same task. The first drug was administered to 124 patients, 18 of whom complained of side effects. The second drug was administered to 98 different patients, 13 of whom complained of side effects. The third drug was administered to 135 different patients, 28 of whom complained of side effects. The company sponsoring the research will decide which of the three drugs to introduce to the market. Should this decision be based, in part, on any purported differences in the number of people who report accompanying side effects?

7-32. Compute the expected frequencies of each cell below from the marginal probabilities given the null hypothesis of independence.

	X	Y	Z	
A				159
B				269
C				338
	259	199	308	

7-33. A polling organization surveyed 229 Washington voters, 177 Oregon voters, and 440 California voters regarding support for a particular piece of legislation. The following table presents their responses.

		State		
		WA	OR	CA
Response	Yes	119	97	248
	No	110	80	192

Does the proportion of people who endorse the issue differ according to state of residence? Answer this question with a

   a. chi-square test, including a statement of the null hypothesis

   b. strength of association index

7-34. A sample of 136 employees were asked if they supported unionization. Possible responses were Yes, No, and No Opinion. The following table presents their responses, classified according to gender.

Unionization

		Yes	No	No Opinion
Gender	**Male**	42	29	7
	Female	31	22	5

Are gender and preference for unionization independent? Answer this question with a

a. chi-square test, including a statement of the null hypothesis

b. strength of association index

7-35. Management at a clothing manufacturer wants to know if preference for a color of jeans is related to gender. A sample of 183 potential consumers chose their favor color of jeans from among Blue, Black, Brown, and Red. The following table presents their responses, classified according to gender.

Color

		Blue	Black	Brown	Red
Gender	**Male**	39	37	8	2
	Female	42	29	12	14

Are gender and color preference independent? Answer this question with a

a. chi-square test, including a statement of the null hypothesis

b. strength of association index

7-36. A sample of 336 employees who commuted downtown were polled regarding their opinion regarding light rail expansion and the subsequent increase in taxes. The transportation mode by which the employees reached their downtown jobs was also recorded.

Light Rail Expansion

		Strongly Agree	Agree	Disagree	Strongly Disagree
Transportation	**Drove Alone**	12	14	36	49
	Car Pooled	17	21	15	12
	Public Trans	58	50	33	19

Are transportation mode and preference for light rail expansion independent? Answer this question with a

a. chi-square test, including a statement of the null hypothesis

b. strength of association index

7-37. A wine producer asked 282 wine tasters to rate a new wine in terms of taste and aroma. The following responses were recorded.

		Aroma		
		Mild	Moderate	Strong
	Poor	18	22	16
Taste	OK	23	41	28
	Great	36	59	39

Are taste and aroma of this wine independent? Answer this question with a

a. chi-square test, including a statement of the null hypothesis

b. strength of association index

7-38. The responses to two questions on a personality questionnaire were recorded. Each question could be answered in terms of Agree, Neither agree nor disagree, or Disagree.

		Question 1		
		Agree	Neither	Disagree
	Agree	87	12	29
Question 2	Neither	18	18	14
	Disagree	34	9	92

Are the responses to the questions independent? Answer this question with a

a. chi-square test, including a statement of the null hypothesis

b. strength of association index

7-39. Management wants to improve plant safety. One aspect of this investigation is to assess when accidents occur. The number of accidents was recorded for different time periods for the last year.

Time	8am–10am	10am–12pm	1pm–3pm	3pm–5pm
# accidents	25	21	27	34

Are accidents more likely to occur at different times throughout the day?

7-40. Scores on a psychological assessment instrument are supposed to be normally distributed with a mean of 50 and a standard deviation of 10. After administering the instrument to 460 employees, the following distribution of scores was obtained.

Score	30–35	35–40	41–45	46–50	51–55	56–60	61–65	66–70
Count	19	41	66	94	86	79	53	22

Is this distribution consistent with the hypothesized distribution?

7-41. For the data in the previous exercise,

Application

a. evaluate the goodness of fit of the distribution to a normal distribution *without* specifying the mean and standard deviation a priori.

b. Determine if this fit is better or worse than the fit in the previous problem with the specified population mean and standard deviation. Why or why not?

7-42. A manager suspects that more employees are likely to call in sick immediately after or before a weekend. To substantiate his claim, the following numbers of absences were recorded for the previous year.

Application

Day	M	Tu	W	Th	F
Count	198	165	149	171	222

The data appear to support his claim, but is this pattern likely the result of a chance statistical fluctuation from an equal number of sick calls each day, or do these results characterize the population as a whole?

7-43. Four machines are used to manufacture a part. The number of parts produced by each machine for one week were recorded.

Application

Machine	M1	M2	M3	M4
Count	545	553	536	585

Is each machine calibrated to produce the same number of parts?

7-44. Analysis of purchasing behavior yielded the following categories based on age: child (under 13), teen (14–19), young adult (20–33), adult (34–45), mature adult (46–60), and older adult (over 61). The proportion of residents in each category for a city of interest was obtained from analysis of the 1990 census. A marketing manager wondered if the proportions had changed in 1996. For each age group, the frequencies for a sample of 250 residents, as well as the proportions derived from the census, are reported in the following table.

Application

	child	teen	young adult	adult	mature adult	older adult
Census Prop	.19	.09	.21	.22	.18	.11
Sample Freq	39	21	51	62	40	37

Did the proportion of people within each group change from the 1990 census?

DISCUSSION QUESTIONS

1. How does an indicator variable relate to the classification of an observation into one of the values of a categorical variable?

2. How are the mean of an indicator variable and a proportion of values of a categorical variable related?

3. What conditions must be satisfied before the distribution of the sample proportion approximates the normal distribution?

4. Why is the sample standard deviation usually *not* given for problems that involve computing a confidence interval around a sample proportion?

5. Why is the t-distribution used to test means and the z-distribution used to test proportions?

6. Why is the hypothesized value of the population proportion used to compute the standard error of the sample proportion?

7. Why is the z-test statistic always used when testing the hypothesis of a single population proportion?

8. What kinds of questions can appear on a survey?

9. What is a two-way contingency table?

10. How does the meaning of the test for homogeneity differ from the meaning of the test of independence?

11. What does a significant χ^2_{obs}, that is, a rejected null hypothesis of no relationship, imply about the size of the strength of association between the variables?

12. How is the goodness of fit of a continuous variable assessed?

13. How is the goodness-of-fit test for a categorical variable applied to analyzing the goodness-of-fit of a continuous variable?

INTEGRATIVE ANALYSIS PROBLEM

The file SURVEY.DAT contains responses of 159 people to the following seven statements. The possible responses and the response codes that appear in the data file are listed next to each statement. The response codes appear in parentheses.

1. Are you Male or Female? Male (M) or Female (F)

2. What is your eye color? Brown (BR), Blue (BL), Green (GN), Gray (GY), or Other (OT)

3. What is your hair color? Brown (BR), Black (BK), Blond (BL), Red (RD), or Other (OT)

4. I would rather have a house: in a sociable suburb (A), in between (B), alone in the deep woods (C)

5. Sometimes I feel a vague danger that I do not understand. yes (A), in between (B), no (C)

6. It would be more interesting working in a business: talking to customers (A), in between (B), keeping office records (C)

7. Sometimes the excitement in my voice is too obvious. yes (A), in between (B), no (C)

   a. Determine if the proportion of males is the same as the proportion of females in the population from which these data were sampled.

   b. Test the hypothesis that 60% of the population has Brown eyes.

   c. Plot a bar graph of eye color.

   d. Determine if the null hypothesis of equal proportions of each eye color across groups is rejected. Ignore the Other category in this test.

   Note: Answer the following questions that assess the relationship between two categorical variables with both a test of the null hypothesis *and* Cramer's V.

e. Is there a relationship between Gender and House Location Preference, which varies from a sociable suburb to alone in the deep woods? That is, do men prefer to live alone more often than women, or vice versa?

f. Is there a relationship between House Location Preference and the Feeling of Vague Danger?

g. Is there a relationship between House Location Preference and Job Preference, which varies from wishing to talk with customers to keeping records?

h. Is there a relationship between House Location Preference and Obvious Voice Excitement?

i. Is there a relationship between the Feeling of Vague Danger and Job Preference?

j. Is there a relationship between the Feeling of Vague Danger and Obvious Voice Excitement?

k. Is there a relationship between Obvious Voice Excitement and Job Preference?

l. Given your responses to g–k, could you group the four statements into two groups of related items?

m. Is this grouping consistent with the meaning of the statements? What aspect of personality does each of these groups of statements seem to be assessing?

8

Describing Relationships between Variables

WHY DO WE CARE?

Different aspects of our world are related: salary to the qualifications and quantity of job applicants, number of new housing starts to interest rate, trading price of a stock to earnings per share, job satisfaction to management's leadership style. When the values of one of these related variables is unknown, regression analysis predicts the *unknown* value from the *known* values of one or more other variables. Examples appear in Table 8-1.

The power to accurately predict leads directly to better decision making. Predicting an increase in new housing construction, a manager at a local construction firm hires new employees before construction falls behind schedule. Predicting a sales increase from a new advertising campaign, a product manager builds inventories to meet anticipated demand.

Regression analysis also explains the extent to which one or more variables influences another variable. With this knowledge, the manager understands the change needed in one variable to obtain a desired amount of change in another variable. How much does a product's price influence sales? Regression analysis both predicts the value of a variable of interest and indicates the extent to which one or more variables influences the variable of interest.

Table 8-1.
Examples of known values from which unknown values can be predicted.

Known	Unknown
Earnings per Share	Price per Share
Interest Rate	New Housing Construction
Interest Rate, Cost of Materials, and Unemployment Rate	New Housing Construction
Participation in Decision Making	Employee Satisfaction
Temperature	Home Power Consumption
Advertising Spending for the Product and Price of Product	Sales of the Product

T he basic concept underlying the relationship between variables is the *function*. The function is presented first, followed by its empirical counterpart, the scatter around the regression line.

8.1 FUNCTIONS AND SCATTERPLOTS

**response variable *Y*
and predictor
variable *X***
*estimate each value
of Y from the
corresponding value
of X*

A regression analysis expresses one variable *Y* as a **response** to one or more **predictor variables** *X*.

Estimating the value of Price per Share (PPS) from Earnings per Share (EPS) is an example of regression analysis with a single predictor variable, sometimes called *simple* regression. A discussion of multiple regression analysis with multiple predictors appears in the following chapter.

The response variable is *Y*, with estimate $\hat{Y}$. Given the value of the predictor variable *X*, the value of $\hat{Y}$ is computed from the regression analysis. A primary goal of regression analysis is for each estimate $\hat{Y}$ to approximately equal the measured value *Y*.

How can, for example, the value of PPS (*Y*) be estimated from EPS (*X*)? To what extent are earnings throughout the year related to the price of a company's stock at the end of the year? The next section introduces the most general technique for this estimation, and then a specific version of regression that assumes linearity is discussed.

Functions

function
*relationship among
variables in which
the value of one
(or more) variable X
determines the
value of another
variable Y*

Consider a classic case of prediction, the prediction of the selling Price per Share (PPS) of a company's stock. One kind of "prediction" follows from investing Canadian money in a U.S. stock. The investor calculates PPS in Canadian dollars from PPS in U.S. dollars. If 1.40 Canadian dollars equal one U.S. dollar, compute the Canadian price in dollars (*Y*) of PPS from the U.S. price in dollars (*X*) as

$$Y = 1.40X.$$

This simple equation relating *Y* and *X* illustrates a concept central to all of mathematics and science—the **function.**

Y-intercept
b_0 **in** $\hat{Y} = b_0 + b_1X$
*value of the response
variable Y when the
predictor variable X
is zero*

The meaning of a functional relationship for two variables is straightforward. If *X* is known, then *Y* can be computed. Often this relationship is expressed as an equation. If $X = 25$ and $Y = 1.40X$, the corresponding value of *Y* is $(1.40)(25) = 35.0$.

The simplest functions are linear functions with two variables, *X* and *Y*, and two parameters that define equations of the form,

$$Y = b_0 + b_1X.$$

slope coefficient
b_1 **in** $\hat{Y} = b_0 + b_1X$
*change in the
response variable Y
for a one-unit
change in the value
of the predictor
variable X*

One parameter is the **Y-intercept** b_0. The second parameter is the **slope coefficient** b_1.

The parameters b_0 and b_1 are constant for any given linear function. Specific values of these parameters define a specific linear function. Setting $b_0 = 0$ and $b_1 = 1.40$ defines the linear function $Y = 1.40(X) + 0$, and $b_0 = 1$ and $b_1 = -6$ defines the linear function $Y = 1 - 6X$. For each of these linear functions, the values of variables *X* and *Y* are free to vary.

X	Y
$16.50	$23.10
$21.63	$30.28
$24.13	$33.78
$32.88	$46.03

Table 8-2.
$Y = 1.40X$ for four values of X.

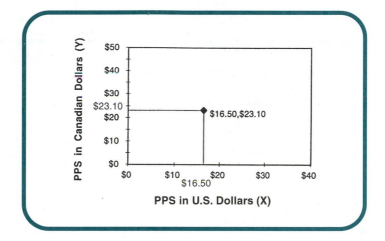

Figure 8-1.
Graph of a single point
<$16.50,$23.10>.

For a functional relationship such as $Y = 1.40(X)$, the value of X exactly determines the value of Y, as illustrated in Table 8-2 for four values of X. Given X, Y is known. For example, a stock trading at $36.50 American dollars trades at $1.40($36.50) = $51.10 Canadian dollars.

The graph of the paired values X and Y is constructed with each point on the graph corresponding to a single paired set of values. As illustrated in Figure 8-1, for the first point <$16.50,$23.10>, the distance of the point on the horizontal axis is the X value, and the distance on the vertical axis is the Y value.

All points for the graph of a function fall on the same curve. For linear functions with two variables, this "curve" is a straight line. Figure 8-2 graphically depicts the four pairs of values for X and Y from the preceding table (the labels for the data values and the first line segment were added separately). Each point on the line corresponds to a pair of values X and Y. For each value of U.S. dollars (X) in Figure 8-2, there is *one and only one* associated value of Canadian dollars (Y).

What is the meaning of the function $Y = 1.40X + 0$? The Y-intercept is the value of Y when $X = 0$, so for this function, $b_0 = 0$ means that when $X = 0$ so does Y. Typically of greater interest for management is the meaning of the slope coefficient b_1, which specifies how fast Y changes when X changes. For every 1-unit

Figure 8-2.
PPS in Canadian dollars is a linear function of PPS in U.S. dollars for a conversion ratio of 1.40.

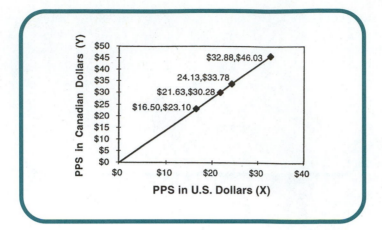

Figure 8-3.
Interpretation of the slope-coefficient b_1.

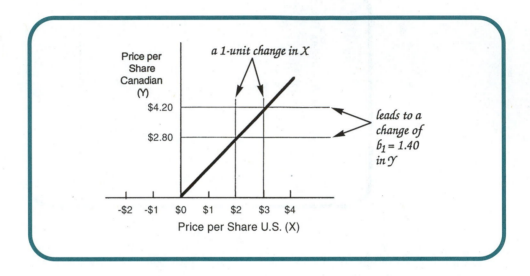

increase in the value of X, the value of Y changes by b_1. In this example, every increase of PPS by $1 U.S. leads to an increase of PPS of $1.40 Canadian, as illustrated in Figure 8-2.

"Estimating" PPS in Canadian dollars from PPS in U.S. dollars is exact but not particularly exciting. We turn next to a more interesting relationship between variables.

Scatterplots

scatterplot
each point in the plot represents a pair of measured values for a single observation

The values of many related variables of interest to the manager are measured instead of computed. The relationship between measured variables is usually not exact, as a graph of the relationship—a **scatterplot**—illustrates.

The scatter in a scatterplot reflects an underlying tendency instead of an exact relationship. Drawing an ellipse around most, but not necessarily all, of the points in the scatterplot demonstrates the *degree* of scatter. The narrower the ellipse, the stronger the relationship. For the exact relationship of a function, this "ellipse" becomes a straight line.

The following illustration shows the scatterplot of two financial variables.

STATISTICAL ILLUSTRATION—Scatterplot

The names of 10 companies[1] and their corresponding 1992 closing values of Earnings per Share (EPS) and Price per Share (PPS) are listed in Table 8-3. The companies are listed in ascending order of their EPS value.

Figure 8-4 presents the scatterplot of PPS and EPS for all 10 companies. An ellipse drawn around most or all of the points in the scatterplot indicates the form of the relationship: As EPS increases, PPS *tends* to increase. The ellipse and the company names were added separately.

The scatterplot of PPS and EPS for *all* 1,402 companies, with the accompanying ellipse that graphically summarizes the relationship, is presented in Figure 8-5 (169, or 12%, of the values of EPS were negative).

The scatter increased in the full sample; some points lie relatively far from the primary tendency summarized by the ellipse drawn around the majority of points.

Company	EPS	PPS
1 IMO INDUSTRIES INC	-3.26	6.50
2 TORO CO	-1.98	13.00
3 CALMAT CO	-0.45	22.50
4 TULTEX CORP	0.56	8.63
5 FAMILY DOLLAR STORES	1.00	17.25
6 PHILADELPHIA SUBURBAN CORP	1.23	16.00
7 RTZ PLC	1.50	41.38
8 TANDY CORP	2.24	24.50
9 OKLAHOMA GAS & ELECTRIC	2.42	34.13
10 NICOR INC	3.83	49.75

Table 8-3.
The illustrative (nonrandom) sample of 1992 data from 10 companies.

1. A small sample of about 10 observations conveniently illustrates the relevant statistical principles and computational methods. However, a randomly drawn sample of this size is too small to indicate reliably any true relationships among the variables. Accordingly, these 10 companies were deliberately (*non*randomly) selected from a larger sample of 1,402 publicly traded companies that paid a cash dividend in 1992. The results of the analyses conducted throughout this and the next chapter on the financial characteristics of these 10 companies approximate the *same* results of the corresponding analysis of the much larger but random sample presented in this and the subsequent chapter.

Figure 8-4.
Scatterplot of PPS
and EPS for the 10
sample companies.

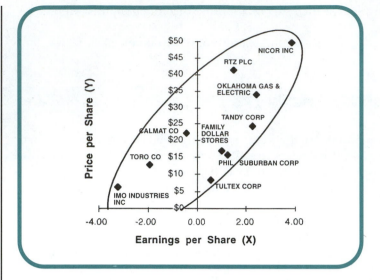

Figure 8-5.
Scatterplot of 1992
PPS and EPS for
1,402 publicly traded
companies that paid
a cash dividend in
1992; two companies
with an EPS just
under −$1 are
highlighted.

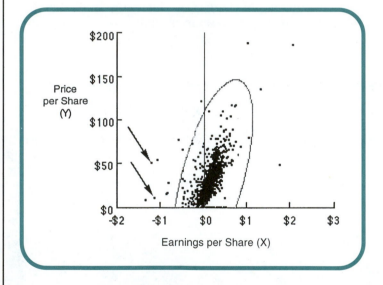

Consider the two companies that have an EPS just under −$1, as illustrated by the arrows in the previous scatterplot. One of the two companies has a corresponding PPS of about $10, yet the other has a much higher PPS of about $50.

A statistic that indicates the degree of scatter in a scatterplot is the correlation coefficient, r, which varies from −1 to 1. For linear relationships, values close to −1 or 1 indicate comparatively little scatter. Values close to 0 indicate much scatter. The correlation in the illustrative small sample in Table 8-3 is $r = .77$, which decreases to $r = .59$ in the full sample. The six scatterplots presented in Figure 8-6 illustrate a range of correlation coefficients from close to −1 to close to 1.

As these six scatterplots illustrate, two attributes describe the linear relationship between two variables: strength and direction.

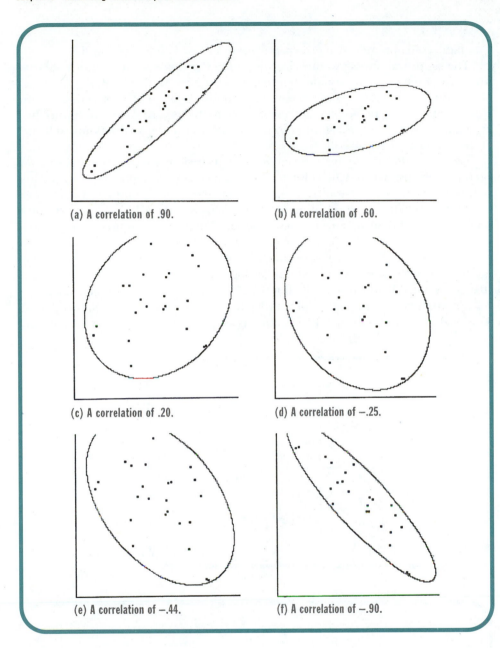

(a) A correlation of .90.   (b) A correlation of .60.

(c) A correlation of .20.   (d) A correlation of −.25.

(e) A correlation of −.44.   (f) A correlation of −.90.

Figure 8-6.
Six scatterplots and associated correlation coefficients.

strength of a relationship
extent of variability of Y about each value of X

direct relationship of two variables
values of the variables change in the same *direction*

indirect (or inverse) relationship of two variables
values of the variables change in the opposite *direction*

The amount of "scatter" in the scatterplot indicates the **strength** of the relationship. A small amount of scatter indicates a strong relationship. When the relationship between *Y* and *X* is perfectly described by a linear function, the "ellipse" is a straight line. At the other extreme, there is no relationship, so the "ellipse" becomes a circle.

The other important characteristic of a linear relationship is direction.

In a **direct relationship,** when *X* gets larger, *Y* gets larger, and when *X* gets smaller, *Y* gets smaller.

In an **indirect relationship,** when *X* gets larger, *Y* becomes smaller and when *X* gets smaller, *Y* becomes larger.

The correlation statistic is formally defined in the following section.

Correlation

The basic concept underlying the correlation statistic is the **cross-product.**

The significant cross-products in computing the correlation are not the cross-products of the original variables but the cross-products of the mean-deviated variables. As shown in Chapter 3, a mean deviation is obtained by subtracting a value from its mean. The mean of a mean-deviated variable is zero. When both variables are mean deviated, the mean of both new variables is zero, so the point (0,0) lies at the center of the scatterplot.

Figure 8-7 illustrates why these cross-products form the basis for evaluating *linear* relationships. In this scatterplot, 92% of the 24 cross-products are positive. Most points lie in the two quadrants in which the mean-deviated X and Y are *both* positive or *both* negative. The resulting cross-product, $(X - \overline{X})(Y - \overline{Y})$, of any of these points in these two quadrants is positive because the product of two positive values is positive, as is the product of two negative values. The resulting sum of these cross-products, $\sum (X - \overline{X})(Y - \overline{Y})$, is relatively large because there are few negative values to reduce the size of the sum. Similar logic applies to variables described by a strong inverse relationship in which most of the cross-products are negative.

For comparison, the scatterplot in Figure 8-8 illustrates a *lack* of correlation. This scatterplot has $6 + 6 = 12$ negative cross-products and $7 + 5 = 12$ positive

Figure 8-7.
The mean-deviated scatterplot with a correlation of .90 for $n = 24$.

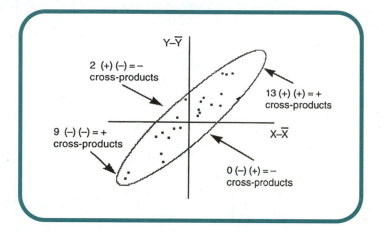

Figure 8-8.
The mean-deviated scatterplot of two variables with an average cross-product and correlation of about .00.

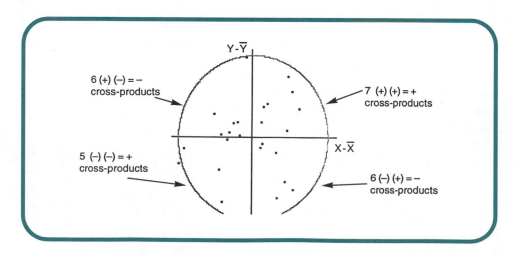

cross-products. The negative and positive cross-products tend to cancel each other out when summed, resulting in a sum of about zero.

For direct relationships, the sum of the positive cross-products is larger than the sum of the negative. For indirect relationships, the negative sum is larger than the positive. Converting this sum to an average results in the **covariance,** a useful statistic for summarizing the strength and direction of linear relationships.

The corresponding sample and population versions of the covariance are

$$s_{xy} \equiv \frac{\sum (X - \overline{X})(Y - \overline{Y})}{n - 1} \quad \text{or} \quad \sigma_{xy} \equiv \frac{\sum (X - \mu_X)(Y - \mu_Y)}{N},$$

> **covariance of variables _X_ and _Y_**
> *average sum of the cross-products of the mean-deviated values*

where n is sample size and N is population size. As with the definition of the variance in Chapter 3, the sample covariance is divided by effective sample size or degrees of freedom instead of actual sample size. Each observation consists of a value of X and a value of Y. Computing the sample mean of each variable, and then using these statistics to compute another statistic from the *same* data, effectively reduce sample size by one observation.

The size of the covariance depends not only on the strength and direction of the relationship between the variables, but also on the sometimes arbitrary units chosen for their measurement. For example, measuring Height in inches yields a dramatically larger covariance with Weight than when measuring Height in feet. The reason for this difference is that measurements in inches are 12 times larger than the corresponding measurements in feet.

When the units of measurement are arbitrary, the values of the original variables X and Y are converted to z-values by dividing each value's mean deviation by the variable's standard deviation. Basing the cross-products on the z-values instead of on ordinary mean deviations constrains the resulting statistic—the **correlation**—to a range between 1 and -1, inclusive.

> **correlation of variables _X_ and _Y_**
> *average cross-product of the corresponding z-values*

This correlation statistic is more formally called the *Pearson product-moment correlation coefficient,* after Karl Pearson's introduction of it in 1900. The sample and population versions of the correlation can be expressed by dividing the covariance by the product of the respective standard deviations,

$$r_{xy} \equiv \frac{s_{xy}}{s_x s_y} \quad \text{or} \quad \rho_{xy} \equiv \frac{\sigma_{xy}}{\sigma_x \sigma_y}.$$

This single division is algebraically equivalent to dividing each individual cross-product by the respective standard deviation. An example follows.

BUSINESS APPLICATION 8.1—Correlation

MANAGERIAL PROBLEM

What is the correlation between Price per Share (PPS) and Earnings per Share (EPS)?

DATA

The data are the PPS and EPS values at the close of 1992 for the 10 companies listed in the following conceptual worksheet. These 20 data values are shaded in gray in that worksheet.

APPLICATION—CONCEPTUAL WORKSHEET

The first step in obtaining the correlation is to calculate the sum of squares and the sum of cross-products for the two variables.

	A	B	C	D EPS dev	E PPS dev	F cross-product	G EPS dev sq	H PPS dev sq
1		EPS	PPS	EPS dev	PPS dev	cross-product	EPS dev sq	PPS dev sq
2	Company	X	Y	$X-\bar{X}$	$Y-\bar{Y}$	$(X-\bar{X})(Y-\bar{Y})$	$(X-\bar{X})^2$	$(Y-\bar{Y})^2$
3	IMO INDUSTRIES INC	-3.26	6.500	-3.97	-16.86	66.93	15.75	284.34
4	TORO CO	-1.98	13.000	-2.69	-10.36	27.86	7.23	107.38
5	CALMAT CO	-0.45	22.500	-1.16	-0.86	1.00	1.34	0.74
6	TULTEX CORP	0.56	8.625	-0.15	-14.74	2.20	0.02	217.19
7	FAMILY DOLLAR ST.	1.00	17.250	0.29	-6.11	-1.78	0.08	37.36
8	PHIL. SUB. CORP	1.23	16.000	0.52	-7.36	-3.84	0.27	54.21
9	RTZ PLC	1.50	41.375	0.79	18.01	14.25	0.63	324.45
10	TANDY CORP	2.24	24.500	1.53	1.14	1.74	2.34	1.29
11	OKLA. GAS & ELECT.	2.42	34.125	1.71	10.76	18.41	2.93	115.83
12	NICOR INC	3.83	49.750	3.12	26.39	82.36	9.74	696.30
13	Sum	7.09	233.625	0.00	0.00	209.13	40.34	1839.11
14	Effective Sample Size	10	10			9	9	9
15	Mean	0.71	23.363			23.24	4.48	204.35
16	SQRT						2.12	14.29

The sum of the cross-product of deviation scores is 209.13. The average of these cross-products, based on $df = n - 1 = 9$, is 23.24, which is the covariance. The correlation is the ratio of the covariance to the product of the standard deviations of 2.12 and 14.29, or 0.77.

APPLICATION—TRADITIONAL NOTATION

Calculate the correlation from the covariance and the two standard deviations. Both statistics are based on mean deviations. For EPS, $\bar{X} = 0.71$, and for PPS, $\bar{Y} = 23.36$. For the first company, Imo Industries Inc., the mean deviations are

$$X - \bar{X} = -3.26 - 0.71 = -3.97 \quad \text{and} \quad Y - \bar{Y} = 6.50 - 23.36 = -16.86.$$

The cross-product is $(X - \bar{X})(Y - \bar{Y}) = (-3.97)(-16.86) = 66.93$.

All 10 cross-products sum to $\sum (X - \bar{X})(Y - \bar{Y}) = 209.13$. The resulting covariance is the average cross-product computed from $df = n - 1$,

$$s_{xy} \equiv \frac{\sum (X - \bar{X})(Y - \bar{Y})}{n - 1} = \frac{209.13}{9} = 23.24.$$

The standard deviations are $s_X = 2.12$ and $s_Y = 14.34$. The correlation is

$$r_{xy} \equiv \frac{s_{xy}}{s_x s_y} = \frac{23.24}{(2.12)(14.29)} = \frac{23.24}{30.27} = 0.77.$$

EXCEL BUILT-IN ANALYSIS

Excel computes the correlation directly with either the Correlation program accessed via the Tools ➤ Data Analysis menu sequence, or the function

$$=\texttt{CORREL(array1,array2)}.$$

The term *array1* refers to the range of values for the first variable, and *array2* refers to the range of values for the second variable. The 10 EPS values in the preceding conceptual worksheet are in Cells C3 to C12, and the 10 PPS values are in Cells D3 to D12. The correlation is obtained from

$$=\texttt{CORREL(C3:C12,D3:D12)},$$

which results in a value of 0.77 in the cell in which the formula is entered. The advantage of the Correlation program found under the Tools ➤ Data Analysis menu sequence is that correlations among many variables can be computed simultaneously.

EXCEL SCATTERPLOT

Begin the graph with the menu sequence

$$\texttt{Insert ➤ Chart...}$$

Step 1—Chart Type. Specify a *XY* (Scatter) chart. Select a format that leaves the points unconnected.

Step 2—Chart Origin. Specify the Data Range to include the cells for both variables, including their labels.

Step 3—Chart Options. Select the Title tab and name the axes. As an option, select the Gridlines tab and uncheck the box that specifies Major gridlines on the *Y*-axis.

Step 4—Chart Location. Specify the location of the chart, either on a new sheet or as an object on the current worksheet.

The result is the following modified chart.

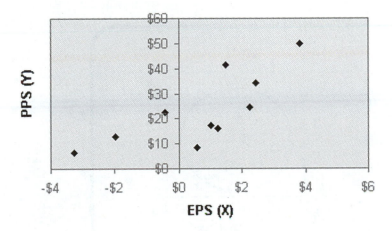

To accomplish these modifications, double-click on the relevant feature and respond to the resulting dialog box. For example, as illustrated in the accompanying Format Axis dialog box, after double-clicking on an axis, choose the Number tab and select the Currency format that displays zero decimal places. Or select the Font tab and then choose the Color for the text displayed next to the axis. Select the Patterns tab and choose the Color for the axis itself.

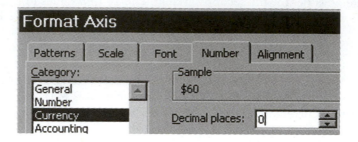

MANAGERIAL INTERPRETATION

As a company's Earnings per Share increases, Price per Share also tends to increase. The variables are related.

The previous example illustrated two highly correlated variables. Two variables are *uncorrelated* when values of one variable are associated with *both* high and low values of another variable. The scatterplot of two uncorrelated variables is circular, as illustrated in Figures 8-9 and 8-10 for Debt Ratio and Dividend per Share. High values of DPS are associated with *both* high and low values of Debt Ratio.

This section demonstrated how to summarize the strength and direction of a relationship between two variables with the correlation coefficient. The next section provides a complementary perspective for describing a relationship between two variables. The basis of this new perspective is the function.

Figure 8-9.
Scatterplot of Debt Ratio and Dividend per Share, $r = .15$, for the illustrative sample of 10 companies.

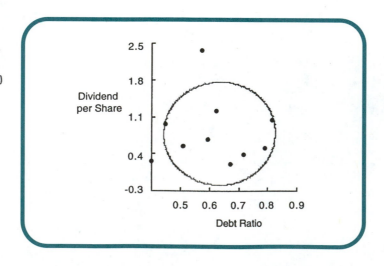

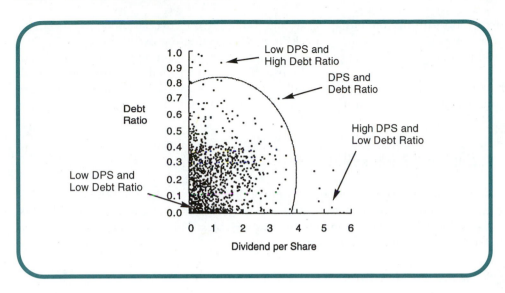

Figure 8-10.
Scatterplot of Debt
Ratio and Dividend per
Share, $r = .07$, for all
1,397 companies from
the full sample of 1,402
with a Debt Ratio less
than 1.0 and Dividend
per Share less than 6.

EXERCISES

8-1. There are 2.54 centimeters per inch.

Mechanical **a.** Specify the function that transforms inches to centimeters. Is the function linear? Why?

b. Plot centimeters as a function of inches for the following adult heights: 60 in, 64 in, 67 in, 72 in, 74 in. Plot the function by connecting the five points.

8-2. The June 1995 *Consumer Reports* listed the Price and Capacity (BTU/Hr) of a variety of air conditioners. Eight of these air conditioners were randomly selected; the data are listed below.

Application

Cost (X)	380	300	250	380
Capacity (Y)	5,800	5,450	5,100	5,600
Cost (X)	420	440	480	360
Capacity (Y)	6,700	7,800	8,600	8,200

a. Draw the scatterplot for these data.
b. Compute the correlation using a conceptual worksheet.
c. Compute the correlation by applying traditional formulas.

d. Compute the correlation with the built-in application of computer software.
e. Interpret the scatterplot and correlation.

8-3. The closing 1992 Debt Ratio and Current Retained Earnings per Share are listed below.

Application

	DR	CRES
Company	X	Y
1 IMO INDUSTRIES INC	0.32	-3.63
2 TORO CO	0.39	-2.46
3 CALMAT CO	0.20	-1.09
4 TULTEX CORP	0.27	0.36
5 FAMILY DOLLAR ST	0.00	0.75
6 PHIL. SUBURBAN CORP	0.42	0.20
7 RTZ PLC	0.22	0.32
8 TANDY CORP	0.11	1.68
9 OKLA. GAS & ELECTRIC	0.32	-0.24
10 NICOR INC	0.18	1.48

a. Draw the scatterplot for these data.
b. Compute the correlation using a conceptual worksheet.
c. Compute the correlation by applying traditional formulas.

d. Compute the correlation with the built-in application of computer software.
e. Interpret the scatterplot and correlation.

8-4. The correlation was defined as the average cross-product of the corresponding

z-values. Compute the correlation between DR and CRES by interpreting the definition literally. That is, compute the corresponding z-values for each of the two variables, then their cross-products, and finally the average cross-product of the z-values. Use $df = n - 1$ to compute the average.

8.2 REGRESSION MODEL

Regression analysis combines the concept of a function, in which the value of Y is known given a value of X, with the concept of scatter in a scatterplot, which illustrates the empirical relation between two variables. This integration of concepts is developed further in this section.

Variability of Y for a Given Value of X

A function specifies the *exact* price in Canadian dollars given the price in U.S. dollars. The relations among measured variables such as PPS and EPS in the day-to-day world of business, however, typically are not exact. PPS, the response or Y variable, is not precisely determined by EPS, the predictor or X variable. Instead, PPS and EPS are only *approximately* related.

The crucial fact is that different companies with the same Earnings per Share typically have different prices.

> For data, the *same* value of X results in different *values of Y*.

In Table 8-4, for example, five values of PPS are obtained for five different companies that all have an EPS of 60¢: $7.38, $8.75, $17.38, $14.00, and $4.63. Instead of a functional relationship with a single value of Y associated with each value of X, a *distribution* of Y values exists for each value of X.

Now consider the issue of estimation. What value of PPS should be estimated from the value of EPS = 60¢? One answer is the mean price for all companies with that value of EPS.

The mean PPS for these five companies in Table 8-4 with EPS = 60¢ is $\hat{Y} = \$10.43$. The **conditional mean** of Y for that value of X is chosen as the estimated value $\hat{Y}$. The estimated value of Y for any company with an EPS of 60¢ is $\hat{Y} = \$10.43$. Defining $\hat{Y}$ across a range of values of the predictor variable defines a function that relates the response and predictor variables.

conditional mean *mean of Y only for those observations with the same value of X*

Each observation has a measured value of Y and a corresponding value $\hat{Y}$ estimated from X, which together define the **residual.** For example, for Brandon Systems Corp., the value of the response variable Y found in Table 8-4 is PPS = $7.38. The residual is calculated as

$$e \equiv Y - \hat{Y} = \$7.38 - \$10.43 = -\$3.05.$$

residual variable *error, the difference between the estimated value and the actual value,* $e \equiv Y - \hat{Y}$

The actual value of Price per Share for this company is $3.05 *below* the estimated value, the conditional mean of $10.43.

The same value of X yields different measured values of Y. For a given value of X, variability of Y around the mean of Y indicates the extent of estimation error. The estimate $\hat{Y}$ is a kind of target. If these values of Y are close to each other, $\hat{Y}$ is close to

Company	EPS X	PPS Y
1 BRANDON SYSTEMS CORP	$0.60	$7.38
2 BUSH INDUSTRIES	$0.60	$8.75
3 TEXAS PACIFIC LAND TRUST	$0.60	$17.38
4 BLOUNT INC	$0.60	$14.00
5 PENOBSCOT SHOE	$0.60	$4.63

Table 8-4. Earnings per Share for 1992 and closing 1992 Price per Share for five companies with EPS = 60¢.

each measured value of Y, with little error of estimation. If the values of Y for a given value of X are widely dispersed, the error of estimation could be considerable.

STATISTICAL ILLUSTRATION—Distribution of Y at a Single Value of X

To illustrate the relationship between EPS and PPS over the range of values from EPS = 60¢ to EPS = 80¢. Table 8-5 shows the analysis of the value of PPS for companies with an EPS of 60¢, 70¢, or 80¢.

Company	X	Y	Statistics
1 BRANDON SYSTEMS CORP	$0.60	$7.38	
2 BUSH INDUSTRIES	$0.60	$8.75	for companies with an EPS of $0.60,
3 TEXAS PACIFIC LAND TRUST	$0.60	$17.38	$\hat{Y} = \bar{Y} = \$10.43$
4 BLOUNT INC	$0.60	$14.00	$s_Y = 5.17$
5 PENOBSCOT SHOE	$0.60	$4.63	
6 CALGON CARBON CORP	$0.70	$17.63	
7 SAMSON ENERGY CO	$0.70	$10.25	
8 MEDIA GENERAL	$0.70	$17.38	for companies with an EPS of $0.70,
9 GENCORP INC	$0.70	$10.63	$\hat{Y} = \bar{Y} = \$14.07$
10 SCIENTIFIC-ATLANTA INC	$0.70	$23.75	$s_Y = 5.79$
11 BAIRNCO CORP	$0.70	$6.75	
12 DANIEL INDUSTRIES	$0.70	$12.13	
13 COLES MYER LTD	$0.80	$25.63	
14 MANITOWOC CO	$0.80	$22.25	for companies with an EPS of $0.80,
15 ROLLINS TRUCK LEASING	$0.80	$12.00	$\hat{Y} = \bar{Y} = \$16.13$
16 CANADIAN MARCONI CO	$0.80	$11.38	$s_Y = 7.30$
17 SPORT SUPPLY GROUP INC	$0.80	$9.38	

Table 8-5. Earnings per Share for 1992 and closing 1992 Price per Share for 17 companies.

Figure 8-11.
Distributions around
the conditional
means of PPS for
three values of EPS:
60¢, 70¢, and 80¢.

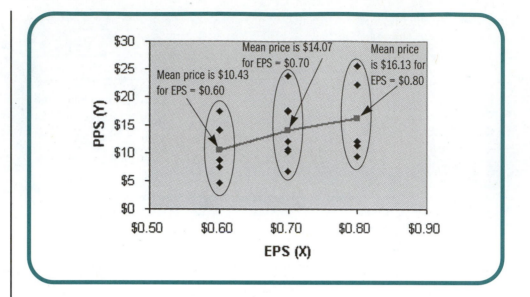

Figure 8-11 displays the scatterplot of EPS and PPS for these 17 companies. The pattern of the conditional means in Figure 8-11, connected by line segments, indicates the general form of the relationship: PPS tends to increase as EPS increases. For EPS = 60¢, mean PPS is $10.43, which increases to $14.07 and $16.13 for EPS of 70¢ and 80¢, respectively. The standard deviation of Y at each level of X is approximately the same, ranging from $5.17 to $7.30.

The pattern of estimated Y values for different values of X can exhibit many forms. Fortunately, the simplest of all functional relationships, a linear relationship between X and Y, describes many situations. The next section introduces regression analysis in which this linearity is assumed.

Regression Models and Residuals

Plotting the mean of Y for each value of X illustrates the relationship between two variables, but this method of regression analysis applies only when there are multiple observations for *each* value of X. In the preceding example, five observations had a value of $X = 60¢$, seven observations had a value of $X = 70¢$, and five observations had a value of $X = 80¢$. If the values of X had not been concentrated at only a few values, the corresponding means could not have been computed directly, because most if not all values of X would occur only once.

When multiple observations are not available for each level of X, the form of the underlying function must be *assumed*. The most common assumption is linearity. Assuming that the conditional means of Y lie on a straight line, regression analysis summarizes the relationship between the variables.

Again, consider the variables Price per Share (PPS) and Earnings per Share (EPS). The graph of PPS and EPS for different companies is a scatterplot with a correlation of $r = .59$ in the sample of 1,402 companies. Even though the relationship is not perfect, linear regression analysis identifies the "best" fitting line through the scatterplot of PPS and EPS. This line indicates that PPS tends to depend on EPS.

The problem in linear regression analysis is estimating the parameters of the linear function that best summarizes the relationship between Y and X. The linear function that provides this estimate is $\hat{Y} = b_0 + b_1 X$. As before, $\hat{Y}$ is the mean of all values of Y for the given value of X—assuming that X and Y are linearly related.

Choosing the values of the **linear regression coefficients** b_0 and b_1 defines a specific linear function, which, when graphed, yields the *regression line*. Given this function, a company's estimated Price per Share $\hat{Y}$ can be estimated from the company's Earnings per Share X.

The function $\hat{Y} = b_0 + b_1 X$ estimates the value of the response variable Y from a specified value of X, $\hat{Y}$. As previously discussed, the estimated slope coefficient b_1 indicates how Y changes on average as the value of X changes. EPS increases \$1. What is the average change in PPS? The answer is b_1.

The goal is to obtain the regression line that best summarizes the relationship between Y and X. To understand the meaning of "best," first consider an arbitrary "trial" regression line, that is, with arbitrarily chosen b_0 and b_1. The scatterplot in Figure 8-12, based on the sample of 10 companies, includes an arbitrary regression line, $\hat{Y} = 12 + 3X$. An estimated value of $\hat{Y}$ for this function falls precisely on this line for each value of X. For Tandy Corporation, with EPS = \$2.24,

$$\hat{Y} = 3X + 12 = 3\,(2.24) + 12 = 6.72 + 12 = 18.72,$$

and for Tultex Corporation with EPS = \$0.56,

$$\hat{Y} = 3X + 12 = 3\,(0.56) + 12 = 1.68 + 12 = 13.68.$$

Given this regression line, *two* values are associated with each company's EPS or X: the actual PPS or Y and the estimated PPS or $\hat{Y}$.

> *The graph of the data, the X's and Y's, is a scatterplot; the graph of the X's and $\hat{Y}$'s is a straight line.*

> **linear regression coefficients**
> Y-intercept b_0 and slope coefficient b_1

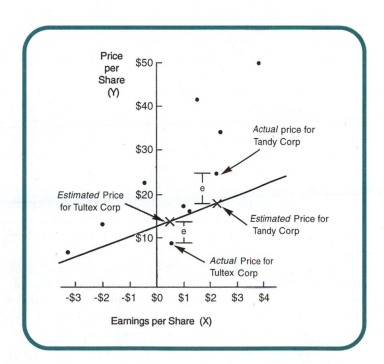

Figure 8-12.
Scatterplot of PPS and EPS for the 10 sample companies around the *arbitrary* regression line $\hat{Y} = 12 + 3X.$

Expressed another way, each value of X always yields a single value of $\hat{Y}$. Because the relationship between X and Y is not perfect, however, different observations with the same value of X generally have *different* values of Y.

Almost all of the points in the scatterplot lie above this arbitrarily chosen regression line, so the line (or corresponding linear equation) does *not* accurately describe the relationship of PPS expressed as a function of EPS. How can this lack of fit be demonstrated statistically? A regression line fits well when each estimated value $\hat{Y}$ is close to the corresponding obtained value of Y, that is, when $Y - \hat{Y} =$ "small" for most observations. Consider the residuals for the Tandy and Tultex Corporations:

$$\text{Tandy Corporation:} \quad e \equiv Y - \hat{Y} = \$24.50 - \$18.72 = \$5.78$$

$$\text{Tultex Corporation:} \quad e \equiv Y - \hat{Y} = \$8.63 - \$13.68 = \text{-}\$5.05.$$

For the Tandy Corporation, actual PPS is \$5.78 *more* than the estimated value. For the Tultex Corporation, actual PPS is \$5.05 *less* than the value estimated by the arbitrary regression line.

regression model for variable Y

Actual (Y) = Estimated $(\hat{Y})$ + Residual (e)

The **regression model** specifies two influences on the value of the variable Y. One influence is the estimated or *explained* component $\hat{Y}$. This component is estimated, such as from a linear regression line, as $\hat{Y} = b_0 + b_1 X$. In the real world, however, X is not the sole influence on Y. Estimation is not perfect. The residual e, which is the difference between the estimated value $\hat{Y}$ and the actual value Y, is a fundamental aspect of regression. The residual variable e represents the *unexplained* influences on the value of Y. The residual e blurs the underlying influence on Y that is predictable from X, mitigating its detection.

The residual reflects a lack of information regarding the value of Y. If more information were available, the residual would be smaller. Some of these unknown influences are other variables related to Y that are omitted from the regression model. Including one predictor variable in the model does not preclude other variables from being viable predictor variables. If these variables are omitted from the model, then their influences on Y are modeled, in part, with the residual variable e. The residual also reflects pure random chance with no specific explanation, analogous to the flip of a coin, for which there is no explanation why a particular flip landed on tails.

Different regression models yield residuals larger than others for the same data. The larger the residuals, the worse the accuracy of estimation. To choose the regression model that yields the smallest residuals (the "best" regression model), a statistic is needed that reflects the size of residuals *across* all observations in the sample. Any one residual may be large or small, positive or negative, but how large do the residuals tend to be over *all* the observations?

To assess the overall size of the residuals, first consider their sum. The problem with this sum is that the negative residuals reduce the size of the overall sum. Imagine two observations with large residuals of exactly the same magnitude. One residual is \$1,000,000 and the other is -\$1,000,000. These two large residuals together equal zero.

To avoid the problem of the positive and negative residuals canceling each other out, the negative signs of each residual e could be removed by either taking the absolute value or by squaring. There is little practical difference between these choices unless outliers are present; outliers tend to have an even more exaggerated effect on the resulting statistic when their values are squared. Because e^2 is more closely related to the normal curve, squaring is the usual choice for removing the negative sign.

For each observation, the residual is the difference of Y and the estimated value $\hat{Y}$, so

$$e \equiv Y - \hat{Y} \quad \text{and} \quad e^2 = (Y - \hat{Y})^2.$$

Once e^2 is obtained for each observation, the **SSE,** or **sum of squared residuals** $\sum e^2$ is computed across all observations.

SSE is the basis for defining the "best" regression line and for evaluating the overall size of the residuals. An example of calculating SSE for an arbitrarily chosen regression model follows.

> sum of the squared residuals (SSE)

STATISTICAL ILLUSTRATION—Residuals for an Arbitrary Regression Model

MODEL

The response variable Y is Price per Share (PPS), and the predictor variable X is Earnings per Share (EPS). The estimated value of Y, $\hat{Y}$ is arbitrarily chosen as $\hat{Y} = 12 + 3X$.

CALCULATION OF SSE

The calculation of SSE follows the general form of the variability table introduced in Chapter 3 for the calculation of the standard deviation. The distinction is that the estimated value of $\hat{Y}$ is the *center* around which each deviation is computed, so the deviations in this table are residuals from the regression line.

	A	B	C	D	E	F
1		Predictor	Response	Center	Deviation from Cntr	Squared Deviation
2		EPS	PPS	Est PPS	Residual	Res Sq
3	Company	X	Y	$\hat{Y} =$ 12 + 3X	$e \equiv Y - \hat{Y}$	e^2
4	IMO INDUSTRIES INC	-3.26	6.500	2.22	4.28	18.32
5	TORO CO	-1.98	13.000	6.06	6.94	48.16
6	CALMAT CO	-0.45	22.500	10.65	11.85	140.42
7	TULTEX CORP	0.56	8.625	13.68	-5.06	25.55
8	FAMILY DOLLAR STORES	1.00	17.250	15.00	2.25	5.06
9	PHIL. SUBURBAN CORP	1.23	16.000	15.69	0.31	0.10
10	RTZ PLC	1.50	41.375	16.50	24.88	618.77
11	TANDY CORP	2.24	24.500	18.72	5.78	33.41
12	OK. GAS & ELECTRIC	2.42	34.125	19.26	14.87	220.97
13	NICOR INC	3.83	49.750	23.49	26.26	689.59
14	Sum	7.09			92.36	**1800.35**

The sum of squared deviations for this arbitrary regression model for these 10 companies is 1,800.35. That is,

$$\text{SSE} \equiv \sum (Y - \hat{Y})^2 \equiv \sum e_i^2 = 1800.35.$$

The statistic SSE indicates the fit of a regression model for a given sample. Calculating SSE for the model $Y = 12 + 3X$ yields a large number, which presumably could be reduced for better fitting models. Our next question is, logically enough, how is the "best" model defined and calculated?

Finding the "Best" Regression Model

> **ordinary least squares criterion (OLS)**
>
> *choose the values of b_0 and b_1 that minimize the sum of squared residuals for the available data*

The usual definition of *best* is expressed in terms of the **ordinary least squares criterion (OLS),** or the sum of *squared* residuals across *all* observations that comprise the available data.

When estimation is perfect, all residuals are zero, so the sum of squared residuals is also zero, SSE = 0. In practice, the best that can be hoped for is to reduce the sum of squared residuals to as small a number as possible.

The one regression model that provides the smallest possible sum of squared residuals SSE is easily obtained with the minimization tools of calculus.

> *Slope coefficient for the OLS regression model:*
> $$b_1 = \frac{s_{XY}}{s_X^2}$$

The OLS estimated slope coefficient is the covariance of the response and predictor variables divided by the variance of the predictor variable.

The estimated Y-intercept b_0 directly follows from the regression coefficient b_1.

> *Y-intercept for the OLS regression model:*
> $$b_0 = \overline{Y} - b_1 X$$

The resulting values of b_0 and b_1 define the regression line that minimizes the sum of squared residuals SSE. Any choice of values for the regression coefficients other than the OLS estimates leads to a larger SSE.

An example of obtaining the OLS regression line follows.

BUSINESS APPLICATION 8.2—Estimated Regression Model

MANAGERIAL PROBLEM

What is the linear equation that predicts a company's Price per Share (PPS) from the company's Earnings per Share (EPS)? How is EPS related to PPS?

DATA

The data are the 1992 PPS and EPS values for the sample of 10 companies listed in Business Application 8.1 on page 340.

APPLICATION—TRADITIONAL NOTATION

To compute SSE, first estimate the OLS regression model from the data for these 10 companies. The covariance of PPS and EPS, s_{XY}, the variance of EPS, s_X^2, and the means, $\overline{X}$ and $\overline{Y}$, were computed in Business Application 8.1:

$$\overline{X} = \$0.709 \quad \text{and} \quad \overline{Y} = \$23.363$$

$$s_{xy} \equiv \frac{\sum (X - \overline{X})(Y - \overline{Y})}{n - 1} = \frac{209.14}{9} = 23.237$$

$$s_X^2 \equiv \frac{\sum (X - \overline{X})^2}{n - 1} = \frac{40.343}{9} = 4.483.$$

From these values, the OLS regression estimates are

$$b_1 = \frac{s_{XY}}{s_X^2} = \frac{23.243}{4.483} = 5.184$$

$$b_0 = \overline{Y} - b_1\overline{X} = 23.363 - 5.184(.709) = 23.36 - 3.68 = 19.69.$$

The model estimated from these data is based on $\hat{Y} = 19.69 + 5.18X$.

APPLICATION—EXCEL BUILT-IN ANALYSIS

Excel estimates the linear regression parameters directly with either the Regression program accessed via the Tools ➤ Data Analysis menu sequence, or the two functions,

```
=INTERCEPT(known_y's,known_x's).
```

```
=SLOPE(known_y's,known_x's).
```

	B	C
2	EPS	PPS
3	X	Y
4	-3.26	6.500
5	-1.98	13.000
6	-0.45	22.500
7	0.56	8.625
8	1.00	17.250
9	1.23	16.000
10	1.50	41.375
11	2.24	24.500
12	2.42	34.125
13	3.83	49.750

The *known_y*'s are the 10 PPS values in Cells C4 to C13. The *known_x*'s are the 10 EPS values in Cells B4 to B13. Obtain the estimated intercept and slope from

```
=INTERCEPT(C4:C13,B4:B13)
```

```
=SLOPE(C4:C13,B4:B13),
```

which result in values of 19.69 and 5.18 in the respective cells in which the formulas were entered.

EXCEL SCATTERPLOT AND REGRESSION LINE

The scatterplot of EPS and PPS for these 10 companies was obtained in Business Application 8.1. To add the regression line to the scatterplot, first compute $\hat{Y}$ for each observation using $b_0 = 19.69$ and $b_1 = 5.18$. Place these estimated values on the worksheet in a new column adjacent to the measured Y values, which is Column D in this example. Select these 10 $\hat{Y}$ values. Move the cursor toward the bottom of the selection until the cursor turns into an arrow. Then click and drag the selection to the scatterplot. Release the mouse button when the cursor is over the scatterplot.

The regression "line" appears as a series of unconnected points. To obtain a smooth line, double-click on one of the unconnected points to edit the data series. Choose the Patterns tab, and then specify a Custom or Automatic line with Marker None. Choosing a custom line allows choice of the color, width, and style of the line. The result is displayed in Figure 8-13, the scatterplot with the regression line added.

RESULTS FOR FULL SAMPLE OF SIZE 1,402

The same analysis for the computation of the OLS regression line was conducted for all 1,402 companies in the much larger sample from which the illustrative sample of only 10 companies was drawn. The analysis of 1,402 companies yielded the following regression line for these 1992 data:

$$\hat{Y} = 19.56 + 5.44X.$$

Figure 8-13.
Scatterplot of PPS and EPS for the 10 sample companies with the OLS regression line
$\hat{Y} = 19.68 + 5.18X.$

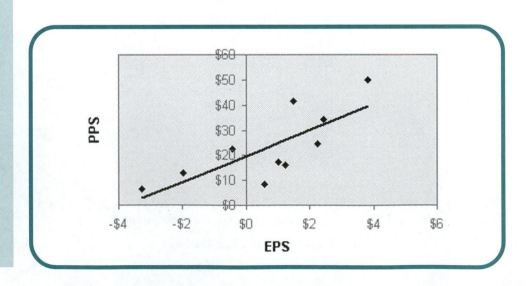

The model $\hat{Y} = 19.56 + 5.44X$ provides the most accurate prediction of PPS from EPS for these 1,402 companies of any other *linear* regression model. As noted earlier in the chapter, the illustrative sample of 10 companies was deliberately chosen nonrandomly to mirror the relationships of the relevant variables in the complete sample.

MANAGERIAL INTERPRETATION

Based on the analysis of 1992 data for 1,402 companies, Earnings per Share is related to stock price. For every dollar increase in Earnings per Share, Price per Share increases an average of $5.44. When Earnings per Share is zero, the average price is around $19.56. Companies with positive earnings add an average of $5.44 to this baseline of $19.56 for every dollar in Earnings per Share, and companies with negative earnings subtract an average of $5.44 for each dollar.

Unfortunately, even for the *best* regression model, the actual value Y and the estimate $\hat{Y}$ differ. Calculate SSE from this difference in Table 8-6.

Summing the squared error term for all 10 companies yields

$$\text{SSE} \equiv \sum (Y - \hat{Y})^2 \equiv \sum e^2 = 755.00.$$

The sum of squared deviations for this OLS regression model, 755.0, is much lower than the 1,800.7 obtained with the arbitrarily chosen regression line. Any other values of b_1 and b_0, that is, any other linear regression model, will yield a higher SSE for these data than the regression line defined by $b_0 = 19.68$ and $b_1 = 5.18$.

Causality

Another important issue regarding the interpretation of a regression model is causality. Sometimes estimation in a regression analysis mirrors a causal relationship. The price of a product or service directly affects the demand for the product

Company	Predictor EPS X	Response PPS Y	Center Est PPS $\hat{Y}=$ 19.69+5.18X	Deviation from Cntr Residual $e \equiv Y - \hat{Y}$	Squared Deviation Res Sq e^2
IMO INDUSTRIES INC	-3.26	6.500	2.79	3.71	13.78
TORO CO	-1.98	13.000	9.42	3.58	12.79
CALMAT CO	-0.45	22.500	17.35	5.15	26.48
TULTEX CORP	0.56	8.625	22.59	-13.97	195.02
FAMILY DOLLAR STORES	1.00	17.250	24.87	-7.62	58.08
PHIL. SUBURBAN CORP	1.23	16.000	26.06	-10.06	101.27
RTZ PLC	1.50	41.375	27.46	13.91	193.55
TANDY CORP	2.24	24.500	31.30	-6.80	46.23
OK. GAS & ELECTRIC	2.42	34.125	32.23	1.89	3.58
NICOR INC	3.83	49.750	39.54	10.21	104.22
Sum	7.09			0.00	**755.00**

Table 8-6.
Calculation of SSE for an OLS regression model.

or service. Regression analysis allows the manager to predict the demand that results from a specified increase or decrease in price. In other situations, the variables are related, but the relationship is not causal. Height does not cause weight, but regression analysis provides identical statistical tools for estimating a person's weight from his or her height as for estimating demand from price. In either case, the forms of the statistical computations and the results are identical.

> *Assigning causality requires more information than can be obtained from the statistical computations of regression.*

The statistical calculations of regression analysis provide for the analysis of the relation between two columns of numbers without any clue about the causal relationships among the variables. Analysis of computer output alone cannot establish causality.

We have defined the linear regression model and showed how to estimate the best version of this model in terms of minimizing the sum of square estimation errors. Next we show how to evaluate the model, including the sizes of the estimation errors and the underlying assumptions of OLS estimation.

EXERCISES

8-5. Consider the model $\hat{Y} = 1.3 + 4.5X$.

Mechanical **a.** Plot this model.

b. For one observation, $X = 3$ and $Y = 20$. What is $\hat{Y}$? What is e? Is $\hat{Y}$ an overestimate or underestimate?

c. For another observation, $X = -1$ and $Y = 2$. What is $\hat{Y}$? What is e? Is $\hat{Y}$ an overestimate or underestimate?

d. Determine which value of Y from (b) or (c) is more accurately estimated.

8-6. A realtor analyzed the relation between size of a house in square feet and market value. He estimated the following OLS regression model:

Concept

$$\hat{Y} = 19.5 + (0.0264)X.$$

a. Use the model to estimate market value for an area of 1,000 square feet.

b. Use the model to estimate market value for an area of 1,001 square feet.

c. Use the model to estimate market value for an area of 1,002 square feet.

d. Determine the difference between the estimated values in (a), (b), and (c).

e. Determine the meaning of the slope coefficient $b_1 = 0.0264$.

8-7. The values of PPS and annual Dividend per Share (DPS) for the sample of 10 companies analyzed in this chapter appear in the following table.

Application

Company	DPS X	PPS Y
1 IMO INDUSTRIES INC	0.38	6.50
2 TORO CO	0.48	13.00
3 CALMAT CO	0.64	22.50
4 TULTEX CORP	0.20	8.63
5 FAMILY DOLLAR STORES	0.25	17.25
6 PHILADELPHIA SUBURBAN CORP	1.03	16.00
7 RTZ PLC	1.18	41.38
8 TANDY CORP	0.56	24.50
9 OKLAHOMA GAS & ELECTRIC	2.66	34.13
10 NICOR INC	2.35	49.75

a. Compute the OLS regression line for PPS as a function of DPS.
b. Plot the OLS regression line through the scatterplot of DPS and PPS.
c. Compute SSE for the OLS regression line.
d. Determine the estimated PPS for a company that paid a Dividend per Share of $1.46.
e. Determine the estimated increase in PPS if the DPS for a company increases $.50.
f. Determine the estimated PPS when DPS = 0.

8-8. For the DPS/PPS data in the previous exercise,

    a. Plot the *arbitrary* regression model $\hat{Y} = 20X + 15$.

b. Compute SSE for the arbitrary regression model in (a).
c. Compare the SSEs for the previous exercise and this exercise. Which is smaller? Why?

8-9. *Consumer Reports* rated large-screen (31 to 35 in) TVs, as reported in the following table (*1994 Buying Guide*, p. 36).

	Rating	Price
Manufacturer	X	Y
1 Quasar SX3130FE	90	$950
2 Toshiba CN3281B	88	$1499
3 Mitsubishi CS-35FX1	86	$2500
4 Panasonic CTP-3180SF	85	$1180
5 Sony KV-32XBR35	84	$1780
6 RCA F35100ST	83	$1880
7 Zenith SJ3275BG	82	$1020
8 GE 31GT656	80	$860
9 Hitachi 31KX6B	79	$890
10 Sears 43958	76	$1500

a. Draw the scatterplot for Rating and Price.
b. Compute the OLS regression line for Price as a function of Rating.
c. Plot the OLS regression line through the scatterplot of Rating and Price. Does the amount of scatter around the line seem adequate for successful prediction?

d. Compute SSE for the OLS regression line.
e. Determine the estimated Price for a TV that has a rating of 81.
f. Determine the estimated change in Price if the Rating score increases two points.

8-10. The following data are the 1992 closing stock price for 24 companies and the Dividend per Share paid by these companies at the end of 1992.

	DPS	PPS
Company	X	Y
LL&E ROYALTY TRUST	0.27	3.50
COL. NATL BANKSHARES	0.27	45.50
COMDISCO INC	0.27	16.13
INTER-REG. FINANCIAL	0.27	17.88
KAUFMAN & BROAD HOME	0.27	15.50
NEVADA POWER CO	1.60	23.63
GEN. PUBLIC UTILITIES	1.60	27.63
PENN. POWER & LIGHT	1.60	27.25
BRIGGS & STRATTON	1.60	44.88
POTOMAC ELCT. POWER	1.60	23.88
SAFECO CORP	1.60	57.25
ALUM. CO OF AMERICA	1.60	71.63
GENERAL MOTORS CORP	1.60	32.25
BANCO DE SANTANDER	2.20	38.38
GOODRICH (B. F.) CO	2.20	48.88
SOUTHERN CO	2.20	38.50
SW PUBLIC SVC CO	2.20	32.63
HERCULES INC	2.20	63.50
OHIO CASUALTY CORP	2.66	63.13
LINCOLN NAT. CORP	2.66	74.00
OK. GAS & ELECTRIC	2.66	34.13
MINN. MINING & MFG CO	3.20	100.63
FINA INC	3.20	60.25
TEXACO INC	3.20	59.75
MOBIL CORP	3.20	63.13

a. Compute the estimated value of PPS for each value of DPS by using the conditional mean as the estimate.

b. On the same graph, (i) plot the scatterplot of PPS and DPS, and (ii) plot the conditional means of PPS and the values of DPS.

c. Determine if there is a relationship between PPS and DPS and why or why not. If there is a relationship, is it linear?

d. Compute the OLS regression model with PPS as the response variable and DPS as the predictor variable.

e. Plot the OLS regression line, and compare this result to the plot of conditional means obtained in (b). Are these results different? Why?

8-11. Consider the following data: the size of a house and the annual cost of heat. Set up the standard spreadsheet for computing SSE that includes columns for X, Y, $\hat{Y}$, e, and

Concept

e^2. At the very beginning of the spreadsheet, however, include space for the two values b_0 and b_1. When entering the linear equation for $\hat{Y}$ in the cells of the relevant column, reference the cells containing b_0 and b_1. The linear function $\hat{Y}$ can now easily be changed by changing the values of the two cells with the values of b_0 and b_1.

Heating Cost	553	621	729	640	714	538	592
Size of House	1250	1800	2430	1550	2280	1390	2100

a. Choose several pairs of values for b_0 and b_1, and compute the corresponding SSE for each pair.

b. Make your best guess for the OLS values of b_0 and b_1.

c. Compute the OLS values of b_0 and b_1.

d. Determine how the OLS values compare with your best guess values. How do the values of SSE compare across the two models?

8.3 ASSESSMENT OF THE REGRESSION MODEL

Constructing a regression model provides a method for describing the relationships among variables and for predicting the unknown from the known. Unfortunately, making a prediction does not guarantee a *good* prediction. As illustrated in Figure 8-14, a regression line can be fit to a scatterplot for either a strong linear relationship between Y and X or for a weak linear relationship. Consider trying to predict SAT Score from Shoe Size. Even the best line would not yield accurate predictions. The correlation between SAT Score and Shoe Size is virtually zero, so knowledge of Shoe Size contains very little information for the prediction of SAT Score or vice versa. Yet a regression line could still be drawn through the resulting scatterplot.

The first task following estimation of b_1 and b_0 is model assessment. What level of accuracy does the prediction equation provide? Is the value of Y expected to be near to or far from the estimated value $\hat{Y}$? The key concept underlying assessment

Figure 8-14.
Two regression lines with the same slope b but different amounts of scatter (residuals) around their respective lines.

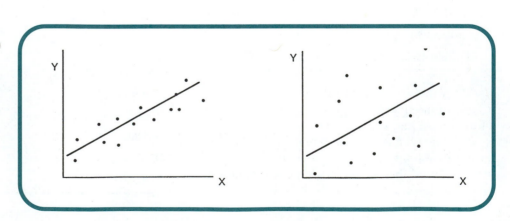

of this fit is the analysis of the residual variable *e*. As Figure 8-14 demonstrates, the magnitude of the residuals in the second diagram is considerably larger than in the first. The analysis of model fit is based on the sum of these squared residuals or SSE across all observations.

Standard Error of Estimate

By itself, SSE is the criterion to optimize, not a general fit index. A larger sample is a worthy goal, but the *sum* of the squared residuals SSE increases as sample size increases simply because the number of residuals increases. To address this problem, consider the **mean squared residual,** similar to the mean square or variance introduced in Chapter 3.

Ideally, the mean square would be computed from all observations in the entire population. The population SSE is typically unavailable, so calculate the mean square from the sample SSE. This mean square is the sum SSE divided by the effective sample size, or the degrees of freedom.

MSE is the mean of the squared residual terms using degrees of freedom *df* as the effective sample size. In the following extension, *npred* is the number of predictor variables in the model. The degrees of freedom for MSE is

$$df = n - (npred + 1)$$

> **mean squared residual (MSE)**
> $$MSE \equiv s_e^2 \equiv \frac{SSE}{df} = \frac{SSE}{n - (npred + 1)}$$
> where *npred* is the number of predictors and *n* is sample size

because there are *npred* + 1 estimates, one for each of the predictor *X* variables and one for the *Y*-intercept b_0. For the one predictor case, $\hat{Y}$ is computed from two sample estimates, b_1 and b_0, so the corresponding degrees of freedom is the sample size reduced by *two, n* − 2. In general, *npred* + 1 statistics must first be estimated to define the sample regression line before s_e can be estimated, in effect reducing the available sample size by *npred* + 1.

As noted in Chapter 3, taking the square root of the variance yields an even more useful variability index that is expressed in the metric of the original variable. The same logic applies to the mean square residual. The **standard error of estimate** s_e is the standard deviation of the residuals, which are assumed to be identical in the population for all values of *X*. For any value of *X*, each value of *Y* differs by the residual *e*, so s_e describes the variability of the observed values *Y* around the sample regression line. The larger s_e is, the larger the scatter of *Y*'s is around each estimated value.

> **standard error of estimate**
> $$s_e \equiv \sqrt{MSE}$$

The standard deviation expresses the variability of values around their mean. In the context of regression analysis, the larger the standard error of estimate, the larger the residuals, and the poorer the prediction of *Y* from *X*.

> *The standard error of estimate s_e indicates the size of the residuals for the sample from which the model was estimated.*

Assuming normally distributed residuals, approximately 95% of a normal distribution falls within two standard errors of the mean. Further, the smallest possible value of s_e, which is zero, occurs when all values of *Y* fall directly on the regression line.

Coefficient of Determination

The standard error of estimate s_e introduced in the previous section gauges the fit of the regression line to the scatterplot of *Y* and *X*. However, no upper limit constrains the size of the residuals, so s_e has no upper bound. Another problem is that changing the units of Y changes the value of s_e. Expressing height in inches yields a larger standard error for the same data than expressing height in feet.

The **coefficient of determination** R^2 complements the standard error of estimate s_e. R^2 equals 0 when the predictor variable does not contribute to the accuracy of prediction, and equals 1 for perfect prediction. Both R^2 and s_e are based on the sum of squared residuals SSE. R^2 also incorporates the sum of squared deviation scores for the variable Y, SSY (defined in Chapter 3, in which each value Y is deviated around the sample mean of all Y's, $\overline{Y}$).

R^2 is a *relative* index. R^2 compares the variability of Y around the conditional mean $\hat{Y}$ for a single value of X to the variability of Y around the mean of all Y, or $\overline{Y}$. Ignoring X, the best guess for the value of Y is $\overline{Y}$. That is, R^2 compares the deviations of two models: the model *with X* to the model *without X*.

> R^2 *indicates the improvement in estimation obtained using the model* $\hat{Y} = b_0 + b_1X$ *versus the model* $\hat{Y} = \overline{Y}$.

Providing an estimate $\hat{Y}$ with less error than $\overline{Y}$ reduces the variability of the deviations around the estimate. Figure 8-15 illustrates this reduced variation.

coefficient of determination

$$R^2 \equiv$$

$$1 - \frac{\sum(Y - \hat{Y})^2}{\sum(Y - \overline{Y})^2}$$

$$\equiv 1 - \frac{\text{SSE}}{\text{SSY}}$$

Figure 8-15a.
A *large* decrease in variability around the regression line compared to variability around the mean, leading to a *large* value of R^2.

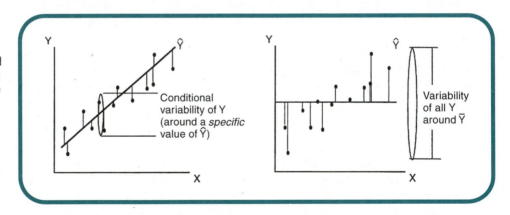

Figure 8-15b.
A *small* decrease in variability around the regression line compared to the variability around the mean, leading to a *small* value of R^2.

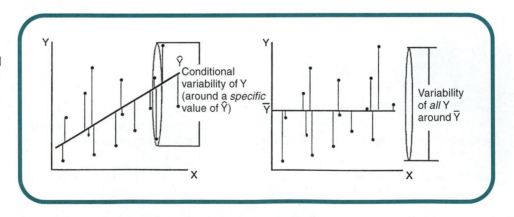

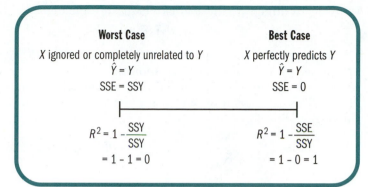

Figure 8-16.
The range of values for
the coefficient of
determination R^2.

The numerator of the ratio that defines R^2 is SSE, obtained from $\hat{Y}$ estimated from knowledge of X. As illustrated in Figure 8-16, if prediction is perfect, then the sum of squared residuals SSE is the smallest possible, or 0, so R^2 equals $1 - 0 = 1$. At the other extreme, if X is not (linearly) related to Y, then SSE = SSY, an equality that occurs when X is ignored, in which case all estimated values of Y are the sample mean $\overline{Y}$. That is, the maximum possible variation of the residuals is the total variation of the variable Y, or SSY. SSY, which serves as a baseline for evaluating the usefulness of the predictor variable, indicates the worst possible prediction.

The following example uses both the standard error of estimate s_e and the coefficient of determination R^2 to assess the efficacy of prediction.

BUSINESS APPLICATION 8.3—Assessing the Size of the Residuals

MANAGERIAL PROBLEM

When predicting Price per Share (PPS) from Earnings per Share (EPS), is the prediction reasonably accurate?

DATA

The data are the 1992 PPS and EPS values for the sample of 10 companies listed in Business Application 8.1 on page 340.

APPLICATION—TRADITIONAL NOTATION

SSE and the corresponding mean squared residual (MSE) are needed for the computation of the standard error of estimate s_e. The degrees of freedom for the mean square is

$$df = n - (npred + 1) = 10 - (1 + 1) = 8.$$

SSE was computed in a previous example as 755.00. MSE is

$$MSE \equiv \frac{\text{SSE}}{df} = \frac{755.00}{8} = 94.38,$$

which leads directly to the standard error of estimate,

$$s_e \equiv \sqrt{\text{MSE}} = \sqrt{94.38} = 9.71.$$

The computation of R^2 depends on the calculation of two sums of squares, the sum of squares of Y around the regression line (SSE) and the sum of squares of Y around the mean of Y (SSY). SSE was previously calculated in this chapter as 755.00. The calculation of SSY for these data was done in Chapter 3, with the result SSY $= 1839.25$.

$$R^2 \equiv 1 - \frac{\sum (Y - \hat{Y})^2}{\sum (Y - \overline{Y})^2} \equiv 1 - \frac{\text{SSE}}{\text{SSY}} = 1 - \frac{755.00}{1839.25} = 0.59.$$

APPLICATION—EXCEL BUILT-IN ANALYSIS

Excel estimates the standard error of estimate s_e and R^2 directly with either the Regression program accessed via the Tools ➤ Data Analysis menu sequence, or the two functions

```
=STEYX(known_y's,known_x's),
=RSQ(known_y's,known_x's).
```

The *known*_y's are the ten PPS values, which are in Cells C4 to C13. The *known*_x's are the ten EPS values, which are in Cells B4 to B13. The estimated values of s_e and R^2 are obtained from

```
=STEYX(C4:C13,B4:B13)
=RSQ(C4:C13,B4:B13),
```

which result in values of 9.715 and 0.589 in the respective cells in which the formulas were entered.

RESULTS FOR FULL SAMPLE SIZE 1,402

The sample statistics SSE, s_e, and R^2 were also computed for the much larger sample of 1,402 companies. These values are compared for both samples in Table 8-7.

SSE is larger for the full sample because, in part, there are many more residuals to cumulate. Also, scatter around the regression line in the full sample is larger,[2] indicated by a larger standard error of estimate s_e and a smaller R^2.

Table 8-7. Comparison of error statistics for the illustrative and full samples.

	SSE	s_e	R^2
Illustrative Sample for $n = 10$	755	$9.71	.59
Full Sample for $n = 1,402$	356,526	$15.96	.35

2. Why are s_e and R^2 so discrepant across the two samples? As noted, the illustrative sample of 10 companies was deliberately chosen nonrandomly to mirror the relationships of the relevant variables in the complete sample. The values for b_0 and b_1 are approximately the same in both samples, but the variability of Price in the full sample is larger, $s_Y = \$19.72$ versus $s_Y = \$14.29$ in the small sample. Or the maximum price in the large sample is $188, compared to $49.75 in the small sample. As a consequence of this reduced variability, obtaining the same strong relationship in a very small sample between EPS and Stock Price requires less scatter around the almost identical regression lines.

MANAGERIAL INTERPRETATION

The obtained coefficient of determination $R^2 = .35$ for the full sample of 1,402 companies indicates that EPS provides useful information regarding the prediction of PPS, but accurate prediction is not possible given the relatively large standard error of estimate $s_e = \$15.96$. There is much scatter around the corresponding regression line.

The coefficient of determination R^2 is a widely used index of model fit that compares variation around the estimated value of Y using the regression model to that obtained not using the model. However, the value of R^2 can be adjusted to provide an even more useful index. The basis of this adjustment, the distinction between sample and population regression lines that forms the basis of statistical inference in regression, is discussed in the next chapter. First, though, we review some of the basic assumptions of OLS and how to detect violations of these assumptions.

Assumptions of OLS

The valid use of OLS for estimating the regression coefficients requires the satisfaction of four assumptions. Analysis of the residuals provides evidence regarding the plausibility of these assumptions.

> *Residuals should only represent chance statistical fluctuations.*

If the residual variable contains any systematic content, one or more of the assumptions is violated. The result is that the model is too simple and should be corrected to model explicitly this systematic information instead of relegating it to the error term. Often this correction includes adding one or more predictor variables, accounting for a nonlinear relationship, or using an estimation procedure other than OLS.

The first assumption is that the mean of the estimation errors over the entire population is zero for any value of X. At each value of X, the errors $Y - \hat{Y}$ should be randomly distributed. This assumption is violated, for example, when incorrectly assuming a linear relationship. If the relationship is not linear, and a linear regression model is specified, the estimated values $\hat{Y}$ tend to overestimate Y for some values of X and underestimate X for other values.

To illustrate, Figure 8-17 displays a relationship in which Y is large only for both small and large values of X. A "best-fitting" curve through these data indicates a quadratic (U-shaped) relationship. Instead of the best-fitting quadratic curve, suppose linearity was falsely assumed, and a sample regression line was obtained. For middle values of X, where the curve is at a minimum, the estimated values $\hat{Y}$ overestimate the value of Y. In the regions of the curve where X is high or low and Y is high, $\hat{Y}$ tends to underestimate Y systematically. At each of these different values of X, the estimation errors are *not* randomly distributed around $\hat{Y}$.

The most obvious method for detecting nonlinearity is to examine the scatterplot of the variables. Or the scatterplot of the residuals and X can be examined to detect a pattern. In this example, the pattern is that low values of X lead to positive residuals, middle values lead to negative residuals, and high values lead

Figure 8-17.
A regression line only indicates the extent of a linear relationship.

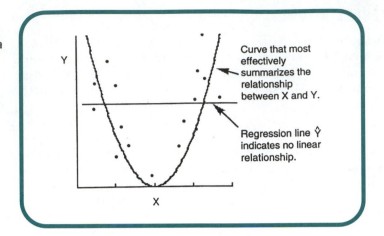

Curve that most effectively summarizes the relationship between X and Y.

Regression line $\hat{Y}$ indicates no linear relationship.

again to positive residuals. If the data are obviously nonlinear, as in Figure 8-17, instead use appropriate nonlinear regression methods explained in more advanced texts.

The second assumption of OLS regression is a constant population standard deviation of the estimation errors at all values of X, the equal variances assumption. The value of Y should be no more or less difficult to predict for different values of X. Any difference in the standard deviation of residuals for different values of X should be attributable only to sampling error. That is, the variability of Y's around each value of X should be the same. The violation of this equal variances assumption is called **heteroscedasticity.**

heteroscedasticity
standard deviation of residuals differs depending on the value of the predictor variable X

When heteroscedasticity occurs, the corresponding standard errors of the regression coefficients and associated confidence intervals, introduced in the next chapter, are also incorrect. A generally effective heteroscedasticity check is a visual examination of the plot of the residuals e against each predictor variable X. The search is for considerably more variability of the residuals at some levels of X than at others. Often the pattern exhibited by heteroscedasticity is a gradually increasing or decreasing variability as X gets larger or smaller.

The third assumption of OLS estimation is that the residuals are uncorrelated with any other variable, including each other. The size of one residual provides no information about the size of a second residual. There should be no trend or pattern exhibited by the residuals, and the residuals should not correlate with the predictor variable. This randomness of the residuals is the same concept illustrated by flipping a coin. If the first flip of a fair coin is a head, the second flip is just as likely to be a head or a tail.

The veracity of this assumption of uncorrelated residuals merits particular attention for the analysis of time-series data. With time-series data, adjacent residuals, which represent adjacent time points, are often correlated. The reason for **autocorrelation** in time-series data is that successive values may follow a specific pattern, such as gradually increasing or gradually decreasing. In data such as these, if one predicted value of Y is an underestimate, then the next value is also likely to yield an underestimate. Knowledge of the sign of one residual yields predictive information about the sign of the next residual, indicating autocorrelation.

autocorrelation
correlation of successive residuals over time

Autocorrelation in time-series data can often be detected visually by plotting the residuals against time. Any emergent pattern indicates a violation of the assumption. Autocorrelation can be quantified by correlating the residuals with a new variable defined by shifting the residuals up or down one or more time points. For example, the residual for the tenth month is paired with the residual for the eleventh month, the residual for the eleventh month is paired with the residual for the twelfth month, and so forth. For the assumption not to be violated, the resulting correlation of the two columns of residuals should be approximately zero.

The fourth assumption of regression, required by statistical inference discussed in the next chapter, is that the estimation errors are normally distributed for each value of X. The same normal distribution should describe the distribution of residuals at each value of X. Although there are more exact methods for assessing shape, an informal assessment of the shape of a distribution can be accomplished with a histogram. Normally distributed residuals more than two standard deviations from their mean should occur less than 5% of the time, and residuals larger than three standard deviations from the mean should rarely occur.

Four assumptions of the model were introduced. For each individual value of X, the population distribution of prediction errors is assumed to be (a) random and (b) normally distributed with a (c) mean of zero and (d) the same standard deviation. An illustration of differing standard errors, the problem of heteroscedasticity, is illustrated next.

STATISTICAL ILLUSTRATION—Heteroscedasticity

DATA

The data consist of 29 pairs of observations, found in the file HETERO.DAT

Obs.	1	2	3	4	5	6	7	8	9	10
X	28.13	18.02	28.33	22.01	20.81	20.61	19.72	26.29	11.88	23.42
Y	14.11	11.23	30.14	23.89	20.06	11.07	8.94	11.84	7.28	14.51

Obs.	11	12	13	14	15	16	17	18	19	20
X	11.73	23.71	8.26	12.87	8.38	17.93	17.13	12.47	27.59	7.50
Y	9.60	10.67	6.67	12.20	10.06	15.32	7.76	6.26	25.13	9.04

Obs.	21	22	23	24	25	26	27	28	29
X	10.66	29.04	18.10	22.28	16.97	28.39	2.42	29.68	24.56
Y	9.94	17.04	9.67	12.95	7.66	12.78	1.99	28.02	21.57

SCATTERPLOT OF *Y* AND *X*

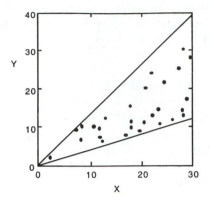

SCATTERPLOT OF RESIDUAL AND *X*

The OLS analysis of these data resulted in the model

$$\hat{Y} = 1.063 + (.650)X.$$

The residuals from this model are plotted with *X* in the following graph.

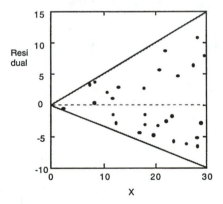

STATISTICAL PRINCIPLE

The heteroscedasticity of variance is evident from the analysis of the scatterplot of *Y* and *X*. However, the pattern is even more apparent in the analysis of the residual plot, which shows the scatter in the data with the linear component $\hat{Y} = b_0 + b_1 X$ removed by subtracting $\hat{Y}$ from *Y*. For these data, as the value of *X* increases, the variance of the residuals at each value also increases. The larger the value of *X*, the greater the uncertainty in predicting *Y*. Also, the OLS estimation procedure assumes unequal variances, so more advanced procedures for estimating the regression weights should replace OLS.[3]

3. Typically, a generalization of OLS called *weighted least squares* or WLS would be used in the presence of heteroscedasticity.

This chapter introduced regression analysis in the context of descriptive statistics. The next chapter presents regression analysis in the context of inferential statistics, examining some consequences of the sampling fluctuations of the estimated regression model from sample to sample.

EXERCISES

8-12. For the prediction of Dividends per Share (DPS) in Exercise 8-7,

a. Compute s_{e_2}
b. Compute R^2
c. Interpret the accuracy of estimation

8-13. For the prediction of Price of large-screen TVs from the *Consumer Report's* Ratings in Exercise 8-9,

a. Compute s_e
b. Compute R^2
c. Interpret the accuracy of estimation

8-14. A manager wanted to study the relationship between the Age in years of a certain model car (*X*) and its Worth in dollars (*Y*). The following data were collected for 12 such cars.

X	1.91	0.91	11.84	5.91	5.64	8.29
Y	16045	16466	11154	14139	15169	14715
X	3.99	2.98	12.32	2.55	3.36	7.63
Y	16235	14572	14510	16035	15275	12745

The corresponding OLS regression model is

$$\hat{Y} = 16501.8 - 311.32\,(X).$$

a. Compute the residuals.
b. Plot the residuals against Age.
c. *Assumption 1.* Do the residuals for approximately equal values of *X* appear to have a mean of zero? Why or why not?
d. *Assumption 2.* Do the residuals appear to have equal variance for all values of *X*? Why or why not?
e. *Assumption 3.* Do the residuals appear to be uncorrelated with each other? Does the value of one residual appear to be predictive of the value of adjacent residuals? Why or why not?
f. *Assumption 4.* Do the residuals appear to be normally distributed?
g. Determine if the OLS estimation of a linear regression model is the appropriate estimation procedure for these data.

8.4 SUMMARY

This chapter presented two primary analyses of the relationship between variables *X* and *Y*: correlation and regression. A regression analysis estimates an equation that summarizes the relationship between variables. Often this equation is linear, of the form $\hat{Y} = b_0 + b_1 X$, where $\hat{Y}$ is the estimated value. The purpose of regression analysis is twofold: to estimate the value of a response variable *Y* from one or more predictor variables *X*, and to explain the extent to which the value of *Y* depends on the values of *X*. Without implying causality, the slope coefficient b_1 is a regression coefficient that indicates the change in *Y* given a unit increase in *X*.

The correlation indicates the amount of scatter in the scatterplot of *Y* and *X* *without* reference to a regression model. For a perfect linear relationship in which the value of *Y* is precisely determined by the value of X, the plot of the values of Y and X is a straight line. However, when the *same* value of X yields *different* values of Y for different observations, knowledge of X provides only approximate knowledge of the value of Y. In this situation, the values of X and Y graph as a scatterplot instead of a straight line (or more generally a curve). The variability of Y around each value of X indicates the amount of scatter.

Regression models computed in practice typically are based on OLS estimates, which minimize the sum of the squared residuals for the data from which the model was estimated. The residual for each observation is the difference between the actual value of Y and the corresponding value $\hat{Y}$ estimated with the regression model. The application of the OLS procedure and the corresponding statistical inference (discussed in the next chapter) assume that the residuals for each value of X are random, with a normal distribution of a mean of zero. The standard deviation of residuals is assumed to be the same across all values of X.

The second task of a regression analysis, following the estimation of the regression model, is an assessment of the model. The two primary indices of the size of the residuals are the standard error of estimate s_e and the coefficient of determination R^2. The standard error of estimate is the square root of the average (or mean) squared residual, and it provides an indication of the size of the residuals in the data from which the model was estimated. The R^2 statistic is a relative index of fit that varies from 0 to 1, with a 1 indicating perfect fit and a 0 indicating no relationship between the predictor variables and the response variable Y. The basis for R^2 is the comparison of the variability of Y around each estimated value for a given level of X, with the larger variability of Y using the sample mean $\overline{Y}$ as the estimated value.

Another form of model assessment is the evaluation of the underlying assumptions: average residual of zero or linearity, constant variability of residuals for all levels of X, independence of residuals, and normality of residuals. The plot of the residuals against each of the predictor variables ideally reveals a purely random pattern. Any violation of randomness indicates that the regression model is missing influential predictor variables or is otherwise inappropriate.

8.5 KEY TERMS

autocorrelation *362*   ordinary least squares criterion (OLS) *350*
coefficient of determination *358*   predictor variable X *332*
conditional mean *344*   regression model *348*
correlation *339*   residual variable *344*
covariance *339*   response variable Y *332*
cross-product *338*   scatterplot *334*
direct relationship *337*   slope coefficient *332*
function *332*   sum of the squared residuals (SSE) *349*
heteroscedasticity *362*   standard error of estimate *357*
indirect(or inverse) relationship *337*   strength *337*
linear regression coefficients *347*   Y-intercept *332*
mean squared residual *357*

8.6 REVIEW EXERCISES

ANALYSIS PROBLEMS

8-15. There are 16 ounces to a pound.

a. Specify the function that transforms ounces to pounds. Is the function linear? Why?

b. Plot pounds as a function of ounces for the following weights: 10 oz, 15 oz, 23 oz, 28 oz. Plot the function by connecting the four points.

8-16. There are 12 inches to a foot.

a. Specify the function that transforms feet to inches. Is the function linear? Why?

b. Specify the function that transforms inches to feet. Is the function linear? Why?

c. Plot feet as a function of inches for the following measurements: 2 in, 5 in, 10 in, 15 in. Plot the function by connecting the four points.

8-17. Consider the model $\hat{Y} = 20.4 + 85.0X$.

a. Plot this model.

b. For one observation, $X = 2$ and $Y = 149$. What is $\hat{Y}$? What is e? Is $\hat{Y}$ an overestimate or underestimate?

c. For another observation, $X = -3$ and $Y = 265$. What is $\hat{Y}$? What is e? Is $\hat{Y}$ an overestimate or underestimate?

d. Determine which value of Y from (b) or (c) is more accurately estimated.

8-18. Consider the model $\hat{Y} = -15 + 43X$.

a. Plot this model.

b. For one observation, $X = 5$ and $Y = 203$. What is $\hat{Y}$? What is e? Is $\hat{Y}$ an overestimate or underestimate?

c. For another observation, $X = 10$ and $Y = 390$. What is $\hat{Y}$? What is e? Is $\hat{Y}$ an overestimate or underestimate?

d. Determine which value of Y from (b) or (c) is more accurately estimated.

8-19. The following table lists the average Prime Rate charged by banks and an index of the Prices of 500 common stocks for 1994 (*Source:* Dept. of Commerce).

	JAN	FEB	MAR	APR	MAY	JUN
Rate	6.00	6.00	6.06	6.45	6.99	7.25
Price	473.9	471.8	463.1	447.3	450.0	454.3

	JUL	AUG	SEP	OCT	NOV	DEC
Rate	7.25	7.51	7.75	7.75	8.15	8.50
Price	451.0	464.4	467.6	463.1	461.1	455.9

a. Draw the scatterplot for these data (ignoring the time dimension).

b. Compute the covariance and the correlation of the Prime Rate and Stock Price index.

c. Determine if the value of the Prime Rate is related to the value of the Stock Price index.

8-20. The May 1995 *Consumer Reports* evaluated the strength of latex condoms. Strength was assessed with a Burst Index, which indicates how much air can be forced into the condom before it bursts, on a scale from 0 to 100 (the percentage of condoms that could be inflated to at least 25 liters). The Burst Index and Cost per condom of eight condoms are listed below.

Cost (X)	1.00	.99	.53	.44	.64	.65	.60	.50
Strength (Y)	100	100	100	98	95	90	82	78

   a. Draw the scatterplot for these data.

   b. Compute the correlation between Cost and Strength.

   c. Determine if the Cost and Strength of a condom are related.

8-21. The values of Price per Share (PPS) and Dividend per Share (DPS) for the 10 companies previously analyzed in Exercise 8-7 appear in the following table.

Application

	Company	DPS	PPS
		X	Y
1	IMO INDUSTRIES INC	0.38	6.50
2	TORO CO	0.48	13.00
3	CALMAT CO	0.64	22.50
4	TULTEX CORP	0.20	8.63
5	FAMILY DOLLAR STORES	0.25	17.25
6	PHILADELPHIA SUBURBAN CORP	1.03	16.00
7	RTZ PLC	1.18	41.38
8	TANDY CORP	0.56	24.50
9	OKLAHOMA GAS & ELECTRIC	2.66	34.13
10	NICOR INC	2.35	49.75

   a. Draw the scatterplot for these data.

   b. Compute the correlation using a conceptual worksheet.

   c. Compute the correlation applying traditional formulas.

   d. Compute the correlation using the built-in application of computer software.

   e. Interpret the scatterplot and correlation.

8-22. The correlation was defined as the average cross-product of the corresponding z-values. Compute the correlation between PPS and DPS from the previous problem by interpreting the definition literally. That is, compute the corresponding z-values for each of the two variables, then their cross-products, and finally the average cross-product of the z-values. Use $df = n - 1$ to compute the average.

Concept

8-23. The 1992 closing stock price for 16 companies and the Book Value per Share of these companies at the end of 1992 appear in the following table.

Application

Company	BVPS	PPS
BUENOS AIRES EMBT	5.45	0.00
SAFECARD SERVICES INC	5.49	7.88
MARRIOTT CORP	5.49	20.75
NORTH AMERICAN MTG CO	5.51	16.25
HOMEPLEX MORTGAGE INVT	5.53	2.38
PLY-GEM INDUSTRIES	10.46	13.00
BRUSH WELLMAN INC	10.47	15.38
BERGEN BRUNSWIG CORP	10.50	19.25
RESORT INCOME INVESTORS	10.50	9.62
KCS ENERGY INC	10.53	19.75
BERLITZ INTERNATIONAL INC	10.54	22.00
LOCTITE CORP	10.54	45.38
MGI PROPERTIES	15.50	11.62
NIPSCO INDUSTRIES INC	15.51	26.50
CASCADE NATURAL GAS CORP	15.54	23.50
CENTRAL & SOUTH WEST CORP	15.54	29.12

a. Compute the conditional mean of PPS for each value of BVPS.

b. On the same graph as (a), (i) plot the scatterplot of PPS and BVPS, and (ii) plot the conditional means of PPS and the values of BVPS, connecting successive conditional means with line segments.

c. Determine if there is a relationship between PPS and BVPS and why or why not. If there is a relationship, is it linear?

8-24. A college admissions officer analyzed final college GPA at graduation (Y) according to SAT (X) score. The following OLS regression estimates were obtained:

$$\hat{Y} = -0.31 + (0.0032)X.$$

a. Use the model to estimate college GPA for an SAT score of 1060.

b. Use the model to estimate college GPA for an SAT score of 1061.

c. Calculate the difference between the estimated values in (a) and (b).

d. Determine the meaning of the slope coefficient $b_1 = 0.0032$.

8-25. The sales manager for an automobile dealer analyzed the relation between hours of time that salespeople worked for a day and gross sales for the day. The following OLS regression model was obtained:

$$\hat{Y} = 213 + (994)X.$$

a. Use the model to estimate sales for 85 sales hours.

b. Use the model to estimate sales for 86 sales hours.

c. Use the model to estimate sales for 87 sales hours.

d. Calculate the difference between the estimated values in (a), (b), and (c).

e. Determine the meaning of the slope coefficient $b_1 = 994$.

8-26. The OLS regression line was computed from the following data (the same as in Exercise 8-2).

Company	Cost X	Actual Capacity Y	X deviation $X - \bar{X}$	Y deviation $Y - \bar{Y}$	product of deviations $(X - \bar{X})(Y - \bar{Y})$	X dev squared $(X - \bar{X})^2$
1 Panasonic CW-606TU	380	5800	a	-856.25	-3210.94	14.06
2 Kenmore 75055	300	5450	-76.25	d	91976.56	5814.06
3 Fedders A3Q05F2A	250	5100	-126.25	-1556.25	f	15939.06
4 Friedrich SQ05H10D	380	5600	b	-1556.25	-3960. 94	h
5 Friedrich SQ06H10D	420	6700	43.75	e	1914.06	1914.06
6 Panasonic CW-806TU	440	7800	63.75	1143.75	72914.06	4064.06
7 Carrier TCA081P	480	8600	103.75	1943.75	g	10764.06
8 Wh.-West. WAC083T7A2	360	8200	-16.25	1543.75	-25085.94	264.06
Sum	3010.00	53250.00	c	0.00	**532687.50**	**38787.50**
	376.25	**6656.25**	0.00	0.00	66585.94	4848.44

a. Fill in the numbers for the corresponding letters in the table above.

b. Compute the OLS regression model.

c. Plot the OLS regression line in the scatterplot of these data.

d. Compute the estimated Capacity for a Cost of $355.

8-27. SSE was computed in the following table from the OLS regression model in the previous exercise.

Company	Cost X	Actual Cap. Y	Estimated Cap. $\hat{Y}$	Residual $e \equiv Y - \hat{Y}$	Residual Squared e^2
1 Panasonic CW-606TU	380	5800	a	-907.75	824011.09
2 Kenmore 75055	300	5450	5609.07	-159.07	e
3 Fedders A3Q05F2A	250	5100	b	177.60	31542.58
4 Friedrich SQ05H10D	380	5600	6707.75	-1107.75	1227111.31
5 Friedrich SQ06H10D	420	6700	7257.09	c	310349.17
6 Panasonic CW-806TU	440	7800	7531.76	268.24	71952.92
7 Carrier TCA081P	480	8600	8081.10	518.90	269258.31
8 Wh.-West. WAC083T7A2	360	8200	6433.08	d	3122003.14
Sum					5881532.39

a.   Fill in the numbers for the corresponding letters in the table above.

b.   Compute MSE.

c.   Compute s_e.

d.   Compute R^2.

Mechanical

8-28.   Hours spent studying for a final and the percentage correct on the final (score) were recorded for four students. The data are presented in the following table.

Hr (X)	Score (Y)
2.00	76.00
3.00	83.00
3.50	81.00
4.50	96.00

a.   Construct the scatterplot for these data.

b.   Draw the following two regression lines in the scatterplot:

$$\hat{Y} = 50 + 5\,(X) \quad \text{and} \quad \hat{Y} = 60 + 7.5\,(X).$$

c.   From a visual inspection of the graph, determine which line fits the best.

Mechanical

8-29.   For the data in Exercise 8-28,

a.   Compute SSE for $\hat{Y} = 50 + 5\,(X)$.

b.   Compute SSE for $\hat{Y} = 60 + 7.5\,(X)$.

c.   Determine which line fits the best and why.

Application

8-30.   For the data in Exercise 8-28, compute the OLS estimates of the linear regression model.

Mechanical

8-31.   For the data in Exercise 8-28 and the model $\hat{Y} = 60 + 7.5\,(X)$,

a.   Compute s_e

b.   Compute R^2

c.   Interpret the accuracy of prediction

Mechanical

8-32.   For the data in Exercise 8-28 and the model $\hat{Y} = 60 + 7.5\,(X)$, compute the estimated Score from studying

a.   3 hours

b.   3.25 hours

c.   6 hours

d.   Determine a primary difficulty with the Score estimated from studying 6 hours.

Concept

8-33.   Consider the following data for predictor variable X and response Y. Set up the standard spreadsheet for computing SSE that includes columns for X, Y, $\hat{Y}$, e, and e^2. At the very beginning of the spreadsheet, however, include space for the two values b_0 and b_1. When entering the linear equation for $\hat{Y}$ in the cells of the relevant column, reference the cells containing b_0 and b_1. The linear function can now easily be changed by changing the values of the two cells that contain the values of b_0 and b_1.

X	32.8	24.9	31.6	34.8	27.9	34.4	28.1	30.1	32.9	15.0	26.2	33.6	38.0	36.7
Y	91.8	70.9	90.5	98.2	84.0	106.5	102.6	89.4	81.6	80.0	31.9	102.5	113.5	91.1

    a. Choose several pairs of values for b_0 and b_1 and compute the corresponding SSE for each pair.

    b. Make your best guess for the OLS values of b_0 and b_1.

    c. Compute the OLS values of b_0 and b_1.

    d. Compare the OLS values to your best guess values. How do the values of SSE compare across the two models?

8-34. A large manufacturing company uses hundreds of one type of machine to assemble its product. What is the relation between maintenance costs of the machine and age of the machine? Maintenance cost and age were collected from a random sample of 20 such machines, as shown in the accompanying table.

Concept

Age	Cost	Age	Cost
2	106.1	6	215.4
6	209.6	4	163.5
5	199.6	3	135.4
6	201.6	3	147.4
5	170.1	5	205.2
6	241.3	6	222.8
5	220.1	4	154.0
5	195.9	6	219.9
3	179.9	5	205.0
4	177.1	5	251.2

    a. Obtain the scatterplot of Age with Cost. Verbally describe the relationship between these two variables.

    b. Compute the conditional means of Cost for each value of Age.

    c. Plot these conditional means, and connect successive values with a straight line.

    d. Compute the conditional standard deviations, which are the standard deviations of Cost for each value of Age.

    e. Determine if the assumption of equal variances is maintained for these data.

    f. Compute SSE for $\hat{Y}$ as the corresponding conditional mean.

8-35. For the Age and Cost data in Exercise 8-34,

Mechanical   **a.** Compute SSE for $\hat{Y} = 75 + 25\,(X)$

    b. Compute SSE for $\hat{Y} = 60 + 30\,(X)$

    c. Determine which line fits the best and why.

8-36. For the data in Exercise 8-34,

   a. Compute the OLS estimates of the linear regression model

   b. Compute s_e

   c. Compute R^2

   d. Interpret the accuracy of prediction

8-37. For the data in Exercise 8-34 and for the regression model

$$\hat{Y} = 75 + 25\,(X),$$

   a. Compute the residuals.

   b. Plot the residuals against Age.

   c. *Assumption 1.* Do the residuals for approximately equal values of X appear to have a mean of zero? Why or why not?

   d. *Assumption 2.* Do the residuals appear to have equal variance for all values of X? Why or why not?

   e. *Assumption 3.* Do the residuals appear to be uncorrelated with each other? Does the value of one residual appear to be predictive of the value of adjacent residuals? Why or why not?

   f. *Assumption 4.* Do the residuals appear to be normally distributed?

   g. Determine if the OLS estimation of a linear regression model is the appropriate estimation procedure for these data.

8-38. For the data in Exercise 8-34 and the model $\hat{Y} = 75 + 25\,(X)$, compute the estimated maintenance Cost from an Age of the machine that is

   a. 4 years old

   b. 4.5 years old

   c. 10 years old

   d. Determine a primary difficulty with the Cost estimated from a machine that is 10 years old.

8-39. The following data were randomly generated from two different distributions.

X	160	142	154	175	161	197	187	149	178	151
Y	67	47	62	67	76	63	72	64	58	67

   a. Compute R^2 using X as the predictor variable and Y as the response variable.

   b. Compare and interpret this statistic, keeping in mind that the data are random numbers.

8-40. Consider the values of the average prime rate charged by banks and the price index of 500 common stocks for 1994 listed in Exercise 8-19.

   a. Construct an OLS regression model that predicts Prime Rate from the stock price index.

   b. Compute the residuals.

   c. Plot the residuals against time.

   d. Determine if the residuals appear to be uncorrelated with each other. Does the value of one residual appear to be predictive of the value of adjacent residuals? Why or why not?

DISCUSSION QUESTIONS

1. What is the key defining characteristic of a function?

2. What are the parameters of a linear function?

3. How does a scatterplot differ from the graph of a function? Why?

4. How does a correlation of −.75 relate to a correlation of .75? Which represents the stronger relationship?

5. What is a cross-product? Why are cross-products the basic component of the definition of the correlation?

6. What is the distinction between correlation and covariance? When is covariance preferred to correlation?

7. What is the relation between conditional means and a regression line?

8. How does the graph of X with Y compare to the graph of X with $\hat{Y}$?

9. What is the meaning of the residual variable e in the regression model?

10. Why is the sum of the squared residuals computed instead of the sum of the residuals?

11. What is the criterion of ordinary least squares?

12. A regression model is appropriately estimated with a random sample. A randomly sampled observation generates a residual of +.5. What value of the residual is predicted for the next observation?

13. What is the meaning of the slope coefficient?

14. When is the assumption of average residuals of zero for any value of X the assumption of linearity?

15. Why is the standard error of estimate a better index of fit than the sum of squared errors?

16. Why is the coefficient of determination R^2 a relative index of fit?

17. If the value of the predictor X is unrelated to the value of the response Y, what is the value of $\hat{Y}$ obtained from the estimated OLS model?

18. Why should the distribution of the residuals from the model not exhibit any systematic pattern?

19. What is heteroscedasticity and how can it be detected?

INTEGRATIVE ANALYSIS PROBLEM

A classic problem in real estate is to estimate the selling price of a property. One simple model, applied to the houses in a single neighborhood or geographical area, predicts a house's selling price from its area in square feet. The data for this problem are found in the file HOUSE.DAT. The variables include Price and Area for 68 observations.

a. Draw the scatterplot for Price and Area. Are the data approximately linear?

b. Compute the correlation between Price and Area. Verbally describe the strength of the linear relationship in terms of the correlation coefficient.

c. Compute the OLS regression model with Price regressed on Area. Verbally describe the strength of the linear relationship in terms of the regression coefficient.

d. Plot the OLS regression line in the scatterplot of these data.

e. Compute the estimated Price for an Area of 355 square feet.

f. Compute s_e.

g.   Compute R^2.

h.   Determine how well the model fits the data in both absolute and relative terms.

i.   *Assumption 1.* Do the residuals for approximately equal values of X appear to have a mean of zero? Why or why not?

j.   *Assumption 2.* Do the residuals appear to have equal variance for all values of X? Why or why not?

k.   *Assumption 3.* Do the residuals appear to be uncorrelated with each other? Does the value of one residual appear to be predictive of the value of adjacent residuals? Why or why not?

l.   *Assumption 4.* Do the residuals appear to be normally distributed?

m.   Determine if the OLS estimation of a linear regression model is the appropriate estimation procedure for these data.

n.   Determine if Area is a good predictor of Price for these data. Should more predictor variables be added to the model? Why? List some possible additional predictor variables.

CHAPTER

9

More on Assessing Relationships

WHY DO WE CARE?

The previous chapter introduced regression analysis as a method for describing the relationship between two variables. From our introduction to statistical inference in Chapter 4, we learned that the real power of statistics is deriving information regarding the entire population from a single sample of data. The obtained OLS regression model is only a sample model rather than the desired, but unknown, population model. From this consideration, several important practical consequences follow. For example, a range of values that likely contains the true population slope coefficient—the confidence interval—should be obtained.

Also, several diagnostic analyses should accompany any regression analysis. The previous chapter showed how to evaluate the adequacy of the four basic assumptions of regression analysis. This chapter extends this analysis by showing the effect of outliers on the estimation of the regression model. One or a few observations with data values substantially different from most other values can affect dramatically the obtained model. Such observations may be valid, but their presence should invoke further study.

Finally, most applications of regression analysis include multiple predictor variables to increase predictive accuracy and understanding. Success achieved with a single predictor variable is usually enhanced by the information provided by additional predictor variables. These topics, which contribute to a much more complete framework for applying regression analysis, are explored in this chapter.

9.1 INFERENCE IN REGRESSION ANALYSIS

The previous chapter showed how to describe the relationship between two variables in a single sample with regression analysis. Unfortunately, the regression model estimated from a sample is not the desired population model that would be obtained if the entire population were available. Statistical inference bridges the gap between sample and population by drawing inferences from the sample about the population.

Sample versus Population Regression Models

The *population* regression model for response Y with predictor X is

$$Y = \hat{Y} + \varepsilon \quad \text{where} \quad \hat{Y} = \beta_0 + \beta_1 X.$$

The true population parameters are β_0 and β_1. The population error ε indicates the difference between the actual value of Y and the estimate from the population regression model. Unfortunately, the true values β_0 and β_1, and by extension, ε, are not known. In practice, the sample estimates b_0, b_1, and e replace the true values.

Figure 9-1 shows a population regression line with population slope coefficient $\beta_1 = 2.85$. Sampling fluctuations result in sample lines with *estimated* slope coefficients that fluctuate around the population value of 2.85. One sample yields a slope coefficient of $b_1 = 1.94$, a second sample yields $b_1 = 3.24$, and a third sample yields $b_1 = 2.99$. The first sample value underestimates β_1, and the second and third values are overestimates.

How close is the sample estimate to the desired population value? As before, the confidence interval answers this question.

Confidence Interval for the Slope Coefficient

The estimated slope coefficient b_1 and the Y-intercept b_0 define the sample version of the one-predictor linear regression model. The slope coefficient is usually of greater interest because it indicates how changes in X relate to changes in Y. The **confidence interval** around b_1 indicates how close the sample estimate b_1 likely is to the unknown population value β_1.

The key value for the analysis of this confidence interval is zero. If zero is in the interval, then no relationship between predictor and response variables is plausible. Once again, the *t*-statistic is the number of estimated standard errors the sample value b_1 lies from the population value β_1. The *t*-distribution is the distribution over repeated sampling of these distances. The size of the 95% confidence interval is the range of 95% of the *t*-values, with 2.5% of the distribution in each tail. The confidence interval is $t_{.025} \approx 2$ standard errors on either side of the sample estimate b_1. The standard error of b_1 is s_{b_1}, so the confidence interval is

$$b_1 \pm t_{.025} s_{b_1}.$$

The exact value of $t_{.025}$ depends on the appropriate degrees of freedom, which is

$$df = n - 2,$$

confidence interval around b_1
range of values that likely contain the true population value β_1

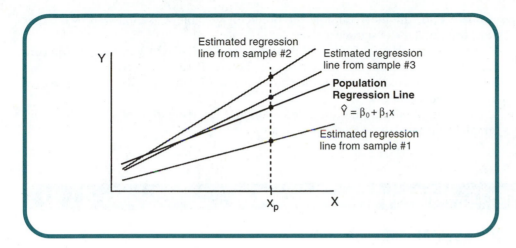

Figure 9-1.
Sample regression lines (defined by sample values b_0 and b_1) around the true population regression line defined by β_0 and β_1.

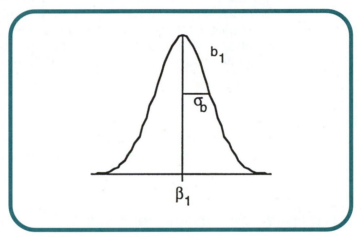

Figure 9-2.
The normal sampling distribution of the estimated slope coefficient b_1 over repeated samples with mean β_1 and standard deviation σ_{b_1}.

because *two* population values b_0 and b_1 are estimated for the one-predictor linear regression model.

What is the meaning of the standard error s_{b_1}? For normally distributed residuals, b_1 is also normally distributed over repeated samples. This sampling distribution is centered on the corresponding population value β_1 with standard deviation σ_{b_1}, as shown in Figure 9-2.

The key to computing the estimated standard error s_b is the standard error of estimate s_e, defined in the previous chapter.

> *Estimated standard error of the sample slope coefficient b_1:*
> $$s_{b_1} = \frac{s_e}{\sqrt{\text{SSX}}}$$

SSX is the variation of X expressed as the sum of squared deviations around its mean, $\sum (X - \overline{X})^2$, as defined in Chapter 3. The smaller the standard error of estimate s_e, or the more variable the predictor variable X as indicated by a larger SSX, the smaller the standard error b_1.

On average, 95 out of 100 confidence intervals calculated with $t_{.025} \approx 2$ will contain the unknown value of β_1. Changing the cutoff value of t from $t_{.025}$ to some other value such as $t_{.05}$ changes the confidence level. For example, $t_{.05}$ sets the confidence level at 90%.

An example illustrating the calculation and interpretation of a confidence interval around the slope coefficient follows.

BUSINESS APPLICATION 9.1—Confidence Interval for a Slope Coefficient

MANAGERIAL PROBLEM

From the full sample of 1,402, the OLS slope coefficient b_1 that predicts Price per Share (PPS) from Earnings per Share (EPS) is $b_1 = 5.44$. This positive value indicates that EPS is related to PPS for this sample. However, management is interested not in the slope coefficient for the sample data but in the value of this coefficient for the *entire* population. What is the range of values that likely contains this unknown population value? Does this range include zero?

DATA

The analysis of 1,402 publicly traded companies that paid a divided in 1992 yielded the following values, where X represents EPS and Y represents PPS: $s_X = 2.13375$, $s_e = 15.96$, and $b_1 = 5.44$.

APPLICATION—TRADITIONAL NOTATION

First, calculate the sum of squares SSX from the standard deviation s_x.

$$s_x = \sqrt{\frac{SSX}{n-1}}, \text{ so } SSX = (n-1)s_X^2 = (1401)(2.13375)^2 = 6378.598.$$

The standard error of the slope coefficient is

$$s_{b_1} = \frac{s_e}{\sqrt{SSX}} = \frac{15.96}{\sqrt{6378.598}} = \frac{15.96}{79.866} = .200.$$

The confidence interval for β_1 is

$$\beta_1 = b_1 \pm t_{.025}s_{b_1}.$$

For a 95% confidence level, the cutoff value of t is $t_{.025} = 1.96$ for this large sample with $df = n - 2 = 1,400$. Accordingly, the value of E, the maximum error of estimation or precision (defined in Chapter 4), is

$$E = t_{.025}s_{b_1} = (1.96)(.200) = 0.39.$$

The resulting interval is $5.44 \pm .39$, so the population regression coefficient β_1 is likely between 5.05 to 5.93, with a 95% level of confidence.

APPLICATION—EXCEL BUILT-IN ANALYSIS

Excel does not have a function for the confidence interval of a slope coefficient. However, the regression program accessed from the Tools ➤ Data Analysis menu sequence does provide this information. The use of this program is illustrated later in the chapter.

MANAGERIAL INTERPRETATION

As Earnings per Share increases, on average so does price. A $1 increase in Earnings per Share likely leads to an average change in Price per Share somewhere between $5 and $6.

The two types of statistical inference are confidence intervals and hypothesis tests. The hypothesis test for the slope coefficient follows.

Hypothesis Test for the Slope Coefficient

The logic of this hypothesis test for β_1 is the same logic of the one-sample test for the population mean (see Chapter 5). Instead of the sample mean $\overline{Y}$ estimating the unknown population mean μ_Y, the sample slope coefficient b_1 estimates the unknown population regression coefficient β_1. If $\beta_1 \neq 0$, then the values of X influence the values of Y. If $\beta_1 = 0$, no such relationship exists, because the model for Y reduces to $Y = b_0 + e$, with the variable X dropping out of the model. When $\beta_1 = 0$, the predicted value of Y ($\hat{Y}$) *does not depend on the value of X*, which means that $\hat{Y}$ remains constant for all values of X.

The usual hypothesis test for β_1 follows from the null hypothesis H_0 that there is no linear relationship between X and Y. The alternative hypothesis H_1 is that some linear relationship exists,

$$H_0: \beta_1 = 0 \quad \text{and} \quad H_1: \beta_1 \neq 0.$$

Values other than zero may be hypothesized, and directional (one-tail) tests may also be performed.

The distance of the sample statistic (b_1) from the hypothesized population value ($\beta_1 = 0$) is evaluated in terms of the estimated standard error of the sample statistic s_{b_1},

$$s_{b_1} = \frac{s_e}{\sqrt{\text{SSX}}} .$$

The resulting t-statistic (see Chapter 5)—the number of estimated standard errors that b lies from the hypothesized value of zero—is

$$t_{b_1} = \frac{b_1 - 0}{s_{b_1}}$$

The degrees of freedom for this test statistic are $df = n - (npred + 1)$, where $npred$ is the number of predictor variables. For one predictor variable X, df reduces to $n - 2$. To evaluate t_{b_1}, calculate either the cutoff value of t, or, following the more contemporary computer-based approach, obtain the p-value. For the alternative hypothesis $\beta_1 \neq 0$, calculate the p-value for a two-tailed, or nondirectional, test.

When $\beta_1 \neq 0$, then X and Y are related, so knowledge regarding X results in generally more accurate predictions about Y than no knowledge about X. A better prediction, however, does not mean a good or acceptable prediction. That is, statistical significance is not practical significance. Other statistics such as the coefficient of determination, (R^2) and the standard error of estimate (s_e) more directly assess the accuracy of the predictions than does a rejection of the null hypothesis test of $\beta_1 = 0$.

BUSINESS APPLICATION 9.2—Hypothesis Test of a Slope Coefficient

MANAGERIAL PROBLEM

From a sample of 1,402 companies, construct a model that predicts Price per Share (PPS) from Earnings per Share (EPS). The OLS slope coefficient is $b_1 = 5.44$. This positive value indicates that EPS is related to PPS for this sample. However, management is more interested in the *population* slope coefficient. Does the range of likely population values include zero?

STATISTICAL HYPOTHESES

Null hypothesis H_0: $\beta_1 = \$0$.
Alternative hypothesis H_1: $\beta_1 \neq \$0$.

APPLICATION—TRADITIONAL NOTATION

Analyses of the data in the previous business application provided the standard error of the slope coefficient as $s_{b_1} = 0.200$. The observed value of t for the null hypothesis that the population slope coefficient is zero is

$$t_{b_1} = \frac{b - 0}{s_{b_1}} = \frac{5.44}{.200} = 27.20.$$

The corresponding p-value is well beyond .001, which renders the null hypothesis that the population slope coefficient is zero extremely unlikely. Reject the null hypothesis; the population slope coefficient is larger than zero.

APPLICATION—EXCEL BUILT-IN ANALYSIS

Excel does not have a function for the hypothesis test of a slope coefficient. However, the regression program accessed from the Tools ➤ Data Analysis menu sequence does provide this information. The use of this program is illustrated in the section on multiple regression later in this chapter.

MANAGERIAL INTERPRETATION

As Earnings per Share increases, on average, so does Price.

The construction of the confidence interval around the sample slope coefficient yields more information than the corresponding hypothesis test. The hypothesis test leads to a conclusion that the population slope coefficient is greater than zero. The confidence level leads to the conclusion that the population slope coefficient is likely somewhere between five and six.

The sampling fluctuations of the parameter estimates b_0 and b_1 have consequences beyond indicating the need for confidence intervals or hypothesis tests. These fluctuations also affect the sizes of the residuals e. Both of the primary indices for assessing fit—the standard error of estimate s_e and the coefficient of determination R^2—require modification to account for these fluctuations. The coefficient of determination is considered first.

Adjusted Coefficient of Determination

The sample residual e is not the population error term of interest, because it also reflects the sampling error in the estimates b_0 and b_1. Change the regression coefficient estimates, and the value of the residual e also changes.

> The estimates b_0 and b_1 minimize SSE for a single sample, but the population values β_0 and β_1 that minimize SSE for the entire population are of primary interest.

The sample statistics b_0 and b_1 are random variables that fluctuate across repeated samples, resulting in a value of SSE minimized only for the sample—*not* for the entire population or other samples.

The fact that SSE is minimized only for the sample from which the model is estimated detracts from using the model for real-world predictions with new data. In practice, the **estimation sample**—the initial sample with known values of both Y and X—provides the data for estimating the regression coefficients. Real-world prediction is done with a subsequent *new* sample of X values for which the corresponding values of Y are initially unknown. This new sample is the **prediction sample.** The regression model computed from the original sample is used for prediction by applying it to the values of X in a new sample.

The problem, as illustrated in Figure 9-3, is that the original regression model from the estimation sample is *not* the optimal OLS regression line for the prediction sample. The model from the estimation sample does not minimize SSE in a new sample. A fit index based on the value of SSE obtained from the estimation sample, such as the coefficient of determination R^2, presents a more favorable picture of fit than actually exists.

estimation sample
sample of known *values of both the predictor variable X and the response variable Y from which the regression model is estimated*

prediction sample
new sample with unknown *values of the response variable Y estimated from* known *values of the predictor variable X according to the estimation sample regression model*

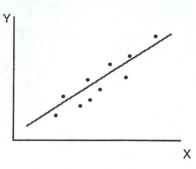 

(a) OLS sample regression line in original
    (estimation) sample with minimized
    SSE.

(b) Original regression line from estimation
    sample applied to new (prediction)
    sample, with larger SSE.

Figure 9-3.
OLS regression line from estimation sample applied to prediction sample.

> *The value of R^2 from the estimation sample decreases when the regression model from that sample is applied to a new sample.*

When predicting the unknown, management is primarily interested in the R^2 obtained by applying the model from the estimation sample to a new sample. Because SSE increases when applying the original model to the new (prediction) sample, R^2 computed from the estimation sample *overestimates* the degree of predictability obtained in practice.

Fortunately, the amount of R^2 shrinkage that results when applying a regression line to new data can be estimated without actually collecting new data. When computing R^2, divide each sum of squares term, SSE and SSY, by its corresponding degrees of freedom. These divisions convert these sums of squares to the corresponding mean squares, MSE and MSY. That is,

$$R^2 \equiv 1 - \frac{\text{SSE}}{\text{SSY}}$$

is adjusted to the following[1]:

adjusted coefficient of determination

average reduced value of R^2 that results from applying the regression model from the estimation sample to the new data in the prediction sample

$$R^2_{\text{adj}} = 1 - \frac{\text{MSE}}{\text{MSY}} \ .$$

This reduced value R^2_{adj} more accurately indicates the true usefulness of the regression model for real-world prediction than does R^2. The adjustment estimates the true predictive efficiency when the regression model derived from one sample is applied to a new sample. Particularly when the sample size n is small relative to the number of predictors *npred*, R^2_{adj} can be considerably smaller than R^2. As the sample size n increases, the value of R^2_{adj} tends to become closer to the value of R^2 because the sampling fluctuations of b_0 and b_1 are reduced.

---

1. A little algebra expresses this adjustment in terms of the original R^2, where *npred* is the number of predictors and n is sample size:

$$R^2_{\text{adj}} = 1 - \left((1 - R^2) \frac{n - 1}{n - (npred + 1)} \right).$$

Statistical Illustration—Adjusted Coefficient of Determination

MODEL OBTAINED FROM ESTIMATION SAMPLE

The OLS regression line for the 10 companies that comprise the estimation sample was obtained in the previous chapter:

$$\hat{Y} = 19.687 + 5.184\,(X).$$

Applying this model to the data resulted in a sum of squared errors around the regression line of SSE = 755.00. The variation of Y in terms of sum of squares around the mean of all Y is SSY = 1,839.25. Together, these values yielded $R^2 = 0.59$. The adjusted value is

$$R^2_{adj} = 1 - \frac{MSE}{MSY} \equiv 1 - \frac{SSE/(n-(npred+1))}{SSY/(n-1)}$$

$$= 1 - \frac{755.00/8}{1,839.25/9} = 0.54.$$

The value of R^2_{adj} is .05 less than R^2.

ESTIMATION MODEL APPLIED TO PREDICTION SAMPLE

The estimation model with $b_0 = 19.687$ and $b_1 = 5.184$ was applied to the EPS values of a new sample of 10 companies, the prediction sample. SSE obtained by applying the estimation model to the prediction sample necessarily resulted in a larger sum of squared errors, SSE = 923.30 instead of the original SSE = 755.00.

	Pred. Sample		Estimation Sample Model			Prediction Sample Model		
	EPS	Actual PPS	Pred. PPS	Resid.	Squared Residual	Pred. PPS	Resid.	d Residu
Company	X	Y	YPred	e	esq	YPred	e	esq
TIMES MIRROR COMPANY	0.44	31.250	21.97	9.28	86.16	18.52	12.73	162.00
CENTRAL FIDELITY BANKS	3.37	42.000	37.16	4.84	23.45	40.23	1.77	3.12
FILTERTEK INC	0.49	9.500	22.23	-12.73	161.98	18.89	-9.39	88.22
PUBLIC SERVICE CO OF NC	1.63	27.250	28.14	-0.89	0.79	27.34	-0.09	0.01
DRESSER INDUSTRIES	0.52	18.875	22.38	-3.51	12.30	19.12	-0.24	0.06
TRANSATLANTIC HOLDINGS	3.13	56.125	35.91	20.21	408.53	38.45	17.67	312.27
BOEING CO	4.57	40.125	43.38	-3.25	10.58	49.12	-9.00	80.98
FLEET FINANCIAL GROUP	1.78	32.750	28.91	3.84	14.71	28.45	4.30	18.48
BARNWELL INDUSTRIES	1.44	14.250	27.15	-12.90	166.46	25.93	-11.68	136.46
DAUPHIN DEPOSIT CORP	1.93	23.500	29.69	-6.19	38.34	29.56	-6.06	36.75
Sum					923.30			838.35

Variability of PPS (Y) for this new data expressed as a sum of squares is SSY = 1778.13. R^2 is

$$R^2 \equiv 1 - \frac{SSE}{SSY} = 1 - \frac{923.30}{1778.13} = 1 - 0.52 = 0.48.$$

This single sample result of $R^2 = 0.48$ is comparable to the estimated reduction of $R^2_{adj} = 0.54$.

MODEL OBTAINED FROM PREDICTION SAMPLE

Later, the actual values of PPS were obtained for the 10 prediction sample companies. For illustrative purposes, calculate the optimal OLS regression line from the prediction sample data,

$$\hat{Y} = 15.262 + 7.410\,(X).$$

SSE is also a random variable that varies from sample to sample, so SSE could be larger or smaller than the original SSE obtained from the estimation sample. By chance, the minimum possible sum of squared errors for these data is larger than the original SSE = 755.00. For these data, the "best" line—the line that minimized SSE—yielded SSE = 838.5 with $R^2 = 0.53$. By necessity, this new value of R^2 is higher than the value of 0.48 obtained by applying the estimation model to the prediction data.

STATISTICAL PRINCIPLE

R^2_{adj} is more useful than R^2 for gauging the efficacy of a regression model for estimating unknown values of Y from X. R^2 presents an overly optimistic picture by failing to account for sampling variability of the estimated regression coefficients. R^2_{adj} accounts for this variability by estimating the value of R^2 when applying the original model to new data.

This example estimated R^2_{adj} by literally applying the regression line from the estimation sample to new data—the prediction sample. Of course, different samples will show different amounts of reductions. More practically, estimate R^2_{adj} by applying a simple formula that adjusts R^2 computed from a single sample downward.

The adjusted coefficient of determination R^2_{adj} is an important piece of information for evaluating the fit of the regression model to the data. Values of R^2_{adj} close to 1.0 indicate that the points in the scatterplot for the new data in the prediction sample are close to the regression line computed from the estimation sample. Values of R^2_{adj} close to 0.0 indicate considerable scatter around the new line.

Which values of R^2_{adj} indicate acceptable fit? Rough guidelines for interpreting R^2_{adj} can be given, but no strict rules are offered because the required precision depends on the situation. Values above .8 or .9 are typically considered excellent, though difficult to obtain in most practical situations. Values of R^2_{adj} above .5 or even .4 are often considered acceptable because useful information regarding Y is obtained from X even though the influence of X on Y is far from complete. Values much below .3 usually indicate that the model fits poorly. However, even an R^2_{adj} in the range of .2 to .3 indicates that the accuracy of predicting Y with knowledge of X is better than predicting Y without this knowledge. A low value of R^2_{adj} indicates that errors around the regression line are almost as large as the errors around the mean of all the values of Y. The estimation model may still have some predictive usefulness even with a low R^2_{adj}, but there is also considerable room for improvement.

The predictive usefulness of the regression model depends on the size of the residuals that the business decision maker is willing to tolerate. To some extent, the standard error of estimate s_e provides this information, but the next section presents an even more appropriate statistic. Confidence intervals, and related intervals called prediction intervals, can be applied to both the estimated value $\hat{Y}$ as well as the slope coefficient b_1, as discussed next.

EXERCISES

9-1. A realtor wanted to assess the relationship between square feet and selling price of houses in a neighborhood of several hundred houses all built at about the same time. A sample of 15 houses revealed the following statistics, where X represents Area in square feet and Y represents Selling Price in \$1,000's: $s_X = 32.7536$, $s_e = 736.48$, $b_0 = 22416.58$, and $b_1 = 87.31$.

a. Compute the 95% confidence interval around the sample slope coefficient.
b. Interpret the meaning of this confidence interval for the business decision maker.

9-2. For the data in the previous exercise,
a. Test the null hypothesis that the population slope coefficient is zero.
b. Determine if the results of the hypothesis test are consistent with the confidence interval computed in the previous problem. Why or why not?

9-3. A sample of 35 quality control specialists revealed the following statistics, in which Number of Years at the job (X) was used to predict Salary (Y) (in 10,000's): $s_X = 3.61$, $s_e = 3.397$, $b_0 = 20.38$, and $b_1 = 1.69$.

a. Compute the 95% confidence interval around the sample slope coefficient.
b. Interpret the meaning of this confidence interval for the business decision maker.

9-4. For the data in the previous exercise,

a. Test the null hypothesis that the population slope coefficient is zero.
b. Determine if the results of the hypothesis test are consistent with the confidence interval computed in the previous problem. Why or why not?

9-5. $SSX = 1209.4$, $s_e = 8.23$, and $b = 2.19$. Does the population slope coefficient equal zero?

9-6. Two exercises from the last chapter, 8-7 and 8-12, involved the prediction of Price per Share from the prediction of Dividends per Share (DPS). Exercise 6-5 provided the data and asked for the regression model, and Exercise 6-11 asked for the standard error of estimate and r-squared.

a. Build on these previous analyses by computing R^2_{adj}.
b. Compare R^2_{adj} to R^2. Is the drop large? How does this new information affect your assessment of the model?

9-7. The prediction of Price of large-screen TVs from the *Consumer Report's* ratings was presented in Exercises 8-9 and 8-13 from the last chapter.

a. Build on these previous analyses by computing R^2_{adj}.
b. Compare R^2_{adj} to R^2. Is the drop large? How does this new information affect your assessment of the model?

9.2 MORE INFERENCE—INTERVALS AROUND THE ESTIMATED VALUE

Consider a specific value of the variable X, denoted as $X = x_p$, such as $X = 5$ or $X = -8.2$. Inserting this specific value x_p into the model yields the corresponding estimate $\hat{Y}$. How much do these estimates $\hat{Y}$ vary from sample to sample for the same predictor value x_p? The answer depends on whether the prediction is for the mean of Y for *all* observations with $X = x_p$, or for a *specific* value of Y with $X = x_p$.

To clarify this discussion, replace the general notation for the estimate $\hat{Y}$ with more precise notation that indicates, for a given value of X, the estimation of the *mean* of Y, or the estimation of an *individual value* of Y. The mean of Y is a point on the regression line, which for a single predictor value x_p is denoted $\hat{Y}_p$. A point in the scatterplot corresponds to a specific individual value of Y for a given value x_p, with estimate denoted $\hat{Y}_{p,i}$. Estimating a mean or a single value from a regression model yields the same estimate, $\hat{Y}$. Whether this estimate is for a mean, $\hat{Y}_p$, or for an individual value, $\hat{Y}_{p,i}$, depends on the context. Consider first the mean.

Confidence Intervals

In the ideal world, a value of Y would be estimated from a single value x_p using population values β_0 and β_1. The result is the true population estimate $\hat{Y}_p$,

$$\hat{Y}_p = \beta_0 + \beta_1 x_p.$$

The population mean of Y for all values of Y with $X = x_p$ is the conditional mean $\hat{Y}_p$, the point on the corresponding population regression line.

In practice, obtain the estimated or sample mean $\hat{Y}_p$ from *sample* regression estimates b_0 and b_1,

$$\hat{Y}_p = b_0 + b_1 x_p.$$

Different samples yield different values of b_0 and b_1, so the sample value of $\hat{Y}_p$ also fluctuates from sample to sample. The value of the unknown population mean likely lies within a confidence interval constructed about the estimated mean. For example, consider the regression model for estimating PPS from EPS:

$$\hat{Y} = 19.687 + (5.184)X.$$

When EPS = \$2.24, the corresponding estimated PPS is $\hat{Y} = \$31.30$. What range of values around \$31.30 for Earnings per Share (EPS) of \$2.24 likely contains the true population estimated value?

The key issue for statistical inference is the variability of the estimated mean $\hat{Y}_p$ across repeated samples, or the standard error $s_{\hat{Y}_p}$. What is the estimated standard error $s_{\hat{Y}_p}$ of the sample mean $\hat{Y}_p$?

> *Estimated standard error of the sample mean $\hat{Y}_p$:*
>
> $$s_{\hat{Y}_p} = s_e \sqrt{\frac{1}{n} + \frac{(x_p - \overline{X})^2}{\text{SSX}}}$$

The 95% confidence interval is then constructed as $t_{.025} \approx 2$ estimated standard errors on either side of the sample statistic, which in this case is the estimated value $\hat{Y}_p$.

Because the expression for the standard error $s_{\hat{Y}_p}$ contains the deviation $x_p - \overline{X}$, the size of $s_{\hat{Y}_p}$ depends on the value of x_p. The farther x_p is from its mean, the larger the standard error is, resulting in wider confidence intervals. This relationship is illustrated in Figure 9-4 for the confidence intervals across the range of EPS (X) values. The heavy lines portray the upper and lower bounds, respectively, of the confidence interval of the estimated mean PPS for *each* value of EPS. The population regression line likely lies within the confidence limit boundaries.

The confidence interval around the sample mean $\hat{Y}_p$ is easily calculated from its standard error $s_{\hat{Y}_p}$.

> *95% confidence interval for estimated mean $\hat{Y}_p$ around x_p:*
> $$\hat{Y}_p \pm t_{.025} s_{\hat{Y}_p}, \quad \text{where } t \text{ has } df = n - (npred + 1)$$

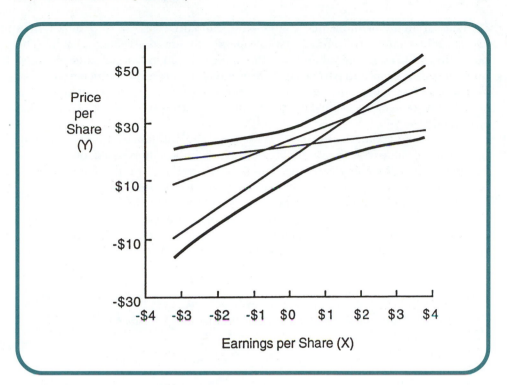

Figure 9-4.
Three possible estimated
regression lines, each
with all $\hat{Y}$ values within
the two heavy lines that
define the upper and
lower bounds of the
confidence interval for
each single value of X.

To obtain this interval, first apply the regression model to calculate the estimated mean $\hat{Y}_p$ from the given x_p. Next, compute the standard error of $\hat{Y}_p$ ($s_{\hat{Y}_p}$) and obtain the cutoff value $t_{.025} \approx 2$ from a t-distribution. As discussed in Chapter 4, different cutoff values yield different confidence levels, such as $t_{.005}$ for a 99% confidence level.

Prediction Intervals

The previous section addressed estimating (i.e., predicting) a point on the regression line: the mean value of Y from a given value of X. This section addresses the prediction of an *individual* value of the variable Y, one data point in the scatterplot. The previous section showed how to construct a confidence interval around the mean estimated PPS for all companies with the same Earnings per Share (EPS) such as $2.24. This section discusses constructing an interval around the estimated price of a single company's stock at a given value of X such as $2.24. For example, what is the variability of prediction for Tandy Corporation's stock across repeated samples?

For each company with EPS = $2.24, predicted PPS is $\hat{Y}_{2.24,i} = \$31.30$, which is also the estimated mean PPS of all these companies.

> *The distinction between predicting an average and predicting a specific value is not the estimated value, but the variability of the predictions over repeated sampling.*

Predicting an *average* value for all Y's at the value x_p, $\hat{Y}_p$, and predicting an *individual* value Y at x_p, $\hat{Y}_{p,i}$, results in the same estimated value of $\hat{Y}$. The key idea here is that even if $\hat{Y}_{p,i}$ were computed from the population regression model, estimation of a single value would still not be perfect.

The variability of individual values—the standard error $s_{\hat{Y}_{p,i}}$—is larger than the variability of the corresponding sample mean—the standard error $s_{\hat{Y}_p}$. Why? The variability of the estimated value Y, whether a mean or an individual value, changes from sample to sample, in part because the estimated regression coefficients change from sample to sample. The random fluctuations of sampling error result in a b_1 estimated from a single sample that does not equal the corresponding population value β_1. Similarly, $b_0 \neq \beta_0$.

However, an additional source of error variability influences the prediction of an individual value of Y: the variability of the individual values of Y around the estimated mean $\hat{Y}_p$ for a single sample. This source of variability is the standard error of estimate s_e. This type of error is due to the failure of the regression model to completely describe the variability of the response variable Y.

The standard error of the prediction of an individual value $s_{\hat{Y}_{p,i}}$ reflects these two independent sources of variability: the sampling error of the estimated regression coefficients and the modeling error resulting from an imperfect regression model.

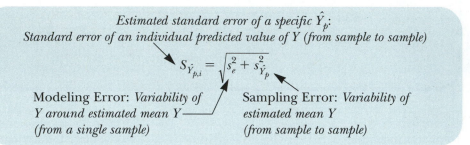

Estimated standard error of a specific $\hat{Y}_p$:
Standard error of an individual predicted value of Y (from sample to sample)

$$S_{\hat{Y}_{p,i}} = \sqrt{s_e^2 + s_{\hat{Y}_p}^2}$$

Modeling Error: *Variability of Y around estimated mean Y (from a single sample)*

Sampling Error: *Variability of estimated mean Y (from sample to sample)*

The variability across repeated samples of the estimated individual value $\hat{Y}$ depends on the variability of individual values of Y around the estimated value, as well as the variability of the estimated value across samples.

Why is the standard error of an individual estimated value of Y ($s_{\hat{Y}_{p,i}}$) of greater interest for gauging the precision of prediction than the standard error of estimate s_e? The standard error of estimate s_e indicates the amount of fluctuation of individual Y's around a value of X for a single sample. The standard error of individual estimated values accounts not only for this within-sample fluctuation, but also the fluctuation of estimated regression coefficients b_0 and b_1 from sample to sample. This across-sample fluctuation must be accounted for when using the model derived from the estimation sample to predict an individual value in a new (prediction) sample. Unfortunately, this more useful $s_{\hat{Y}_{p,i}}$ is larger than the standard error of estimate s_e, reflecting the additional source of error.

How does $s_{\hat{Y}_{p,i}}$ depend on sample size n? Unlike the standard error of the estimated mean, which converges to zero as the sample size increases, the standard error of estimate does not.

The standard error of an estimated individual value cannot be smaller than the standard error of estimate.

Increasing sample size minimizes the fluctuations of b_0 and b_1 from sample to sample but does not decrease s_e. The only method for reducing s_e is to develop a better model.

This interval constructed around a single value of Y is called a prediction interval.

$$95\% \text{ prediction interval for estimating } \hat{Y}_p \text{ from } x_p:$$
$$\hat{Y}_p \pm t_{.025} s_{\hat{Y}_{p,i}}, \text{ where } t \text{ has } df = n - (npred + 1)$$

This prediction interval has the same form as a confidence interval, plus and minus the cutoff value of t multiplied by the corresponding standard error. The distinction is that a confidence interval estimates a population value, and the prediction interval estimates an individual value.

An example illustrating these two types of intervals follows.

BUSINESS APPLICATION 9.3—Intervals around the Predicted Value

MANAGERIAL PROBLEM

Previous analysis of 1992 data for 1,402 companies demonstrated that Earnings per Share (EPS) is related to stock Price per Share (PPS). For every dollar increase in earnings, stock price increases an average of $5.44. Without any earnings, the average PPS is around $19.56. Given an established relationship between EPS and PPS, management now seeks to evaluate the precision of the resulting prediction. How precisely can mean PPS be estimated for *all* companies with a given level of EPS? Also, how precise is the prediction of PPS for a *single* company from that company's EPS?

DATA

The data are the values of EPS (X) and PPS (Y) for large ($n = 1,402$) and small ($n = 10$) samples of publicly traded companies that paid a dividend in 1992. The data for the small sample appear in Table 9-1.

APPLICATION—CONCEPTUAL WORKSHEET

Step 1. First enter the data, the values of X and Y, into the worksheet as shown in the shaded area in Table 9-1. For convenience, this worksheet was constructed using cell names, as shown in Chapter 1.

Table 9-1.
Confidence intervals and prediction intervals for estimating PPS from EPS for a sample of 10 companies.

	EPS	PPS			Conf. Intervals				Pred. Intervals		
	X	Y	YPred	StdPred	CILo	CIHi	CIWidth	StdInd	PILo	PIHi	PIWidth
1	-3.26	6.500	2.79	6.80	-12.90	18.48	31.38	11.86	-24.56	30.14	54.70
2	-1.98	13.000	9.42	5.13	-2.41	21.26	23.68	10.99	-15.91	34.76	50.67
3	-0.45	22.500	17.35	3.55	9.18	25.53	16.36	10.34	-6.49	41.20	47.70
4	0.56	8.625	22.59	3.08	15.49	29.69	14.21	10.19	-0.91	46.09	47.00
5	1.00	17.250	24.87	3.10	17.71	32.03	14.32	10.20	1.35	48.39	47.04
6	1.23	16.000	26.06	3.17	18.74	33.38	14.64	10.22	2.50	49.63	47.13
7	1.50	41.375	27.46	3.30	19.85	35.08	15.23	10.26	3.80	51.12	47.32
8	2.24	24.500	31.30	3.86	22.39	40.21	17.81	10.45	7.19	55.41	48.22
9	2.42	34.125	32.23	4.04	22.93	41.54	18.61	10.52	7.97	56.49	48.52
10	3.83	49.750	39.54	5.68	26.45	52.63	26.18	11.25	13.60	65.49	51.89

Table 9-2.
Labels and corresponding statistics.

n	SdX	MeanX	slope	inter	SEE	SSX	t.025
10	2.12	0.71	5.18	19.69	9.71	40.34	2.31

Table 9-3.
Description and worksheet formulas for each of the descriptive statistics and *t*-value found in Table 9-2.

Description	Stat Symbol	Worksheet Name	Worksheet Formula
Sample size	n	n	=COUNT(X)
Standard deviation	s_X	SdX	=STDEV(X)
Mean	$\bar{X}$	MeanX	=AVERAGE(X)
Slope coefficient	b_1	slope	=SLOPE(Y,X)
Y-Intercept	b_0	inter	=INTERCEPT(Y,X)
Standard error of estimate	s_e	SEE	=STEYX(Y,X)
Sum of squares of X	SSX	SSX	=(n-1)*SdX^2
t-cutoff value	$t_{.025}$	t.025	=TINV(0.05,n-2)

Step 2. Next enter the labels in Table 9-2 for the descriptive statistics and the *t*-value needed for the computation of the confidence and prediction intervals.

The formulas for calculating the statistics in Table 9-2 have been presented throughout the text. For review, the specific formulas entered into this worksheet for each of these statistics is found in Table 9-3.

Step 3. Now enter the formulas for the standard errors and intervals. The confidence and prediction intervals for all 10 values of EPS for the 10 sample companies are provided in Table 9-1, with corresponding formulas and descriptions provided in Table 9-4. The farther the value of EPS from its mean, the wider the corresponding interval.

APPLICATION—TRADITIONAL NOTATION

The sum of squares for X (SSX) is needed to compute the confidence and prediction intervals. SSX is easily obtained from the standard deviation,

$$s_X = \sqrt{\frac{\text{SSX}}{n-1}}, \text{ so SSX} = (n-1)s_X^2.$$

For $n = 10$, SSX $= (9)(2.117^2) = 40.343$. For $n = 1402$, SSX $= (1401)(2.134^2)$ $= (1401)(4.553) = 6378.753$.

Table 9-4.
Descriptions and
worksheet formulas
for the computation
of the confidence
and prediction
intervals around
predicted values.

Description	Symbol	Worksheet	Worksheet
Predicted value	$\hat{Y}$	YPred	=inter+slope*X
Estimated standard error of predicted mean	$s_{\hat{Y}p}$	StdPred	=SEE*SQRT((1/n)+(X-MeanX)^2/SSX)
Lower bound of confid. int.		CILo	=YPred-(t.025*StdPred)
Upper bound of confid. int.		CIHi	=YPred+(t.025*StdPred)
Width of confidence interval		CIWidth	=CIHi-CILo
Estimated standard error of a specific prediction	$s_{\hat{Y}p,i}$	StdInd	=SQRT(SEE^2+StdPred^2)
Lower bound of prediction int.		PILo	=YPred-(t.025*StdInd)
Upper bound of prediction int.		PIHi	=YPred+(t.025*StdInd)
Width of prediction interval		PIWidth	=PredHi-PredLo

Confidence Intervals

The standard deviation of predicted values $s_{\hat{Y}_p}$ around the corresponding conditional mean for all companies in this sample of 10 is

$$s_{\hat{Y}_p} = s_e\sqrt{\frac{1}{n} + \frac{(x_p - \overline{X})^2}{\text{SSX}}} = 9.715\sqrt{\frac{1}{10} + \frac{(x_p - 0.709)^2}{40.343}}.$$

The standard error $s_{\hat{Y}_p}$ for *all* companies with an EPS of $2.24 is

$$s_{\hat{Y}_p} = 9.715\sqrt{\frac{1}{10} + \frac{(2.24 - 0.709)^2}{40.343}} = 9.715\sqrt{.158} = 3.863.$$

The t-cutoff value is based on $df = n - 2$, so $df = 8$. For a confidence level of 95%, the cutoff value of t is 2.31.

The 95% confidence interval can now be computed for EPS = $2.24. The distance from the predicted value $\hat{Y} = 31.30$ to either end of the interval (the precision or maximum error of estimation E) is 2.31 standard errors, which is

$$E = t_{.025}s_{\hat{Y}_p} = (2.31)(3.863) = 8.924.$$

Obtain the confidence interval by adding and subtracting 8.91 from $\hat{Y}$.

Lower Bound: $\hat{Y} - 2.31 \, (s_{\hat{Y}_p}) = \$31.30 - \$8.92 = \$22.39$

and

Upper Bound: $\hat{Y} + 2.31 \, (s_{\hat{Y}_p}) = \$31.30 + \$8.92 = \$40.21.$

The population mean of PPS for all companies with an EPS of $2.24 is likely between $22.39 and $40.21, with a 95% level of confidence. This interval is $17.82 wide.

Prediction Intervals

The standard error $s_{\hat{Y}_{p,i}}$ describes the variability of the predicted value of any individual company. For an EPS of $2.24, such as for Tandy Corp, this standard error is

$$s_{\hat{Y}_{p,i}} = \sqrt{s_e^2 + s_{\hat{Y}_p}^2}$$

$$= \sqrt{9.715^2 + 3.863^2} = \sqrt{94.381 + 14.923} = \sqrt{109.304} = 10.45.$$

The t-cutoff value is based on $df = n - 2 = 8$. For a confidence level of 95%, $t_{.025} = 2.31$.

Now calculate the 95% prediction interval for an individual company. The distance from the predicted (estimated) value $\hat{Y} = 31.30$ to either end of the interval (the precision or maximum error of estimation E) is 2.31 standard errors:

$$E = t_{.025}s_{\hat{Y}_{p,i}} = (2.31)(10.45) = 24.11.$$

Obtain the prediction interval by adding and subtracting 24.11 from $\hat{Y}$.

$$\text{Lower Bound: } \hat{Y} - 2.31\,(s_{\hat{Y}_{p,i}}) = \$31.30 - \$24.11 = \$7.19$$

and

$$\text{Upper Bound: } \hat{Y} + 2.31\,(s_{\hat{Y}_{p,i}}) = \$31.30 + \$24.11 = \$55.41.$$

Based on this analysis of only 10 companies, the population value of PPS for a single company with an EPS of $2.24 is probably between $7.19 and $55.41, with a 95% level of confidence. This interval is $48.22 wide.

Table 9-1 provides similar calculations for 10 different values of EPS. The predicted price for companies with negative earnings (e.g., EPS = -$3.26) is positive (e.g., $2.79), but the corresponding prediction interval includes negative values. Negative PPS values are not possible in practice. However, PPS could be well below the predicted value, all the way down to zero. The widths of these prediction intervals varies from 47.00 to 54.70, a considerably larger width than that provided only by the standard error $s_e = 9.71$. Two standard errors on either side of $\hat{Y}$ yield a width of only 38.84.

ANALYSIS OF FULL SAMPLE FOR $N = 1,402$

The same calculations were also done for these 10 companies as part of the larger sample of 1,402 companies. Table 9-5 lists the needed statistics. Shaded values were calculated elsewhere and entered as constants into the worksheet.

Table 9-6 presents the results. In Table 9-6, the confidence intervals around the estimated means are considerably smaller with the much larger sample size. Because the standard error of estimate $s_e = 15.96$ is larger for the full sample than the $s_e = 9.72$ obtained for the nonrandom sample of 10 companies, the larger sample yields wider prediction intervals.

APPLICATION—EXCEL BUILT-IN ANALYSIS

Excel does not provide built-in programming for the calculation of confidence and prediction intervals around the predicted value from a regression model.

Table 9-5.
Statistics for
$n = 1,402$

n	SdX	MeanX	slope	inter	SEE	SSX	t.025
1402	2.134	1.487	5.436	19.561	15.958	6380.09	1.96

	EPS	PPS			Conf. Intervals				Pred. Intervals		
	X	Y	YPred	StdPred	CILo	CIHi	CIWidth	StdInd	PILo	PIHi	PIWidth
1	-3.26	6.500	1.84	1.04	-0.20	3.88	4.08	15.99	-29.53	33.21	62.74
2	-1.98	13.000	8.80	0.81	7.20	10.39	3.19	15.98	-22.55	40.14	62.69
3	-0.45	22.500	17.11	0.58	15.99	18.24	2.26	15.97	-14.21	48.44	62.65
4	0.56	8.625	22.61	0.46	21.69	23.52	1.82	15.96	-8.71	53.92	62.63
5	1.00	17.250	25.00	0.44	24.14	25.85	1.72	15.96	-6.32	56.31	62.63
6	1.23	16.000	26.25	0.43	25.41	27.09	1.68	15.96	-5.07	57.56	62.63
7	1.50	41.375	27.72	0.43	26.88	28.55	1.67	15.96	-3.60	59.03	62.63
8	2.24	24.500	31.74	0.45	30.85	32.62	1.77	15.96	0.42	63.05	62.63
9	2.42	34.125	32.72	0.47	31.80	33.63	1.83	15.96	1.40	64.03	62.63
10	3.83	49.750	40.38	0.63	39.14	41.62	2.48	15.97	9.05	71.71	62.66

Table 9-6.
Confidence intervals
and prediction
intervals for
predicted mean PPS
for the 10 companies
in the full sample of
1,402 companies.

PLOT OF THE INTERVALS AROUND THE REGRESSION LINE FOR $N = 10$

Assessing the Excel Output

The considerable width of the two sets of intervals around the regression line in Figure 9-5 vividly illustrates the lack of confidence in predictions of PPS from EPS—particularly for predictions of individual companies. The graph also illustrates that the farther the value of X is from its mean, the larger the corresponding standard error will be.

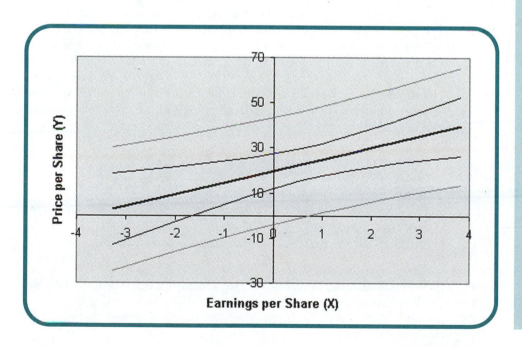

Earnings per Share (X)

Figure 9-5.
Confidence intervals
(regular line) and
prediction intervals
(light gray line)
about the regression
line (heavy line)
computed from the n
$= 10$ sample.

Obtaining the Graph

Insert ➤ Chart...

Step 1—Chart Type. Specify an *XY* Scatter chart, which is for a numeric horizontal axis. Select the format that connects the points with line segments, or the format that joins them with a smooth curve.

Step 2—Chart Source. Specify the cells for the Data Range, which initially includes the EPS values in Cells C6 through C16 and the estimated PPS values in Cells E6 through E16. These columns are not adjacent, so use a discontiguous selection to select them both. Choose one column of cells, hold down the Control key (Windows) or the Command key (Mac), and then select the second column of cells. Or just type the relevant cell references, separating the EPS cell range from the predicted PPS cell range with a comma.

Data range: =Sheet1!$C$6:$C$16,Sheet1!$E$6:$E$16|

Step 3—Chart Options. Click the Legend tab and uncheck the Show legend box. Click the Titles box to provide the titles for the *X* and *Y* axes.

Step 4—Chart Location. Specify a new sheet for the chart or a starting cell for the chart in the current worksheet.

Now add the curves for the upper and lower confidence and prediction intervals to the regression line. For each curve, select the cells that contain the corresponding values, release the mouse, and then move the cursor to the edge of the selection. At the edge, when the cursor turns to an arrow, hold the mouse button down, drag the data values to the graph, and release. The Paste Special dialog box appears, which indicates that a new series is to be added to the graph. Click OK, and one or more additional columns of data are added to the chart, with one resulting curve per column.

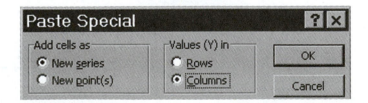

To help distinguish among the various curves, change their appearance. Double-click on one of the curves, which calls up the Format Data Series dialog box. Select the Patterns tab, as shown in the accompanying illustration, and then choose a style, color, and weight of the line.

Change the formatting of the values on an axis by first double-clicking the axis, which results in the Format Axis dialog box. Then select the Number tab and choose the desired number of Decimal places, which is zero in this example.

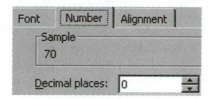

Figure 9-5 displays the resulting graph from the sample of 10 companies.

STATISTICAL PRINCIPLE

Larger sample sizes result in smaller confidence intervals around the predicted values. The variability of the conditional means from sample to sample becomes smaller as the sample size grows. Unfortunately, a larger sample size does not decrease the variability of the individual observations, so the error of the prediction of the value of Y for an individual observation does not diminish to zero for increasingly larger sample sizes.

MANAGERIAL INTERPRETATION

Previous analyses had established that Earnings per Share is (linearly) related to Price per Share. Knowing the corresponding earnings allows a better estimate of price than not knowing this information. Further, on a per share basis, if mean price is predicted for all companies with a specified earnings, then a large sample size can provide reasonably accurate prediction. Unfortunately, if the focus is on the stock of a single company, increasing sample size offers limited gains in predictive accuracy from this model. For the companies considered in these samples, very wide prediction intervals were obtained, around $60 for the sample of 10 and $71 for the 1,402 sample. On a per share basis, earnings is related to price, but not to the extent that accurate predictions can be made of a single price from earnings.

The previous example provided confidence intervals and prediction intervals only for values of EPS present in the data. Part of the appeal of regression analysis is that a value of Y such as PPS may be predicted from *any* value of the predictor variable that is *within* the range of values in the data from which the regression model was estimated. For example, in the sample of 10 companies analyzed above, the values of EPS range from –3.26 to 3.83, so PPS can be predicted for any value of EPS between –3.26 and 3.83, and the associated confidence interval or prediction interval can be calculated. However, **extrapolation**—applying the model to values outside the range of the predictor variable included in the analysis—can be misleading.

Values outside of the range were not analyzed, so no evidence regarding their relationship to the response variable Y has been observed. There is no guarantee, for example, that the relationship between Y and X is even linear over these ranges of the predictor variable X. In the absence of all other information, extrapolation provides a predicted value of Y, but this value should be treated more as a guess and less as a formal prediction.

A common extrapolation error in the interpretation of some regression models is the interpretation of the intercept estimate b_0. When the range of X values does not include zero, the predicted value of Y when $X = 0$ (b_0) cannot be properly interpreted. A literal interpretation may even lead to a nonsensical conclusion. If a regression equation shows that the number of cars sold per month increases when more salespeople are working, this equation can be extrapolated to include $X = 0$, which literally means that there are no salespeople to sale cars. Typically this regression line would cross the vertical (Y) axis at some nonzero value, such as 15. Interpreted literally, the result is often an absurd conclusion such as, "The number of cars sold when there are no salespeople to sale cars is 15."

Extrapolation is an improper application of a regression model. The next section presents other problems that can arise from the application of regression analysis.

extrapolation

application of the regression model to values of the predictor variables outside of the range of data used to estimate the model

EXERCISES

 9-8. For the prediction of PPS (Y) from the Dividends per Share (X) Exercise 8-7 in the previous chapter, the OLS regression model is

$$\hat{Y} = (13.05)X + 10.67,$$

with $n = 10$, $X = 0.973$, $s_X = 0.868$, and $s_e = 9.245$.

a. For DPS = \$1, compute the confidence interval for predicted PPS.
b. For DPS = \$1, compute the prediction interval for predicted PPS.
c. Determine which of the intervals is wider and why.

 9-9. Consider the prediction of PPS (Y) from DPS (X) for the full sample of 1,402 companies. The OLS regression model esti-

mated from these data is $\hat{Y} = 10.62(X) + 17.95$, with $\overline{X} = 0.913$, $s_X = 0.825$, and $s_e = 17.68$.

a. For DPS = \$1, compute the confidence interval for PPS.
b. For DPS = \$1, compute the prediction interval for PPS.

 9-10. Compare the results of the previous two problems.

a. Are either of the *confidence* intervals dramatically wider? Why?
b. Are either of the *prediction* intervals dramatically wider? Why?

 9-11. For the prediction of the Price (Y) of large-screen TVs from the *Consumer Report's* ratings (X) Exercise 8-12 from the previous chapter, $\hat{Y} = 24.11X - 601.99$, with $n = 10$, $\overline{X} = 83.30$, $s_X = 4.24$, and $s_e = 554.197$.

a. For Rating = 85, compute the confidence interval for Price.

b. For Rating = 90, compute the confidence interval for Price.

c. Determine which of the intervals is wider and why.

9.3 OUTLIERS IN REGRESSION ANALYSIS

The previous chapter demonstrated how to obtain ordinary least squares (OLS) estimates of the parameters of a regression model, how to assess the fit of the model, and how to analyze the residuals from the model to assess the validity of the four basic assumptions. This section extends the previous discussion of residuals. The focus here is on the various types of problems and interpretive issues that may arise when applying regression analysis to real world problems. We begin with a discussion of outliers.

Outliers

As defined in Chapter 3, an *outlier* is a value considerably different from most values in the distribution. If the outlier was sampled from a population different from that which produced most of the remaining data, the corresponding observation should be removed from the analysis. Consider the five salaries in Table 9-7.

The first four salaries are from support staff, and the last salary is the CEO's. The mean of these salaries is $284,090, a value that is neither representative of the support staff salaries nor the CEO's. Drop the largest value from this small distribution and the mean plummets all the way down to $42,030.

The crucial issue is not the deviant value per se but that processes different from those that influenced the remaining values may have generated the outliers. The process by which a person is compensated more than a million dollars, such as with stock investments, is different from the process in which an hourly employee earns a salary below $50,000. A simultaneous analysis of all five salaries in Table 9-7 leads to a description that applies to *neither* the lower income group nor to the CEO.

Figure 9-6 illustrates that the same principle applies both to the analysis of the mean and to regression analysis (i.e., conditional means). One or just a few outliers in the data may dramatically influence the results. If the process that generated the values for outliers is different from the process that generated the remaining observations, a different regression model should be applied to the majority of the data values than that applied to the outliers.

Examining the outliers can reveal why the corresponding prediction was so far off. Perhaps a bus was 30 minutes late due to an accident that shut down the highway, so that specific bus arrival time was dramatically underpredicted. Dropping this one value from an analysis restricts the generalization of the results to bus

Table 9-7.
Five illustrative salaries with one outlier.

1	2	3	4	5
$35,250	$38,840	$45,280	$48,750	$1,252,330

Figure 9-6.
Dramatic impact of two outliers on the estimation of a regression line.

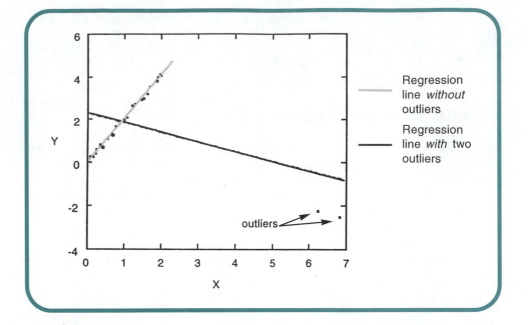

arrival times *not* delayed by a relatively rare event such as a major accident. The resulting benefit is that estimates of the remaining values more accurately describe the relationships among the variables under more normal circumstances.

When constructing a regression model, first follow the steps already presented in this and the previous chapter: Estimate the regression coefficients, estimate the associated standard errors, and assess the fit of the model. An analysis of outliers and a possible reanalysis with the outliers removed should then be conducted. Different ways of detecting outliers potentially present in a regression analysis are discussed next.

Detecting Residual Outliers

A regression analysis does not estimate most values of *Y* exactly, so most residuals are generally smaller or larger than zero. However, some residuals may be particularly large relative to the remaining residuals; these are called **residual outliers.** A very large residual may indicate that the corresponding *X* and *Y* values do not belong with the remaining values. Perhaps the observation was sampled from a different population, or perhaps a data coding error occurred.

> **residual outlier of an observation**
> *large residual e relative to the remaining residuals*

How are large residuals identified? Chapter 3 introduced the concept of a standardized value: the number of standard deviations a value is from the mean. Knowing that a residual is –25.88 does not provide much information regarding the position of this residual relative to the remaining residuals. Knowing that the corresponding *standardized* residual is –1.14 indicates that the residual lies a little more than one standard deviation below the mean. A value such as –25.88 may seem large, but if the residuals are approximately normally distributed, then many more residuals lie beyond 1.14 standard deviations on either side of the mean.

> **standardized residual of an observation**
> $$Z_e \equiv \frac{e}{s_e}$$

The mean of a distribution of residuals from an OLS regression analysis is always zero. Accordingly, the **standardized residual** is the residual divided by the standard error of estimate. The population mean and standard deviation of Z_e are 0 and 1, respectively.

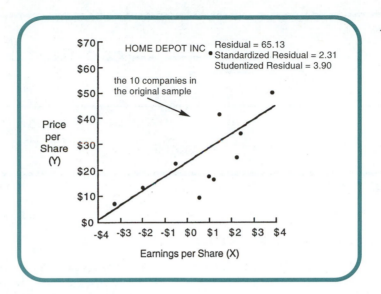

Figure 9-7.
The residual analysis for
Home Depot, Inc.

Values of Z_e from a normal distribution larger than 3 or smaller than −3 are likely outliers, generated by a process different from the process that generated most of the remaining values. Values larger than 2 or smaller than −2 could also be outliers. If the residuals are normally distributed, less than 5% of the residuals should be more than two standard errors on either side of zero.

An outlier can substantially affect the values of the estimated regression coefficients. Yet the initial analysis that yielded a large standardized residual included the outlier, and the regression coefficients are calculated so as to minimize the size of this and all other (squared) residuals. The more relevant issue is the size of the residual for regression coefficients estimated *without* the deviant observation, an issue addressed by the Studentized residual.

The **Studentized residual** shows how large the residual is without the influence of the observation on the estimation of the model; it is typically larger than the unmodified standardized error. To illustrate, Figure 9-7 displays the scatterplot and regression line of PPS and EPS for the original sample of 10 companies plus an additional company, Home Depot, Inc. The company has a large Studentized residual, 3.90, which indicates that Home Depot is an outlier. The Studentized residual is larger than the standardized residual (2.31), indicating that this observation substantially affects the estimation of the regression coefficients.

An example of analyzing the distribution of residuals to identify outliers follows.

> **Studentized residual of an observation**
> *standardized residual from the regression model estimated with the observation deleted from the data*

BUSINESS APPLICATION 9.4—Analysis of Residual Outliers

MANAGERIAL PROBLEM

Regression analysis of 1,402 companies demonstrated that Earnings per Share (EPS) is related to Price per Share (PPS). Diagnostics that address the validity of the analysis and the usefulness of the corresponding substantive conclusions are based on the analysis of the residuals from the regression. Is the derived regression equation valid, or do the results depend on nonrepresentative data values?

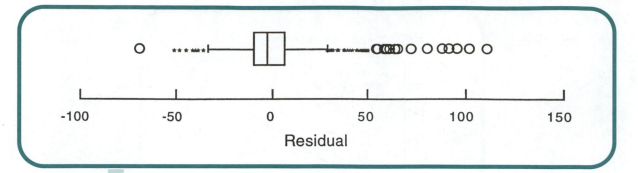

Residual

Figure 9-8.
Box plot of 1,402
residuals from
estimating PPS
from EPS.

BOX PLOT OF RESIDUALS

The initial data for the analysis are the Earnings per Share and Price per Share of the sample of 1,402 companies from 1992 year-end data. The box plot of the residuals (Chapter 3 extension), displayed in Figure 9-8, indicates a relatively large number of large residuals and a very large dispersion from the smallest to the largest residual.

The demarcation between a potential outlier and an actual outlier (Chapter 3) shown on the preceding box plot is just slightly above 50 or below –50. A characteristic of many of these residuals becomes apparent in the residual plot in Figure 9-9. This plot illustrates the importance of examining the residuals plotted against the predictor variable. Most points lie in a circle bounded by EPS = –5 and EPS = 9, with only about 3% of the points scattered outside of this circle. Many of these points outside of the circle are residual outliers, with values above 50 or below –50.

Figure 9-9.
Plot of 1,402
residuals from
estimating PPS from
EPS.

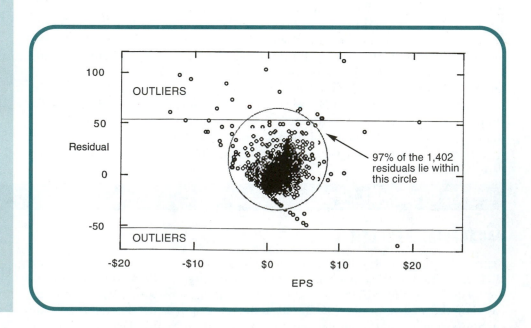

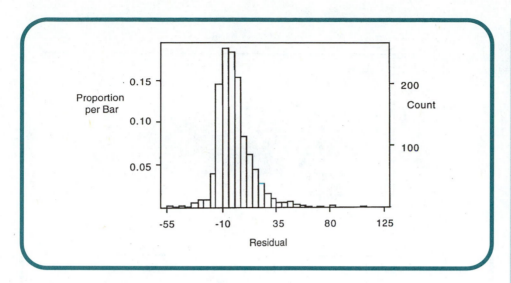

Figure 9-10.
Histogram of 1,385
residuals from
predicting PPS
against the
predictor variable
EPS (between −5
and 9).

RESIDUAL VERSUS PREDICTOR VARIABLE PLOT

These outliers may represent different underlying processes from that which produced those observations in which EPS is between −5 and 9. *If* a different process can be identified for these observations, the outliers should be deleted, though the results then only generalize to observations that fit the EPS criteria between −5 and 9. To illustrate the statistical effects of this deletion in Figure 9-10, the range of EPS values in the following analyses was restricted to consider only the 1,385 companies with an EPS between −5 and 9.

DISTRIBUTION OF RESIDUALS FOR THE RESTRICTED VALUES

Except for the presence of several very large residuals, the distribution of residuals is roughly normal.

RESIDUAL VERSUS PREDICTOR VARIABLE PLOT
FOR THE RESTRICTED VALUES

The residuals should be randomly distributed for all values of EPS; in other words, they should have the same variability at each value of EPS. Unfortunately, as seen from Figure 9-11, most of the negative residuals exist primarily at small values of EPS, which corresponds to relatively few overpredictions at these values.

MANAGERIAL INTERPRETATION

First, observations with extreme values of EPS (less than −$5 and greater than $9) are potential outliers and *possibly* should be deleted from the analysis given further

Figure 9-11.
Plot of 1,385
residuals from
predicting PPS
against the
predictor variable
EPS (between −5
and 9).

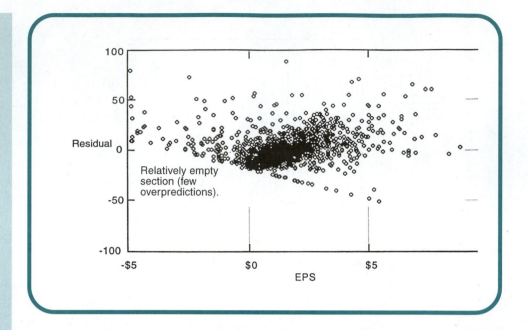

substantive analysis. Many of these observations generated large residuals, which means that they did not conform very well to the regression model. Second, for values of EPS less than approximately $1, and particularly less than −$1, negative residuals are relatively sparse. Only infrequently is PPS overpredicted for small values of EPS. Potential reasons for this disparity should be further investigated.

When an observation has a larger Studentized than standardized residual, the observation has a substantial effect on the estimation of the regression coefficients. Direct methods for estimating this influence are considered next.

Detecting Influential Observations

There are several statistics for gauging the impact of a single observation on the estimation of the regression coefficients.

If you remove an **influential observation** from the analysis, the estimated values of the regression coefficients and intercept dramatically change. One consideration in the assessment of the influence of an observation is the extent to which the values of the predictor variables X are unusual. Another consideration is the extent to which the residuals, and their standardized or Studentized versions, indicate that the response Y is unusual.

Cook's Distance explicitly indicates the level of influence of an observation's X values and Y value on the calculation of the regression coefficients. In practice, Cook's Distance for each observation is not actually calculated by subtracting the estimated regression coefficients from the analyses with and without the observation of interest. Fortunately, a more efficient expression reveals that Cook's Distance depends on both the value of the residual as well as the distance of the value

influential observation
disproportionate influence on the estimated values of the regression coefficients

Cook's Distance c of an observation
distance between the regression coefficients calculated with the observation included and deleted in the analysis

of X from the mean of X. This distance indicator is called *leverage*, which—for the one-predictor model only—is defined as

$$h = \frac{1}{n} + \frac{(x_p - \overline{X})^2}{SSX}.$$

This expression previously appeared in the definition of the standard error of the estimated conditional mean ($s_{\hat{Y}_p}$). Cook's Distance (c) for an observation is defined from the residual e and leverage h for that observation, and from MSE for the overall analysis. For models with a single predictor variable,

$$c = \frac{e^2}{MSE\,(npred + 1)} \left(\frac{h}{(1 - h)^2} \right).$$

The larger the observation's residual or leverage, the larger the Cook's Distance.

Deleting observations with a large influence substantially changes the estimated regression coefficients, and, consequently, the predicted value for many of the observations. What value of Cook's Distance indicates a large influence? The answer is a judgment call based on two considerations.

First, the value should generally be reasonably large. In practice, values of Cook's Distance above approximately .8 are typically considered large. Also, the value should be considerably larger than most other distances. These large values are generally found in analyses with small or moderate sample sizes. For large samples, even moderately deviant observations have little influence on the calculation of the regression coefficients.

An example follows.

BUSINESS APPLICATION 9.5—Unusual Observations in Regression Analysis

MANAGERIAL PROBLEM

The model that expresses Price per Share (PPS) in terms of Earnings per Share (EPS) has been estimated. Are there any unusual observations in the data that could render the estimates misleading?

DATA

The data include 1992 PPS and EPS for the previously described sample of 10 companies, plus two additional companies, CBS Inc. and 1st Empire State Corp. For purposes of this illustration, the available data relating EPS to PPS are from these 12 companies.

ANALYSIS

The OLS regression model estimated from these 12 observations is

$$\hat{Y} = 18.864 + 10.634X.$$

The analysis of the residuals and influence statistics follows.

Company	EPS	Actual PPS	Predicted PPS	Residual	Residual Sq.	Standard Res.	Student. Res.	Cook's Distance
	X	Y	$\hat{Y}$	e	e^2	Z_e		c
1 IMO INDUST. INC	-3.26	6.500	-15.80	22.30	497.42	0.91	1.03	0.15
2 TORO CO	-1.98	13.000	-2.19	15.19	230.78	0.62	0.66	0.04
3 CALMAT CO	-0.45	22.500	14.08	8.42	70.92	0.34	0.35	0.01
4 TULTEX CORP	0.56	8.625	24.82	-16.19	262.25	-0.66	-0.67	0.03
5 FAM. DOL. ST	1.00	17.250	29.50	-12.25	150.01	-0.50	-0.50	0.01
6 PHIL. SB. CORP	1.23	16.000	31.94	-15.94	254.21	-0.65	-0.66	0.02
7 RTZ PLC	1.50	41.375	34.82	6.56	43.03	0.27	0.27	0.00
8 TANDY CORP	2.24	24.500	42.68	-18.18	330.66	-0.74	-0.76	0.03
9 OK. GAS & ELT.	2.42	34.125	44.60	-10.47	109.69	-0.43	-0.43	0.01
10 NICOR INC	3.83	49.750	59.59	-9.84	96.87	-0.40	-0.40	0.01
11 CBS INC	10.51	188.000	130.63	57.37	3291.62	2.33	6.18	1.99
12 1ST EMPIRE STATE CORP	13.41	134.500	161.47	-26.97	727.16	-1.09	-1.79	1.55

Sum of squared residuals: SSE   6,064.66

Mean squared residuals: MSE   606.47

STATISTICAL PRINCIPLE

The scatterplot with regression line in Figure 9-12 visually indicates that CBS and 1st Empire are unusual observations. Quantitative analysis confirms this impression. The largest Cook's Distance of the original 10 companies is only .15, but the respective Cook's Distances for these two companies are 1.99 and 1.55, both values well above .8. Similarly, the Studentized residuals are considerably larger for these two companies.

Figure 9-12.
Scatterplot and regression line of PPS and EPS for the 10 sample companies, plus an additional two unusual observations.

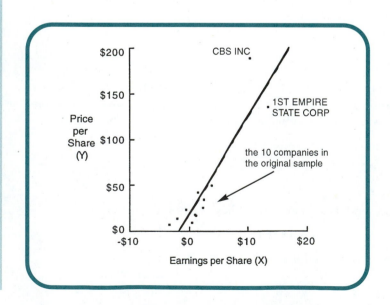

The deletion of these two outliers substantially changes the model. The estimated slope coefficient b is 10.63 from these $n = 12$ data, but it is almost half of this size, 5.18, from the analysis of only the original 10 companies.

MANAGERIAL INTREPRETATION

Inclusion of CBS and 1st Empire in the analysis substantially affects the estimation of the regression line. These companies are outliers and probably should not be included in the same analysis as the other 10 companies, particularly if the processes that generated their EPS and corresponding PPS are shown to be different from the process that generated these values for the 10 companies in the original sample. Deleting the outliers limits generalization of the results to companies with EPS less than $10, but this limitation is necessary because different regression models likely represent the relationship between PPS and EPS for these two sets of companies.

We have now accomplished four objectives. First, we have shown how to estimate an OLS regression model that predicts Y from a single predictor X. Second, we have shown how to assess the amount of error around this line. Third, we demonstrated statistical inference by building confidence intervals around the slope coefficient and by building confidence and prediction intervals around the estimated value $\hat{Y}$. Fourth, we have shown how to perform some diagnostics for identifying outliers and influential observations and for examining the pattern of residuals. The next section extends the analysis to regression models with more than a single predictor.

EXERCISES

9-12. The following OLS analysis is from the prediction of Price of large-screen TVs from the *Consumer Report's* ratings exercise (8-9) in the previous chapter.

Rating	Price	Residual	Stdnt. Res.	Cook's Dist
90.00	$950	-617.40	-1.52	0.60
88.00	$1,499	-20.19	-0.04	0.00
86.00	$2,500	1029.02	2.67	0.34
85.00	$1,180	-266.88	-0.49	0.02
84.00	$1,780	357.23	0.66	0.03
83.00	$1,880	481.33	0.91	0.05
82.00	$1,020	-354.56	-0.65	0.03
80.00	$860	-466.36	-0.91	0.09
79.00	$890	-412.25	-0.82	0.10
76.00	$1,500	270.06	0.62	0.16

a. Interpret the residuals and Studentized residuals.
b. Interpret Cook's Distance.
c. Determine if any observations are problematic. What action do you recommend?

9-13. The following tables contain the 29 Studentized residuals and the 29 Cook's Distances from the heteroscedasticity example at the end of the previous chapter.

Studentized residuals							
-1.13	-0.32	2.52	1.87	1.16	-0.70	-1.03	-1.36
-0.31	-0.37	0.19	-1.23	0.05	0.58	0.77	0.54
-0.93	-0.61	1.34	0.67	0.41	-0.62	-0.65	-0.54
-0.93	-1.48	-0.15	1.73	0.96			

Cook's Distance							
0.06	0.00	0.26	0.07	0.03	0.01	0.02	0.07
0.00	0.00	0.00	0.04	0.00	0.01	0.03	0.01
0.02	0.01	0.08	0.08	0.01	0.02	0.01	0.01
0.02	0.10	0.00	0.17	0.03			

a. Does the analysis of the Studentized residuals suggest any outliers?

b. Does the analysis of the Cook's Distances suggest any influential observations?

c. Does the analysis of these statistics replace the plot of residuals with the predictor variable for detecting heteroscedasticity? Why or why not?

9.4 MULTIPLE REGRESSION

Multiple regression is regression analysis with two or more predictor variables. Multiple regression extends the one-predictor model by accounting for the value of Y with the additional information inherent in the multiple predictor variables. In practice, the number of predictors (*npred*) typically varies from 1 to 6 or so, though models with more number of predictors are occasionally developed.

> *Multiple regression model*
> $$Y = b_0 + b_1 X_1 + b_2 X_2 + \ldots + b_{npred} X_{npred} + e$$

As with the single-predictor model, the multiple regression model is

$$Y = \hat{Y} + e.$$

The observed Y is the sum of the systematic component of the model ($\hat{Y}$) and the residual (e), which represents the cumulative effect of all influences on Y not accounted for by the predictor variables.

Many of the previously presented expressions such as that for R^2_{adj} were already defined for the more general case of multiple regression. In these equations, the expression for the number of predictor variables *npred* was included, so these equations may be applied to the simpler one-predictor models with *npred* = 1 as well as to the more general multiple regression models.

Multiple Predictor Variables

Why add more predictor variables to the model? More predictor variables potentially, though not necessarily, lead to smaller residuals and more useful slope coefficients. Consider estimation first. The interpretation of regression coefficients in multiple predictor and single predictor models differs.

> *Each regression coefficient b in the multiple regression model specifies the influence of the corresponding predictor variable on Y, with all other predictor variables in the model* held constant.

The multiple regression model isolates the effect of a predictor variable X on the response variable Y from changes in the other predictor variables.

Adding predictor variables to a model generally changes the values of the estimated coefficients, and these changes are often considered an improvement. The slope coefficient in a simple (one-predictor) model is generally not equal to the coefficient of the *same* predictor variable in a multiple regression model. Also, adding predictor variables to a regression model generally changes the values of the coefficients of each of the original predictor variables in the model as well.

Another reason to add variables to the model is that, under the right circumstances, the size of the residuals decreases.

> *The size of the residuals decreases the most when a new predictor variable is correlated with the response variable Y but not with the remaining predictor variables.*

Adding a new predictor variable ideally adds *new* information to the model.

Ordinary least squares (OLS) also applies to the estimation of the regression coefficients in multiple regression models. As with single predictor models, the estimated regression coefficients minimize the sum of squared errors,

$$\text{SSE} = \sum (Y - \hat{Y})^2 \equiv \sum e_i^2,$$

for the given data. The geometry of this minimization occurs in three or more dimensions depending on the number of predictor variables. Two-predictor variable models contain three variables including Y, so the plot of the resulting regression model requires three dimensions. The best-fitting regression line becomes a regression plane—the plot of a linear function in three dimensions. The regression surfaces become increasingly abstract as the number of predictor variables increases.

An application of multiple regression follows. The expression for SSE, s_e, and R^2_{adj} remain the same as previously presented for single predictor models. In this example, the intermediate calculations for the estimated regression coefficients and the confidence and prediction intervals are not provided. These calculations are expressed in the language of matrix algebra, and the calculations are correspondingly more complex and tedious than for the simple (one-predictor) regression model.

BUSINESS APPLICATION 9.6—Multiple Regression

MANAGERIAL PROBLEM

In previous analyses throughout this and the previous chapter, Earnings per Share (EPS) was shown to be linearly related to Price per Share (PPS), but this relationship is far from perfect. Prediction of PPS is enhanced by knowledge of EPS, but the resulting prediction is likely to be inaccurate. Both predictive accuracy and estimation may be improved by adding one or more predictor variables to the model.

Management considered a new predictor variable called BookValue per Share (BVPS), calculated by dividing Common Equity by the Total Number of Shares. BVPS indicates how much each share of stock represents of the company's common equity. Shares with a large BookValue represent a greater proportion of common equity than do shares with a low BookValue.

DATA

The data are the small ($n = 10$) and large ($n = 1,402$) samples of PPS and related variables analyzed throughout this and the previous chapter.

APPLICATION—EXCEL BUILT-IN ANALYSIS

Displaying the Numerical Output

The standard regression statistical output is displayed in three sections. Under the heading Regression Statistics, some of the error indices such as the standard error of estimate s_e are presented. Note that s_e is ambiguously labeled Standard Error rather than Standard Error of Estimate.

Regression Statistics	
Multiple R	0.90
R Square	0.81
Adjusted R Square	0.76
Standard Error	7.03
Observations	10

R^2
R^2_{adj}
s_e standard error of estimate
n

The next regression output, labeled ANOVA, is the analysis of a variance table (which is discussed in more detail in the next chapter). Included in the ANOVA table is the sum of squares of the response variable SSY, as well as two more error indices: the sum of squared errors SSE and the mean squared error MSE.

ANOVA					
	df	SS	MS	F	Significance F
Regression	2	1492.88	746.44	15.09	0.00
Residual	7	346.23	49.46		
Total	9	1839.11			

SSE   SSY   MSE

The last section of the standard statistical output contains the estimated regression model and associated estimated standard errors and confidence intervals for each of the coefficients of the model.

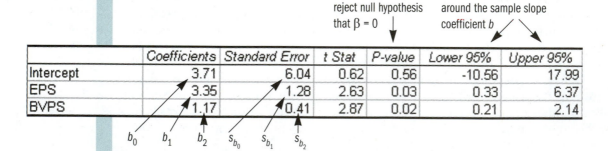

Less than .05 means reject null hypothesis that $\beta = 0$

95% confidence interval around the sample slope coefficient b

	Coefficients	Standard Error	t Stat	P-value	Lower 95%	Upper 95%
Intercept	3.71	6.04	0.62	0.56	-10.56	17.99
EPS	3.35	1.28	2.63	0.03	0.33	6.37
BVPS	1.17	0.41	2.87	0.02	0.21	2.14

b_0 b_1 b_2 s_{b_0} s_{b_1} s_{b_2}

The OLS regression model estimated from these data is

$$\hat{Y} = 3.71 + 3.35X_{\text{EPS}} + 1.17X_{BVPS}.$$

The confidence intervals for both slope coefficients contain only positive values, and the *p*-values for the corresponding hypothesis tests of zero slope coefficients are less than 0.05. We conclude that both unknown population slope coefficients are larger than zero, so both predictor variables in this model, EPS and BVPS, are simultaneously related to the response variable PPS.

As an option, the residuals and standardized residuals are also displayed.

RESIDUAL OUTPUT			
Obser vation	Predicted PPS	Residuals	Standard Residuals
1	9.571	-3.071	-0.495
2	10.063	2.937	0.474
3	19.912	2.588	0.417
4	12.176	-3.551	-0.572
5	12.771	4.479	0.722
6	22.379	-6.379	-1.029
7	29.211	12.164	1.961
8	33.067	-8.567	-1.381
9	38.071	-3.946	-0.636
10	46.403	3.347	0.540

The largest residual is for the seventh company, 12.164. The corresponding standardized residual, however, is still under 2.0. We conclude that the residual analysis does not reveal any outliers.

Displaying the Residual Plots

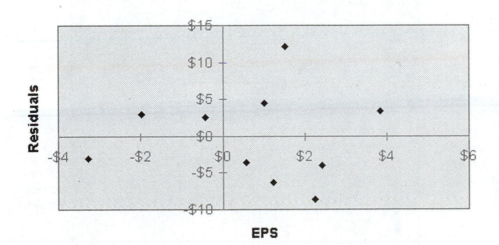

EPS Residual Plot

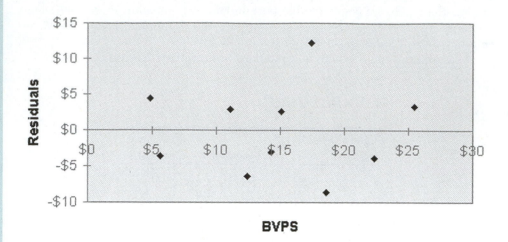

There is no apparent structure or pattern in either residual plot. That is, the residuals are apparently reflecting random, statistical noise, which is a necessary condition for the interpretation of the regression analysis to proceed.

Obtaining the Output

Tools ➤ Data Analysis... ➤ Regression

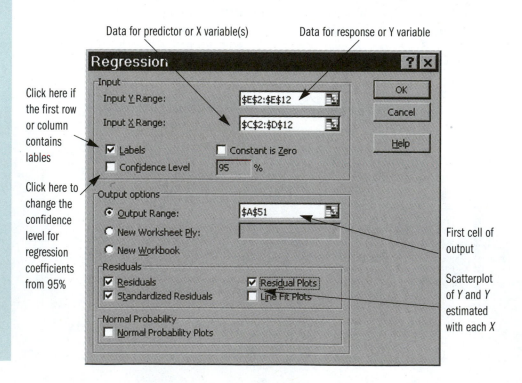

Table 9-8.
Predicted values
and residuals
based on
$\hat{Y} = 3.71 + 3.35X_{EPS}$
$+ 1.17X_{BVPS}$

Company	EPS X_1	BVPS X_2	Actual PPS Y	Predicted PPS $\hat{Y}$	Residual $e \equiv Y - \hat{Y}$	Residual Squared e^2
1 IMO INDUSTRIES INC	-3.26	14.31	6.500	9.53	-3.03	9.19
2 TORO CO	-1.98	11.07	13.000	10.03	2.97	8.84
3 CALMAT CO	-0.45	15.09	22.500	19.86	2.64	6.99
4 TULTEX CORP	0.56	5.61	8.625	12.14	-3.51	12.35
5 FAMILY DOLLAR STORES	1.00	4.86	17.250	12.75	4.50	20.27
6 PHILADELPHIA SUB. CORP	1.23	12.39	16.000	22.32	-6.32	40.00
7 RTZ PLC	1.50	17.44	41.375	29.14	12.24	149.74
8 TANDY CORP	2.24	18.61	24.500	32.98	-8.48	71.98
9 OKLA. GAS & ELECTRIC	2.42	22.36	34.125	37.98	-3.85	14.84
10 NICOR INC	3.83	25.43	49.750	46.29	-3.46	11.99
Sum						346.19

APPLICATION—CONCEPTUAL WORKSHEET FOR SUM OF SQUARED ERRORS

The sum of squared errors for this multiple regression model is SSE = 346.19. This value is considerably less than SSE = 755.00, which was obtained for the single predictor regression model that estimated PPS from EPS only.

Confidence Intervals and Prediction Intervals around the Predicted Value

Excel does not provide for the calculation of the confidence intervals and prediction intervals around the predicted value. Moreover, these calculations require the use of matrix algebra for the more general multiple regression models. Accordingly, these values were computed with another statistics program and included below for completeness.

Both the confidence intervals and the prediction intervals are smaller for the multiple regression model than for the one-predictor model. For example, from the previous analysis with EPS as the only predictor variable, the maximum width confidence and prediction intervals were $31.38 and $54.70, respectively. For this analysis with *both* predictor variables, the respective maximum width intervals decreased to $25.84 and $42.12. The same conclusion follows from the analysis of the data in the full sample.

RESULTS FOR FULL SAMPLE OF SIZE 1,402

The same analysis for the calculation of SSE, s_e, and R^2 was conducted for all 1,402 companies in the much larger sample from which the illustrative sample of only

Company	EPS X_1	BVPS X_2	Actual PPS Y	Predicted PPS $\hat{Y}$	Confidence Intervals			Prediction Intervals		
					Lower	Upper	Width	Lower	Upper	Width
1 IMO ...	-3.26	14.31	6.50	9.57	-3.35	22.49	25.84	-11.49	30.63	42.12
2 TORO CO	-1.98	11.07	13.00	10.06	1.26	18.87	17.61	-8.76	28.89	37.65
3 CALMAT CO	-0.45	15.09	22.50	19.91	13.49	26.34	12.85	2.08	37.75	35.67
4 TULTEX CORP	0.56	5.61	8.63	12.18	2.11	22.24	20.13	-7.27	31.62	38.89
5 FAMILY ...	1.00	4.86	17.25	12.77	1.49	24.06	22.57	-7.33	32.88	40.21
6 PHIL. SUB ...	1.23	12.39	16.00	22.38	16.16	28.60	12.44	4.62	40.14	35.52
7 RTZ PLC	1.50	17.44	41.38	29.21	23.38	35.05	11.67	11.58	46.84	35.26
8 TANDY CORP	2.24	18.61	24.50	33.07	26.30	39.84	13.54	15.11	51.03	35.92
9 OKLA. G&E	2.42	22.36	34.13	38,07	29.66	46.49	16.83	19.43	56.72	37.29
10 NICOR INC	3.83	25.43	49.75	46.41	35.16	57.65	22.49	26.33	66.48	40.15

Table 9-9.
Confidence intervals and prediction intervals with two predictors.

10 companies was drawn. The estimated model for the full sample of 1,402 companies is

$$\hat{Y} = 3.41X_{\text{EPS}} + 0.75X_{\text{BVPS}} + 10.66.$$

The standard errors of the regression coefficients are 0.191 for b_{EPS}, 0.032 for b_{BVPS}, and 0.587 for the constant. None of the 95% confidence intervals constructed around the regression coefficient for the full sample includes zero. Table 9-10 compares the results from the analysis of 1,402 companies to those from the illustrative sample.

As with the single predictor case, SSE is considerably larger for the full sample because of considerably more residuals to cumulate. But why are s_e and R^2 so discrepant across the two samples? The values for b_0 and b_1 are approximately the same in both samples because the illustrative sample of 10 companies was deliberately chosen to mirror the relationships of the relevant variables in the complete sample. Choosing a small sample nonrandomly leads to a better prediction model than that obtained with the full sample.

Table 9-10.
Comparison of error statistics for the illustrative and full samples.

	SSE	s_e	R^2	R^2_{adj}
Illustrative Sample for $n = 10$	346.10	7.03	.81	.76
Full Sample, $n = 1,402$	258155.69	13.58	.53	.53

STATISTICAL PRINCIPLES

The original model only used EPS to predict PPS. Adding a second predictor BVPS greatly enhances the accuracy of prediction: The standard error of estimate decreased from 15.96 to 13.58, and R^2 increased from .35 to .53. Consistent with the improved model, the size of the confidence intervals and prediction intervals decreased.

MANAGERIAL INTERPRETATION

Regression models of Price per Share (PPS) were developed that include one or two predictor variables. A company's Earnings per Share (EPS) and Book Value per Share (BVPS) predict PPS more accurately than EPS alone. A simultaneous consideration of current earnings and past equity investment in the company better reflects the potential for future price than a consideration only of earnings.

The meaning of the slope coefficients in multiple regression models and simple regression models is discussed next, as we further explore the implications of the previous example.

Meaning of Regression Coefficients

One of the most intriguing and potentially confusing aspects of regression analysis is that the slope coefficient for a variable changes as other predictor variables are added to or deleted from a model. In the one-predictor model, a $1 increase in EPS tends to increase PPS by $5.44. In the multiple regression model, a $1 increase leads to a 3.41 average increase in PPS when the value of BVPS is held constant. How can these coefficients for the same variable in different models be interpreted? Is any one of the coefficients better than the others? Why do these coefficients change? What are the managerial implications of these changes?

Answering these questions illuminates the meaning of the slope coefficients. Consider first the simple (one-predictor) regression model. The slope coefficient of X indicates the change in Y that results from a one-unit change in X. However, the single predictor variable X is typically correlated with many other variables not included in the model.

> *When the value of the predictor variable X is changed, the values of many other potential predictor variables* not *included in the model but correlated with X also change.*

Changes in these other variables also lead to changes in Y. The slope coefficient in the one-predictor model such as $5.44 for EPS reflects the cumulative impact of *all* these changes on Y. Some changes in Y result directly from a change in X, and other changes in Y result from the associated changes in many other potential predictor variables that change with X.

A slope coefficient from a *multiple* regression analysis indicates the influence of the corresponding predictor variable X on the response variable Y when holding each of the remaining predictor variables in the model constant. The effect of the variation of X on Y can then be estimated without the extraneous influences from

Table 9-11.
Regression model for different values of BVPS.

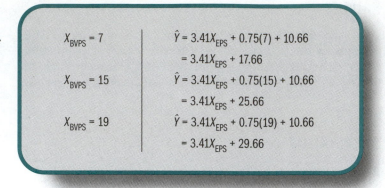

$$X_{BVPS} = 7 \qquad \hat{Y} = 3.41 X_{EPS} + 0.75(7) + 10.66$$
$$= 3.41 X_{EPS} + 17.66$$
$$X_{BVPS} = 15 \qquad \hat{Y} = 3.41 X_{EPS} + 0.75(15) + 10.66$$
$$= 3.41 X_{EPS} + 25.66$$
$$X_{BVPS} = 19 \qquad \hat{Y} = 3.41 X_{EPS} + 0.75(19) + 10.66$$
$$= 3.41 X_{EPS} + 29.66$$

other variables. For this reason, the multiple regression coefficient for predictor variable X such as \$3.41 for EPS is also called a *partial* regression (or slope) coefficient. The effects of the other predictor variables on the response Y that result from a change in X are removed from the analysis.

To illustrate, consider the preceding multiple regression model,

$$\hat{Y}_{PPS} = 3.41 X_{EPS} + 0.75 X_{BVPS} + 10.66.$$

Table 9-11 lists the specific model for three different values of BVPS.

For the linear multiple regression model, the influence of EPS on PPS is the same for all values of BVPS. According to the model, for all companies with the same value of BVPS, a \$1 increase in EPS results in an average price increase of \$3.41. Figure 9-13 portrays these three parallel regression lines, each with a slope of 3.41. Lines with larger values of BVPS are higher in the graph than lines with smaller values of BVPS, but the effect of EPS on PPS is the same.

Virtually any predictor variable of interest is correlated with many other variables. A change in the value of a predictor X results in a change of all of these other correlated variables as well. Potentially inadvertent changes in the values of these other variables lead to additional changes in the value of response Y. The result is that the value of the corresponding slope coefficient indicates the change in Y from two different sources. The first source is the change in Y resulting from a direct change in predictor X. The second source of change in Y is a result of all the indirect changes that occur in all variables correlated with X that are not already included in the multiple regression model.

If the goal is to understand the direct causal impact of predictor X on response Y—that is, how a predictor variable X affects response Y with only the value of X changing—then these other influences should be included in the model as additional predictor variables. If these other variables correlated with X do not appear in the model, their impact on Y will be inadvertently included in the estimate of the slope coefficient of X. However, if the goal is to assess the overall change, with all the values of all correlated variables also changing to some extent as well as X, then the one-predictor model regression coefficient provides the desired estimate.

A consequence of these extraneous correlated variables with predictor X is that the slope coefficients of the same predictor variable from the one-predictor and multiple regression models generally differ. Which interpretation is preferred? The answer depends on the question asked. Does management want to focus on

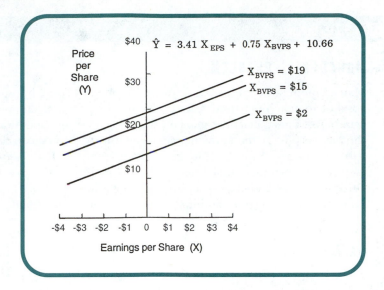

Figure 9-13.
The prediction of PPS
from EPS and BVPS for
three values of BVPS.

the effect of a change in *X* on *Y* for all other variables held constant, or should this effect be assessed with the other predictors freely varying?

Next, a potential problem that can result from constructing multiple regression models is discussed.

Collinearity

A standard method for obtaining more accurate prediction and estimation is to add predictor variables to the model. In the previous application, both Book Value (BVPS) and Earnings per Share (EPS) predicted Price per Share (PPS) better than EPS alone. Unfortunately, benefits do not automatically accrue from the addition of more predictor variables.

Adding more predictor variables to the regression model enhances predictive accuracy when the predictor variables are uncorrelated with each other *and* each predictor variable is correlated with the response variable. Ideally, each predictor variable is related to the response variable and contributes "new" information to the regression model. For some regression models, however, two or more predictor variables are highly correlated; that is, they demonstrate a high degree of **collinearity.**

The information supplied by these collinear predictor variables is redundant. Little gain in predictive efficiency results from the addition to the model of a new predictor variable that correlates with an existing predictor variable. Conversely, dropping one of the redundant variables from the model does not substantially diminish predictive accuracy.

What is the influence of collinearity on estimation? The problem is that collinearity increases the standard errors of the slope coefficients for the correlated predictor variables. Consider the extreme case, illustrated in the following example, in which two predictor variables are almost perfectly correlated. Estimation of the corresponding regression coefficients requires estimating the *separate* effects of a unit change in either predictor variable on the dependent variable. When both predictor variables simply represent different names for the same concept, the standard errors of the estimates are inflated because the effects cannot be easily disentangled.

**collinearity of
predictor variables**
*occurs when a
predictor variable
can be linearly
predicted from one
or more of the
remaining predictor
variables*

BUSINESS APPLICATION 9.7—Collinearity

MANAGERIAL PROBLEM

Management seeks to understand the factors that contribute to the maintenance costs of its machines used to manufacture its product. One consideration is the number of days a machine runs until a breakdown occurs. At a meeting to discuss the various possibilities, one manager suggests that the Age of the machine is a contributing factor. Another manager suggests that the Time actually used to manufacture the product since the machine was purchased is the critical variable. During any given week, a machine could be idle most if not all of the time. Yet another manager suggests simultaneously studying both variables.

DATA

The data for the analysis (in file BREAK.DAT) consist of the Age (in days), Time Used (in days), and Days to Breakdown from purchase or the last repair. All 10 machines are of the same type.

Age	Time Used	Days to Breakdown
2014	1812	703
1938	1776	1214
2289	2072	1271
1447	1275	20
1831	1646	169
1293	1117	39
2014	1771	466
1889	1721	707
1889	1669	941
1889	1717	560

MULTIPLE REGRESSION

The multiple regression model for predicting the number of days between Breakdowns from the Age in days and the number of days the machine is Used is

$$\hat{Y} = -2.45 \text{ Age} + 3.88 \text{ Used} - 1297.97.$$

The two predictor variables, Age and Time Used, correlate .99.

The accuracy of predictability using this model is a considerable improvement over using no model at all, as indicated by $R^2 = .69$ and $R^2_{\text{adj}} = .57$. Unfortunately, the estimated slope coefficients $b_{\text{AGE}} = -2.45$ and $b_{\text{USED}} = 3.88$ are unstable, as is evident from their respective standard errors, 3.96 and 4.14. These estimates result in extremely wide 95% confidence intervals of -11.40 to 6.50 and -5.48 to 13.24 (for $t_{.025} = 2.26$ at $df = 9$), respectively. The corresponding population slope coefficients β likely lie anywhere within these large intervals.

Both of these intervals include zero, indicating that values for the population regression coefficients of zero are plausible. Neither population slope coefficient may be differentiated from zero.

SIMPLE REGRESSIONS

The corresponding separate regression models for predicting the number of days between Breakdowns from the Age in days or the number of days the machine is Used are

$$\hat{Y} = 1.25 \, \text{Age} - 1700.36$$

$$\hat{Y} = 1.33 \, \text{Used} - 1596.41.$$

The precision of predictability using these one-predictor models is reasonable; it is equivalent to the precision obtained from the multiple regression models, as indicated by the respective R^2_{adj} of .58 and .61. The estimated slope coefficients $b_{\text{AGE}} = 1.25$ and $b_{\text{USED}} = 1.33$ are considerably more stable, given the dramatically reduced standard errors of .34 and .35. The considerably smaller 95% confidence intervals around the estimated slope coefficients, again computed from $t_{.05} = 2.26$ for $df = 9$, are 0.48 to 2.02 and .54 to 2.12. Neither interval includes zero.

b = 1.25	b = 1.33
.48 ┼ 2.02	.54 ┼ 2.12

Both Age and Used apparently are related to Breakdown.

STATISTICAL PRINCIPLE

Age of machine and Time the machine was Used are almost perfectly correlated— $r = .99$. Using both of these variables as predictors in a regression model to predict the time until the next machine breakdown results in a collinear model. The estimated slope coefficients are unstable because the model attempts to portray the separate effects of each predictor variable on time between Breakdowns, yet the two predictor variables are essentially two names for the same concept. Using both predictors simultaneously in the model does not improve the accuracy of prediction over the use of either one of the variables alone, and it also yields highly unstable, unusable estimates of the resulting slope coefficients.

MANAGERIAL INTERPRETATION

The regression model for predicting time between breakdowns should be estimated with either one of the predictor variables, Age of machine or Time the machine has been Used. Both predictor variables should *not* be used simultaneously.

Collinearity exists whenever one of the predictor variables can be approximated as a linear function of one or more of the remaining predictor variables. How can collinearity be detected in practice? One method is to regress each predictor variable on all of the remaining predictor variables. To accomplish this, calculate the **tolerances** of the predictor variables. Tolerance values close to zero indicate high collinearity. Tolerance is close to zero when R^2 is close to one, which indicates a high degree of overlap between the predictor variable in question and the remaining variables.

An even simpler procedure for detecting some forms of collinearity is to examine all of the correlations among the predictor variables. If a predictor variable can be approximated by a linear function of one of the remaining variables, then the two variables are highly correlated. In the previous example, the correlation between the two predictor variables, time between Breakdowns and Age of machine, was an extraordinarily high .99.

A particularly useful strategy for detecting and avoiding collinearity is presented next.

> **tolerance of a predictor variable**
> *1 minus the coefficient of determination (R^2) from a regression model in which the predictor variable is the response predicted by all remaining predictor variables*

Stepwise Regression

One goal of model building is *parsimony:* Use as few predictor variables as possible to achieve the desired level of explanation. Adding more predictor variables to a model generally lowers the size of the residuals, but only with diminishing returns. Moreover, simpler models tend to be more understandable and more likely to avoid problems with collinearity. For these reasons, most useful models encountered in practice have no more than five or six predictor variables.

A predictor variable by itself may provide useful information for estimating the response variable, but when added to an already existing model, the predictor may not contribute much *incremental* information. One strategy for building regression models tends to minimize the number of predictor variables by avoiding redundant predictor variables.

Stepwise regression evaluates redundancy among the predictor variables. One criterion for evaluating the change in fit attributable to a predictor variable is R^2, but other criteria can also be used. A variable *added* to a model that does not substantively increase R^2 either is not related to Y, or the new information regarding Y is redundant with the information provided by the original predictors. Similarly, a variable *deleted* from a model that does not decrease R^2 beyond a trivial amount is either not related to Y or the information the new predictor conveys regarding Y is redundant (collinear) with the information provided by the remaining predictors.

Most regression analysis computer programs also offer one or more forms of stepwise regression. A regression analysis is recomputed at each addition or deletion of a predictor variable to or from a model. If the criterion is based on R^2, forward selection begins by adding the variable that provides the largest R^2 value. The next variable added provides the largest increase in R^2 from the value obtained with only the first predictor. This process continues until only trivial increases in R^2 are obtained as new predictor variables are added to the model.

The decision to add or delete a variable according to the incremental value of R^2 or similar fit index is based solely on statistical criteria, and therein lies a potential problem.

> **stepwise regression model building strategy**
> *either selectively add predictor variables to a model until large increases in model fit do not occur (forward selection), or delete variables until large decreases in fit do occur (backward selection)*

Relying exclusively on statistical methods for model construction, particularly for small sample sizes, can result in models that are statistical artifacts.

A statistical artifact is a result based more on the vagaries of random statistical fluctuations than on stable population characteristics. Use another sample, and a completely different model would be created from the very same statistical criterion. Only in large samples with a reasonably small number of predictor variables will stepwise regression construct stable models that would continue to be selected from different samples of the same size. Most analysts, for example, are comfortable using stepwise regression with 5 predictor variables and 300 observations but are very uncomfortable with 10 predictor variables and 50 observations. Particularly for small samples, substantive considerations regarding the meaning of the variables should also guide model construction.

The forward selection strategy of model building is illustrated in the following application. This method can be reasonably applied to these data given the large sample size of 1,402 companies.

BUSINESS APPLICATION 9.8—Stepwise Regression

MANAGERIAL PROBLEM

Management wants to predict stock Price per Share (PPS) from a variety of predictor variables:

BVPS, Book Value per Share

EPS, Earnings per Share

DPS, Dividend per Share

EBITPS, Earnings per Share before Income and Taxes

LEV, Leverage, portion of the company's operation financed by debt

DATA

The data for this analysis are the financial indices of the 1,402 companies analyzed throughout this and the previous chapter.

ANALYSIS

A stepwise regression analysis constructed a series of models by successively adding the predictor variable that provided the largest increase in R^2, as shown in Table 9-12.

MANAGERIAL INTERPRETATION

The more predictor variables in the model, the better is the prediction of PPS. As usual, however, when more and more variables are added to the model, returns

Table 9-12.
Prediction of PPS
from different sets
of predictor
variables.

Predictor variables	R^2_{adj}	s_e
BVPS	.42	15.04
BVPS, EPS	.53	13.58
BVPS, EPS, DPS	.55	13.18
BVPS, EPS, DPS, EBITPS	.56	13.01
BVPS, EPS, DPS, EBITPS, LEV	.57	12.98

diminish. Little predictive gain is obtained beyond that provided by two predictor variables, EPS and BVPS.

This example concludes our study of collinearity and stepwise regression. The next chapter considers regression models with a single categorical predictor variable. Each value of the predictor variable defines a group, and the analysis tests the equality of the corresponding group means.

EXERCISES

9-14. A college admissions officer is interested in predicting College GPA (0 to 4.0) at graduation from High School GPA (0 to 4.0) and SAT scores divided by 1000 (0 to 1.2). (For convenience and numerical accuracy, the admissions officer divided SAT by 1000 so that all variables entered into the model were on approximately equal scales.) The resulting model is

$$\hat{Y} = 8.0\,(X_{SAT}) + 1.3\,(X_{HSGPA}) - 10.$$

a. Sally has a High School GPA of 3.5 and an SAT score of 1135. What is Sally's predicted College GPA?
b. Joe has a High School GPA of 2.9 and an SAT score of 1050. What is Joe's predicted College GPA?
c. What is the increase in the predicted College GPA if High School GPA increases by 1.0 and the SAT score stays the same?
d. What is the increase in the predicted College GPA if SAT score increases by 150 and High School GPA stays the same?
e. What is the regression model for all students with an SAT score of 1150?

9-15. A realtor wanted to analyze the following data to predict the selling Price of a house in a particular neighborhood dependent on its Size and Age.

Size (100s of sq ft)	Age (years)	Price (1,000s of $)
24.0	2	215
18.0	8	165
19.5	0	200
15.0	1	135
25.0	5	220
11.0	0	120
30.0	4	235
22.5	10	150

In the past, the realtor has used two different regression models to predict price.

a. Obtain the SSE, s_e, and R^2_{adj} for $\hat{Y} = 7.2X_{SIZE} - 4.1X_{AGE} + 46.3$.

b. Obtain the SSE, s_e, and R^2_{adj} for $\hat{Y} = 8.8X_{SIZE} - 2.9X_{AGE} + 41.7$.

c. Using a computer program, obtain the OLS regression model for these data along with SSE, s_e, and R^2_{adj}.

d. Determine which model yields the best prediction for these data and why.

9-16. Two variables, X_1 and X_2, were used to estimate Y for 42 observations. With both X_1 and X_2 in the model, the following results were obtained.

Regression Statistics	
Multiple R	0.641
R Square	0.410
Adj. R Square	0.380
Standard Error	13.337
Observations	42

	Coefficients	Standard Error
Intercept	-14.431	12.621
X1	4.174	10.143
X2	4.258	2.770

With only X_1 in the model, the following results were obtained.

Regression Statistics	
Multiple R	0.612
R Square	0.375
Adj. R Square	0.359
Standard Error	13.563
Observations	42

	Coefficients	Standard Error
Intercept	4.239	3.488
X1	18.662	3.813

a. Construct the 95% confidence intervals for the X_1 slope coefficients in the two-predictor model and the one-predictor model. What conclusion can be drawn about the relation of X_1 to Y from each of these analyses in isolation from the other analysis?

b. Compare the indices of fit for the two models. Does the addition of X_2 increase fit?

c. Determine whether the correlation between X_1 and X_2 is high, medium, or low.

d. Determine how many predictor variables would be included in the model if a stepwise regression analysis was performed on these data. Why?

e. Identify which problem in regression analysis this example demonstrates. What is the practical response to this problem?

9.5 SUMMARY

Regression analysis is simultaneously simple and complex. The underlying idea is straight-forward—choose estimates of the Y-intercept and slope coefficients of a linear model that minimize the sum of the squared prediction errors. Moreover, virtually any computer program for statistics performs these computations. However, application of this concept results in a variety of sometimes subtle interpretational difficulties such as the effects of collinear-ity or heteroscedasticity. Entire books have been written on regression analysis, including in-terpretational issues and the analysis of the residuals.

Three different types of variability for the response variable Y were identified in the con-text of a regression analysis. The variability of the actual values of Y for a given value of X is the standard deviation of the residuals (s_e). The standard deviation of the predicted values of Y for a given value of X across different samples is $s_{\hat{Y}_{p,i}}$. The standard deviation of the pre-dicted values of the mean of Y for a given value of X across different samples is $s_{\hat{Y}_p}$.

The initial goal of regression analysis is to estimate the regression model for the popu-lation as a whole. The question of primary interest is not how well the regression model fits the original sample, which is answered by R^2 and s_e, but how well the model predicts with new data. This latter question is addressed by the adjusted coefficient of determination R^2_{adj}, which is generally preferred over the unadjusted R^2 as an index of model fit.

A confidence interval can be constructed around an estimated regression coefficient from a one-predictor model, sometimes called simple regression, or a multiple predictor model, called multiple regression. Confidence intervals can also be constructed around an estimated predicted mean response for a given value of X. The interval around a predicted individual response is called a prediction interval, and is often considerably larger than the interval around the mean response.

Analysis of the residuals $e = Y - \hat{Y}$ provides a wealth of diagnostic information. The residuals, the standardized residuals, and the Studentized residuals all provide useful information. A Studentized residual resembles the standardized residual except that the corresponding observation has been removed from the analysis. Examination of the overall distribution of residuals reveals potential outliers.

Cook's Distance provides a related diagnostic analysis. Cook's Distance is the distance between the regression coefficients calculated with the observation included and deleted in the analysis. Ideally, any one observation contributes to the stability of the estimated regression coefficients by reducing their standard errors, but no single observation should have too much influence on the estimated values. A high value of Cook's Distance indicates an observation that has a disproportionate influence on the calculation of the regression coefficients.

Most applications of regression analysis involve multiple predictor variables. Adding predictor variables to the model can potentially increase the accuracy of prediction, resulting in a lower s_e, as well as more realistically portray the relationship between each predictor variable and the response variable. However, interpretational problems may occur as well. Collinearity occurs in a multiple regression model when one of the predictor variables can be (linearly) predicted from one or more of the remaining variables. The problem is that adding a collinear predictor does not increase predictive accuracy very much if at all, and it inflates the standard errors of the collinear regression coefficients. The result is a likely inaccurate estimation of the regression coefficients. Stepwise regression is a model building strategy that tends to avoid collinear models by selecting only nonredundant predictor variables that are related to the response variable.

9.6 KEY TERMS

adjusted coefficient of determination *384*	prediction sample *383*
collinearity *417*	residual outlier *400*
confidence interval *378*	standardized residual *400*
Cook's Distance *404*	stepwise regression *420*
estimation sample *383*	Studentized residual *401*
extrapolation *398*	tolerance *420*
influential observation *404*	

9.7 REVIEW EXERCISES

ANALYSIS PROBLEMS

Application

9-17. A manager wanted to estimate labor cost for a week from the volume of production during that week. A sample of 25 weeks revealed the following statistics, where X represents Number of Assemblies and Y represents Labor Cost: $s_X = 40.826$, $s_e = 591.25$, $b_0 = 2103.02$, and $b_1 = 8.26$.

a. Calculate the 95% confidence interval around the sample slope coefficient.

b. Interpret the meaning of this confidence interval for the business decision maker.

9-18. For the data in Exercise 9-17,

a. Test the null hypothesis that the population slope coefficient is zero.

b. Determine if the results of the hypothesis test are consistent with the confidence interval calculated in the previous problem and why.

9-19. For the data in Exercise 9-17, given that SSE = 8,040,382.834 and SSY = 10,767,810.30,

a. Calculate R^2.

b. Calculate R_{adj}^2.

c. Compare R_{adj}^2 to R^2. Is the drop large? How does this new information affect your assessment of the model?

9-20. For the data in Exercise 9-17, given that $\overline{X} = 487.14$,

a. For Production Volume = 450, calculate the confidence interval for predicted Labor Cost.

b. For Production Volume = 450, calculate the prediction interval for predicted Labor Cost.

c. Determine which of the intervals is wider and why.

9-21. For the data in Exercise 9-17, given that $\overline{X} = 487.14$,

a. For Production Volume = 500, calculate the confidence interval for predicted Labor Cost.

b. For Production Volume = 500, calculate the prediction interval for predicted Labor Cost.

c. Compare the size of the confidence and prediction intervals at Production Volume = 500 with the intervals from the previous problem with Production Volume = 450. Determine which of the two confidence intervals and which of the two prediction intervals are larger and why.

9-22. A sample of 65 machinists revealed the following statistics, in which Number of Years on the job (X) was used to predict Salary (Y) (in 10,000s): $s_X = 4.42$, $s_e = 2.347$, $b_0 = 12.85$, and $b_1 = 0.98$.

a. Calculate the 95% confidence interval around the sample slope coefficient.

b. Interpret the meaning of this confidence interval for the business decision maker.

9-23. For the data in the previous exercise,

a. Test the null hypothesis that the population slope coefficient is zero.

b. Determine if the results of the hypothesis test are consistent with the confidence interval computed in the previous problem and why.

9-24. A product manager at a consumer goods company was predicting Sales of a product from Price and Advertising costs. Sales was measured on a saturation scale from 0 to 10. She used the following regression model,

$$\hat{Y}_{SALES} = 12.2 + 3.8\,(X_{PRICE}) + 4.1\,(X_{ADVERT}).$$

a. If Price is $4.80 and Advertising saturation is 4.0, what is predicted Sales revenue?

b. If Price is $5.30 and Advertising saturation is 3.5, what is predicted Sales revenue?

c. What is the increase in predicted Sales if Price increases by 1.0 and Advertising saturation stays the same?

d. What is the increase in predicted Sales if Price increases by 2.0 and Advertising saturation stays the same?

e. What is the regression model for all levels of Price when Advertising saturation is 5.0?

9-25. A college dean investigated the relationship between hours Studying (X_{STDY}), hours spent watching TV (X_{TV}), and GPA (Y). The data are reported in the following table.

Application

STDY	11.70	8.80	9.60	8.30	12.50	5.30	14.00	12.10
TV	1.40	8.90	0.80	0.50	5.00	0.70	4.40	10.60
GPA	3.75	3.25	3.60	3.21	3.80	3.10	3.95	3.10

In the past, the administration used two different multiple regression models to predict GPA.

a. Calculate SSE, s_e, and R^2_{adj} for $\hat{Y} = .102X_{STDY} - .053X_{TV} + 2.967$.

b. Calculate SSE, s_e, and R^2_{adj} for $\hat{Y} = .133X_{STDY} - .049X_{TV} + 1.998$.

c. Determine which model yields the best prediction for the new data and why.

9-26. Use the data in the previous exercise. With both Study and TV in the model, the following OLS results were obtained.

Application

Regression Statistics	
Multiple R	0.892
R Square	0.796
Adusted R Square	0.715
Standard Error	0.183
Observations	8

	Coefficients	Standard Error
Intercept	2.493	0.263
X1	0.115	0.027
X2	-0.050	0.019

With only Study in the model, the following results were obtained.

Regression Statistics	
Multiple R	0.715
R Square	0.512
Adjusted R Square	0.430
Standard Error	0.259
Observations	8

	Coefficients	Standard Error
Intercept	2.573	0.369
X1	0.087	0.035

a. Construct the 95% confidence intervals for the regression (slope) coefficients for Study in the two-predictor model and in the one-predictor model.

What would be concluded about the relation of Study to GPA from each of these analyses in isolation from the other analysis?

b. Compare the indices of fit for the two models. Does the addition of TV increase fit?

c. Construct the 95% confidence interval for the slope coefficient of TV.

d. State the meaning of the negative sign for the slope coefficient for TV.

e. Make a guess about how many predictor variables would be included in the model if a stepwise regression analysis was performed on these data. Explain your answer.

9-27. Consider the data and model from the two previous exercises that included only one predictor variable, X_{STDY}. Also, $\overline{X} = 10.29$, and $s_X = 2.82$.

Application

a. Determine the predicted GPA for five hours of studying.

b. Calculate the confidence interval of the conditional mean for this predicted value for $X_{STDY} = 5$.

c. Calculate the prediction interval of an individual predicted value for $X_{STDY} = 5$.

d. Determine which interval is larger and why.

e. Explain how these results are consistent with the analysis from Exercise 9-26.

9-28. An analyst attempted to construct a regression model predicting Y from three predictor variables: X_1, X_2, and X_3. A model was estimated with all three predictors included and also separately for each of the predictors. The results of these analyses are presented below.

Mechanical

Regression Statistics	
Multiple R	0.865
R Square	0.749
Adusted R Square	0.623
Standard Error	27.449
Observations	10

	Coefficients	Standard Error
Intercept	-129.239	56.973
X1	-5.352	5.202
X2	16.311	8.310
X3	0.905	0.396

Regression Statistics	
Multiple R	0.580
R Square	0.336
Adusted R Square	0.253
Standard Error	38.623
Observations	10

	Coefficients	Standard Error
Intercept	-42.662	52.359
X1	5.572	2.767

Regression Statistics	
Multiple R	0.703
R Square	0.495
Adj. R Square	0.431
Standard Error	33.706
Observations	10

	Coefficients	Standard Error
Intercept	-111.206	62.065
X2	10.773	3.850

Regression Statistics	
Multiple R	0.655
R Square	0.429
Adj. R Square	0.357
Standard Error	35.837
Observations	10

	Coefficients	Standard Error
Intercept	21.951	19.183
X3	1.201	0.490

a. Calculate the confidence intervals for the OLS regression weights for X_1, X_2, and X_3 from the multiple regression. Do any intervals include zero? How do you interpret the negative regression (slope) coefficient for X_1?

b. Calculate the confidence intervals for the OLS regression weights for X_1, X_2, and X_3 from the three respective single predictor regression models. Do any intervals include zero?

c. Account for the different results from (a) and (b) above.

d. Determine which variables should be included in the model.

Application

9-29. The following data have been extensively analyzed throughout the last two chapters. The OLS regression model for predicting PPS from EPS is $\hat{Y} = 5.18X + 19.68$, and the residuals from this model are listed below.

		Actual	Predicted	
	EPS	PPS	PPS	Residual
Company	X	Y	$\hat{Y}$	$e \equiv Y - \hat{Y}$
1 IMO INDUSTRIES INC	-3.26	6.50	2.79	3.71
2 TORO CO	-1.98	13.00	9.42	3.58
3 CALMAT CO	-0.45	22.50	17.36	5.14
4 TULTEX CORP	0.56	8.63	22.59	-13.96
5 FAMILY DOLLAR STORES	1.00	17.25	24.87	-7.62
6 PHILADELPHIA SUBURBAN CORP	1.23	16.00	26.06	-10.06
7 RTZ PLC	1.50	41.38	27.46	13.92
8 TANDY CORP	2.24	24.50	31.30	-6.80
9 OKLAHOMA GAS & ELECTRIC	2.42	34.13	32.23	1.90
10 NICOR INC	3.83	49.75	39.53	10.21

a. Calculate the standardized residuals.

b. Determine if any outliers are present and why.

Application

9-30. The following is a plot of the Residuals and Book Value per Share (BVPS) from the regression model that predicted PPS from BVPS.

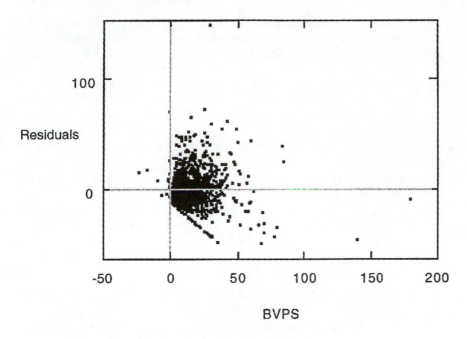

BVPS

a. Do outliers appear to be present?

b. What evidence of violation of any of the four basic assumptions of the regression model discussed in the previous chapter does this plot indicate?

9-31. An analyst constructed a model that predicted Y from X_1 and X_2. The OLS analysis for this model and the model with only Y and X_1 are presented below.

Concept

Regression Statistics	
Multiple R	0.780
R Square	0.609
Adjusted R Square	0.497
Standard Error	2.355
Observations	10

	Coefficients	Standard Error
Intercept	0.152	1.933
X1	0.492	0.367
X2	0.762	0.273

Regression Statistics	
Multiple R	0.415
R Square	0.172
Adjusted R Square	0.069
Standard Error	3.204
Observations	10

	Coefficients	Standard Error
Intercept	3.431	2.089
X1	0.638	0.494

a. Construct the confidence intervals for the three OLS estimates, b_0, b_1, and b_2. Which of the corresponding estimates—b_0, b_1, or b_2—is most likely *not* zero?

b. Determine if the result from the single predictor model consistent with your conclusion from the multiple predictor model in (a) and explain.

    c. Determine if the estimates for the regression coefficients should be interpreted without examining the corresponding standard errors. What is the interpretational problem with avoiding the standard errors?

9-32. This problem requires a computer program for generating random data, such as the Excel Random Number Generation program, which is called up from the Data Analysis option from the Tools menu.

Concept

    a. Generate 10 normally distributed observations for eight predictor variables and a response variable. Set the mean to 50 and the standard deviation to 10 for each of the variables.

    b. Identify the population correlations among the nine variables. What are the population slope coefficients?

    c. Calculate the sample correlations among the nine variables. How many of the correlations are above .50? How can this be, given that the data are randomly generated?

    d. Calculate the multiple regression. Compare the values of R^2 and R^2_{adj}. Why is R^2 so high and R^2_{adj} so low?

    e. Determine which fit index, in real-life data analysis, provides the most useful assessment of model fit, R^2 or R^2_{adj}.

    f. Draw a conclusion about the need for large samples when analyzing multiple regression models with many predictor variables.

DISCUSSION QUESTIONS

  1. What is the meaning of the standard error of the slope coefficient?

  2. What is the purpose of constructing a confidence interval around an estimated regression coefficient, such as a slope coefficient?

  3. What happens to the interpretation of the regression coefficient when the associated confidence interval includes zero?

  4. How is the adjusted coefficient of determination R^2_{adj} related to statistical inference?

  5. What is the purpose of the prediction sample? Why is the prediction sample different from the estimation sample?

  6. A regression analysis revealed a coefficient of determination $R^2 = .92$. Is this high value indicative of a causal relationship?

  7. Why is the adjusted coefficient of determination R^2_{adj} preferred to the unadjusted value R^2?

  8. Why is R^2 never smaller than the corresponding R^2_{adj}?

  9. How do you explain the difference between the information provided by R^2 and R^2_{adj} and the information provided by the estimated regression coefficients b and their associated standard errors?

10. If the linearity assumption is correct, what is the estimated value $\hat{Y}$ for a given value of X equal to?

11. What is the difference between a confidence interval around $\hat{Y}$ and a prediction interval around $\hat{Y}$?

12. What is the source of variability for the size of confidence interval around $\hat{Y}$?

13. What two sources contribute to the size of a prediction interval around $\hat{Y}$?

14. Why does increasing the sample size not eventually bring the size of the prediction interval down to zero?

15. What is the problem with extrapolation?

16. How dramatically can one or two outliers affect the estimation of a regression line?

17. What is the advantage of a Studentized residual over the standardized residual?

18. What is an influential observation?

19. How does Cook's Distance indicate the influence of an observation?

20. What is the advantage of multiple regression over single predictor regression models?

21. Why does the slope coefficient from a single predictor model usually differ from the corresponding coefficient from a multiple regression model?

22. When is a stepwise regression used?

23. How can the estimated regression coefficient be 3.9 in a simple regression analysis with a single predictor variable, and yet drop in value to $b = 2.1$ in a corresponding multiple regression model?

24. The model featured throughout this and the previous chapter—the estimation of Price per Share from Earnings per Share—is only modestly successful. What other variables added to this model are contenders for increasing the success of the model?

INTEGRATIVE ANALYSIS PROBLEM

A college president wants to understand the basis for the salaries paid to tenured professors at the university. A fundamental aspect of this investigation is to construct a regression model that accounts for Salary as a function of the relevant predictor variables. The file SALARY.DAT contains the following variables for 38 faculty members, all of whom are full professors in the business school.

1. Salary

2. Gender (0 for Male, 1 for Female)

3. Years Experience since Ph.D.

4. Years Employed at the university

5. Number of Publications in referred journals

6. Number of Citations in the social science citation index for the previous five years

    a. Construct a regression model of Salary using only Gender as a predictor variable.

    b. Construct a regression model of Salary using all five predictor variables.

    c. Determine if the slope coefficient for Gender changes across the two models. Interpret each coefficient separately, and account for the difference between the values.

    d. Determine which of the predictor variables in the full model using all five predictors are not significantly different from zero.

    e. Run the regression model with the nonsignificant variables removed from the model.

    f. Calculate the correlations among the predictor variables with each other as well as with the response variable.

    g. Use the correlations to help explain why some of the predictor variables were nonsignificant. Is collinearity present?

    h. Determine if results with the new reduced model differ from the original model. Compare R^2, s_e, and the remaining slope coefficients. How do you account for these results?

    i. Analyze the residuals and Studentized residuals of the model for outliers. Determine if outliers are present, and explain your answer.

chapter 10

Evaluating Differences among Many Groups

WHY DO WE CARE?

Comparing the performance of one group with another on variables such as product share, satisfaction, cost, salary, or time is a central concern of management. Which training session is most effective? Which version of the product do customers prefer? Which production method yields the lowest cost? the highest quality? How does sales growth differ for different regions of the country? Managers are continually asking and seeking answers to questions such as these. We have presented inferential statistics for answering these questions when comparing two groups with each other. This chapter extends this analysis to as many groups as specified.

The crucial statistical aspect of these comparisons is that the sample means of the variable of interest for each group differ, but the manager wants to evaluate potential differences among the *unknown* population means. Sample means differ even when the population group means are equal. Inferential statistics can provide evidence that differences among sample means are large enough to conclude that the population means probably also differ. The new way of manufacturing parts really does lead to higher quality. Customers really do prefer this brighter package color. This other training method really is more effective.

Managers often want to move beyond simply evaluating group differences to attributing causality. A group difference may exist—sales may be higher for red packaging than for yellow packaging—but does the color of the package actually *cause* higher sales? Perhaps product in the red package was shipped to more appropriate retail outlets than product in the yellow package. Perhaps had the yellow packages been sent to the same outlets, sales for yellow would have been just as high or higher. The procedures presented in this chapter let the manager evaluate the group differences and then uncover the underlying causal influences that lead to these differences.

This chapter is about differences among group means. It shows how to evaluate the null hypothesis of equal group means for as many groups as specified.

> When evaluating differences among group means, the values of a categorical variable define the groups for a measured numeric variable that is compared across the groups.

The categorical variable Gender defines two groups of people, Male and Female. Many numeric variables such as Salary, Height, or Job Satisfaction can be compared across groups of men and women. Other categorical variables define more than two groups. The variable Undergraduate Class defines Freshmen, Sophomores, Juniors, and Seniors, and the variable Package Color defines a set of available colors such as Red, Yellow, Orange, and Blue.

The evaluation of group differences has two main applications. One goal is to demonstrate a *difference* in population means for the different groups. The other, more ambitious, goal is to identify group membership as the *cause* of the difference. The analysis of cause and effect takes place within the context of an experiment, discussed next.

10.1 EXPERIMENTAL DESIGN

One of the most basic questions managers or anyone else can ask is, "What are the causes of something?" Cause-and-effect questions are as crucial to everyday life as they are to the professional manager. For the models presented in this chapter, the causal agent is membership in a group defined by a value of a categorical predictor variable, and the effect is represented as a response variable.

What manager does not want to know the production method that leads to the highest quality of the finished parts? Or the color of the package that leads to the most sales? Or the training procedures that lead to the best job performance? The manager is asking: How do changes in the predictor variable—Training Procedure, Production Method, or Color—lead to changes in the response variable—Job Performance, Precision, or Sales?

Previous chapters presented regression analysis as a primary statistical tool for investigating the relationships among variables. This chapter introduces a form of regression analysis called *analysis of variance* or, more simply, ANOVA.

> ANOVA is a form of regression analysis that uses categorical predictor variables to analyze population mean differences.

The analysis focuses on the differences in the response variable (such as Sales) across the groups that are defined by the values of the categorical variable (such as Package Color: Red or Yellow). Categorical predictor variables that define preexisting groups are also called *grouping variables* because each value of the predictor variable defines a group.

Statistical procedures such as regression analyze relationships among variables, but even the correct use of these procedures does not necessarily allow for the attribution of causality.

> *Regression analyses such as ANOVA answer questions about how variables are related, but the analyst cannot deduce from the statistical analysis per se if the relationships are causal.*

If X causes Y, then X and Y are correlated, and statistical analysis will detect this correlation. However, the fact that X and Y are correlated does not imply that X caused Y. The more fire engines at the fire, the larger the fire damage, but fire engines do not cause the damage. Instead, a third variable—size of the fire—causes both the number of fire engines at the scene and the fire damage. A regression model could be constructed and analyzed in which the number of fire engines predicted fire damage, or a model could be built in which fire damage predicted the number of engines. However, the resulting slope coefficients from either analysis would not describe a causal relationship.

Identifying a relationship as causal depends not only on the correct use of statistical procedures but also on the method of data collection. The primary method for collecting data to uncover causal relationships is the experiment, which is the subject of this section. The analysis of data from an experiment, in conjunction with the statistical procedure of ANOVA, forms a powerful strategy for analyzing the causal effects of one or more variables on another variable.

There are many different **experimental designs,** ranging from the simple to the complex and esoteric. Entire textbooks are devoted to explaining the possible sampling plans and the corresponding statistical analysis of the resulting data. Implementation of an appropriate experimental design allows the analyst systematically to vary one or more potential causal influences and then use ANOVA to assess the corresponding effect on the response variable.

> **experimental design**
> *sampling plan for gathering and analyzing groups of data*

One-Way Designs

The simplest experimental design yields samples from two groups. The corresponding statistical analysis is of the *single* mean difference of the response variable. Does an observed sample mean difference generalize to the population mean difference? Choose one variable, such as Supplier, with two different values, and gather a sample of Delivery Times for each Supplier. The variable Supplier is a categorical predictor variable with two values, and Delivery Time is the response variable. Does the observed difference in delivery times generalize to the population as a whole?

In general, the categorical predictor variable—or **treatment variable**—may have any specified number of levels. Delivery Time, for example, can be compared among four different suppliers instead of just two. The generic response variable is Y, with generic treatment variable A. The values, or levels, of the treatment variable A are $A1$, $A2$, and so forth. An arbitrary level of A is a. The generic number of values of A is p, which defines p groups.

> **treatment variable**
> *predictor variable of substantive interest in the context of ANOVA*

The observations within each of the p groups have the same value of the predictor (treatment) variable. When comparing the Supplier Delivery Time of two companies, the predictor variable is Supplier, with two levels, Supplier $S1$ and Supplier $S2$. In a study of the differences in Sales depending on the Color of the package, the predictor variable is Color, with values that are specific colors. A sample

Figure 10-1.
Layout for a one-way
independent groups
design with three levels
of the predictor variable
($p = 3$) and, in this
example, four values
of the response
variable per group
($n_1 = n_2 = n_3 = n_y$).

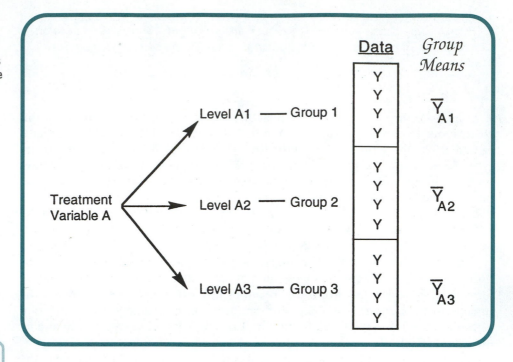

of Sales amounts is gathered at different stores for each Color, and the mean differences are compared for the different groups.

The simplest experimental designs have only a single predictor variable—the treatment variable—and a single response variable. The structure of a **one-way independent groups design** appears in Figure 10-1. The specific design in Figure 10-1 has three values, or levels, of the treatment variable. These three levels could be, for example, three different suppliers in an experiment that assesses differences among supplier delivery time.

When a single predictor variable has only two levels, the single mean difference is analyzed using one of two closely related statistical procedures: ANOVA or independent samples t-test of a mean difference. With data from designs with more than two levels, such as in Figure 10-1, ANOVA is used. As discussed in the following chapter, more sophisticated versions of ANOVA analyze the simultaneous effect of many predictor variables on the response variable.

Random Assignment

The predictor variable defines at least two different groups. In a true experiment, each individual observation, such as a person or company or store, is randomly assigned to one of the groups. This process is called **randomization.** Random assignment is a key characteristic of an **experiment.**

In a true experiment, the experimenter actively manipulates and sets the values of the treatment variable. Consider the assessment of the effectiveness of different Training Programs. The experimenter manipulates the value of the treatment variable Training Program for each employee. The employee shows up at the designated time and then the experimenter assigns the employee to a training program. Before the experiment began, the value of the treatment variable for this employee was undefined. The experimenter then sets this value for the employee by randomly assigning him or her to one of the Training Programs.

The purpose of randomization is to average out the effect of other extraneous variables on the response variable across the different groups.

> *After random assignment to groups, the only variable that distinguishes observations within the different groups is the value of the treatment variable.*

For example, the employees in one group should be, on average, no taller or shorter than employees in the other groups. If the employees in one training program were taller than the employees in the other program, the analyst would not know which variable—Training Program or Height—contributed to any mean differences in the response variable.

A true one-way independent groups design defines an experiment with random assignment to the p groups. In practice, manipulation of the values of the treatment variable by random assignment is not always possible. In this situation, the values of the treatment variable have been set *before* the experiment begins and membership in the p groups reflects preexisting differences, such as for the variable Gender. The statistical analysis is identical whether the analysis is of data from a design with random assignment or the analysis is of preexisting differences. The difference is in the interpretation of the results: Causal inferences are possible only for the true experiment.

For example, the value of the predictor variable Gender is not assigned to each person in a study of pay differences for men and women. Variables such as Gender represent naturally occurring differences that the analyst does not control.

> *Lack of random assignment does not invalidate an inference of population mean differences, but it does diminish the ability to establish a causal influence.*

The causal influence in question is the potential effect of changes in the value of the predictor variable on values of the response variable.

To illustrate the difficulty of attributing causality without random assignment, consider the evaluation of pay differences among men and women in a hypothetical company. In that company, men may be paid on average more than women, but they also have more job experience, for whatever reason. Because of the lack of random assignment, any demonstrated statistical difference in pay levels cannot be unequivocally attributed to differences in the value of the predictor variable Gender. If Gender is correlated with Job Experience, then distinguishing between people on the basis of Gender may result in Salary differences, but Gender did not necessarily *cause* the Salary differences in this particular case. If may be, for example, that no difference in average salary of men and women exists for employees with the same amount of job experience.

An example of a one-way sampling design follows.

BUSINESS APPLICATION 10.1—One-Way Sampling Design

MANAGERIAL PROBLEM

The vehicle maintenance manager who oversees a large fleet of company cars wants to maximize gas mileage for the fleet. His concern is the causal influence of Engine Oil on Miles per Gallon (MPG) of gasoline. Do the three different engine oils ($A1$, $A2$, and $A3$) lead to different gasoline mileage?

DATA

The manager selected three different engine oils to examine their potential effect on MPG. The same model car will be used for each of the tests, with 16 different measurements of MPG. Because different drivers and cars get different mileage, 16 drivers and cars will be randomly assigned to each of the three types of engine oils—four sets of cars and drivers to each of the oil types. The resulting MPGs after one month of normal driving will be recorded.

The resulting sampling plan is presented in the accompanying figure. Each "?" represents a data value, a value of the response variable Y, that will be measured after the drivers complete their routes.

Driver	Oil	MPG
1	A1	?
2	A1	?
3	A1	?
4	A1	?
5	A2	?
6	A2	?
7	A2	?
8	A2	?
9	A3	?
10	A3	?
11	A3	?
12	A3	?

ANALYSIS

The sample means of the response variable for the three groups will differ, but will the differences be sufficiently large to suggest that the underlying population means differ? The statistical analysis of the data for this sampling plan is a one-way ANOVA. The categorical predictor variable has three groups, with four observations per group. Because of random assignment, the explanation for any differences in the population group means of MPG will be due to differences attributable to different types of motor oil.

MANAGERIAL INTERPRETATION

The interpretation awaits the statistical analysis of the data, which is provided later in the chapter.

The next section introduces the statistical procedure of ANOVA for the evaluation of differences among any number of groups.

EXERCISES

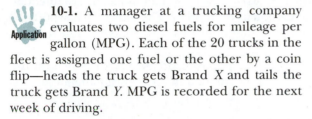

10-1. A manager at a trucking company evaluates two diesel fuels for mileage per gallon (MPG). Each of the 20 trucks in the fleet is assigned one fuel or the other by a coin flip—heads the truck gets Brand *X* and tails the truck gets Brand *Y*. MPG is recorded for the next week of driving.

a. What is the treatment variable? What are the levels of the treatment variable?
b. What is the response variable?
c. Does this study represent an experiment? Why or why not? If not, name a variable other than the treatment variable that could account for any differences in the response variable means.
d. If the null hypothesis of equal group population means is rejected, what can the manager conclude?

10-2. A personnel manager investigated the relationship between Education and Salary. Employees at the company were classified into three groups: no college degree, bachelor's degree, master's degree. Salaries were then compared across the three groups.

a. What is the treatment variable? What are the levels of the treatment variable?
b. What is the response variable?
c. Does this study represent an experiment? Why or why not? If not, name a variable other than the treatment variable that could account for any differences in the response variable means.
d. If the null hypothesis of equal group population means is rejected, what can the manager conclude?

10.2 ONE-WAY ANOVA

A purchasing manager wants to evaluate the time lag between ordering materials from each of *four* different suppliers and receiving those materials. A vehicle maintenance manager who oversees a large fleet of company cars wants to study the effect of *three* different engine oils on gasoline mileage. A personnel manager wants to compare the job satisfaction of employees at *five* different manufacturing plants. Each of these investigations requires comparing the mean of a response variable across three or more groups. The independent groups *t*-test (Chapter 6) is the statistical analysis for comparing two group means. ANOVA is the statistical analysis for comparing two or more group means.

The **one-way ANOVA** analyzes data from the one-way independent groups design with a single categorical predictor variable *A*—the treatment variable—and the response variable *Y*. In general, variable *A* has *p* values that define *p* independent groups, such as a group of cars for each of three different engine oils, or a group of orders for each of four different suppliers. The sample mean of the ath group is $\overline{Y}_a$, such as the mean of the first group, $\overline{Y}_1$.

one-way ANOVA
evaluates the equality of population mean differences of the response variable for independent groups, with each group corresponding to a value of a single predictor variable

Although the sample means do not equal each other, are the population means equal? The null hypothesis specifies equal population means for all groups,

$$H_0: \mu_1 = \mu_2 = \ldots = \mu_p.$$

For the analysis of engine oil, the null hypothesis specifies that all three engine oils have the same effect on mileage. That is, the null hypothesis states that the type of oil does *not* influence gasoline mileage.

The alternative hypothesis H_1 is that *at least one* of the population group means does not equal another population group mean,

$$H_1: \text{not all population means are equal.}$$

The alternative hypothesis is true if all except two population means are unequal, or if none of the population means equals each other. The alternative hypothesis is true if at least one of the engine oils either improves or worsens gasoline mileage when compared to the others.

The statistical evaluation of this null hypothesis with ANOVA is based on the different types of variation of Y that can be defined in an experimental design.

Types of Variation in One-Way Designs

This section presents a different perspective underlying the independent samples *t*-test for two groups. This new perspective focuses on identifying and analyzing different types of variation, a perspective that easily generalizes to the analysis of mean differences from two groups to many groups. Reanalyzing a mean difference from this new perspective also fosters a deeper understanding of the meaning of these hypothesis tests.

grand mean μ or $\overline{\overline{Y}}$
mean of the response variable for all values of Y

Variation of the response variable Y within an experimental design is expressed in four general ways. One type is simply the variation of Y across the entire design. The underlying deviations are computed around the **grand mean,** which is the mean of *all* the data. The sample mean of a group is $\overline{Y}$. The sample mean of all of the data is $\overline{\overline{Y}}$. Ignoring the different groups, the variability of all values of Y is the **total variation sums of squares,** or SSY. Variability of Y is expressed in terms of the sum of squared deviations around the mean of Y, as introduced in Chapter 3. The distinction is that the mean of all the data is called the grand mean $\overline{\overline{Y}}$ in the context of ANOVA.

total variation sums of squares SSY.
variability of the response variable Y around the grand mean

STATISTICAL ILLUSTRATION—Sum of Squares of Total Variation

DATA

Data are collected according to a one-way independent groups design illustrated in the following table. Treatment variable A defines three groups, and three data values are obtained for each of the three groups. The sample group means are $\overline{Y}_1 = 4$, $\overline{Y}_2 = 6$, and $\overline{Y}_3 = 8$. The grand mean is $\overline{\overline{Y}} = \frac{54}{9} = 6$. The first two columns of the following table contain the data, which yield SSY = 48.

SUM OF SQUARES OF TOTAL VARIATION

Treat ment (A)	Res ponse (Y)	Grand Mean	Resid ual	Res Sq
A1	2	6	-4	16
A1	4	6	-2	4
A1	6	6	0	0
A2	4	6	-2	4
A2	6	6	0	0
A2	8	6	2	4
A3	6	6	0	0
A3	8	6	2	4
A3	10	6	4	16
Sum	54		0	48
Mean	6			SSY

STATISTICAL PRINCIPLE

The total sum of squares SSY is the total variation of the individual data values around the grand mean in terms of squared deviation scores. This is just the sum of the squared deviations for all of the data, ignoring group structure.

ANOVA expresses the total variation of the response variable SSY as a sum of the three other types of variation: between groups, within groups, and interaction. These types of variation of Y follow from the group structure specified by the design. Between-group and within-group variability are involved in the analysis of data obtained from one-way independent groups designs. Interaction variation is described in the following chapter.

VARIABILITY AMONG GROUP MEANS. The independent-samples t-test that evaluates the null hypothesis of two *equal* population means is expressed as

$$t_{\overline{Y}_1 - \overline{Y}_2} = \frac{\text{sample mean difference}}{\text{estimated standard error of the mean difference}}.$$

However, the t-test cannot be applied to the analysis of more than two groups. The numerator is a single value, the difference between two group means, $\overline{Y}_1 - \overline{Y}_2$. Shifting from two to three groups, however, means a shift from one to three sample mean differences,

$$\overline{Y}_1 - \overline{Y}_2, \overline{Y}_1 - \overline{Y}_3, \text{ and } \overline{Y}_2 - \overline{Y}_3.$$

Again, however, the numerator of $t_{\overline{Y}_1 - \overline{Y}_2}$ provides for only a single mean difference. Fortunately, there is a solution to this problem.

A single value that simultaneously reflects the differences among all group means is their variance. To obtain this variance, use the deviation of each group mean $\overline{Y}$ from the mean of *all* the data, $\overline{\overline{Y}}$. The deviation of a group mean from the grand mean indicates the size of the effect on response Y of the corresponding group. Interpretation of this **treatment effect** is crucial to the managerial implications

> **treatment effect for a^{th} level of treatment A**
>
> *population:*
> $$\beta_a = \mu_a - \mu$$
> *sample estimate:*
> $$\beta_a = \overline{Y}_a - \overline{\overline{Y}}$$

of the entire analysis. For example, b_1 is the treatment effect for level 1, or, to be more explicit, b_{A1} is the treatment effect for level 1 of Treatment A.

The number of groups in this context is traditionally called p. Consider another example of $p = 3$ groups of the same size with means of $\overline{Y}_1 = 15$, $\overline{Y}_2 = 20$, and $\overline{Y}_3 = 100$. The mean of all Y values is $\overline{\overline{Y}} = 45$. What effect does membership in each group have on the value of the response variable Y? The answer to this question uses the overall grand mean as a baseline for comparison. The three corresponding treatment effects given $\overline{\overline{Y}} = 45$ are

$$b_1 = \overline{Y}_1 - \overline{\overline{Y}} = 15 - 45 = -30,$$
$$b_2 = \overline{Y}_2 - \overline{\overline{Y}} = 20 - 45 = -25$$
$$b_2 = \overline{Y}_3 - \overline{\overline{Y}} = 100 - 45 = 55.$$

For these sample data, the effect of membership in the first group is to lower the mean response for each value of Y by 30 units below the overall mean. Membership in the second group lowers the response of the value of Y by 25 units. Membership in the last group *raises* the mean value of Y by 55 units.

The key idea underlying the sum of the squared treatment effects is that each observation within the same group experiences the same level of the treatment variable. All parts in the group come from the same supplier, all employees in the group attended the same training session, all companies in the group have the same earnings per share.

> *The one-way ANOVA model specifies that all values of the response variable Y within the* same *group are raised above or lowered below the grand mean to the* same *extent.*

For example, each observation in the group defined by the first level of Treatment A has the treatment effect $(\overline{Y}_1 - \overline{\overline{Y}}) \equiv b_1$.

To calculate the variance of the group means, first calculate the sum of squared Treatment A effects for each of N observations,

$$\text{SSA} \equiv \sum (\overline{Y}_a - \overline{\overline{Y}})^2 \equiv \sum b_a^2$$

over all N observations in the analysis. However, sums of squares get larger when more data are analyzed. Accordingly, the *mean* of the squared deviations is a more appropriate gauge of variability.

The mean of these squared deviation scores is called the **mean square between groups,** or MSA, for the groups defined by Treatment A. MSA is the sum of squares divided by the effective sample size. Although the total number of observations is N, there are only p unique group effects b_a, one for each of the p groups. Further, computing SSA uses the grand mean $\overline{\overline{Y}}$ previously computed from the same data. As explained in Chapter 3, the *effective* sample size or degrees of freedom is the number of freely varying data values after accounting for any previously used statistics calculated from the same data. The degrees of freedom for the treatment sum of squares SSA computed from p unique means is $p - 1$.

The larger the differences among the group means, the larger the MSA.

Variance estimated from group means is *between* group variation, one of the four basic types of variance in ANOVA. The computation of MSA follows.

mean square between groups (MSA) for p levels of Treatment A

$$MSA \equiv \frac{\text{SSA}}{df_A}$$
$$\equiv \frac{\sum b_a^2}{p - 1}$$

STATISTICAL ILLUSTRATION—Mean Square between Groups

DATA

Data are collected according to a one-way independent groups design, and they appear in the shaded area of the following table. Treatment A defines three groups; three data values are obtained for each of the three groups. The sample group means are $\overline{Y}_1 = 4$, $\overline{Y}_2 = 6$, and $\overline{Y}_3 = 8$. The grand mean is

$$\overline{\overline{Y}} = \frac{(2+4+6)+(4+6+8)+(6+8+10)}{9} = 6.$$

MSA

The estimated treatment effects are deviations of the corresponding group means from the grand mean of $\overline{\overline{Y}} = 6$:

$$b_1 = \overline{Y}_1 - \overline{\overline{Y}} = 4 - 6 = -2,$$
$$b_2 = \overline{Y}_2 - \overline{\overline{Y}} = 6 - 6 = 0,$$
$$b_3 = \overline{Y}_3 - \overline{\overline{Y}} = 8 - 6 = 2.$$

The treatment effects and squared treatment effects, as well as the sum of squares, are presented below.

Treatment (A)	Response (Y)	Treatment Mean	Treatment Effect	Trt Eft Sq
A1	2	4	-2	4
A1	4	4	-2	4
A1	6	4	-2	4
A2	4	6	0	0
A2	6	6	0	0
A2	8	6	0	0
A3	6	8	2	4
A3	8	8	2	4
A3	10	8	2	4
Sum	54		0	24
Mean	6			SSA

For degrees of freedom,

$$df_A = p - 1 = 3 - 1 = 2;$$

the mean square *between* groups is

$$MSA \equiv \frac{SSA}{df_A} = \frac{24}{2} = 12.$$

STATISTICAL PRINCIPLE

The estimated effect of membership in the first group with these sample data lowers the grand mean by two units. The estimated third group effect increases the grand mean by two units. Membership in the second group has no effect on the overall mean. Compute the sum of squared treatment effects across all observations. The three different treatment effects, one for each group, result in $p - 1 = 2$ degrees of freedom.

The previous example computed MSA from the original data. MSA can also be calculated directly from the group means and sample sizes. There is only one treatment effect $\overline{Y}_a - \overline{\overline{Y}}$ for each group or treatment level, so the sum of the treatment effects for the n_a observations in Group a is just $n_a(\overline{Y}_a - \overline{\overline{Y}})$. Summing this expression over all p groups yields the following alternate expression for the sum of squares SSA,

$$SSA = \sum n_a (\overline{Y}_a - \overline{\overline{Y}})^2 \text{ over all } p \text{ groups.}$$

Applying this expression to the preceding example,

$$SSA = n_1 (\overline{Y}_1 - \overline{\overline{Y}})^2 + n_2 (\overline{Y}_2 - \overline{\overline{Y}})^2 + n_3 (\overline{Y}_3 - \overline{\overline{Y}})^2$$
$$= 3(-2)^2 + 3(0)^2 + 3(2)^2 = 12 + 0 + 12 = 24.$$

Dividing SSA by the degrees of freedom $p - 1 = 2$ yields the mean square between groups MSA $= 12$.

The mean square between groups for Treatment A reflects, in part, variability due to any existing population mean differences for the different groups. The larger the differences among the population group means, the larger the expected differences among the sample group means, which indicates larger treatment effects. How large must these effects be before the null hypothesis of equal means is rejected? The answer is based on the comparison of the mean square between groups with the mean square statistic introduced next.

STATISTICAL NOISE. A key aspect of a model is the random error term that reflects the magnitude of the statistical noise around the estimated value. The variability of this random error is the basis for assessing the fit of the model to the data. The model for one-way ANOVA specifies that each value of Y is accounted for by three distinct sources: the grand mean, the effect of the corresponding group or treatment level, and random error.

> *Model for one-way ANOVA:*
> $Y = $ *grand mean $+$ group effect $+$ random error*

This model is written in terms of population values or sample estimates, respectively, as

$$Y = \mu + \beta_a + \varepsilon \quad \text{or} \quad Y = \overline{\overline{Y}} + b_a + e.$$

The individual terms of this model are explained next.

The grand mean μ or $\overline{\overline{Y}}$ is the baseline, the constant common to all the values of Y. The group effect β_a or b_a indicates how far up or down membership in a particular group shifts the respective group mean from the grand mean. For example, b_1 is the group effect for level 1, or, to be more explicit, b_{A1} is the group effect for level 1 of Treatment A. As illustrated in more detail at the end of the following chapter, the value of the corresponding predictor variable A is coded as a 1 when b_a refers to the group of which Y is a member. Instead of $(b_a)(1)$, we simply include the coefficient b_a in the model.

A statistical model expresses the value of the response variable Y partly in terms of the explained (what is known) and partly in terms of the unexplained. The unexplained is the error, estimated by the observed residual e, which is the difference between the observed Y and the known component, the estimated $\hat{Y}$. The most generic version of this model for the measured value Y is

$$Y = \hat{Y} + e.$$

For the one-way ANOVA model, the estimated value $\hat{Y}$ is

$$\hat{Y} = \overline{\overline{Y}} + b_a.$$

The model accounts for the value of the response variable Y in terms of the grand mean and the associated treatment effect. All observations in the same group have the same estimated value.

What is the value of the estimate $\hat{Y}$? The estimated treatment effect b_a is the deviation of the corresponding group mean $\overline{Y}_a$ from the grand mean. So, the estimated value of Y is

$$\hat{Y} = \overline{\overline{Y}} + b_a \equiv \overline{\overline{Y}} + (\overline{Y}_a - \overline{\overline{Y}}) = \overline{Y}_a.$$

> *The estimated value of the response variable Y with the one-way ANOVA model is the corresponding group mean.*

All values of Y in the same group have the same estimate because all observations in the same group experience the same level of the predictor (treatment) variable.

The values of the response variable Y within the same group, however, generally differ. The deviation of a value from its own group mean represents a source of variation *unexplained* by the model. That is, the one-way ANOVA model does not account for any variation of responses within the same group. Instead, the omnipresent statistical noise is modeled as the random error component e. This error contributes to the differences among values of Y even among observations in the same group. An error, or residual, is the deviation from this estimated value,

$$e \equiv Y - \hat{Y} = Y - \overline{Y},$$

where $\overline{Y}$ is the group mean for the value Y. The population error is ε and the sample estimate is e, the residual unique to each individual value. The residuals e always sum to zero in any one sample.

The assessment of error variability for all observations is expressed as a mean, which is the variance of the error component s_e^2. This mean is computed using the effective sample size—the actual sample size N minus the number of statistics previously estimated from the same data. Each value of Y is deviated from its own group mean, so the calculation of SSE uses all p group means. The error degrees of freedom (df_E) is $N - p$. Calculate the **mean squared error,** or MSE, from the sum of the squared errors (SSE) for all values of the response variable Y.

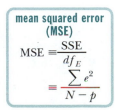

mean squared error (MSE)

$$MSE \equiv \frac{SSE}{df_E}$$

$$= \frac{\sum e^2}{N - p}$$

All values of the response variable Y in the same group have the same estimated value, so error is the only source of variation for values in the same group. This within-group variation MSE is one of the four basic types of variation in ANOVA. In the context of a one-way ANOVA, within-group variability MSE is error variability, the variability of response Y at a *single* value of categorical variable A.

> *Error variance is statistical noise that obscures the detection of existing population mean differences.*

If the observations within each group are highly variable, then the differences between the observed means must be substantial before the null hypothesis of the equality of population means can be rejected.

An illustration of the calculation of this error variability follows.

STATISTICAL ILLUSTRATION—Mean Squared Error for One-Way ANOVA

DATA

Data are collected according to a one-way independent groups design. One treatment variable A has three different values that define three groups. Three data values are obtained for each of the three groups. The sample group means are $\overline{Y}_1 = 4$, $\overline{Y}_2 = 6$, and $\overline{Y}_3 = 8$. The grand mean is $\overline{\overline{Y}} = 6$.

MSE

Treatment (A)	Response (Y)	Y Estimated	Residual	Res Sq
A1	2	4	-2	4
A1	4	4	0	0
A1	6	4	2	4
A2	4	6	-2	4
A2	6	6	0	0
A2	8	6	2	4
A3	6	8	-2	4
A3	8	8	0	0
A3	10	8	2	4
Sum	54		0	24
Mean	6			SSE

The sum of squared errors is SSE = 24. The mean square *within* groups is the error variance,

$$\text{MSE} = \frac{\text{SSE}}{df_E} = \frac{24}{9-3} = \frac{24}{6} = 4.$$

STATISTICAL PRINCIPLE

Error variability is computed as the sum of squared errors for all observations in the analysis. This variability is within-group variance, one of the four fundamental forms of variability in ANOVA.

The previous discussion demonstrated how to calculate SSE directly from the data. SSE can also be calculated from the group standard deviations and sample sizes. In fact, the pooled variance s_{avg}^2 from the independent samples t-test is simply another name for MSE. As defined in Chapter 6, this within-group variance is the average of the group variances s_1^2 and s_2^2 weighted by their degrees of freedom,

$$\text{MSE} = s_{avg}^2 = \frac{df_1 s_1^2 + df_2 s_2^2}{df_1 + df_2}.$$

The weighted average is easily extended to any number of groups, such as $p = 3$,

$$\text{MSE} = s_{avg}^2 = \frac{df_1 s_1^2 + df_2 s_2^2 + df_3 s_3^2}{df_1 + df_2 + df_3}.$$

Once MSA and MSE are obtained, either from the original data or from the summary statistics of these data, the one-way ANOVA can be completed. This analysis is shown in the next section.

Logic of ANOVA

Any ANOVA, including the one-way ANOVA introduced in this section, is based on analysis of different types of the sums of squares. Three types of variation, illustrated in Figure 10-2, have already been presented: total variation (SSY); between-group variation across levels of Treatment A (SSA); and within-group variation (SSE). Fundamental to the logic of ANOVA, all three types of variation are related by a simple expression.

> *Partitioning of the total sum of squares:*
> SSY = SSA + SSE

This relationship follows directly from the underlying model,

measurement = grand mean + treatment effect + error,

or

$$Y = \mu + \beta_a + \varepsilon,$$

which is estimated with

$$Y = \overline{\overline{Y}} + (\overline{Y}_a - \overline{\overline{Y}}) + (Y - \overline{Y}).$$

To obtain SSY = SSA + SSE, subtract the grand mean $\overline{\overline{Y}}$ from each side of this expression, square both sides, and sum all observations.

The ANOVA evaluation of mean differences compares variability between the group means $\overline{Y}$ to the statistical noise of random error variability. The one-way ANOVA compares the two variance estimates to test the null hypothesis of equal population group means. If the null hypothesis is true—no population

Figure 10-2.
Three types of variation based on the one-way independent groups design, with three groups and four responses per group.

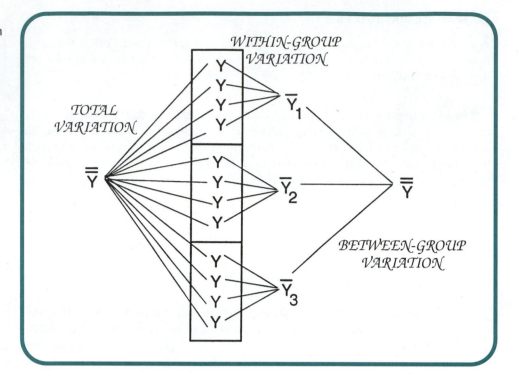

group differences exist—then MSA estimates the same random noise variability estimated by MSE. However, if group differences do exist, then MSA tends to be larger than MSE because MSA reflects random noise variability as well as the differences among population means.

How does the size of SSE affect the rejection of the null hypothesis of no difference among population means? The answer is revealed in the following example. This analysis is based on the previously discussed independent samples *t*-test (Chapter 6) but exactly the same results (*p*-values) are obtained with ANOVA.

STATISTICAL ILLUSTRATION—Within-Group Variation and Statistical Significance

OVERVIEW

The following three data samples each contain six values, three values for Group *A*1 and three values for Group *A*2. The mean of the *A*1 values is always 54 and the *A*2 mean is always 56; these are the respective estimated values within each group. For each data sample, the hypothesis test evaluates the same observed sample mean difference of $54 - 56 = -2$.

The distinction between each of the samples is the variability of the values within each group, which is the unexplained random error. For Sample 1, the standard deviation of the three values is a very small .10. This within-group variability increases for Sample 2, which has a within-group standard deviation of .9, and again for Sample 3, with a within-group standard deviation of 2.0.

DATA, SCATTERPLOT, AND ANALYSIS

1.

Group	Y	$\hat{Y}$	e	e^2
A1	53.9	54.0	-0.10	0.01
A1	54.0	54.0	0.00	0.00
A1	54.1	54.0	0.10	0.01
A2	55.9	56.0	-0.10	0.01
A2	56.0	56.0	0.00	0.00
A2	56.1	56.0	0.10	0.01

0.04 SSE

Group	n	Mean	SD		
A1	3	54	0.10	t =	-24.495
A2	3	56	0.10	df =	4
				p =	0.000

Conclusion: population means not equal.

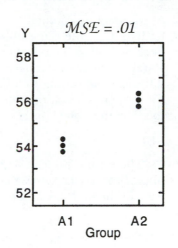

$\mathcal{MSE} = .01$

2.

Group	Y	$\hat{Y}$	e	e^2
A1	53.1	54.0	-0.90	0.81
A1	54.0	54.0	0.00	0.00
A1	54.9	54.0	0.90	0.81
A2	55.1	56.0	-0.90	0.81
A2	56.0	56.0	0.00	0.00
A2	56.9	56.0	0.90	0.81

3.24 SSE

Group	n	Mean	SD		
A1	3	54	0.90	t =	-2.72
A2	3	56	0.90	df =	4
				p =	0.053

Tentative Conclusion: population means are equal.

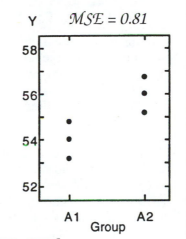

$\mathcal{MSE} = 0.81$

3.

Group	Y	$\hat{Y}$	e	e^2
A1	52.0	54.0	-2.00	4.00
A1	54.0	54.0	0.00	0.00
A1	56.0	54.0	2.00	4.00
A2	54.0	56.0	-2.00	4.00
A2	56.0	56.0	0.00	0.00
A2	58.0	56.0	2.00	4.00

16.00 SSE

Group	n	Mean	SD		
A1	3	54	2.00	t =	-1.22
A2	3	56	2.00	df =	4
				p =	0.288

Conclusion: population means are equal.

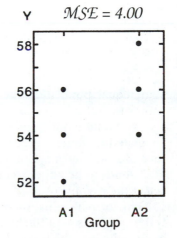

$\mathcal{MSE} = 4.00$

STATISTICAL PRINCIPLE

As within-group variability *increases*, indicated by MSE $= s_{avg}^2$ increasing from .01 to 0.81 to 4.00, the same observed mean difference of $\overline{Y}_1 - \overline{Y}_2 = -2$ becomes *less* likely to lead to the rejection of the null hypothesis H_0: $\mu_1 - \mu_2 = 0$. The hypothesis test of mean differences, *t*-test or ANOVA, analyzes the observed sample group difference according to a baseline that reflects the variability within each group. The larger this within-group variability, the larger the error and the more difficult to reject the null hypothesis of equal population means.

The error variance (MSE) is variance unexplained by the model. The variation of the actual data values Y around the corresponding estimated value $\hat{Y}$ forms the basis of the evaluation of a regression model, including ANOVA models.

> *Differences among the population means of independent groups likely exist if the sample group mean differences are large relative to the differences among the observations within each group.*

Both the independent-samples *t*-test and the corresponding one-way ANOVA compare the differences among the means of the groups to the baseline established by the variability within each sample. MSE reflects the variation of Y within the groups.

The formal hypothesis test that compares the between- and within-group variability estimates is introduced next.

F-TEST. MSA estimates variability from differences among the group sample means. What contributes to this variation? The answer depends on whether the null hypothesis of equal population group means is true or false. Under the null hypothesis, all population group means μ_a equal each other as well as the grand mean μ. With equal population means, the resulting sample means tend to be close to one another in value. The only reason the sample estimates of group mean $\overline{Y}_a$ and grand mean $\overline{\overline{Y}}$ are not equal for a true null hypothesis is random sampling error, the unexplained fluctuations that manifest as within-group variation.

> *For a true null hypothesis of equal population means, both MSA and MSE estimate the same population variance.*

F-statistic for predictor *A*

$$F = \frac{\begin{pmatrix} \textit{estimated pop.} \\ \textit{variance from the} \\ \textit{sample means} \end{pmatrix}}{\begin{pmatrix} \textit{estimated pop.} \\ \textit{variance from the} \\ \textit{original values} \end{pmatrix}}$$

$$= \frac{\text{MSA}}{\text{MSE}}$$

With equal population means, the random variation of sampling error alone causes the differences among the corresponding sample means, so MSA $\approx$ MSE.

With a false null hypothesis, however, the population means differ so that the estimated treatment effects reflect both the differences among population group means as well as sampling error. The result of different population means is that MSA tends to be larger than MSE. If MSA is much larger than the baseline MSE, reject the null hypothesis of equal population means.

The formal evaluation of the null hypothesis of equal population group means is the comparison of the between-group variance estimate to the within-group variance estimate, which gives us the **F-statistic.** The purpose of the *F*-test, the ratio

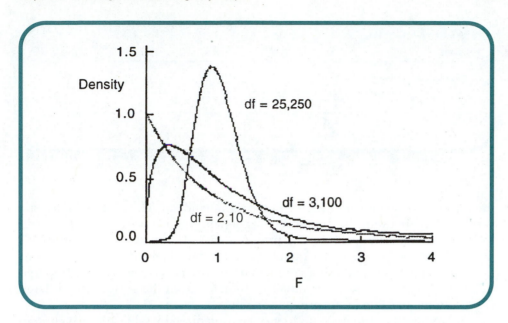

Figure 10-3.
Three different sampling
distributions of the
F-statistic assuming the
null hypothesis of equal
population means.

of two variance estimates, is to infer the equality or inequality of the population group means.

To evaluate the null hypothesis of equal group means, compare the observed value of *F* to the sampling distribution of *F* consistent with the null hypothesis. If the null hypothesis is true, what is the distribution of the *F*-statistic over repeated sampling? As with the family of *t*-distributions, there are many *F*-distributions. The specific distribution depends on both the degrees of freedom for the numerator df_A and the degrees of freedom for the denominator df_E, as illustrated in Figure 10-3. Each degrees of freedom is written as $df_{\text{num,den}}$.

The *F*-test is a one-tailed test that determines whether MSA is much larger than MSE—assuming equal within-group variances. As illustrated in Figure 10-4, all of

Figure 10-4.
Five percent upper-tail
cutoff for an
F-distribution assuming
a true null hypothesis.

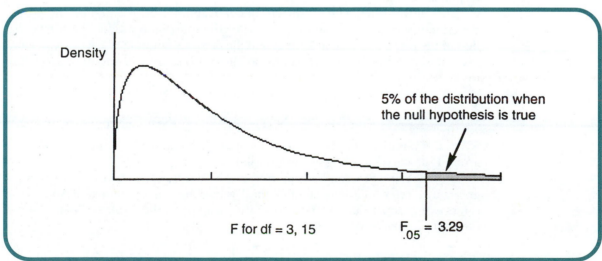

Table 10-1.
The one-way ANOVA
summary table for
evaluating the effect of
p levels of Treatment A
on response variable Y.

Source	SS	df	MS	F	p
Treatment A (Between)	$\sum b_a^2$	$p - 1$	SSA/df_A	MSA/MSE	<.05?
Error (Within)	$\sum e^2$	$N - p$	SSE/df_E		
Total	SSY	$N - 1$			

the rejection region is concentrated in the right-hand tail. The obtained F-statistic is then compared with the appropriate right-hand tail cutoff value of the corresponding F-distribution, such as $F_{.05}$ from Appendix D, the value that cuts off 5% of the distribution of the upper right-hand tail. If the obtained value of F exceeds the cutoff, the null hypothesis is considered unlikely and is rejected. Such a large value of F is obtained when the variance estimated from the group mean is large relative to the baseline within-group variability.

The results of the analysis of variance are organized in Table 10-1, which summarizes the statistics for each source of variation. The one-way ANOVA has three sources of variation: total; between, corresponding to Treatment A; and within, corresponding to error.

STRENGTH OF ASSOCIATION. Evaluating the null hypothesis is evaluating whether the predictor (treatment) and response variables are related. The *strength* of the relationship between these variables should also be assessed. This assessment was provided in Chapter 8 in the context of linear regression. The R^2 statistic provides an estimate of the strength of the relationship between the predictor variable and the response variable. In the context of ANOVA, the treatment variable is a categorical predictor variable, that is, a variable with qualitative, nonnumeric data values. Does the same logic developed for the relationship between two numeric variables apply to the relationship between a categorical predictor variable and a numeric response variable?

The answer is yes. The coefficient of determination R^2 is based on the two independent sources of variation specified by the regression model: the total variation in the response variable Y (SSY) and the error variation (SSE). The expression presented in Chapter 8 for R^2 compares these two sources of variation according to

$$R^2 \equiv 1 - \frac{\sum (Y - \hat{Y})^2}{\sum (Y - \overline{Y})^2} \equiv 1 - \frac{\text{SSE}}{\text{SSY}}.$$

SSY is the variation of Y around the mean of all Y's, and SSE is the variation of Y around the corresponding estimated value $\hat{Y}$.

Both SSY and SSE can be expressed in ANOVA notation. In the context of regression, $\overline{Y}$ refers to the mean of all the Y values, but in the context of ANOVA, $\overline{Y}$ refers to a group mean and $\overline{\overline{Y}}$ refers to the mean of all the Y values. So in ANOVA the sum of squares of Y is expressed as

$$\text{SSY} = \sum (Y - \overline{\overline{Y}})^2.$$

Similarly, SSE is the sum of the squared deviations of each value of the response variable Y around the corresponding estimated value $\hat{Y}$. In ANOVA each estimated value is the corresponding group mean, so SSE is written as

$$SSE = \sum (Y - \overline{Y})^2.$$

The same concepts developed in regression that define R^2—comparing variability around the estimated value to variability around the overall mean—apply also to ANOVA[1].

As discussed in Chapter 9, R^2 describes the relationship between predictor and response variables in the sample but *not* in the population. Applying the model developed in one sample to a new sample lowers R^2. This lower value is of greater interest because it more accurately reflects the *population* relationship between predictor variables and response variable. The following adjustment of R^2 for linear regression,

$$R^2_{adj} = 1 - \frac{MSE}{MSY},$$

also applies to ANOVA[2]. This adjusted statistic estimates the proportion of total variance in the population attributable to the group classifications or treatment levels. R^2_{adj} in this context estimates the strength of the relation in the population of between-group membership to the resulting value of the response variable Y.

Omega squared $(\hat{\omega}^2)$, a statistic analogous to R^2_{adj}, applies specifically to models with categorical predictor variables, where N is the total sample size, df is the predictor degrees of freedom, and F is the value of the F-statistic.

Both R^2_{adj} and $\hat{\omega}^2$ have the same intent, to estimate the population relation between the predictor and response variable, and their values will generally approximate each other, with $\hat{\omega}^2$ slightly smaller. However, $\hat{\omega}^2$ is used more frequently than R^2_{adj} to assess the strength of relationship in ANOVA. Generally accepted guidelines for interpreting the size of $\hat{\omega}^2$ are that values larger than about .14 indicate a large association, and any value around .01 indicates a small association. Values around .06 indicate a medium association.

An example follows that illustrates a one-way analysis of variance.

> estimated omega squared $\hat{\omega}^2$ for **Predictor A**
>
> $$\hat{\omega}^2 = \frac{(df)(F-1)}{(df)(F-1)+N}$$

BUSINESS APPLICATION 10.2—One-Way ANOVA

MANAGERIAL PROBLEM

The vehicle maintenance manager who oversees a large fleet of company cars wants to save his company money by maximizing the fleet's gas mileage. His concern is the causal influence of Engine Oil on Miles per Gallon (MPG) of gasoline. Do the three different engine oils ($A1$, $A2$, and $A3$) lead to different gasoline mileage?

---

1. R^2 is also called $\hat{\eta}^2$ (estimated eta squared) in the context of ANOVA, but the more familiar R^2 label already introduced in Chapter 6 is used here for both regression and ANOVA.

2. R^2_{adj} is computed from R^2 according to $1 - \left((1 - R^2) \frac{N-1}{N-p} \right)$.

STATISTICAL HYPOTHESES

Null hypothesis H_0: $\mu_1 = \mu_2 = \mu_3$.
Alternative hypothesis H_1: some means are not equal.

DATA

The manager selected three different engine oils to examine their potential effect on MPG. The same model car was used for each of the tests, with 12 different measurements of MPG. Because different drivers and cars get different mileage, 12 drivers and cars were randomly assigned to each of the three types of engine oils—four sets of cars and drivers to each of the oil types. The resulting MPG's after one month of normal driving were recorded.

Driver	Oil	MPG
1	A1	27.2
2	A1	23.8
3	A1	27.2
4	A1	20.5
5	A2	27.8
6	A2	28.4
7	A2	34.9
8	A2	26.3
9	A3	30.4
10	A3	28.0
11	A3	33.5
12	A3	23.1

The resulting sample means are

$$\overline{Y}_1 = 24.68, \overline{Y}_2 = 29.35, \text{ and } \overline{Y}_3 = 28.75.$$

Although sample means differ, are the differences sufficiently large to suggest that the underlying *population* means differ?

EXCEL GRAPHICAL ANALYSIS

Assessing the Excel Output
The data, which appear in Figure 10-5, appear amenable to further analysis. No outliers or other oddities characterize these data. The within-group variation appears approximately equal for each of the groups.

Obtaining the Output

Insert ➤ Chart...

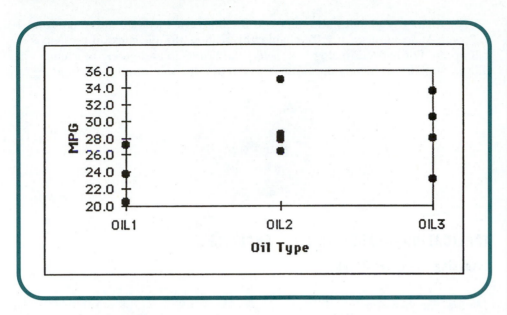

Figure 10-5.
Plot of MPG by Type
of Engine Oil.

Step 1—Chart Type. Specify an *X Y* Scatter chart, which is for a numeric horizontal axis. Select the format that leaves the points unconnected.

Step 2—Chart Source. Specify the cells for the Data Range, which includes the columns that contain the values for Oil and MPG as well as the corresponding labels. The value of Oil must be numerical. For example, 1 is the value of Oil for each driver in the first group.

Data range: =Sheet1!$B$1:$C$13

Step 3—Chart Options. Click the Legend tab and uncheck the Show legend box. Click the Titles box to provide the titles for the *Y* and *X* axes.

Step 4—Chart Location. Specify that the chart be placed on a new worksheet or the current worksheet.

To enhance readability, the values on the horizontal axis should range from 1 to 3, with Major unit set at 1. To change this scaling, double-click on the *X*-axis to call up the Format Axis dialog box. Select the Scale tab and enter the changes as shown. Similarly, reformat the vertical axis so that the minimum value is 20.

Value (X) axis scale

Auto

☐ Mi̲nimum: 1

☐ Ma̲ximum: 3

☐ Ma̲jor unit: 1

APPLICATION—EXCEL BUILT-IN ANALYSIS

Assessing the Excel Output

Anova: Single Factor

SUMMARY

Groups	Count	Sum	Average	Variance
Oil1	4	98.7	24.675	10.316
Oil2	4	117.4	29.350	14.470
Oil3	4	115	28.750	19.257

ANOVA

Source of Variation	SS	df	MS	F	P-value	F crit
Between Groups	51.762	2	25.881	1.763	0.226	4.256
Within Groups	132.128	9	14.681			
Total	183.889	11				

The *p*-value is greater than .05, so the null hypothesis of equal population means is *not* rejected.

Obtaining the Output

The data for the Excel ANOVA analysis are organized differently than for the plot of the data by group. The responses for each type of oil (treatment level) appear in a separate column.

	E	F	G
1	Oil1	Oil2	Oil3
2	27.2	27.8	30.4
3	23.8	28.4	28.0
4	27.2	34.9	33.5
5	20.5	26.3	23.1

Given the required formatting of the data, call up the Excel one-way ANOVA program with the following menu sequence.

Tools ➤ Data Analysis... ➤ Anova: Single Factor

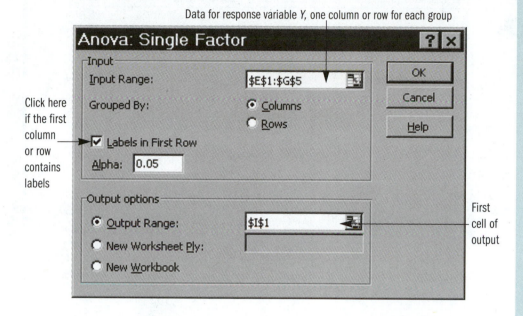

Data for response variable Y, one column or row for each group

Click here if the first column or row contains labels

First cell of output

APPLICATION—SUM OF SQUARES CONCEPTUAL WORKSHEET

Estimated Values, Effects, and Residuals

The grand mean is $\overline{\overline{Y}} = 27.59$. The estimated value for each observation is the sum of the respective Oil effect and the grand mean. That is, how far up or down does the level of Oil move the response value? For example, Observation 1 is in the first group, which has a treatment effect of $b_a = -2.92$, so

$$\hat{Y} = \overline{\overline{Y}} + b_a = 27.59 - 2.92 = 24.68.$$

The actual MPG for Observation 1 is 27.2, so the residual is

$$e \equiv Y - \hat{Y} = 27.2 - 24.68 = 2.53.$$

The estimated values, residuals, squared residuals, and also the squared group effects are displayed in Table 10-2 for all observations.

APPLICATION—TRADITIONAL NOTATION

Mean Squares

Degrees of freedom for error is

$$df_E = df_1 + df_2 + df_3 = (n_1 - 1) + (n_2 - 1) + (n_3 - 1)$$
$$= (n_1 + n_2 + n_3) - (1 + 1 + 1) = N - p = 12 - 3 = 9.$$

Estimate of the variability *within* each group is

$$\text{MSE} = \frac{\text{SSE}}{df_E} = \frac{132.12}{9} = 14.68.$$

Predictor	Response	Target (group)	Deviation from Trgt	Deviation Squared	Target (residual)	Deviation from Trgt	Deviation Squared
Oil Type	Actual MPG	Grand Mean	Oil Effect	Oil Efct Squared	Estimated MPG	Residual	Residual Squared
A	Y	$\overline{\overline{Y}}$	$b_a \equiv \overline{Y} - \overline{\overline{Y}}$	b_a^2	$\hat{Y} = \overline{Y}$	$e \equiv Y - \hat{Y}$	e^2
A1	27.2	27.59	-2.92	8.51	24.68	2.53	6.38
A1	23.8	27.59	-2.92	8.51	24.68	-0.88	0.77
A1	27.2	27.59	-2.92	8.51	24.68	2.53	6.38
A1	20.5	27.59	-2.92	8.51	24.68	-4.18	17.43
A2	27.8	27.59	1.76	3.09	29.35	-1.55	2.40
A2	28.4	27.59	1.76	3.09	29.35	-0.95	0.90
A2	34.9	27.59	1.76	3.09	29.35	5.55	30.80
A2	26.3	27.59	1.76	3.09	29.35	-3.05	9.30
A3	30.4	27.59	1.16	1.34	28.75	1.65	2.72
A3	28.0	27.59	1.16	1.34	28.75	-0.75	0.56
A3	33.5	27.59	1.16	1.34	28.75	4.75	22.56
A3	23.1	27.59	1.16	1.34	28.75	-5.65	31.92
Sum	331.10		0.00	51.76		0.00	132.12
Mean	27.59			SSA			SSE

Table 10-2.
Estimated values (of MPG) and residuals for the one-way independent groups design with three groups (Oil Type).

Estimate of the mean square *between* groups is

$$\text{MSA} \equiv \frac{\text{SSA}}{df_A} = \frac{\text{SSA}}{p-1} = \frac{51.76}{3-1} = 25.88.$$

Summary Table

The obtained F-statistic is

$$F \equiv \frac{\text{MSA}}{\text{MSE}} = \frac{25.88}{14.68} = 1.76.$$

For degrees of freedom 2 and 9, Appendix D lists the cutoff value for $F_{.05}$ as 4.26, so the obtained value of $F = 1.76$ is not sufficiently deviant under the null hypotheses to merit rejection of the equality of population group means.

The p-value for $F = 1.76$ is obtained with the Excel FDIST function,

$$\text{=FDIST(Fvalue,df}_A\text{,df}_E\text{)}$$

In this case

$$\text{=FDIST(1.76,2,9)}$$

returns 0.226.

Source	df	SS	MS	F	p
Oil (A)	2	51.76	25.88	1.76	0.226
Error (E)	9	132.13	14.68		
Total	11	183.89			

The p-value of .226 is considerably larger than the 0.05 criterion needed to reject the null hypothesis of no difference of population group means.

Strength of Association

$$R^2 = 1 - \frac{\text{SSE}}{\text{SST}} = 1 - \frac{132.12}{183.89} = .281$$

$$R^2_{\text{adj}} = 1 - \frac{\text{MSE}}{\text{MSY}} = 1 - \frac{132.12/9}{183.89/11} = .122$$

$$\hat{\omega}^2 = \frac{(df)(F-1)}{(df)(F-1)+N} = \frac{(3-1)(1.76-1)}{(3-1)(1.76-1)+(4)(3)} = .113$$

As expected, R^2_{adj} and $\hat{\omega}^2$ approximately equal each other, with $\hat{\omega}^2$ slightly lower, and both are lower than the sample description provided by R^2. The large drop from R^2 to the population estimates R^2_{adj} and $\hat{\omega}^2$ is due in part to the small sample size.

MANAGERIAL INTERPRETATION

Although the sample mean MPG's varied from 24.68 to 29.35 for the three types of oil, these differences are not large enough to conclude that they generalize to the population as a whole. Repeating the study could reverse the ranking of the Engine Oils in terms of MPG. For example, for these data the second type of oil yielded the best gasoline mileage, an average of 29.35 mpg. Because the null hypothesis was not rejected, however, the highest ranking for this type of oil may be due only to chance. In a new study, this type of oil may be the worst performer instead of the best performer.

Differences in population means could not be detected from this study, but neither can the opposite conclusion of no differences be drawn. First, the sample size is too low, yielding an hypothesis test of little power. There could be real differences in population means that this test was not powerful enough to detect. Second, the model underlying the design of the study accounts only for potential differences in oil. In particular, the model does not account for any natural variations of drivers and/or cars, so this variation becomes random error variance. The more random error variance there is, the more difficult it is to detect differences when they exist.

The strength of association between Type of Engine Oil and MPG is estimated as reasonably large. Additional work may include a larger sample as well as a different experimental design that removes from the error term the variance due to drivers and/or cars. Both of these changes would contribute to a more powerful test of the hypothesis of equal group means, and could possibly indicate MPG differences for different types of Engine Oil.

Relation of *t* and *F* Statistics. The similarity of the *t*-test of a mean difference and the corresponding *F*-test is evident when a single mean difference is analyzed using both methods. First, the *p*-values of the two tests are identical. Second, the resulting obtained *F*-statistic is the square of the corresponding *t*-statistic $t_{\bar{Y}_1 - \bar{Y}_2}$ under the null hypothesis of no difference for a nondirectional (two-tailed) test, assuming equal within-group variances. The same relation holds true for the corresponding cutoff values. For example, consider two groups with a sample size of 26 in each group, $df_E = 50$, and $df_A = 1$. The cutoff value of *t* is

$$t_{.025} = 2.009 \text{ for } df = 50.$$

The corresponding cutoff from the *F*-distribution is

$$F_{.05} = 4.03 = 2.009^2 = t_{.025}^2 \text{ for } df = 1,50.$$

As we have seen, however, the *t*-test offers some additional flexibility over its *F*-test counterpart. The *t*-test may evaluate a nonzero difference between population means and it may be directional (or one-tailed); also, a version exists that does *not* assume equal variances.

This section has outlined the procedure for conducting a one-way ANOVA. The next section describes the procedure to follow when the null hypothesis of equal population means is rejected. When the equality of all population means is in doubt, the next task is to identify the pattern of mean differences. Are all population group means different from each other? Is just one population group mean different from the others? Or is there some other pattern that describes the mean differences.

EXERCISES

 10-3. Provide the following cutoff values of the *F*-distribution from Appendix D.

a. $F_{.05}$ for 3 groups, 5 observations per group
b. $F_{.05}$ for 3 groups, 4 observations in the first group, 6 in the second group, and 7 in the third group
c. $F_{.05}$ for 5 groups, 3 observations per group
d. $F_{.05}$ for 2 groups, 10 observations in the first group and 12 in the second

 10-4. Complete the following one-way ANOVA summary table.

Source	SS	df	MS	F	p
Temp	380.200	4	c.	d.	0.075
Error	a.	15	35.867		
Total	918.200	b.			

 10-5. For the statistics presented in the ANOVA table in the previous exercise,

a. How many groups were in this study?
b. How many experimental units (e.g., people) were in this study?
c. Is the null hypothesis of equal group means rejected or not rejected? Why or why not?
d. Calculate R^2, R_{adj}^2, and $\hat{\omega}^2$. How strong is the effect between the predictor variable *A* and the response variable *Y*?

10-6. A manager intent on improving the quality of a manufacturing process wants to evaluate the strength of a new material depending on the temperature at which the material was processed—either 200°F, 300°F, or 400°F. The resulting strength was recorded for each of five pieces of the material randomly assigned to each temperature.

Temp	Strength
200	3.5
200	3.1
200	4.7
200	4.2
200	3.3
300	6.5
300	6.7
300	4.5
300	4.8
300	7.1
400	6.3
400	9.3
400	5.0
400	6.3
400	5.5

a. Does processing temperature affect strength?
b. How strong is the estimated relationship between temperature and strength?
c. What are the estimated treatment effects?
d. What is the estimated strength for each temperature?
e. Why cannot the independent-samples *t*-test be used to examine group differences for these data?

10-7. A large retail company is considering opening an outlet in a particular city. The company will choose the final location from two locations within the city. One of the factors in the decision is the average annual family income in the areas immediately surrounding each potential location. The accompanying table lists the family income (in thousand of dollars) of five families, each randomly sampled from a radius of two miles from the potential locations.

Area	Income
A1	39,760
A1	41,390
A1	43,290
A1	37,230
A1	67,420

Area	Income
A2	43,860
A2	44,180
A2	56,120
A2	88,130
A2	68,900

a. Do an independent-samples *t*-test of the mean difference to evaluate the equality of the population means.
b. Do an *F*-test from a one-way ANOVA of the mean difference to evaluate the equality of the population means.
c. Determine the relation between the test statistics (observed *t* and observed *F*) and the *p*-values from the two analyses.
d. Calculate the sample mean difference. Is this difference large enough to lead to the rejection of the null hypothesis of equal population means? Why or why not?

10-8. An oil company manager needs to buy some meters for measuring oil flow. Seventeen meters representing four different brands are evaluated for accuracy, with a grand mean of −.20. The group summary statistics appear in the accompanying table. The error in measurement is calibrated in gallons per minute, under or over the ideal of perfect measurement represented by zero. For example, a group mean of −1.86 indicates that the average error underestimates the correct flow by 1.86 gallons per minute. The one-way ANOVA of these data did *not* reject the null hypothesis of equal group means.

Group	Size	Mean	SD
A1	6	−1.86	2.65
A2	4	−1.40	2.79
A3	3	1.73	6.58
A4	4	2.05	3.20

a. Perform the one-way ANOVA from these data, demonstrating the nonsignificant *F*-test.
b. Given group means that range from −1.86 to 2.05, give your opinion about why the null hypothesis was not rejected.
c. Make a recommendation to management regarding the assessment of the accuracy of these meters.

10.3 ISOLATING THE SOURCE OF THE MEAN DIFFERENCES

The one-way ANOVA F-test described in the previous section tests the null hypothesis that population means for all of the groups are equal. If the null hypothesis is rejected, then some pairs of population group means are apparently not equal. From the F-test alone, however, no further conclusion regarding the difference of means is warranted.

> *A significant one-way ANOVA F-test indicates only that at least one of the population group means differs from the others; it does not specify the particular pairs of means that differ.*

Perhaps all population group means differ from each other, or perhaps only one mean differs from the others. When the null hypothesis of equal population group means is rejected, we need some procedure that isolates the population means that differ from the others.

One procedure that does *not* work is to do an independent-samples t-test or confidence interval on all pairs of mean differences to identify groups with different population means. Each individual confidence interval around a sample mean difference has a specified probability, usually $\alpha = .05$, of *not* containing the true population mean difference. Unusual events, however, do occur. Even though each individual interval has a confidence level of 95% and an associated error rate of $\alpha = .05$, the probability that one of many such intervals does not contain the true mean difference is larger than .05.

familywise error rate for a confidence interval

probability that one or more confidence intervals does not contain the true mean difference per set (family) of related tests

Some method for controlling the **familywise error rate** for the entire family of comparisons is needed. This need is particularly acute given the large number of possible mean comparisons for even a relatively small number of groups, as illustrated in Table 10-3. The more mean comparisons, the more likely that one of the confidence intervals does not contain zero even when there is no corresponding mean difference in the population. That is, even if all population group means are equal, some confidence intervals may falsely indicate a difference, particularly when the number of comparisons is large.

Another unsuccessful procedure for identifying the specific population mean differences is to wait until the data are analyzed and then use an independent-samples t-test or confidence interval to compare the larger sample group means with the smaller sample group means. Even if all population group means are equal, sample means will differ. As the number of mean comparisons grows, the chance difference that separates the smallest and largest sample group means gets larger. Comparing the two groups simply because a large sample mean difference was

Table 10-3.
The number of possible mean comparisons depending on the number of means (groups).

Means	2	3	4	5	6	7	8
Pairs of Means	1	3	6	10	15	21	28

found is an example of *data snooping,* and typically will yield the conclusion that population differences exist even when they do not.

To address these problems, many specific procedures have been developed for comparing means *after* the ANOVA has been performed. These procedures do not take undue advantage of chance, and they provide a specified error rate across the entire set of comparisons. Of these many procedures, perhaps the most generally useful is the Tukey HSD procedure.[3] The HSD (honestly significant differences) procedure holds the familywise error rate equal to a specified value such as .05 for all possible mean difference comparisons. That is, the analyst is free, without worrying about data snooping, to compute the HSD confidence intervals around all sample group mean differences. With HSD intervals, the probability that one or more intervals will not contain the true mean difference is held at a constant, specified value.

Beginning with a specified familywise error rate, such as 5%, the HSD test adjusts this error rate downward for each individual confidence interval. The downward adjustment increases the size of each interval just enough to ensure that the familywise error rate stays at the specified value. A crucial aspect of this adjustment is provided by the appropriate distribution of the Studentized range statistic q, which replaces the t-distribution when searching data for mean differences. As seen in Appendix D, there is a separate distribution of q depending on the number of group means p and degrees of freedom df_E. Similar to the family of F-distributions, only the right-hand tail of the relevant distribution is of interest, so use the .05 cutoff value to specify an error rate of $\alpha = .05$.

To construct the confidence interval, we first need the standard error. The estimated standard error for the corresponding q-distribution follows.

$$\textit{HSD standard error for } \overline{Y}_i - \overline{Y}_j:$$
$$s_{\text{HSD}} = \sqrt{\frac{\text{MSE}\left(\dfrac{1}{n_i} + \dfrac{1}{n_j}\right)}{2}}$$

If the sample sizes n_i and n_j are equal, this standard error is more simply expressed as

$$\sqrt{\frac{\text{MSE}}{n}},$$

obtained by substituting a single $\frac{1}{n}$ in the general expression.

The confidence interval constructed around a mean difference when searching for patterns of mean differences follows the same general procedure as that for a confidence interval around a single mean difference, as presented in Chapter 4. When examining differences among many means, however, the cutoff value is specified according to a familywise error rate such as .05, and the distribution from which the cutoff value is obtained is q (Appendix E) instead of t.

$$\textit{HSD confidence interval for a 5\% familywise error rate:}$$
$$\overline{Y}_i - \overline{Y}_j \pm q_{.05} s_{\text{HSD}}$$

3. This test was invented by John Tukey in 1953, the same Tukey who developed the box plot described in Chapter 3.

Figure 10-6.
Convenient display for
the presentation of an
HSD analysis of all
possible sample mean
comparisons.

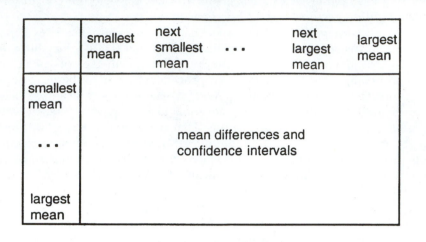

The confidence interval can be computed for all possible familywise sample mean differences. As is true of the interpretation of any confidence interval around a sample mean difference, if the interval contains zero, then a population mean difference cannot be substantiated from the data. If all values of the interval are positive or all values are negative, however, then a difference between population means is concluded to exist.

When you are systematically searching for all possible sample mean differences, the results can be conveniently displayed in a rectangular table. The means are ordered from smallest to largest along the rows and columns of the table. The body of the table contains the mean differences and confidence intervals of the individual comparisons. This table facilitates the recognition of patterns of means that are equal or unequal. For a one-way ANOVA with $p = 5$ groups, for example, the two smallest means may equal one another and the largest three means may equal one another, a pattern that would be readily identified from Figure 10-6.

An example follows of computing HSD confidence intervals for a systematic search of all mean differences.

BUSINESS APPLICATION 10.3—HSD Search of all Mean Differences

MANAGERIAL PROBLEM

A realtor wants to compare Housing Prices for five different neighborhoods. A sample of four houses was gathered for each Area. Are all of the prices the same for the different neighborhoods? If not, what patterns of similarity and dissimilarity describe the prices?

DATA

Area	Price
A1	179
A1	161
A1	144
A1	168
A2	197
A2	198
A2	169
A2	187
A3	160
A3	142
A3	162
A3	156

Area	Price
A4	174
A4	162
A4	168
A4	172
A5	185
A5	182
A5	196
A5	195

ONE-WAY ANOVA

Source	df	SS	MS	F	p
Area	4	3719	930	8.37	0.001
Error	15	1666	111		
Total	19	5385			

$$R^2_{\text{adj}} = .61 \quad \text{and} \quad \hat{\omega}^2 = .60$$

The null hypothesis of equal population means is rejected. Further, Area and Price are strongly related. The price of a house depends to some extent on the area in which the house is located.

APPLICATION—TRADITIONAL NOTATION

To illustrate the computation of the HSD confidence intervals, calculate the interval for the mean difference between the two smallest means, $\overline{Y}_3$ and $\overline{Y}_1$:

$$\overline{Y}_3 - \overline{Y}_1 = 155.00 - 163.00 = -8.00.$$

The HSD standard error is

$$s_{\text{HSD}} = \sqrt{\dfrac{\text{MSE}\left(\dfrac{1}{n_i} + \dfrac{1}{n_j}\right)}{2}},$$

which, for equal sample sizes, reduces to

$$s_{HSD} = \sqrt{\frac{MSE}{n}} = \sqrt{\frac{111.07}{4}} = \sqrt{27.77} = 5.27.$$

For $p = 5$ and $df_E = 15$, the Studentized range statistic cutoff value from Appendix E for a familywise error rate of $\alpha = .05$ is $q_{.05} = 4.37$. The precision or maximum error for the confidence interval is 4.37 standard errors, which is

$$E = q_{.05}s_{HSD} = (4.37)(5.27) = 23.03.$$

The HSD confidence interval is $\overline{Y}_i - \overline{Y}_j \pm q_{.05}s_{HSD}$,

$$\text{Lower Bound: } -8.00 - 23.03 = -31.03$$

and

$$\text{Upper Bound: } -8.00 + 23.03 = 15.03.$$

This interval includes zero, so no difference between the population means of Group 1 and Group 3 can be concluded.

The HSD confidence intervals in thousands of dollars for all mean comparisons are presented in Table 10-4 for a familywise error rate of .05, and then again for .15 in Table 10-5. Intervals that do not include zero are displayed in boldface, which represent comparisons with a population mean difference other than zero.

STATISTICAL PRINCIPLE

Controlling the familywise error rate α for all mean difference comparisons leads to a wide confidence interval around each sample mean difference. The smaller the familywise error rate, the smaller the error rate α for each individual comparison. For familywise $\alpha = .05$, the individual α is .007. Increasing the familywise α to .15 increases the individual α to a still low .026.

In neither situation can the prices for Areas 1 and 3 be shown to be different; the same is true for the prices for Areas 2 and 5. When familywise $\alpha = .05$, Area 4

Table 10-4.
HSD confidence intervals (thousands of $) around all sample group means, with the familywise error rate set at .05 and the resulting individual error rate at .007.

	$\overline{Y}_3 = 155.00$	$\overline{Y}_1 = 163.00$	$\overline{Y}_4 = 169.00$	$\overline{Y}_2 = 187.50$	$\overline{Y}_5 = 189.50$
$\overline{Y}_3 = 155.00$	—				
$\overline{Y}_1 = 163.00$	-31.03 15.03	—			
$\overline{Y}_4 = 169.00$	-37.03 9.03	-29.03 17.03	—		
$\overline{Y}_2 = 187.75$	**-55.78** **-9.72**	**-47.78** **-1.72**	-41.78 4.28	—	
$\overline{Y}_5 = 189.50$	**-57.53** **-11.47**	**-49.53** **-3.47**	-43.53 2.53	-24.78 21.28	—

	$\bar{Y}_3 = 155.00$	$\bar{Y}_1 = 163.00$	$\bar{Y}_4 = 169.00$	$\bar{Y}_2 = 187.50$	$\bar{Y}_5 = 189.50$
$\bar{Y}_3 = 155.00$	–				
$\bar{Y}_1 = 163.00$	-26.39 10.39	–			
$\bar{Y}_4 = 169.00$	-32.39 4.39	-24.39 12.39	–		
$\bar{Y}_2 = 187.75$	**-51.14** **-14.36**	**-43.14** **-6.36**	**-37.14** **-0.36**	–	
$\bar{Y}_5 = 189.50$	**-52.89** **-16.11**	**-44.89** **-8.11**	**-32.89** **-2.11**	-20.14 16.64	–

Table 10-5.
HSD confidence intervals (thousands of $) around all sample group means, with the familywise error rate set at .15 and the resulting individual error rate at .026.

prices cannot be differentiated from the prices of any of the other areas. When familywise $\alpha = .15$, the individual confidence intervals are reduced in size, with the result that Area 4 prices are differentiated from the prices for Areas 2 and 5. For familywise $\alpha = .15$, the mean prices form two distinct groups, Areas 1, 3, and 4 and Areas 2 and 5.

MANAGERIAL INTERPRETATION

The observed differences in Housing Prices in the five different Areas are real—price does vary according to area. The mean prices for Areas 1 and 3 are the same or similar, as are the prices for Areas 2 and 5. The mean prices for Area 4 could not be differentiated from the other areas with as much confidence, but they are probably different from the mean prices for Areas 2 and 5 and similar to Areas 1 and 3.

There is a price to be paid for the increased protection provided by a constant familywise error rate such as $\alpha = .05$, where an "error" refers to a confidence interval that fails to contain the population mean difference. Holding the familywise error rate constant implies that the error rate for the individual intervals *diminishes*. The more mean comparisons, the larger the decrease in α for each individual interval, which leads to a wider confidence interval. That is, the way to reduce the probability that the confidence interval will miss the true mean difference is to increase the width of the confidence interval, which diminishes the precision of estimation. A very wide confidence interval may include zero, so the null hypothesis of no difference would not be rejected, when in fact a difference could exist.

Once again, there is no free lunch. To obtain better precision, or equivalently, to minimize the probability of failing to reject a false null hypothesis, some analysts set the familywise error rate at a value higher than $\alpha = .05$, such as .10. Only so much information is available in any data set, and there is no way to avoid all possible errors. The best you can do is to be aware of the possible tradeoffs of each decision and the ways in which that decision may not be correct.

The discussion of HSD analysis of means for pinpointing group differences concludes our discussion of one-way ANOVA. One-way ANOVA is ANOVA with a single predictor variable called a treatment variable. The next chapter presents designs and corresponding versions of ANOVA that include *multiple* predictor variables.

EXERCISES

10-9. A one-way ANOVA with four groups and 10 observations per group yielded sample means of $\overline{Y}_1 = 47.9$, $\overline{Y}_2 = 41.8$, $\overline{Y}_3 = 46.2$, and $\overline{Y}_4 = 48.5$. MSE for this study is 2.8 and the *p*-value is 0.04.

a. Determine if an a posteriori analysis of mean differences should be conducted for these data.
b. If yes, compute and interpret the HSD confidence intervals for these groups.

Mechanical

10-10. Exercise 10-6 presents a one-way ANOVA with three groups.

Application

a. Determine if an a posteriori analysis of mean differences should be conducted for these data.
b. If yes, compute and interpret the HSD confidence intervals for these groups.

10.4 SUMMARY

The motivating question for all of the models introduced in this text is, "What causes variation in the response variable *Y*?" Statistics is the study of variation, and models are a primary vehicle for studying variation. This chapter introduced a model for independent samples experimental designs with one categorical predictor (treatment) variable and one response variable. The experimental design is a sampling plan for collecting data and a template for the statistical analysis of that data. Each value of the predictor (treatment) variable defines a group from which data are collected. The statistical analysis assesses the relation between the predictor variable and the response variable.

A true experiment includes manipulation of the values of the predictor or treatment variable with random assignment of the observations, such as people. If the data were collected as part of a true experiment, then changes in mean response values, depending on the value of the predictor variable, can be accounted for in terms of cause and effect. *If* changes are made in the level of the predictor variable, *then* predictable changes in the response variable will also occur. Unless the analyst creates the values of the predictor variable, the relations between the variables can still be properly analyzed, but causal inferences should not be made.

The statistical procedure that generalizes the analysis of two mean differences to many mean differences is the one-way ANOVA, which assumes equal within-group variances. The predictor variable for a one-way ANOVA may have two or more values that define the corresponding number of independent samples. The underlying model specifies that the value of a response variable depends on the grand mean of all of the values of the response variable, the effect of the group in terms of movement up or down from the grand mean, and random error that results in variation within each group. The pooled within-group variance s_{avg}^2 from the independent-samples *t*-test that estimates the population variance of *Y* for each group is another example of this within-group or conditional variability.

ANOVA is a family of related procedures that identifies up to four different sources of variation for the data collected according to an experimental design. The one-way ANOVA includes three of these sources of variation: total, between, and within. Total variation is computed ignoring group structure. Between-group variation reflects random error and any differences among population means. Within-group variation reflects only random error, the extent to which values within the same group vary around their own group mean. The estimated response value for each observation is the group mean, so within-group variation is error variation. The F-test of the one-way ANOVA is the ratio of the between-group variation to the within-group variation. The larger the value of F, the more likely that the null hypothesis of equal population means is false.

In the one-way ANOVA, the strength of the relation between the predictor or treatment variable and the response variable is summarized with an R^2 type of statistic. This chapter demonstrated how both R^2 and R^2_{adj} from regression analysis can be calculated in the context of a one-way ANOVA. A third statistic developed specifically for ANOVA with the categorical predictor variable is the estimated omega squared $\hat{\omega}^2$.

A significant F indicates that at least one pair of population means likely differs, but it does not identify the specific means that differ. When the null hypothesis of equal population means is rejected, all means may differ from each other, or only one mean may differ from the others. Tukey's honestly significant difference (HSD) test identifies patterns of mean differences *after* the data have been collected. The problem that results from these comparisons is that large differences can occur by chance, and when many comparisons are made, some population means may appear different when they are not. Tukey's HSD test is one of many available procedures for controlling the familywise error rate that results from these multiple comparisons.

10.5 KEY TERMS

experiment *436*
experimental design *435*
familywise error rate *462*
F-statistic *450*
grand mean *440*
mean squared error *445*
mean square between groups *442*

omega squared *453*
one-way ANOVA *439*
one-way independent groups design *436*
randomization *436*
total variation sums of squares *440*
treatment effect *441*
treatment variable *435*

10.6 REVIEW EXERCISES

ANALYSIS PROBLEMS

10-11. Provide the following cutoff values of the F-distribution.

Mechanical

a. $F_{.05}$ for 4 groups, 6 observations per group

b. $F_{.05}$ for 4 groups, 10 observations in the first group, 16 in the second group, and 12 in the third group

c. $F_{.05}$ for 3 groups, 6 observations per group

d. $F_{.05}$ for 2 groups, 29 observations in the first group and 22 in the second

10-12. Provide the following cutoff values of the F-distribution.

Concept

a. $F_{.05}$ for 2 groups, 10 observations per group

b. $F_{.05}$ for 3 groups, 10 observations per group

c. $F_{.05}$ for 4 groups, 10 observations per group

    d. $F_{.05}$ for 5 groups, 10 observations per group

    e. Draw conclusions about the size of the cutoff value and the number of groups in the study.

10-13. A restaurant manager investigated the relationship between menu display and sales. Two different menus were randomly handed out to customers throughout an entire week, with all customers at the same table receiving the same menu. All sales receipts were recorded with menu type.

    a. What is the treatment variable? What are the levels of the treatment variable?

    b. What is the response variable?

    c. Does this study represent an experiment? Why or why not? If not, name a variable that could account for any differences in the response variable means other than the treatment variable.

    d. If the null hypothesis of equal group population means is rejected, what can the manager conclude?

10-14. An independent polling service conducted a survey to see if men and women rated the president differently. One hundred men and 100 women rated the president on a 10-point scale with 10 being most favorable.

    a. What is the treatment variable? What are the levels of the treatment variable?

    b. What is the response variable?

    c. Does this study represent an experiment? Why or why not? If not, name a variable that could account for any differences in the response variable means other than the treatment variable.

    d. If the null hypothesis of equal group population means is rejected, what can the manager conclude?

10-15. The dean asked that two instructors who taught the same course and the same content administer a common final. The dean then compared final test scores across the two groups to evaluate teacher effectiveness.

    a. What is the treatment variable? What are the levels of the treatment variable?

    b. What is the response variable?

    c. Does this study represent an experiment? Why or why not? If not, name a variable that could account for any differences in the response variable means other than the treatment variable.

    d. If the null hypothesis of equal group population means is rejected, what can the manager conclude?

10-16. Complete the following one-way ANOVA summary table.

Source	SS	df	MS	F	p
Treatment	a.	2	1083.89	d.	0.02
Error	11065.84	b.	263.47		
Total	13233.62	c.			

    a. How many groups were in this study?

    b. How many experimental units (e.g., people) were in this study?

    c. Is the null hypothesis of equal group means rejected or not rejected? Why or why not?

Application

Application

Application

Mechanical

d. Calculate R^2, R^2_{adj}, and $\hat{\omega}^2$. How strong is the effect between the treatment variable A and the response variable Y?

10-17. Complete the following one-way ANOVA summary table.

Source	SS	df	MS	F	p
Treatment	18.32	b.	6.11	0.35	d.
Error	1343.68	76	c.		
Total	a.	79			

10-18. For the statistics presented in the ANOVA table in the previous exercise,

a. How many groups were in this study?

b. How many experimental units (e.g., people) were in this study?

c. Is the null hypothesis of equal group means rejected or not rejected? Why or why not?

d. Calculate R^2, R^2_{adj}, and $\hat{\omega}^2$. How strong is the effect between the predictor variable A and the response variable Y?

10-19. [*Complete data appear in Exercise 6-26.*] Two different methods of instruction were used in a management training program. Managers were randomly assigned to either the traditional Classroom-Lecture method (CLM) or the Computer Assisted Instruction method (CAI). None of the managers was familiar with the material at the beginning of training, and at the end of training a test was administered to all of the participants to evaluate their learning. For the 52 CLM managers, the mean score was 85.81 with standard deviation 8.58. For the 38 CAI managers, the mean score was 78.5 and the standard deviation was 8.67. Is there sufficient evidence to conclude that the two designs lead to different levels of learning?

10-20. [*Complete data appear in Exercise 6-3.*] A company was considering relocating to one of two midwestern cities. One factor in the decision is the amount of each city's annual snowfall. Over the last ten years, City A received an average of 39.2 inches of snow with a standard deviation of 8.0, and City B received an average of 48.8 inches of snow with a standard deviation of 11.3. Is there sufficient evidence to conclude that the two cities have differing amounts of snowfall?

10-21. [*Same data found in the Integrative Analysis Problem for Chapter 6.*] The owner of two restaurants wanted to compare the average cost of a meal at Restaurant A to the average cost of a meal at Restaurant B. Thirty-eight receipts at Restaurant A and 42 Restaurant B receipts were recorded. Assuming equal population variances, can a difference between population values be detected?

Restaurant A costs

14.66	9.47	13.85	15.98	11.46	15.70	13.18	11.60
12.88	14.71	2.94	10.34	15.18	18.12	17.25	16.95
17.60	12.60	12.77	10.88	7.25	11.12	12.76	9.81
7.91	16.33	16.13	12.16	16.11	12.36	12.08	10.12
8.79	10.75	13.69	13.29	8.55	12.66		

Restaurant B costs

12.95	19.59	8.38	13.53	7.78	16.21	13.97	12.22
15.41	10.93	10.07	14.45	5.35	10.01	10.31	10.80
6.20	7.93	14.52	9.58	13.26	20.26	14.09	11.20
8.87	13.59	10.12	13.32	12.30	7.83	13.32	14.04
11.12	11.16	13.52	13.44	9.17	13.11	9.63	9.53
11.88	10.68						

Application

10-22. [*Same as Exercise 6-28.*] Starting salaries were compared for graduating students from two M.B.A. programs. One of the programs recently began to emphasize quality management and the other program retained the traditional content. The respective mean starting salaries for the programs with and without quality management content are $43,740 ($n = 28$, $SD = \$3125$) and $41,688 ($n = 31$, $SD = \$3767$). Is there a difference in program means for all graduating student salaries in the two programs?

Application

10-23. Management wanted to assess the relative job satisfaction of its men and women employees. Using a job satisfaction inventory that yielded scores from 0 to 100 for maximum satisfaction, the data showed that 241 men averaged 88.2 with a standard deviation of 4.3, and 202 women averaged 87.8 with a standard deviation of 5.1. Is there a difference in job satisfaction for men versus women?

Application

10-24. A new manager who is a strong advocate of quality and customer service was assigned to a local bank. After collecting data on 150 customers, he discovered the unpleasant fact that these customers had to wait an average of 2.4 minutes for service with a standard deviation of .5 minutes. He immediately instituted a new personnel policy that provided for more tellers. After the policy implementation, a random check on 110 customers yielded an average wait time of 1.9 minutes with a standard deviation of .4 minutes. Did the policy make a difference?

Application

10-25. A consumers group compared the price of the most common size of automobile battery at three types of outlets in an urban area: discount stores that sell a variety of products, automobile repair shops, and automobile tire shops.

Store	Price
Disc.	47
Disc.	45
Disc.	41
Disc.	34
Repair	45
Repair	60
Repair	59
Repair	52
Tire	65
Tire	66
Tire	59
Tire	47

    a.   Does price vary by type of retail outlet?

    b.   How strong is the estimated relationship between retail outlet and price?

    c.   If the answer to (a) is yes, can any differences of knowledge attributable to specific types of retail outlets be concluded?

    d.   What is the estimated value for each store?

    e.   What is the residual for each value of the response variable?

Application

10-26. Management wanted to assess the effectiveness of different techniques used to teach the company's new employee relations policy. Before beginning the expensive task of educating the thousands of employees, sixteen employees were randomly selected and randomly assigned to one of four teaching methods, though one of the employees in the second teaching method left the company before his test score was obtained. One week after the class, employees were tested on their knowledge of the new policies. The percentage correct was recorded for each employee.

Class	Score
A1	93
A1	89
A1	93
A1	90
A2	96
A2	85
A2	88
A2	?
A3	89
A3	94
A3	90
A3	95
A4	99
A4	98
A4	97
A4	95

    a.   Does teaching method affect knowledge of the new policy as reflected by the test score?

    b.   How strong is the estimated relationship between teaching method and knowledge?

    c.   If the answer to (a) is yes, can any differences of knowledge attributable to specific teaching methods be concluded?

Application

10-27. A chemical engineer wanted to maximize the hardness of a rubber compound. The data from three different batches of chemical mixtures were evaluated for hardness, with a grand mean of 27.68 (the higher the number, the harder the object). The group summary statistics appear in the accompanying table.

Group	Size	Mean	SD
A1	16	24.25	7.79
A2	13	26.91	6.35
A3	19	31.09	8.96

a. Is the chemical mixture related to hardness?

b. If your answer to (a) is correct, which group differences can be detected using HSD confidence intervals?

Mechanical

10-28. A one-way ANOVA with three groups and fifteen observations per group yielded sample means of $\overline{Y}_1 = 76.49$, $\overline{Y}_2 = 85.09$, and $\overline{Y}_3 = 93.49$. MSE for this study is 263.47, and the p-value is 0.02.

a. Determine if an a posteriori analysis of mean differences should be conducted for these data and why or why not.

b. If yes, compute and interpret the HSD confidence intervals for these groups.

Application

10-29. Employees were to be trained on a new task. To facilitate this training, the written directions for part of the task need to be as clear as possible. Four different versions of the directions were written, and each of one of the versions was randomly administered to each of 44 employees. The amount of time needed to complete successfully the corresponding form was recorded, as reported in the following table.

Form 1	Form 2	Form 3	Form 4
10.28	17.64	18.50	19.45
19.25	10.47	13.49	23.37
9.23	24.97	16.36	14.61
23.92	22.78	34.98	30.86
20.02	24.23	19.18	29.89
16.97	15.12	23.35	15.27
22.52	17.31	22.88	32.21
14.71	21.10	13.32	24.12
13.21	22.89	24.14	26.24
20.85	19.05	19.11	21.29
4.99	23.23		16.92
13.12			

a. Does the amount of time needed to complete the form vary by type of form?

b. How strong is the estimated relationship between completion time and type of form?

c. What is the estimated completion time for each form?

    d.   If the answer to (a) is yes, can any differences of knowledge attributable to specific forms be concluded?

10-30. A product manager for a new brand of laundry detergent needed to choose a color for the box from among yellow, red, or green. Potential consumers were randomly assigned to one of three groups, eight per group, and asked to walk down a mock-up of a store aisle that contained the detergent in one of the three colors, plus a variety of competing detergents. The response variable was the amount of time in seconds that each person gazed at the detergent of interest, as recorded in the following table.

Yellow	Red	Green
4.56	2.98	2.77
4.31	4.96	3.37
3.58	4.87	4.26
4.11	3.63	4.14
4.02	4.57	2.70
0.99	3.24	3.95
4.71	5.61	4.25
5.34	5.25	6.56

    a.   Does the amount of time looking at the detergent vary by type of color?

    b.   How strong is the estimated relationship between gaze time and color?

    c.   What is the estimated gaze time for each color?

    d.   If the answer to (a) is yes, can any differences of knowledge attributable to specific colors be concluded?

10-31. This problem requires a computer program for generating random data. You might try Excel's Random Number Generation program, which is called up from the Data Analysis option in the Tools menu.

    a.   Generate three groups of 10 normally distributed observations, each with a population standard deviation of 15. Set the respective population means at 50, 60, and 70.

    b.   Determine if the null hypothesis of equal population means is correct. Conduct a one-way ANOVA on these three groups of data. Is the null hypothesis rejected?

    c.   Generate another three groups of 10 normally distributed observations, now each with a population standard deviation of 3. Again set the respective population means at 50, 60, and 70.

    d.   Conduct a one-way ANOVA on these three groups of data. Is the null hypothesis of equal population means correct? What is the result of the ANOVA? Is the null hypothesis rejected?

    e.   Explain the disparity of results in (b) and (d).

    f.   State how your explanation tempers any conclusions you might draw regarding the results of an ANOVA that did *not* lead to rejection of the null hypothesis.

DISCUSSION QUESTIONS

1. What is an experimental design?

2. When can causality be legitimately inferred in a statistical analysis?

3. When assessing causality with ANOVA, what variable is the cause and what variable is the effect?

4. Why is randomization of observations into groups crucial to the inference of cause and effect?

5. Why is the variable that defines the groups in a one-way ANOVA called a *predictor* variable?

6. What are the four sources of variation analyzed by an ANOVA?

7. How does the analysis of the variation of group means result in an estimate of the variance of the response variable within each group?

8. What is a treatment effect?

9. What is the model underlying a one-way ANOVA?

10. Why is the within-group sum of squares defined as the error variance?

11. How is the variance of the group means in one-way ANOVA analogous to the difference between the two group means in the independent groups t-test?

12. What effect does a false null hypothesis of no group mean differences have on the variability of group means?

13. What is an F-test?

14. Why cannot the largest difference between group means be identified and then analyzed for significance with an independent-samples t-test?

15. What is a familywise error rate? Why should it be controlled?

16. What is an honestly significant difference?

17. When conducting a Tukey HSD test, what method of displaying all combinations of sample mean differences facilitates identifying patterns of differences among the population means?

INTEGRATIVE ANALYSIS PROBLEM

A marketing manager was interested in assessing the relative effectiveness of three different television ads for her company's primary product. To conduct the assessment, 45 consumers were randomly assigned to three different groups. Consumers in each group viewed one of the ads, along with some distracting material. The next day, each person was evaluated on his or her recall of the ad. Higher scores indicate better recall. The variables Ad and Group appear in the data file ADS.DAT.

a. Identify the treatment variable. What are the levels of the treatment variable?

b. Identify the response variable.

c. Determine if this study represents an experiment and why or why not. If not, name a variable that could account for any differences in the response variable means other than the treatment variable.

d. Plot recall scores for each of the three groups on the same graph.

e. Calculate the sample standard deviation for each group. Does the assumption of equal population variances across the three groups appear reasonable?

f.   Conduct the one-way ANOVA for these data.

g.   Determine if the null hypothesis of equal population group means is rejected and why or why not.

h.   Determine if a causal relationship can be established between treatment variable and response variable and why or why not.

i.   Determine if an a posteriori analysis of means is appropriate and why or why not.

j.   If appropriate, conduct the a posteriori analysis of means and interpret the results.

k.   State the primary conclusions of this study.

Multiple Predictor Variable Designs

WHY DO WE CARE?

The previous chapter introduced the intertwined concepts of the experimental design or data collection plan that defines the group structure, as well as the accompanying statistical analysis guided by the underlying model. These designs and analyses were limited to documenting the effect of a single predictor variable, the treatment variable, on the response variable. The models underlying more potentially useful designs include multiple predictor variables. These more sophisticated models provide two distinct advantages over one-predictor variable models.

The data from experimental designs are analyzed according to a specific model. The value of the response variable should be close to the value predicted by the underlying model; otherwise, the accompanying statistical analysis will have little power to detect genuine group differences. Predictor variables can be added to a model solely to reduce the size of the errors. These additional variables themselves need not be of intrinsic interest, but their inclusion in the model can provide a more powerful statistical analysis for studying the group differences of primary interest.

Managers often want to understand the *simultaneous* influences of multiple predictor variables on the response variable of interest. In this situation, the predictor variables are treatment variables, which are of substantive interest. How do advertising revenue *and* package color jointly influence sales? How do tire pressure *and* type of gasoline jointly influence mileage? How do type of training *and* managerial style affect job satisfaction? Statistical procedures introduced in this chapter provide the manager with the tools to build and evaluate models that use multiple predictor variables, whether all of the predictor variables are of substantive interest or they are included simply to reduce the amount of error in the analysis.

A
s discussed in the previous chapter, for ANOVA the variables that predict the response *Y* are categorical variables. Each value of one of these categorical variables defines a group, a distinct population from which values are sampled according to the sampling plan specified by the experimental design. Designs in the previous chapter included a single predictor variable *A* and a single response variable *Y*. The data from these designs could be analyzed with the independent-samples *t*-test for two groups defined by variable *A* and the one-way ANOVA for two or more groups.

This chapter introduces experimental designs with more than a single predictor variable. The first type of design that includes another predictor variable adds the variable solely to reduce error variance so that the first predictor variable, the treatment variable, can be studied more effectively. Later in the chapter, two-predictor variable models are studied in which both predictors are treatment variables of substantive interest.

11.1 RANDOMIZED BLOCK DESIGN

For an independent-samples design, the order of the data for each group could be randomly shuffled because data in one group were not linked to data in the other group or groups. Data for dependent samples, however, are collected in blocks. As defined at the end of Chapter 6, each block is a set of *matched data* across the groups. Each data value in one group has a matching data value in another group, so that a block could consist of two or more measures of the same employee, graduating college GPA of college students with the same entering SAT score, or a husband and wife's scores on a marital satisfaction questionnaire.

The dependent-samples *t*-test (Chapter 6) allows any number of blocks but only two groups. For example, one group of scores could consist of assembly times by employees using the standard assembly method. The second group of scores could consist of assembly times by the same employees using a proposed revised method. For analysis with a dependent-samples *t*-test, the study could include the assembly times of 10, 20, or a 100 employees (blocks) but only two groups of scores defined by two treatment levels: Standard Procedure and Revised Procedure.

The ANOVA generalization of the dependent-samples *t*-test, the **randomized block design,** allows for more than two groups. For example, performance could be evaluated for three different assembly procedures—the standard procedure and two proposed alternatives. In this design, each value of the response variable *Y*, assembly time, is matched with another value of *Y* in each of the remaining two groups.

The layout of a randomized block design with three levels appears in Figure 11-1. Contrast this layout with the layout in the previous chapter of the corresponding one-way independent groups design with three levels. In the design in Figure 11-1, the data are organized according to blocks, and each of the three observations in a block are randomly assigned to one of the three treatment levels: *A*1, *A*2, or *A*3. For example, if the treatment variable Assembly Method is defined by three assembly methods, then the order in which each employee used each method would be randomly determined. The first employee might be assigned the second method first, the third method second, and the first method last. The second employee would likely perform the assemblies in an entirely different order.

The analyst usually sets the *p* values of the treatment variable. The types of teaching methods, the suppliers of the critical part, or the temperature settings of

randomized block design

sampling plan in which observations (e.g., people) are assigned to blocks, and then each observation in a block is randomly assigned to one of the p levels of a single treatment variable

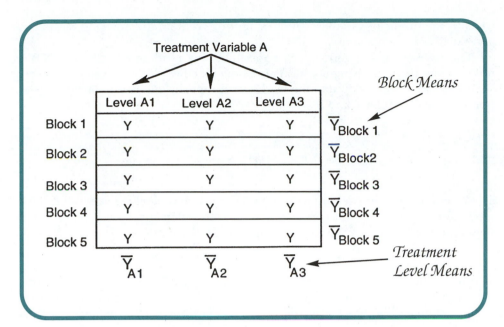

the oven are explicitly chosen before data collection. A replication of the study with new data would use the same values of the treatment variable. The values of the blocking variable, however, are typically random. Employees may be matched by test scores across the design, but the employees were not chosen in advance of the study. Instead, the employees were randomly sampled, and then a new set of employees would be obtained if the study were repeated.

Corresponding to the randomized block design is the statistical procedure for analysis of the resulting data. This design answers exactly the same question addressed by the one-way independent groups design: Do the population means of the response variable differ across treatment levels? As with the dependent-samples *t*-test, the **randomized block ANOVA** removes from the error term the corresponding systematic variation due to differences in blocks. When the blocking variable—employee, entering SAT score, or marital unit—is related to the response variable, the size of the error variation can be greatly reduced. For example, some employees simply assemble parts faster than do other employees.

> *This smaller error term resulting from removing variation due to the blocking variable yields a more powerful test for detecting differences across levels of the treatment variable.*

An appropriate blocking variable yields a test more sensitive to uncovering differences among treatment means of the response variable.

The analysis of the randomized block design also provides a test of the equality of group means for each block, but that test is incidental. The differences among means of the response variable for different blocks should be significant, because if the blocking variable did not relate to the response variable, it would not be included as part of the design. The purpose of including the blocks is not to analyze the blocks per se, but to provide a more effective analysis of the treatment variable,

> **randomized block ANOVA**
> *evaluates differences among population means of the response variable for two or more levels of a single treatment variable, with a blocking variable to minimize error*

which is the predictor variable of interest. For this reason, the blocking variable is also called a *nuisance variable*.

The assessment of random error variability for randomized block ANOVA follows from the underlying model. This model specifies that each value of the response variable Y is accounted for by the grand mean, the effects of the corresponding treatment level and block, and random error.

> *Model for randomized block ANOVA:*
> $Y = grand\ mean\ +\ trt\ level\ effect\ +\ block\ effect\ +\ random\ error$

The two predictor variables are treatment variable A and blocking variable K. This model for a value of response variable Y in the ath group and the kth block is, for population parameters or sample estimates, respectively,

$$Y = \mu + \beta_a + \beta_k + \varepsilon \quad \text{or} \quad Y = \overline{\overline{Y}} + b_a + b_k + e.$$

The grand mean μ or $\overline{\overline{Y}}$ is the common influence on all values of Y. Just as the treatment effect β_a or b_a indicates how far a treatment level moves the group mean from the grand mean, the block effect β_k or b_k indicates how far a particular block is from the grand mean. The definition of a block effect follows the same form as the definition of a treatment effect:

$$\beta_k = \mu_k - \mu \quad \text{or} \quad b_k = \overline{Y}_k - \overline{\overline{Y}}.$$

That is, how far is the kth block mean from the grand mean $\overline{\overline{Y}}$? The values of Y in some blocks are higher than the grand mean, and the values in other blocks are lower. For example, because some employees generally assemble parts faster than other employees do, those with a positive block effect are faster than average, and those with a negative block effect are slower than average.

The *estimated* value $\hat{Y}$ of the response variable in a randomized block ANOVA model consists of the combined effects of the grand mean, treatment level, and block:

$$\hat{Y} = \overline{\overline{Y}} + b_a + b_k$$
$$\equiv \overline{\overline{Y}} + (\overline{Y}_a - \overline{\overline{Y}}) + (\overline{Y}_k - \overline{\overline{Y}}).$$

After accounting for $\hat{Y}$, what is left over? The answer is error—ε in the population and sample estimate e—the residual unique to each value of the response variable Y. Errors are deviations from the estimated value $\hat{Y}$,

$$e \equiv Y - \hat{Y}.$$

Any variation unexplained by the predictable component of the model is due to variation of the error component s_e^2 or MSE. An error score is calculated for each observation, so MSE is computed from the sum of squares for error SSE across all values of Y. The degrees of freedom for the error term is

$$df_E = (p - 1)(k - 1).$$

As before, MSE is the ratio of SSE to df_E.

Why bother with the added complexity of adding a blocking variable to the design? The answer is the same as the reason for moving from a regression model with a single predictor to multiple regression, as discussed in Chapter 9: adding a blocking variable related to the response variable Y reduces error variability.

Table 11-1.
Randomized block
ANOVA summary table.

Source	SS	df	MS	F	p
Treatment A (Between)	$\sum b_a^2$	$p - 1$	SSA/df_A	MSA/MSE	<.05?
Blocks K (Between)	$\sum b_k^2$	$k - 1$	SSA/df_K	MSK/MSE	<.05?
Error (Interaction)	$\sum e^2$	$(p - 1)(k - 1)$	SSE/df_E		
Total	$\sum (Y - \bar{\bar{Y}})$	$N - 1$			

The addition of the blocking variable as a new predictor further partitions the error sum of squares from the one-way ANOVA into variation due to blocks (SSK) and the new, reduced error variation (SSE). Summing the components of the model for Y across all observations, along with some algebraic manipulations, leads to the following partitioning of variance.

$$
\begin{array}{cccccc}
\text{Total variation} & & \text{Variation} & & \text{Variation} & & \text{Error} \\
\text{of the response} & = & \textit{between} \text{ levels of} & + & \textit{between} & + & \text{variation} \\
\text{variable } Y & & \text{treatment } A & & \text{blocks} &
\end{array}
$$

or

$$
\text{SST} \quad = \quad \text{SSA} \quad + \quad \text{SSK} \quad + \quad \text{SSE}
$$

For the one-way ANOVA, the error sum of squares SSE is the within-group variability. For a randomized block ANOVA, the sum of the squared errors is another one of the four basic expressions of variability in ANOVA: an *interaction* variability. The meaning and interpretation of an interaction is further explored in the next section. We identify SSE as an interaction here for the sake of completeness, because each source of variation in any ANOVA table is one of the four fundamental forms.

The computation of the sum of squares for the predictor variable SSA follows exactly the same between-group procedure as the one-way independent groups design. The blocks sum of squares SSK is also a between-group sum of squares, so its calculation also follows this form,

$$
\text{SSK} \equiv \sum (\overline{Y}_k - \overline{\overline{Y}})^2
$$

for *all* N observations in the analysis, where $\overline{Y}_k$ is the mean of the kth block. The degrees of freedom for blocks is the number of blocks minus one, $df_K = k - 1$. The complete summary appears in Table 11-1.

The purpose of the analysis is to evaluate the relation between each source of variation on the resultant response variable variation. One aspect of this investigation is the test of the two null hypotheses, one for the treatment and one for blocks. The strength of association between predictor (treatment) variable A and the response variable Y for the randomized block designs is assessed by estimated omega squared ω^2. This fit index is defined exactly as in the previous chapter for the one-way independent groups design,

$$
\hat{\omega}_A^2 = \frac{(df_A)(F_A - 1)}{(df_A)(F_A - 1) + N} ,
$$

where N is the total number of observations in the analysis, df_A is the degrees of freedom for the treatment variable, and F_A is the F-statistic for the treatment variable. With the blocks removing systematic variance out of the error term, ω^2 for the treatment variable from the randomized block design is higher than that obtained from the one-way independent groups design.

Evaluation of specific pairs of mean differences for the predictor variable *after* the data are collected and analyzed follows the same procedure for the one-way ANOVA introduced in the previous chapter. The Tukey HSD standard error for the mean difference $\overline{Y}_i - \overline{Y}_j$ in the randomized block ANOVA is the same as that presented for the one-way ANOVA,

$$s_{\mathrm{HSD}} = \sqrt{\frac{\mathrm{MSE}}{n}}.$$

The HSD confidence interval around a mean difference at a 5% familywise error rate is computed as before,

$$\overline{Y}_i - \overline{Y}_j \pm q_{.05} s_{\mathrm{HSD}}.$$

Degrees of freedom for the $q_{.05}$ statistic is $df = (p - 1)(n - 1)$.

An example of a randomized block ANOVA follows. For purposes of comparison, this example uses exactly the same data as that from the one-way ANOVA example from the previous chapter. For this example, the values of the response variable Y are separated into blocks, with each driver/car combination experiencing all three groups.

BUSINESS APPLICATION 11.1—Randomized Block ANOVA

MANAGERIAL PROBLEM

The vehicle maintenance manager who oversees a large fleet of company cars wants to maximize gas mileage for the fleet. His concern is the causal influence of Engine Oil on Miles per Gallon (MPG) of gasoline. Do the three different engine oils (1, 2, and 3) lead to different gasoline mileage?

STATISTICAL HYPOTHESIS

Null hypothesis H_0: $\mu_1 = \mu_2 = \mu_3$.
Alternative hypothesis H_1: some means are not equal.

DATA

Three different engine oils were selected to examine their potential effect on MPG. The same model car was used for each of the tests, with 16 different measurements of MPG. Because different drivers and cars get different mileage, four drivers and cars were randomly assigned to each of the three types of engine oils. The resulting MPG's after one month of normal driving are presented opposite.

Driver	Oil A1	Oil A2	Oil A3	Mean
1	27.2	27.8	30.4	28.47
2	23.8	28.4	28.0	26.73
3	27.2	34.9	33.5	31.87
4	20.5	26.3	23.1	23.30
Mean	24.68	29.35	28.75	27.59

EXCEL GRAPHICAL ANALYSIS

Excel Output

The plot suggests distinct differences among drivers, with Driver 3 able to obtain the best gas mileage and Driver 4 obtaining the least gas mileage. To the extent that these differences generalize to the population, Driver would be an effective blocking variable for reducing the size of the random errors, yielding a more sensitive test for detecting potential differences among Oil Types.

OBTAINING THE OUTPUT

Insert ➤ Chart...

Step 1—Chart Type. Specify a Line chart, which is for a categorical horizontal axis. Select a format that connects the points.

Figure 11-2. Plot of MPG depending on type of Engine Oil for the four different drivers.

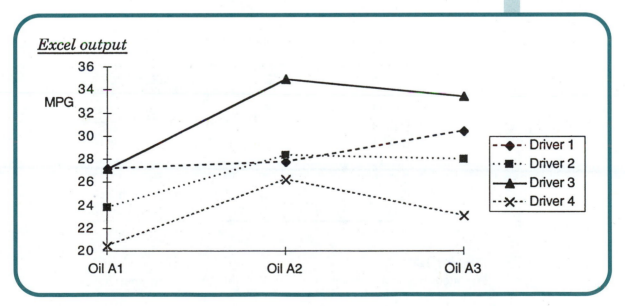

Step 2—Chart Source. For the Data Range, specify the cells that include the data. Include the labels D1, D2, D3, and D4 as well as Oil1, Oil2, and Oil3 in the specification. Also, specify that the series be displayed in rows.

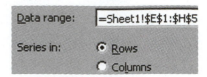

Step 3—Chart Options. Under the Titles tab, name the *X* and *Y* axes.

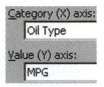

Step 4—Chart Location. Specify the location of the chart, either on a new sheet or as an object on the current worksheet.

APPLICATION—EXCEL BUILT-IN ANALYSIS

Group and Marginal Means

The ANOVA statistical output is displayed in two sections. The section labeled SUMMARY presents the descriptive statistics for level of blocks and treatment variables.

Anova: Two-Factor Without Replication				
SUMMARY	Count	Sum	Average	Variance
Driver1	3	85.40	28.47	2.89
Driver2	3	80.20	26.73	6.49
Driver3	3	95.60	31.87	16.82
Driver4	3	69.90	23.30	8.44
Oil1	4	98.70	24.68	10.32
Oil2	4	117.40	29.35	14.47
Oil3	4	115.00	28.75	19.26

Summary Table

The second part of the statistical output is the ANOVA summary table.

Drivers
(Blocks)

Oil →
(Treatment)

ANOVA						
Source of Variation	SS	df	MS	F	P-value	F crit
Rows	114.59	3	38.20	13.07	0.00	4.76
Columns	51.76	2	25.88	8.85	0.02	5.14
Error	17.54	6	2.92			
Total	183.89	11				

The Output

Tools ➤ Data Analysis ➤
Anova: Two-Factor Without Replication

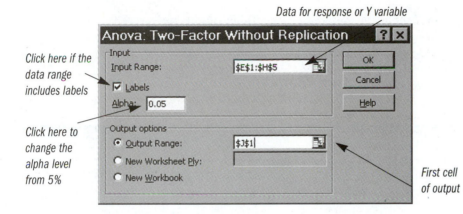

Data for response or Y variable

Click here if the data range includes labels

Click here to change the alpha level from 5%

First cell of output

APPLICATION—SUM OF SQUARES CONCEPTUAL WORKSHEET

The grand mean of gas mileage is $\overline{\overline{Y}} = 27.59$. The estimated value for each observation is the sum of the respective Oil and Driver effects on the grand mean. That is, how far up or down do the levels of Oil and the Driver move the response value? For Observation 1, which is in Group 1 with Driver 1, subtract the grand mean from the treatment mean to obtain the treatment effect of the first level of the treatment, Oil 1.

$$\text{Effect of Oil 1: } \overline{Y}_{A1} - \overline{\overline{Y}} = 24.68 - 27.59 = -2.92$$

To obtain the block effect of Driver 1, subtract the grand mean from the block mean for Driver 1.

$$\text{Effect of Driver 1: } \overline{Y}_{K1} - \overline{\overline{Y}} = 28.47 - 27.59 = 0.88.$$

Calculate the estimated value of the response variable for the first observation from these estimated effects:

$$\hat{Y} = \overline{\overline{Y}} + b_a + b_k = 27.59 - 2.92 + 0.88 = 25.55.$$

The actual MPG for Observation 1 is 27.2, so the residual is the estimated value subtracted from the measured value:

$$e \equiv Y - \hat{Y} = 27.2 - 25.55 = 1.65.$$

The estimated values, deviations, and squared deviations appear in Table 11-2 across all observations for three different sums of squares, SSA, SSK, and SSE.

APPLICATION—TRADITIONAL NOTATION

Mean Squares

Estimate of error variability is

$$\text{MSE} \equiv \frac{\text{SSE}}{df_E} = \frac{17.54}{(p-1)(k-1)} = \frac{17.54}{6} = 2.92.$$

Estimate of the mean square between Types of Oil is

$$\text{MSA} \equiv \frac{\text{SSA}}{df_A} = \frac{51.76}{p-1} = \frac{51.76}{2} = 25.88.$$

Table 11-2. Predicted values (of response variable MPG) and residuals for the randomized block design, with three groups (Oil Type) and four blocks (Drivers), $\hat{Y} = 27.59 + b_a + b_k$.

Trt	Block	Respns							
Oil	Driver	Actual MPG	Oil Effect	Driver Effect	Pred MPG	Residual	Residual Squared	Oil Efct Squared	Drv Efct Squared
A	K	Y	b_a	b_k	$\hat{Y}$	e	e^2	b_a^2	b_k^2
A1	K1	27.2	-2.92	0.88	25.55	1.65	2.72	8.53	0.77
A1	K2	23.8	-2.92	-0.86	23.82	-0.02	0.00	8.53	0.74
A1	K3	27.2	-2.92	4.28	28.95	-1.75	3.06	8.53	18.32
A1	K4	20.5	-2.92	-4.29	20.38	0.12	0.01	8.53	18.40
A2	K1	27.8	1.76	0.88	30.23	-2.43	5.88	3.10	0.77
A2	K2	28.4	1.76	-0.86	28.49	-0.09	0.01	3.10	0.74
A2	K3	34.9	1.76	4.28	33.63	1.28	1.63	3.10	18.32
A2	K4	26.3	1.76	-4.29	25.06	1.24	1.54	3.10	18.40
A3	K1	30.4	1.16	0.88	29.63	0.77	0.60	1.35	0.77
A3	K2	28.0	1.16	-0.86	27.89	0.11	0.01	1.35	0.74
A3	K3	33.5	1.16	4.28	33.03	0.48	0.23	1.35	18.32
A3	K4	23.1	1.16	-4.29	24.46	-1.36	1.85	1.35	18.40
	Sum	331.10	0.00	0.00		0.00	17.54	51.76	114.59
	Mean	27.59					SSE	SSA	SSK

Estimate of the mean square between Drivers is

$$MSK \equiv \frac{SSK}{df_K} = \frac{114.59}{k-1} = \frac{114.59}{3} = 38.20.$$

The F-statistic for the treatment variable Oil Type is

$$F_A \equiv \frac{MSA}{MSE} = \frac{25.88}{2.92} = 8.85$$

with a p-value of 0.016. The F-statistic for the blocks (Drivers) is

$$F_K \equiv \frac{MSK}{MSE} = \frac{28.20}{2.92} = 13.07$$

with a p-value of 0.005. That is, the Driver has an effect on mileage, as anticipated by including this variable in the design as a blocking variable.

Strength of Association

$$\hat{\omega}^2 = \frac{(p-1)(F_A-1)}{(p-1)(F_A-1)+np} = \frac{(3-1)(8.85-1)}{(3-1)(8.85-1)+(4)(3)} = .567.$$

STATISTICAL PRINCIPLE

Because of the systematic differences among the drivers, the randomized block design is more powerful at detecting real differences among the treatment levels—the Types of Oil—than is the corresponding one-way ANOVA (from an application in the last chapter). The advantage of the randomized block design is that the variance in the response variable due to Drivers is partialled out of the error term. This more expansive model identifies a distinct source—Driver—for what was previously modeled as statistical noise. The reduced statistical noise SSE yields both a more powerful F-test for evaluating differences among Oil Types, as well as indicates a stronger relationship between Oil Type and MPG.

In the one-way ANOVA, SSE is 132.13 with $df = 9$. The resulting MSE is 14.68. In this randomized block ANOVA of the same data organized with four blocks of drivers,

$$SSK + SSE = 114.589 + 17.538 = 132.13,$$

$$df_K + df_E = 3 + 6 = 9.$$

Adding Blocks of Drivers as a new predictor variable literally pulls the sum of squares due to individual Drivers out of the error sum of squares. The result is a smaller error term SSE and, consequently, MSE, which is the denominator of the F-test. Also, the strength of the relationship between the treatment variable Oil Type and the response variable MPG, as indicated by $\hat{\omega}^2$, increased from .113 all the way to .567.

MANAGERIAL INTERPRETATION

Oil Type affects MPG. Some engine oils lead to better gas mileage than do other engine oils.

As stated previously, the dependent-samples *t*-test analyzes data from a randomized block design with two groups. What happens if a randomized block ANOVA is also used to analyze blocked data from this same design? As with the independent-samples *t*-test and the one-way ANOVA applied to data from a one-way design, the results are equivalent—for both analyses the exact same *p*-value is obtained, with the corresponding value of *F* equal to the square of the obtained value of *t*.

We have seen that the one-way independent groups design from the last chapter can be improved upon by adding another predictor variable—a blocking variable—to the model. The next section presents another generalization of the one-way ANOVA design: the addition of another predictor of substantive interest to the model, another *treatment variable*.

EXERCISES

11-1. Complete the following randomized block ANOVA summary table.

Mechanical

Source	df	SS	MS	F	p
Trt	a.	62.35	31.18	d.	0.055
Block	4	b.	11.17	1.52	e.
Error	8	58.69	7.34		
Total	14	c.			

11-2. For the statistics presented in the ANOVA table in the previous exercise,

Mechanical

a. How many groups were in this study?
b. How many blocks were in this study?
c. Is the null hypothesis of equal group means rejected or not rejected? Why or why not?
d. Was the blocking variable worthwhile? Why or why not?
e. Calculate $\hat{\omega}^2$ for treatment variable *A*. How strong is the effect between Treatment *A* and response variable *Y*?

11-3. [*Same problem from Chapter 6.*] The manager of a weight-reduction program weighed 10 participants before the program began and then again after the program was successfully completed. The following weights were recorded.

Person	1	2	3	4	5	6	7	8	9	10
Before	220	187	265	314	219	172	183	202	298	174
After	206	189	254	289	215	163	180	202	291	163

Evaluate the effectiveness of the program with a randomized block ANOVA.

11-4. A manufacturer of cold breakfast cereal was concerned that the location of product on the shelf from the end of the aisle to the middle might influence sales. To test this idea, she had three different distances noted on standard grocery shelves: the end, between the end and middle, and the middle. To control for variation in sales at different stores, five different stores served as blocks. Sales in cartons of the cereal boxes were recorded over one week.

Trt	Blk	Y
Dist	Store	Sales
1	1	10
1	2	12
1	3	12
1	4	17
1	5	17
2	1	10
2	2	11
2	3	16
2	4	16
2	5	13
3	1	11
3	2	17
3	3	17
3	4	20
3	5	16

a. Does distance from the end of the shelf affect purchases?

b. How strong is the estimated relationship between distance and number of purchases?

c. Was the blocking variable effective?

d. What are the estimated group effects?

e. What is the predicted number of purchases for each distance?

11.2 FACTORIAL DESIGNS AND INTERACTION

The last chapter introduced the one-way independent groups design and corresponding ANOVA. The model underlying this design has a single predictor variable: the treatment variable. The randomized block design from the last section generalized further by adding another predictor variable to the model: the blocking variable. The current section generalizes from the one-way model of the last chapter by adding a second predictor variable to the design, but the additional variable is another treatment variable. These designs and their associated statistical analysis allow simultaneous study of the effect of several treatment variables on the response variable.

A primary advantage of including multiple treatment variables is the ability to study the interaction between the two variables. To illustrate, consider the rather plebeian example of the tastiness of a peanut butter and jelly sandwich. The response variable in this little experiment is Tastiness and the treatment variables are sandwich ingredients: Peanut Butter and Jelly. Each treatment variable has two levels: present and absent. This experiment has four groups of observations: some people eat only Plain Bread, others have only Peanut Butter on the bread, others have only Jelly on the bread, and some have both Peanut Butter and Jelly on the bread. After munching a few bites, each person rates his or her sandwich for the response variable Tastiness on a scale from 0 to 50. The resulting group means are presented in Figure 11-3.

What are the results of this hypothetical investigation? By itself, plain bread rates an average tastiness score of only 10. Peanut Butter alone makes the sandwich much tastier than plain bread. On the average, Peanut Butter by itself contributes 8 points to the Tastiness rating, for a score of 18. Jelly by itself with the bread is also much tastier than plain bread. On the average, Jelly contributes 12 tastiness points, for an average score of 22.

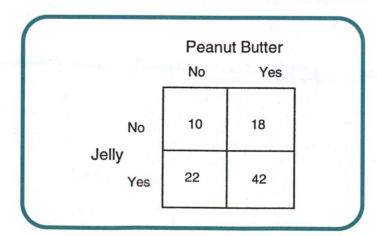

Figure 11-3.
Group means for each of the four combinations of Peanut Butter and Jelly.

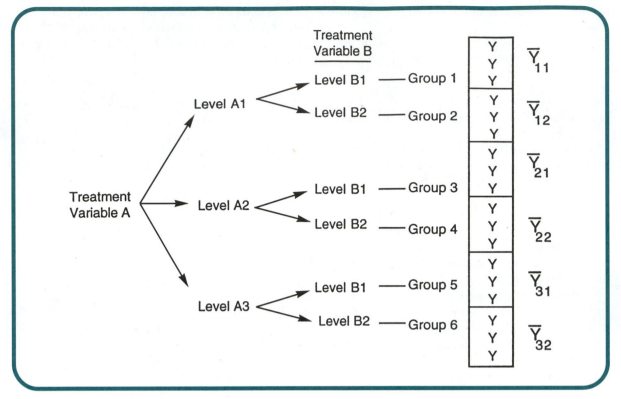

Figure 11-4.
Layout for a completely crossed factorial design, with three levels of Treatment *A*, two levels of Treatment *B*, and, in this example, three values of the response variable *Y* per group.

completely randomized factorial design
sampling plan in which observations are randomly assigned to groups, one group for each combination of p levels of one treatment variable and q levels of another treatment variable

What is an interaction? Consider Peanut Butter and Jelly together. The tastiness of this combination is much more than expected from adding together the separate effects of Peanut Butter and Jelly. If there is *no* interaction, Peanut Butter and Jelly together would result in an average Tastiness increase over plain bread that is the sum of their individual effects, $8 + 12 = 20$, for a total Tastiness score of $10 + 20 = 30$. However, most of us know that an increase of 20 on a scale from 0 to 50 is not enough. Instead, Peanut Butter and Jelly *interact*—the combination of ingredients results in more than the addition of their separate contribution, resulting in an average Tastiness value of a whopping 42. Peanut Butter is good, Jelly is good, but Peanut Butter and Jelly together are awesome!

As with the Peanut Butter and Jelly example, the simplest factorial design is defined by two treatment variables. Each possible combination of treatment levels defines a group of observations. A key characteristic of the **completely randomized factorial design** is *completely crossed* treatment variables—each level of one treatment variable occurs once with each level of the other treatment variable. An example of a completely crossed factorial design appears in Figure 11-4, where $p = 3$ and $q = 2$. For example, Group A1 occurs with each of the two levels of Treatment B, represented by Groups 1 and 2 in the following diagram. Each observation is randomly assigned to one of the groups.

To introduce the analysis of the data obtained from a completely crossed factorial design for Treatment variables *A* and *B*, consider the means obtained from a one-way independent groups design, as illustrated in Figure 11-5. The one-way design has one treatment variable, *A*, with $p = 3$ levels, but in this analysis Treat-

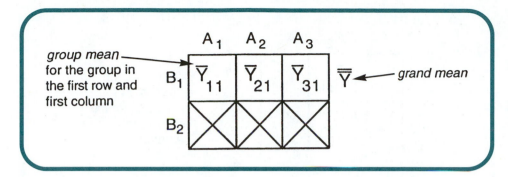

Figure 11-5.
The means for a one-way independent groups design with three levels in the context of a completely crossed factorial design, with three levels of one treatment and two levels of the other treatment variable.

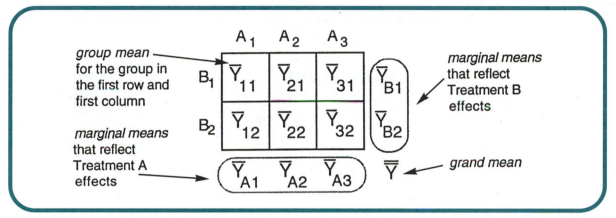

Figure 11-6.
The means for a completely crossed factorial design.

ment B only has one level. All observations have the same value of Treatment B, a constant for this analysis. The one-way design generates three group means and one grand mean of all of the data. The one-way ANOVA for the analysis of these data compares the between-group variability of group means around the grand mean to the within-group variability of each value around the corresponding group mean.

Now consider the additional information when Treatment B with two levels enters the design as another predictor variable. This completely crossed factorial design has $3 \times 2 = 6$ groups and corresponding group means, as presented in Figure 11-6, with $\overline{Y}_{ab}$ the mean for Group $A_a B_b$. As with the one-way designs, there is only one grand mean. However, another set of means is included in the analysis of factorial designs.

The **marginal means** are the means at the margins of the table. The notations for group means, marginal means, and the grand mean are shown in Figure 11-6. For example, the marginal mean $\overline{Y}_{A1}$ is the average of all values of the response variable Y at the first level of Treatment A. These values are from the groups at both the first and second levels of Treatment B.

How are these data analyzed? One purpose of the **two-way factorial ANOVA** is exactly the same as for the one-way ANOVA and randomized block ANOVA already introduced: Do the population means of each of the treatment variables differ? Also, the concept of interaction must be considered. Unlike the one-way ANOVA,

marginal mean of a treatment level
mean of the response variable Y for all values of the treatment level, which are averaged over all levels of the remaining treatment variable

two-way factorial ANOVA
evaluates differences among population means of the response variable for all possible combinations of the levels of two treatment variables

Figure 11-7.
Estimate of a main
effect $\overline{Y}_{A1} - \overline{\overline{Y}}$ for the
first level of Treatment A
averaged over the levels
of Treatment B.

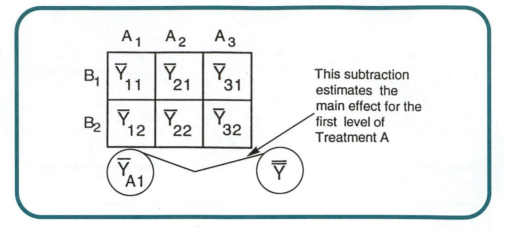

factorial designs should have the same number of observations within each group, or the analysis becomes considerably more complicated.

To evaluate the effect of a level of Treatment A in a one-way ANOVA, the grand mean is subtracted from the corresponding group mean, $\overline{Y}_a - \overline{\overline{Y}}$. In a factorial design, however, several groups all have the same value of the treatment variable. One method for assessing the effect of a level of Treatment A is to average across all values of the response variable Y at that level. That is, compare the marginal mean to the grand mean. Specifically, the **main effect** of a treatment level is evaluated by subtracting the corresponding marginal mean from the grand mean. For example, the effect of the first level of Treatment A is estimated as $\overline{Y}_{A1} - \overline{\overline{Y}}$. Figure 11-7 illustrates the main effect.

The effect of a single group can also be evaluated in a factorial design, as is done in a one-way ANOVA. Evaluate the **simple main effect** of the group by subtracting a group mean from the corresponding marginal mean at the same level of the other treatment variable. Figure 11-8 illustrates a simple main effect.

There is also an interaction effect in the analysis of a factorial design, which also includes total variation, between-group variation, and within-group variation. Before introducing this effect, we discuss the simpler two-way factorial ANOVA in the context of data that exhibit no interaction.

> **main effect of a
> treatment level**
> *average over all
> levels of the other
> treatment variable
> minus the grand
> mean*

> **simple main effect of
> a group**
> *mean of Y for the
> group minus the
> average of a single
> level of the other
> treatment variable*

Two Treatment Variables with No Interaction

If the data exhibit no interaction, then the value of a group mean is estimated from knowledge of the grand mean and both treatment effects. Without interaction, the only source of variation left from the influence of the grand mean and the group effects is the random error exhibited by within-group variation.

> *Additive model for two-way factorial ANOVA:*
> $Y = $ *grand mean* $+$ *Trt A effect* $+$ *Trt B effect* $+$ *random error*

The additive model for this factorial design involves only the grand mean and the treatment effects. The additive model for the population and sample, respectively, is

$$Y = \mu + \beta_a + \beta_b + \varepsilon \quad \text{or} \quad Y = \overline{\overline{Y}} + b_a + b_b + e \quad [\textit{no interaction}].$$

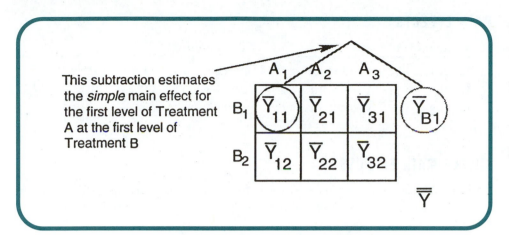

This subtraction estimates the *simple* main effect for the first level of Treatment A at the first level of Treatment B

Figure 11-8.
Estimate of a *simple* main effect $\overline{Y}_{11} - \overline{Y}_{B1}$ for the first level of Treatment *A* at the first level of Treatment *B*.

In this model, Y refers to the value of the response variable for an observation in the ath group of Treatment variable A and the bth group for Treatment variable B. The ath group effect for A is represented by β_a or b_a, and the bth group effect for B is represented by β_b or b_b.

The factorial design permits the simultaneous study of the effect of two treatment variables on the response variable. An example without interaction follows.

STATISTICAL ILLUSTRATION—Two-Way Factorial Design without Interaction

DATA

To illustrate the lack of an interaction in the absence of the blurring effects of sampling error, population data are used. Figure 11-9 presents the means and accompanying graph.[1] The same principles apply to real data with sampling error but all group means would only approximate the population values implied by the model.

Figure 11-9.
Means and plot of means for a two-way factorial design with no interaction.

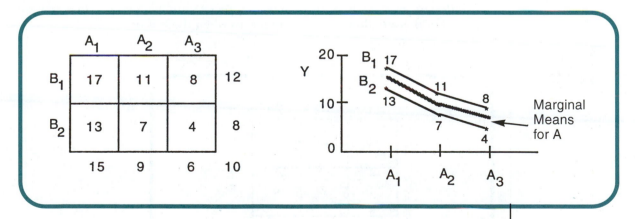

1. In Chapter 2, we noted that the points in the graph for a categorical variable (such as a predictor variable in ANOVA) should not be connected by a straight line, which indicates continuity. However, the means from a plot of the results of an ANOVA are traditionally connected by these lines, even though the values of the variable are categorical.

MAIN EFFECTS

Treatment A		Treatment B	
Level 1:	$\overline{Y}_{A1} - \overline{\overline{Y}} = 15 - 10 = 5$	Level 1:	$\overline{Y}_{B1} - \overline{\overline{Y}} = 12 - 10 = 2$
Level 2:	$\overline{Y}_{A2} - \overline{\overline{Y}} = 9 - 10 = -1$	Level 2:	$\overline{Y}_{B2} - \overline{\overline{Y}} = 8 - 10 = -2$
Level 3:	$\overline{Y}_{A3} - \overline{\overline{Y}} = 6 - 10 = -4$		

SIMPLE MAIN EFFECTS

All of the simple main effects are exactly the same as the corresponding main effects. For example, the simple main effects for Level 1 of Treatment A are

$$\text{at Level 1 of Treatment } B: \overline{Y}_{11} - \overline{Y}_{B1} = 17 - 12 = 5$$

$$\text{at Level 2 of Treatment } B: \overline{Y}_{21} - \overline{Y}_{B2} = 13 - 8 = 5,$$

and the corresponding main effect also equals 5. That is, the simple main effects for A are *same* at *each* level of B. The same relationship between simple main effects and main effects applies for Treatment B.

Figure 11-10 illustrated another aspect of the similarity between the simple main effects and the main effects. Differences between adjacent row and column means, including the marginal means, are constant.

ESTIMATED VALUES

Consider Group A_1B_2, with $\overline{Y} = 13$. According to the additive model, the estimated value is the grand mean of 10 plus the effect of the Treatment A main effect of 5 plus the Treatment B main effect of -2:

$$\hat{Y} = 10 + 5 - 2 = 13.$$

The estimated value is the group mean. This result occurs with all of the six groups in this design. That is, the additive model, without sampling error, completely explains all of the variation of the group means when there is no interaction.

Figure 11-10.
Differences between
adjacent means.

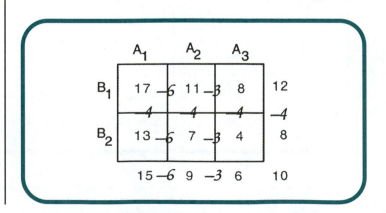

STATISTICAL PRINCIPLE

Because Treatment variables A and B do not interact, the same effects are observed at each level of the other variable. This is the essence of the lack of interaction. If Level 2 of Treatment B has an effect of -2, then that same effect occurs for all levels of Treatment A. Expressed another way, whatever the effect of the Treatment A level, the effect of Level 2 of Treatment B is -2; the Treatment B effect simply adds to the Treatment A effect. The graphical result of this additive process is a series of parallel curves when the group means and the marginal means are plotted.

In the absence of interaction, the group mean can be *exactly* predicted if the grand mean and the two main effects are known. Marginal means contain all of the information necessary for the reconstruction of the group means when there is no interaction. The difference between two marginal means is the same difference between corresponding group means; simple main effects are the same as the corresponding main effect.

The next section introduces the full two-way factorial model with an interaction term. For real data, the estimated interaction effects will not be exactly zero. The significant question is whether the sample interaction effect is large enough to conclude that the *population* interaction effect is larger than zero.

Two Treatment Variables with Interaction

Evaluate a treatment effect by comparing the corresponding marginal means. Evaluate an **interaction** effect by examining patterns of group means. Even without sampling error, when two treatment variables interact the group means cannot be recovered from knowledge of only the grand mean and main effects.

In the previous statistical illustration without interaction, Level 1 of Treatment A increased the value of the response variable Y by 5 units, *regardless* of the level of the other treatment variable, B. If Treatment variables A and B interact, the magnitude of effect for Level 1, or potentially any other level, of A depends on the level of B. If A and B interact, Level 1 of A could have an effect of 5 units at Level 1 of B, and an effect of 15 units at Level 2 of B.

> **two-way interaction of predictor variables**
> *effect of one treatment variable on the response variable depends on the level of the other treatment variable*

To illustrate, return to the peanut butter and jelly example that began this section. The interaction is shown by nonparallel lines when the group means are plotted in Figure 11-11.

> *An interaction is a difference in mean differences.*

For example, in the graph in Figure 11-11, the two levels of Peanut Butter, Absent (No) or Present (Yes), appear on the horizontal axis, and the values of the response variable appear on the vertical axis. Each level of Jelly is represented by a separate curve. Because the effects of Peanut Butter differ at each level of Jelly, the two curves have different slopes.

The interaction effect for each observation is the same for all observations within a group. To compute this interaction effect, begin with the joint effect of Treatment variables A and $B,$ defined as the difference between the group mean and the grand mean,

$$\text{joint effect} = \mu_{ab} - \mu.$$

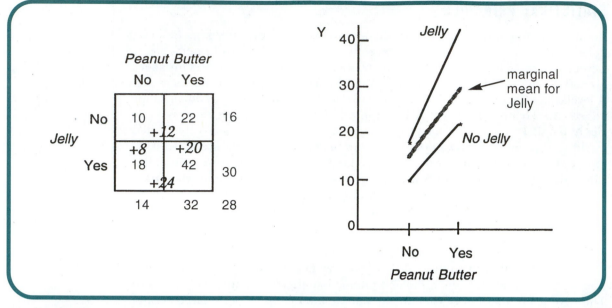

Figure 11-11.
Group means and graph
of the Tastiness means
for the peanut butter
and jelly example.

The **interaction effect** for a single observation is the joint effect of the treatment variables minus the separate, individual effects of Treatment *A* and Treatment *B*.

The corresponding interaction effect sum of squares is the sum of these squared effects over *all observations*,

$$\text{SSAB} = \sum b_{ab}^2 \quad \text{summed over } \textit{all N} \text{ observations.}$$

For the two-way factorial analysis, the number of terms in this summation is *pqn*, the number of groups *pq* times the number of observations in each group *n*.

The general model underlying a completely crossed factorial design includes the interaction effect.

**interaction effect of
*a*th level of *A* and
*b*th level of *B***

population:
$\beta_{ab} = (\mu_{ab} - \mu) - (\mu_a - \mu) - (\mu_b - \mu)$
sample estimate:
$b_{ab} = (\overline{Y}_{ab} - \overline{\overline{Y}}) - (\overline{Y}_a - \overline{\overline{Y}})(\overline{Y}_b - \overline{\overline{Y}})$

> *Full model for the two-way factorial ANOVA:*
> $Y = grand\ mean\ +\ Trt\ A\ effect\ +\ Trt\ B\ effect\ +\ int\ effect\ +\ error$

This model for Treatments *A* and *B* is

$$Y = \mu + \beta_a + \beta_b + \beta_{ab} + \varepsilon \quad \text{or} \quad Y = \overline{\overline{Y}} + b_a + b_b + b_{ab} + e,$$

for the respective population values or the corresponding sample estimates. The treatment effects, β_a and β_b, are subscripted only once because they each refer to the effects of a single treatment variable averaged across the response variable for all levels of the other treatment variable. Similarly, the grand mean μ has no subscripts because it is averaged across all values of the response variable. The interaction effect β_{ab} has two subscripts because it is a property of a single group defined by a combination of two treatment levels.

As is true of all ANOVA models, the partitioning of the sums of squares follows directly from straightforward algebraic manipulations of the underlying model. The result is that sums of squares are calculated for the two main effects, one in-

Source	SS	df	MS	F	p
Treatment A (Between)	$\sum b_a^2$	$p - 1$	SSA/df_A	MSA/MSE	<.05?
Treatment B (Between)	$\sum b_b^2$	$q - 1$	SSAB/df_B	MSB/MSE	<.05?
A × B (Interaction)	$\sum b_{ab}^2$	$(p - 1)(q - 1)$	SSAB/df_{AB}	MSAB/MSE	<.05?
Error (Within)	$\sum e^2$	$N - p$	SSE/df_E		
Total	$\sum (Y - \bar{\bar{Y}})$	$N - 1$			

Table 11-3.
The ANOVA summary table for the completely crossed factorial design, with p and q levels for Treatment variables *A* and *B*, respectively, and $pqn = N$ total observations.

teraction effect, and the average within-group error term. Together, all of these sums of squares add up to the total sums of squares,

$$SST = SSA + SSB + SSAB + SSE.$$

The sum of squares for each treatment effect is calculated from the variation of the relevant marginal means around the grand mean. The within-group sum of squares SSE is also calculated, just as in a one-way ANOVA, as the sum of deviations around each group mean for all groups.

Because a degrees of freedom corresponds to each sum of squares, a variance estimate, a mean square, can be computed for each effect. The degrees of freedom have been presented for the main effects and error sum of squares. The interaction sum of squares SSAB has degrees of freedom,

$$df_{ab} = (p - 1)(q - 1).$$

The form of the complete summary appears in Table 11-3. The two-way ANOVA contains all four fundamental forms of variation: total, between, within, and interaction.

A primary purpose of the analysis is to evaluate the three hypotheses that correspond to the two main effects and the interaction effects. After calculating the sums of squares and degrees of freedom, calculate the mean squares. The within-group mean square is the denominator of the F ratio for both main effects as well as the interaction effect.

Interpretation of the main effects is problematic in the presence of a significant interaction. By definition, if the null hypothesis of no interaction is rejected, the effect of each treatment variable on the response variable *differs* at different levels of the other treatment variable. With an interaction, no one main effect describes all situations; a main effect calculated from the marginal means is not representative of all simple main effects. In the extreme case, the simple main effects could be completely opposite each other, as illustrated in Figure 11-12, canceling each other out in the computation of the marginal means and the main effects.

In addition to testing the null hypothesis of each of the effects in the design, this analysis can assess the strength of association between the effect and the response variable. The strength of association for each effect on the response variable is gauged with estimated omega squared, $\hat{\omega}^2_{\text{effect}}$, which could be computed for either of the treatment variables as well as for the interaction. The expression of

Figure 11-12.
A crossed interaction in
which the Treatment *A*
effects at one level of
Treatment *B* lead to an
increase in *Y*, and the
effects at the other level
of *B* lead to a decrease
in *Y*.

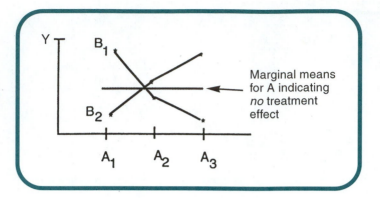

this index of association follows the same form as that of the randomized block and one-way ANOVA:

$$\hat{\omega}^2_{\text{effect}} = \frac{(df_{\text{effect}})(F_{\text{effect}} - 1)}{(df_{\text{effect}})(F_{\text{effect}} - 1) + N}$$

where N is the total number of observations in the analysis, which for the two-way factorial design is $N = npq$.

Evaluation of specific pairs of mean differences after the data are collected and analyzed follows the same procedure for the one-way ANOVA introduced in the previous chapter. The Tukey HSD standard error for $\overline{Y}_i - \overline{Y}_j$ for equal group sample sizes is virtually the same as that presented for the one-way ANOVA. The only distinction is that for a two-way factorial design, the differences are evaluated for the marginal means instead of for the group means. Accordingly, the expression of the standard error reflects the group size as well as the number of levels of the other treatment variable that are averaged to obtain the marginal mean. The standard error for the one-way ANOVA,

$$s_{\text{HSD}} = \sqrt{\frac{\text{MSE}}{n}},$$

becomes, for the evaluation of Treatment *A* means,

$$s_{\text{HSD}} = \sqrt{\frac{\text{MSE}}{nq}},$$

and, for the evaluation of the Treatment *B* means,

$$s_{\text{HSD}} = \sqrt{\frac{\text{MSE}}{np}}.$$

The HSD confidence interval around a mean difference at a 5% familywise error rate is computed as before,

$$\overline{Y}_i - \overline{Y}_j \pm q_{.05} s_{\text{HSD}},$$

except that $\overline{Y}_i$ and $\overline{Y}_j$ are marginal means, in the context of a two-way ANOVA. Degrees of freedom for the $q_{.05}$ statistic is $df = pq(n - 1)$.

The following example illustrates the full two-way factorial ANOVA. The data in this example are related to the data in the previous example. The marginal means in the two examples are identical, though the group means differ.

BUSINESS APPLICATION 11.2—Two-Way Factorial ANOVA with Interaction

MANAGERIAL PROBLEM

A company was considering adopting open offices, with only partitions separating employees from each other. The noise level in the open office environment is considerably higher than the level with separate offices. A manager was concerned with the effects of noise on the ability to work. Can employees concentrate with the distraction of additional noise? Does the impact of the distraction depend on the complexity of the work?

STATISTICAL HYPOTHESIS

Distraction null hypothesis: $\mu_{D1} = \mu_{D2} = \mu_{D3}$
Complexity null hypothesis: $\mu_{C1} = \mu_{C2}$
Interaction null hypothesis for each combination of levels for Distraction and Complexity:

$$(\mu_{dc} - \mu) = (\mu_d - \mu) + (\mu_c - \mu)$$

EXPERIMENTAL DESIGN

Studying the relevant psychological and organizational literature on the topic, the manager discovered a research article that investigated how ability to Learn (response variable) depends on Environmental Distraction and Task Complexity (treatment variables). Each employee in the study was instructed to read the new employee relations manual. Learning was operationalized by a test of how well each employee learned the new policies. Distraction was operationalized by the amount of noise transmitted through a pair of headphones. Complexity refers to one of two versions of the manual: regular and more difficult reading complexity.

Distraction	Complexity
D_1: None	C_1: Easy
D_2: Low	C_2: Difficult
D_3: High	

The three levels of Distraction are crossed with the two levels of Complexity—a completely randomized factorial design with two treatment variables, one with $p = 3$ levels and the second with $q = 2$ levels. This example has $3 \times 2 = 6$ groups. For example, Group D_3C_1 refers to the group that is at the third level of Distraction and the first level of Complexity.

DATA

Each of the six groups contains the minimum number of observations, $n = 2$.

D	1	1	2	2	3	3	1	1	2	2	3	3
C	1	1	1	1	1	1	2	2	2	2	2	2
Y	13	15	10	14	9	11	13	19	5	7	0	4

APPLICATION—EXCEL BUILT-IN ANALYSIS

The ANOVA statistical output is displayed in two sections.

Descriptive Statistics

Anova: Two-Factor With Replication			
SUMMARY	Easy	Hard	Total
No Distraction			
Count	2	2	4
Sum	28	32	60
Average	14	16	**15**
Variance	2	18	8
Low Distraction			
Count	2	2	4
Sum	24	12	36
Average	12	6	**9**
Variance	8	2	15.333
High Distraction			
Count	2	2	4
Sum	20	4	24
Average	10	2	**6**
Variance	2	8	24.667
Total			
Count	6	6	
Sum	72	48	
Average	**12**	**8**	
Variance	5.6	47.2	

Distraction Marginals

Complexity Marginals

The grand mean $\overline{\overline{Y}}$ is not provided by this Excel analysis. The separately calculated value is $\overline{\overline{Y}} = 10.00$.

Summary Table

Distraction (rows)

ANOVA						
Source of Variation	SS	df	MS	F	P-value	F crit
Sample	168	2	84	12.6	0.007	5.143
Columns	48	1	48	7.2	0.036	5.987
Interaction	56	2	28	4.2	0.072	5.143
Within	40	6	6.667			
Total	312	11				

Complexity

Obtaining the Output

Tools ➤ Data Analysis... ➤
ANOVA: Two-Factor With Replication

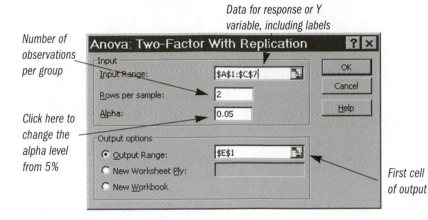

*Data for response or Y
variable, including labels*

*Number of
observations
per group*

*Click here to
change the
alpha level
from 5%*

*First cell
of output*

EXCEL GRAPHICAL ANALYSIS OF MEANS

Assessing the Excel Output

Compute and plot the three group means of Distraction for each level of complexity, Easy or Hard.

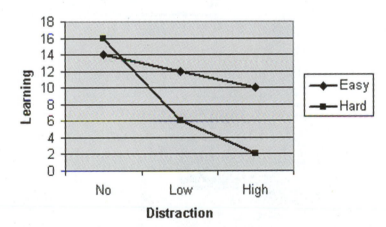

Because the two lines are not parallel, Complexity and Distraction interact for this sample. The meaning of this interaction is that distraction lowers learning more for complex tasks than for easy tasks, but for the tasks used in this study, both tasks resulted in the same amount of learning when no distraction was present. Does the interaction observed in this sample data generalize to the population?

Obtaining the Output

The first step to plotting the means is to create a table of means from the ANOVA output. In the SUMMARY output, Excel lists the means in the rows labeled Average. Either re-enter these means somewhere else in the worksheet or copy them somewhere else. Include in this new table the labels of each of the levels of the treatment variables, as illustrated below.

	A	B	C
10		Easy	Hard
11	No	14	16
12	Low	12	6
13	High	10	2

To create the graph from these means,

$$\text{Insert} \blacktriangleright \text{Chart...}$$

Step 1—Chart Type. Specify a Line chart, which is for a categorical horizontal axis. Select a format that connects the points.

Step 2—Chart Origin. Specify the cells that include the data, which are the group means. Include the labels in the Data Range.

Data range:	=Sheet1!$A$10:$C$13

Step 3—Chart Options. Under the Titles tab, add the titles to the X and Y axes.

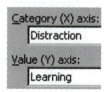

Step 4—Chart Location. Specify the location of the chart, either on a new worksheet or as an object on the current worksheet.

APPLICATION—SUM OF SQUARES CONCEPTUAL WORKSHEET

Estimated Values, Effects, and Residuals

Each estimated value is the corresponding group mean, which is expressed in terms of the underlying effects. For example, for Group $D_1 C_2$ the main effects (as computed in the previous example) are

Main Effect for Level 1 of Distraction: $\overline{Y}_{D1} - \overline{\overline{Y}} = 15 - 10 = 5$

Main Effect for Level 2 of Complexity: $\overline{Y}_{C2} - \overline{\overline{Y}} = 8 - 10 = -2.$

The interaction effect for Group $D_1 C_2$ is

$$(\overline{Y}_{12} - \overline{\overline{Y}}) - (\overline{Y}_{D2} - \overline{\overline{Y}}) - (\overline{Y}_{C2} - \overline{\overline{Y}}) = (16 - 10) - (15 - 10) - (8 - 10)$$

$$= 6 - 5 + 2 = 3,$$

which indicates that the sample mean for this group is three units larger than is expected from the effect of the two treatment variables considered separately.

The estimated value for each observation in this group is the sum of these three effects and the grand mean:

$$\hat{Y}_{12} = \overline{Y}_{12} = \mu + b_d + b_c + b_{dc} = 10 - 2 + 5 + 3 = 16.$$

Calculations for the effects and estimated value, as well as the residual $e \equiv Y - \hat{Y}$, are provided below for each of the 12 observations.

z	B	Respns									
Dst	Cmpl	Actual Learn	Dst Effect	Cmpl Effect	Int Effect	Pred Learn	Res	Res Sq	Dst Eft Sq	Cpl Eft Sq	Int Eft Sq
D	C	Y	b_d	b_c	b_{dc}	$\hat{Y}$	$e \equiv Y - \hat{Y}$	e^2	b_d^2	b_c^2	b_{dc}^2
D1	C1	13	5	2	-3	14	-1	1	25	4	9
D1	C1	15	5	2	-3	14	1	1	25	4	9
D2	C1	10	-1	2	1	12	-2	4	1	4	1
D2	C1	14	-1	2	1	12	2	4	1	4	1
D3	C1	9	-4	2	2	10	-1	1	16	4	4
D3	C1	11	-4	2	2	10	1	1	16	4	4
D1	C2	13	5	-2	3	16	-3	9	25	4	9
D1	C2	19	5	-2	3	16	3	9	25	4	9
D2	C2	5	-1	-2	-1	6	-1	1	1	4	1
D2	C2	7	-1	-2	-1	6	1	1	1	4	1
D3	C2	0	-4	-2	-2	2	-2	4	16	4	4
D3	C2	4	-4	-2	-2	2	2	4	16	4	4
	Sum	120	0	0	0		0	40	168	48	56
	Mean	10						SSE	SSD	SSC	SSDC

APPLICATION—TRADITIONAL NOTATION

Mean Squares

The estimate of error variability is

$$\text{MSE} \equiv \frac{\text{SSE}}{df_E} = \frac{40}{N - pq} = \frac{60}{12 - 6} = 6.67.$$

The variance estimate of the mean square between Distraction groups is

$$\text{MSD} \equiv \frac{\text{SSD}}{df_D} = \frac{168}{p - 1} = \frac{168}{3 - 1} = 84.00.$$

The variance estimate of the mean square between Complexity groups is

$$\text{MSC} \equiv \frac{\text{SSC}}{df_C} = \frac{48}{q-1} = \frac{48}{2-1} = 48.00.$$

The variance estimate provided by the interaction mean square is

$$\text{MSDC} \equiv \frac{\text{SSDC}}{df_{DC}} = \frac{56}{(p-1)(q-1)} = \frac{56}{(3-1)(2-1)} = 28.$$

The three corresponding F-statistics and p-values for Distraction are

$$F_D \equiv \frac{\text{MSD}}{\text{MSE}} = \frac{84.00}{6.67} = 12.60,$$

with a p-value of 0.007. The F-statistic for Complexity is

$$F_C \equiv \frac{\text{MSC}}{\text{MSE}} = \frac{48.00}{6.67} = 7.20,$$

with a p-value of 0.036. The F-statistic for the interaction of Distraction and Complexity is

$$F_{DC} \equiv \frac{\text{MSDC}}{\text{MSE}} = \frac{28.00}{6.67} = 4.20$$

with a p-value of 0.072. The null hypothesis of no Distraction effect is rejected, as is the corresponding null hypothesis for the effect of Complexity.

Strength of Association

$$\hat{\omega}_D^2 = \frac{(df_D)(F_D - 1)}{(df_D)(F_D - 1) + N} = \frac{(2)(12.60 - 1)}{(2)(12.60 - 1) + (2)(3)(2)} = 0.659$$

$$\hat{\omega}_C^2 = \frac{(df_C)(F_C - 1)}{(df_C)(F_C - 1) + N} = \frac{(1)(7.20 - 1)}{(1)(7.20 - 1) + (2)(3)(2)} = 0.341$$

$$\hat{\omega}_{DC}^2 = \frac{(df_{DC})(F_{DC} - 1)}{(df_{DC})(F_{DC} - 1) + N} = \frac{(6)(4.20 - 1)}{(6)(4.20 - 1) + (2)(3)(2)} = 0.348$$

STATISTICAL PRINCIPLE

The interaction of Distraction and Complexity approaches significance at $p = .072$. Literally interpreted, the interaction is not significant at $\alpha = .05$, though three considerations mitigate acceptance of this conclusion. First, the p-value is very close to .05. Second, the graph of the means indicates a crossed interaction for this sample, that is, the lines actually cross each other. Third, $\hat{\omega}_{DC}^2 = 0.348$, which is reasonably large, indicating a strong effect. Accordingly, we conclude that the variables interact even though the p-value is close to but does not exceed $\alpha = 0.05$. This interaction means that learning particularly deteriorates when the person attempts to learn a complex task in the presence of interaction.

MANAGERIAL INTERPRETATION

Learning markedly decreases as environmental distraction increases. To a lessor extent, learning also decreases as the complexity of the task increases. However, for a task of high complexity, distraction leads to a more profound decrease in learning than for a less complex task. To the extent that the results of this study generalize to the office environment, ideally distraction should be minimized, but special effort should be made to ensure that work that requires much concentration be performed with relatively few distractions.

This example presented a two-way factorial ANOVA of the model with main effects and an interaction effect. The next section introduces a different model that can be applied to the same data.

Additive Model for Two Treatment Variables

What if the analyst has prior evidence that no interaction is present? How should the ANOVA proceed with the specification of no interaction? The answer is to specify and analyze the additive model by dropping the interaction term from the model. If the model does not explicitly account for the interaction effect, then any interaction becomes part of the error term. Interaction sum of squares are relegated to the error sum of squares SSE, and the interaction degrees of freedom become part of the error degrees of freedom.

Is there an advantage to not specifying an interaction term in the two-way ANOVA model? If the interaction sum of squares SSAB only represents sampling error, then SSAB is small, so merging SSAB with SSE only slightly increases SSE. The corresponding increase of the degrees of freedom is relatively large, with all $(p-1)(q-1)$ interaction degrees of freedom added to the error degrees of freedom. Dividing SSE by a larger df leads to a smaller MSE, which is the denominator of the respective F-tests for the null hypothesis that the population marginal means of each treatment variable are equal. That is, the smaller error variance MSE results in a more sensitive test of the main effects for each treatment variable.

If no interaction term is specified and the interaction effect is real, then having the interaction effect absorbed by the error term leads to a substantially increased SSE. The degrees of freedom will also decrease, but the net effect raises the corresponding mean squared error MSE, resulting in less powerful tests of the main effects. In the absence of knowledge regarding the interaction effect, or if the interaction effect is known to exist, then the full model should be specified.

The following illustration is of an ANOVA based on an additive model.

STATISTICAL ILLUSTRATION—Two-Way ANOVA, Additive Model

DATA AND ANALYSIS

The data are from the previous example of the effect of Task Complexity and Distraction on Learning. The group effects are computed as before. For the additive model, the predicted value for each observation in this group is computed from

Table 11-4.
Calculation of sum of squares for two group effects

A	B	Respns							
Dst	Cmpl	Actual Learn	Dst Effect	Cmpl Effect	Pred Learn	Res	Res Sq	Dst Eft Sq	Cpl Eft Sq
D	C	Y	b_d	b_c	$\hat{Y}$	e	e^2	b_d^2	b_c^2
D1	C1	13	5	2	17	-4	16	25	4
D1	C2	15	5	2	17	-2	4	25	4
D2	C3	10	-1	2	11	-1	1	1	4
D2	C4	14	-1	2	11	3	9	1	4
D3	C1	9	-4	2	8	1	1	16	4
D3	C2	11	-4	2	8	3	9	16	4
D1	C3	13	5	-2	13	0	0	25	4
D1	C4	19	5	-2	13	6	36	25	4
D2	C1	5	-1	-2	7	-2	4	1	4
D2	C2	7	-1	-2	7	0	0	1	4
D3	C3	0	-4	-2	4	-4	16	16	4
D3	C4	4	-4	-2	4	0	0	16	4
.	Sum	120	0	0		0	**96**	**168**	**48**
	Mean	**10**					SSE	SSD	SSC

only the two group effects and the grand mean. This calculation is illustrated for the observations in the group for no Distraction (first level) and high Complexity (second level):

$$\hat{Y}_{12} = \overline{Y}_{12} = \mu + b_d + b_c$$
$$= 10 + 5 - 2 = 13.$$

The calculation of the effects and estimated value, as well as the calculation of the residual, $e \equiv Y - \hat{Y}$, is provided in Table 11-4 for each of the 12 observations.

The degrees of freedom for the additive model error term is the sum of the within-group df plus the interaction df. The estimated error variability is

$$\text{MSE} \equiv \frac{\text{SSE}}{df_E} = \frac{96}{(N-p)+(p-1)(q-1)} = \frac{96}{6+(2)(1)} = 12.$$

The variance estimate of the mean square between Distraction groups is

$$\text{MSD} \equiv \frac{\text{SSD}}{df_D} = \frac{168}{p-1} = \frac{168}{3-1} = 84.00.$$

The variance estimate of the mean square between Complexity groups is

$$\text{MSC} \equiv \frac{\text{SSC}}{df_C} = \frac{48}{q-1} = \frac{48}{2-1} = 48.00.$$

COMPLETELY RANDOMIZED FACTORIAL ANOVA

Source	SS	df	MS	F	p
Distraction	168	2	84	7.0	.018
Complexity	48	1	48	4.0	.080
Error	96	8	12		
Total	312	11			

Table 11-5.
The additive model
ANOVA summary table
for the completely
crossed factorial
design.

STATISTICAL PRINCIPLE

Because these data exhibit an interaction, as shown in the previous example, in practice the additive model would not be appropriate. For comparison purposes, however, the same data were analyzed with both the full and the additive models. Dropping the interaction effect from the model resulted in adding the interaction sum of squares SSDC = 56 from the previous example to the error sum of squares. Because the interaction effect does exist, the resulting tests of the null hypotheses of equal population group means for each treatment variable were less powerful than when analyzed with the full model. The corresponding F's are larger, as are the p-values. Moreover, the null hypothesis of equal Complexity means cannot be rejected with this additive model analysis as $p \approx .080$, but in the previous example the null hypothesis of equal population means was rejected for both treatment variables.

However, had the interaction sum of squares been small and attributable only to sampling error, then the additive model would have resulted in more powerful tests of the treatment variable null hypotheses.

The additive model of the data from a two-way factorial design is a version of the same model for the randomized block model presented in the previous section. The randomized block ANOVA can be thought of as a two-way factorial analysis with no replications per group. In this situation, the error term consists only of the interaction between the treatment variable and the blocking variable. The randomized block ANOVA has no within-group variation estimate because there is only one observation for every combination of treatment level and blocks.

Consideration of the additive model illustrates that the type of sampling plan specified by the experimental design does not completely determine the model analyzed by the statistical procedure of ANOVA. Data resulting from the completely crossed factorial design could be analyzed with the complete two-way factorial model or with the additive model. As designs become more complex, there are increasingly more competitive models that could be analyzed with the same data.

The complexity of the experimental design is limited only by the creativity of the analyst. Experimental designs are not limited to only two treatment variables. There can be three, four, or as many as specified, although the practical upper limit seems to be about five treatment variables. With three treatment variables, for example, there are three main effects, three two-way interaction effects, and one three-way interaction among three treatment variables. A significant three-way interaction means that the two-way interaction between two of the treatment variables is different at different levels of the third variable. For four treatment variables, there are three three-way interactions and one four-way interaction.

Blocking variables can also be added to designs with multiple treatment variables. Designs can have some treatment variables in which observations (or blocks) are matched across levels of the variable, and other treatment variables where there are different observations in each level. Another distinction is that in some designs, the treatment variables are not crossed but are hierarchical. And there can be more than one response variable. For any of these designs, the analysis is more complicated if each group does not have the same number of observations.

All of the ANOVAs used to analyze the data from any of the designs are forms of regression analysis with categorical treatment variables. Up until now, we have presented the underlying regression models and computed the sum of squared errors SSE for ANOVA just as we did for the analysis of regression models in Chapters 8 and 9. We have not, however, shown how data from an experimental design can actually be analyzed with a regression program instead of an ANOVA program. We will show such an analysis with the most basic design with one two-level treatment variable.

EXERCISES

11-5. Finish this completely randomized factorial ANOVA summary table.

Mechanical

Source	df	SS	MS	F	p
Treatment A	a.	2	53.37	7.95	0.021
Treatment B	99.475	1	c.	e.	0.008
A × B	b.	2	1.93	0.29	f.
Error	40.30	6	d.		
Total	250.37	11			

11-6. For the statistics presented in the ANOVA table in the previous problem,

Mechanical

a. How many levels does Treatment *A* have?
b. How many levels does Treatment *B* have?
c. How many observations are in each group?
d. Is the null hypothesis of equal group means for Treatment *A* rejected or not rejected? Why or why not?
e. Is the null hypothesis of equal group means for Treatment *B* rejected or not rejected? Why or why not?

f. Calculate $\hat{\omega}^2$ for Treatment *A*, Treatment *B*, and the interaction. Is the interpretation of this statistic for each effect the same as the interpretation of each corresponding *p*-value? Why or why not?

11-7. The data and analysis at the top of the following page were obtained for a completely crossed factorial design with two levels of one treatment variable, two levels of the other treatment, and three observations per group.

Concept

a. Construct the ANOVA summary table.
b. Compute and interpret $\hat{\omega}^2_{effect}$ for each of the three effects.
c. For the first level of Treatment *B*, plot the values of the response variable *Y* for each level of Treatment *A*. Repeat for the second level of *B*.
d. Explain why an additive model is appropriate for these data.
e. Compute SSE for the additive model.
f. Construct the ANOVA summary table for the additive model.
g. Explain how the results compare between the full model and the additive model.

Treatment (A)	Treatment (B)	Response (Y)	Trt A Mean	Trt A Effect	Trt A Eft Sq	Trt B Mean	Trt B Effect	Trt B Eft Sq	Group Mean	Int Effect	Int Eft Sq	Y Estimated	Residual	Res Sq
1	1	22.65	22.80	-1.854	3.44	23.25	-1.40	1.97	20.83	-0.56	0.32	20.83	1.82	3.30
1	1	19.37	22.80	-1.854	3.44	23.25	-1.40	1.97	20.83	-0.56	0.32	20.83	-1.46	2.14
1	1	20.48	22.80	-1.854	3.44	23.25	-1.40	1.97	20.83	-0.56	0.32	20.83	-0.35	0.12
1	2	25.22	22.80	-1.854	3.44	26.06	1.41	1.98	24.76	0.55	0.31	24.76	0.46	0.21
1	2	26.82	22.80	-1.854	3.44	26.06	1.41	1.98	24.76	0.55	0.31	24.76	2.06	4.24
1	2	22.24	22.80	-1.854	3.44	26.06	1.41	1.98	24.76	0.55	0.31	24.76	-2.52	6.35
2	1	26.85	26.51	1.856	3.44	23.25	-1.40	1.97	25.67	0.57	0.32	25.67	1.18	1.38
2	1	24.74	26.51	1.856	3.44	23.25	-1.40	1.97	25.67	0.57	0.32	25.67	-0.93	0.87
2	1	25.43	26.51	1.856	3.44	23.25	-1.40	1.97	25.67	0.57	0.32	25.67	-0.24	0.06
2	2	25.18	26.51	1.856	3.44	26.06	1.41	1.98	27.35	-0.57	0.32	27.35	-2.17	4.71
2	2	26.58	26.51	1.856	3.44	26.06	1.41	1.98	27.35	-0.57	0.32	27.35	-0.77	0.59
2	2	30.29	26.51	1.856	3.44	26.06	1.41	1.98	27.35	-0.57	0.32	27.35	2.94	8.64
Sum		296		0	41.29		0	23.69		0	3.80		0	32.63
Mean	24.65				SSA			SSB			SSAB			SSE
	GM													

11-8. A business school dean was interested in the starting salary of his recent M.B.A. graduates. What are the sources of the considerable variation in starting salary? The dean considered two factors that could account for some of the differences in the data listed in the accompanying table.

Major	Exp	Salary
MGMT	No	37.72
MGMT	No	41.80
MGMT	No	40.83
ACCT	No	46.53
ACCT	No	44.51
ACCT	No	39.95
FINC	No	43.65
FINC	No	45.97
FINC	No	44.39
MGMT	Yes	45.05
MGMT	Yes	43.44
MGMT	Yes	45.32
ACCT	Yes	45.49

Major	Exp	Salary
ACCT	Yes	41.52
ACCT	Yes	47.14
FINC	Yes	52.12
FINC	Yes	51.85
FINC	Yes	54.56

Major: Management, Accounting, or Finance
Prior Work Experience: No or Yes

The dean studied the influence of Major and Prior Work Experience using a 3×2 crossed ANOVA with three observations for each of the six groups.

a. Plot the salary for each of the three majors, once for those graduates with prior work experience and once for those without prior experience.
b. Construct the ANOVA summary table for these data.
c. Compute $\hat{\omega}^2_{\text{effect}}$ for each of the three effects.
d. Using evidence from your answers to all three previous questions, determine if the treatment variables interact.
e. State the managerial interpretation, free of statistical jargon, for these data.

11.3 EVALUATING MEAN DIFFERENCES WITH REGRESSION

Throughout this and the last chapter, ANOVA has been defined as a regression procedure with categorical predictor variables, either treatment variables or blocking variables. This section continues to develop this similarity by demonstrating how OLS regression provides yet another statistical procedure for evaluating mean differences.

When doing a *t*-test or ANOVA to evaluate mean differences, the labels used to describe the values of the predictor variable are somewhat arbitrary, usually chosen to communicate effectively the meaning of the groups. For two groups, typical predictor variable values are Graduate or Undergraduate for the variable Student, Old or New for the variable Machine, or Male or Female for the variable Gender. When the mean differences between groups are evaluated with an OLS regression analysis, the values of the predictor variable are numeric and must be chosen with care.

Consider the simplest model, one predictor variable with two values. The regression coefficient b_1 indicates the change in the response variable Y for a unit change in the value of the predictor variable X.

> *When using regression analysis to evaluate mean differences, choose values of the predictor variable so that the slope coefficient b is the difference between the group means.*

Consider what happens when the two values of the predictor variable are 0 and 1. The estimated value of each group is the group mean, so the estimated value is calculated as

$$\hat{Y} = \overline{Y} = b_0 + b_1 X.$$

When $X = 1$,

$$\hat{Y} = \overline{Y}_1 = b_0 + b_1 (1) = b_0 + b_1,$$

and when $X = 0$,

$$\hat{Y} = \overline{Y}_2 = b_0 + b_1 (0) = b_0.$$

Subtracting these equations yields

$$\overline{Y}_1 - \overline{Y}_2 = b_1.$$

The slope coefficient b_1 is the difference of the group means when the values of the predictor variable are 0 and 1.

There is also a correspondence between regression analysis and ANOVA for the hypothesis test of the population difference of the group means. The resulting *t*-test of the null hypothesis H_0: $\beta = 0$ provides the same *t*-value and associated *p*-value as does the equivalent independent-samples *t*-test. Regression analysis assumes equal group variances, as does the traditional independent-samples *t*-test.

To illustrate the use of regression to evaluate a mean difference, the following application reanalyzes the data presented in the application of the independent groups *t*-test from Chapter 6.

BUSINESS APPLICATION 11.3—Testing a Mean Difference with Regression

MANAGERIAL PROBLEM

Modern manufacturers attempt to minimize the time lag between ordering materials from suppliers and receiving those materials. At one firm with two suppliers, is the delivery of materials longer for one supplier than for the other? The delivery times last year for all 19 shipments from Company A and all 15 shipments from Company B were recorded.

STATISTICAL HYPOTHESIS

Null hypothesis H_0: $\mu_A - \mu_B = 0$.
Alternative hypothesis H_1: $\mu_A - \mu_B \neq 0$.

DATA

The delivery times for Company A and Company B follow. To facilitate a causal inference that any detected population mean difference is due to the type of supplier, orders were randomly assigned to each of the suppliers. Because of random assignment, no average differences in orders on any other variable, such as weight or dollar value of the shipment, should exist between the two groups except for the choice of supplier.

A	7.3	9.1	9.0	9.1	9.2	10.2	9.9	9.4	10.5	8.3	10.7
	8.4	7.7	11.1	10.5	13.7	8.7	10.4				
B	8.4	9.9	10	8.9	9.7	8.1	7.8	5.2	9.4	5.7	7.9
	6.5	9.8	7.8	6.2							

Company is the predictor variable. For the purposes of the regression analysis, the predictor variable is coded in the data matrix in a second row or column with a 0 to indicate Company A and a 1 to indicate Company B.

APPLICATION—EXCEL BUILT-IN ANALYSIS

Assessing the Excel Output

Regression Statistics	
Multiple R	0.45
R Square	0.20
Adjusted R Square	0.18
Standard Error	1.51
Observations	34

Sample Mean Difference   t-test of Mean Difference   Confidence Interval of Mean Difference

	Coefficients	Standard Error	t Stat	P-value	Lower 95%	Upper 95%
Intercept	9.57	0.35	27.64	0.00	8.87	10.28
Source	-1.49	0.52	-2.85	0.01	-2.55	-0.42

Note: The use of the Excel regression procedure was explained in detail in Chapter 9. The following example illustrates evaluating a mean difference with regression and displays only the data and the relevant output needed to compare these results with those obtained with the *t*-test for independent samples.

APPLICATION—TRADITIONAL NOTATION

The OLS regression model computed for these 34 observations is

$$\hat{Y} = -1.49X + 9.57.$$

The predicted value for Company *A* is

$$\hat{Y} = -1.49\,(0) + 9.57 = 9.57,$$

which is the mean delivery time for Company *A*. Similarly, the predicted value for Company *B* is

$$\hat{Y} = -1.49\,(1) + 9.57 = 8.08,$$

which is the mean delivery time for Company *B*. The difference of these group means is the estimated slope coefficient, $b = -1.49$.

Assessing fit, $R^2 = .20$, which shrinks to $R^2_{adj} = .18$, with $s_e = 1.51$. The *t*-value of the regression coefficient, assuming the null hypothesis $H_0: \beta_1 = 0$, is $t = -2.85$ with a two-tailed *p*-value of .01. Reject the hypothesis of no relationship between the predictor variable Company (X) and Delivery Time (Y). The confidence interval varies from −2.55 days to −0.42 days.

GRAPHICAL ANALYSIS

Figure 11-13.
The scatterplot and regression line of Delivery Time on Company.

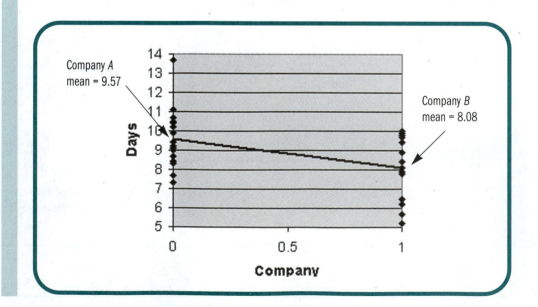

STATISTICAL PRINCIPLE

Evaluation of the difference between two population means can be accomplished with any of these increasingly general inferential procedures: independent-samples *t*-test, one-way ANOVA, or regression analysis. The results of this regression analysis are identical to the *t*-test and ANOVA results. For example, the *t*-test of no difference between the group means in Chapter 6 yielded an observed value of $t = -2.85$ with $p = .01$, the identical values obtained testing the difference of the slope coefficient from zero with this regression analysis. More generally, regression analysis can evaluate both continuous and categorical predictor variables when appropriate values are specified for one or more predictor variables.

MANAGERIAL INTERPRETATION

The average delivery time Company *A* is about half a day to 2½ days longer than the delivery time for Company *B*.

The previous example applied regression analysis to the simplest possible test for the evaluation of mean difference—a single predictor variable with only two values. This example can be generalized in order to define regression models to analyze mean differences in the context of *any* experimental design and associated ANOVA. The proper choice of coded values for the predictor variables allows more complex ANOVA models to be analyzed through a regression analysis. More advanced statistical texts extend the logic of this section to more complex models.

The equivalence of ANOVA with OLS regression results is conceptually interesting. However, when the sample sizes in a factorial design are not equal, the similarity is a practical necessity. Special adjustment procedures have been developed to account for unequal sample sizes, but the only statistically sound procedure is to do a formal OLS regression analysis of the data from a factorial design in place of ANOVA. Computer programs generally provide this procedure under the term *general linear model*. These programs can automatically generate the correct coded values of the predictor variables, and then provide the OLS regression analysis that generates the group comparisons of interest.

Estimating a regression model, and then testing specific hypotheses based on these estimates, forms the basis for many of the elaborate statistical procedures found in more advanced texts. These general linear model analyses form a fundamental principle underlying much of modern statistics. The material in this section serves only as a brief introduction to a wealth of available material.

EXERCISES

11-9. A company was considering relocating to one of two midwestern cities. One factor in the decision is the amount of each city's annual rainfall, presented in the following table for the last ten years.

City A	45.91	55.14	31.81	45.62	35.99
City B	46.64	28.61	52.53	59.70	60.04
City A	35.62	38.26	36.38	27.06	40.27
City B	41.39	58.47	32.46	56.15	52.01

Use regression analysis to answer the question, Is there sufficient evidence to conclude that the two cities have differing amounts of rainfall?

11-10. During a recent week, consumer gasoline prices for regular unleaded at the pump were compared for the West Coast and the East Coast. The data from several randomly sampled gasoline stations are reported below.

Application

W	W	W	W	W	W	W	W
131.9	129.9	131.9	124.9	131.9	122.9	121.9	126.9

E	E	E	E	E	E	E
131.9	134.9	127.9	133.9	130.9	128.9	127.9

Use regression analysis to answer the question, Is there sufficient evidence to conclude that gasoline prices differ on the two coasts?

11.4 SUMMARY

This chapter and the previous chapter introduced three basic related concepts: *experimental designs,* statistical *models* of the data gathered from these designs, and the *statistical procedures* for analyzing the data. The motivating question for all of the models introduced in this text is, "What causes variation in the response variable Y?". Statistics is the study of variation. The concepts introduced in these last two chapters illustrate how statistical analysis identifies sources of variation.

The models in this and the previous chapter focus on group differences in the response variable. The experimental design is the sampling plan that specifies the populations from which the data are sampled. Each group of observations is sampled from a potentially distinct population. The underlying statistical model specifies the components that contribute to the value of the response variable; these are the sources of variation across multiple observations. The form of the model is the explained or predictable component plus the unexplained component—error. The component explained by the model is the sum of the values of the predictor variables weighted by their respective slope coefficients. For ANOVA models, the values of the predictor variables can be either zero or one, indicating membership status in a specific group. Consequently, the ANOVA models can be written including only the slope coefficients, as was done throughout this and the previous chapter.

We studied the three most widely used designs: completely randomized with one treatment variable (from the previous chapter), completely randomized with two crossed treatment variables, and randomized block with one treatment variable and one blocking variable. The last two designs, presented in this chapter, include multiple predictor variables. These designs, and associated models and analyses, are summarized in Table 11-6.

A blocking variable is a predictor variable included in the design to reduce the error sum of squares. This reduction results in a more powerful test of the null hypothesis of no population group differences defined by the variable of interest: the treatment variable. The values of the blocking variable are typically random and would vary across future replications of the study. In contrast, the values of a treatment variable are typically chosen specifically by the analyst before the study begins, and they would be repeated for future replications of the study.

If there is large variation in values of the response variable Y across observations, then the dependent-samples test is preferred over the corresponding independent-samples test. The reason for this is the increased power of the dependent-samples test. The same conclusion also applies to the more general one-way ANOVA for independent samples and the randomized block ANOVA for dependent samples. Blocking variables, which yield dependent samples, always provide a more powerful test with a smaller error sum of squares when the blocking variable is related to the response variable.

Design	Treatment Variables	Blocking Variables	Population Model	Statistical Analysis
One-Way	1	0	$Y = \mu + \beta_a + \varepsilon$	One-way ANOVA (also independent-samples t-test for $p = 2$)
Random blocks	1	1	$Y = \mu + \beta_a + \beta_k + \varepsilon$	randomized block ANOVA (also dependent-samples t-test for $p = 2$)
Crossed factorial	2	0	$Y = \mu + \beta_a + \beta_b + \beta_{ab} + \varepsilon$ $Y = \mu + \beta_a + \beta_b + \varepsilon$	two-way factorial ANOVA

Table 11-6.
Experimental designs with associated models and statistical analyses presented in this and the previous chapter.

The two-way factorial ANOVA is the statistical procedure for the simultaneous analysis of two treatment variables. When two treatment variables are of interest, the two-way ANOVA is always preferred over two separate one-way ANOVAs because of potential interaction between the treatment variables. An interaction occurs when the effects of one treatment variable on the response variable differ depending on the level of the other treatment variable. That is, there is no one general effect, called the *main effect,* that can be summarized by the averages across the other groups. Instead, the effect of each treatment variable must be qualified by the level of the other treatment variable, the *simple main effect.* Because of this qualification, interpretation of general treatment effects is not recommended in the presence of interaction. This recommendation is particularly applicable when the effects at different levels of the other variable are in opposite directions.

One important topic at the core of much contemporary statistical analysis is the generality of regression analysis. Regression is the most general statistical procedure presented in this text; it actually subsumes tests of mean differences. The example presented in this chapter demonstrated that regression analysis provides the same analysis as that provided by a t-test or ANOVA for evaluating the difference between the means of two groups. More advanced texts show how regression analysis can be used for the analysis of *any* experimental design that would otherwise be analyzed with ANOVA. The basic requirement of this generalization is to carefully code each of the groups so that the regression coefficients represent mean differences.

The formal equivalence of ANOVA and regression is interesting from a conceptual perspective but also necessary when the number of observations is not the same from group to group in factorial designs. In that situation, standard ANOVA programs cannot be used for data analysis. Instead, use more general regression programs that automatically code the categorical variables in the model.

11.5 KEY TERMS

completely randomized factorial design *492*
interaction *497*
interaction effect *498*
main effect *494*
marginal mean *493*

randomized block ANOVA *481*
randomized block design *480*
simple main effect *494*
two-way factorial ANOVA *493*

11.6 REVIEW EXERCISES

ANALYSIS PROBLEMS

Mechanical

11-11. Complete the following randomized block ANOVA summary table.

Source	df	SS	MS	F	p
Trt A	2	a.	82.01	2.94	d.
Block	b.	163.26	c.	1.95	0.223
Error	6	167.21	27.87		
Total	11	e.			

Mechanical

11-12. For the statistics presented in the ANOVA table in the previous exercise,

a. How many groups were in this study?

b. How many blocks were in this study?

c. Is the null hypothesis of equal group means rejected or not rejected? Why or why not?

d. Was the blocking variable worthwhile? Why or why not?

e. Calculate $\hat{\omega}^2$ for Treatment variable A. How strong is the effect between Treatment A and the response variable Y?

Application

11-13. [*Same data as Exercise 6-31.*] To determine if tires manufactured with new materials last longer than tires manufactured the old way, a tire manufacturer had nine test cars outfitted with identically sized tires. One randomly chosen front wheel of each car had one type of tire and the other front wheel had the other type. All nine cars were driven for tens of thousands of miles on a test machine, and the mileage at which each tire reached 1/16" tread was recorded.

Car	1	2	3	4	5	6	7	8	9
Old	42771	42534	43858	43538	44063	38840	40458	41840	42481
New	45010	44446	45749	46031	46215	41547	42677	43326	44476

Is tire wear affected by the choice of materials?

a. Analyze these data graphically. What do you conclude?

b. Analyze these data with a randomized block ANOVA. What do you conclude?

11-14. [*Same data as Exercise 6-19.*] A long distance telephone company claimed that by switching to its services, customer costs would decrease. To evaluate this claim, the manager responsible for making this decision had samples of the last eight monthly company phone bills analyzed. The actual costs from using the current phone company and the costs claimed by the new company are listed on the opposite page to the nearest dollar.

Month	1	2	3	4	5	6	7	8
Current	$7420	$6493	$7234	$8334	$6216	$6149	$8337	$7209
New	$7336	$6421	$7298	$8314	$6228	$6151	$8329	$7177

Evaluate the effectiveness of the program with a randomized block ANOVA.

11-15. A manager for a leading laundry detergent manufacturer wanted to compare the retail price of his firm's detergent with the prices offered by two competitors. The manager gathered the prices of the three detergents from seven different stores.

Store	1	2	3	4	5	6	7
Ours	$3.14	$2.99	$3.09	$2.99	$3.29	$3.13	$2.99
Comp1	$3.12	$2.99	$3.15	$2.89	$3.15	$3.20	$2.97
Comp2	$3.10	$2.99	$3.19	$2.89	$3.19	$3.29	$2.99

Is there a difference in the price of the three brands of detergent?

a. Analyze these data graphically. What do you conclude?

b. Analyze these data with a randomized block ANOVA. What do you conclude?

11-16. A marketing manager of a new laundry detergent wanted to study the influence of Package Color on Sales. Choices of color were Blue, Orange, and Green. Each color choice was tested at each store during three successive weeks. Because overall levels of sales are different at different stores, Store is a blocking variable. Number of units sold at each store and for each package color are shown below.

Store	Blue	Orange	Green
1	16	25	20
2	4	5	5
3	23	39	18
4	29	26	15
5	31	39	23
6	18	22	11

a. Does Package Color affect Sales?

b. Is Store properly considered a blocking variable? That is, does choice of Store affect Sales?

11-17. A fertilizer company wanted to evaluate the effectiveness of three new blends: *A, B,* and *C.* Each fertilizer was tested for growing corn on four different plots of land. Because overall yields are different on different plots,

Plot is a blocking variable. Overall yield in bushels of corn for each blend at each plot is shown below.

Plot	BlendA	BlendB	BlendC
1	38	43	55
2	29	27	31
3	65	59	61
4	43	41	47

a.   Does Fertilizer Blend affect Yield?

b.   Is Plot properly considered a blocking variable? That is, does choice of Plot affect Yield?

Application

11-18.   A sales manager wanted to know how the background of a salesperson affected his or her ability to sell. The manager defined background in terms of three types of college majors: Business (e.g., marketing, accounting, management, finance), Social Science (e.g., psychology, sociology, political science), and the Natural Sciences (e.g., mathematics, physics, and chemistry). The manager then identified blocks of salespeople who all had similar GPAs, one for each of the three types of majors. Gross sales, in thousands, during the last month were recorded for each salesperson.

Block	Busin.	Social Science	Natural Science
1	11.4	10.9	9.5
2	9.2	8.4	8.1
3	13.9	14.1	12.7
4	10.5	9.9	10.2

a.   Does Background affect Sales?

b.   Is GPA properly considered a blocking variable? That is, does GPA affect Sales?

11-19.   Finish this completely randomized factorial ANOVA summary table.

Mechanical

Source	df	SS	MS	F	p
Trt A	a.	3.10	3.10	f.	0.2610
Trt B	1	c.	6.02	2.840	g.
A*B	b.	0.19	0.19	0.088	0.7737
Error	8	16.96	e.		
Total	11	d.			

11-20. For the statistics presented in the ANOVA table in the previous exercise,

Mechanical

a.   How many levels does Treatment A have?

b.   How many levels does Treatment B have?

c.   How many observations are in each group?

d.   Is the null hypothesis of equal group means for Treatment A rejected or not rejected? Why or why not?

e.   Is the null hypothesis of equal group means for Treatment B rejected or not rejected? Why or why not?

f.   Is the null hypothesis of the interaction of Treatment A with Treatment B rejected or not rejected? Why or why not?

g.   Calculate $\hat{\omega}^2$ for Treatment A, Treatment B, and the interaction. Is the interpretation of this statistic for each effect the same as the interpretation of each corresponding p-value? Why or why not?

11-21. Finish this completely randomized factorial ANOVA summary table.

Mechanical

Source	df	SS	MS	F	p
Trt A	a.	5.07	2.54	0.605	e.
Trt B	1	24.64	c.	d.	0.0321
A*B	2	b.	8.64	2.060	f.
Error	12	50.31	4.19		
Total	17	97.30			

11-22. For the statistics presented in the ANOVA table in the previous exercise,

Mechanical

a.   How many levels does Treatment A have?

b.   How many levels does Treatment B have?

c.   How many observations are in each group?

d.   Is the null hypothesis of equal group means for Treatment A rejected or not rejected? Why or why not?

e.   Is the null hypothesis of equal group means for Treatment B rejected or not rejected? Why or why not?

f.   Is the null hypothesis of the interaction of Treatment A with Treatment B rejected or not rejected? Why or why not?

g.   Calculate $\hat{\omega}^2$ for Treatment A, Treatment B, and the interaction. Is the interpretation of this statistic for each effect the same as the interpretation of each corresponding p-value? Why or why not?

11-23. The following data and analysis were obtained for a completely crossed factorial design with two observations per group.

Mechanical

a.   Construct the ANOVA summary table.

A	B	Respns	A Effect	B Effect	AB Effect	Pred Rsp	Res	Res Sq	A Eft Sq	B Eft Sq	AB Eft Sq
A	B	Y	b_a	b_b	b_{ab}	$\hat{Y}$	$e \equiv Y - \hat{Y}$	e^2	b_a^2	b_b^2	b_{ab}^2
1	1	35.41	−4.68	−3.03	−1.13	35.48	−0.06	0.00	21.89	9.19	1.28
1	1	35.54	−4.68	−3.03	−1.13	35.48	0.07	0.00	21.89	9.19	1.28
2	1	47.73	−0.40	−3.03	2.57	43.46	4.27	18.23	0.16	9.19	6.62
2	1	39.19	−0.40	−3.03	2.57	43.46	−4.27	18.23	0.16	9.19	6.62
3	1	44.04	5.08	−3.03	−1.44	44.92	−0.88	0.77	25.76	9.19	2.09
3	1	45.79	5.08	−3.03	−1.44	44.92	0.88	0.77	25.76	9.19	2.09
1	2	41.93	−4.68	3.03	1.13	43.80	−1.87	3.48	21.89	9.19	1.28
1	2	45.66	−4.68	3.03	1.13	43.80	1.86	3.48	21.89	9.19	1.28
2	2	41.91	−0.40	3.03	−2.57	44.38	−2.47	6.08	0.16	9.19	6.62
2	2	46.84	−0.40	3.03	−2.57	44.38	2.47	6.08	0.16	9.19	6.62
3	2	49.55	5.08	3.03	1.44	53.87	−4.32	18.62	25.76	9.19	2.09
3	2	58.18	5.08	3.03	1.44	53.87	4.32	18.62	25.76	9.19	2.09
		531.77	0.00	0.00	0.00		0.00	**94.35**	**191.26**	**110.23**	**39.93**
		44.31	GM					SSE	SSA	SSB	SSAB

b. Compute and interpret $\hat{\omega}^2_{\text{effect}}$ for each of the three effects.

c. For the first level of Treatment B, plot the values of the response variable Y for each level of Treatment A. Repeat for the second level of B.

d. Explain why the full model is appropriate for these data.

11-24. Analyze the additive model for the data in the previous exercise.

Mechanical

a. Compute SSE for the additive model.

b. Construct the ANOVA summary table for the additive model.

c. Determine how the results compare for the full model and the additive model.

11-25. The following data and analysis were obtained for a completely crossed factorial design with two observations per group.

Mechanical

a. Construct the ANOVA summary table.

b. Compute and interpret $\hat{\omega}^2_{\text{effect}}$ for each of the three effects.

c. For the first level of Treatment B, plot the values of the response variable Y for each level of Treatment A. Repeat for the second level of B.

d. Determine if an additive model is appropriate for these data and why or why not.

A	B	Respns	A Effect	B Effect	AB Effect	Pred Rsp	Res	Res Sq	A Eft Sq	B Eft Sq	AB Eft Sq
A	B	Y	b_a	b_b	b_{ab}	$\hat{Y}$	$e \equiv Y - \hat{Y}$	e^2	b_a^2	b_b^2	b_{ab}^2
1	1	8.0	−0.51	−0.71	0.13	6.57	1.43	2.05	0.26	0.50	0.02
1	1	6.5	−0.51	−0.71	0.13	6.57	−0.07	0.00	· 0.26	0.50	0.02
1	1	5.2	−0.51	−0.71	0.13	6.57	−1.37	1.87	0.26	0.50	0.02
2	1	9.4	0.51	−0.71	−0.12	7.33	2.07	4.27	0.26	0.50	0.02
2	1	5.1	0.51	−0.71	−0.12	7.33	−2.23	4.99	0.26	0.50	0.02
2	1	7.5	0.51	−0.71	−0.12	7.33	0.17	0.03	0.26	0.50	0.02
1	2	8.4	−0.51	0.71	−0.12	7.73	0.67	0.44	0.26	0.50	0.02
1	2	6.5	−0.51	0.71	−0.12	7.73	−1.23	1.52	0.26	0.50	0.02
1	2	8.3	−0.51	0.71	−0.12	7.73	0.57	0.32	0.26	0.50	0.02
2	2	8.9	0.51	0.71	0.13	9.00	−0.10	0.01	0.26	0.50	0.02
2	2	9.9	0.51	0.71	0.13	9.00	0.90	0.81	0.26	0.50	0.02
2	2	8.2	0.51	0.71	0.13	9.00	−0.80	0.64	0.26	0.50	0.02
		91.9	0.00	0.00	0.00		0.00	**16.96**	**3.10**	**6.02**	**0.19**
		44.31	GM					SSE	SSA	SSB	SSAB

11-26. A fleet manager was interested in any potential effect of Type of Gasoline
and Tire Pressure on Miles per Gallon. She evaluated two types of gasoline,
A and *B*, and two tire pressures, LO and HI.

Gas	Tire Prs	MPG
A	LO	26.3
A	LO	26.5
A	LO	25.2
B	LO	29.4
B	LO	25.1
B	LO	27.5
A	HI	27.3
A	HI	26.5
A	HI	28.3
B	HI	30.4
B	HI	28.5
B	HI	30.9

a. Plot MPG for each of the two gasolines, once for LO pressure and once for HI pressure.

b. Construct the ANOVA summary table for these data.

c. Compute $\hat{\omega}^2_{\text{effect}}$ for each of the three effects.

d. Using the results from all three previous steps, determine if the predictor variables interact.

e. State the managerial interpretation, free of statistical jargon, for these data.

11-27. A completely crossed factorial design yielded data for six groups. Four of these means appear in the following table.

	A_1	A_2	A_3
B_1	55	61	70
B_2	49	a.	b.

a. Determine the value of $\overline{Y}_{22}$ if there is *no* interaction sum of squares.

b. Determine the value of $\overline{Y}_{32}$ if there is *no* interaction sum of squares.

c. Plot the resulting six means that exhibit no interaction among the two predictor variables.

d. Identify the characteristic of this graph that demonstrates the lack of interaction.

11-28. [*Same data in Exercise 6-5.*] A record company executive wants to know if the average play length of rock and roll singles differs from that of country and western singles. To provide an answer to this question, she selects 10 country and western singles and 9 rock and roll singles.

C&W	3.80	3.30	3.43	3.30	3.03	4.18	3.18	3.83	3.22	3.38
R&R	3.88	4.13	4.11	3.98	3.98	3.93	3.92	3.98	4.67	

Use regression analysis to answer the question, Is there sufficient evidence to conclude that the average play length differs between rock and roll and country and western singles?

11-29. [*Same data presented in the Integrative Analysis Problem in Chapter 6.*] The owner of two restaurants wants to compare the average cost of a meal at Restaurant A with the average cost of a meal at Restaurant B. Thirty-eight receipts at Restaurant A and 42 Restaurant B receipts were recorded.

Restaurant A costs

14.66	9.47	13.85	15.98	11.46	15.70	13.18	11.60
12.88	14.71	2.94	10.34	15.18	18.12	17.25	16.95
17.60	12.60	12.77	10.88	7.25	11.12	12.76	9.81
7.91	16.33	16.13	12.16	16.11	12.36	12.08	10.12
8.79	10.75	13.69	13.29	8.55	12.66		

Restaurant B costs

12.95	19.59	8.38	13.53	7.78	16.21	13.97	12.22
15.41	10.93	10.07	14.45	5.35	10.01	10.31	10.80
6.20	7.93	14.52	9.58	13.26	20.26	14.09	11.20
8.87	13.59	10.12	13.32	12.30	7.83	13.32	14.04
11.12	11.16	13.52	13.44	9.17	13.11	9.63	9.53
11.88	10.68						

Use regression analysis to answer the question, Is there sufficient evidence to conclude that the average cost of a meal differs between the two restaurants?

DISCUSSION QUESTIONS

1. What is a block?

2. How does randomization proceed in a design that uses blocks?

3. What is the advantage of analyzing data collected with a dependent-samples test rather than with an independent-samples test?

4. Which of the four sources of variation in ANOVA are present in a randomized block ANOVA?

5. How does a randomized block ANOVA relate to a dependent-samples t-test?

6. Why is omega squared of interest for the predictor variable but not for the blocking variable in a randomized block ANOVA?

7. What are the types of predictor variables in an ANOVA? What is the purpose of including each type of predictor variable?

8. What is a marginal mean?

9. What is a main effect? a simple main effect?

10. In a factorial design, when are main effects the same as the simple main effects?

11. How could you detect an interaction simply from a graph? What is the purpose of the interaction hypothesis test if the graph indicates an interaction?

12. What is a crossed interaction?

13. Why does the presence of an interaction cloud the interpretation of the main effects?

14. What is the additive model? When would this model be used in data analysis?

15. Why must the groups be coded numerically when using a regression analysis to analyze mean differences?

16. How is the test of the null hypothesis from an independent groups t-test performed when using regression analysis to analyze a mean difference?

INTEGRATIVE ANALYSIS PROBLEM

A consumer testing group evaluated the cleaning power of four detergents, A, B, C, and D, at three levels of water hardness, Soft, Medium and Hard. The response variable was evaluated on a 100-point scale of how effectively the clothes were cleaned. Each group in the design, representing a specific combination of detergent and water hardness, had five observations. The data are found in the file CLEAN.DAT.

a. Compute and plot the group means. Plot the cleanness scores for each level of detergent across the three levels of water hardness.

b. Draw conclusions from the pattern of group means about these sample data.

c. Compute the group standard deviations. Is the assumption of equal group variances plausible for these data?

d. State your conclusion if the data were only available for one level of water hardness, Soft. Answer this question with a one-way ANOVA.

e. State your conclusion if the data were only available for the cleaning power of the detergents. Answer this question with a one-way ANOVA.

f. Compute the two-way ANOVA on these data. What is your conclusion regarding the cleaning power of the detergents?

g. Determine if there is an interaction in these data. If so, interpret the interaction.

h. Determine if the descriptive analysis of the sample data agrees with the inferential analysis.

i. Identify how the two-way ANOVA is a more comprehensive analysis than the one-way ANOVA that did not consider the hardness of water at all.

j. Identify how the two-way ANOVA is a more comprehensive analysis than the one-way ANOVA that only considered Soft water.

12

Forecasting the Future from the Past

WHY DO WE CARE?

Every business must plan for the future. Many management decisions depend on an estimate of the value of one or more variables at some future time. What are the monthly sales projections for the next three months? How many employees will our company have at this time next year? What is the estimated interest rate two months from now? How large will inventory be during the summer months? Some of these questions, such as the estimated interest rate, involve forecasting a single value. Inventory, however, might consist of thousands of different items, each one requiring a specific forecast. Planning for the future in such a company literally involves thousands of forecasts.

Understanding how the process performed in the past is the key to forecasting how it might perform in the future. If sales have been steadily increasing every month for the last two years, and this trend is expected to continue, then a forecast of future sales can project this trend into the next three months. Successful forecasting is the successful search for patterns, the ability to separate random noise and irregular statistical fluctuations from underlying structure. Although noise obscures forecasts, structure and pattern can be projected into the future. The construction of models by searching for pattern buried among noise and instability is not only central to forecasting, it is crucial to statistical thinking in general.

Chapters 8 and 9 on regression analysis demonstrated how a set of predictor variables X predicts the value of a response variable of interest Y. These regression models are sometimes called *explanatory* models because explanation and prediction of the variable of interest Y are accomplished with different variables: the predictor variables. Values of Y and the predictor variables were measured for different observations—different companies, different people, or different instances of whatever the unit of analysis is.

In this chapter, the value of the variable Y at some particular time is estimated from the values of the *same* variable Y at earlier times. This chapter focuses on time-series or historical data (Chapter 1), the values of a variable at different points in time, usually measured at specific intervals, such as every month or every year. The measurements are all of the same variable Y, but the observations are at different points in time. The resultant models are called *time-series models* or *forecasting models* to differentiate them from the explanatory models discussed in the previous chapters.

As illustrated in Figure 12-1, for variable of interest Y, Y_t indicates the value of Y at time period t. Time period t usually refers to the current time period. The previous time period is $t-1$, with value of Y indicated by Y_{t-1}. The time period that follows the current time is $t+1$, and the value of Y at that time is Y_{t+1}. Of course, the value of Y_{t+1} is currently unknown. The predicted or forecasted value of Y_{t+1} is $\hat{Y}_{t+1}$. Likewise, $\hat{Y}_{t+3}$ indicates the forecasted value of Y three time periods into the future.

The adequacy of the regression models presented in previous chapters were evaluated in terms of how close the actual value of Y was to the predicted or estimated value ($\hat{Y}$) for each observation. The same concept applies to time-series models. The effectiveness of a forecasting model is evaluated according to how well it forecasts, which is measured by the **forecasting error.**

Large values of e indicate poor forecasts, and small values indicate accurate forecasts. Calculate an index of the adequacy of the forecasting model by combining the forecasting errors over many different time periods into a single statistic, such as the sum of the squared errors.

If needed, adjust the values of Y at different time points so that they are directly comparable with each other.

> *Time-series data should be properly adjusted so that the values of Y are comparable at different time periods.*

forecasting error e
difference between actual and forecasted value,
$$Y_{t+1} - \hat{Y}_{t+1} \equiv e_{t+1}$$

Figure 12-1.
Notation that indicates the time period in relation to the present, and the actual and forecasted values of Y.

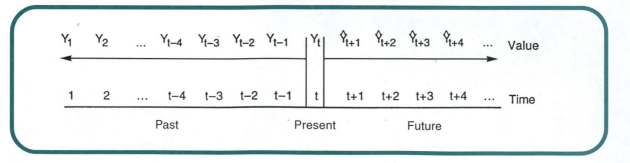

For example, inflation changes the value of a dollar at different times, so a time series beginning in 1980 and ending in 1994 might express all values in terms of 1980 dollars.

As with the explanatory regression models presented in the previous chapters, random chance and instability in the data contribute to forecasting errors. A goal of many time-series analyses is to uncover and separate any underlying systematic pattern of the values of Y over time from the random sampling fluctuations that obscure this underlying pattern. The types of patterns found in time-series data were presented in Chapter 3: trend, cycle, and seasonal.

12.1 RANDOM WALK

One method for obtaining a forecast is to express the forecasted value in terms of past values. One of the simplest such time-series models is called a **random walk.** For time-series data generated by a random walk, no trend, cyclical, or seasonal component underlies the data. For random walk data, the only underlying component is random error, which is added to the current value of the series Y_t.

The next data value of a random walk model is the current value plus the influence of random error. The only term left after removing the random error e is Y_t, which is the forecast,

$$\hat{Y}_{t+1} = Y_t.$$

The population mean of e is zero, so the next value of Y is just as likely to increase as decrease. This forecast is the simplest possible: The current value of Y is the forecasted value.

The random walk model is not only simple but also useful. Many financial forecasters maintain that the behavior of general stock market indices over time, such as the Dow-Jones Industrial Average and many individual stocks as well, is best characterized by a random walk. Interpreting random walk data is, however, not always straightforward. Data generated by a random walk model with an average error of zero display no trends over time. The time series "meanders," moving up and down, sometimes misleadingly appearing to follow a pattern over a small number of trials. Some of these misleading patterns are demonstrated in the following example.

> **random walk**
> *process that generates the time series* $Y_{t+1} = Y_t + e$

STATISTICAL ILLUSTRATION—Random Walk

DATA

The data for this illustration were generated by a random walk model with an average population error equal to zero. The error assumed a value of 1 with a probability of .5 and a value of −1 with a probability of .5. That is, the value of Y at the next time period was as likely to be one unit higher as one unit lower. The four data sets were not chosen because they exhibited certain patterns. Instead, four

Figure 12-2.
Four different random
walk time series and the
misleading "apparent"
tendencies ascribed to
the four time series.

random walks of 25 time periods each were generated in succession, shown in Figure 12-2.

RANDOM WALK TIME-SERIES PLOTS

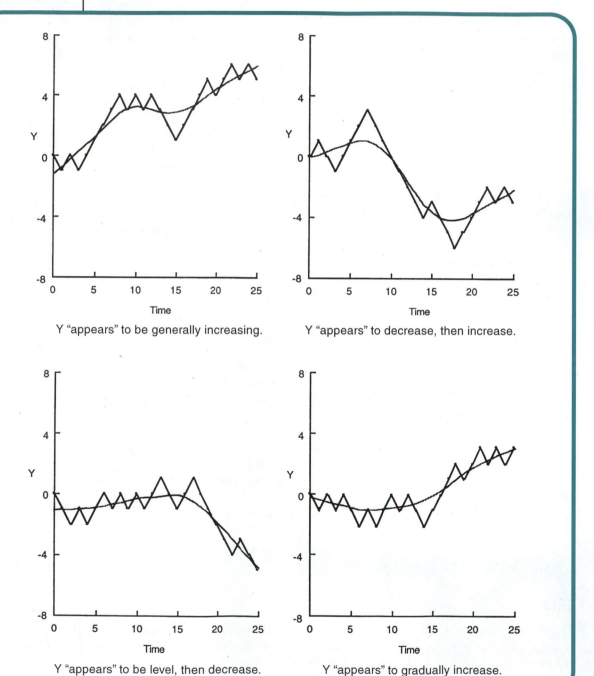

Y "appears" to be generally increasing.

Y "appears" to decrease, then increase.

Y "appears" to be level, then decrease.

Y "appears" to gradually increase.

STATISTICAL PRINCIPLE

Through each of the four plots, a smooth curve is drawn that best summarizes the apparent relationships. A pattern can be incorrectly identified for each of the four time series. Any apparent pattern is only a statistical artifact of a small sample size because all four time series were generated with a random walk. If the time periods were increased from 25 to 50 or 100, the patterns observed in these time series would likely not be repeated in the longer sequences.

As discussed in the material on quality control in Chapter 4 Extension, management should avoid the trap of ascribing long-term patterns when none exists. A random walk contains a random component, but what occurs next is *predictable* from what is currently occurring. The forecasted value is the current value. A time series accurately described by a random walk meanders and drifts but not in a predictable direction. The search for an underlying stable, long-term pattern in random walk data is futile.

How can a set of time-series data be identified as a random walk? The key to identifying a random walk follows from the definition of the underlying model;

$$Y_{t+1} = Y_t + e.$$

Subtracting values at two successive time periods yields

$$Y_{t+1} - Y_t = e.$$

For a random walk time series, the only distinction between successive observations is random error.

A test for random walk data is the systematic analysis of these differences for all successive values of the original data Y. Calculating these differences for all values yields the **differenced time series.** Analysis of the ΔY time series indicates whether the original time series Y is a random walk. If the differences are nothing more than random error that exhibits no pattern or structure whatsoever, then the original time series Y is a random walk. No more search need be conducted to uncover an underlying structure of a random walk time series such as trend or seasonality.

> **differenced time series ΔY**
> *difference of successive observations from the original time series Y,*
> $\Delta Y_t = Y_t - Y_{t-1}$

Examination of the forecasting errors for patterns follows the same general principle as the analysis of the errors from explanatory regression models discussed in the regression chapters. If the model correctly identifies the underlying structure, and if this structure is removed from the data, then all that remains $(Y_t - \hat{Y}_t)$ is random error.

> *Random forecasting errors indicate that the model accurately describes any stable pattern underlying the data.*

For a random walk process, differences between successive values of the time series implies that the model

$$Y_{t+1} = Y_t + e$$

accurately describes the data. Because of the presence of random error, identifying the underlying process described by the model does not guarantee accurate prediction, but knowing this process is prerequisite for achieving predictive accuracy. Accurate prediction also requires relatively small errors.

BUSINESS APPLICATION 12.1—Random Walk

MANAGERIAL PROBLEM

The Dow-Jones Industrial Average is perhaps the most widely cited index of stock market performance. Can future values of this index be forecasted?

DATA

The time series of the individual values of the differenced Dow-Jones average, Figure 12-3, demonstrates that the differences between successive values are largely random.

MANAGERIAL INTERPRETATION

Differences between successive values are largely random. However, the October 1987 market plummet is a brief downward trend that exceeds the expectation of chance. Also, the differences in the postcrash market exhibit larger variance than the differences in the precrash market. A random walk model explains much but not all of the behavior of the Dow-Jones Industrial Average.

Figure 12-3.
Time series of the monthly differenced Dow-Jones Industrial Average.

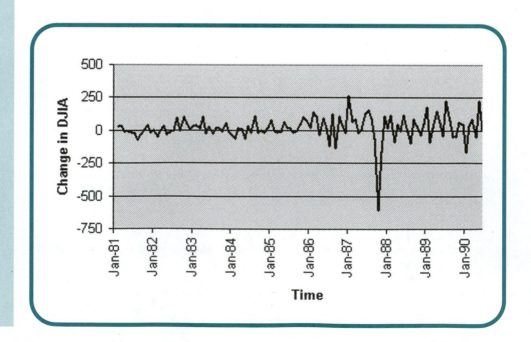

The forecasting models considered in the next section require more than just the current value of Y. These models also base the forecast on the values of Y at *previous* times as well as the current time.

EXERCISES

Mechanical

12-1. A forecasting model resulted in the following errors for time periods 1 to 25.

0.07	2.30	-0.72	-0.20	1.68	-0.36	-0.97
1.01	-0.74	-2.31	-1.69	0.89	-0.75	-0.79
0.83	0.71	-0.12	0.22	-0.18	-0.52	1.16
-1.71	0.26	0.19	-0.22			

a. The first observation is $Y_0 = 10$. Plot the time series for a random walk model.
b. The first observation is $Y_0 = -10$. Plot the time series for a random walk model.

c. Identify the differences between the two time series in (a) and (b).
d. Compute the differenced time series. How does this new time series demonstrate that the data were generated by a random walk process?

Application

12-2. The following data represent the differenced time series ΔY_t of the monthly stock price index reported by the U.S. Department of Commerce from January 1992 until April 1995.

Does this graph provide evidence that the time series Y_t is a random walk? Why?

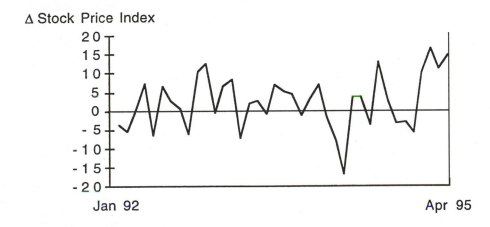

Δ Stock Price Index

Jan 92   Apr 95

12.2 FORECASTING THE FUTURE BY AVERAGING THE PAST

One relatively simple but widely used family of forecasting methods is based on a technique called *smoothing*. A **smoothing method** predicts the future by averaging the past. The average is computed without isolating the trend, cyclical, or seasonal components of the time series. Instead, the past is directly projected into the future by averaging. Smoothing models express the forecasted value $\hat{Y}_{t+1}$ of the next time period as a *weighted* mean of some or all of the previous values.

> **smoothing method of forecasting**
> *forecasted value is a weighted average of the previous values*

Smoothing method forecast:
$$\hat{Y}_{t+1} = b_t Y_t + b_{t-1} Y_{t-1} + b_{t-2} Y_{t-2} + \ldots + b_1 Y_1, \sum b = 1.$$

Any set of weights—b_t, b_{t-1}, and so on—may be chosen as long as their sum is 1, though the weights usually follow a pattern in which the present and immediate past are weighted more than the distant past. That is, the weights are typically chosen so that $b_t \geq b_{t-1} \geq b_{t-2} \geq \ldots \geq b_1$.

A specific smoothing model provides a specific set of weights, such as

$$\hat{Y}_{t+1} = (.6)Y_t + (.3)Y_{t-1} + (.1)Y_{t-2} + (0)Y_{t-3} + \ldots + (0)Y_1.$$

In this model, the forecast for the value of Y at the next time period $\hat{Y}_{t+1}$ is the value of Y at the current time period (Y_t) multiplied by .6, plus the value of Y at the previous time period (Y_{t-1}) multiplied by .3, plus the value of Y at two time periods ago (Y_{t-2}) multiplied by .1. All values of Y at earlier time periods are ignored. The sum of the weights is

$$.6 + .3 + .1 + 0 + \ldots + 0 = 1,$$

so the condition that the weights sum to 1 is satisfied.

Each smoothing method produces a different set of weights. The methods for choosing the values of the weights for specific smoothing methods are discussed next.

Moving Averages Smoothing Method

n-period moving average forecasting method

forecast $\hat{Y}_{t+1}$ is the average of the n previous values of Y

The simplest of all smoothing forecasting methods—the **n-period moving average**—relies on a simple average. For example, a forecast of the next time period $\hat{Y}_{t+1}$, computed as the average of the current and two previous time periods, is a 3-period moving average:

$$\hat{Y}_{t+1} = \frac{Y_t + Y_{t-1} + Y_{t-2}}{3} = \frac{1}{3}Y_t + \frac{1}{3}Y_{t-1} + \frac{1}{3}Y_{t-2}.$$

The weights for the 3-period moving average are $b_t = \frac{1}{3}$, $b_{t-1} = \frac{1}{3}$, $b_{t-2} = \frac{1}{3}$, $b_{t-3} = 0, \ldots, b_1 = 0$. The present and immediate past two time periods are weighted one-third, and all earlier time periods are ignored, as illustrated in Figure 12-4.

Four-period moving average forecasts and 5-period moving average forecasts are similarly defined. The weights for the 4-period moving average are .25 for the last four weights and 0 for all previous times, as illustrated in Figure 12-5.

Figure 12-4.
Smoothing weights for a 3-period moving average for the forecast of the next time period.

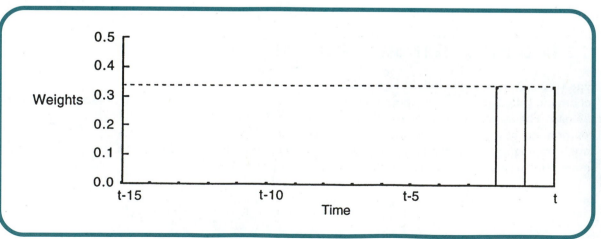

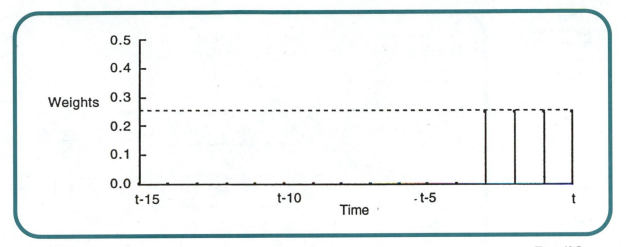

Figure 12-5.
Smoothing weights for a
4-period moving average
for the forecast of the
next time period.

This forecasting method is called *moving averages* because the average "moves" forward as the "next" period becomes the "current" time period. Consider the following data.

Time	1	2	3
Y	28	31	29

The forecasted value based on a 3-period moving average is

$$\hat{Y}_4 = \frac{Y_1 + Y_2 + Y_3}{3} = \frac{28 + 31 + 29}{3} = 29.33.$$

The forecast of the fifth time period is possible using a moving average model when the data for the fourth time period becomes available.

Time	1	2	3	4
Y	28	31	29	25

The average "moves forward" according to

$$\hat{Y}_5 = \frac{Y_2 + Y_3 + Y_4}{3} = \frac{31 + 29 + 25}{3} = 28.33.$$

This process of moving forward is repeated as new data become available, and the forecast is revised by moving ahead one time period.

The moving averages models presented above are examples of a *simple* moving average. These models may be extended by allowing the weights to assume different values. The following smoothing model considers only the present and previous two time periods, as does the 3-period moving average illustrated above. This weighted average model, however, weights the present more than the previous time period, which in turn is weighted more than the next previous time period.

$$\hat{Y}_{t+1} = \tfrac{3}{6}Y_t + \tfrac{2}{6}Y_{t-1} + \tfrac{1}{6}Y_{t-2}.$$

Figure 12-6.
The Dow-Jones Industrial Average and the corresponding 4-period moving average from March of 1988 to December of 1990.

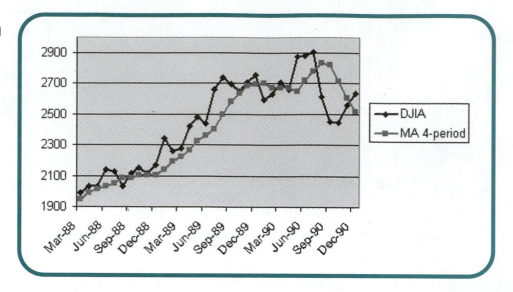

The weights for all previous time periods sum to 1, so the forecast $\hat{Y}_{t+1}$ is a weighted average.

To choose the weights, first choose a preliminary set of weights that follows the desired pattern, and then sum these preliminary weights. An actual weight is the corresponding preliminary weight divided by the sum. For example, a set of preliminary weights for a 4-period moving weighted average is 12, 9, 5, and 1. The sum of these preliminary weights is

$$12 + 9 + 5 + 1 = 27.$$

The resulting forecast is

$$\hat{Y}_{t+1} = \frac{12}{27}Y_t + \frac{9}{27}Y_{t-1} + \frac{5}{27}Y_{t-2} + \frac{1}{27}Y_{t-3}.$$

The weights for all time periods sum to $\frac{27}{27} = 1$.

Why are these forecasts based on averages of past data called smoothing methods? The answer is illustrated in Figure 12-6, in which the Dow-Jones Industrial Average and the corresponding 4-period moving average is plotted monthly from March 1988 to December 1990. The moving average plot is smoother, less jagged.

The smoothing of the historical data averages out some of the influence of the random sampling fluctuations, providing a more stable basis for forecasting the next value in the series.

A forecast from a smoothing method isolates and extends the smooth trend by filtering the noise from the data.

By chance, the random error for the current time period could be positive, resulting in an observed Y_t larger than expected from the underlying stable pattern. Similarly, the random error for the previous time period could be negative, so that the observed Y_{t-1} is smaller than expected. Averaging Y_t and Y_{t-1} together tends to cancel out these two opposing errors, generally yielding a more accurate prediction for the future $\hat{Y}_{t+1}$.

Evaluating a Forecasting Method

The previous section presented a variety of weight schemes: 3-period moving average, 4-period moving average, and a weighted moving average. Actually, the number of weighting patterns that could define different moving average models is limitless. How does the analyst choose from among the various competing weighting schemes?

The "best" weighting scheme chosen from a set of plausible alternatives is the set of weights that minimizes some function of the errors. The technique for obtaining these errors is to use the alternative models to "forecast" what is already known. How well do the different models predict the known value of Y_t from earlier time periods? The value of Y_t is known, but it can also be "forecasted" from the value of Y at earlier times. Or, extending this logic further, how well can the different models predict Y_{t-1} from earlier time periods? Or Y_{t-2}? Or Y_{t-3}? The accuracy of prediction for each model is gauged by comparing the forecasted value from earlier time periods with the actual, known value. The chosen forecasting model is the model that has the smallest fit statistic, such as the sum of the squared forecasting errors, among all alternative models.

The sum of the squared errors SSE was discussed in detail throughout Chapter 8. For regression analysis, the sum of the squared errors, or some related statistic such as the mean squared error MSE or its square root $s_e = \sqrt{\text{MSE}}$, is the criterion of primary interest because the regression weights are derived so as to minimize SSE. The weights that define a specific moving average forecasting model are not chosen explicitly to minimize SSE, so other criteria for model evaluation are also applied to forecasting models.

An alternative to MSE or $\sqrt{\text{MSE}}$ is computed not from the sum of the squared errors but from the sum of the absolute value of the forecasting errors. This fit statistic is called the **mean absolute deviation.** The MAD statistic is analogous, and often approximately equal, to $\sqrt{\text{MSE}}$. To compute MAD, compute the *absolute value* of each error, and then obtain the average of this new variable. To compute $\sqrt{\text{MSE}}$, compute the average of the *square* of each error, and then take the square root of the average.

An example illustrating the use of various sets of weights for generating a forecast, and then choosing the "best" set of weights, is presented next.

> **mean absolute deviation or MAD** *average absolute value of the forecasting errors (deviations)*

BUSINESS APPLICATION 12.2—Moving Averages

MANAGERIAL PROBLEM

Management needs to forecast sales for the next month, January.

DATA

Sales data are available for the last 12 months. These 12 data values ($10,000s) appear in the following conceptual worksheet, shaded in gray.

APPLICATION—CONCEPTUAL WORKSHEET

Simple 3-Period Moving Average

Each moving average is the average of the previous three months, so calculate the first 3-period moving average for the fourth month, April. Continue this calculation for all remaining months. The average calculated over the last three months is the forecast for the subsequent months.

	A	B	C	D	E	F
2	Weights	0.333	0.333	0.333	1.000	
3		Wt1	Wt2	Wt3	WtTotal	
4						
5	Month	Sales	Forecast	Error	SqError	AbsErr
6	Jan	5.6				
7	Feb	9.3				
8	Mar	12.1				
9	Apr	11.6	9.00	2.60	6.76	2.60
10	May	13.5	11.00	2.50	6.25	2.50
11	Jun	20.3	12.40	7.90	62.41	7.90
12	Jul	16.2	15.13	1.07	1.14	1.07
13	Aug	19.4	16.67	2.73	7.47	2.73
14	Sep	14.1	18.63	-4.53	20.55	4.53
15	Oct	20.1	16.57	3.53	12.48	3.53
16	Nov	22.5	17.87	4.63	21.47	4.63
17	Dec	19.8	18.90	0.90	0.81	0.90
18	Forecast		**20.80**			
19	Sum				139.34	30.40
20	Mean				15.48	**3.38**
21	Sq Root				**3.93**	

The formulas for the first row of calculations, Row 9, are shown below. The forecasted sales in Column C is the average of the previous three monthly sales. The error in Column D is the forecast subtracted from the actual sales, which is then squared in Column E, and any minus sign is deleted in Column F.

	A	B	C	D	E	F
5	Month	Sales	Forecast	Error	SqError	AbsErr
6	Jan	5.6				
7	Feb	9.3				
8	Mar	12.1				
9	Apr	11.6	=(Wt1*B8+Wt2*B7+Wt3*B6)/WtTotal	=Sales-Forecast	=Error^2	=ABS(Error)

For this forecasting model, $\sqrt{\text{MSE}} = \$39{,}300$ and MAD $= \$33{,}800$, with a January forecast of \$208,000.

Weighted 3-Period Moving Average

	A	B	C	D	E	F
1	Pattern	3	2	1		
2	Weights	0.500	0.333	0.167	1.000	
3		Wt1	Wt2	Wt3	WtTotal	
4						
5	Month	Sales	Forecast	Error	SqError	AbsErr
6	Jan	5.6				
7	Feb	9.3				
8	Mar	12.1				
9	Apr	11.6	10.08	1.52	2.30	1.52
10	May	13.5	11.38	2.12	4.48	2.12
11	Jun	20.3	12.63	7.67	58.78	7.67
12	Jul	16.2	16.58	-0.38	0.15	0.38
13	Aug	19.4	17.12	2.28	5.21	2.28
14	Sep	14.1	18.48	-4.38	19.21	4.38
15	Oct	20.1	16.22	3.88	15.08	3.88
16	Nov	22.5	17.98	4.52	20.40	4.52
17	Dec	19.8	20.30	-0.50	0.25	0.50
18	Forecast		**20.75**			
19	Sum				125.86	27.25
20	Mean				13.98	**3.03**
21	Sq Root				3.74	

Calculate the weights in Row 2 from the pattern specified in Row 1.

	A	B	C	D	E
1	Pattern	3	2	1	
2	Weights	=B1/SUM($B$1:$D$1)	=C1/SUM($B$1:$D$1)	=D1/SUM($B$1:$D$1)	=SUM(B2:D2)
3		Wt1	Wt2	Wt3	WtTotal

Given the weights, calculate the weighted mean forecast for a month from sales for the previous three months in Column C. The formulas are the same as those presented for the simple 3-period moving average.

The forecast for the next January sales from this weighted averages model is $207,500, with $\sqrt{\text{MSE}} = \$37,400$ and MAD = $30,300.

APPLICATION—TRADITIONAL NOTATION

3-Period Moving Average

The forecasted value for April (in $10,000s) is

$$\hat{Y}_{\text{Apr}} = \frac{Y_{\text{Mar}} + Y_{\text{Feb}} + Y_{\text{Jan}}}{3} = \frac{5.6 + 9.3 + 12.1}{3} = \frac{27.0}{3} = 9.0.$$

Similar calculations are applied to the succeeding months. The average for the last three months is the forecast of *next* month's sales $\hat{Y}_{t+1}$, $208,000. Once all the moving average forecasts are available, calculate the forecasting errors. For example, the error for the April forecast is

$$e_{\text{Apr}} \equiv Y_{\text{Apr}} - \hat{Y}_{\text{Apr}} = 11.6 - 9.0 = 2.6.$$

The squared errors and absolute value of the errors are readily obtained from these forecasting errors.

Weighted 3-Period Moving Average

Calculate the weighted moving average according to the pattern 3, 2, and 1, which translates into weights of $\frac{3}{6} = .5$, $\frac{2}{6} = .33$, and $\frac{1}{6} = 0.17$. For example, the following expression calculates this weighted average forecast of April (in $10,000s) from the previous three months,

$$\hat{Y}_{\text{Apr}} = \frac{(3)Y_{\text{Mar}} + (2)Y_{\text{Feb}} + (1)Y_{\text{Jan}}}{6} = \frac{(3)12.1 + (2)9.3 + (1)5.6}{6}$$

$$= \frac{186.9}{6} = 10.08.$$

EXCEL GRAPHICS

Figure 12-7 presents a time-series (line) plot of the data and the forecasted values based on the simple 3-period average. The latter represent a smoothed version of the actual data. The technique for plotting multiple columns of data on the same graph is described in detail in Business Application E4.1 in Chapter 4 Extension.

STATISTICAL CONCLUSION

Comparing the weighted and unweighted models on the basis of the accuracy of past prediction results in choosing the weighted averages model. Both statistical indices of forecasting error, $\sqrt{\text{MSE}}$ and MAD, were less for the weighted averages

Figure 12-7.
Time series plot of data and the three-period average forecast.

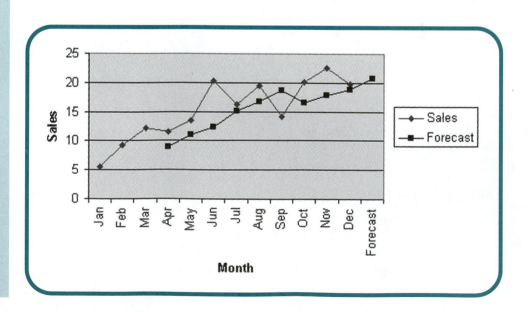

model. However, the actual forecasts barely differed. The preferred weighted averages forecast of next January sales is $207,500, whereas the simple averages model forecasted a sales of $208,000.

MANAGERIAL INTERPRETATION

The January sales forecast is about $208,000.

In the previous example, the weighted averages model, in which more weight is placed on recent time periods than on more distant time periods, was more accurate in forecasting the next value of Y than was the unweighted or simple moving averages model. Another version of a weighted averages model is introduced next.

Exponential Smoothing Method

Of the many time-series forecasting methods, including many not discussed in this chapter, exponential smoothing is perhaps the most widely used. Exponential smoothing provides a set of weights for calculating a weighted average so that the next forecast is explicitly adjusted according to the current forecasting error. The forecast is self-adjusting in that if the current forecast $\hat{Y}_t$ is too large, the next forecast $\hat{Y}_{t+1}$ is smaller than the current forecast. Or, if the current forecast $\hat{Y}_t$ is too small, the next forecast $\hat{Y}_{t+1}$ is larger.

The forecasting error from the current forecast is $Y_t - \hat{Y}_t$. A positive difference indicates that the model underpredicted Y_t so that the next forecast should be increased. A negative difference indicates that the next forecast should be decreased. The exponential smoothing forecast $\hat{Y}_{t+1}$ results from adding this correction to the previous forecast $\hat{Y}_t$. The adjustment made for the next forecast is some proportion of this forecasting error. Adjusting the next forecast by the entire amount of the random error causes the model to overreact in a futile attempt to model error.

The **damping factor α** may assume any value from 0 to 1, although in practice α typically ranges from .1 to .3. This damping factor α is also called the *smoothing parameter* or the *smoothing constant*. The **exponential smoothing** forecast adds this error correction to the current forecast.

$$\boxed{\hat{Y}_{t+1}} \quad = \quad \boxed{\hat{Y}_t} \quad + \quad \boxed{\alpha(Y_t - \hat{Y}_t)}$$

| next forecast | current forecast | adjustment for error in current forecast |

damping factor α
specifies a proportion of the forecasting error according to $\alpha(Y_t - \hat{Y}_t)$, where $0 \le \alpha \le 1$

A little algebraic rearrangement of the above expression yields the computationally simpler expression for generating forecasts displayed in the marginal term box.

For a given value of the damping factor α, the next forecast is calculated from the current value of Y and the current forecasted value of Y. To illustrate, suppose that $\alpha = .3$, the current forecast $\hat{Y}_t = \$128$, and the actual value was $Y_t = \$133$. Calculate the forecast for the next value as

exponential smoothing forecasting method
forecast $\hat{Y}_{t+1}$ is $\hat{Y}_{t+1} = (\alpha)Y_t + (1-\alpha)\hat{Y}_t$, where $0 \le \alpha \le 1$

$$\hat{Y}_{t+1} = (\alpha)Y_t + (1 - \alpha)\hat{Y}_t$$

$$= (.30)\$133 + (.70)\$128 = \$39.90 + \$89.60 = \$129.50.$$

The current forecast of \$128 was \$5 below the actual value of \$133. Accordingly, the new forecast was raised by $.3(\$133 - \$128) = (.3)(\$5) = \$1.50$. The new forecast of \$129.50 partially compensates for this difference from the forecasted and actual.

Why is this model a smoothing model? That is, how can the exponential smoothing model be related to the moving averages models discussed in the previous section? An exponential smoothing model for a given value of a produces a set of weights for each previous time period, just as do the moving averages models. To identify these weights, consider the model for the next forecast:

$$\hat{Y}_{t+1} = (\alpha)Y_t + (1 - \alpha)\hat{Y}_t.$$

Now project the model back one time period to obtain the current forecast $\hat{Y}_t$:

$$\hat{Y}_t = (\alpha)Y_{t-1} + (1 - \alpha)\hat{Y}_{t-1}.$$

Now substitute this expression for $\hat{Y}_t$ back into the model for the next forecast:

$$\hat{Y}_{t+1} = (\alpha)Y_t + (1 - \alpha)[(\alpha)Y_{t-1} + (1 - \alpha)\hat{Y}_{t-1}].$$

A little algebra reveals that the next forecast can be expressed in terms of the current and previous time period as

$$\hat{Y}_{t+1} = (\alpha)Y_t + \alpha(1 - \alpha)Y_{t-1} + (1 - \alpha)^2\hat{Y}_{t-1}.$$

Moreover, this process can be repeated for each previous time period. Moving back two time periods from $t + 1$, the model is expressed as

$$\hat{Y}_{t-1} = (\alpha)Y + t - 2 + (1 - \alpha)\hat{Y}_{t-2}.$$

Substituting the value of $\hat{Y}_{t-1}$ into the previous expression for $\hat{Y}_{t+1}$ yields

$$\hat{Y}_{t+1} = (\alpha)Y_t + \alpha(1 - \alpha)Y_{t-1} + (1 - \alpha)^2[(\alpha)Y_{t-2} + (1 - \alpha)\hat{Y}_{t-2}].$$

Working through the algebra results in an expression for the next forecast in terms of the current time period and the two immediately past time periods:

$$\hat{Y}_{t+1} = (\alpha)Y_t + \alpha(1 - \alpha)Y_{t-1} + \alpha(1 - \alpha)^2Y_{t-2} + (1 - \alpha)^3\hat{Y}_{t-2}.$$

In each of the above expressions for the forecast $\hat{Y}_{t+1}$, the forecast is a weighted sum of some past time periods plus the forecast for the last time period considered. Table 12-1 shows the specific values of the weights over the current and 10 previous time periods for four different values of α. Note that the forecast is made according to $(\alpha)Y_t + (1 - \alpha)\hat{Y}_t$, so these weights are not actually computed to make the forecast but are *implicit* in the forecast. Also, more than 10 previous time periods are necessary for the weights for $\alpha = .1$ and $\alpha = .3$ to sum to 1.00.

The reason for the word *exponential* in the name of this smoothing method is demonstrated by the following plots of the smoothing weights for three different values of α. Each set of weights in Figures 12-8, 12-9, and 12-10 exponentially decreases from the current time period back into previous time periods. The larger the value of α, the more relative emphasis placed on the current and immediate time periods.

What value of α should be chosen for a particular model in a particular setting? The basis for choosing a value of α is partly empirical and partly theoretical. The theoretical reason follows from the previous table and graphs that illustrate the smoothing weights for different values of α. Larger values of α give more weight to the current and immediate past than do smaller values. If the time series is relatively free from random error, then a larger value of α permits the series to adjust more quickly to any underlying changes. For time series that contain a substantial

Time	Weights	$\alpha = .1$	$\alpha = .3$	$\alpha = .5$	$\alpha = .7$
t	$b_t = \alpha$	.100	.300	.500	.700
$t-1$	$b_{t-1} = \alpha(1-\alpha)^1$	.090	.210	.250	.210
$t-2$	$b_{t-2} = \alpha(1-\alpha)^2$	.081	.147	.125	.063
$t-3$	$b_{t-3} = \alpha(1-\alpha)^3$	.073	.103	.063	.019
$t-4$	$b_{t-4} = \alpha(1-\alpha)^4$	.066	.072	.031	.006
$t-5$	$b_{t-5} = \alpha(1-\alpha)^5$	.059	.050	.016	.002
$t-6$	$b_{t-6} = \alpha(1-\alpha)^6$	.053	.035	.008	.001
$t-7$	$b_{t-7} = \alpha(1-\alpha)^7$	.048	.025	.004	.000
$t-8$	$b_{t-8} = \alpha(1-\alpha)^8$	.043	.017	.002	.000
$t-9$	$b_{t-9} = \alpha(1-\alpha)^9$	.039	.012	.001	.000
$t-10$	$b_{t-10} = \alpha(1-\alpha)^{10}$	.035	.008	.000	.000
	Sum	0.687	.0979	1.000	1.001

Table 12-1.
Weights from exponential smoothing models for $\alpha = .1$, .3, .5, and .7 for the present value of Y and the previous ten values of Y.

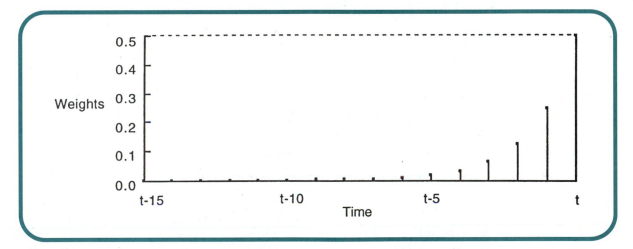

Figure 12-8.
Smoothing weights with $\alpha = .5$ for the forecast of the next time period.

random error component, however, smaller values of α should be used so as not to "overreact" to the random sampling fluctuations inherent in the data.

This advice regarding the choice of α is useful, but more information is needed in order to select this value. How is the usefulness of one value of α compared to the usefulness of another? The answer is based on the same technique illustrated in the previous section: Compute $\sqrt{\text{MSE}}$ or MAD, and choose the smoothing model—exponential smoothing or some other weighting method such as simple averages—that minimizes these values.

One problem in computing these error indices for an exponential smoothing model is that the current forecast is needed to compute the next forecast. What

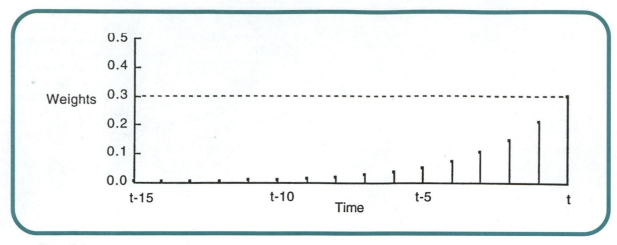

Figure 12-9.
Smoothing weights with
$\alpha = .3$ for the forecast
of the next time period.

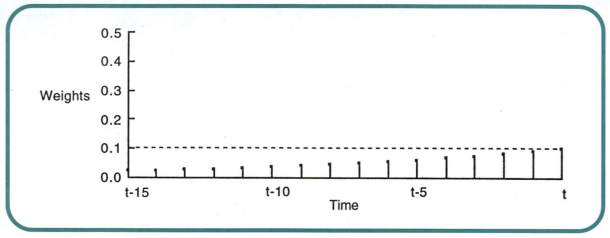

Figure 12-10.
Smoothing weights with
$\alpha = .1$ for the forecast
of the next time period.

value should be used for the forecast of the first time period in which no previous forecasts exist? One technique is to set the first forecast equal to the first data value. Another technique is to set the first forecast equal to the average of the first four or five data values.

An example of choosing the value of the smoothing parameter α follows.

BUSINESS APPLICATION 12.3—Exponential Smoothing

MANAGERIAL PROBLEM

Management needs to forecast sales for the next month, January. Previous forecasts were obtained with simple and weighted moving averages, but now management wants to evaluate exponential smoothing.

DATA

Sales data are available for the last 12 months. These 12 data values appear in the following conceptual worksheet. Their time-series plot appears in Business Application 12.2.

APPLICATION—TRADITIONAL NOTATION

Calculate exponential smoothing forecasts with $\alpha = .2$ according to

$$\hat{Y}_{t+1} = (\alpha) Y_t + (1 - \alpha) \hat{Y}_t = .2 Y_t + .8 \hat{Y}_t.$$

To begin these calculations, let the initial sales forecast be the first month sales. Calculate the forecast for February sales as

$$\hat{Y}_{\text{Feb}} = .2 Y_{\text{Jan}} + .8 \hat{Y}_{\text{Jan}} = (.2)5.6 + (.8)5.6 = 5.6.$$

Similarly, calculate the March sales forecast as

$$Y_{\text{Mar}} = .2 Y_{\text{Feb}} + .8 \hat{Y}_{\text{Feb}} = (.2)9.3 + (.8)5.6 = 6.34.$$

The April forecasting error is the difference between actual and forecasted:

$$E_{\text{Apr}} = Y_{\text{Apr}} - \hat{Y}_{\text{Apr}} = 11.6 - 7.49 = 4.11.$$

The following worksheet illustrates these calculations for all relevant time periods.

APPLICATION—EXCEL ANALYSIS

Worksheet for a Single Value of Alpha

The following Excel worksheet computes the room mean square residual (RMSR) from the specified value of the damping factor, Alpha. Forecasting errors were not computed for the first three months in order to facilitate the comparison with the moving averages forecasts made in the previous example, in which forecasts could not be made for the first three months. Also, the forecast for the first month does not exist, so it was arbitrarily set to the sales for the first month. Skipping the errors for the first few months mitigates the effect of this arbitrariness in the computation of $\sqrt{\text{MSE}} = \$61,100$ and $\text{MAD} = \$54,200$.

When you change the value of Alpha in Cell B1, the new RMSR in Cell E18 is automatically computed. The first prediction in Cell C4 is just the initial sales, that is, sales for January. The following predictions are based on the expression for exponential smoothing,

$$\hat{Y}_{t+1} = (\alpha) Y_t + (1 - \alpha) \hat{Y}_t,$$

which is the weighted average of the previous value plus the previous forecasted value.

The given data from which the analysis proceeds is shaded in gray. Cell A1 is named Alpha, and Cell E18 is named RMSR. To name a cell, select both the name next to the cell and the cell itself, and then use the menu sequence

Insert ➤ Name ➤ Create...

	A	B	C	D	E
1	Alpha	0.2			
2					
3	Month	Sales	Forecast	Error	SqError
4	Jan	5.6	5.60		
5	Feb	9.3	5.60		
6	Mar	12.1	6.34		
7	Apr	11.6	7.49	4.11	16.88
8	May	13.5	8.31	5.19	26.90
9	Jun	20.3	9.35	10.95	119.88
10	Jul	16.2	11.54	4.66	21.71
11	Aug	19.4	12.47	6.93	47.99
12	Sep	14.1	13.86	0.24	0.06
13	Oct	20.1	13.91	6.19	38.36
14	Nov	22.5	15.15	7.35	54.09
15	Dec	19.8	16.62	3.18	10.14
16	Forecast		17.25		
17					
18				RMSR	6.11

Annotations on the worksheet:
- Row 4 Forecast ← *B4*
- Row 5 Forecast ← *Alpha *B4 + (1 − Alpha)*C4*
- Row 7 Error ← *= B7 − C7*
- Row 7 SqError ← *= D7^2*
- Row 18 ← *=SQRT(AVERAGE(E7:E15))*

Worksheet for a Range of Values of Alpha

The previous worksheet that yielded a single RMSR given a single value of Alpha can be extended using the Excel Table feature. This feature automatically computes the value of RMSR for an entire *range* of Alpha values. The key to setting up the table is to specify the range of values for Alpha, and then instruct Excel to provide RMSR for each value of Alpha.

Enter labels in G1 and H1 to improve readability. Next, skip a line and enter the first value of Alpha, 0.0, in G3. Use the Edit ➤ Fill ➤ Series . . . menu sequence to specify the remaining values, such as in .1 increments, until the largest possible value of Alpha of 1.0 is reached.

	G	H
1	Alpha	RMSR
2		
3	0.0	
4	0.1	
5	0.2	
6	0.3	
7	0.4	
8	0.5	
9	0.6	
10	0.7	
11	0.8	
12	0.9	
13	1.0	

Next, provide Excel the formula for computing the desired value from the previously constructed worksheet. This is done by setting Cell H2 to the desired expression, which is =RMSR, or $E$18. To enhance readability, the cell can be formatted to appear blank: Invoke the Format ➤ Cells . . . menu sequence, select the Number tab, select Custom under Category, and then insert three semicolons for Type.

Now provide Excel the value to input into this formula. Select the cell range G2:H13, and formally define the table with the following menu sequence.

Data ➤ Table...

In the resulting dialog box, enter Alpha as the input cell for a column of values.

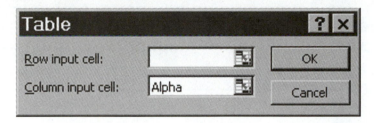

Excel calculates the resulting values of RMSR and enters them into the table.

	G Alpha	H RMSR
1	Alpha	RMSR
2		
3	0.0	12.41
4	0.1	8.32
5	0.2	6.11
6	0.3	4.91
7	0.4	4.27
8	0.5	3.94
9	0.6	3.81
10	0.7	3.79
11	0.8	3.85
12	0.9	3.97
13	1.0	4.14

← = RMSR

Graph for a Range of Values of Alpha

A graph of these paired values of Alpha and RMSR is easily constructed, beginning with the following menu sequence.

Insert ➤ Chart...

Step 1—Chart Type. Specify an $X\,Y$ (Scatter) chart for the plot of two continuous variables. Select a format that connects the points with a smoothed curve.

Step 2—Chart Source. Specify a Data Range of cells that includes the data for the two variables, Alpha and RMSR.

Step 3—Chart Options. Unclick the Show legend checkbox to remove the redundant legend. Select the Titles tab and name the *X* and *Y* axes as well as the chart.

Step 4—Chart Location. Specify the location of the chart, either on a new sheet or as an object on the current worksheet.

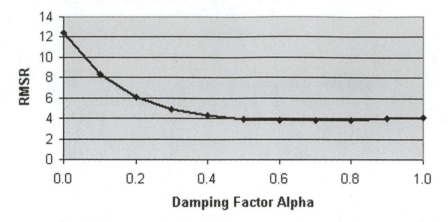

Worksheet for the Optimal Value of Alpha

Examination of the previous graph indicates that the value of Alpha that yields the lowest RMSR for this one sample is between 0.6 and 0.8. Excel can locate the specific value of Alpha that minimizes the error index, RMSR. Begin with the optimization program called Solver found under the Tools menu.

Tools ➤ Solver...

Calling up this program results in the following dialog box. Set Target Cell to the value of RMSR, which is Cell E18. Specify the Min option for minimization, and change the cell corresponding to the value of Alpha, which is Cell B1.

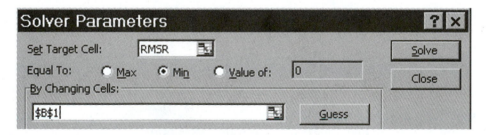

In the next dialog box, select the Keep Solver Solution option.

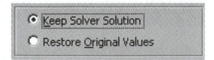

The optimized value of α, 0.67, and the corresponding minimized value of RMSR, 3.79, both appear on the spreadsheet.

	A	B	C	D	E
1	Alpha	0.67			
2					
3	Month	Sales	Forecast	Error	SqError
4	Jan	5.6	5.60		
5	Feb	9.3	5.60		
6	Mar	12.1	8.07		
7	Apr	11.6	10.76	0.84	0.71
8	May	13.5	11.32	2.18	4.75
9	Jun	20.3	12.77	7.53	56.63
10	Jul	16.2	17.80	-1.60	2.54
11	Aug	19.4	16.73	2.67	7.12
12	Sep	14.1	18.51	-4.41	19.46
13	Oct	20.1	15.57	4.53	20.54
14	Nov	22.5	18.59	3.91	15.27
15	Dec	19.8	21.20	-1.40	1.96
16	Forecast		20.27		
17					
18				RMSR	**3.79**

Remember that this optimized value of the smoothing constant α is optimized only for the one sample of data entered into the worksheet. Of greater interest is the optimized value of α for the entire population from which the sample was obtained. The confidence interval and associated standard error for estimating this population value are available only from statistical methods more advanced than those presented here.

STATISTICAL PRINCIPLE

In practice, the value of α typically varies from .1 to .3. In this brief example, the value for α of .67, did the best job of forecasting over past time periods, with MAD = 3.20, compared to the values of 3.59 for $\alpha = .4$ and 5.42 for $\alpha = .2$. Why do the results of this example run counter to the established practice of using relatively small values of α? The reason is that, in practice, the analysis usually includes many more than 12 data values. With only 12 data values, the initial value of the forecast assumes the weight needed so that all weights sum to 1.00. With a small value of α, the weight for the initial value is relatively large in this example. Yet the initial value Y_{Jan} is considerably smaller than the average of the time-series values or of the more recent values. A value of .6 for α leads to a pattern of weights that virtually ignores Y_{Jan}, leading to lower values of $\sqrt{MSE}$ or MAD.

MANAGERIAL INTERPRETATION

Based on the technique that provided the most accurate forecasts from existing data, the forecasted sales revenue for the next month is $202,700.

The methods used to generate forecasts from time-series data presented up to this point combine one or more values of the time series to forecast the next value. Next, we'll examine some forecasting methods that base the forecast on an analysis of the underlying trend and seasonal components of a time series.

EXERCISES

12-3. The following table lists the number of building permits for new private housing over 15 years, scaled so that 1987 = 100 (Source: Department of Commerce).

Year	1980	1981	1982	1983	1984
Permits	78.6	65.1	65.7	106.7	109.6
Year	1985	1986	1987	1988	1989
Permits	112.4	114.9	100.0	94.2	87.6
Year	1990	1991	1992	1993	1994
Permits	72.9	61.4	71.2	78.3	86.4

For these data, compute

a. The 3-period simple moving average, MAD, and $\sqrt{\text{MSE}}$.
b. The 4-period simple moving average, MAD, and $\sqrt{\text{MSE}}$.
c. The weighted moving average with .6, .3, and .1 weights; MAD; and $\sqrt{\text{MSE}}$.
d. Forecast the number of permits for 1995.

12-4. Plot the data in Exercise 12-3 as well as the forecasted values for the method that yielded the best forecasts over these 15 years.

12-5. The following monthly data were analyzed with exponential smoothing in the preceding business application with the three different values of the smoothing parameter α of .2, .4, and .6.

Jan	Feb	Mar	Apr	May	Jun
5.6	9.3	12.1	11.6	13.5	20.3

Jul	Aug	Spt	Oct	Nov	Dec
16.2	19.4	14.1	20.1	22.5	19.8

For each analysis in the preceding application, the initial forecast was chosen as the initial data value of 5.6. Compute the forecasted value for the succeeding January with initial values of 10 and 30 for

a. $\alpha = .2$
b. $\alpha = .4$
c. $\alpha = .6$
d. Compare the nine forecasted values obtained with the three different smoothing parameter values α and the three initial values. How do the values of α and the initial forecast values influence the January forecast?

12.3 ANALYZING THE COMPONENTS OF A TIME SERIES

In Chapter 3, the trend, cyclical, and seasonal components underlying time-series data were discussed. Forecasting with smoothing methods does not identify and use these components. However, knowledge of these components provides an enhanced theoretical understanding of the processes that generate the values of the time series, as well as facilitate forecasting future values. This section begins by generating a forecast from a time series described only by a trend component plus error. Following is the description of the more complicated process of forecasting from a time series characterized by trend *and* seasonality plus error.

Forecasting from the Trend Component

As explained at the end of Chapter 3, the trend component of a time series is a long-term steady increase or decrease over time. The trend can appear in a variety of different forms, the simplest of which is linear. The variable Trend represents the trend component and t represents time periods such as 1, 2, 3, … With this notation, a linear trend is expressed as

$$\text{Trend} = b_1 t + b_0.$$

If the underlying time series has neither cyclical nor seasonal components, each data value Y is generated from only the trend and error components. If trend is the only stable component, the forecast can be based exclusively on this trend, as is demonstrated in the following example.

BUSINESS APPLICATION 12.4—Forecasting from Linear Trend

MANAGERIAL PROBLEM

The number of employees of a growing computer software company has been steadily increasing since the company's founding in 1980. As part of a new business plan, management needs to forecast the number of employees for the next year, 1999.

DATA

Year	1979	1980	1981	1982	1983	1984	1985	1986	1987	1988
Employees	0	30	39	31	64	73	88	75	121	148

Year	1989	1990	1991	1992	1993	1994	1995	1996	1997	1998
Employees	152	144	156	183	180	199	191	248	227	243

ANALYSIS

Visual examination of the time-series data Y in Figure 12-11 indicates linear growth with no apparent cyclical components. Accordingly, the data Y were regressed on the time periods t, beginning with $t = 1$ and ending with $t = 20$. The result is expressed in the following OLS regression equation:

$$\text{Trend} = 12.611t - 2.811.$$

The large adjusted R-square of $R^2_{adj} = .968$ indicates that this linear regression model explains the data very well, so more complicated models are unnecessary. The corresponding graph and predicted values of Y based on this linear trend are presented in Figure 12-11.

Using the estimated regression model, the forecast for the following year, 1995 or Time Period 21, is

$$\hat{Y} = 12.611\,(21) - 2.811 \approx 262.$$

The number of employees forecast for 1999 by extrapolating linear trend is 262.

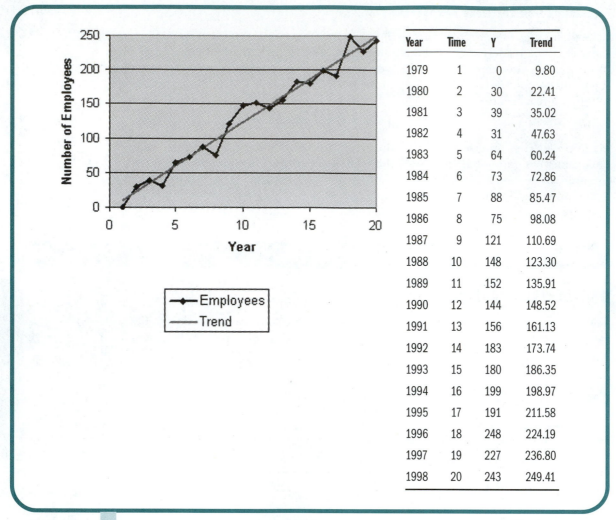

Year	Time	Y	Trend
1979	1	0	9.80
1980	2	30	22.41
1981	3	39	35.02
1982	4	31	47.63
1983	5	64	60.24
1984	6	73	72.86
1985	7	88	85.47
1986	8	75	98.08
1987	9	121	110.69
1988	10	148	123.30
1989	11	152	135.91
1990	12	144	148.52
1991	13	156	161.13
1992	14	183	173.74
1993	15	180	186.35
1994	16	199	198.97
1995	17	191	211.58
1996	18	248	224.19
1997	19	227	236.80
1998	20	243	249.41

Figure 12-11.
Time series *Y*
(number of
employees) and the
underlying linear
trend.

MANAGERIAL INTERPRETATION

Unless there is a major structural change in the business environment, such as the entrance of a major new competitor or the acquisition of a new automated software generator, plans for next year's staffing should include an increase of 19 employees from this year's 243 employees, for a total of 262.

The data in the previous example closely followed a linear growth trend. Many businesses also encounter seasonal influences on important variables such as sales or number of employees. The next section deals with this more complex scenario.

Isolating the Seasonal Components

Many time series are characterized by both trend and seasonality. Consider a swimsuit manufacturer. Each year sales tend to increase over the previous year, but demand for swimwear is always larger in the summer than in winter. The corresponding time-series data show a steady upward progression modulated by the seasonal ups and downs and the ever present random error. Forecasts of future values must not only account for the gradual upward trend, but also for the specific season for which the forecast is made.

The forecasting method that accounts for both trend and seasonality is an extension of the method discussed in the previous section that considered only trend. In this more complex situation, the effect attributed to each season, such as a 12% increase above the yearly average for summer sales, first needs to be identified and then removed. Removal of the seasonal effects leaves only the trend and cyclical components plus random error. In the absence of a cyclical component, the remaining trend component is forecast into the future by following the procedure described in the last section: Regress the time-series data onto time, except here use the data with the seasonal effects removed. This extrapolation of the underlying trend is then adjusted according to the previously isolated seasonal effects. For example, if summer sales tend to be 12% more than the yearly average, then the trend forecast of summer sales should be increased 12%.

Forecasts based on trend and seasonality are generated by identifying and removing the seasonal influences, extrapolating the linear trend such as with regression, and then adjusting the forecasts according to the seasonal influences.

In essence, seasonality is removed, and then the trend is extrapolated and adjusted for seasonality.

Identifying the seasonal component of a time series, such as the systematic up-and-down fluctuations within a year, requires the analyst first to identify the seasons. A year could be broken into four quarters: Winter, Spring, Summer, and Fall. Another common alternative is to divide the year into 12 months. The number of seasons with which the data are analyzed depends on the judgment of the analyst and the time interval between adjacent values in the time series. Quarterly data rule out a monthly analysis.

Once you've established the number of seasons, remove the seasonal fluctuations with a moving average that has the number of periods equal to the number of seasons. For example, four seasons per year leads to the computation of a 4-period moving average. An average of Y across four consecutive quarters—Winter, Spring, Summer, and Fall—averages out the seasonal influences.

Seasonal fluctuations are removed from a time series with n seasons per year by calculating an n-period moving average for each value of Y.

Calculating this moving average for each data value removes the fluctuations of seasonality from the entire time series. With the seasonal fluctuations removed, each actual value of Y for a season can be compared to the corresponding averaged value. For example, if the data value for the third quarter tends to be consistently larger than the corresponding yearly average computed around each third quarter, then the seasonality effect for the third quarter boosts Y above the yearly average.

Calculate the first moving average as the average of the first year's sales,

$$\overline{Y} = \frac{Y_1 + Y_2 + Y_3 + Y_4}{4}.$$

With which season does this moving average correspond? This value can be thought of as representing the middle of the year, but because the number of quarters (seasons) is an even number, there is no middle quarter. The middle of the year is represented not by a single quarter but by the last half of Quarter 2 and the first half of Quarter 3.

Similarly, calculate the second moving average from the second quarter of the first year to the first quarter of the second year, the fifth data value:

$$\overline{Y} = \frac{Y_2 + Y_3 + Y_4 + Y_5}{4}.$$

This average corresponds to the last half of Quarter 3 and the first half of Quarter 4.

As illustrated in Figure 12-12, averaging these two moving averages yields a value, called the **centered moving average,** that matches the complete third quarter—first half and second half—with the fluctuations due to seasonal influences removed.

The extra step of computing centered moving averages from the moving averages is only necessary when the number of seasons per year is an even number, such as quarters or months. With an odd number of seasons per year, the initially computed moving averages already match the seasons of the year, so the additional centering is unnecessary.

The centered moving average provides a value for each quarter free from seasonal fluctuations. The key to estimating the seasonal effects is to compare each actual data value to the corresponding smoothed value. The type of comparison depends on the type of model—additive or multiplicative—as described in Chapter 3. With the additive model, this comparison is accomplished by subtracting the smoothed value from the actual value. With the multiplicative model, the comparison is made by dividing the actual value by the smoothed value. The result is an estimate of the effect of seasonality for that particular season in that particular year.

This adjustment isolates the seasonal and error components. How should the influence of random error be removed: Calculate the *initial seasonal index* for a particular season which is the average of the indices for that season across all years. For the additive model, these seasonal indices must sum to zero. For the multiplicative model, the indices should average one. Sometimes the seasonal indices need to be adjusted to conform to this requirement. For the multiplicative model, adjust each seasonal index by multiplying the initial index by the number of seasons and then dividing this result by the sum of the initial or unadjusted seasonal indices.

$$\text{Seasonal Index} = \frac{\text{initial seasonal index} * \text{number of periods per year}}{\text{sum of initial seasonal indices}}$$

The result is the seasonal index for each season.

An example illustrating this process is presented next.

centered moving average
average of two successive moving averages

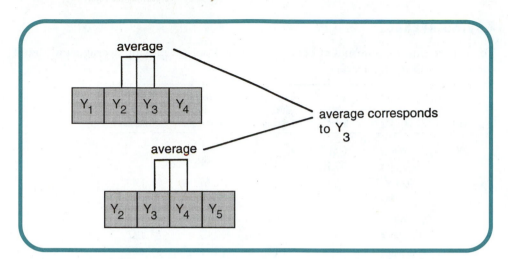

Figure 12-12.
The (centered moving) average of the two averages corresponds to the third time period.

BUSINESS APPLICATION 12.5—Seasonal Data I, Seasonal Indices

MANAGERIAL PROBLEM

Although annual sales for a swimwear company have been increasing, managers have noticed a considerable (though not unexpected) fluctuation for each of the four seasons of the year. Sales appear to peak in summer and are depressed in winter. To better understand these seasonal fluctuations, management wants to estimate the effect of each season on sales (in $10,000s).

Figure 12-13.
Time-series plot of quarterly sales data (in $10,000s).

DATA

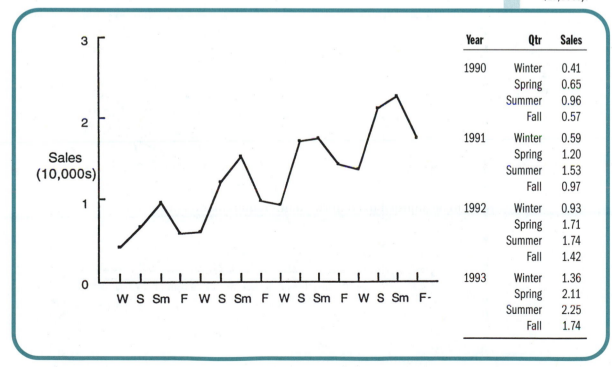

Year	Qtr	Sales
1990	Winter	0.41
	Spring	0.65
	Summer	0.96
	Fall	0.57
1991	Winter	0.59
	Spring	1.20
	Summer	1.53
	Fall	0.97
1992	Winter	0.93
	Spring	1.71
	Summer	1.74
	Fall	1.42
1993	Winter	1.36
	Spring	2.11
	Summer	2.25
	Fall	1.74

MOVING AVERAGE

To average out the seasonal effects, calculate a 4-period moving average and then the centered moving average.

Year	Qtr	Sales	4-Period Moving Average	Centered Moving Average	Specific Seasonal Index
1990	Winter	0.41			
	Spring	0.65	0.65		
	Summer	0.96	0.69	0.67	1.43
	Fall	0.57	0.83	0.76	0.75
1991	Winter	0.59	0.97	0.90	0.66
	Spring	1.20	1.07	1.02	1.17
	Summer	1.53	1.16	1.12	1.37
	Fall	0.97	1.29	1.22	0.80
1992	Winter	0.93	1.34	1.31	0.71
	Spring	1.71	1.45	1.40	1.23
	Summer	1.74	1.56	1.50	1.16
	Fall	1.42	1.66	1.61	0.88
1993	Winter	1.36	1.78	1.72	0.79
	Spring	2.11	1.87	1.82	1.15
	Summer	2.25	1.53		
	Fall	1.74			

The plot of the centered moving average and the original time-series data appears in Figure 12-14.

Figure 12-14. Quarterly sales and the corresponding centered moving averages.

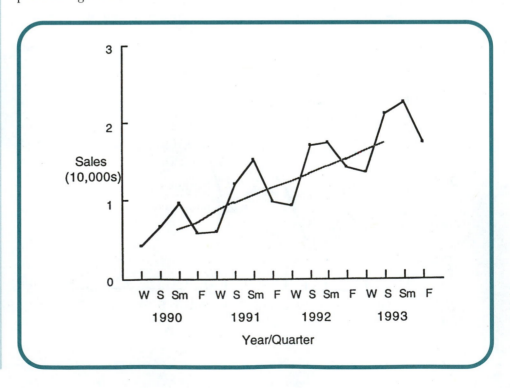

Table 12-2.
Initial seasonal
indices

Qtr	Specific Seasonal Indices	Unadjusted Index
W	0.66, 0.71, 0.79	0.72
S	1.17, 1.23, 1.15	1.18
Sm	1.43, 1.37, 1.16	1.32
F	0.75, 0.80, 0.88	0.81
		4.03

SEASONAL INDICES

To compute the specific summer seasonal index for 1990, consider sales for Summer 1990, which were $9,600. The average sales for all four quarters of 1990, centered over Summer 1990, is $6,700. The specific seasonal index is

$$\text{Specific Seasonal Index for Summer 1990} = \frac{\$9,600}{\$6,700} = 1.43.$$

Summer 1990 sales were 43% more than that expected without considering seasonality.

Sales each summer are larger than the corresponding year average. For 1990 through 1992, the respective specific summer indices are 1.43, 1.37, and 1.16. The average of these three numbers provides a better estimate of the general summer index than does any of the individual values:

$$\text{Initial Summer Index} = \frac{1.43 + 1.37 + 1.16}{3} = \frac{3.96}{3} = 1.32.$$

Repeating this averaging for all four indices yields the initial or unadjusted seasonal indices in Table 12-2.

The problem with these initial indices is that, to maintain the interpretability of the indices as percentages above or below the overall average, their average must be 1.00, which specifies that their sum is 4.00. In this case, the sum is slightly larger: 4.03. The initially derived seasonal indices are adjusted by multiplying each initial index by 4 and dividing by the sum of the initial indices, which is 4.03.

$$\text{Quarterly Seasonal Index} = \frac{4*\text{Unadjusted Index}}{\sum \text{Unadjusted Indices}}$$

Applying this adjustment leads to the seasonal indices in Table 12-3.

Of course, this expression for the adjustment of the seasonal indices is modified for seasons of different lengths. Adjusting monthly indices requires multiplying each unadjusted index by 12.

MANAGERIAL INTERPRETATION

Sales of swimwear fluctuate throughout the year according to the four seasons. During winter, sales are 29% below the overall average. Spring sales are 18% above

Table 12-3.
Adjusted seasonal indices

Qtr	Seasonal Index
W	0.71
S	1.18
Sm	1.31
F	0.80
	4.00

the overall average as consumers begin to purchase swimwear for the upcoming swim season. The primary selling season is summer, when sales are 31% larger than the overall annual average. As the swimming season ends in the fall, sales drop to 20% below the overall average, but not as low as they do in winter, perhaps because many people take advantage of end-of-the-year Fall specials.

The forecast for the next value is obtained using these seasonal components, as shown in the next section.

Forecasting from the Trend and Seasonal Components

deseasonalized time series
time series with the seasonal effects removed

Once the seasonal indices are known, the fluctuations of the seasonal effects can be removed, creating a **deseasonalized** time series. For the multiplicative model, deseasonalizing is accomplished by dividing each data value of the time series by the corresponding seasonal index. For example, if summer sales were $10,000, and the summer seasonal index is 1.31, then the deseasonalized value is computed as follows.

$$\text{Deseasonalized } Y_t = \frac{Y_t}{\text{seasonal index}} = \frac{\$10,000}{1.31} = \$7634.$$

If summer sales were equal to the yearly average, then summer sales would not be $10,000 but $7,634.

If no cyclical component is present, deseasonalizing the time series leaves trend as the only remaining stable aspect of the series. This trend can be identified and projected into the future using the method discussed in the previous section. Regressing the deseasonalized time series onto time identifies a trend line for forecasting the next value $\hat{Y}_{t+1}$. The actual forecast is the trend projection adjusted by the relevant seasonality index.

BUSINESS APPLICATION 12.6—Seasonal Data II, Forecasting

MANAGERIAL PROBLEM

Management wants to forecast sales (in $10,000s) for each of the next four quarters.

DATA

The data for this problem are the same data listed in Business Application 12.5, which calculated the seasonal indices.

DESEASONALIZATION

First deseasonalize the data. Using the multiplicative model, divide each data value Y_t by the corresponding seasonal index. Consider the first data value, $Y_1 = .41$, which represents Winter 1990 sales of $4,100. From the previous business application, the Winter seasonal index is .71, so the deseasonalized value is larger than .41, computed as follows.

$$\text{Deseasonalized Winter 1990 Sales} = \frac{.41}{.71} = .58.$$

Similar computations are done for all values of Y_t, using the seasonal indices computed in the previous example: Winter = .71, Spring = 1.18, Summer = 1.31, and Fall = .80. The deseasonalized time series is presented in Table 12-4 and Figure 12-15.

EXTRAPOLATING LINEAR TREND

From these deseasonalized data, the regression equation is computed as

$$\hat{Y} = (.104)t + .383.$$

Year	Qtr	Sales	Deseasonalized Sales
1990	Winter	0.41	0.58
	Spring	0.65	0.55
	Summer	0.96	0.73
	Fall	0.57	0.71
1991	Winter	0.59	0.83
	Spring	1.20	1.02
	Summer	1.53	1.17
	Fall	0.97	1.21
1992	Winter	0.93	1.31
	Spring	1.71	1.45
	Summer	1.74	1.33
	Fall	1.42	1.77
1993	Winter	1.36	1.91
	Spring	2.11	1.79
	Summer	2.25	1.72
	Fall	1.74	2.17

Table 12-4.
Deseasonalized time series.

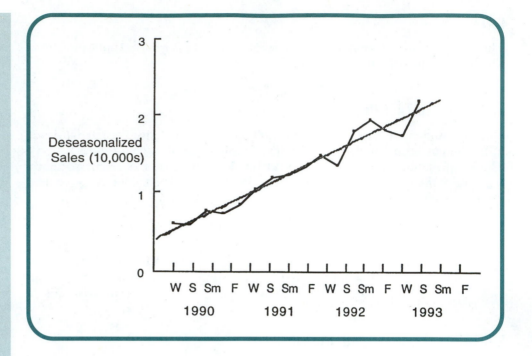

Qtr	Y pred from trend
17	2.151
18	2.255
19	2.359
20	2.463

The corresponding adjusted R-square of $R^2_{\text{adj}} = .947$ indicates that the linear model provides an excellent fit to these data. The four quarters of 1994 are Quarters 17, 18, 19, and 20. Based on this regression equation, the values predicted by trend only appear in Table 12-5.

ADJUSTING FOR SEASONALITY

The seasonal indices were computed for Winter, Spring, Summer, and Fall in the preceding application as 0.71, 1.18, 1.31, and 0.80, respectively. For example, Winter sales are forecasted to be 71% below the linear trend. Multiplying each prediction from the linear trend by the corresponding seasonal index results in the forecasts in Table 12-6 for each of next year's seasons.

Qtr	Seas. Index	Predicted from trend	Forecast
17	0.71	2.151	1.527
18	1.18	2.255	2.661
19	1.31	2.359	3.090
20	0.80	2.463	1.970

Table 12-6. Forecasts for next year's seasons.

MANAGERIAL INTERPRETATION

Management needs to be prepared for sales of over $30,000 for the coming summer, the largest forecast in company history. The smallest sales are forecast for winter quarter, with only about half of the summer value, a little more than $15,000. Spring sales should increase to $26,610 and drop down to under $20,000 for fall.

As is true of most topics discussed in this text, we have only introduced the subject of the chapter, in this case the time-series models and some corresponding statistical analyses. Much more sophisticated techniques exist, but the relatively simple models introduced in this chapter are both useful and understandable without extensive statistical training. For our purposes, the study of time-series models is complete.

EXERCISES

Application

12-6. The following time series represents the monthly money supply (M2) from January 1992 to April 1995, in 1987 billions of dollars.

2848.8	2858.3	2850.4	2840.5	2833.8	2823.4	2818.1
2819.4	2819.0	2817.4	2813.3	2807.7	2796.0	2783.1
2776.6	2770.8	2782.2	2787.6	2785.8	2785.9	2791.5
2782.5	2785.6	2784.5	2788.7	2777.8	2780.1	2781.9
2780.0	2769.0	2768.9	2756.8	2749.8	2742.4	2741.3
2738.7	2739.4	2727.9	2727.5	2726.7		

a. Plot the time series.
b. Determine why a linear trend forecast appears plausible. Does there appear to be any seasonality in these data?

c. Forecast the value of the series for the next quarter based on a linear trend.

12-7. The sales forecasting technique used by one company is to extend the deseasonalized trend line and then adjust for seasonality. The trend line for one company's sales (in $10,000s) is

$$\text{Trend} = .55t + 1.23 \text{ for the past 15 time periods.}$$

The four seasonal indices follow.

W	Sp	Sm	F	Sum
0.86	1.12	1.35	0.67	4.00

Forecast sales volumes for the next four years by multiplicatively combining this trend and seasonality data.

12-8. The following net incomes were obtained for a company (in $1,000s). The data consist of quarterly sales over the last two years. The data exhibit trend and seasonality.

-167	-829	1697	253	-374	923	-230
2833	2325	948	1303	1938	2063	1145
537	2681	3284	1647	2507	4210	4865
1773	3613	3593	3180	3052	3467	5114
3597	2507	4246	7258	5460	3520	3218
7946	7147	3896	2592	7935		

a. Plot the data. How many seasons per year are exhibited by these data?

b. Compute the centered moving averages.

c. Estimate the seasonal indices from the specific seasonal indices.

d. Deseasonalize the data.

e. Estimate the trend line from the deseasonalized data.

f. Forecast the next four quarterly values by adjusting the trend projections for seasonality.

12.4 SUMMARY

Time-series analysis is a statistical technique for forecasting future values of a variable. Distinct from the explanatory model regression analysis procedures discussed in Chapters 8 and 9, a forecast from a time-series analysis extrapolates the past into the future. An underlying pattern is identified by removing the random statistical fluctuations or noise from the data. This pattern is then projected into the future.

The underlying pattern is an additive or multiplicative composite of up to three types of basic patterns: trend, cycles, and seasons, initially introduced in Chapter 3. Trend is the long-term upward or downward movement. Cycles are long-term, often irregular swings. Seasons are comparatively short-term, regular fluctuations corresponding to, for example, the four seasons of the year. The actual data consist of the composite of these basic patterns embedded in statistical fluctuations.

However, one of the most widely used time-series methods—weighted averages or smoothing—does not use these basic patterns. Instead, statistical noise is removed by simple averaging of past values. All of these smoothing techniques can be expressed as a weighted sum of all past values. The simplest such methods are moving averages. The weights for exponential smoothing methods follow a pattern of exponential decay. The calculation of these weights depends on choosing a value of the smoothing parameter, which can vary from zero to one. Smaller values lead to the relatively large influence of values from the distant past, and larger values lead to most of the influence being placed on the immediate past.

Examples of forecasting methods that explicitly identify and use the underlying basic patterns were also presented. If only a linear trend is present, the OLS regression of Y regressed onto time can provide the basis for the forecast. If seasonality is also present, a forecasting method was discussed that first identified and then removed the effect of seasonality, used OLS regression to project the trend into the future, and then modified the projected trend by adjusting for the previously identified seasonality effects.

The choice of different forecasting models is often based on the analysis of the accuracy of the models for data that already exists. A model is evaluated by "forecasting" previous values from which the actual value is already known. The model with the smallest root mean squared error, or the smallest mean absolute deviation, is generally chosen.

12.5 KEY TERMS

centered moving average *554*   forecasting error *528*
damping factor *541*   mean absolute deviation *537*
deseasonalized *558*   *n*-period moving average *534*
differenced time series *531*   random walk *529*
exponential smoothing *541*   smoothing method *533*

12.6 REVIEW EXERCISES

ANALYSIS PROBLEMS

12-9. Consider the following monthly data.

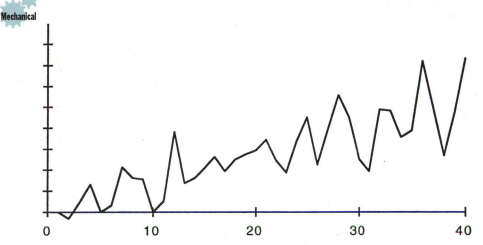

Hand sketch the

a. trend component

b. cyclical component

c. seasonal component

12-10. Management used a time-series analysis to estimate a multiplicative model. At a specific time, the trend component is 508. At that time period, the model estimates a seasonal component of .95 and an error component of 1.22. No cyclical component was present.

a. Does the seasonal component raise or lower the data value around the underlying trend? Why? What is the combined effect of trend and seasonality at that time period?

b. Does the error component raise or lower the data value around the underlying trend and seasonal component? What is the value of Y at that time period?

12-11. The following table lists quarterly GNP (1987 dollars) from January 1992.

1	2	3	4	5	6
4929.1	4955.5	4997.2	5061.0	5083.9	5110.1

7	8	9	10	11	12
5148.4	5218.7	5262.7	5310.5	5359.9	5416.0

For these data, compute

a. The 3-period simple moving average, MAD, and $\sqrt{\text{MSE}}$.

b. The 4-period simple moving average, MAD, and $\sqrt{\text{MSE}}$.

c. The weighted moving average with .7, .2, and .1 weights; MAD; and $\sqrt{\text{MSE}}$.

d. Forecast GNP for first quarter 1995.

12-12. Using the GNP data from Exercise 12-11, compute the exponential smoothing forecasts and associated MAD and $\sqrt{\text{MSE}}$ for

a. $\alpha = .2$

b. $\alpha = .4$

c. $\alpha = .6$

d. Determine which exponential smoothing model you would use to forecast 1995 GNP and why.

12-13. The pattern of annual gross revenues (in 1,000s of dollars) for a growing business are provided below for the last 40 years (random errors were removed for clarity).

1.02	2.82	4.23	3.24	2.56	6.12	9.88	8.97
9.20	17.25	23.28	18.69	18.60	35.12	44.98	31.90
24.32	35.28	40.22	27.41	21.46	31.05	32.46	19.44
12.78	26.50	38.10	31.40	29.64	51.74	65.62	49.84
47.22	85.30	104.96	71.77	52.94	74.48	82.56	54.82

For these data, compute

a. The 3-period simple moving average, MAD, and $\sqrt{\text{MSE}}$.

b. The 4-period simple moving average, MAD, and $\sqrt{\text{MSE}}$.

c. The weighted moving average with .7, .2, and .1 weights; MAD; and $\sqrt{\text{MSE}}$.

d. Forecast GNP for first quarter 1995.

e. Determine if this time series is best described by an additive model or a multiplicative model and why.

12-14. Using the GNP data from the previous problem, calculate the exponential smoothing forecasts and associated MAD and $\sqrt{\text{MSE}}$ for

a. $\alpha = .2$

b. $\alpha = .4$

c. $\alpha = .6$

d. Determine which exponential smoothing model you would use to forecast 1995 GNP and why.

12-15. The following table lists the number of building permits for new private housing over 15 years, scaled so that 1987 = 100 (Source: Department of Commerce).

Year	1980	1981	1982	1983	1984	1985	1986	1987
Permits	78.6	65.1	65.7	106.7	109.6	112.4	114.9	100.0

Year	1988	1989	1990	1991	1992	1993	1994
Permits	94.2	87.6	72.9	61.4	71.2	78.3	86.4

Exercise 12-3 asked for the plot and several different weighted means forecasts based on these data. Now compute from these data the exponential smoothing forecasts and associated MAD and $\sqrt{\text{MSE}}$ for

a. $\alpha = .2$

b. $\alpha = .4$

c. $\alpha = .6$

d. Determine the optimum value of α you would use to forecast 1995 number of building permits.

12-16. Consider the building permit data in Exercise 12-15.

a. Forecast the number of 1995 building permits based on the linear trend.

b. Determine whether the model also appears to fit the best exponential smoothing model from Exercise 12-15.

c. From an analysis of the statistics and of the appearance of the plot of the data, determine which forecasting method you would choose. Given a choice of available techniques, what is your forecast for number of 1995 building permits?

12-17. The following time series contains a company's gross earnings in $10,000 units for the last 20 quarters.

0.34	-0.25	0.49	0.89	0.48	0.43	0.18	0.34
0.66	1.38	1.18	1.12	1.52	1.12	2.04	1.75
1.92	1.29	2.41	2.14				

a. Plot the time series.

b. Explain why a linear trend forecast appears plausible. Does there appear to be any seasonality in these data?

c. Forecast the value of the series for the next quarter based on a linear trend.

12-18. The sales forecasting technique used by one company extends the deseasonalized trend line and then adjusts for seasonality. The trend line for one company's sales (in $100,000s) is,

Trend = .63t + .84 for the past 20 time periods.

The four seasonal indices follow.

W	Sp	Sm	F	Sum
1.23	0.56	0.75	1.46	4.00

Forecast the sales volumes for the next four years by combining this trend and seasonality data with a multiplicative model.

12-19. Consider the following annual U.S. merchandise trade deficit (in billions of 1992 dollars).

Year	1983	1984	1985	1986	1987	1988	1989
Trade Deficit ($ bil)	57.5	107.9	132.1	152.7	152.1	118.6	109.6

Year	1990	1991	1992	1993	1994	1995	
Trade Deficit ($ bil)	101.7	65.4	84.5	115.6	151.1	159.6	

    a. Create a time-series plot of Trade Deficit.

    b. Calculate the underlying trend line.

    c. Determine the forecast for 1996 and 1997 based on the trend line.

    d. Briefly describe the pattern of this variable over time. Do you think that the trend line will provide an accurate forecast?

12-20. Consider the following GNP data (in billions of 1992 dollars).

Year	1980	1981	1982	1983	1984	1985	1986	1987
GNP	12,226	13,547	13,961	14,998	16,508	17,529	18,374	19,323
Year	1988	1989	1990	1991	1992	1993	1994	1995
GNP	20,605	21,984	22,979	23,416	24,447	25,373	26,589	27,541

    a. Create a time-series plot of GNP.

    b. Calculate the underlying trend line.

    c. Determine the forecast for 1996 and 1997 based on the trend line.

    d. Briefly describe the pattern of this variable over time. Do you think that the trend line will provide an accurate forecast?

12-21. The sales forecasting technique used by one company is to extend the deseasonalized trend line and then adjust for seasonality. The trend line for one company's sales (in $10,000s) is

$$\text{Trend} = .29t \text{ for the past 15 time periods.}$$

The four seasonal indices follow.

W	Sp	Sm	F	Sum
0.67	1.15	1.29	0.89	4.00

Forecast the sales volumes for the next four years by combining this trend and seasonality data with a multiplicative model.

12-22. The following sales data were obtained for a promising new manufacturer of summerwear (in $10,000s). The data consist of quarterly sales over the last two years. The data exhibit trend and seasonality.

14.09	7.72	12.39	19.17	17.77	12.16	9.03	23.73
27.09	15.46	13.95	28.99	24.98	15.24	18.65	33.98
33.09	15.14	19.88	37.43	36.42	13.73	20.07	43.80

a.   Plot the data. How many seasons per year are exhibited by these data?

b.   Compute the centered moving averages.

c.   Estimate the seasonal indices from the specific seasonal indices.

d.   Deseasonalize the data.

e.   Estimate the trend line from the deseasonalized data.

f.   Forecast the next four quarterly values by adjusting the trend projections for seasonality.

DISCUSSION QUESTIONS

1.   What is the distinction between explanatory models and time-series models?

2.   What is the effect of the error component on the shape of the time series?

3.   Are all time-series data characterized by error?

4.   What is a potential mistake in interpreting random walk data?

5.   How can a random walk time series be identified?

6.   What well-known type of time-series data is approximately characterized as a random walk?

7.   What is a moving average forecasting method?

8.   What is the difference between a simple moving average and a weighted moving average?

9.   Why is the parameter α in exponential smoothing called a damping factor?

10. How does the value of the parameter α in exponential smoothing affect the forecast in terms of the influence of past time values?

11. Why is exponential smoothing a weighted average forecasting method?

12. What is the difference between MAD and $\sqrt{MSE}$? Why is MAD directly compared to $\sqrt{MSE}$ instead of to MSE?

13. How do seasonal components influence the data in a multiplicative model?

14. When is a centered moving average used in time-series analysis?

15. How are the initial seasonal indices adjusted to obtain the final indices?

16. How are data deseasonalized?

17. How are trend projections adjusted for seasonality?

INTEGRATIVE ANALYSIS PROBLEM

Management at a furniture manufacture was interested in forecasting sales for the next three months from past sales performance. Quarterly sales data for the last five years are found in the file SALES.DAT.

a.   Plot the time series of quarterly sales.

b.   From a visual examination of the plot, describe the trend, seasonal, and error components.

c.   Determine whether the underlying model is additive or multiplicative and why.

d.   Calculate the differenced time series.

e.   Determine if a random walk model accounts for these data and why or why not.

f.   Calculate the 3-period simple moving average, MAD, and $\sqrt{MSE}$, and forecast sales for the next time period.

g.   Calculate the weighted moving average with .7, .2, and .1 weights and MAD, $\sqrt{MSE}$, and forecast sales for the next time period.

h.   Calculate from these data the exponential smoothing forecasts and associated MAD and $\sqrt{MSE}$ for $\alpha = .4$, and forecast sales for the next time period.

i.   Calculate from these data the optimal value of α for an exponential smoothing forecast. Then calculate the associated MAD, $\sqrt{MSE}$, and forecast sales for the next time period.

j.   Calculate the centered moving averages.

k.   Estimate the seasonal indices from the specific seasonal indices.

l.   Deseasonalize the data.

m.   Estimate the trend line from the deseasonalized data.

n.   Forecast the next four quarterly values by adjusting the trend projections for seasonality.

o.   Identify which forecasting method you believe is most appropriate for these data and why.

p.   Forecast values of sales for the next four quarters.

APPENDICES—TABLES

APPENDIX A—STANDARD NORMAL CUMULATIVE PROBABILITIES

Each table entry is the probability that a standard normal random variable Z is less than the specified value.

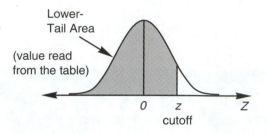

Z	Cumul. Prob.	Z	Cumul. Prob.	Z	Cumul. Prob.	Z	Cumul. Prob.
-4.00	0.0000	-2.37	0.0089	-2.12	0.0170	-1.87	0.0307
-3.50	0.0002	-2.36	0.0091	-2.11	0.0174	-1.86	0.0314
-3.00	0.0013	-2.35	0.0094	-2.10	0.0179	-1.85	0.0322
-2.80	0.0026	-2.34	0.0096	-2.09	0.0183	-1.84	0.0329
-2.70	0.0035	-2.33	0.0099	-2.08	0.0188	-1.83	0.0336
-2.65	0.0040	-2.32	0.0102	-2.07	0.0192	-1.82	0.0344
-2.60	0.0047	-2.31	0.0104	-2.06	0.0197	-1.81	0.0351
-2.55	0.0054	-2.30	0.0107	-2.05	0.0202	-1.37	0.0853
-2.54	0.0055	-2.29	0.0110	-2.04	0.0207	-1.36	0.0869
-2.53	0.0057	-2.28	0.0113	-2.03	0.0212	-1.35	0.0885
-2.52	0.0059	-2.27	0.0116	-2.02	0.0217	-1.34	0.0901
-2.51	0.0060	-2.26	0.0119	-2.01	0.0222	-1.80	0.0359
-2.50	0.0062	-2.25	0.0122	-2.00	0.0228	-1.79	0.0367
-2.49	0.0064	-2.24	0.0125	-1.99	0.0233	-1.78	0.0375
-2.48	0.0066	-2.23	0.0129	-1.98	0.0239	-1.77	0.0384
-2.47	0.0068	-2.22	0.0132	-1.97	0.0244	-1.76	0.0392
-2.46	0.0069	-2.21	0.0136	-1.96	0.0250	-1.75	0.0401
-2.45	0.0071	-2.20	0.0139	-1.95	0.0256	-1.74	0.0409
-2.44	0.0073	-2.19	0.0143	-1.94	0.0262	-1.73	0.0418
-2.43	0.0075	-2.18	0.0146	-1.93	0.0268	-1.72	0.0427
-2.42	0.0078	-2.17	0.0150	-1.92	0.0274	-1.71	0.0436
-2.41	0.0080	-2.16	0.0154	-1.91	0.0281	-1.70	0.0446
-2.40	0.0082	-2.15	0.0158	-1.90	0.0287	-1.69	0.0455
-2.39	0.0084	-2.14	0.0162	-1.89	0.0294	-1.68	0.0465
-2.38	0.0087	-2.13	0.0166	-1.88	0.0301	-1.67	0.0475

Z	Cumul. Prob.	Z	Cumul. Prob.	Z	Cumul. Prob.	Z	Cumul. Prob.
-1.66	0.0485	-1.26	0.1038	-0.90	0.1841	-0.54	0.2946
-1.65	0.0495	-1.25	0.1056	-0.89	0.1867	-0.53	0.2981
-1.64	0.0505	-1.24	0.1075	-0.88	0.1894	-0.52	0.3015
-1.63	0.0516	-1.23	0.1093	-0.87	0.1922	-0.51	0.3050
-1.62	0.0526	-1.22	0.1112	-0.86	0.1949	-0.50	0.3085
-1.61	0.0537	-1.21	0.1131	-0.85	0.1977	-0.49	0.3121
-1.60	0.0548	-1.20	0.1151	-0.84	0.2005	-0.48	0.3156
-1.59	0.0559	-1.19	0.1170	-0.83	0.2033	-0.47	0.3192
-1.58	0.0571	-1.18	0.1190	-0.82	0.2061	-0.46	0.3228
-1.57	0.0582	-1.17	0.1210	-0.81	0.2090	-0.45	0.3264
-1.56	0.0594	-1.16	0.1230	-0.80	0.2119	-0.44	0.3300
-1.55	0.0606	-1.15	0.1251	-0.79	0.2148	-0.43	0.3336
-1.54	0.0618	-1.14	0.1271	-0.78	0.2177	-0.42	0.3372
-1.53	0.0630	-1.13	0.1292	-0.77	0.2206	-0.41	0.3409
-1.52	0.0643	-1.12	0.1314	-0.76	0.2236	-0.40	0.3446
-1.51	0.0655	-1.11	0.1335	-0.75	0.2266	-0.39	0.3483
-1.50	0.0668	-1.10	0.1357	-0.74	0.2296	-0.38	0.3520
-1.49	0.0681	-1.09	0.1379	-0.73	0.2327	-0.37	0.3557
-1.48	0.0694	-1.08	0.1401	-0.72	0.2358	-0.36	0.3594
-1.47	0.0708	-1.07	0.1423	-0.71	0.2389	-0.35	0.3632
-1.46	0.0721	-1.06	0.1446	-0.70	0.2420	-0.34	0.3669
-1.45	0.0735	-1.05	0.1469	-0.69	0.2451	-0.33	0.3707
-1.44	0.0749	-1.04	0.1492	-0.68	0.2483	-0.32	0.3745
-1.43	0.0764	-1.03	0.1515	-0.67	0.2514	-0.31	0.3783
-1.42	0.0778	-1.02	0.1539	-0.66	0.2546	-0.30	0.3821
-1.41	0.0793	-1.01	0.1562	-0.65	0.2578	-0.29	0.3859
-1.40	0.0808	-1.00	0.1587	-0.64	0.2611	-0.28	0.3897
-1.39	0.0823	-0.99	0.1611	-0.63	0.2643	-0.27	0.3936
-1.38	0.0838	-0.98	0.1635	-0.62	0.2676	-0.26	0.3974
-1.33	0.0918	-0.97	0.1660	-0.61	0.2709	-0.25	0.4013
-1.32	0.0934	-0.96	0.1685	-0.60	0.2743	-0.24	0.4052
-1.31	0.0951	-0.95	0.1711	-0.59	0.2776	-0.23	0.4090
-1.30	0.0968	-0.94	0.1736	-0.58	0.2810	-0.22	0.4129
-1.29	0.0985	-0.93	0.1762	-0.57	0.2843	-0.21	0.4168
-1.28	0.1003	-0.92	0.1788	-0.56	0.2877	-0.20	0.4207
-1.27	0.1020	-0.91	0.1814	-0.55	0.2912	-0.19	0.4247

Z	Cumul. Prob.	Z	Cumul. Prob.	Z	Cumul. Prob.	Z	Cumul. Prob.
-0.18	0.4286	0.18	0.5714	0.54	0.7054	0.90	0.8159
-0.17	0.4325	0.19	0.5753	0.55	0.7088	0.91	0.8186
-0.16	0.4364	0.20	0.5793	0.56	0.7123	0.92	0.8212
-0.15	0.4404	0.21	0.5832	0.57	0.7157	0.93	0.8238
-0.14	0.4443	0.22	0.5871	0.58	0.7190	0.94	0.8264
-0.13	0.4483	0.23	0.5910	0.59	0.7224	0.95	0.8289
-0.12	0.4522	0.24	0.5948	0.60	0.7257	0.96	0.8315
-0.11	0.4562	0.25	0.5987	0.61	0.7291	0.97	0.8340
-0.10	0.4602	0.26	0.6026	0.62	0.7324	0.98	0.8365
-0.09	0.4641	0.27	0.6064	0.63	0.7357	0.99	0.8389
-0.08	0.4681	0.28	0.6103	0.64	0.7389	1.00	0.8413
-0.07	0.4721	0.29	0.6141	0.65	0.7422	1.01	0.8438
-0.06	0.4761	0.30	0.6179	0.66	0.7454	1.02	0.8461
-0.05	0.4801	0.31	0.6217	0.67	0.7486	1.03	0.8485
-0.04	0.4840	0.32	0.6255	0.68	0.7517	1.04	0.8508
-0.03	0.4880	0.33	0.6293	0.69	0.7549	1.05	0.8531
-0.02	0.4920	0.34	0.6331	0.70	0.7580	1.06	0.8554
-0.01	0.4960	0.35	0.6368	0.71	0.7611	1.07	0.8577
0.00	0.5000	0.36	0.6406	0.72	0.7642	1.08	0.8599
0.01	0.5040	0.37	0.6443	0.73	0.7673	1.09	0.8621
0.02	0.5080	0.38	0.6480	0.74	0.7704	1.10	0.8643
0.03	0.5120	0.39	0.6517	0.75	0.7734	1.11	0.8665
0.04	0.5160	0.40	0.6554	0.76	0.7764	1.12	0.8686
0.05	0.5199	0.41	0.6591	0.77	0.7794	1.13	0.8708
0.06	0.5239	0.42	0.6628	0.78	0.7823	1.14	0.8729
0.07	0.5279	0.43	0.6664	0.79	0.7852	1.15	0.8749
0.08	0.5319	0.44	0.6700	0.80	0.7881	1.16	0.8770
0.09	0.5359	0.45	0.6736	0.81	0.7910	1.17	0.8790
0.10	0.5398	0.46	0.6772	0.82	0.7939	1.18	0.8810
0.11	0.5438	0.47	0.6808	0.83	0.7967	1.19	0.8830
0.12	0.5478	0.48	0.6844	0.84	0.7995	1.20	0.8849
0.13	0.5517	0.49	0.6879	0.85	0.8023	1.21	0.8869
0.14	0.5557	0.50	0.6915	0.86	0.8051	1.22	0.8888
0.15	0.5596	0.51	0.6950	0.87	0.8078	1.23	0.8907
0.16	0.5636	0.52	0.6985	0.88	0.8106	1.24	0.8925
0.17	0.5675	0.53	0.7019	0.89	0.8133	1.25	0.8944

Z	Cumul. Prob.	Z	Cumul. Prob.	Z	Cumul. Prob.	Z	Cumul. Prob.
1.26	0.8962	1.61	0.9463	1.96	0.9750	2.31	0.9896
1.27	0.8980	1.62	0.9474	1.97	0.9756	2.32	0.9898
1.28	0.8997	1.63	0.9484	1.98	0.9761	2.33	0.9901
1.29	0.9015	1.64	0.9495	1.99	0.9767	2.34	0.9904
1.30	0.9032	1.65	0.9505	2.00	0.9772	2.35	0.9906
1.31	0.9049	1.66	0.9515	2.01	0.9778	2.36	0.9909
1.32	0.9066	1.67	0.9525	2.02	0.9783	2.37	0.9911
1.33	0.9082	1.68	0.9535	2.03	0.9788	2.38	0.9913
1.34	0.9099	1.69	0.9545	2.04	0.9793	2.39	0.9916
1.35	0.9115	1.70	0.9554	2.05	0.9798	2.40	0.9918
1.36	0.9131	1.71	0.9564	2.06	0.9803	2.41	0.9920
1.37	0.9147	1.72	0.9573	2.07	0.9808	2.42	0.9922
1.38	0.9162	1.73	0.9582	2.08	0.9812	2.43	0.9925
1.39	0.9177	1.74	0.9591	2.09	0.9817	2.44	0.9927
1.40	0.9192	1.75	0.9599	2.10	0.9821	2.45	0.9929
1.41	0.9207	1.76	0.9608	2.11	0.9826	2.46	0.9931
1.42	0.9222	1.77	0.9616	2.12	0.9830	2.47	0.9932
1.43	0.9236	1.78	0.9625	2.13	0.9834	2.48	0.9934
1.44	0.9251	1.79	0.9633	2.14	0.9838	2.49	0.9936
1.45	0.9265	1.80	0.9641	2.15	0.9842	2.50	0.9938
1.46	0.9279	1.81	0.9649	2.16	0.9846	2.51	0.9940
1.47	0.9292	1.82	0.9656	2.17	0.9850	2.52	0.9941
1.48	0.9306	1.83	0.9664	2.18	0.9854	2.53	0.9943
1.49	0.9319	1.84	0.9671	2.19	0.9857	2.54	0.9945
1.50	0.9332	1.85	0.9678	2.20	0.9861	2.55	0.9946
1.51	0.9345	1.86	0.9686	2.21	0.9864	2.60	0.9953
1.52	0.9357	1.87	0.9693	2.22	0.9868	2.65	0.9960
1.53	0.9370	1.88	0.9699	2.23	0.9871	2.70	0.9965
1.54	0.9382	1.89	0.9706	2.24	0.9875	2.80	0.9974
1.55	0.9394	1.90	0.9713	2.25	0.9878	3.00	0.9987
1.56	0.9406	1.91	0.9719	2.26	0.9881	3.50	0.9998
1.57	0.9418	1.92	0.9726	2.27	0.9884	4.00	1.0000
1.58	0.9429	1.93	0.9732	2.28	0.9887		
1.59	0.9441	1.94	0.9738	2.29	0.9890		
1.60	0.9452	1.95	0.9744	2.30	0.9893		

APPENDIX B—CUTOFF VALUES OF SELECTED t-DISTRIBUTIONS

Each entry in this table is a cutoff value of t that corresponds to the probability that an observed value of t is larger than the cutoff value, that is, the area in the upper tail of the t-distribution. For example, for $df = 10$, $P(t > 2.228) = .025$.

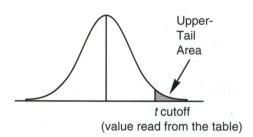

Upper-
Tail
Area

t cutoff
(value read from the table)

df = n − 1	Area in Upper Tail						
	0.400	0.250	0.100	0.050	0.025	0.010	0.005
1	0.325	1.000	3.078	6.314	12.706	31.821	63.657
2	0.289	0.816	1.886	2.920	4.303	6.964	9.925
3	0.277	0.765	1.638	2.353	3.182	4.541	5.841
4	0.271	0.741	1.533	2.132	2.776	3.747	4.604
5	0.267	0.727	1.476	2.015	2.571	3.365	4.032
6	0.265	0.718	1.440	1.943	2.447	3.143	3.707
7	0.263	0.711	1.415	1.895	2.365	2.998	3.499
8	0.262	0.706	1.397	1.860	2.306	2.896	3.355
9	0.261	0.703	1.383	1.833	2.262	2.821	3.250
10	0.260	0.700	1.372	1.812	2.228	2.764	3.169
11	0.260	0.697	1.363	1.796	2.201	2.718	3.106
12	0.259	0.695	1.356	1.782	2.179	2.681	3.055
13	0.259	0.694	1.350	1.771	2.160	2.650	3.012
14	0.258	0.692	1.345	1.761	2.145	2.624	2.977
15	0.258	0.691	1.341	1.753	2.131	2.602	2.947
16	0.258	0.690	1.337	1.746	2.120	2.583	2.921
17	0.257	0.689	1.333	1.740	2.110	2.567	2.898
18	0.257	0.688	1.330	1.734	2.101	2.552	2.878
19	0.257	0.688	1.328	1.729	2.093	2.539	2.861
20	0.257	0.687	1.325	1.725	2.086	2.528	2.845
21	0.257	0.686	1.323	1.721	2.080	2.518	2.831
22	0.256	0.686	1.321	1.717	2.074	2.508	2.819
23	0.256	0.685	1.319	1.714	2.069	2.500	2.807
24	0.256	0.685	1.318	1.711	2.064	2.492	2.797
25	0.256	0.684	1.316	1.708	2.060	2.485	2.787
26	0.256	0.684	1.315	1.706	2.056	2.479	2.779
27	0.256	0.684	1.314	1.703	2.052	2.473	2.771
28	0.256	0.683	1.313	1.701	2.048	2.467	2.763
29	0.256	0.683	1.311	1.699	2.045	2.462	2.756
30	0.256	0.683	1.310	1.697	2.042	2.457	2.750
40	0.255	0.681	1.303	1.684	2.021	2.423	2.704
50	0.255	0.679	1.299	1.676	2.009	2.403	2.678
60	0.254	0.679	1.296	1.671	2.000	2.390	2.660
80	0.254	0.678	1.292	1.664	1.990	2.374	2.639
100	0.254	0.677	1.290	1.660	1.984	2.364	2.626
150	0.254	0.676	1.287	1.655	1.976	2.351	2.609
200	0.254	0.676	1.286	1.653	1.972	2.345	2.601
500	0.253	0.675	1.283	1.648	1.965	2.334	2.586
1000	0.253	0.675	1.282	1.646	1.962	2.330	2.581
Normal Curve	0.253	0.674	1.282	1.645	1.960	2.326	2.576

APPENDIX C—CUTOFF VALUES OF SELECTED CHI-SQUARE DISTRIBUTIONS

df	Area in Upper Tail					
	0.40	0.25	0.15	0.10	0.05	0.01
1	0.708	1.323	2.072	2.706	3.841	6.635
2	1.833	2.773	3.794	4.605	5.991	9.210
3	2.946	4.108	5.317	6.251	7.815	11.345
4	4.045	5.385	6.745	7.779	9.488	13.277
5	5.132	6.626	8.115	9.236	11.070	15.086
6	6.211	7.841	9.446	10.645	12.592	16.812
7	7.283	9.037	10.748	12.017	14.067	18.475
8	8.351	10.219	12.027	13.362	15.507	20.090
9	9.414	11.389	13.288	14.684	16.919	21.666
10	10.473	12.549	14.534	15.987	18.307	23.209
11	11.530	13.701	15.767	17.275	19.675	24.725
12	12.584	14.845	16.989	18.549	21.026	26.217
13	13.636	15.984	18.202	19.812	22.362	27.688
14	14.685	17.117	19.406	21.064	23.685	29.141
15	15.733	18.245	20.603	22.307	24.996	30.578
16	16.780	19.369	21.793	23.542	26.296	32.000
17	17.824	20.489	22.977	24.769	27.587	33.409
18	18.868	21.605	24.155	25.989	28.869	34.805
19	19.910	22.718	25.329	27.204	30.144	36.191
20	20.951	23.828	26.498	28.412	31.410	37.566
25	26.143	29.339	32.282	34.382	37.652	44.314
30	31.316	34.800	37.990	40.256	43.773	50.892
40	41.622	45.616	49.244	51.805	55.758	63.691
60	62.135	66.981	71.341	74.397	79.082	88.379
80	82.566	88.130	93.106	96.578	101.879	112.329
100	102.946	109.141	114.659	118.498	124.342	135.807
120	123.289	130.055	136.062	140.233	146.567	158.950
150	153.753	161.291	167.962	172.581	179.581	193.207

APPENDIX D—CUTOFF VALUES OF SELECTED *F*-DISTRIBUTIONS

df for Den	cut off	df for Numerator								
		1	2	3	4	5	6	7	8	9
2	.05	18.51	19.00	19.16	19.25	19.30	19.33	19.35	19.37	19.38
	.01	98.50	99.00	99.16	99.25	99.30	99.33	99.36	99.38	99.39
3	.05	10.13	9.55	9.28	9.12	9.01	8.94	8.89	8.85	8.81
	.01	34.12	30.82	29.46	28.71	28.24	27.91	27.67	27.49	27.34
4	.05	7.71	6.94	6.59	6.39	6.26	6.16	6.09	6.04	6.00
	.01	21.20	18.00	16.69	15.98	15.52	15.21	14.98	14.80	14.66
5	.05	6.61	5.79	5.41	5.19	5.05	4.95	4.88	4.82	4.77
	.01	16.26	13.27	12.06	11.39	10.97	10.67	10.46	10.29	10.16
6	.05	5.99	5.14	4.76	4.53	4.39	4.28	4.21	4.15	4.10
	.01	13.75	10.92	9.78	9.15	8.75	8.47	8.26	8.10	7.98
7	.05	5.59	4.74	4.35	4.12	3.97	3.87	3.79	3.73	3.68
	.01	12.25	9.55	8.45	7.85	7.46	7.19	6.99	6.84	6.72
8	.05	5.32	4.46	4.07	3.84	3.69	3.58	3.50	3.44	3.39
	.01	11.26	8.65	7.59	7.01	6.63	6.37	6.18	6.03	5.91
9	.05	5.12	4.26	3.86	3.63	3.48	3.37	3.29	3.23	3.18
	.01	10.56	8.02	6.99	6.42	6.06	5.80	5.61	5.47	5.35
10	.05	4.96	4.10	3.71	3.48	3.33	3.22	3.14	3.07	3.02
	.01	10.04	7.56	6.55	5.99	5.64	5.39	5.20	5.06	4.94
11	.05	4.84	3.98	3.59	3.36	3.20	3.09	3.01	2.95	2.90
	.01	9.65	7.21	6.22	5.67	5.32	5.07	4.89	4.74	4.63
12	.05	4.75	3.89	3.49	3.26	3.11	3.00	2.91	2.85	2.80
	.01	9.33	6.93	5.95	5.41	5.06	4.82	4.64	4.50	4.39
13	.05	4.67	3.81	3.41	3.18	3.03	2.92	2.83	2.77	2.71
	.01	9.07	6.70	5.74	5.21	4.86	4.62	4.44	4.30	4.19
14	.05	4.60	3.74	3.34	3.11	2.96	2.85	2.76	2.70	2.65
	.01	8.86	6.51	5.56	5.04	4.69	4.46	4.28	4.14	4.03
15	.05	4.54	3.68	3.29	3.06	2.90	2.79	2.71	2.64	2.59
	.01	8.68	6.36	5.42	4.89	4.56	4.32	4.14	4.00	3.89
16	.05	4.49	3.63	3.24	3.01	2.85	2.74	2.66	2.59	2.54
	.01	8.53	6.23	5.29	4.77	4.44	4.20	4.03	3.89	3.78
17	.05	4.45	3.59	3.20	2.96	2.81	2.70	2.61	2.55	2.49
	.01	8.40	6.11	5.19	4.67	4.34	4.10	3.93	3.79	3.68
18	.05	4.41	3.55	3.16	2.93	2.77	2.66	2.58	2.51	2.46
	.01	8.29	6.01	5.09	4.58	4.25	4.01	3.84	3.71	3.60
19	.05	4.38	3.52	3.13	2.90	2.74	2.63	2.54	2.48	2.42
	.01	8.18	5.93	5.01	4.50	4.17	3.94	3.77	3.63	3.52

df for Den	cut off	df for Numerator								
		10	12	15	20	24	30	60	120	inf
1	.05	241.88	243.90	245.95	248.02	249.05	250.10	252.20	253.25	254.32
2	.05	19.40	19.41	19.43	19.45	19.45	19.46	19.48	19.49	19.50
	.01	99.40	99.42	99.43	99.45	99.46	99.47	99.48	99.49	99.50
3	.05	8.79	8.74	8.70	8.66	8.64	8.62	8.57	8.55	8.53
	.01	27.23	27.05	26.87	26.69	26.60	26.50	26.32	26.22	26.13
4	.05	5.96	5.91	5.86	5.80	5.77	5.75	5.69	5.66	5.63
	.01	14.55	14.37	14.20	14.02	13.93	13.84	13.65	13.56	13.46
5	.05	4.74	4.68	4.62	4.56	4.53	4.50	4.43	4.40	4.37
	.01	10.05	9.89	9.72	9.55	9.47	9.38	9.20	9.11	9.02
6	.05	4.06	4.00	3.94	3.87	3.84	3.81	3.74	3.70	3.67
	.01	7.87	7.72	7.56	7.40	7.31	7.23	7.06	6.97	6.88
7	.05	3.64	3.57	3.51	3.44	3.41	3.38	3.30	3.27	3.23
	.01	6.62	6.47	6.31	6.16	6.07	5.99	5.82	5.74	5.65
8	.05	3.35	3.28	3.22	3.15	3.12	3.08	3.01	2.97	2.93
	.01	5.81	5.67	5.52	5.36	5.28	5.20	5.03	4.95	4.86
9	.05	3.14	3.07	3.01	2.94	2.90	2.86	2.79	2.75	2.71
	.01	5.26	5.11	4.96	4.81	4.73	4.65	4.48	4.40	4.31
10	.05	2.98	2.91	2.85	2.77	2.74	2.70	2.62	2.58	2.54
	.01	4.85	4.71	4.56	4.41	4.33	4.25	4.08	4.00	3.91
11	.05	2.85	2.79	2.72	2.65	2.61	2.57	2.49	2.45	2.40
	.01	4.54	4.40	4.25	4.10	4.02	3.94	3.78	3.69	3.60
12	.05	2.75	2.69	2.62	2.54	2.51	2.47	2.38	2.34	2.30
	.01	4.30	4.16	4.01	3.86	3.78	3.70	3.54	3.45	3.36
13	.05	2.67	2.60	2.53	2.46	2.42	2.38	2.30	2.25	2.21
	.01	4.10	3.96	3.82	3.66	3.59	3.51	3.34	3.25	3.17
14	.05	2.60	2.53	2.46	2.39	2.35	2.31	2.22	2.18	2.13
	.01	3.94	3.80	3.66	3.51	3.43	3.35	3.18	3.09	3.00
15	.05	2.54	2.48	2.40	2.33	2.29	2.25	2.16	2.11	2.07
	.01	3.80	3.67	3.52	3.37	3.29	3.21	3.05	2.96	2.87
16	.05	2.49	2.42	2.35	2.28	2.24	2.19	2.11	2.06	2.01
	.01	3.69	3.55	3.41	3.26	3.18	3.10	2.93	2.84	2.75
17	.05	2.45	2.38	2.31	2.23	2.19	2.15	2.06	2.01	1.96
	.01	3.59	3.46	3.31	3.16	3.08	3.00	2.83	2.75	2.65
18	.05	2.41	2.34	2.27	2.19	2.15	2.11	2.02	1.97	1.92
	.01	3.51	3.37	3.23	3.08	3.00	2.92	2.75	2.66	2.57
19	.05	2.38	2.31	2.23	2.16	2.11	2.07	1.98	1.93	1.88
	.01	3.43	3.30	3.15	3.00	2.92	2.84	2.67	2.58	2.49

(continued)

APPENDIX D—(*Continued*)

df for Den	cut off	df for Numerator								
		1	2	3	4	5	6	7	8	9
20	.05	4.35	3.49	3.10	2.87	2.71	2.60	2.51	2.45	2.39
	.01	8.10	5.85	4.94	4.43	4.10	3.87	3.70	3.56	3.46
21	.05	4.32	3.47	3.07	2.84	2.68	2.57	2.49	2.42	2.37
	.01	8.02	5.78	4.87	4.37	4.04	3.81	3.64	3.51	3.40
22	.05	4.30	3.44	3.05	2.82	2.66	2.55	2.46	2.40	2.34
	.01	7.95	5.72	4.82	4.31	3.99	3.76	3.59	3.45	3.35
23	.05	4.28	3.42	3.03	2.80	2.64	2.53	2.44	2.37	2.32
	.01	7.88	5.66	4.76	4.26	3.94	3.71	3.54	3.41	3.30
24	.05	4.26	3.40	3.01	2.78	2.62	2.51	2.42	2.36	2.30
	.01	7.82	5.61	4.72	4.22	3.90	3.67	3.50	3.36	3.26
25	.05	4.24	3.39	2.99	2.76	2.60	2.49	2.40	2.34	2.28
	.01	7.77	5.57	4.68	4.18	3.85	3.63	3.46	3.32	3.22
26	.05	4.23	3.37	2.98	2.74	2.59	2.47	2.39	2.32	2.27
	.01	7.72	5.53	4.64	4.14	3.82	3.59	3.42	3.29	3.18
27	.05	4.21	3.35	2.96	2.73	2.57	2.46	2.37	2.31	2.25
	.01	7.68	5.49	4.60	4.11	3.78	3.56	3.39	3.26	3.15
28	.05	4.20	3.34	2.95	2.71	2.56	2.45	2.36	2.29	2.24
	.01	7.64	5.45	4.57	4.07	3.75	3.53	3.36	3.23	3.12
29	.05	4.18	3.33	2.93	2.70	2.55	2.43	2.35	2.28	2.22
	.01	7.60	5.42	4.54	4.04	3.73	3.50	3.33	3.20	3.09
30	.05	4.17	3.32	2.92	2.69	2.53	2.42	2.33	2.27	2.21
	.01	7.56	5.39	4.51	4.02	3.70	3.47	3.30	3.17	3.07
40	.05	4.08	3.23	2.84	2.61	2.45	2.34	2.25	2.18	2.12
	.01	7.31	5.18	4.31	3.83	3.51	3.29	3.12	2.99	2.89
50	.05	4.03	3.18	2.79	2.56	2.40	2.29	2.20	2.13	2.07
	.01	7.17	5.06	4.20	3.72	3.41	3.19	3.02	2.89	2.78
60	.05	4.00	3.15	2.76	2.53	2.37	2.25	2.17	2.10	2.04
	.01	7.08	4.98	4.13	3.65	3.34	3.12	2.95	2.82	2.72
80	.05	3.96	3.11	2.72	2.49	2.33	2.21	2.13	2.06	2.00
	.01	6.96	4.88	4.04	3.56	3.26	3.04	2.87	2.74	2.64
120	.05	3.92	3.07	2.68	2.45	2.29	2.18	2.09	2.02	1.96
	.01	6.85	4.79	3.95	3.48	3.17	2.96	2.79	2.66	2.56
inf	.05	6.63	4.61	3.78	3.32	3.02	2.80	2.64	2.51	2.41
	.01	3.84	3.00	2.60	2.37	2.21	2.10	2.01	1.94	1.88

df for Den	cut off	df for Numerator								
		10	12	15	20	24	30	60	120	inf
20	.05	2.35	2.28	2.20	2.12	2.08	2.04	1.95	1.90	1.84
	.01	3.37	3.23	3.09	2.94	2.86	2.78	2.61	2.52	2.42
21	.05	2.32	2.25	2.18	2.10	2.05	2.01	1.92	1.87	1.81
	.01	3.31	3.17	3.03	2.88	2.80	2.72	2.55	2.46	2.36
22	.05	2.30	2.23	2.15	2.07	2.03	1.98	1.89	1.84	1.78
	.01	3.26	3.12	2.98	2.83	2.75	2.67	2.50	2.40	2.31
23	.05	2.27	2.20	2.13	2.05	2.01	1.96	1.86	1.81	1.76
	.01	3.21	3.07	2.93	2.78	2.70	2.62	2.45	2.35	2.26
24	.05	2.25	2.18	2.11	2.03	1.98	1.94	1.84	1.79	1.73
	.01	3.17	3.03	2.89	2.74	2.66	2.58	2.40	2.31	2.21
25	.05	2.24	2.16	2.09	2.01	1.96	1.92	1.82	1.77	1.71
	.01	3.13	2.99	2.85	2.70	2.62	2.54	2.36	2.27	2.17
26	.05	2.22	2.15	2.07	1.99	1.95	1.90	1.80	1.75	1.69
	.01	3.09	2.96	2.81	2.66	2.58	2.50	2.33	2.23	2.13
27	.05	2.20	2.13	2.06	1.97	1.93	1.88	1.79	1.73	1.67
	.01	3.06	2.93	2.78	2.63	2.55	2.47	2.29	2.20	2.10
28	.05	2.19	2.12	2.04	1.96	1.91	1.87	1.77	1.71	1.65
	.01	3.03	2.90	2.75	2.60	2.52	2.44	2.26	2.17	2.06
29	.05	2.18	2.10	2.03	1.94	1.90	1.85	1.75	1.70	1.64
	.01	3.00	2.87	2.73	2.57	2.49	2.41	2.23	2.14	2.03
30	.05	2.16	2.09	2.01	1.93	1.89	1.84	1.74	1.68	1.62
	.01	2.98	2.84	2.70	2.55	2.47	2.39	2.21	2.11	2.01
40	.05	2.08	2.00	1.92	1.84	1.79	1.74	1.64	1.58	1.51
	.01	2.80	2.66	2.52	2.37	2.29	2.20	2.02	1.92	1.80
50	.05	2.03	1.95	1.87	1.78	1.74	1.69	1.58	1.51	1.44
	.01	2.70	2.56	2.42	2.27	2.18	2.10	1.91	1.80	1.68
60	.05	1.99	1.92	1.84	1.75	1.70	1.65	1.53	1.47	1.39
	.01	2.63	2.50	2.35	2.20	2.12	2.03	1.84	1.73	1.60
80	.05	1.95	1.88	1.79	1.70	1.65	1.60	1.48	1.41	1.32
	.01	2.55	2.42	2.27	2.12	2.03	1.94	1.75	1.63	1.49
120	.05	1.91	1.83	1.75	1.66	1.61	1.55	1.43	1.35	1.25
	.01	2.47	2.34	2.19	2.03	1.95	1.86	1.66	1.53	1.38
inf	.05	1.83	1.75	1.67	1.57	1.52	1.46	1.32	1.22	1.00
	.01	2.32	2.18	2.04	1.88	1.79	1.70	1.47	1.32	1.00

APPENDIX E—CUTOFF VALUES OF SELECTED STUDENTIZED RANGE DISTRIBUTIONS

df	Errorcut off	Number of Means (p) 2	3	4	5	6	7	8	9	10
2	.05	6.08	8.33	9.80	10.90	11.70	12.40	13.00	13.50	14.00
	.01	14.00	19.00	22.30	24.70	26.60	28.20	29.50	30.70	31.70
3	.05	4.50	5.91	6.82	7.50	8.04	8.48	8.85	9.18	9.46
	.01	8.26	10.60	12.20	13.30	14.20	15.00	15.60	16.20	16.70
4	.05	3.93	5.04	5.76	6.29	6.71	7.05	7.35	7.60	7.83
	.01	6.51	8.12	9.17	9.96	10.60	11.10	11.50	11.90	12.30
5	.05	3.64	4.60	5.22	5.67	6.03	6.33	6.58	6.80	6.99
	.01	5.70	6.98	7.80	8.42	8.91	9.32	9.67	9.97	10.24
6	.05	3.46	4.34	4.90	5.30	5.63	5.90	6.12	6.32	6.49
	.01	5.24	6.33	7.03	7.56	7.97	8.32	8.61	8.87	9.10
7	.05	3.34	4.16	4.68	5.06	5.36	5.61	5.82	6.00	6.16
	.01	4.95	5.92	6.54	7.01	7.37	7.68	7.94	8.17	8.37
8	.05	3.26	4.04	4.53	4.89	5.17	5.40	5.60	5.77	5.92
	.01	4.75	5.64	6.20	6.62	6.96	7.24	7.47	7.68	7.86
9	.05	3.20	3.95	4.41	4.76	5.02	5.24	5.43	5.59	5.74
	.01	4.60	5.43	5.96	6.35	6.66	6.91	7.13	7.33	7.49
10	.05	3.15	3.88	4.33	4.65	4.91	5.12	5.30	5.46	5.60
	.01	4.48	5.27	5.77	6.14	6.43	6.67	6.87	7.05	7.21
11	.05	3.11	3.82	4.26	4.57	4.82	5.03	5.20	5.35	5.49
	.01	4.39	5.15	5.62	5.97	6.25	6.48	6.67	6.84	6.99
12	.05	3.08	3.77	4.20	4.51	4.75	4.95	5.12	5.27	5.39
	.01	4.32	5.05	5.50	5.84	6.10	6.32	6.51	6.67	6.81
14	.05	3.03	3.70	4.11	4.41	4.64	4.83	4.99	5.13	5.25
	.01	4.21	4.89	5.32	5.63	5.88	6.08	6.26	6.41	6.54
16	.05	3.00	3.65	4.05	4.33	4.56	4.74	4.90	5.03	5.15
	.01	4.13	4.79	5.19	5.49	5.72	5.92	6.08	6.22	6.35
20	.05	2.95	3.58	3.96	4.23	4.45	4.62	4.77	4.90	5.01
	.01	4.02	4.64	5.02	5.29	5.51	5.69	5.84	5.97	6.09
24	.05	2.92	3.53	3.90	4.17	4.37	4.54	4.68	4.81	4.92
	.01	3.96	4.55	4.91	5.17	5.37	5.54	5.69	5.81	5.92
30	.05	2.89	3.49	3.85	4.10	4.30	4.46	4.60	4.72	4.82
	.01	3.89	4.45	4.80	5.05	5.24	5.40	5.54	5.65	5.76
40	.05	2.86	3.44	3.79	4.04	4.23	4.39	4.52	4.63	4.73
	.01	3.82	4.37	4.70	4.93	5.11	5.26	5.39	5.50	5.60
60	.05	2.83	3.40	3.74	3.98	4.16	4.31	4.44	4.55	4.65
	.01	3.76	4.28	4.59	4.82	4.99	5.13	5.25	5.36	5.45
120	.05	2.80	3.36	3.68	3.92	4.10	4.24	4.36	4.47	4.56
	.01	3.70	4.20	4.50	4.71	4.87	5.01	5.12	5.21	5.30
inf	.05	2.77	3.31	3.63	3.86	4.03	4.17	4.29	4.39	4.47
	.01	3.64	4.12	4.40	4.60	4.76	4.88	4.99	5.08	5.16